Fishing the Great Lakes

Robert von Neumann, *Great Lakes Fishermen* or *Trapnet Fishing on the Great Lakes,* 1943, lithograph. (Courtesy David T. Prosser, Jr.)

Fishing the Great Lakes

AN ENVIRONMENTAL HISTORY
1783–1933

Margaret Beattie Bogue

The University of Wisconsin Press

The University of Wisconsin Press
2537 Daniels Street
Madison, Wisconsin 53718

3 Henrietta Street
London WC2E 8LU, England

1 3 5 4 2

Printed in the United States of America

Library of Congress Cataloging-in-Publication Data

Bogue, Margaret Beattie, 1924–
Fishing the Great Lakes : an environmental history,
1783–1933 / Margaret Beattie Bogue.
464 p. cm.
Includes bibliographical references and index.
ISBN 0-299-16760-7 (cloth: alk. paper)
ISBN 0-299-16764-X (paper: alk. paper)
1. Fisheries—Great Lakes—History.
2. Fishery policy—Great Lakes—History.
3. Fisheries—Environmental aspects—Great Lakes. I. Title.
SH219.6.B64 2000
333.95′613′0977—dc21 00-008601

To the younger generations

Sue, Margaret, Paul,

Ellie, Steve, Alex,

and Rachelle

Contents

Illustrations ix
Tables xi
Preface xii
Acknowledgments xvii

1. Legacies from the Wilderness 3

PART I. THE RISE OF COMMERCIAL FISHING, 1800–1893

2. Lake Ontario Salmon in an Early Agricultural-Commercial Economy 19
3. Patterns of Growth through 1872 28
4. The Expansive Heyday, 1875–1893 44
5. A. Booth and Company Bids for Great Lakes Dominance 59
6. Fishers of the Great Lakes, 1850–1893 74
7. The Fishers and the Fish 89

PART II. GREAT LAKES WATERS IN A DEVELOPING DRAINAGE BASIN, 1815–1900

8. Agriculture, Lumbering, Mining, and the Changing Fish Habitat 113
9. Commerce, Community Growth, Industrial-Urban Development, and the Changing Fish Habitat 137
10. The Fish React: Changing Species in Changing Waters 149

Part III. Policy Makers and the Great Lakes Fisheries, 1801–1896

11. The First Regulators: The Provinces and the States 175
12. Changing Ideas: The United States and the Great Lakes Fishery 195
13. Canada's Regulated Fishery, 1868–1888 204
14. Charles Hibbert Tupper and the New Broom, 1888–1896 216
15. To Save the Fish: The Crisis of the 1890s and the Canadian–American Joint Commission of 1892 238

Part IV. Toward Lamprey Eve: The Great Lakes Fisheries, 1896–1933

16. Commercial Fishing: From Prosperity to Recession 253
17. Policy Makers and the Ever-Widening Stain 279
18. Public Policy and the Declining Fish Resource 297
19. The End of an Era 321

20. Reflections 331

Notes 341
Glossary of Fish Species 393
Bibliography 395
Index 413

Illustrations

	Robert von Neumann, *Great Lakes Fishermen*	*frontispiece*
1.1.	Paul Kane, Indians spearfishing by torchlight	7
1.2.	Political division of the Great Lakes	13
2.1.	Atlantic salmon	20
3.1.	William Henry Bartlett, "Wellington, Prince Edward County, Lake Ontario"	32
3.2.	William Henry Bartlett, "Fish Market, Toronto"	33
3.3.	Green Bay pound net	39
3.4.	Gill net drying on a reel	40
3.5.	Mackinaw boats, Collingwood, Ontario	41
4.1.	Fishing boats, Erie, Pennsylvania	50
4.2.	Interior of a fish-packing plant	52
5.1.	Lake Superior and northern Lake Michigan, with Booth company operations	63
6.1.	Fishing station, Fitzwilliam Island	82
6.2.	Chippewa village, Sault Sainte Marie	82
6.3.	Fishing village, Jones Island	84
6.4.	Ice fishermen bringing home the catch on dogsleds	87
7.1.	Concentration of pound nets in western Lake Erie	95
7.2.	Crew of a stake boat driving stakes for a pound net	96
7.3.	Crew of a pound-net boat lifting the pot of a pound net	96
8.1.	Natural wealth of the Great Lakes basin	115
8.2.	Cutover and burned-over forestland	123
8.3.	Bird's-eye view of the Quincy, Pewabic, and Franklin mines	131
9.1.	Growth of Milwaukee and its harbor	140
10.1.	Lake whitefish	150
10.2.	Lake trout	153
10.3.	Lake herring	156

10.4. Lake sturgeon 158
10.5. Alewife 162
10.6. Carp 165
11.1. Federal hatchery, Northville, Michigan 183
13.1. Bird's-eye view of the Newcastle Hatchery 209
14.1. "Battle of Lake Erie (1894)" 232
16.1. W. F. Colby and Company gill-net steamer and the Kolbe fishing docks 254
16.2. Bay of Quinte fishermen 259
16.3. Expensive, effective technology of the harvest 260
16.4. Jabs at the powerful A. Booth and Company 270–271
16.5. Charles Livingston Bull, poster for the United States Food Administration 277
17.1. Industrial waste discharge 282
18.1. Hatchery and steamer *Shearwater* 300
18.2. Patrol cruiser *Vigilant* 310
18.3. David Starr Jordan and Edward Ernest Prince 314–315
19.1. Gill-net steamer *Earl Bess* with herring 325
19.2. Sea lamprey invasion of the Great Lakes 328
19.3. Sea lamprey attached to a lake trout and feeding 329

Tables

4.1. Total fish production, Canada and the United States, 1868–1893 46
4.2. Size and value of fish harvest, 1872–1889 48
7.1. Average size and value of catch, per fisherman, the United States and Canada, 1880–1890 90
10.1. Lake whitefish production, 1879–1899 151
10.2. Lake trout production, 1879–1899 155
10.3. Lake herring production, 1879–1899 157
10.4. Lake sturgeon production, 1879–1899 160
10.5. Great Lakes production by species groups, 1880–1903 170
16.1. Total major commercial species production, 1879–1930 256
16.2. Production of all Great Lakes fisheries by species groups, Canada and the United States, 1879–1930 257
16.3. Average catch, average value, and average investment, per fisherman, Canada and the United States, 1899–1922 262

Preface

Historians have written at length about the economic development of the Great Lakes region, stressing the role of its rich natural resources in making it one of the nation's prominent wealth producers. The growth of the fur trade, the expansion of agriculture, and the exploitation of timber and mineral resources have attracted substantial interest. Yet scholars have given tangential and piecemeal treatment to the fish and water resources of the Great Inland Seas, as nineteenth-century enthusiasts liked to call the Great Lakes. They, too, deserve careful study as part of the natural wealth that contributed to regional and national development, and as a showcase of the intricacy of natural and human relationships.

From the perspective of the Great Lakes as a geographic unit, this book recounts the history of human use of the fish resources of these waters, analyzing the changing nature of the fish population, especially the decline of the species that came to be preferred in the commercial markets: Atlantic salmon of Lake Ontario, whitefish, trout, herring, and sturgeon. These developments are best understood in the context of the mainstream of historical experience in Canada and the United States, of which they were an integral part. In seeking the explanation for change and decline, this study considers the complex interaction between physical alterations in the Great Lakes basin and the fish resource as humans adapted the natural wealth of the lakes to serve their needs. It examines the rise of an aggressive, exploitative commercial-fishing industry in which fishers who were close to the resource and entrepreneurial dealers who handled its collection, storage, and marketing competed for livelihoods, profits, and even fortunes. The third and fourth ingredients considered in this interactive composite are the policy makers who were responsible for regulating and conserving the fish resources and the marine scientists who, beginning around 1900, gathered basic information to help guide the policy makers. In probing the relationships among these four groups, this book takes into account the influences of human attitudes toward natural resources, political heritages of Americans and Canadians, the economic systems and policies of the United States and Canada, and the cultural and ethnic orientations of producers and consumers. Because this study addresses the Great Lakes as a whole, it permits a comparison of American and Canadian behavior, attitudes, and policies related to the fish resource in shared waters and the efforts of the two nations to achieve joint management.

The origins of this book stem from my work in the 1970s with the University of Wisconsin Sea Grant College Program when its director decided that the upcoming bicentennial called for humanistic input into a basically scientific-technical program. Publications and special program offerings could stimulate public interest in the past, present, and future of the Great Lakes as a way to build support for protecting and conserving the waters and marine life, he believed. Responding to these ideas, I secured Sea Grant College funds to do basic library research and fieldwork for two books written for the general public in the form of guides to the historic locations around the shores of Lakes Superior and Michigan.[1] In preparing historical essays on the main themes in the economic development of the lakes, I quickly found that the fisheries have been treated in only a piecemeal fashion in scattered articles in professional journals, have received short shrift in most local histories, and have inspired relatively few books. The very truncated treatment of the fish resource in the American Lakes Series, edited by Milo M. Quaife and published in the 1940s, seemed surprising offhand, but not on second thought, considering how heavily the authors relied on secondary literature when treating a subject that was obscure.[2] Only one author who contributed to the series, Grace Lee Nute, whose research interests in the fur trade had led her to study the early commercial fisheries of Lake Superior, gave the subject more than passing notice in her *Lake Superior.*[3]

Two books that deal with the history of the Great Lakes fishery that were published before the inauguration of the Sea Grant bicentennial projects are notable in different ways. Frank Prothero's *Good Years* is a popular social and economic history, written to honor Canada's Lake Erie fishermen. It emphasizes the uncertainty and rigorous nature of their lives and the problems created by declining harvests.[4] The other, *Fisherman's Beach,* is a novel by George Vukelich. Drawing on a storehouse of remembered family experiences, Vukelich wrote insightfully about the lives of the LeClairs, a fishing family in Two Rivers, Wisconsin, who face the total ruin of their century-old business by the spread of the sea lamprey, delineating their rigorous lives and their attitudes about Lake Michigan's fish resources.[5]

The invasion of the sea lamprey and the general concern about the environmental deterioration of the Great Lakes inspired other books, from the late 1970s to 1990. Thomas C. Kuchenberg and Jim Legault, in *Reflections in a Tarnished Mirror,* were concerned primarily with pollution problems, changing fish populations, and policy making in the wake of sea lamprey devastation.[6] William Ashworth picked up the theme of spoliation in *The Late, Great Lakes,* which deals very broadly with the causes of pollution and, to only a minor extent, with the fish population.[7] Alan B. McCullough's *Commercial Fishery of the Canadian Great Lakes,* a study done for Environment Canada, is the first historical account to describe the evolution of the fisheries industry topically by exploring its structure and regulation, technology, labor, fish stocks, federal problems, international jurisdiction, and conservation for all of Canada's waters. It is a very important contribution to the body of knowledge about the Great Lakes fisheries, and it provided real help in writing this book.[8] Timothy C. Lloyd and Patrick B. Mullen's *Lake Erie Fishermen,* a folklore and social history study based primarily on oral interviews and documentary photographs, sheds valuable light on the lives and thinking of Lake Erie fishermen in the late 1980s.[9] Finally, Robert Doherty, in *Disputed Waters,* examined both the struggle of the Ojibwes and Ottawas of Michigan during the 1970s and 1980s to exercise their treaty rights to fish and the accompanying legal battles.[10]

In addition to these books, journal articles, chapters in edited books, a few unpublished master's theses, and government publications relate parts of the history of the Great Lakes fisheries. Articles in historical journals—from Grace Lee Nute's excellent study of the American Fur Company's Lake Superior enterprise in the 1830s and 1840s to Stephen Bocking's analysis of Ontario's Great Lakes fishery policy from the 1920s to the present—provide valuable insights into aspects of the larger history.[11]

To date, there is no comprehensive history of the Great Lakes fisheries that traces economic, environmental, and policy-making themes from the wilderness period through the early twentieth century. This book suggests the legacies passed from the age of the seventeenth-and eighteenth-century explorers, fur traders, and empire builders to that of the nineteenth-century settler-developers of the Great Lakes basin. The major part of the study is organized around the relationships between the fish population and the fishers, human developmental activity in the lakes basin, and policy makers and scientists. These relationships are divided into two periods: from 1800 to 1893, when the commercial fishery developed, reached its zenith, and faced a crisis; and from 1896 to 1933, when the commercial fishery based on lake whitefish, trout, sturgeon, and herring as the old reliables declined. The book does not deal with all species of fish, but concentrates on the big four and on the changing species profile.

In considering the impact of developmental change in the drainage basin on the marine habitat of the Great Lakes, this study focuses on the sources of and reasons for declining water quality. The sources are treated in generalized categories. Known, measured specifics of pollution are scarce and relate to small areas of water, such as river mouths, streams, and harbors. The findings here are "probabilities" or "possibilities," and their tentative nature is so designated.

This study emphasizes the relationship between fish and humans in their many roles as fishers, policy makers, entrepreneurial fish dealers, marine scientists, consumers, conservationists, environmentalists, sport-fishing enthusiasts, politicians, creators of ever more efficient harvest technology, and inventors of a network of arbitrary governing jurisdictions unrelated to the realities of the natural world. The time frame designated in the title begins in 1783, the date of the first major political division of Great Lakes waters, and ends in 1933, the year when the sea lamprey made its way into Lake Huron, wreaking devastation on the lake trout population, and when, in disillusionment, the Great Lakes states and Ontario abandoned their efforts to develop uniform regulations for Lake Erie, a goal that had been sought for more than a half century.

This study has been a large undertaking, perhaps too ambitious given the vast differences in the physical conditions in the lakes, with their twenty identified ecoregions, each exhibiting its own set of variations,[12] and given the complex relationships among fish life, water pollution, intruded species, a market-driven commercial-fishing industry, scientific research, democratic politics, and changing public attitudes about the resource. Undoubtedly, future studies will make the many nuances apparent, but meanwhile a general picture based on commonalities among regions can reveal much about past human experience as part of the natural world of the Great Lakes at a time when marine resources in the oceans, lakes, and rivers of the world are a major concern.

A former chairman of the Wisconsin Natural Resources Board said that he was glad I was writing this book because he had found it very difficult to gain an understanding of the history of the Great Lakes fisheries: "Fish are here and there and everywhere, but in no particular context in the literature."[13] A marine biologist who lives on the Keweenaw Peninsula of Michigan, when told about the project and startled by its size, remarked, "It's like the rise and fall of the Roman Empire!" One historian said that it was not worth the effort, but most environmental historians have been supportive. As an environmental historian, I believe it highly important to study the ways in which people have interacted with the physical world around them, seeking very specific knowledge of how humans used resources, why they utilized them as they did, and what the consequences of that use were. The story of the commercial exploitation of the Great Lakes fisheries is one part of that relationship, significant as environmental history, as history of economic development in the North American midcontinent, and as part of a tradition of using aquatic resources that stretches back for centuries.[14]

Acknowledgments

Many archives, libraries, institutions, and people have helped make this study possible. To the University of Wisconsin College Sea Grant Program, I am especially indebted for the research funding in the 1970s that introduced me to the possibilities for research on the Great Lakes fisheries. Later the University of Wisconsin's sabbatical program and the Graduate School's grant of salary support and travel funds enabled me to gather widely scattered archival materials in order to lay a foundation for this study.

To the staffs of the National Archives of the United States and the National Archives of Canada, I am especially grateful for assistance in locating relevant collections of documents essential for this study. I owe a special thanks to the archivists and librarians of the Minnesota Historical Society, the Minnesota State Archives, the State Historical Society of Wisconsin, the Michigan State Archives, the Michigan State Library, the Wisconsin Maritime Museum, the Chicago Historical Society, the Milwaukee County Historical Society, the Baker Library at the Harvard University Graduate School of Business Administration, the J. J. Talman Regional Collection of the D. B. Weldon Library at the University of Western Ontario, the Green and Law Libraries at Stanford University, and the University of Wisconsin–Madison libraries, especially Steenbock Memorial, Geography, Map and Air Photo, Biology, Memorial, Law, and Health Sciences.

Among the people who proved outstandingly helpful were the group in Bayfield, Wisconsin, including Nancy Reiten Bainbridge, Marjorie Benton, Richard Bodin, Eleanor Knight, and Sheree Peterson, who in the early 1990s shared their knowledge of fisheries history. I am especially grateful to David L. Snyder, former historian at the Apostle Islands National Lakeshore, who made extraordinary efforts to facilitate research in the Apostle Islands historical records and to identify contacts in the community. Norman W. Larson of Cornucopia, Wisconsin, generously supplied leads to source materials he found while studying the Cornucopia fishing business. Isco Valli, director of the Wisconsin Maritime Museum, strongly supported this research effort and helped broaden and deepen my understanding by naming me as a consultant to the museum's projects on Great Lakes maritime history generally and the commercial fisheries specifically.

Others who lent exceptional help to the project over an extended period of time are Loraine Adkins, Ellen Burke, John Peters, and Donna Sereda, of the State Historical Society of Wisconsin, and the late Kathy Jones, my able staff assistant at the University of Wisconsin for a quarter century. Trish Canaday, Thomas R. Huffman, and Mark Marlaire contributed significantly to search tasks. To the many staff members of the environmental agencies of Canadian, United States, and state governments, I am indebted for their interest and helpful recommendations about sources of information. Special thanks are due to Jan Lindquist of the Ontario Ministry of the Environment, to Dr. John M. Casseslan of the Ontario Ministry of Natural Resources, and to William Horn, Larry Lynch, and Karl Scheidegger of the Wisconsin Department of Natural Resources. Among the members of a very supportive University of Wisconsin College Sea Grant Program, I am much indebted to Mary Lou Reeb and Robert A. Ragotzkie. Credit for the excellence of the maps goes to two people especially: Onno Brouwer and Juliet Landa of the Cartographic Laboratory, University of Wisconsin–Madison.

For moral and scholarly support, I am grateful to Allan G. Bogue, Jane T. Schulenburg, and Michael Conzen. For his dedication to rigorous, intensive, and meticulous research in new fields of study, the late Paul W. Gates, who directed my doctoral work at Cornell University long ago, remains an inspiration. Two young scholars who critically read the manuscript for the University of Wisconsin Press, Kurkpatrick Dorsey of the University of New Hampshire and Stephen Bocking of Trent University, have helped immeasurably with their suggestions for change and improvement.

Historians who venture into the unfamiliar territory of other disciplines need help. Lee T. Kernen, retired director of Wisconsin fisheries for the Wisconsin Department of Natural Resources, helped me by critiquing the manuscript and making many valuable suggestions.

Particularly do I wish to express my gratitude to a good friend, the late Louise Wyatt, who delighted in fielding numerous questions about this manuscript through her diligent research in the library in London,

Ontario, and who followed the Canadian press for reports on the status of the Great Lakes fisheries in Canada and forwarded the clippings. Mary Elizabeth Braun, formerly acquisitions editor at the University of Wisconsin Press, through her intellectual interest in and advocacy of this study, helped immeasurably to make its publication a reality, as did Scott Lenz, senior editor of the press who skillfully shepherded the book through the rigors of publication.

Fishing the Great Lakes

I

Legacies from the Wilderness

Dexterity and Strength Are Needed

In the late nineteenth century, fishers, public officials charged with conserving fish resources, and many people in the Great Lakes region expressed concern about the decline of choice commercial species in Great Lakes waters. They spoke alarmingly of crises, danger lines, and extinction. Most believed that the problem had developed in the preceding few decades, and they blamed the fishers. In reality, its roots extended to the wilderness period of the seventeenth and eighteenth centuries. At that time, human activity to sustain life, policy decisions inherent in intercolonial rivalries, and commerce set long-lasting precedents whose effects lingered for hundreds of years, significantly shaping the contours of Great Lakes commercial fishing as it developed. To understand the relationships between fish and people in the following centuries, this study begins with an examination of legacies from the wilderness era, first addressing the physical legacy of lakes and fish.

THE LAKES AND THE FISH

No matter how you consider them, whether looking at a satellite photograph, viewing them from high in the air, or pondering their measurements, the Great Lakes are an impressive expanse of water, the largest body of freshwater in the world. Their beauty and utility have impressed people for thousands of years. Among the very early recorded reactions was that of Father Claude Dablon, a Jesuit missionary. In October 1655, he found the entrance to Lake Ontario an inspiring sight, and he later described how he had felt when his canoe propelled and guided by Indians entered the lake along the northern shore: "Such a scene of awe-inspiring beauty I have never beheld,—nothing but islands and huge masses of rock, as large as cities, all covered with cedars and firs." After crossing to the southern side, the missionary's party passed "through a multitude of Islands, large and small, after which we saw nothing but water on all sides."[1]

The Great Lakes cover 94,250 square miles and hold 5,439 cubic miles of water stretching from Kingston, Ontario, on the east to Duluth, Minnesota, on the west, approximately 780 miles away, and from Gary, Indiana, on Lake Michigan's southern shore to Nipigon, Ontario, on Lake Superior's northern shore 500 miles away. The shorelines stretch for 10,210 miles. Lake Superior is the largest, coldest, and deepest of the Great Lakes, averaging 483 feet and plunging to as much as 1,330 feet, and Erie is the warmest and shallowest, averaging 62 feet in depth. Retention time, the length of time it would take for the water in a lake to flow out, calculated from volume and mean rate of outflow, varies: 191 years for Superior, 99 for Michigan, 22 for Huron, 6 for Ontario, and 2.6 for Erie. The lakes are very different in appearance as well as in physical characteristics. Moreover, the land area of the Great Lakes basin, covering 201,460 square miles, falls into distinctive northern and southern segments whose climates, soils, topography, original vegetation, and animal life have produced two major living environments. The northern part (Lake Superior and northern Lakes Huron and Michigan) has a colder climate, granite bedrock, thin acidic soils, original land cover dominated by conifer forests, and rocky lake shorelines. In 1600, the southern portion of the Great Lakes basin (Lakes Erie and Ontario and southern Lakes Huron and Michigan) was covered mainly by deciduous forests, with some areas of grassland and woodland intermixed. Deeper, more fertile soils, warmer temperatures, and a longer growing season made it more habitable than the northern area. Animal life differed between the two regions, being far more plentiful in the south where both game and fish abounded. In the north, fish were plentiful and game animals more scarce. Land cover of the basin remained minimally disturbed, and the lake waters were a relatively stable habitat for marine life in 1600.[2]

From the writings of seventeenth-century explorers, fur traders, and missionaries come the earliest descriptions of fish life in the Great Lakes and their tributary rivers and streams. Very large mature trout and whitefish in Lake Superior, large Atlantic salmon in Lake Ontario, and giant sturgeon in all the lakes particularly drew attention. Gabriel Sagard wrote from his observations in 1623 and 1624 about both the abundance of fish caught in nets in Lake Huron in November and the amazing size of some:

"For indeed in this Fresh-water Sea there are sturgeon, *Assihendos* [white-fish], trout, and pike of such monstrous size that nowhere else are they to be found bigger, and it is the same with many other species of fish that are unknown to us here [in France]." [3]

Similarly Antoine Cadillac, French commandant of Michilimackinac, found the fish and fishing very impressive. About the settlement of the Ottawas there in 1695, he remarked, "The great abundance of fish and the convenience of the place for fishing have caused the Indians to make a fixed settlement in those parts. It is a daily manna, which never fails." He spoke of the pleasure of seeing fishermen "bring up" a net filled with "as many as a hundred whitefish." He rated that species the most delicate in the lake. The Ottawas also caught trout as large as fifty pounds, sturgeon, pike, herring, and walleye, "and a hundred different kinds of fish abound at this part of the lake."[4]

Instructed to record what they observed about the physical world around them and the Indian peoples they hoped to convert to Christianity, the Jesuit missionaries often did so in considerable detail, frequently marveling at the abundance of fish and game and commenting on their size and the Indian methods of fishing, leaving for posterity their observations in the *Jesuit Relations.*[5] Yet given seventeenth-century descriptions of Great Lakes fish life, it is impossible to identify all the species in the lakes at the time of European contact or to estimate accurately the volume of fish life. We can safely assume that the lakes were not overfished or the large mature fish so often mentioned by the Europeans would not have been as plentiful as they apparently were. The seventeenth-century Europeans observed the lakes at a time when the land cover was relatively undisturbed and the drainage basin supported a small population. Wilderness conditions with substantial areas of oxygen-rich lake waters must have been optimal for the Atlantic salmon, lake whitefish, trout, sturgeon, and herring so attractive to latter-day arrivals.

THE FIRST FISHERS

For thousands of years before the coming of European explorers, the Indians depended on the fish of the Great Lakes for food. They were the first fishers. According to archaeological evidence, by 3000 to 2000 B.C. they used a broad range of fishing gear developed and adapted over long periods of time, including spears, gaffs, hooks and lines, and weirs in the upper Great Lakes. In the lower Great Lakes as early as 2500 B.C., these implements were supplemented by nets, probably an adaptation of nets used in hunting, while net fishing apparently began later in the northern segment, sometime between 300 and 200 B.C. While fish supplemented game and plants as important sources of food in the southern parts of the basin, in the northern Great Lakes, given the less abundant animal and plant food, fish became a major food source. Anthropologist Charles E. Cleland, a leading authority on the inland shore fishery of the northern Great Lakes, believes that this "unique" prehistoric fishery "provides the most important single organizing concept for understanding the cultural development of this region." Widely dispersed through lake waters through most of the year, the fish became a "regular, predictable" food source during the spring and fall spawning seasons. That spawning cycle, Cleland believes, is "the key to understanding the evolution of subsistence and settlement systems of the upper Great Lakes Indians."[6]

Harold Hickerson also emphasizes the importance of fish as a source of food among the precontact Indians, who before 1620 occupied the upper Great Lakes shoreline area to the north and west of Sault Sainte Marie and along the North Channel of Lake Huron eastward to Lake Nipissing, living in primarily "self-sufficient and self-contained" groups of perhaps as many as 100 to 150.[7]

In the seventeenth century, incoming Europeans found the Indians of the Great Lakes using the technology developed over the past thousands of years. Samuel de Champlain described gill-net fishing through the ice in Georgian Bay in 1615, and Henri Joutel wrote of gillnetting at Mackinac in open water in 1687.[8]

Ojibwe hoop-net fishing in the rapids of the St. Mary's River, spectacular and easily observed, caught the attention of those passing between Lakes Huron and Superior from the seventeenth until the early twentieth century. Father Claude Dablon noted in 1669 that at the foot of the rapids, "even amid those boiling waters," from spring to winter the Indians caught the plentiful whitefish, which were "very white," "very excellent," and a major source of food. He observed:

> Dexterity and strength are needed for this kind of fishing: for one must stand upright in a bark canoe, and there, among the whirlpools, with muscles tense, thrust deep into the water a rod, at the end of which is fastened a net made in the form of a pocket, into which the fish are made to enter. One must look for them as they glide between the rocks, pursue them when they are seen; and when they have been made to enter the net, raise them with a sudden strong pull into the canoe.[9]

Whether fishing the rapids of the St. Mary's River or the calmer rivers and inshore waters of the Great Lakes, the Indians of the northern Great Lakes used the birch-bark canoe, a craft so skillfully designed that it has drawn the admiration of the earliest incoming Europeans as well as the praise of canoeists through the centuries since. The construction materials used were white cedar for the structure; white birch bark for the covering;

Figure 1.1. Paul Kane made the sketch for this painting of Indians spearfishing by torchlight on the Fox River, southwest of Green Bay, Wisconsin, on his way west. He commented that "by night, this has always been a very picturesque appearance, the strong red glare of the blazing pine knots and roots in the iron frame, or light-jack, at the bow of the canoe throwing the naked figure of the Indians into wild relief upon the dark water and sombre woods." (From Paul Kane, *Wanderings of an Artist among the Indians of North America* [London: Longman, Brown, Green, Longmans and Roberts, 1859], 31; photograph courtesy Royal Ontario Museum, Toronto)

coarse thread made from the roots of tamarack, spruce, and jack pine for sewing; and pine pitch with charcoal added for sealing the seams.[10]

Incoming Europeans commented particularly on night spearfishing. Using torchlight to spot the fish, the Indian fisher stood in the bow of the canoe and wielded a harpoon-like spear (figure 1.1). In the 1650s, a Jesuit missionary spoke of this method, which continued to draw attention in the nineteenth century and to arouse bitter controversy in the twentieth. It was common along the northwestern shore of Lake Ontario in the 1830s and in the Fox River of Green Bay a decade later.[11]

At the time of European contact, Great Lakes Indians fished cooperatively within families, bands, and clans. The work roles were clearly defined: women gathered the nettles and hemp to make fibers into fine cord for netting by spinning and twisting it "on their bare thighs," and men apparently made the gill nets; men fished, and women preserved and stored the catch.[12] Indians fished primarily for food and, to some extent, used fish for barter in their trade networks.[13]

From her extensive research done in preparation of the *Atlas of Great*

Lakes Indian History, Helen Hornbeck Tanner concluded that by around A.D. 1000 the Indians of the region, after centuries of experimentation, had developed four major subsistence patterns. Those located in the southern Great Lakes basin relied mainly on domesticated plants. Indian groups to the north and northeast of the Great Lakes placed major emphasis on hunting. Wild rice provided the mainstay of the third subsistence pattern followed by Indians who lived in the deciduous–coniferous forest to the west of Lake Michigan and stretching north to Lake Superior's southern and western shores. Great Lakes fish provided the main sustenance for Indians in the fourth subsistence category: Ottawas, Ojibwes, and some of the Hurons of northern Lakes Michigan and Huron and eastern Lake Superior. In no case was the mainstay of a subsistence pattern the sole source of food; rather, the principal one combined with other available resources. Indian inshore fishing occurred around the shores of all the Great Lakes. Tanner concluded that "the evidence suggests that a stable balance was reached in which population, group size, seasonal movements, and the division of labor combined to produce a successful accommodation to specific sets of environmental resources."[14]

With the coming of European explorers, traders, and missionaries in search of empire, wealth, and Christian converts, the patterns of subsistence culture changed somewhat in the seventeenth century and more so in the eighteenth. Indians bartered fish, furs, and other products of their labor for trade goods. Later they also supplied soldiers of the French and British colonial powers in Detroit, Sault Sainte Marie, Green Bay, and Michilimackinac. Yet according to Richard White's study, the Indians in the Great Lakes region retained and used the skills of subsistence life to a far greater degree during the French period than has been supposed in much scholarship on the fur trade.[15]

Remnants of the subsistence patterns long remained in those parts of the Great Lakes basin where a sparse population and agricultural, lumbering, and mining development did not destroy them. For example, the Ottawas in the northern parts of the Lower Peninsula of Michigan clung to traditional subsistence activity, combining it with seasonal wage labor in the late nineteenth century.[16]

Did the Great Lakes Indians at the time of European contact intentionally conserve fish resources? Logically the answer is yes, because they relied on them for sustenance. As many have suggested, Indian fishing technology and population size in relation to the fish resource could have produced a conservative use pattern without a conscious effort to conserve. Very practical considerations, such as transporting large quantities of fish for a long distance, would tend to discourage overfishing, even taking into account the use of fish as a trade item. Practically speaking, why take more fish than could be used?

Moreover, Indian animistic beliefs encouraged a conservative exploitation of natural food sources. As Christopher Vecsey has explained the human–animal relationship at the time of European contact, Ojibwes believed that humans, animals, plants, and inanimate entities possessed souls. Indians were one part of the cosmos and not superior to others. They tried to cultivate positive, respectful relationships with the manitos, very powerful spirits, principal among them the Four Winds, the Underworld Manito, the Thunderbirds, and the Owners of Nature, all of whom controlled food sources and the ability of the Indians to sustain life. In the Nanabashu creation myth, Nanabashu established the right of the Indians to hunt in order to survive, an activity in which, regretfully, animals sacrificed their lives to provide subsistence for humans. *Subsistence* was the object. While "it was the duty of the manitos to keep the Ojibwa alive and healthy," the Indians also had obligations to the Owners of Nature, each of whom was responsible for the well-being of an animal group. They had to treat animal life with respect, which required performing rituals, preserving animal bones, offering tobacco, thanking the Owner for the kill, and the like. Alienate the Owners of Nature—by incorrectly conducting rituals, violating taboos, indiscriminately killing animals, torturing animals before killing them, or bestiality—and failure in the food quest or outbreak of disease would follow. If one accepts as evidence critically analyzed writings of European observers at the time of contact, and traditions and legends that probably originated in the prehistoric period, this system of belief must have tempered the ways in which the Indians used plant and animal life, including fish.[17]

Those beliefs and values, as understood in 1600, would be challenged by Europeans, with their very different ideas about religion and the wealth of the natural world. Where, when, and how Indian ideas changed remains a matter of controversy.[18]

DIVIDING THE LAKES AND THE FISHES

Wilderness conditions and the pattern of Indian subsistence fishing around the shores of Lakes Ontario and Erie gradually changed in the late eighteenth century as a result of a series of British and American political decisions that encouraged the development of the eastern Great Lakes basin. The governments acted in response to their continuing rivalries after the American Revolution and the pressures of a growing population that had spilled west beyond the Allegheny Mountains even before 1776. While the policies dealt with immediate problems of governance, they had a long-term influence on the marine resources of the lakes and the adjacent Indian population. The principal components of the United States formula that transformed the wilderness into an early agricultural and commercial economy were the Treaty of Paris of 1783, the Land Ordinance of 1785, the Northwest Ordinance and the Constitution, both drafted in 1787, and an aggressive policy of subduing rebellious Indians by means of military force, treaties of land cession, and removal put in place to counter British influence and to encourage white settlement. Survey of land and its sale to settlers and investors followed.

The process was somewhat different in British North America, but the results were the same. Assistance after 1783 in the form of land, tools, and clothing given to British Loyalists who were leaving the United States to reestablish themselves under the jurisdiction of the Crown led to a nucleus of settlements in the Kingston–Bay of Quinte area at the eastern end of Lake Ontario and to another group of settlements on the Niagara Peninsula in the mid-1780s. By 1789, the population of all these communities, in the area later known as Ontario, had grown to about 10,000. The Constitutional Act of 1791, which separated the province of Quebec into Upper and Lower Canada and gave each jurisdiction a two-house legislature, served as another milestone in British policy that encouraged development in the wilderness around Lakes Ontario and Erie as a bulwark against expansive Americans. John Simcoe, the first governor of Upper Canada, encouraged the new legislature to make the province a model of the British system, with English common law as the rule for controversies over property and civil rights. The creation of counties, surveying and selling land at low prices, road construction, and publicity extolling the area as a prime farming region were all parts of Simcoe's policy from 1792 to 1796, which encouraged agriculture before 1800.[19]

The British and American common goal of agricultural development in the Great Lakes region led to the influx of people, early removal of the original land cover and exposure of soils to erosion, destruction of the moisture-retaining qualities of the trees and grasses sacrificed for cropland, and damming of streams and rivers to harness waterpower to operate mills, all of which made an impact on natural waters and, in the case of dams, impeded the migration of fish from lakes to upstream spawning grounds. These changes along the shores of Lakes Ontario and Erie by the turn of the nineteenth century were small, to be sure, but they marked the beginning of an early agricultural-commercial economy that grew to real significance a quarter century later. Moreover, the American assertion of authority over the Indians in the Ohio country before 1800 set the pattern for negotiated treaties, land cessions, reservations, and removals that so severely circumscribed the Indians' ancient, already modified yet enduring subsistence pattern of Great Lakes fishing.

Other influences arising in the political-diplomatic cauldron of the late eighteenth century ultimately had devastating consequences for the Great Lakes water and fish resources.[20] In 1783, the American and British commissioners meeting in Paris to draft a peace treaty drew a boundary between the United States and British North America using an accepted principle of international law: when nations border on bodies of water, the boundary should run through the middle of the lake, river, or bay. The British favored an interpretation of the "middle" formula, according to which the boundary was drawn equidistant from the opposite shores, unless this line would divide islands in two. The Americans agreed with this idea for the Great Lakes, but wanted to use a newly emerging principle in international law for dividing the rivers that connected them. What came to be known as the thalweg principle appealed to the Americans because it used the main navigable channel as the boundary rather than a line equidistant from either shore. In the nineteenth century, the United States and Great Britain finally settled the river boundaries by a series of conventions that employed the thalweg formula.[21]

The Great Lakes international boundary divided the waters roughly through the middle of Lakes Ontario, Erie, Huron, and Superior, giving approximately one-third of the total water surface to Canada and two-thirds to the United States. In an age innocent of the idea of managing naturally unified land and water resources as a whole to conserve them, treaty makers did not consider the desirability of drawing boundaries that conformed with nature's reality. Nor did they think about the consequences of the division of lake waters for marine life. A strong sense of territoriality, with each side striving for the more generous settlement, dominated negotiations. More divisions of lake waters followed.

Once the young republic had devised a policy, outlined in the Northwest Ordinance of 1787, for the governance of the area west of the Allegheny Mountains and north of the Ohio River, and running west to the Mississippi River and north to the Great Lakes, the stage was set for further boundary complications. Anxious to avoid the kind of problems that Great Britain had encountered by failing to devise a satisfactory system of administering the unsettled frontier areas to the west of the Atlantic coastal colonies, the authors of the ordinance drafted a document that assured a system of government on the outer fringes of settlement compatible with the fundamental principles of the state and national governments and a process of moving from territory to statehood that guaranteed newly created states equality with the older states. The ordinance stipulated that "not less than three nor more than five" states would be carved from the Northwest Territory, and five eventually were: Ohio was admitted in 1803; Indiana, in 1816; Illinois, in 1818; Michigan, in 1837; and Wisconsin, in 1848. When Congress drew up the enabling acts for the admission of the states, each law included the portions of the Great Lakes adjacent to the state's boundaries. Thus Ohio's northern border coincided with the international boundary in Lake Erie by a system that projected the state's eastern and western borders on land due north to the Canadian–American division of Lake Erie. A different example of divided waters occurs in Lake Michigan, which is located entirely within the United States. The enabling acts divided the lake between Michigan and Wisconsin, but gave small parts of it to Indiana and Illinois.[22]

In Canada, the Great Lakes have always been within a single governing jurisdiction. Title to the waters and beds of the Great Lakes, which lie within Ontario, is vested in the Crown in the right of the province and not in the Dominion of Canada, which was created by the British North America Act of 1867. This proprietary right existed before the establishment of the dominion and was not affected by it, but the act gave the authority to regulate fisheries to the dominion parliament.[23] After many years of tussling between Ottawa and Toronto, Ontario had assumed the management of its fisheries by the late 1920s.

In 1787, the same year that Congress enacted the Northwest Ordinance, the delegates to the Constitutional Convention met in Philadelphia to restructure the national government. When they finished their work, the authority to regulate fisheries was not designated as an enumerated power of Congress. Thus the states interpreted it as a power reserved for them under the Tenth Amendment, and so it remains. That seemed very appropriate in 1787, for each colony had regulated fishing during the colonial period. Each of eight Great Lakes states—New York, Pennsylvania, Ohio, Indiana, Illinois, Michigan, Wisconsin, and Minnesota—still makes fishery rules for its Great Lakes waters.

The balkanizing of the Great Lakes into a complex pattern of ownership in the eighteenth and early nineteenth centuries endures today, with a total of nine governments in two countries making fishery rules and regulations, no two of them the same, despite repeated efforts to achieve uniformity (figure 1.2). The international division of the lakes in 1783 and the system conceived in 1787 by the United States while the Great Lakes region was still a wilderness have left present-day marine conservationists with a major impediment to unified management and regulation.

HOW TO SAVE THE FISH

One further legacy from the wilderness era with long-term repercussions on the Great Lakes fish population originated in British colonial policy. By the seventeenth century, the British had developed a set of ideas about the fisheries in the waters adjacent to the British Isles that ranged from the recognition of their national importance to the legal relationship of the Crown and British subjects to fish and fishing. These included the beliefs that Parliament should regulate the fisheries and conserve fish as a valuable source of food, that commercial fishing was a significant way to

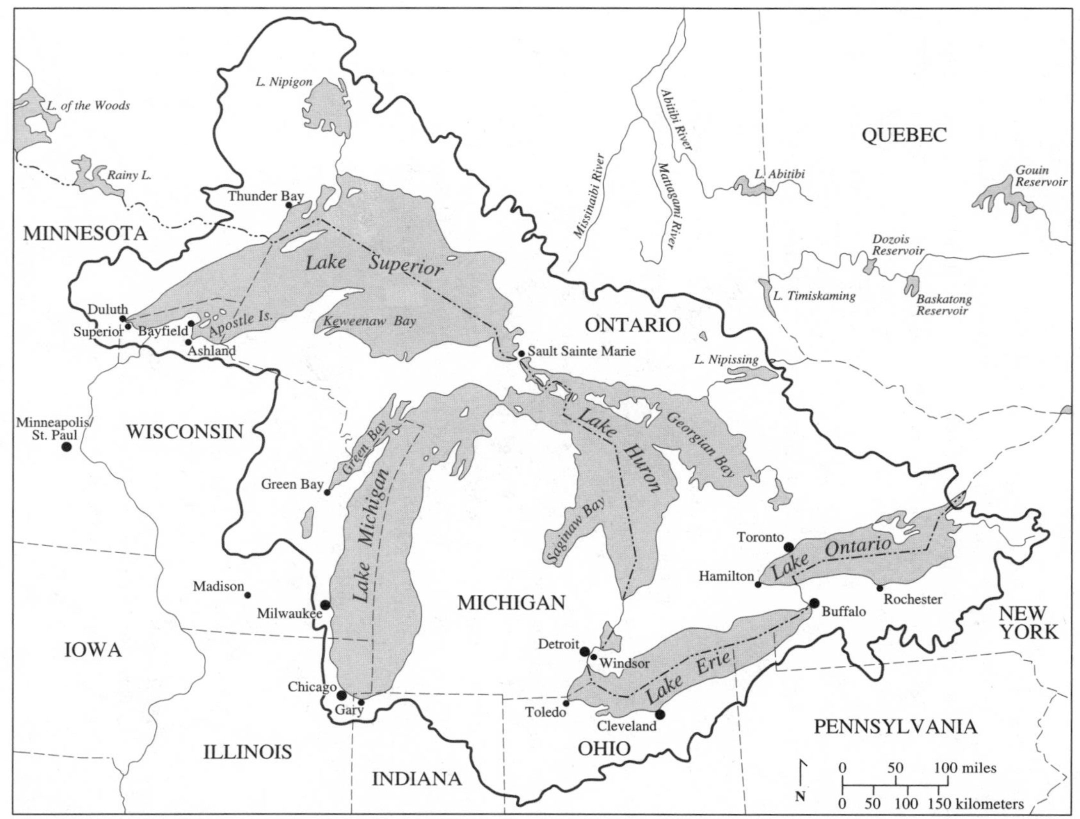

Figure 1.2. Political division of the Great Lakes. This patchwork of jurisdictions created multiple policy makers for the fisheries: eight states, one province, and two national governments. (Cartographic Laboratory, University of Wisconsin–Madison)

enhance national wealth and interests, and that sea fishing was "a nursery for our seamen." In the era of North American colonization, common law held that all British subjects had the right to use the public fisheries of the seas and the navigable rivers of the British Isles. The fish were common property, although subject to regulation designed to conserve them for the nation as a whole. From Magna Carta in the twelfth century through the eighteenth century, British fishery laws expressed these ideas, which, not coincidentally, are strikingly similar those used by the Great Lakes states, the province of Ontario, and the dominion government to conserve the lake fisheries in the nineteenth and early twentieth centuries. These ideas passed from England to the British colonies and provinces of North America, and, once legally established on the Atlantic seaboard, the precedents passed into the legal codes of the states of the Great Lakes region, as newly organized governments borrowed directly and heavily from the established codes of the states and provinces that bordered the Atlantic.

By the time settlement spread to the shores of the Great Lakes, seventeenth- and eighteenth-century eastern legislators had developed a remarkable series of rules designed to preserve the fish, or, in more modern language, to sustain the yield. While no state or province had enacted a systematic body of protective legislation and none consistently enforced its laws, taken in toto these laws subscribed to most of the conservation ideas found in fishery policies for the Great Lakes developed by the states, the United States, the province of Ontario, and the Dominion of Canada until the mid-twentieth century: open passageways for fish in spawning streams, closed seasons, prohibitions on the possession or sale of species taken in the closed season, protected areas, special rules for favored species, regulation of net and seine use (time, place, mesh size, depth of set), limits on the number of legal fishing days per week, permit requirements, limits on the size and use of the catch, restrictions on nonresidents, limits on the amount and kind of gear and equipment used, prohibitions on the dumping of fish offal and ship ballast into fishing waters, prohibitions on the use of poison to enhance the catch, encouragement to stock the waters, and, finally, support of interstate cooperation in regulating fisheries in shared waters. These protective measures, along with a track record of little success in fishery conservation, were transferred by legal codes and accepted practice into the Great Lakes region. Yet the idea of managing the fish for long-term use would surface repeatedly, making its appearance on the statute books of New York and Upper Canada very early in the nineteenth century, as the transition from wilderness to an agricultural-commercial economy around the shores of Lake Ontario began in earnest, and the lake's Atlantic salmon became a casualty of development.[24]

Legacies from the Wilderness

By 1800, human experience during the centuries-long wilderness period had left Euro–North Americans with visions of the Great Lakes as grand avenues of transportation, an entrée to the midcontinent, and as suppliers of a limitless store of fish, a never-ending source of food for Indian subsistence fishers and explorers, missionaries, and fur traders. British traditions and colonial rivalries in the eighteenth century had left the great water resource politically divided, with the potential for further divisions, and threatened because of a history of weak regulation to conserve the fish resources. That legal heritage lived on during the next two centuries, influencing fish, fishers, and policy makers for Great Lakes marine resources. In the wilderness period, two use patterns for Great Lakes fish coexisted: the Indian subsistence pattern, which left the Great Lakes fish resource in a healthy condition at the turn of the nineteenth century, and the western European commercial-fishing pattern, introduced along with the fur trade, which changed and developed during the nineteenth century in highly destructive ways and contributed to the declining quality of Great Lakes commercial fish populations, despite the efforts of conservationists and policy makers to stem the tide. The fur trade itself left a heritage of unlimited commercial exploitation of a free natural resource, the beavers. With the devastation of these dam-building creators of ponds and swampy areas went a wilderness legacy of eroded wetlands, which in the long run made an impact on the Great Lakes fish habitat.[25] Thus the wilderness era left a heritage of ideas, political decisions, and economic behavior that would long influence the way people transformed the rich wilderness of land, lake, and animal and marine life.

Part I

The Rise of Commercial Fishing 1800–1893

Commercial fishing on the Great Lakes evolved slowly until the mid-nineteenth century, when in response to population growth, wider markets, improved transportation, and new techniques of harvest and preservation, it escalated, reaching a climax in 1889 in an atmosphere of concern about the future of the industry. The following six chapters analyze the growth of the commercial-fishing industry, showing how a complex of historical developments had devastating repercussions on the Great Lakes fish resource and how people's relation to and attitudes about the resource changed.

2

Lake Ontario Salmon in an Early Agricultural-Commercial Economy

The Murder on the Spawning Grounds

The salmon of Lake Ontario (*Salmo salar*), a landlocked Atlantic salmon, are unique in the annals of Great Lakes commercial fishing. Prized as food and environmentally very sensitive, they survived settlement and development for only a short time, becoming the first of the large commercial species to be decimated (figure 2.1). Legislators in Canada and the United States made them the first target for regulation in the early nineteenth century. Contemporaries left for posterity a larger store of recorded information about *Salmo salar* and their relationship to humans than about any other species in the Great Lakes. In the process, they delineated the ways in which both Indians and Euro-Americans living around Lake Ontario made the transition from subsistence to commercial fishing, a change that is extremely difficult to document. Finally, the early destruction of the Atlantic salmon is the most dramatic and devastating example of the impact of environmental change and commercial fishing on Great Lakes species during the nineteenth century, containing most of the elements of the general scenario of decline that followed.

Long an important food for the Indians of the Lake Ontario–St. Lawrence drainage basin, salmon nurtured the French in the seventeenth cen-

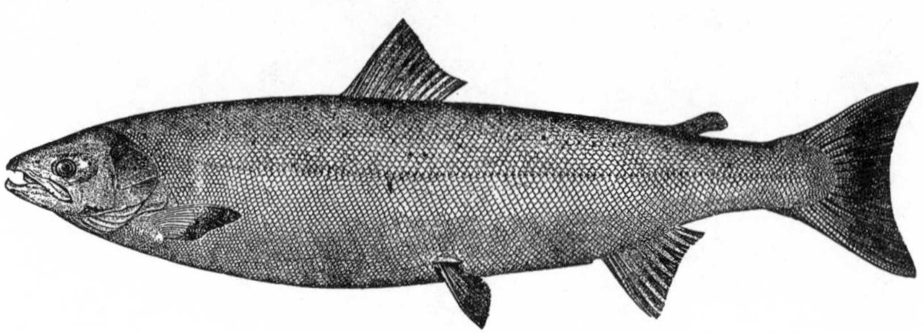

Figure 2.1. Atlantic salmon (*Salmo salar)*. (From Ontario, *Sessional Papers,* 1892, no. 79, pl. 19)

tury and subsequent Europeans in the wilderness. During the wilderness and pioneering era, by all accounts, salmon abounded in the lower St. Lawrence and its tributaries. Above the tide line at Trois Rivières, Quebec, they frequented the St. Francis River and via the Richelieu made their way into Lake Champlain. Caught at Cape Vincent, Chaumont, and Kingston at the juncture of Lake Ontario and the St. Lawrence, they ascended the rivers flowing into the Bay of Quinte, including the Salmon. To the west along the northern shore of Lake Ontario every fall at spawning time, they jostled and crowded into the Don, Humber, Rouge, and Credit Rivers until their waters were literally alive. They sought the clear, cool gravel-bottomed shallows of lesser streams and creeks as well. Fishers found large numbers of salmon in Toronto and Burlington Bays. Artist Paul Kane watched fishermen take them by torchlight and spear in Toronto Bay during his youth in the early nineteenth century. Along the southern shore of Lake Ontario, the Salmon, Oswego, and Genesee were major salmon rivers. As on the northern shore, minor streams tributary to the lake furnished spawning beds. The Niagara River lacked such places, and the falls deterred the fish from moving into Lake Erie.[1]

What manner of fish population was this: the Atlantic salmon (*Salmo salar*) or a close relative? How extensive was its population? What were the lake salmon's physical characteristics, life-cycle patterns, and habitat needs? Relying on the writings of those who knew the salmon of Lake Ontario, from the Jesuits of the seventeenth century to the settler-developers of the nineteenth, a reasonably accurate image can be created.

For want of an actual count of Lake Ontario's salmon population, consider the clues left by a number of early-nineteenth-century travelers and residents. They recounted that, on both the northern and southern shores of Lake Ontario, spawners swarmed up rivers and creeks in such numbers that settlers could catch them without fishing gear. The Superintendent of Fisheries for Upper Canada stated in a report written in 1859:

"I have seen them from 1812 to 1815, swarming the rivers so thickly, that they were thrown out with a shovel, and even with the hand." A fish dealer in Pulaski, New York, on the Salmon River, whose fishing experience there spanned the years 1825 to 1880, told of two fishermen having caught 230 salmon in four hours one night in October 1836, while two others pulled in 200: "Twelve skiffs in one night have taken an average of three hundred Salmon each." During his fishing experience, he noted, "we have had fifteen hundred fresh Salmon in the fish-house at one time."[2]

Silas Davis, a settler in Mexico Township, Oswego County, New York, recalled how every autumn his family would catch fifteen to twenty barrels of salmon. B. E. Ingersoll of Oswego, New York, told investigating commissioners of the Canadian and United States governments that his father and uncle had speared salmon on the river: "There was one store here which made a bargain with them to take what salmon they could catch at 2 cents a pound, and at the end of 10 days the man offered them $50 if they would let him back out." Samuel Wilmot, Canada's pioneer fish culturist, reported in 1869 that older settlers near Wilmot's Creek, a relatively small stream emptying into Lake Ontario forty miles east of Toronto, recalled catches of as many as 1,000 in one night thirty to forty years earlier. He later cited his memory of a harvest by canoe and torchlight of 2,000 pounds of salmon in one night at the juncture of Wilmot's Creek and Lake Ontario.[3] John Barret Van Vlack recalled large runs up the Credit River every spring in the 1840s. Before settlement, an early pioneer in the area told him, the Indians caught salmon by the thousands "for their own use" and hung them to dry along the banks of rivers and creeks.[4]

Their size and quality made the Lake Ontario salmon highly desirable as table fare to incoming Euro-Americans. They ranged from about eight pounds for a young adult to as much as thirty to forty pounds. The largest ever caught in the Salmon River of New York, according to a fisherman with fifty-five years' experience there, weighed 44.75 pounds.[5] Despite statements of their detractors, who portrayed them as a pale reflection of *Salmo salar* caught in the Atlantic Ocean, these were sizable fish.

While only scanty evidence remains about variations in physical appearance, there were variations. One astute observer, a longtime fisher who lived in Pulaski, New York, noted that an experienced fisherman could easily tell the difference between the salmon taken from Grindstone Creek, Deer Creek, and the Salmon River: "In Deer Creek the fish were long and slim, in Grindstone short and chubby, and in Salmon River large and heavy."[6] Their flesh varied in color with the season. The salmon were sleek, silvery, strong, and swift when they entered rivers, streams, and creeks in springtime. Speaking of a June run of salmon in the Oswego River, Ingersoll described them for Canadian and American investigators in 1894: "They were of a silvery color; they would shine like a silver dollar, and the meat was as red as a cherry. The longer they were here the darker they got, and the paler the flesh got." Remembering the salmon of the Humber River, Wilmot noted in 1871 that fish caught in April and May "were bright and silvery in color, rich and fat in flesh, in prime condition." These spring salmon contrasted greatly with fall salmon, which "were dark in color, lean and lank in flesh, out of condition, being at that season of the year engaged in the work of spawning."[7]

The life cycle of the Lake Ontario salmon intrigued nineteenth-century fishermen, naturalists, fish culturists, and biologists. Familiar as they were with the Atlantic salmon, which matured to adulthood in the ocean and returned to the freshwater streams of their birth to spawn, they wondered if the Lake Ontario salmon were also anadromous. Did they seek the salt water of the Atlantic as smolts and return to the lake to spawn? Or were they a landlocked variety that had come into the lake by way of the St. Lawrence River, acclimated to freshwater, and remained, using the lake as their sea and migrating into its tributary rivers, lakes, and streams to spawn? The debate went on throughout the nineteenth and early twentieth centuries until it came to a scientific conclusion in 1938, when A. A. Blair, a Canadian marine biologist, analyzed scales taken from the few existing museum specimens. He concluded that the Lake Ontario salmon were landlocked *Salmo salar.* Marine biologists still maintain this position and have concluded that landlocked salmon of North America and Europe adjacent to the Atlantic Ocean are true Atlantic salmon, not a separate and distinct species of the salmonoids, as nineteenth-century scientists were inclined to think.[8]

Their life cycle made the Lake Ontario salmon highly vulnerable to changing conditions of water and land. They required the food found in the lake: crustaceans, small fish, and insects. They needed free-flowing, unobstructed rivers and streams with clear, clean, cool water and gravel-bottomed areas for spawning. They thrived in relatively moderate summers and reproduced well in autumn seasons of gradually falling temperatures and plenty of rain. The lightly populated Lake Ontario drainage basin, with its largely undisturbed vegetation cover, provided these conditions as long as the Indians were its main inhabitants. They harvested fish for food and for trade with other Indian groups to secure things they did not produce themselves. The Jesuits described their methods of taking Lake Ontario salmon in the mid-seventeenth century. They speared them by torchlight from canoes on lake waters. On streams and rivers, they caught them by use of dam and sluice structures.[9] While their harvesting methods worked very well, the Indians did not take enough salmon to threaten the resource. Nor did the changes they wrought in the vegetation cover by burning the brush and by tilling the soil around the lake disturb the land enough to alter water quality significantly.

Once Euro–North Americans' commercially oriented culture came to dominate the region, the natural world changed so rapidly and drastically that the salmon lived on borrowed time. By words and actions, the latecomers clearly revealed their attitude toward both the Lake Ontario salmon and the larger natural world. The Jesuit missionaries of the mid-seventeenth century thought of salmon as an important source of food, as did the Indians. But they regarded themselves as the centerpiece of creation and the fish as given to them by God specifically for their sustenance as they spread Christianity among the Indians. A Jesuit missionary in Iroquois country on the southern shore of Lake Ontario expressed the idea clearly in 1656: "I might say that He filled the rivers anew with fish expressly for us." Claude Dablon recorded that, in 1655, a group of Iroquois had pleased the Jesuits with a welcoming ceremony that invited "the salmon, brill, and other fish, to leap into our nets, and to fill that river for our service only."[10]

Settlers began to occupy the shoreline areas of Lake Ontario in the late eighteenth century. For the most part Christian, these newcomers operated from a set of assumptions about the natural world that differed from that of the Indian fishers already on the scene. Humans are the centerpiece in the account of creation set forth in Genesis 1:28–30. The settlers believed that they had scriptural justification to subdue the earth. They had dominion over fish, birds, everything that moved, as well as plant life. Motivated by a desire to create fuller, better lives and homes for themselves, they regarded the natural resources around them as a means to that end. They functioned in a commercial world, and while for a short time they might catch salmon only as food for subsistence to allow them to survive in a remote, lightly populated setting, salmon soon became articles of commerce for them.

The real-estate interests on both sides of Lake Ontario recognized that these fish made their lands more valuable. A speculative land investor in the Pulaski, New York, area, writing in 1792, emphasized salmon as one of the principal assets of the region for the incoming settlers and pointed to the commercial value of the fish as well: "The salmon is generally salted and sold for 4 pounds the barrel." A notice in a Toronto newspaper announcing a farm sale in 1798 extolled the property: "above all, it affords an excellent salmon fishery, large enough to support a number of families, which must be conceived a great advantage in this infant country."[11]

Settlers caught Lake Ontario salmon in rivers and creeks from spring through November and salted them for winter use. They became a year-round staple and an important item of survival. A pioneer settler on Lake Ontario's southern shore reminisced in 1864 about early hardships, especially about a winter spent in a cabin where the family scraped by on potatoes and salted salmon: "Some may say, if they could get salmon they would live highly—Would they like broiled salt salmon, no butter, no lard?"[12]

As for their commercial value to settler-farmers, Ingersoll told Canadian and American fishery experts: "They [salmon] were sold through the country—all through this section and the town of Richland; that was the only way they [his father and uncle] had of getting ready money. They used to take them to Utica and all around." The trade in salted and pickled salmon grew to such proportions in the Salmon River area that in 1818 the New York legislature appointed fish inspectors for the towns of Richland and Orwell. There owners with riparian rights combined fishing operations for market, and "as much as two miles of shore were operated by some companies." Fishery officers for the Canadian Department of Marine and Fisheries corroborated settlers' commercial uses of the Lake Ontario salmon. In a special report prepared in 1868 on the salmon of Wilmot's Creek, located east of Toronto, they noted, "Settlers bought and paid for farms and built houses from the sale of salmon."[13] The fish became sufficiently important as an item of trade that some entrepreneurs hired Indians to take salmon during the closed season. As early as 1823, the province of Upper Canada prohibited the practice.[14]

A popular item in the markets of towns around Lake Ontario from their earliest history, salmon found their way into a wider stream of commerce. From the market in Rochester, New York, boats could carry them east and west along the Erie Canal. While no record of Canadian commercial totals remains, some reliable contemporary comments do. As late as 1856, salmon caught commercially at Port Credit reportedly numbered more than 200,000, according to the Superintendent of Fisheries for Upper Canada. An experienced fisheries overseer who knew the western end of Lake Ontario well told the House of Commons in 1869 about a Port Credit fisherman who "has repeatedly taken . . . with his seine in one haul, one thousand Salmon . . . while the fish were waiting their time to enter the Credit river to spawn." In the late 1860s, when the days of the Lake Ontario salmon were numbered, many salmon taken in the Bay of Qunite area with spears and nets supplied American markets. One member of parliament was so galled by the loss of these Canadian fish resources to Americans that in the course of debate he confronted the Minister of Marine and Fisheries with the demand "to prevent these encroachments by foreigners."[15]

By all accounts, the vulnerability of these excellent fish at spawning time led to a massive onslaught in the early decades of the nineteenth century. Along the banks of Wilmot's Creek, on the northern shore of Lake Ontario, in the 1820s, "they were so plentiful . . . that men slew them with clubs and pitchforks—women seined them with flannel petticoats. . . . Later they were taken by nets and spears, over one thousand being often caught in the course of one night." From the Salmon River–Salmon Creek area of New York, accounts of the crude harvest were much the same. One scientist studying the salmon of the St. Lawrence River cites evidence from 1817 of the destruction of 100,000 salmon at the base of an early dam across the Genesee River at Rochester, where they were speared, clubbed, and pitchforked, but he fails to identify his source. Whatever the case, contemporary accounts add up to evidence of a callous slaughter of Lake Ontario salmon in the early developmental period. Regrets came afterward, as expressed by Silas Davis, who late in life "reflected on how unwise the early settlers were in their reckless slaughter of native fish, birds, and beasts."[16]

When economic development of the Great Lakes region responded to the general prosperity of the years 1853 to 1857, commercial fishing took on larger dimensions, and the commercial harvest of the Lake Ontario salmon reached levels that threatened to exterminate them. Introduced on the American side of Lake Ontario in 1850 and set along the shoreline near the mouths of rivers and streams that the salmon ascended, trap nets virtually cleaned them out in about five years, in the opinion of Seth Green, a fisherman and fish dealer on Lake Ontario and later a noted fish culturist, who had dressed and marketed tons of salmon in the quarter century before 1861.[17]

In the mid-nineteenth century, legislators—prodded by their constituents, sportfishing enthusiasts, and fishery experts—sounded the alarm about the decline of the Atlantic salmon in North American waters. Indeed, during the first decade of the century, the need to conserve the salmon of Lake Ontario had sparked the first regulations for the Great Lakes fish population when both Upper Canada and New York State enacted laws to restrict the use of seines, nets, weirs, and other devices to prevent fish from ascending to their spawning grounds. In 1857, Richard Nettle, the Superintendent of Fisheries for Lower Canada and an advocate of fish culture who at the time was experimenting with the artificial propagation of brook trout and salmon in Quebec City, made a plea for the protection and restoration of the salmon fisheries of the St. Lawrence in a book dedicated to the governor general and pleading for his attention and help. He lamented that salmon, once so abundant, were becoming scarce and "that, which the beneficent creator has provided for the many, is being destroyed by the few." He lashed out against "Man, the destroyer, man," who was engaged in a war of extermination. Only three years later there appeared *Salmon-Fishing in Canada by a Resident,* edited by James

Edward Alexander, a book primarily for sportfishermen. The author, nevertheless, took time to lament that the "extermination" of the St. Lawrence salmon seemed a certainty. Their near demise spoke ill of the country's legislators for allowing the wanton and reckless destruction of the fish. The appendix included essays on the disappearing salmon written by well-educated observers with a great interest in sportfishing. They joined the chorus of regrets, similar to those heard over the loss of salmon in rivers in New England and New Brunswick, which was attributed primarily to dam construction and pollution from lumbering operations.[18]

The lament over the salmon had very strong cultural as well as the more obvious economic roots. As W. B. Scott and E. J. Crossman have observed, "Few animals, whether fish, bird, or beast, have attracted as much attention through the ages as has the Atlantic salmon. Prized by the Gauls, then by the Romans, an abundant commercial fish in the British Isles, mentioned in the Magna Charta, revered by the sportsman and esteemed by gourmets, its relation with man has been truly unique."[19]

One man deeply concerned about the disappearing salmon population of Lake Ontario, Samuel Wilmot, decided to do something about it. Wilmot was "an acute student of natural history," a successful farmer and merchant in Newcastle, Ontario, and a college-educated community leader who took an active part in local government and organized religion.[20] As a boy on the family farm near the shores of Lake Ontario, Wilmot had known the salmon in the period when they still flourished. He became Canada's pioneer fish culturist in an age when fishery experts inclined more and more to restocking streams, rivers, and lakes as the solution to seriously dwindling fish populations. Wilmot decided to repair the damage by rejuvenating the salmon population of Lake Ontario, and so he began in his home basement using a very small stock of salmon found in waters adjacent to Wilmot Creek. He started his work with the belief that the salmon of Lake Ontario could be rehabilitated through an artificial hatchery and stocking program, if the "systematic destruction" of the past could be prevented by law in the future: "The overfishing, the murder on the spawning grounds, the trap-net fishing along the shores of the lake and the estuaries of the streams, and the excessive demand and greed for the fish has done this work." By 1881, he had broadened his assessment of the causes of destruction to include environmental changes on land combined with hot weather and lowered lake levels. The salmon's congenial habitat had been destroyed. Removal of trees, cultivation of land, runoff from farms, construction of dams, and the addition of industrial and human sewage to natural waters had taken their toll. In the same year, after sixteen years of effort, he gave up trying to rehabilitate Lake Ontario's salmon, lamenting that "I cannot disguise from myself that the time is now gone by forever for the growth of salmon and speckled trout in the frontier streams of Ontario."[21]

Only a half century of early agricultural-commercial development around the shores of Lake Ontario destroyed the salmon, a resource that the Indians had used for centuries. The fate of these fish marked the beginning of a century of deterioration for the lake whitefish, trout, sturgeon, and herring populations, which became the mainstays of commercial fishing on the Great Lakes. Because of their widespread distribution and their large populations, coupled with changes in the marine habitat emanating from development of the drainage basin in different parts of the lakes at different times, these species took longer than the salmon to weaken seriously. However, all the elements of decline significant from 1850 to 1930 were present in the case of the salmon: changes in the land- and waterway-use pattern in the drainage basin, the rise of strong market demand, improvements in fishing technology, ineffective protective measures to save the fish, the absence of scientific knowledge necessary to make effective laws, and the prioritizing of economic activity in a developing region that assigned minor value to the fish resource. The demise of the salmon foreshadowed the general decline of Great Lakes commercial fishing, which finally captured public attention in 1925 with the herring debacle in Lake Erie.

3

Patterns of Growth through 1872

Like a Bright Cloud Moving Rapidly through the Water

Growth patterns of commercial fishing in the Great Lakes in the nineteenth century varied considerably in place and time, conditioned by market demand and access. Early in the century along the shores of Lakes Ontario and Erie, new residents in undeveloped areas who came primarily in search of farms and not as prospective fishermen caught fish for barter and sale. As noted in the case of Lake Ontario salmon, fish first provided subsistence and soon became items for trade in small local markets, a pattern repeated in newly settled lands around all the lakes. Commercial fishing grew with communities and their general mercantile businesses that resold fish taken in barter locally or traded them with distant suppliers for needed goods. As the population grew, some residents made an important part of their livelihoods by fishing to supply a community market, selling their catch directly to consumers. At the same time, a more extensive trade in fish originated in the businesses of provision merchants in established and growing centers of trade and population, such as Detroit and Toronto.

THE EARLY YEARS, 1800–1850

In his study of commercial fishing in the Canadian waters of the Great Lakes, Alan B. McCullough noted that it is generally believed that the industry on the Great Lakes began "on the American side of Lake Ontario in Chaumont Bay, near the Maumee River on Lake Erie, and on the Detroit River at about the time of the War of 1812." Both American and Canadian fisheries in the waters connecting Lake Erie and Lake Huron long associated with the fur trade grew, their catch going to an expanding salted fish market in Detroit. Other examples of early commercial fisheries can be cited from the 1820s, such as that at Sandusky Bay. In 1830, Sandusky, Ohio, destined to become "the largest market for fresh-water fish in the world" late in the century, boasted two fish dealers, each with a small-scale business. The city council developed regulations for fishing in the Toronto Islands in the mid-1830s.[1]

The expansive years of the 1830s are the first period of notable growth of Great Lakes commercial fishing, a period of experimentation. On all five lakes, entrepreneurs large and small tested the wealth of the waters. Until that time, the very sparse population in most areas adjacent to the lakes limited local consumption, and transportation to distant markets was difficult and costly. Yet the heady mixture of nationwide prosperity, speculative investment in transportation improvements and public lands, and accelerated movement of settlers into the lands surrounding Lakes Ontario and Erie, into the Lower Peninsula of Michigan, and around the southern shore of Lake Michigan created an optimistic assessment of the salability of Great Lakes fish. Surely a vastly expanded regional market for fish was at hand. The advent of steamboats on the Great Lakes in the 1820s; the opening in 1825 of the Erie Canal, which connected Lake Erie and New York City by way of the Hudson River; the completion in 1833 of the first Welland Canal, which bypassed Niagara Falls; and the promise of projected new canal systems taken together greatly increased the potential markets for Great Lakes fish.

The growth of commercial fishing in the 1830s emanated in part from the expanding business community in Detroit. Already experienced in handling salted, barreled fish incident to the fur trade, Detroit merchants with venture capital eyed the growing population along the lakeshores poorly accessed by land transportation as consumers for their goods and services. Lake shipping could carry needed goods to them and on the return journey bring cargoes of salted fish for sale. The merchants also regarded company fishing ventures in the virtually untapped lake waters as part of the trade pattern. Fishing and commerce would work hand in hand.

In the summer of 1837, for example, John P. Clark, a Detroit merchant, fish dealer, and shipbuilder, established a fishing business along the Lake Michigan shoreline near Manitowoc, Wisconsin, a fledgling frontier community, to exploit the waters so richly endowed with whitefish. Clark began the fishery shortly after a test seining by two Green Bay venturers, who are said to have cast their seines close to shore at that location and, in the first haul, harvested 10 barrels, or 2,000 pounds, of whitefish. Clark operated in 1838 with a company schooner, the *Gazelle,* twenty men, and fishing apparatus. The Green Bay and Detroit entrepreneurs formed a partnership that reportedly harvested 2,000 barrels, or 400,000 pounds, of Lake Michigan fish annually. Clark's company continued the fishing business for fifteen years "with unfailing success," accumulating "considerable wealth" from fishing in its own right and from buying fish from others for the Detroit market. Early in its fishing operation on Lake Michigan, the company assumed a year-round presence at the fishery sites by reducing its employees to six or eight during the winter. They mended nets and cut cordwood to ship east early in the spring. The company's Great Lakes fleet of sailing vessels carried settlers, provisions, and clothing from Detroit into the developing Great Lakes region to the west. By the 1850s, rough lumber and grain as well as fish traveled east on the return journey.[2]

Nor was the Lake Michigan venture of the J. P. Clark Company an isolated case. Other Detroit entrepreneurs exploited Canadian waters during the 1830s. They fostered a gill-net fishery involving canoes, small sailboats about twelve feet long, and homemade hand-knitted linen nets in Georgian Bay, Canada's finest Great Lakes fishing ground, which was richly endowed with whitefish and trout. Detroit traders brought schooners to the fishing stations to collect the catch and to supply needed salt and barrels. The fishermen took general supplies in payment for the salted catch.[3] The fishers who established themselves on Thunder Bay and the Middle Islands in Lake Huron and along the Lower Peninsula of Michigan and elsewhere on the Lake Huron coast in the mid-1830s supplied the Detroit market. So did the harvests from the Detroit River, Lake St. Clair, the St. Clair River, and western Lake Erie.

Entrepreneurial hustle characterized early commercial-fishing operations by Canadians in Canadian waters. Consider the example of ship's captain Alexander MacGregor of the newly founded settlement of Goderich, Ontario. In 1831, he discovered an unusually bountiful population of whitefish and herring around the Fishing Islands adjacent to the Bruce Peninsula, where they came in great schools at spawning time. He hastily assembled the essential workers, nets, salt, barrels, drying racks, schooners, and rowboats, and in short order built a fishing station on Main Station Island, as it came to be known. The small community of Goderich could not absorb the enormous catch. MacGregor contracted with a

Detroit merchant to sell him a minimum of 3,000 barrels, or 600,000 pounds, of fish annually, at $1 a barrel, and as many more as he could supply on the understanding that the dealer would accept them.[4] The methods of MacGregor's fishery afford a rare detailed glimpse of commercial-fishing operations of the 1830s. A son who assisted with the fisheries and other contemporaries, including John Evans, a Methodist missionary, left descriptions of the harvest. A spotter watched for the approach of the school of fish: "The shoal when sighted seemed like a bright cloud moving rapidly through the water." The fishermen quickly manned a large rowboat that was loaded with a massive seine. They maneuvered to surround the school and then laboriously hauled the net to shore, where workers threw the fish onto the beach. There "they formed a splendent mass, flapping and gasping life away."[5]

Among the suppliers of the hundreds of thousands of pounds of salted fish that descended on the Detroit market in the 1830s were two large fur-trading companies: the Hudson's Bay Company and the American Fur Company. Both launched commercial-fishing ventures on Lake Superior, hoping to bolster earnings in an area where the fur trade was on the wane. The Hudson's Bay Company marketed its salted, barreled catch in Detroit in 1835 and 1836, and continued its fishing operations on Lake Superior to fill its needs and to sell in the lower lakes until 1860. In 1834, the American Fur Company launched an effort that was larger and shorter lived than that of the Hudson's Bay Company, but very well documented.[6]

The beginnings of large commercial catches on the Great Lakes in the 1830s were just that, beginnings. Notable growth awaited the dissipation of hard times, which lasted from the Panic of 1837 into the 1840s. We have no figures showing the total volume of production and only a spotty and episodic knowledge of the early industry. Evidence of the operations of large-scale entrepreneurs remains, yet they represented only one segment of the early industry. In the 1830s, small-scale commercial fishermen worked the waters around the Toronto Islands, in the Point Pelee area, near Weller's Beach in Prince Edward County, in Chaumont Bay, and on the southern shore of western Lake Erie as well as fished the Detroit and St. Clair Rivers and Lake St. Clair, to mention but a few of the most obvious locations (figure 3.1).[7] Nevertheless, the developments of the 1830s deserve scrutiny, for with the advantage of hindsight, they reveal many characteristics of the industry in its heyday in the late nineteenth century. In the 1830s, people regarded the fishery resource as a way to survive, to acquire farms, and to accumulate wealth free for the taking. Exploitation for quick profit characterized commercial fishing, as did a lack of concern about the consequences of such exploitation for the fish population in the future. That attitude is easily understandable because

Figure 3.1. William Henry Bartlett, "Wellington, Prince Edward County, Lake Ontario," 1838. Workers in a small-scale commercial fishery are using seines to harvest salmon and whitefish. (From N. P. Willis, *Canadian Scenery* [London: Virtue, 1842], 2:facing 61; photograph courtesy Toronto Reference Library)

the Great Lakes region was vast and very sparsely populated and contained seemingly boundless natural wealth. By the accepted norm of the day, people should develop this wilderness for their benefit. There was plenty for everyone. As for the fish, they counted for little except for human use. The destructive nature of fishing with seines, as practiced by MacGregor off the Fishing Islands, carried over into the future, just as it had become part of human ways in the 1830s from ages past.

In the1830s, many of the structural characteristics of the future industry took shape. Primary market centers emerged to which the catch was sent from very considerable distances for redistribution. The system of merchant-dealers who both gathered the catch from remote locations and developed their own fishing enterprises evolved. The industry developed with some very large as well as small merchant-dealer entrepreneurs, with units of production ranging widely in size, and with many small fishermen, some of whom worked independently while others worked in units of production that were organized and supplied by merchant-dealers—characteristics that permeated its nineteenth- and early-twentieth-century history. The practice of fishing part-time as a way to supplement the earnings from a principal occupation became common in these early

Figure 3.2. William Henry Bartlett, "Fish Market, Toronto," 1838. (From N. P. Willis, *Canadian Scenery* [London: Virtue, 1842], 1:facing 88; photograph courtesy Toronto Reference Library)

years, and it would continue to characterize a sizable group of Great Lakes fishermen for more than a century. The spirit of aggressive entrepreneurship evident in the 1830s rose to new heights later in the nineteenth century.

In that decade, as in the future, market access and market demand shaped the industry, sending entrepreneurs in search of new buyers and new ways of transporting fish to the open, unregulated, and highly competitive markets. Market as place also assumed a special meaning. Before the close of the decade, merchant-entrepreneurs in Detroit made the city into the largest primary market for salted Great Lakes fish, and as such it exerted a great influence on the fortunes of the fishermen as a place to trade and a source of credit. Toronto, a fast-growing community of 9,254 in 1834, the year it officially became a city, regulated its fisheries. It soon emerged as the principal commercial fish market for Canadian Great Lakes waters (figure 3.2).[8] Largely because of marketing costs and proximity, Americans exploited Canadian fish resources during this first period of fishery expansion. The loss of this Great Lakes fish resource to American poachers and to American merchant-dealers who knew how to circumvent Canadian law initiated a long period of friction between the fishing interests of the two countries that extended well into the twentieth century.

GROWTH: THE PATTERN OF EXPANSION

In the late 1840s, the Great Lakes fisheries entered a period of further expansion that was characterized by more intensive harvests, growing regional markets, and better means of transportation to a widening national market. Economic growth, whose dimensions went unmeasured in any systematic way until the late 1860s, revived in the prosperous years of the 1850s and accompanied the spread of railroads into the southern Great Lakes region. That decade marked the beginning of more systematic large-scale fishing in western Lake Erie and in Lake Michigan, around whose shores the growing regional populations readily absorbed much of the marketable catch and newly built rail connections were at hand to carry the balance to more distant markets. In Milwaukee, Chicago, Detroit, Sandusky, Cleveland, Toronto, Buffalo, and other Great Lakes ports, merchant-dealers who specialized in fish took their place in the community business profile. The depression of the late 1850s temporarily dampened the midcentury surge. The industry took on new life during the Civil War to supply civilians with a substitute for meat, which was needed to feed the Union Army. From the late 1860s to the end of the century, harvests from Great Lakes waters escalated, reaching a record high in 1899.[9]

Like much American industrial growth in the nineteenth century, Great Lakes fishing rested on a rich natural resource base and a largely domestic market, but not exclusively so. Some Great Lakes whitefish appeared in the London and Liverpool markets.[10] The natural increase in native-born people and the addition of millions of foreign-born immigrants to the United States and Canada in the latter half of the century created more consumers. Many incoming western Europeans, given their dietary preferences and their religious practices, found fish a very acceptable food. Moreover, the expansion of the urban working class gave fish sales an impetus. Compared with meat, fish was cheap and thus offered a more affordable way of putting protein on the family table, a reality that the Canadian Department of Marine and Fisheries used to justify government experiments in fish propagation and stocking. Fish was "food for the masses."[11]

For Chicago's immigrant working class, the bounteous fish market in the city required no lures. The same attraction held for low-income people in the fishing ports and urban centers all around the lakes, especially noticeable in those where industry and commerce employed sizable work forces: Milwaukee, Detroit, Toledo, Cleveland, Sandusky, Erie, Buffalo, Rochester, Toronto, and Hamilton. In Cleveland, the retail market for fish clearly reflected class lines. In his survey of the Great Lakes fisheries, written in 1879, Frederick W. True noted, "There are two retailers who supply the wealthy class. They sell only the very best varieties, and receive proportionately high prices. The other dealers sell cheaper grades, and receive the patronage of less opulent citizens."[12] In company-operated lumbering camps and mining communities around the Great Lakes, fish became a staple in workers' diets. In well-developed agricultural areas, local peddlers fanned out from fishing ports with horse-drawn wagons carrying fish to the rural population.

Aggressive Great Lakes fish dealers harnessed the spreading railroad network and relied on innovations in methods of preservation and modes of transportation to make Great Lakes fish available to a growing and more distant body of consumers. In 1888, when pioneer Michigan geologist Bela Hubbard wrote *Memorials of a Half-Century,* he commented on the wide market for Great Lakes whitefish: "Now this 'deer of the lakes'—par excellence—is not only universally known, but is procurable cheaply, at all seasons, both fresh and salted, from the lakes to the Gulf, and from the Mississippi to Cape Cod. It has even overleaped these bounds and is shipped direct to Liverpool."[13]

THE INDUSTRY IN 1872 AND THE MILNER REPORT

In 1872, Canada and the United States recorded the magnitude of commercial fishing on the Great Lakes. This was the first time that both countries gathered data on the size of an industry that had been developing since the 1830s. The harvest in Canadian and American waters totaled 39,330,000 pounds, with a value of $1,819,849. Of that total, Canadian authorities reported 7,080,000 pounds and American officials, the balance.[14] The American production figures, compiled for the newly created Commission of Fish and Fisheries, probably understated the 1872 catch by as much as 25 percent. The Canadian count, an established government procedure since 1868, was probably far more accurate, but it, too, is deceiving because American fishermen worked in Canadian waters and American fish dealers developed contractual arrangements with Canadian fishermen that resulted in their harvests going directly to American ports. Thus American production totals included millions of pounds of fish from Canadian waters.

Under the direction of Spencer Baird, the first Commissioner of Fish and Fisheries, James Milner, a biologist in Waukegan, Illinois, prepared a special report on the American Great Lakes fishing industry in 1872. The report provides the earliest official portrait of Great Lakes commercial fishing, especially significant because it was written at a critical point in the industry's history, on the eve of massive changes over the next two decades. In evaluating the status of the fishery, Milner gathered information by extensive fieldwork, observation, investigation, interviews, study of local records, and correspondence. He visited Lakes Superior, Huron, Michigan, and Erie, and the Detroit River. He observed the habits of various species, collected specimens, and made dredgings to determine food sources, paying particular attention to whitefish, the most valuable of the commercial species, whose spawn he collected and placed in a Michigan hatchery. He investigated fishing grounds, collected testimony from fishermen, studied their harvest methods, and gathered the production data for the 1872 season. Milner examined the fisheries of Lake Michigan more intensively than those of the other lakes. He appealed to state legislatures to enact laws to protect the fish resource. The report, written after two decades of very substantial growth in the commercial fisheries, revealed a competitive industry spreading into ever larger areas of the Great Lakes as lake steamers and railroads made market connections possible.

Milner's findings shed light on the three major operations in the industry: harvesting, processing, and marketing. The fishermen-harvesters, the men in the boats, tended the nets in all kinds of weather from April through late November. In some localities, they worked during the winter, fishing hook lines, spears, and nets through the ice. Among them were those who owned their own gear and supervised their fisheries—independents, as they styled themselves. Most often, the independents were organized as partnerships and, according to Milner's estimates, had an investment of $300 to $20,000 in nets, boats, and shore properties. They earned up to $7,000 from fish sales in a season. In fishermen's pecking order, they ranked high. Others, lacking the capital to outfit themselves, worked for wages or fished on shares. While some worked for the independents, many worked with the dealers.[15]

Dealers performed the other two operations in the commercial-fishing industry: processing and marketing. They greatly influenced the fortunes of all fishermen who depended on them to purchase their catch, often to process it for market, and to funnel it into the market network to secondary locations for broader distribution. They acted as a control on fishing, for the dealers set the price they would pay fishermen based on their own expenses and the going market price, establishing a margin of profit for themselves. Competition among dealers, theoretically, acted as a check on them. They insisted on quality standards, such as size and freshness, and paid or refused to pay accordingly. They tried to establish territories where one dealer would serve as the sole carrier from all fishing stations to market, using steamers to collect the fish. Many collected fish from remote locations and supplied isolated fishermen with food, clothing, fishing gear, and other necessities. Their steamers were a floating version of the company store so common in many work environments in the late nineteenth century.

By 1872, some dealers owned as much as $20,000 to $30,000 worth of nets that they offered to fishermen for use on shares, or they hired fishermen to bring in the catch. Thus they were directly involved in harvesting as well as processing and marketing the catch. Over and above the capital they had invested in fishing gear and collecting steamers, dealers had spent very sizable amounts of money on warehouses, processing sheds, ice houses, and freezers. They used working capital to cover the costs of shipping containers, inspections, freight charges, repairs, and supplies incident to transporting the catch to distant markets. Dealers who packed, shipped, and marketed the catch made more money than fishermen, according to Alan B. McCullough, historian of the Canadian commercial-fishing industry in the Great Lakes. By the early 1870s, there were dozens of dealerships ranging in size from very small businesses that handled the catch of local fishermen in the local market to larger ones that sent their fish to regional and national markets. The precise number of dealers and size of their investments are not known. Yet some suggestion of size might be gleaned from data on Sandusky, Ohio, a major fishing port on Lake Erie. In 1870 to 1872, nine firms handled an average of 8.5 million pounds of fish. Of these nine, three were considered the major ones.[16]

Fish dealers were so entrenched in the industry's structure that Milner surveyed them in 1872 to make an estimate of the production of American fisheries in the Great Lakes. The survey revealed Chicago, Detroit, Toledo, Sandusky, Huron, Cleveland, and Buffalo as major market and distribution centers. Chicago and Buffalo, which were dominated by large dealerships, were the giants of the market. In 1872, these centers marketed 7.5 million and 6.4 million pounds of fish, respectively.[17]

The preeminence of Chicago and Buffalo resulted from a combination of excellent steamship and railroad connections that enabled merchant-dealers to collect the catch from producers and distribute it to far-flung markets. Chicago by 1870 was a rail hub for the nation, rapidly increasing its tributary commercial territory in all directions. Buffalo's railroad connections made New York City and the northeastern industrial areas readily accessible and linked it with areas to the south, north, and west as well. The Erie Canal also carried vary large quantities of fish to markets. Great Lakes fish went by rail in large quantities to New York City from both Buffalo and Chicago. Newly developed systems for freezing made it possible to ship fresh-frozen Great Lakes whitefish and trout by rail to Cincinnati, St. Louis, Omaha, Washington, D.C., and intervening cities as well as to the New York market, Milner noted in his report. Toronto, on Lake Ontario, by virtue of its rapidly growing population and excellent railroad connections to the east, west, and north, developed as Canada's major Great Lakes fish market and principal seat of wholesale and retail dealerships.[18]

The larger dealers gave considerable thought to and spent much time devising strategies for marketing fish in the most efficient and cost-effective way. They worked out special contracts with railroad carriers and rented and constructed storage facilities at strategic locations in their marketing territory. They advertised their fish and negotiated working agreements with retail merchants. The marketing function, the one least alluded to in Milner's report, had begun evolving along these lines by 1872. It became much more clearly delineated and more aggressively developed in the ensuing quarter century.

Milner on the Technology of the Harvest

As Milner reported, in the early 1870s, the working units of production used a variety of small sailboats, nets, and manpower, adapted to widely varied fishing grounds and conditions. To understand the fortunes of the commercial-fishing industry and the exploitation of the fish resource, the technology needs careful review, for it was key to the rapid rise of the industry and the serious erosion of Great Lakes fish resources. While seining implemented by rowboats dominated the early commercial-fishing operations from the 1830s to 1850, when fish in large numbers came into shallow shoreline waters and rivers in relatively undeveloped areas to feed and to spawn, by midcentury fishermen found sailboats and pound and gill nets to be essential to the harvest.

The seine was the simplest and least expensive of the nets. It was fine meshed and ranged in length up to 900 to 1,000 or more feet. Shaped like a sling, the seine used corks at the top and lead weights at the bottom: "One end is fastened to the shore, and the fishermen, awaiting an opportune time to inclose a school of fish, row out into the lake with the other end, and, making a wide sweep, bring it to shore, inclosing whatever fish may be within its sweep." Men drew it to shore, or, in some instances, a treadmill fitted with a capstan and powered by horses hauled it in.[19]

As the yield from seines diminished, inshore fishermen turned to the pound net, which had been "developed in Scotland and introduced to North America in the 1830s." Connecticut River fishermen, part of the great New England westward exodus, used it in Black River Bay on Lake Ontario in 1850, in the shallow western end of Lake Erie, and in Saginaw Bay on Lake Huron at about the same time. Over the next two decades, more and more fishermen adopted it. More complex and expensive than the early seines, the pound net consisted of a leader, a tunnel, and a pot (figure 3.3). The leader was a net positioned at a right angle to the shore. Leaders used in 1879 measured from 500 to 1,400 feet in length. The leader guided fish toward the core of the net, a heart-shaped enclosure from where they passed through a tunnel into the pot of the net. Usually

Figure 3.3. Green Bay pound net. (Drawn by L. Kumlien; from Hugh M. Smith and Merwin-Marie Snell, "Review of the Fisheries of the Great Lakes in 1885," U.S. Commission of Fish and Fisheries, *Report,* 1887, Appendix, 50th Cong., 2d sess., 1889, H. Misc. Doc. 133 [Serial 2661], facing 108)

a twenty- to forty-foot-square enclosure, the pot was rigged to allow fishermen to enter it with a pound-net boat, a flat-bottomed sailboat, and scoop up the fish. Pound nets were often set at depths of thirty to fifty feet and sometimes deeper. Average depth in 1879 was thirty-five feet; the deepest then known, ninety-seven feet. Because they were held in place by stakes driven into the lake bottom, pound nets were seldom used at great depths, nor were they suitable on gravelly or rocky bottoms. Milner noted that the average value of 284 pound nets used on Lake Michigan was $500, and pound-net boats averaged $50. The western end of Lake Erie contained the greatest concentration of pound nets on the lakes. In Canadian waters, fishermen used very few pound nets in 1872. There, the gill net, the other mainstay of harvest, predominated.[20]

Fishermen relied very extensively on gill nets for fishing in deeper waters. Developed and used for centuries by the Indians of the Great Lakes region, gill nets were fished commercially in the 1830s by the American Fur Company on Lake Superior. Fishermen on Georgian Bay who supplied Detroit traders with salted fish used gill nets fished from canoes and small boats, but their widespread use dates from the mid-nineteenth century, when early development along the shorelines of the southern Great Lakes diminished the inshore fish harvest. The gill net was a simple device, a lightweight net suspended in the water like a curtain, with weights on the bottom and floats at the top (figure 3.4). Fish swimming into it got their gills entangled when they tried to get out, and there they remained until fishermen lifted the nets and removed them. The size of net

Figure 3.4. Gill net drying on a reel. (From Hugh M. Smith and Merwin-Marie Snell, "Review of the Fisheries of the Great Lakes in 1885," U.S. Commission of Fish and Fisheries, *Report,* 1887, Appendix, 50th Cong., 2d sess., 1889, H. Misc. Doc. 133 [Serial 2661], facing 74)

mesh determined the size of fish caught. Fishermen increasingly relied on these nets as the century progressed because they worked well in deeper waters far from shore where the declining numbers of fish could be found. The smallest gill-net rig was less expensive than a pound net and pound-net boat. Milner noted in his report that the price of a light gill-net rig on Lake Michigan averaged $225 and the Mackinaw boat to tend it cost about $100, compared with $500 for a pound net and $50 for a simple, roughly built pound-net boat. In addition, pound-net fishing required a scow fitted with a pile driver to set the stakes that supported the nets. On Lake Michigan in 1872, nets for heavy gill-net rigs averaged $725 and the boat to set and tend them cost around $500.[21] Seine, pound, and gill nets worked very effectively as fish traps. By their design and the ways fishermen used them, all three types wasted millions of tons of fish.

In the early 1870s, the majority of gill-net fishermen on Lakes Michigan, Huron, Superior, and Ontario used Mackinaw boats, usually twenty-two to twenty-six feet in length, varying somewhat in design from location to location (figure 3.5). To this famous craft, Milner paid an

Figure 3.5. Mackinaw boats, Collingwood, Ontario, 1870. (Photograph courtesy Wisconsin Maritime Museum, Manitowoc)

enthusiastic tribute in 1872. He noted that the Mackinaw boat had been in use longer and had a better safety record on the upper lakes than any other: "She is fairly fast, the greatest surf-boat known, and with an experienced boatman will ride out any storm, or, if necessary, beach with greater safety than any other boat." Fishermen used two other sailboats, the square-sterned Huron boat and the Norwegian boat, with large gill-net rigs, but neither in numbers comparable with that of the Mackinaw.[22]

When Milner conducted his survey of the commercial-fishing industry in 1872, he reported only a few gill-net steamers in use with heavy rigs. They had been introduced on Lake Michigan in 1869: the *Kittie Gaylord,* of Washington Island, and the *Pottawattomie,* near Green Bay. They would become key to the vast expansion of the fisheries from the mid-1870s through the 1880s.[23]

Significance of the Milner Report

James Milner's profile of the commercial-fishing industry in 1872 illuminates its development, reflecting the changes during the preceding twenty years and establishing a benchmark from which to measure changes during the next twenty years. The young scientist delineated the technology of Great Lakes fishing at a turning point in its history. Seining, the earliest and least expensive technique, was on the wane, and pound-net and gill-net fishing using wind power had come to dominate harvesting methods. During the next fifteen years, steam would revolutionize the industry, making it much more capital intensive, more efficient, and far more destructive of the fish population. Milner's survey showed how railroad construction had widened the market for whitefish and trout. That expansion would continue for the balance of the century as rail connections reached more and more communities.

The report also made it very clear that the newly patented system of freezing fresh fish had expanded their marketability far and wide. The system involved freezing the fish in covered metal trays packed in ice and salt and then storing or shipping them. Patented in 1869 by W. Davis of Detroit, the system appealed to fish dealers in all the important American cities on the Great Lakes. They purchased rights and built freezing and preserving houses in the early 1870s. Railroad refrigerator cars, an innovation of the late 1860s developed to serve the meat-packing industry, also widened the potential market for fresh and fresh-frozen fish. So did the use of fish cars, double-sided boxes with two-inch packing space between the sides mounted on four-wheeled iron trucks with iron tongues at one end. They made it possible to send fresh fish for long distances "in perfect condition." A fishing business on Mackinac Island used fish cars as early as 1845 to transport fresh fish to Cleveland. The fish cars of the late nineteenth century were twice as large, with a capacity of 4,000 pounds. Using these refrigeration methods, more and more of the catch went to market fresh.[24]

Milner fully and clearly documented one other characteristic of the industry in 1872 that continued to threaten the fortunes of fishermen and dealers for the rest of the nineteenth century and in the twentieth: the specter of a vanishing resource. Only two decades after the beginning of extensive commercial fishing on the Great Lakes, many feared that the resource was declining and in danger of further erosion. Milner noted, "The impression prevails that there is an alarming diminution of the food-fishes of the lakes. This is the ordinary feeling among dealers, a majority of the fishermen, and the people generally."[25] Thus Milner's profile reveals an expansive but uneasy Great Lakes fishing industry in 1872. It was primarily an industry of small producers, competing for a resource that was free for the taking in American waters and available with the payment of a small license fee in Canadian. Many fishermen with a modest investment in a Mackinaw boat and gill nets or in a pound-net operation braved the elements, the uncertainties of yield, and the very hard work essential for a living on the lakes. During the next two decades, technological change would revolutionize production. Led by aggressive entrepreneurs, the Great Lakes commercial-fishing industry would become much like the other large business enterprises in late-nineteenth-century North America. Dealers, several steps removed from daily life on the lakes and the hands-on work of the harvest, would come to dominate production. They regarded fish as merely one cost factor on the balance sheet.

4

The Expansive Heyday 1875–1893

Nets by the Mile . . . Catch by the Ton

Rapid change permeated the Great Lakes fishing industry between 1875 and 1893. Production grew, reaching a high point in 1889 with a 146,284,000-pound harvest, a record exceeded only in 1899 and 1915, both exceptional seasons, and rarely even approached during the twentieth century. The escalation of harvest tonnage to record heights followed by the onset of a long-term irregular downward trend characterized this "heyday" of commercial fishing. In many ways, it was akin to the production patterns in the Great Lakes regional fur trade, lumbering, and mining, yet another example of a highly competitive, virtually unregulated, and wasteful exploitation of a natural resource for profit that over time seriously eroded its commercial utility. In an age of laissez-faire liberalism and public approval and encouragement of the rapid development of the continent, entrepreneurs stepped forward to harness their capital, abundant and cheap labor, and a resource that was free in American waters and regulated in Canadian waters after 1858 (yet virtually free, for enforcement was lax). As Alfred Booth, a Chicago millionaire fish dealer, shrewdly observed in 1885: "It did not take long for capital to see the rewards which might be gained by reaping the fields which Nature had so abundantly supplied with a crop [Great Lakes fish] that cost nothing for the sowing or raising, and but little for the reaping."[1]

During the period 1875 to 1893, an intensive application of steam and refrigeration technology and larger capital investments in the harvesting, processing, and marketing of the catch were integral components of expanding production. A larger work force, larger units of production, and the grouping of small fishing enterprises into loosely associated units for marketing purposes also characterized the era of expansion. Dealer-entrepreneurs rose to new heights of power and control as they directed the growing industry, combining labor, capital, technology, and the skills of marketing to deliver fish to a growing nationwide consumer population. In their quest for greater profits, they provided the driving force for escalating American operations in the Canadian waters of the Great Lakes and for establishing American dominance in marketing the Canadian catch. The years of greatest expansion and optimism were 1880 to 1885. During the second half of the decade and continuing to the onset of the Panic of 1893, the industry corrected for the excesses of boom times and for a noticeable decline in the most valuable commercial species. As the catch diminished, fishermen introduced more efficient methods of harvest. Then came further declines, and the adoption of newer technologies to sustain the catch. This scenario emerged as a pattern for the future, a downward cycle contributing heavily to the demise of the era of the commercial fishing of whitefish, trout, herring, and sturgeon in the Great Lakes.

MEASUREMENTS OF CHANGE

Production

Examining these trends more closely, first consider the production record. While only incomplete data remain, they show larger and larger harvests from the 39,300,000 pounds for all Great Lakes waters in 1872 to 146,284,000 pounds in 1889. Had systematic records been kept in the United States as well as they were in Canada, a far better picture of the escalating catch would remain. As it is, we have significant guideposts, but no record of annual fluctuations in the harvest.

In 1868, under the newly created dominion government, Canada began to collect and report the annual catch. The United States did not systematically gather such data until 1914, but it did make a series of special studies of its Great Lakes fisheries. These reviews make it possible to compile poundage figures for all waters in 1872, 1879, 1880, 1885, 1889, 1890, and 1893.

The Great Lakes fisheries of the United States waters are probably the most studied American fisheries in the nineteenth century for several reasons. First, Spencer Baird, the first United States Commissioner of Fish

Table 4.1. Total fish production from Canadian and U.S. Great Lakes waters, 1868–1893

Year	Canada	United States	Total
1868	5,698,900	[22,796,000]	[28,494,900]
1872	7,080,000	32,250,000	39,330,000
1876	10,185,400	[40,740,000]	[50,925,400]
1879	10,098,400	64,459,230	74,557,630
1880	11,356,800	68,742,000	80,098,000
1885	27,378,180	99,842,076	127,220,256
1889	29,198,359	117,085,568	146,283,927
1890	26,937,453	113,898,531	140,835,984
1893	26,610,452	96,619,671	123,230,123

Sources: The figures from Canada were compiled from Canada, *Sessional Papers,* 1869, 1873, 1877, 1880, 1881, 1891, 1892, and 1894; the figures for the United States are in James W. Milner, "Report on the Fisheries of the Great Lakes: The Result of Inquiries Prosecuted in 1871 and 1872," in U.S. Commission of Fish and Fisheries, *Report,* 1872–1873, Appendix A, 42d Cong., 3d sess., 1872, S. Misc. Doc. 74 (Serial 1547), 7; Frederick W. True, "The Fisheries of the Great Lakes," in George Brown Goode, *The Fisheries and Fishing Industries of the United States,* Section 2, 47th Cong., 1st sess., 1881, S. Misc. Doc. 124 (Serial 1999), 633; Hugh M. Smith, "The Fisheries of the Great Lakes," in U.S. Commission of Fish and Fisheries, *Report,* 1892, Appendix, 53d Cong., 2d sess., 1893, H. Misc. Doc. 209 (Serial 3264); and U.S. Commission of Fish and Fisheries, *Report,* 1895, 54th Cong., 2d sess., 1896, H. Doc. 104 (Serial 3518), 97.

Note: The numbers in brackets for the years 1868 and 1876 were derived by using a rough estimate of 20 percent of the total catch having come from all Canadian and 80 percent from American waters of the Great Lakes. There are no actual figures for the United States for those years. The 20 percent is based on an analysis of the ratios between the Canadian and the American harvests in 1872, 1879, 1880, 1885, 1889, 1890, and 1893, for which the yields are recorded.

and Fisheries, undertook a general status assessment of American fisheries in the early 1870s. Baird, deeply concerned about declining fish populations, particularly along the Atlantic coast, sought documentation of the state of the fisheries and hoped to devise policies to restore them. James Milner's study of the Great Lakes fish population, published in 1872, was an outgrowth of Baird's larger concerns. With documentation thus begun, the United States Commission of Fish and Fisheries continued to track the industry, sometimes in cooperation with the national decennial census, as in 1879, and sometimes to compile data to use in negotiations with Canada about commercial matters, as in 1885, or to respond to pressure for investigations from state and local sources.

Combining United States production figures found in these special studies with similar figures for Canada, seven totals show an enormous increase in the harvest from 1872 to 1893 (table 4.1). Using the known figures for the Canadian harvest and analyzing the relationship between the size of harvests for the two nations, estimates have been made for

United States production in 1868 and 1876. With those and the actual figures, it is possible to suggest rough production estimates at intervals of no more than five years for the period 1868 to 1893. All the data, actual and estimated, should be viewed with caution. Much of the harvest from Canadian waters went directly to the American market and was reported in the American totals. Contemporary authorities agreed that the reported totals were smaller than the real harvest. Given the nature of the industry, much of the catch went unreported. Thus the existing data understate the number of fish taken. How much of an underestimate is mere guesswork. For all their flaws, the figures do reflect a very expansive industry.

Noting growth between the documented guideposts, the 1872 harvest was smaller by 40 million pounds than the figures reported for 1880. In 1885, the catch surpassed the 1880 total by more than 47 million pounds. Figures for 1889 exceeded the 1885 harvest by more than 19 million. While the 1880s were the decade of greatest expansion, it is clear from descriptive records that escalation became notable after 1875, when some of the worst effects of the Panic of 1873 began to dissipate.

Capital Investment, Labor Force, and Value of Product

The earliest clue about capital investment in commercial fishing in American waters comes from Milner's study of Lake Michigan. He estimated that in 1871 the fishing interests of that lake had invested $430,000 in nets, boats, and shore properties and another $150,000 in working capital. In all Canadian waters of the Great Lakes, where the fisheries were less developed, the value of boats, nets, and materials employed in the same year totaled $106,306. This figure is an understatement, for not all the fishery officers reported, and is a poor comparison with the Lake Michigan figures, which include investments in shore properties and working capital. A much better idea of the amount of capital invested in fishing in all Great Lakes waters is available for 1880, when a conservative estimate showed $1.5 million. Five years later, that figure had jumped to $4.9 million. In 1890, it stood at $5.9 million.[2] Yet considering that the 1880 value was 100 in the Warren and Pearson United States wholesale price index, which used 1910 to 1914 as a base period, the increase is very real but not as great as it appears. The index figures for 1885 and 1890 were 85 and 82 percent, respectively.[3]

The number of workers employed in fishery production grew. Again, existing records are an underestimate. In 1871, Milner found 1,989 men employed on Lake Michigan. The Canadian Department of Marine and Fisheries reported 1,527 for all its Great Lakes waters in that year. In 1880, the total for all the Great Lakes was approximately 7,000. In 1885,

Table 4.2. Size and value of Great Lakes fish harvest, 1872–1889

Year	Pounds	Value (current U.S. $)	Indexed Value
1872	39,330,000	$1,950,768	$2,653,360
1880	80,215,000	1,925,160	1,925,160
1885	127,220,256	3,307,727	2,811,567
1889	146,283,927	3,262,132	2,642,326

Sources: James W. Milner, "Report on the Fisheries of the Great Lakes: The Result of Inquiries Prosecuted in 1871 and 1872," in U.S. Commission of Fish and Fisheries, *Report,* 1872–1873, Appendix A, 42d Cong., 3d sess., 1872, S. Misc. Doc. 74 (Serial 1547), 7; Hugh M. Smith, "The Fisheries of the Great Lakes," in U.S. Commission of Fish and Fisheries, *Report,* 1892, Appendix, 53d Cong., 2d sess., 1893, H. Misc. Doc. 209 (Serial 3264), 366; U.S. Commission of Fish and Fisheries, *Report,* 1895, 54th Cong., 2d sess., 1896, H. Doc. 104 (Serial 3518), 96; Department of Commerce, Bureau of the Census, *Historical Statistics of the United States: Colonial Times to 1970,* Bicentennial ed., 93d Cong., 1st sess., 1973, H. Doc. 93-78, Part 1, 201.

Note: Most of the Canadian catch went to American markets and sold at American prices. The value of Canadian dollars was almost equal to that of American dollars, and thus the value of the Canadian and American harvests were very close, given the exchange rate. The indexed value is based on the Warren and Pearson Index of wholesale prices, 1910–1914 = 100.

it had grown to nearly 13,000. This total included 1,239 shoresmen and preparators in the United States figures, whereas the United States figure for 1880 did not include them. By 1890, the number employed had dropped to 12,500, including 1,614 workers in fish houses in the United States, but none in Canada. These incomplete data show that 78 percent of the work force was American and 22 percent was Canadian in 1890. Available data reveal 1885 as the high point in the number of workers employed and a distinct decline by 1890, a trend that continued in the twentieth century.[4]

One other set of figures gathered by the American and Canadian governments, estimating the value of the fish taken from the Great Lakes, help to give an idea of the industry's fortunes between 1872 and 1889 (table 4.2). In 1872, the estimated value of the total harvest was $1,950,768.[5] Adjusted to the 1910 to 1914 United States wholesale price index, the value was $2,653,360; in 1880, it had fallen to $1,925,160; in 1885, it slightly surpassed the 1872 value, reaching $2,811,567; and in 1889, the banner harvest year, the catch was valued at $2,642,326, just slightly less than the 1872 harvest. But what a vast difference in poundage: 39,330,000 in 1872 compared with 146,283,927 in 1889.

The enormous expansion in the size of the harvests resulted from the efforts of fishermen and dealers alike to maintain and possibly even to improve wages and profits in the face of market realities. The catch changed in composition with a decline in some of the more valuable species, especially whitefish and sturgeon. While fishers pursued these species relentlessly, they turned to large harvests of commercially less valuable ones. In addition, the poundage harvested in general contained more and more small fish, which brought lower prices. Therefore, more fish had to be caught and sent to market. Such economic pressures on the resource, in turn, seriously eroded the ability of the fish to reproduce. Fishermen and dealers were caught in a seemingly endless downward cycle, and the fish population suffered severely.

THE TECHNOLOGY OF MASSIVE HARVESTS

The tools of the great catch between 1875 and 1889 were basically the net, boat, and preservation systems developed earlier and in use when Milner wrote his report, but technically improved and applied much more intensively. The expansion of the fleet of gill-net steamers, equipped with gill-net lifters; the use of many more and finer-meshed nets; and the increased use of freezing techniques introduced in 1869 made such enormous harvests physically possible. The significant advance to ammonia refrigeration for freezing and storing fish came in 1892, introduced in Sandusky, Ohio.[6]

Gill-net steamers, so central to the expanded harvests, enabled fishermen to work the waters at greater distances from home port and far out into the lakes; to carry much greater lengths of netting; and, using the manually operated gill-net lifter, to fish at greater depths (figure 4.1). About 1890, at the end of the great expansive period, the introduction of the steam-powered net lifter greatly enhanced harvest capabilities. By 1885, gill-net steamers had revolutionized the harvest on Lake Michigan, where fishermen used them more than on the other four lakes. They set gill nets "farther and farther from shore, until now [1885] the ends of those belonging to fishermen of opposite sides nearly meet at the center," according to the United States Commission of Fish and Fisheries.[7]

In the three highly productive parts of the Great Lakes—Lake Michigan, Georgian Bay, and Lake Erie—the increased use of gill-net steamers followed somewhat different scenarios. Lake Michigan, the second most productive of the lakes—given its location and physical characteristics, market demand, and aggressive industry leadership—developed the earliest and most extensive fleet of gill-net steamers. It grew from five in 1873 to thirty in 1880 and eighty-two in 1885, and then declined to forty-eight boats five years later. This drop reflected an exodus to more productive waters, notably Georgian Bay, Canada's richest Great Lakes fishing ground. There in 1875, 6 tugs worked the waters along with 264 sailing craft, using 2.6 million feet of gill nets. By 1894, the gill-net fleet had

Figure 4.1. Fishing boats: rowboat (*left*) and three gill-net steamers (*center and right*), Erie, Pennsylvania. (From Pennsylvania, State Commissioners of Fisheries, *Report,* 1895, facing 194)

expanded to 32 tugs (about half the total reported for all Canadian Great Lakes waters) and the number of sailboats to 345. Together, they used 11.2 million feet, or 2,121 miles, of gill nets. The most rapid growth of the steam-powered fleet occurred between 1885 and 1890.[8]

On Erie, the most productive of the Great Lakes, not until 1881 and 1882 did fishermen try gill-net steamers successfully at the eastern end of the lake. In 1885, Erie, Pennsylvania, with its fine, protected natural harbor, boasted seventeen gill-net steamers valued at $40,000. Fishermen harvested the waters "30 to 40 miles in each direction from their home port and across the lake to within 8 miles of the Canadian shore." Five years later the number of gill-net steamers working Lake Erie waters had doubled. Considering the Great Lakes as a whole, the gill-net steamer fleet grew from 58 boats in 1880 to 183 in 1890.[9] The application of steam power and the intensive use of pound nets and gill nets played a major role in overtaxing the fish resources.

EXPANSION AND THE WHOLESALE FISH DEALERS

The movers and shakers of expansion in the Great Lakes fishing industry in the late 1870s and the 1880s, the wholesale dealers in Great Lakes fishing communities, shaped the pattern of exploitation. Long a part of the industry, they refined and specialized their business practices in ways that made them an even more potent force than James Milner had found them in 1872. In many ways, they were like the vast body of American business entrepreneurs of the late nineteenth century: ambitious; hustling; ingenious in combining capital, labor, and raw materials to create marketable products; eager to tap natural resources; profit hungry; influential in politics; impatient of government interference or restraints, but glad to have a benevolent government assist them. While they claimed to advocate laissez faire, open competition, and free enterprise, they favored tariff regulations advantageous to them, a lax immigration policy, tax breaks, and large government hatchery and stocking programs. Many of the very successful dreamed of creating a monopoly or at least becoming a major part of a commercial oligopoly. Profits were the bottom line.

To maximize their income and profits from a declining resource, the wholesale dealers embarked on in-house fishing ventures in larger numbers than ever, expanding their operations into the least harvested and/or most productive fishing grounds. They augmented and improved their fleets on northern Lake Michigan, on Superior and Huron. As successful businessmen in Great Lakes shoreline communities, they either possessed or borrowed the capital necessary to invest in the newest and best of steam and freezing technology, gill-net steamers, steam-powered collection boats, steam-powered pile drivers for setting pound-net stakes, and freezers to enable them to hold part of the harvest from market until they could receive an advantageous price for it. Such equipment cost far more than individual fishermen could afford. For instance, freezer plants based on the technology introduced in the late 1860s cost $8,000 to build in 1880. Gill-net steamers weighing from five to thirty tons cost from $2,000 to $10,000 apiece.[10] To make such investments cost effective, operations had to be on a far larger scale than they had been when wind power dominated the industry. Dealer-owned fishing companies sometimes achieved economies of scale by hiring fishermen to operate their equipment, or they contracted with fishermen to use it for a share of the catch. They often bought out small fishermen and added them to the company work force. At other times, they achieved economies of scale by organizing marketing units of "independent" fishermen who owned their boats and equipment, picking up their catch and taking it to market. Sometimes they employed all these methods simultaneously, as they planned and organized larger units of production to supply the market in a way that maximized their profits.

The wholesale dealers on the Great Lakes tended to operate in clearly defined areas, carved out in competition with one another. On Lake Erie, for example, dealers in Cleveland controlled the fisheries of Lorain and Cuyahoga Counties. Those in Sandusky, the "world's largest market for fresh fish," dominated the fisheries of Sandusky Bay, the Bass Islands, the

Figure 4.2. Interior of a fish-packing plant, showing a fish-cleaning gang at work, Sandusky, Ohio. (From Hugh M. Smith and Merwin-Marie Snell, "Review of the Fisheries of the Great Lakes in 1885," U.S. Commission of Fish and Fisheries, *Report,* 1887, Appendix, 50th Cong., 2d sess., 1889, H. Misc. Doc. 133 [Serial 2661], facing 266)

shore between Port Clinton and Huron, and, to the ire of the Canadians, much of the pound-net fishing grounds in Ontario's Lake Erie waters (figure 4.2).[11] Dealers in Sault Sainte Marie, Michigan, controlled the catch of eastern Lake Superior in waters in reality belonging to Canada. At Killarney, Ontario, on Georgian Bay, one large dealership spread a wide net of control over the northern part of the bay, Manitoulin Island, and the adjacent smaller islands. "Control" was the verb used again and again in the study of the Great Lakes commercial-fishing industry conducted in 1885 by the United States Commission of Fish and Fisheries when referring to firms that handled the fish trade of particular cities. For the fisherman, dealer control included prices, market access, fish quality, and very often credit. For the independents who did not join forces with large operators, it also meant sometimes being forced out of customary fishing grounds.[12]

In 1885, fifty wholesale dealers controlled the fish trade of Lake Erie, an "enormous" trade by the standards of the day, "surpassing that of any other lake," and marketed products valued at nearly $2 million. The principal markets were Toledo, Port Clinton, Sandusky, Huron, Cleveland, Erie, and Buffalo. Dealers in Chicago "practically" controlled the entire catch from Lake Michigan and handled fish from other lakes as well. In Detroit, where several firms operated fisheries "on a large scale, in all parts of the lakes," six wholesale dealers handled 12.2 million pounds brought to market, and in Buffalo, three purchased almost 3.4 million pounds of fresh fish, largely from Canadian waters. In 1885, an estimated total of ninety wholesale dealers handled the harvest from the American Great Lakes. Many of them headed branch dealerships for large companies or, while ostensibly independent, worked under formal and informal agreements to supply large wholesalers.[13]

In his study written in 1879, one astute observer, Frederick W. True, described the tendency toward larger units of production at work in the Straits of Mackinac. From there, a catch totaling 3.3 million pounds went principally to Chicago, Detroit, Sandusky, and Cleveland. Speaking of those engaged in producing that harvest, he noted that they ranged from poor fishermen to "the wealthy merchant who owns extensive grounds and fishes by proxy. The tendency, however, is toward concentration of interests." The small operators sold out to the wealthier firms and became their hired employees.[14]

In 1885, looking back over thirty-five years of experience in the Great Lakes fishing industry, Alfred Booth reflected about the changing technology, the growth of larger production units, and the triumph of the dealer-entrepreneurs. The fisherman's apparatus had been much simpler and business had been far less systematic and much less sophisticated in 1850: "There was not a steam tug on the Lakes which was then exclusively employed in the business; the little sail boats of the fishermen constituted the only means of carrying, setting and tending the nets; and, very often, the means of transporting the catch to market." Change came, he believed, because the opportunity to make money attracted ambitious men who had capital to invest. Booth observed, "The bulk of the fish are now taken by moneyed individuals or companies, who use every possible means to facilitate the work; who measure their nets by the mile, their catch by the ton; who employ perhaps hundreds of men, and put into requisition, besides the old-fashioned sail boats, numbers of fast-running tugs."[15]

AMERICAN ENTREPRENEURS AND EXPANSION INTO CANADIAN WATERS

The American exploitation of Canadian waters dated from the beginning of commercial fishing on the Great Lakes. During the 1870s and 1880s, American entrepreneurs sought the wealth of Canadian waters as never before. Responding to an increasing market demand and an eroding whitefish population in American waters, they looked to the better stocked Canadian Great Lakes to keep their businesses profitable. There, commercial fishing was less fully developed and the dominion government tried to ensure the long-term use potential of the fishery by licensing fishermen and appointing officers to enforce rules and regulations. Spearheading the northward expansion, the wholesale dealers developed a series of techniques for tapping Canadian resources. The most obvious and widely practiced of these was to take boats and gear into Canadian waters and go fishing, a practice that became increasingly dangerous as the Department of Marine and Fisheries in the late 1880s and 1890s initiated cruiser patrols to arrest American poachers. One could gamble and plan on evasive action, frequent areas difficult to search, and learn about the timing of surveillance and evade it. Americans who fished illegally did all of these. As early as 1873, the Department of Marine and Fisheries criticized American dealers for creating a demand and offering high prices for fresh fish, a direct encouragement for Canadians to fish in remote areas that were difficult to supervise.[16]

There were more subtle and less obviously illegal ways of achieving the same end. American companies sent their collection steamers to Canadian fishing ports, where they bought fish at a higher price than Canadian fishermen could get in the home market, but that system had its limitations. Beginning in 1869, the Canadian government required its nationals to secure commercial-fishing licenses. No foreigners need apply. American wholesale fish companies worked out arrangements with Canadian fishermen whereby they supplied them with the money to buy licenses and furnished them with nets, boats, and all necessary gear on the understanding that the fishermen would deliver the catch to company collection steamers for an agreed-on price per pound.[17] Some American fish dealers established companies with Canadian partners who supervised operations in the dominion and saw to it that the fish went to American markets and that the business methods passed legal muster. They induced established Canadian companies to enter working arrangements with them. Large firms like Post and Company of Sandusky had one partner live in Canada to look after company interests. American dealers sometimes moved part of their production operations to Canada. The United States Commissioner of Fish and Fisheries reported in 1892 that the number of men employed and the capital investment in the fisheries of the Duluth, Minnesota, area had declined because some "extensive" American dealers had transferred their processing plants to the Canadian side of Lake Superior. These dealers believed that the fish had deserted American for Canadian waters.[18] The American presence in the fisheries of the Canadian Great Lakes became so pervasive that one member of the

House of Commons lamented in 1894, in the wake of the commercial "invasion," that "in Canada there are just a few fish firms, and these are mostly composed of Americans."[19]

United States tariff regulations played a major role in helping American dealers achieve dominance in Canadian waters. The tariff law of 1883, which put lake fish on the free list, posed no impediment to importing Canadian fish into the American market for either Canadian or American dealers. But with the enactment of the McKinley Tariff in 1890, American dealers gained the advantage. That tariff placed a duty of three-quarters of a cent per pound on fresh fish imported into the United States unless the importer could prove that the fish were caught with American-owned equipment. After October 1, 1890, the importer had to take an oath to that effect. Many American dealers had already adopted the system of furnishing Canadian fishers with equipment, and those who had not done so "purchased or furnished the apparatus of the Canadian fishermen from whom they obtained fish."[20] Or, as the Canadians charged, they presented paper evidence of dummy sales to satisfy the United States customs authorities. Canadian dealers, however, had to pay the duty, which made the fish they sent to the United States noncompetitive in a very competitive market. The United States tariff laws presented no threats to American fish dealers bringing in Canadian fish. As one member of the House of Commons noted bitterly, the McKinley Tariff had the effect of placing "the control of our inland fisheries, or a large portion of them, in the hands of the American dealer, and to take them out of the hands of the Canadian dealer."[21]

Large American companies in Detroit and Buffalo, noted one member of the House of Commons in 1891, had taken control of the principal fisheries of Lake Huron and Georgian Bay. Edward E. Prince, the well-trained British fisheries biologist recently brought to Canada by the Minister of Marine and Fisheries, confirmed this view one year later. So did the findings of the Dominion Fishery Commission on the status of fisheries in Ontario.[22]

The dealers in Sandusky, Ohio, owned and controlled much of the pound-net fishery on the Canadian side of Lake Erie. The report on the Great Lakes issued by the United States Commission of Fish and Fisheries in 1890 recognized extensive American control in a segment headed "Canadian fisheries of Lake Erie controlled by Sandusky dealers": "Several firms now control important pound-net fisheries on the northern shore of Lake Erie. Over 100 pound nets are there employed, and 3 steamers are engaged in transporting the catch to Sandusky." Their businesses employed 156 workers in 1890, utilized $86,225 worth of boats and apparatus, and produced 3,098,267 pounds of fish valued at $40,522. Between 1881 and 1890, the Canadian fish imported to Sandusky ranged between

1 million and 6 million pounds. The average for the ten years was 2.8 million.[23]

Canadian perceptions of the way the structure of the Great Lakes fisheries industry had changed in the latter 1880s were quite accurate. By 1893, three large groups of dealers controlled the harvesting and marketing of most of the Great Lakes catch: dealers in Cleveland and Sandusky monopolized that of western Lake Erie; dealers in Buffalo, principally the Buffalo Fish Company, controlled the yield from parts of eastern Lake Erie, Lakes Huron and Ontario, and Georgian Bay, and most of that from the connecting waters of Lakes Huron and Erie; and in Chicago, the A. Booth Packing Company controlled the catch from most of Lakes Michigan and Superior.

EXPERIMENTATION AND INNOVATION

While the entrepreneurial wholesale fish dealers relied heavily on the expansion of fishing to maximize their profits, they also looked to technical innovation to achieve the same end. For example, they sought to develop new products and to devise new ways of using formerly wasted parts of the catch. They fostered and supplied the sturgeon-processing industry. A few experimented with canning fish, a notable example being a Cleveland firm that canned artificially stained herring and marketed it as "canned salmon." Some expanded their product lines to include smoked fish. Others ventured into producing fish oil, which was used in tanning leather and as an ingredient in printing ink, lubricants, and greases. The detailed figures on the wholesale fish trade of Lake Erie compiled in 1885 give some perspective on the value of the products derived from fresh, frozen, and salted fish that fish dealers sent to market compared with the value of smoked and canned fish, caviar, oil, and isinglass. The fresh, frozen, and salted category was worth $1.5 million; the specialized products, $271,200.[24]

Dealer-entrepreneurs displayed a keen interest in experimenting with fishing methods other than the well-known and successful adaptations of tugs as gill-net steamers. In 1873, one tried to introduce the beam trawl from England into the Lake Michigan fishery, but quickly found that the irregular lake bottom caught the net and fouled its operation. Other experiments involved the use of set-lines or trawls. The Connable Fishing Company of Chicago reported in 1894 that a member of the firm had invented a gill-net lifting machine. One had been built and was in test operation on a tug: "It is run by a separate rotary engine and will take the nets from almost any depth of water at an average speed of about 15 minutes per box; will do this when the water is rough or smooth, without damage to the nets or to the fish." While these examples do not exhaust the list of efforts of the large dealer-producers to try new ways of enhancing production, they do illustrate their innovative turn of mind.[25]

Yet for all their ingenuity in organizing and dominating the industry at its height in the 1880s, in creating competitive market strategies, in developing and adapting the most efficient technologies of harvest, and in recognizing the advantages that railroad transportation using fast freight and refrigerator cars gave them in reaching distant markets, the dealer-entrepreneurs knew that the best times in the Great Lakes fisheries were quickly passing. The ratio between capital invested and value of the catch had shifted markedly between 1880 and 1890. Considering the figures for American production, in 1880 for $1 of capital invested, the harvest yielded $1.23; in 1885, the ratio had fallen to 73 cents; and in 1890, it had dropped to 46 cents. These figures obviously reveal only part of the picture, leaving out labor, management, and marketing costs.[26]

Even without the benefit of these comparative official data at hand, fish dealers knew that they could do far better in newer, unexploited waters. They followed the mobile pattern characteristic of fur traders and trappers, lumbermen, miners, and farmers searching for newer, richer resources to tap. In the mid- to late 1880s, the more venturesome of them actively sought the bountiful whitefish and sturgeon of Lake of the Woods, which straddles parts of Minnesota, Ontario, and Manitoba, and Lake Winnipeg, in Manitoba. In these remote areas, wholesale dealers from the Great Lakes basin developed direct and indirect ties to secure supplies necessary to maintain their trade. A dealer in Irving, New York, spoke candidly about his relocation plans in 1894, noting that after seventeen years of business on Lake Erie, fish had become scarce and profits had declined. He proposed to move to Rainy Lake to fish for sturgeon, taking a colony of fishermen with him, he hoped as many as 300. Samuel Corson, a fisherman from Collingwood, Ontario, with a quarter century of experience on the lakes, believed that Lake Winnipeg and Lake Winnipegosis provided great opportunities: "You can go up there with one hundred dollars worth of nets and catch more lbs. of fish in 6 weeks than you can catch here in 6 months with five hundred dollars worth of nets."[27]

Well aware of the declining fish harvests, dealers approved of hatcheries and stocking programs and even contributed to those efforts, but they resisted regulation as a way to conserve the resource. Of the humans interacting with Great Lakes fish, the entrepreneurial wholesale fish dealers of the late nineteenth century were the most powerful. They wielded enough political influence to shape national and local policy in both Canada and the United States. Their motivations, thoughts, feelings, and business practices contributed greatly to the decline of the resource. Control of fishermen, price fixing, and intense competition among them led to overfishing the most valuable commercial species: whitefish, trout, herring, and sturgeon.

The depression beginning in 1893 and the declining resources caused a monumental shake-up in fish dealerships. Several experienced large dealers noted in 1894 that the industry was producing at dangerously high levels, far beyond market demand, and experiencing serious loss. Louis Streuber, a very influential dealer in Erie, Pennsylvania, who pioneered in introducing gill-net tug fishing there in 1881, observed that the industry's principal problem was "the great number of lakes, the great amount of fish, and the great number of people that are at it." A dealer in Huron, Ohio, observed, "I don't believe I would be a false prophet if I should say that half the people now in the fishing business will go out of it within a couple of years."[28]

While some businesses failed, the largest of them, with a history spanning the years 1850 to 1985, A. Booth and Company, came forward to order, regulate, and, it was hoped, monopolize the Great Lakes fishing industry. The company's business strategies and tactics affected the fish resource during the nineteenth century as the firm gained control of fish production on Lakes Michigan and Superior.

5

A. Booth and Company Bids for Great Lakes Dominance

There Were No Wealthy Fishermen

Among the Great Lakes wholesale fish dealers in the United States and Canada, the entrepreneur with the grandest vision of how the industry should be organized was Alfred Booth, an English-born Chicago merchant. The labors of his lifetime culminated in 1898 with the organization of "The New Fishery Trust" as the *New York Times* called it, formally A. Booth and Company, a $5.5 million "consolidation of the principal fisheries of the great lakes."[1] An examination of this leading business among the Great Lakes wholesale fish dealers provides valuable insights into the workings of the commercial-fishing industry, particularly the ways in which the dealers functioned, related to the fish resource, wielded their influence to control fishermen and policy makers, and applied their organizing skills to maximize profits in a highly competitive industry.

Beyond these perspectives, the Booth company's business history suggests how its operations affected the fish resources of the Great Lakes and how its large presence in Canadian waters exasperated and troubled many Canadians and the Canadian government. Such information is hard to come by, for few nineteenth-century dealers' records remain. The Booth company's records, too, apparently have been destroyed. Yet enough bits and pieces from American and Canadian documents, court records, newspapers, a smattering of company publications, and a variety of nineteenth-century Chicago business directories, social registers, histories, and biographical albums remain to provide a small but significant body of knowledge about the company's operations on the Great Lakes. In addition, the wealthy and influential Booth served on innumerable committees and commissions, and, as a result, the press quoted him from time to time. At the request of the *American Field,* he wrote a series of articles for its November 1885 issues, stating his ideas about the resource, the fishermen, and fishery policy.

EARLY YEARS IN CHICAGO

Born in Glastonbury, England, Alfred Booth migrated to the United States in 1848, at the age of twenty. After living briefly near Kenosha, Wisconsin, he moved to Chicago. In 1850, on the eve of the city's great commercial expansion, he opened a small store and traded in fish and vegetables. Before the Panic of 1857, the business had moved to more up-scale quarters, a twenty- by forty-foot three-story brick building at the corner of Dearborn and Madison Streets. If, as legend has it, he began by buying fish from Lake Michigan fishermen and distributing them through the streets of Chicago on a cart, then seven years wrought a wonderful change in his business fortunes. A picture taken on opening day in front of the new store shows him in a high hat, surveying the new quarters and four small, horse-drawn delivery wagons parked in front. His first two decades in business paralleled the early period of notable growth in the Great Lakes commercial-fishing industry. Without question, Booth had embarked in the food supply business in Chicago at a very auspicious time. Following the city's commercial growth in the 1850s came the economic stimulus of the Civil War. Ambitious, successful, hard driving, and considered by some "a clever fine fellow," Booth thought big about the future of the wholesale food industry. Commercial ratings show his business with a capital of $8,000 to $10,000 in 1862. By 1871, it had moved into the $100,000 to $250,000 rating category. By 1883, A. Booth and Sons—as the firm became known when Booth's sons, Alfred B. and William, acquired partnership interests in 1880—had risen into the next bracket: $300,000 to $500,000. The company showed a consistently good credit rating from 1859 to 1897.[2]

Before 1871, Booth had acquired several operating locations in Chicago. His investments grew to include a salmon-canning operation on the

Sacramento River in California and the properties of an East Coast oyster merchant, D. D. Mallory. Whatever the precise sequence of growth, in 1885 A. Booth and Sons could portray the company empire in an elaborate letterhead showing the oyster-packing house in Baltimore; the salmon canneries in Astoria, Oregon; and the impressive four-story headquarters at Lake and State Streets in Chicago, and could list no fewer than twelve major locations of company activity, including St. Paul; St. Louis; Louisville; Indianapolis; Escanaba and Manistique, Michigan; Washburn, Wisconsin; San Francisco and Collinsville, California; and Pittsburgh. Alfred T. Andreas's *History of Chicago* characterized the Booth business as "the most extensive oyster, fish and fruit dealers in the West."[3]

Booth could rightly consider himself as one of Chicago's merchant princes. He belonged to the appropriate social clubs. His residence at 1638 Michigan Avenue stood among those of Chicago's wealthy and successful elite. He was listed in the *Social Register* and the *Chicago Blue Book*. The *New York Tribune*'s list of American millionaires published in June 1892 included Alfred Booth among the 276 in Chicago who were worth at least $1 million, along with such well-known entrepreneurs as George M. Pullman, Potter Palmer, Marshall Field, and Cyrus H. McCormick. He was unique among American millionaires, the only one in the *Tribune*'s national roster to accumulate such wealth through the "sale and packing of fish, oysters, etc." An Episcopalian who served as president of the St. George Benevolent Association of Chicago from 1873 to 1877, he was proud of his English origins and often returned to his place of birth, Glastonbury, the ancient cathedral town.[4]

In all likelihood, Booth used these visits to further company business. He may have been looking at the fishing industry of the British Isles for ideas, for in 1873 he imported a beam-trawl from England for trial on Lake Michigan. Booth may have sought English capital for his business ventures. When plans for a consolidation of the company's "most important concerns" in Great Lakes fishing were under way in 1896 through 1898, at first English capital was central to the proposal. Ultimately, American capital financed the merger, once the British funds pledged earlier failed to materialize. Booth, like many late-nineteenth-century businessmen, saw commercial merit in winning awards for company products at expositions abroad and at home. The banner "Highest Medals and Awards—England, France, Germany, and the United States" was added to the company's letterhead in the 1880s. This scanty evidence suggests the possibility of a strong overseas dimension to Booth's business success, long before the firm became involved in fishing operations in international waters.[5]

EXPANSION IN THE GREAT LAKES

Lake Michigan

Booth's involvement in buying fish from the Great Lakes dated from his beginnings in Chicago in 1850 and grew rapidly, at first to supply the Chicago market and later, as the city's national rail hub developed, to supply increasingly larger and far-flung markets. As Chicago assumed the position of dominant marketplace for Lake Michigan fish, Booth's wholesale fish business developed into the city's largest among a dozen or more similar ventures. The company's collection steamers and fishing operations initially worked the southern part of the lake. Fishing boats out of Chicago, remarked Booth in 1885, until very recent years could bring in all the whitefish they wanted by going no farther north than Milwaukee. That was no longer the case. In pursuit of whitefish, A. Booth and Sons worked out a system of harvesting the bounteous waters of the northern part of the lake. In 1880, the company built a freezer plant in Escanaba, Michigan. Shortly afterward, it added another in Manistique. When the United States Commission of Fish and Fisheries made its elaborate study of the Great Lakes fisheries in 1885, A. Booth and Sons was firmly entrenched in the area of northern Lake Michigan, from where two company steamers carried the catch to Chicago. A tug and a sailboat operated a gill-net fishery, and the company owned pound nets near Naubinway, as well. In addition to fishing on its own account, the firm bought fish from fishermen along the whole arc of the northern Lake Michigan shoreline from Point Detour to St. Helena Island, near the Straits of Mackinac, and in the Beaver and Manitou Islands. Shipments of fresh and frozen fish from the company's plant in Escanaba in 1884 totaled over 1 million pounds.[6]

Lake Superior

Bayfield, Wisconsin

With its Lake Michigan operations well established, A. Booth and Sons laid plans to expand into Lake Superior (figure 5.1). The completion of the Chicago, St. Paul, Minneapolis, and Omaha Railroad to Bayfield, Wisconsin, in 1883 had spurred development, opening a new avenue for Lake Superior fish into the growing trans-Mississippi markets. During the 1885 season, the company began testing the feasibility of opening operations in Bayfield, adjacent to the Apostle Islands in Lake Superior, noted for centuries as a very rich fishing ground. There three other operators in addition to Booth employed "several hundred men nearly all year around," according to the *Bayfield County Press*. Their combined catch

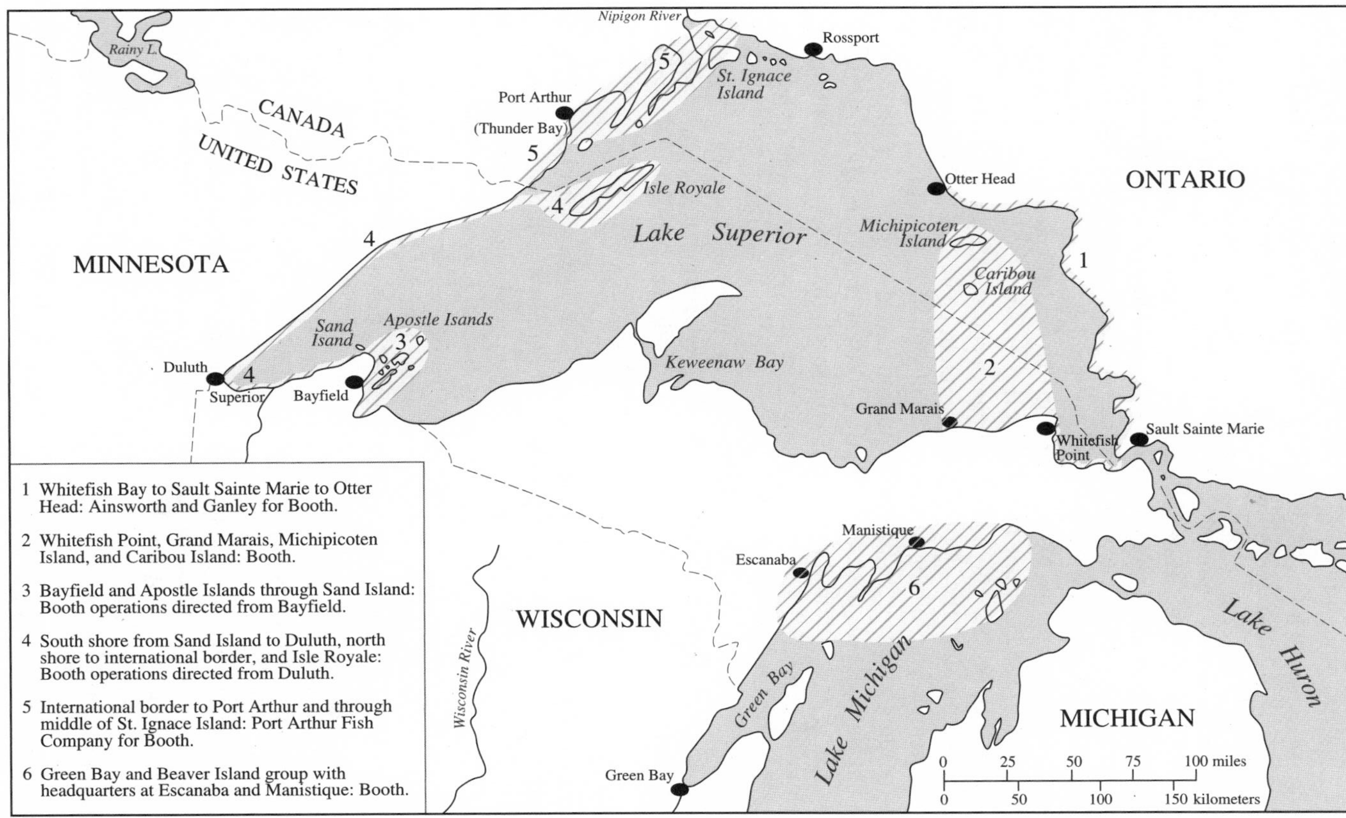

Figure 5.1. Lake Superior and northern Lake Michigan, showing major sectors of the fishing and collecting operations of the A. Booth Packing Company, 1894. (Cartographic Laboratory, University of Wisconsin–Madison)

was 2.5 million pounds in 1885, a somewhat smaller harvest than in preceding years.[7] During the next decade, both the pound-net and gill-net fisheries escalated and then slumped. By 1894, fishermen and dealers in Bayfield unanimously complained of a declining catch of whitefish. The findings of the Joint Commission Relative to the Preservation of the Fisheries in Waters Contiguous to Canada and the United States, appointed in 1892, reveal the extent and nature of the Booth company's gill-net fishing operations based in Bayfield. When interviewed in 1894, Booth's local agent, M. B. Johnson, estimated that the number of gill-net fishers had declined by one-third in his six years in Bayfield because of the poor catches. Booth used just one tug there in 1894. Seine fishing had been all but abandoned because there was no longer a run of fish along the shores. In Johnson's opinion, the gloomy outlook might be improved if fishermen were prevented from taking too many small whitefish. To him, this was a long-standing problem going back through decades of seining that resulted in wagon loads of small unmarketable whitefish being dumped on the beach to rot. In addition, he was convinced that pound-net fishing, which destroyed large quantities of undersize fish, should be suspended along the Wisconsin shore for five years to give the small fish a chance to mature and reproduce. Then the resource would return to its former bounty. Such a move on the part of the state legislature, a goal the company had worked for but failed to achieve in the winter of 1893/1894, along with "the good work that the Duluth Hatchery is doing," would turn the tide.

The opposition of the A. Booth Packing Company, as it came to be known in 1885, to pound netting roused the ire of pound netter Joseph La Belle, a "bright, intelligent fisherman, of French birth," who had come from Quebec to Bayfield twenty-five years earlier. The principal pound-net owner in the area, he operated sixteen nets on Chequamegon Bay and on Stockton Island and employed twenty fishermen. La Belle told Richard Rathbun, an American member of the Joint Commission, that "all those big parties want to do away with the pound nets in order to get all the chance to kill the rest of the fish with gill nets; that is what they are after." Johnson deplored the Indian treaty rights, which granted the Ojibwes freedom to fish in Lake Superior without regulation. He praised the Canadian system of licensing and regulating mesh size for all nets, but did not advocate such a system in American waters. Aside from curbing the pound-net fishers, he did not have a clearly defined plan of regulation and offered many reasons why regulation would not work. The Booth company's experience in Bayfield during the height of commercial fishing on the Great Lakes in the late nineteenth century reveals not only the firm's ideas, but the typical commercial fishers' view of how state and national government could help by subsidized restocking and how state regulation could help by establishing rules that hampered the operations of their competitors.[8]

Sault Sainte Marie, Michigan

Operations in Bayfield were the beginning of Booth's dominance on Lake Superior. By the early 1890s, the A. Booth Packing Company had control of the largest share of Lake Superior's catch in both Canadian and American waters. In addition to Bayfield, key centers of fishing and collecting operations were Sault Sainte Marie and Whitefish Point, Michigan; Duluth, Minnesota; and Port Arthur, Ontario, each with its own large sector served by steam-powered collection vessels. In Sault Sainte Marie, the A. Booth Packing Company developed a marketing arrangement with Ainsworth and Ganley, the major fishing firm at that location, that ensured delivery of its fish to Booth's Chicago distribution facilities. Ainsworth and Ganley dominated the southern shore of Whitefish Bay from the Tahquamenon River east to Sault Sainte Marie and the eastern shore of Lake Superior as far north as Otter Head.[9]

Ainsworth and Ganley organized its business to accommodate the realities of Canadian fishery regulations and dominant American markets. C. E. Ainsworth was an American from Cape Vincent, New York, and Joseph Ganley was a Canadian from the Lake Huron fishing town of Collingwood on southern Georgian Bay. Ganley operated a fishing tug, looked after Canadian commercial-fishing licenses, and supervised fishing at the eight stations on the Canadian shore, where "they have practically no opposition." In 1894, after eleven years of successful operations, the company fished twice as much apparatus as it had six or eight years earlier, using hired fishermen principally from Sault Sainte Marie. Ganley piloted the collection steamer to the fishing stations, collected the catch, and delivered it to the company's fish house in Sault Sainte Marie. The plant expanded in size by one-third between 1889 and 1894.[10]

On November 10, 1893, Joseph Ganley explained the Ainsworth and Ganley business to the Dominion Fisheries Commission, which was investigating the Ontario fisheries. The company's fish went directly to Chicago by boat: "We pay no duty on our fish; they go in as American fish, but all are caught in Canada by Canadian fishermen in Canadian boats and under Canadian licenses. The actual duty is ¾ of a cent on Canadian fish going into the United States, unless got in by some arrangement by which the duty is taken off." The arrangement in the case of this company was very simple. It was an American business by legal definition, fishing in Canadian waters. It furnished the fishermen with the tools of the harvest, thus making the fish duty free by the terms of the McKinley Tariff. Ganley noted that the company bought 100 tons from fifteen fishermen and from Indian boats, consigning all its catch to Chicago, principally the

A. Booth Packing Company. He explained: "*We could not establish our own agency to send fish in a profitable way, as the other dealers are too strong for us to compete with. The trade is all in their hands. . . . I do not know of any Canadian agents who buy or deal in fish in the United States.*"[11]

Whitefish Point, Michigan

The other component of the A. Booth Packing Company's operations on eastern Lake Superior centered on Whitefish Point, Michigan, where in 1892 it established a fishing station in competition with E. Endress and Sons, which had fished there continually for thirteen years. Both companies worked the shore from Grand Marais to Whitefish Point. The A. Booth Packing Company also counted Caribou Island and Michipicoten Island as part of its eastern Lake Superior collection sphere, with a company steamer serving Whitefish Point and the islands. Endress operated three fishing tugs, and Booth operated two. They went to Whitefish Point from northern Lake Michigan, where they had fished until late May or mid-June. In addition, the Booth interests came to an agreement with the lighthouse keeper at Whitefish Point, who owned seines and claimed the sole right to use them on the shore. The company furnished the labor and boats and made the catch, which it divided with the lighthouse keeper. Rathbun found Booth's men seining every day, all day, weather permitting, during his visit in the summer of 1894. Booth also operated pound nets on the inside shore of Whitefish Point under the supervision of a very experienced fisherman. Some of the pounds were set 100 feet deep in the water with covers over the pots, making them technically trap nets—efficient, destructive, and outlawed in Canada.

Endress had been established since 1879 at Whitefish Point when the Booth company made its bid for a share of the catch. He told representatives of the Joint Commission that the arrival of Booth threatened to ruin the fishery: "When we had this ground here entirely to ourselves we never overdid the business. Years ago we might have caught more fish than we did, but we tried to preserve it and make it last a long time, when the Booth people came here we had to go in for our share." The contest at Whitefish Point is an excellent example of how the highly competitive nature of commercial fishing contributed to overfishing.[12]

One other firm sought a piece of the whitefish resource in that region. The Connable Fishing Company of Chicago, whose general headquarters were in Petoskey, Michigan, sometimes ran its operations out of Grand Marais, Michigan, where it fished on its own and bought fish from small fishermen. This firm moved its gill nets and tugs from place to place on the Great Lakes, "seldom fishing at one point exclusively for an entire season." This system, rather widely used in the age of intensive steam technology and declining resources, made sense for roving gill-net steamer captains, but it irritated the local fishermen in whose grounds the interlopers chose to set their nets.[13]

Duluth, Minnesota

Moving clockwise around Lake Superior from Whitefish Point, the next center of Booth activity, in Bayfield and the Apostle Islands, has already been discussed. Farther west in Duluth, at the head of the lake, the A. Booth Packing Company established a branch house in 1886, from where it shipped fish west and southwest by rail. In 1894, the fisheries tributary to the Duluth market included those of the southern shore from Sand Island in the Apostles west to Duluth, which was served by Booth's passenger and freight steamer, *S. B. Barker;* the Minnesota shore; Isle Royale; and the Canadian shore north almost to Port Arthur. The company's experience here clearly illustrates the competition among wholesale dealers, the unpredictable and volatile nature of commercial fishing, and the uneasy business relationships between the Booth company and fishermen. The beginning of the company's presence in Duluth are related to the decision of J. E. Cooley to quit the commercial-fishing business after more than a decade of braving northeasters, probing the mysteries of a fish population that changed locations rapidly, suffering the wreck and repair of a fishing tug, and, finally, losing the tug at Isle Royale. In 1886, he sold out to the A. Booth Packing Company, "well satisfied that the surest way to make money in the fish business is to keep out of it."

John Coventry, the Booth manager in Duluth, commented extensively on the trials and tribulations of fishermen in his interview with Richard Rathbun in 1894. They were experiencing real difficulty in paying for gill nets and pound nets purchased on credit from dealers. Fishermen had to plan on at least three months of "hard fishing" to retire the debt on gill-net rigs, which cost $200 to $250. A stormy spring could prolong that time period, making it well into autumn before they could begin making money for themselves. To minimize the problem, they had developed an alternative that combined gill-net and hook-line fishing, a system, noted Coventry, that had been working quite well in recent years. He believed that they had taken the idea of balancing fishing methods from their farming experience, for most of the Minnesota North Shore fishers were part-time farmers and part-time fishermen: "They have figured out (from their experience) that mixed farming pays better than wheat farming alone, and now instead of taking a $200 gillnetting rig, they will take probably half of that, and will take $50 worth of hooks and lines. They will run both kinds of gear at the same time." When one apparatus did not work, the other usually did. Coventry noted, "One man last year started out with hooks and lines that did not exceed $50 in value. He fished all through the season, paid his men and his grocer's bill, and came home in the fall with between $700 and $800 in his pocket." The only problem with the hooks and lines, he noted, was that the fishermen brought him too many large, very large trout. The hotels liked them, but families did not.

The performance record of pound nets, which were far more expensive than gill nets, in this segment of the lake had become so uneven that the old system of the company's owning the nets and hiring them fished was no longer economically feasible. Now the Booth company insisted that fishermen own the nets and take their chances with the catch. Coventry cited the case of one fisherman who had bought a set of pound nets from Booth for $2,500. After four years of fixing, repairing, and fishing them, he still owed $400, but the company deeded them anyway on the understanding that he would pay when he could. To Rathbun, Coventry portrayed the fishermen as wasters of the resource. He spoke of repeatedly being offered catches of undersize whitefish, which he rejected as unmarketable, and of hundreds of tons of undersize whitefish being dumped on the beaches of the southern shore of the lake. The superintendent of the federal fish hatchery in Duluth, noted Coventry, had worked hard to teach as many fishermen as possible how to fertilize fish eggs and return them to the water. He got little cooperation: "Where I have found one that would do it, I would find 20 who would not." One wonders if Coventry thought about the way in which competition among wholesale fish dealers, fish prices, and fishermen's income contributed to overfishing, waste, and little interest in the long-term productivity of the resource. The relations between the fish dealers and the fishermen was by its nature adversarial, akin to those between labor and management in business and industry generally.

Episodes of friction between Coventry and fishermen are evident in the case of the Isle Royale fishermen. The log of the Menagerie Islet lighthouse keeper noted that on June 18, 1890, the fishermen had gone on strike and produced no fish for the Booth company's steamer *Dixon* to pick up. By the end of the month, a new contract had been signed. The interviews conducted in 1894 in Duluth by members of the Joint Commission cite another instance of differences between Booth's agent, Coventry, and the fishermen of Isle Royale. There in 1894, approximately fifty fishermen using twenty-three or twenty-four small boats and gill nets caught primarily trout. As did those in other isolated locations on the Great Lakes, the majority of Isle Royale fishermen moved from the mainland to their fishing grounds at the beginning of the season and returned to the mainland in late November or early December. In the winter, many worked in the woods and in the mines. The waters around Isle Royale produced far more fish than did the fishing grounds along the Minnesota shore. Isolated on the island for eight months, the fishermen depended on steamers to supply them and to take the catch to market.

According to S. P. Wires, the superintendent of the federal fish hatchery in Duluth, the Booth company sent the *Dixon* twice a week to pick up the catch from Isle Royale and that from along the Minnesota shore until the spring of 1894, when the Isle Royale fishermen staged a revolt. They refused to accept Booth's price and asked for more money. Booth refused to pay more, and the majority of the fishermen began to send the catch to a new firm in Duluth: Stone-Ordean. The company's manager, M. F. Kalmbach, knew his fishermen well. He came from a pioneer fishing family on Washington Island in Lake Michigan. The details of how the contest ended are not known, but the A. Booth Packing Company regained control and, in the early twentieth century, continued to dominate the lives of the Isle Royale fishermen.[14]

In her charming account of life on Isle Royale and the North Shore in the early twentieth century, Ingeborg Holte tells us about the dependence of the fishers on the Booth firm:

> Unfortunately, for many years, this was the only company that bought fish from the fishermen all along the north shore and on Isle Royale. I expect it is unnecessary to add that there were no wealthy fishermen. Each fisherman's supplies and freight were delivered on account at the beginning of the season. As the fisherman sold fish to the company through the season, his credit was merely deducted from his account. Rarely did the fisherman or his family see cash. He was considered fortunate if his catches for the season covered the account of supplies laid in for the summer.[15]

Fishermen in isolated places along the Great Lakes similar to Isle Royale experienced the same problem with a fish buyer-supplier monopoly.

Port Arthur, Ontario

Because of a scarcity of whitefish needed to meet market demands, the A. Booth Packing Company began operations in Canadian waters to the north of the Pigeon River boundary between Canada and the United States. The experience in Port Arthur, Ontario, in the 1890s provides a rich example of Canadian fishermen's exasperation with Americans' exploitation and the company's competitive practices. About 1890, the Booth company opened a branch in Port Arthur, from which its boats operated south to the international boundary and north to the middle of St. Ignace Island. When a representative of the Joint Commission visited Port Arthur in July 1894, Joseph Brunson of the Port Arthur Fish Company, as the Canadian operation of the Booth business was called, reported that the company operated two tugs and three sailboats. It fished from twelve- to twenty-pound nets, taking whitefish that averaged two to five pounds and some as large as ten pounds. According to Brunson, "Directly there are about 15 men employed, although the Booth Company buys fish of all other parties fishing here under contract," an arrangement that the manager did not describe. The tugs and sailboats conducted gill-net fishing at a considerable distance from shore using approximately 150 nets during June and from August to November, the beginning of the closed season. The nets were lifted every third day. The fishermen landed 95 percent of the gill-net catch in marketable condition, but Brunson shared the opinion of many fishermen that the pound-net catch was preferable because the fish were caught live and "always in good condition." All the fish were marketed fresh. The Booth steamer *Dixon* transported the greater part of the total catch at Port Arthur to Duluth. Two Booth and four other tugs operated from the Port Arthur dock.[16]

When interviewed by the Dominion Fisheries Commission, Port Arthur fishermen revealed their uneasiness with the business methods of the Port Arthur Fish Company. Some of them entered into contracts at the beginning of the season to sell their fish exclusively to that firm at a set price that, the company explained, was less than the price they could receive in Canada because the fish were going to the United States and thus were subject to a duty, according to Henry Servais. Testifying on October 26, 1893, in the midst of the fall season, he added, "Sometimes we strike for higher prices as at this time." Servais and his brother fished eleven-pound nets. They owned several tugs. "If the duty was paid by us there was nothing made out of them [the fish]," noted Servais. Canadian fishermen resented this: "Our fishermen say hard things . . . we think it unfair towards Canadians." Another Port Arthur fisherman, E. J. Nuttall, who along with his brother fished both gill and pound nets, held the same view. The company used the tariff argument to explain its low price, 3½ cents a pound, and at times took a temporary assignment of ownership of nets and gear by bill of sale in order to circumvent the duty. Nuttall had his doubts about the company's arrangements. According to him, the Booth company insisted on such assignments or a fisherman would receive three-quarters of a cent less per pound for his catch. He added, "I think there is many in this region that do not assign their nets over and get the same as those that do." Right or wrong, the testimony illustrates tensions between the American company and the Port Arthur fishermen.[17]

One year later, strong criticism of Booth's business methods surfaced, leading to an investigation by the Department of Marine and Fisheries. In early June 1895, Brunson wrote to the local dominion fishery overseer, D. F. Macdonell, that an "illwilled fisherman" had complained about his nets at Nipigon Bay. Macdonell undertook to defend Brunson in a letter to the Department of Marine and Fisheries. Brunson, said he, "is always anxious to observe the fishery laws." Captain E. Dunn of the department's fisheries patrol vessel, *Petrel,* had a very different view, claiming that Brunson was fishing pound nets for which he had no license.[18]

In the last week of June, W. A. Beebe, a fisherman with twenty years of experience and the captain of a fishing tug at Port Arthur, perhaps the "illwilled fisherman," entered the fray. He charged that Brunson, on behalf of the Booth interests, had broken the law in a number of ways. He was fishing some pound nets without a license. He had circumvented the intent of Canadian law with Macdonell's knowledge by taking out pound-net licenses in the names of several of his employees and then hired fishermen to set them, tend them, and bring in the catch for the Booth interests. Moreover, justice was hard come by, since Macdonell's brother was a member of the House of Commons. Being privy to the plans of the Department of Marine and Fisheries to send the *Petrel* to Port Arthur, he had kept the overseer informed about the time the patrols would be made, alleged Beebe. Ten days later, impatient with government delay, he wrote to Dunn, demanding action or he would take his complaint to the newspapers: "To think that the Dept. will allow a foreign Company to due [*sic*] them up to the disadvantage of their own subjects . . . is too much."

The Department of Marine and Fisheries opted to investigate and sent the *Petrel* under Dunn's command to Port Arthur. In early September, Beebe lodged a formal complaint against Brunson for fishing "at least two pound nets" without a license. Brunson was summoned to appear before Dunn to give evidence and, on September 9, immediately pled guilty, stating that he, with Macdonell's knowledge, was fishing fourteen pound nets for which he had formally sought license, expecting that official permission would materialize. To Dunn's consternation, the guilty plea cut off the possibility of quizzing others who were involved and had been summoned to appear. Brunson was fined; Macdonell was dismissed; and the A. Booth Packing Company continued to fish out of Port Arthur.[19]

The Fisheries Protection Service of the Dominion of Canada had instructed Dunn to find proof that the Port Arthur Fish Company was really controlled by the A. Booth Packing Company. He did manage to produce several pieces of evidence confirming what the local fishermen considered to be common knowledge. One reveals some of the tactics that the company used to gain an upper hand. In 1894, a former employee of the Booth company, as proprietor of the Rossport Fish Company, began to buy fish in competition with the Chicago firm. The manager of the A. Booth Packing Company wrote to Brunson that in the spring of 1895 the company would send a tug from Sault Sainte Marie, Michigan, station it at Rossport, and have the captain buy fish at high prices. Dunn reported to his superiors the effect of Booth's business practices on the local fishermen. Favoritism to Booth inclined the company "to disregard the laws."

"This foreign firm" was allowed to fish fourteen pound nets, "whereas, they [the fishermen] were refused five."[20] Thus in the opinion of the Department of Marine and Fisheries, the A. Booth Packing Company emerged from the Port Arthur episode with a bad image as a foreign company that took the bulk of the catch and whose conduct in manipulating the Canadian system left the local fishermen disgusted with Canadian laws designed to encourage long-term yields from Great Lakes waters.

These vignettes of the Booth company's activities on Lake Superior that are found in the unpublished government documents of Canada and the United States illustrate some main themes in the company's struggle to organize and control the commercial fisheries of the Great Lakes. In a broader sense, they provide very specific on-site examples of major characteristics of the commercial-fishing industry of the Great Lakes in the late nineteenth century.

The example of Booth's relationship with Ainsworth and Ganley in Sault Sainte Marie shows how the A. Booth Packing Company gained indirect control over the fish yield of the Canadian waters of eastern Lake Superior. By agreement, Ainsworth and Ganley's fish went to Booth in Chicago. More broadly, Joseph Ganley's testimony revealed American entrepreneurial dominance in the Great Lakes wholesale fish trade. The materials clearly reflect the keen competition for the resource among large wholesale companies and between them and local fishing businesses in Whitefish Point, Bayfield, Duluth, and Port Arthur. They highlight the frictional and dependent relationships between fishermen and wholesale dealers in Duluth, Isle Royale, and Port Arthur, where ill feeling emanated from class differences, resentment over exploitation of the local resource by nonresidents, and a revulsion for monopoly. The company's practices in Duluth reveal technical adjustments in the harvest to compensate for the unpredictable and volatile nature of fishing. Throughout, the materials show the general popularity of government hatchery and restocking programs and distaste for industry regulation. In Port Arthur, the presence of a large American corporation that threatened to control Canadian fishermen's use of the Canadian resource added a nationalistic element to the local fishermen's protest. Perhaps most important, the records provide very specific working examples of an industry in which the intensity of fishing generated by competition to maximize profits and to make a living wage played havoc with the resource. Waste and overfishing took a heavy toll.

During the 1890s, the A. Booth Packing Company expanded its influence in the Great Lakes region, gathering into its fold fishing dealerships that had failed in the depression following the Panic of 1893. By 1898, the time had come to take the next steps toward industry control:

the formation of A. Booth and Company, a corporation worth $5.5 million that consolidated under Illinois law "the principal fisheries of the great lakes." In July 1899 came the incorporation of the Dominion Fish Company, a consolidation of Great Lakes and Manitoba fishing operations under Canadian law.[21] This drive for dominance had tragic consequences for the Great Lakes fish resources in the twentieth century.

6

Fishers of the Great Lakes 1850–1893

They Doubly Earn Every Dollar

Key to understanding how human activity affected the Great Lakes fish population are the fishermen and their families, those people in closest daily contact with the resource and dependent on it for a livelihood. The fishermen were legendary for their love of independence and their hard labor on the water, whatever the weather. They engaged the forces of nature in a struggle to make a living from the lakes' bountiful supply of fish, which was free for the taking if the will, daring, sense of adventure, discipline, ingenuity, and endurance to face physical hardships and uncertain results year in and year out were theirs. These qualities were the stuff of the fishermen's self-image, revealed in reminiscences and stories of their routine work and not-so-routine times of peril on the Great Lakes.[1]

Nineteenth-century fishers told many tales of harrowing escapes from death on stormy waters, from drowning when the ice broke up, and from nearly freezing to death in sudden late-autumn cold. One good example appeared in the *Ashland* [Wisconsin] *Press* on November 30, 1872, involving the Boutins, a prominent fishing family in Bayfield, Wisconsin, and formerly of Two Rivers, Wisconsin, on Lake Michigan. Benjamin Boutin told the editor about a harrowing trip from Duluth to Bayfield in a Mackinaw boat loaded with "gill nets, camp equipment, and his family." All was well when they set sail, but near Bark Pointe Bay, "the wind shifted to northeast, creating a heavy sea, compelling him to throw a portion of his load overboard, to keep the boat from swamping." Unable to ride the heavy swells, he made a run for the beach and landed the boat safely, but "full of water and everything in it wet through, the weather cold and ice making fast and his children nearly frozen." Thus began five miserable days on a windswept island in the midst of a blizzard with only a few pounds of sugar to sustain them. Finally, when the family was nearly starved, the storm ceased and they sailed home in a few hours. Concluded the editor of the *Ashland Press,* "Such is a fisherman's life. — They doubly earn every dollar received for their labor."[2] Bravery, daring, great physical strength, resourcefulness, and skill were the personal qualities the fishermen projected in accounts of life on the inland seas. To many, it was a way of life they loved as well as a livelihood. It had no equal.

While fishermen's accounts of their adventures on the Great Lakes glorified and enriched their lives, for most the bottom line remained: fishing to make a living. Nineteenth-century fishermen left relatively few personal records relating to their work, yet a variety of contemporary materials help reveal who they were, why and how they fished, and what they earned for their efforts. They also help explain their attitudes toward the resource and the way a changing economic structure of the industry and an unregulated, unprotected market affected fish and fishers.

Most fishers working the boats and nets on Great Lakes waters in the historic period down to the present have been men, yet the tasks involved in harvesting the fish and preserving them for consumption or readying them for market sometimes were a team effort, involving men, women, and children. While women and children's work cannot be quantified, vignettes of their labors emerge from diaries and government documents, contemporary writings, and the work of archaeologists and anthropologists. Indian women from the early pre-contact era on cleaned; smoked, dried, or otherwise preserved; and cooked the fish that the men harvested from the lakes, and the women's work included gathering the firewood needed for preserving and cooking.

During the nineteenth century, when many full-time fishers lived around the lakes in family households, fishing was a family enterprise. The more close knit the family, the more its energies focused on fishing. For example, in the French settlement at Two Rivers, on Washington Island, Wisconsin, and in the community on Jones Island in Milwaukee, boys at an early age helped on the water while learning to fish. Mothers and daughters from diverse cultural backgrounds made nets and helped with the catch as needed as well as cared for a home and reared a new generation of fishers. In the many families who combined fishing and farming, women assisted with the fishery as well as the farm work. At peak work times, such as the herring harvest on Lake Superior in November, which was conducted under very cold and stormy conditions, all the family members helped.[3]

With the development of the system of wholesale dealers and ever-improved methods of refrigeration and delivery, some of the functions carried out by the fisher families declined in the late nineteenth century, particularly in areas where large packing facilities operating with hired labor could handle the catch, such as the region around Toledo, Sandusky, and Cleveland, Ohio. In rather isolated Bayfield, Wisconsin, the large fish packers hired townspeople, men and women alike, to work at the docks during the November herring harvest, picking the fish from the nets, "to behead, gut, salt, and pack the herring, usually in half-barrels."[4]

Moreover, the women in some fisher families worked on the water. This is difficult to document, but examples are a matter of record for the twentieth century, and the practice probably extended back well into the nineteenth. For example, the wives of the Hockenson brothers, who fished and farmed in the Red Cliff Reservation area on the southern shore of Lake Superior from the second decade of the twentieth century into the 1950s, went out on the boats to work with their husbands, just as they joined them in doing the farmwork.[5] They may have felt as did Sandy Anderson of Milwaukee, who in the early 1990s performed many tasks for the family enterprise. As she put it, "I am Jill of all trades and master of none." She has worked all her life as a regular crew member on a fishing tug. "It's heavy work," she said. "It's not really for a woman to do, but a woman can do it and we do it. We have to prove it, and we do it. I do it."[6]

The fisher people of the Great Lakes were a racially and ethnically mixed group whose composition changed markedly from the seventeenth through the nineteenth century, particularly in the nineteenth century with the influx of population in the lands surrounding the lakes. One segment remained a constant throughout those 300 years: the region's Indians. The Ojibwes of Lake Superior in 1893 symbolized that long continuous Indian presence as they fished the rapids of the St. Mary's River with scoop nets and canoes, as had their predecessors when the French came upon them in the mid-seventeenth century using the catch for food and barter. The Indian population around the lakes changed markedly in composition and numbers under the impact of Euro–North American culture. They were fewer in number in 1893 than they had been around 1600. The tribal mix had changed through the centuries of fur trade, warfare, treaties, and removals. But Native North Americans were still present, especially in the northern parts of Lakes Huron and Michigan, and in the western areas of Lake Superior as far north as Grand Portage. Most notable were the Ojibwes, who had the largest amount of reservation land located on and near the lakes in Canada and the United States. They continued to rely on fish harvested in traditional ways for food and, to a certain extent, for trade in kind or cash.

Practical people who were always adjusting to the changing world around them, the Native Americans adapted to the commercial-fishing industry. With the areas where they could pursue traditional hunting and fishing for a livelihood more and more circumscribed, they had little choice. The lumbering industry laid waste to millions of acres of timber, destroying the habitat for fish and wildlife, by both the removal of trees and the subsequent outbreak of devastating fires. Reservation lands could not supply enough fish and game to sustain resident Indians, nor did most government programs to encourage farming and lumbering succeed in producing adequate livelihoods for them. They worked in the commercial-fishing businesses of the American Fur Company and the Hudson's Bay Company on Lake Superior and may have operated small fishing boats independent of either in the 1840s, suggests Robert Doherty. His research in the federal census records revealed that in 1860, as the fishing operations of the Hudson's Bay Company on Lake Superior were drawing to a close, 112 of 190 fishermen in Mackinac County, Michigan, were Indians, "mostly mixed-bloods," nearly 40 percent of whom owned no property and the balance, modest amounts. They were small poor fishermen, on the whole less well off than their white counterparts. Obviously, the propertyless group worked as fisher-laborers or fished on shares for commercial fishers. To the south in the Little Traverse Bay region, families of the Odawa band of Ottawas engaged on their own account in commercial fishing as a principal source of cash in the mid-nineteenth century.[7]

The profile of fishers in Mackinac County changed remarkably during the 1860s, with the arrival of fishermen from outside the area, possessed of varied amounts of capital and, in some cases, bringing their workmen with them to exploit the riches of northern Lake Michigan waters. The industry there plainly was shifting from small-scale fishing toward the dealer-entrepreneur organizations. With this transition, some Indians in the northern Great Lakes worked by agreements with the larger commercial wholesale companies. For example, in the 1890s, the Ainsworth and Ganley firm of Sault Sainte Marie, which bought fish from Indians, supplied Indian fishers with gill nets. At Batchawana Bay, the Indians also cut ice for the company's icehouse and cordwood for its tug. The company offered jobs to "any Indian on the North Shore who wishes to work."[8]

Well-kept records of the Canadian Department of Marine and Fisheries reveal such arrangements when they led to problems with the enforcement of the fishery laws. In one case, evidence clearly pointed to James and Charles Noble of Killarney, Ontario, very influential commercial fishermen. They were involved in furnishing the Indians of Manitoulin Island with illegal nets and equipment and encouraging them to fish during the closed season for a share of the catch.[9]

The exploitation of the local Indians by the Noble brothers is matched by the activities of another commercial-fishing company that operated on the St. Clair River in 1894. The report of an investigation by the Department of Marine and Fisheries of destructive sturgeon fishing at Walpole Island during the spawning season, in May and June, stated that reservation Indians caught sturgeon and delivered them daily for $1 apiece to a tug sent from Sandusky, Ohio, that towed them live in a sunken scow to the processing plant. "Yankees," fulminated one fishery overseer, were furnishing the Indians with hooks and lines to fish for them. The dominion Indian agent at Walpole Island indicated that some thousands of dollars came to these impoverished people from the sturgeon harvest. Clearly, commercial interests took advantage of their poverty.

In this case, the Department of Marine and Fisheries zealously protected the fishery resource. Investigating overseer Fred Kerr reported in early 1894 that at Walpole Island he had found forty to fifty Indians each using 1,000 to 2,000 hooks attached about eighteen inches apart to ropes that were stretched across channels. Each morning, the Indian fisher pulled in his lines and towed the trapped sturgeon with gaff hooks to live pounds. "According to my information the fish are most cruelly and roughly handled from the times they are caught until they are slaughtered in the Sandusky fish market," reported Kerr. Surely, the sturgeon of Lake St. Clair faced annihilation if this continued. Kerr vented his outrage: "No kind of fish can stand this mode of fishing and multiply. Just imagine 3,000 fish caught in the act of spawning with the spawn ripe ready to be impregnated, the fish in the act of mating, male and female coming thither for that purpose. . . . The process of reproduction being done by rolling together at the bottom thereby coming in contact with the numerous hooks set there by the design of man."[10]

The on-site overseer, J. C. Pollock, reported in May 1894 that this kind of sturgeon fishing had been going on for a full decade. A month later, he noted that the Canadian customs service had caught the American tug taking the sturgeon from the Indians. Ordered to seize the lines and hooks and fine the Indians, he did: "I took up and destroyed 47,000 yards of line and 44,000 hooks. . . . [N]early all the lines and hooks *belong to Americans*."[11]

The incident merits reporting at length because it illustrates two general themes in the history of the Great Lakes fishery aside from rivalries between Canada and the United States for the resource: commercial exploitation of Indian fishers, and a rise in objections to fishing by Native

North Americans at the end of the nineteenth century when commercial overfishing had weakened the resource. Deny as it might having anti-Indian attitudes, the Department of Marine and Fisheries waxed very officious when Indians were involved. In this case, its administrative files stressed the brutal sturgeon-fishing methods used by the Indians, but Euro–North Americans used the same methods and were fully as brutal without receiving such severe criticism.

In the 1890s, without question, that department showed a negatively critical attitude and legal unfairness to Indians in administering its regulations, insisting that the fishery laws applied to Indians as well as non-Indians, treaty rights not withstanding. Samuel Wilmot, Charles Hibbert Tupper, and Edward E. Prince—the three key people in the department—claimed that there was just too much evidence of commercial interests exploiting the Indians and encouraging them to fish year round to supply the markets. The oft-repeated official position was that "Indians and Whitemen alike are required to observe the law, but any special case of grievance or injustice will always have just consideration."[12] For example, the case of the Ojibwes of the Saugeen Reserve in 1894 and 1895 shows the conflict between treaty rights and Department of Marine and Fisheries regulations. The department at first denied the Ojibwes' treaty rights to fish on Lake Huron and then, once convinced that the Ojibwes sorely needed help to feed the hungry and that commercial interests could not benefit in this instance, honored the treaty.[13]

The Canadians were not alone in this kind of prejudicial behavior. The A. Booth Packing Company's agent in Bayfield, Wisconsin, denounced Indian treaty rights as a burden on the fishery because the Indians could be manipulated to use the rights to furnish commercial fishermen with a catch forbidden under state regulations, a highly ironic comment in view of the behavior of other Booth agents. Like the Department of Marine and Fisheries, newly created fish and game departments in the Great Lakes states sought to compel Indians to fish according to state rules, no matter how their rights were defined in federal treaties. Both Wisconsin and Michigan took this stance. Protest as they might, the Indians engaged in a discouraging battle until a renewed struggle by Native North Americans to assert their legal rights through the courts beginning with and following the civil rights movement of the 1960s produced some positive results.[14]

It seems more than ironic that the first fishers of the Great Lakes, the masters of a technology that allowed them to secure a major part of their food needs from fishing, found themselves at the turn of the twentieth century being harassed by state and dominion authorities and denied their fishing rights to make way for sport- and commercial fishermen.

Even more ironic, local residents perceived any rights given to the Indians by treaty as very unfair because they led to unequal access to the resource. It should be equally available to all.[15] The capital-intensive commercial fishery of the late nineteenth and early twentieth centuries required investments in boats and gear far beyond those that most Indian fishermen could muster, and they found themselves relegated to low-income jobs in the industry's hierarchy and, like other small fishermen, poor.

The new nineteenth-century fishermen came from the ranks of the people who moved into the Great Lakes basin and gradually but surely displaced the Indian population. While some migrants came with plans to fish the well-endowed lake waters, most who became fishermen chose the occupation as one among other possibilities available in a newly developing region. Fishing had very special attractions for lakeshore residents. In the mid-nineteenth century, fishing gear required only a modest investment, far less than farming, and the fish belonged to the people, free for the taking. Westward-moving Canadians and Americans became fishermen of the Great Lakes as well as farmers, businessmen, merchants, day laborers, skilled tradesmen, and professionals in newly developing communities. When at mid-century thousands of European immigrants to the United States made their homes in the Great Lakes region, they, too, found fishing an acceptable choice.

With the development of a large domestic market for Great Lakes fish in the post–Civil War years, the ranks of fishermen grew to include thousands from varied national origins. During the 1870s and 1880s, many immigrants among the tens of thousands who made new homes in the region found work in the fisheries. Some tasks required no special skills; others could be learned on the job; and special skills came with years of experience. Incoming immigrants and Canadian- and American-born workers alike fished for daily or monthly wages and contracted to fish on shares using equipment furnished by dealers, frequently with the option of buying it at the end of the season. Many tried and some succeeded in getting a start as "independent" fishermen through such arrangements.

By 1880, the Great Lakes fisheries had attracted a heterogeneous work force of fishermen, owners, managers, and dealers representing many nationalities. Referring to American waters, Ludwig Kumlien observed in 1880 that American-born fishermen were most numerous, and of the foreign-born, Germans and French Canadians were the largest groups. He noted further:

> The Scandinavian nations are also well represented. In some localities, particularly at the west end of Lake Superior and in the vicinity of Sault Ste. Marie, the Straits of Mackinac, and Saginaw Bay, many pure and half-breed Indians are

employed. At Sault de Ste. Marie, Indians are the principal fishermen. In the majority of the towns the nationalities are very much mixed. A catalogue would include Americans, English, French, Germans, Norwegians, Swedes, Russians, Poles, Belgians, Swiss, Dutch, Irish, and Indians.[16]

In 1885, on the crest of a period of great expansion in fishing, the United States Commission of Fish and Fisheries made an elaborate survey of the Great Lakes commercial-fishing industry, the most detailed of those done in the late nineteenth century. Field-workers for Lake Michigan reported a change in the nationality of the fishermen on that lake. They noted that the country had "gradually filled up with foreigners," many of whom turned to fishing, "and the industry is now practically in their hands, the Germans, Scandinavians, Irish, and French Canadians predominating. The few Americans are men who became interested in the work at an early date, or members of their families who have grown up in the business."[17] The fishers of Door Peninsula on Lake Michigan were a veritable smorgasbord of northern European immigrants who learned early on that to sustain themselves on the thin soils of the Niagara escarpment they had to combine fishing with farming and timber harvesting, often for cordwood and shingles.

In Canada, the fishermen were principally Canadian-born—second generation of British Isles origin, French Canadians, métis, and Indians—most of whom fished the waters of Lakes Huron and Superior. When the Dominion Fishery Commission interviewed Great Lakes fishermen in 1892 and 1893, most of those who participated in the investigation identified themselves as Canadians either by birth or by naturalization. Some gave their nationality as Scottish, English, or Irish. The Scottish fishermen of Goderich and Georgian Bay, Ontario, were the most numerous of the foreign-born interviewees.[18] The rosters of persons securing fishing licenses in the 1890s found in the unpublished records of the Department of Marine and Fisheries confirm the dominance of Canadian-born fishermen of British Isles extraction and French Canadians in the ranks of Great Lakes fishermen and the frequent presence of Native North Americans (figure 6.1).

National and cultural diversity produced diverse fishing communities. In lakeshore Indian reservation communities such as L'Anse, Michigan, on Keweenaw Bay; Red Cliff, Wisconsin, on the Lake Superior shore; Sault Sainte Marie; and Wikwemikong on Manitoulin Island, Georgian Bay, generations of fishermen passed their skills from father to son, as in centuries past (figure 6.2). Other groups of Great Lakes Indians lived in shoreline villages or in separate neighborhoods within towns pursuing fishing for a living. Such was the case in Harbor Springs, Cross Village, and Good Hart, Michigan.[19]

Figure 6.1. Fishing station, Fitzwilliam Island, Georgian Bay. Note the fisherman's wife and children and the family's dog in front of the fishing shanty. (From Ontario, *Sessional Papers,* 1903, no. 31, 15)

Figure 6.2. Chippewa village, Sault Sainte Marie, Michigan, 1850. (Photograph courtesy State Archives of Michigan, Lansing; negative no. 01438)

In Two Rivers, Wisconsin, a French Canadian fishing community took root in the 1840s, located at the mouth of the two rivers. It became known as "Canada," distinctly different from the balance of this lumbering and ship-building community, where the French-speaking families lived lives attuned to their customs and to the fortunes of fishing on Lake Michigan, on which they depended for a livelihood. Kumlien, who gathered materials about the community in 1880, noted, "Their profession is handed down from father to son. The boys assist in fishing when very young and develop into good fishermen and skillful boatmen." He elaborated on the family nature of the business: "the women and children spend most of the winter in making nets for local supply and for shipment to other fishing towns on Lake Michigan." Frederick W. True observed, "Most of the older fishermen were in good circumstances, but when their business is very prosperous they are all apt to live extravagantly and expend a large part of their gains. Intemperance, which was formerly quite prevalent here, has almost entirely disappeared." These fishermen were noted for their hard work, their skill, their close family life, and their faith in the teachings of the Catholic Church.[20]

Other notable examples of fishing communities with a distinctive ethnic base include the Scottish in Goderich and Kincardine, Ontario; the Irish on Beaver Island in Lake Michigan; the Scandinavians on Isle Royale; and the French Canadian farmer-fishermen along the shore of Lake Erie from the mouth of the Detroit River to Toledo. Other ethnic communities included the German fishermen in "fish town," at the mouth of the Detroit River at Saugatuck, Michigan; the fifty fishers of French descent and their families, living year round on scows on the St. Clair River in Michigan and making a living by catching sunfish, perch, and muskrats; the Dutch in Oostburg, Wisconsin; the French Canadians at French Settlement, south of Bayfield, Ontario; the Kashubes from the West Prussian peninsula of Hel and Germans from Pomerania on Jones Island, south of downtown Milwaukee (figure 6.3); the Belgian farmer-fishermen in the area around Dyckesville and Namur, Wisconsin, on Green Bay; the Icelanders on Washington Island, at the tip of the Door Peninsula; the Finns at Portage Entry on the Keweenaw Peninsula; and the métis communities of northern Georgian Bay. These groups and dozens more like them added another dimension to the nineteenth-century ethnic enclaves familiar in rural and urban areas of the Midwest, in this case with commercial fishing as their raison d'être. Ruth Kriehn has depicted, with great depth and much detail, the flavor of life in one such community in *The Fisherfolk of Jones Island,* an informal social, cultural, and economic history.[21]

The presence of varied national and racial groups affected the Great Lakes fishing industry in a number of ways. The influx of immigrants after the Civil War provided a large, readily available, low-cost labor supply for

Figure 6.3. Fishing village, Jones Island, Milwaukee, Wisconsin, 1888. (Photograph courtesy Milwaukee County Historical Society)

the entrepreneurial fishing companies and dealers in the expansive 1870s and 1880s. Newcomers to the Great Lakes region brought with them methods of fishing and ways of processing the catch that played a part in the expansion of the industry. For example, folklorist Timothy Cochrane has pointed out that the Scandinavian fisher people of Isle Royale adapted old-country methods of hook-line fishing to trout fishing on Lake Superior. Their boat-building skills were "grafted onto American ways of making Mackinaw boats and herring skiffs." Norwegian boats, noted for their stability and dryness, were used in a number of places, notably in the St. Joseph area of Lake Michigan, where storms were sudden and violent. Pound nets of Scottish origin were brought into the Great Lakes region by Connecticut River fishermen who moved to the eastern end of Lake Ontario. Alfred Booth, the millionaire Chicago fish and produce dealer, imported and tried to adapt the beam-trawl of his native England. After a captain who was experienced in surface set-line fishing for salmon in the Baltic Sea demonstrated the method successfully at Milwaukee in 1885, crews on gill-net steamers adopted it to enhance the catch.[22] Most obvious of all in this catalog of ethnic contributions to fishing methods, the Indians, the first fishers of the Great Lakes, developed over the centuries fishing gear that worked well for them: hook and line, weir, sluice, seine, hoop net, gill net, and spear. While many of these methods of fishing were common to western Europe as well as indigenous to the Indians of the Great Lakes, the demonstrated fishing skill of the Native North Americans on the lakes and their tributary rivers gave an invaluable applied knowledge to newcomers.

Before 1860, fishermen considered sturgeon to be worthless pests and destroyed them. That changed when Siemon Schacht, a German immigrant, settled in Sandusky and developed a business in preparing smoked sturgeon, caviar, isinglass, and oil. From very modest beginnings, it had grown into a "large and profitable industry" by 1872.[23] German, principally Prussian, dealer-processors assumed preeminence in the production of smoked fish in the late nineteenth century. To labor and technological innovation add entrepreneurial skill in the case of people like Schacht and Alfred Booth as a major contribution of foreign-born Americans in the Great Lakes fishing industry.

Considering the large number of northern European immigrants at work in the commercial-fishing industry, as a group they did contribute to the heavy pressure on the fish population. Caught up in the machinery of the commercial market as they tried to make a living, fishermen responded to low prices and dealer domination by fishing for a maximum catch. Yet this general view fails to take into account individual differences and special cases. About the influx of Scandinavian fishermen to Isle Royale in the mid-1880s, Cochrane concluded that the labor-intensive, small-scale technology they used and their awareness of the island's finite limits led them to "steward their resources carefully. . . . Island fishermen did not overfish. Instead they bequeathed to future generations an unequaled genetic reservoir of lake trout. Nowhere else in the Great Lakes are lake trout doing as well."[24] Perhaps he overstated his case, yet it is undeniable that in the ranks of Great Lakes fishermen, there were thoughtful, concerned fishers who wished to conserve the resource, but who had little chance of doing so given the physical characteristics of the grounds they fished, the pressure on them for a livelihood, and the number of competitors they had.

Diversity in the people who fished the Great Lakes waters extended far beyond race, gender, and nationality. Fishing included a wide range of work combinations. A majority of the fishermen reported in the Canadian and American federal fishery records in the 1880s either worked full time as fishermen or devoted the major part of their time to fishing and considered it the main source of their income. For example, in 1885, at the height of employment in the industry, of the 9,116 fishermen in American waters (exclusive of shoresmen and preparators), 62 percent considered themselves full time or primarily fishermen in occupation, while 38 percent combined fishing and some other employment.[25]

Farmer-fishermen who divided their energies between tilling the soil and catching fish to make a living were familiar types in Canada and the United States on all the lakes, although least so on Lake Superior. The possibilities for agriculture around that lake were quite limited, but farming was done in the Apostle Islands, on the North Shore of Minnesota, and in the Thunder Bay area. Vast differences characterized this subgroup of farmer-fishermen. In the fruit-growing regions of southern Lake Michigan and around Lakes Erie and Ontario, for example, fruit farmers with lake frontage made their living from both the land and the lake. Some had very substantial farming and fishing enterprises, while others were small-scale fisher-farmers who made a very modest living by hedging against a harvest failure on either land or water.[26]

The extent to which farmers fished varied widely. Some simply fished for family needs, whereas others fished to sell the catch either in local markets or to the fish dealers who supplied the national markets. The intensity of their fishing changed with their needs and especially with economic conditions. One very experienced Georgian Bay fisherman, Captain Larry King, remarked in 1894 that in Thessalon, Ontario, none of the fishermen farmed, but, he added, "they should, however. I think if I can catch hold of a piece of land I will hang on[to] it. Fishermen make lots of money, but they spend lots too."[27]

Workers in the areas around northern Lakes Michigan, Huron, and Superior, many of them young itinerant laborers, combined part-time fishing with lumbering and mining, job packages that worked well given the complimentary seasonal nature of the industries. Once the fishing season was over in Collingwood, Ontario, on Georgian Bay, some of the fishermen "go to work at whatever they can get to do." Some "will do a little ship carpentering or boat-building, but generally when they are not fishing they are preparing their nets or doing nothing."[28]

Longshoremen, sailors, and laborers in Buffalo, New York, turned to ice fishing once traffic on Lake Erie ceased for the season (figure 6.4). From around December 1, when the water froze, to the end of March, an estimated 800 to 1,000 fished principally through the ice for blue pike and yellow perch, and for walleye, lake trout, herring, and sturgeon during the 1880s. The fishery produced about 1 million pounds of fish annually, valued at $50,000. Other estimates have placed the total catch much higher. The special report on the fisheries of the Great Lakes prepared in 1885 described the Buffalo ice fisherman's workday, which began at dawn with a one- to ten-mile ride from shore using dog sleds, most plain and some fancy, about 175 of them, drawn mainly by Newfoundlands, and ended at dark with the sleds carrying "large loads of fish," at times with both dog and man in harness. The 1887 season—a long, quite profitable, and very hazardous one in Buffalo—paid the fishermen well for their efforts. For a good day's catch of from 60 to 200 pounds, the fishermen earned $3 to $10. Noted the authors of the report, "From these figures something of an idea may be obtained of the importance of this winter industry, by which Lake Erie gives subsistence to many families."[29]

In the years 1857 to 1875, line fishing through the ice on Green Bay attracted about eighty men every winter, including many locals and others from as far as Milwaukee. Whitefish were abundant, and a veritable vil-

Figure 6.4. Ice fishermen bringing home the catch on dogsleds, Buffalo, New York. (From Hugh M. Smith and Merwin-Marie Snell, "Review of the Fisheries of the Great Lakes in 1885," U.S. Commission of Fish and Fisheries, *Report,* 1887, Appendix, 50th Cong., 2d sess., 1889, H. Misc. Doc. 133 [Serial 2661], facing 290)

lage on ice sprang up that was serviced by merchants and fish dealers. Entire families took up residence to help with the harvest and to keep the nets in repair. In the 1880s, ice fishing helped earn income during the winter for approximately forty fishermen, farmers, sailors, and lumbermen on the Door Peninsula who used nets and movable shanties, sometimes sail-powered sleds, but more commonly a horse and wagon to travel to and from the fishing area. The catch, harvested from January to March, averaged $75 to $100 per fisher each season. Across Lake Michigan on Grand Traverse Bay, the ice fishermen used five-pronged, seven-foot spears to harvest trout, operating from sheds fitted with stoves and bunks. They earned an estimated $16 a week. In Hamilton, Ontario, city residents, farmers, and twelve to fourteen fishermen speared pike and bass. "A couple of hundred or more" houses five to six feet square placed on wheels or runners and fitted with stoves and bunks dotted the ice of Burlington Bay. Ice fishing made good sense as a way for fishermen to extend their harvests to nearly year-round work and for people with other seasonal occupations to earn income in the winter.[30]

When considering the commercial fishermen of the Great Lakes, it is easy to overlook urban dwellers with low incomes, who usually were employed in the manufacturing and service sectors. For many of them, the fish resource meant income and/or table fare. Living in the shadow of large fish dealers' establishments, many of the poorer people of Cleveland depended on ice fishing with hook and line for winter income. Near Toronto, hook-and-line fishing greatly benefited the poor, according to O. B. Sheppard, the Dominion Inspector of Fisheries. He advised that no net licenses be issued for the Humber River, "a small river very near the City of Toronto. . . . [V]ery many poor people go there to fish with hook and line and even the small and inferior fish caught by them are of great value to them for food." From the piers in south Chicago, "not a few men" made a living by catching large marketable fish and eels with hand lines and dip nets. Many others who worked in city factories and in low-paying jobs in transportation and commerce fished simply for home consumption. Periods of depression and unemployment swelled their ranks.[31]

The fishers of the Great Lakes formed a heterogeneous, loosely structured group among the working people of the North American midcontinent. Ranked in pecking order, the full-time, long-term "professional" fishermen who owned gear and boats stood at the top. Next came part-time fishers who owned gear and boats, followed by hired fishers who owned little or no equipment and were paid by wage or share of the catch. The men who tended the nets ranked beneath the tugboat captains, agents, and dealers. The most prestigious of all in the Great Lakes commercial-fishing industry, the dominant A. Booth Packing Company stood at the top of the economic and social pyramid. Hard-working people in pursuit of a living and an improved economic status as a group overfished the resource.

7

The Fishers and the Fish

I Live Here and I Will Do All I Can to Save the Fish

The changing attitudes of Great Lakes fishers toward the resource varied widely during the nineteenth century. From the era of frontier plenty through the Civil War, few questioned its long-term durability. After that, doubts grew, shaped and influenced by individuals' short- and long-term expectations for working the water, perceptions of the abundance and durability of the resource over time, changing economic conditions in the industry, the rigors of the fisherman's work, and pressures to make a livelihood.

INCOME IN A COMPETITIVE MARKET

To evaluate the relationship between the resource and full-time fishermen, who made up the majority of fishers in the United States and Canadian census counts, both their incomes and the ways the industry's expansion affected them have to be considered. One of the biggest voids in contemporary records are data on the incomes of fishers. Neither the Canadian nor the American government gathered occupational income figures, but scattered evidence in government reports reveals a wide range of earnings. When Ludwig Kumlien did fieldwork around the American shores of the Great Lakes in 1879 as part of his research for a special report, he found it virtually impossible to gather data on fishermen's income systematically. But he did record what he could discover about fishers' economic status in the places where he conducted interviews. He generalized that pound-

Table 7.1. Average size and value of catch per fisherman, for the United States and Canada, 1880–1890

	U.S.			Canada		
		Value			Value	
Year	Pounds	Current	Indexed	Pounds	Current	Indexed
1880	13,612	$328	$328	5,911	$215	$215
1885	10,952	295	251	10,821	501	426
1890	14,253	309	253	9,878	686	563

Sources: Frederick W. True, "The Fishes of the Great Lakes," in George Brown Goode, *The Fisheries and Fishing Industries of the United States,* Section 2, 47th Cong., 1st sess., 1881, S. Misc. Doc. 124 (Serial 1999), 633; Hugh M. Smith, "The Fisheries of the Great Lakes," in U.S. Commission of Fish and Fisheries, *Report,* 1892, Appendix A, 53d Cong., 2d sess., 1893, H. Misc. Doc. 209 (Serial 3264), 366; U.S. Commission of Fish and Fisheries, *Report,* 1895, 54th Cong., 2d sess., 1896, H. Doc. 104 (Serial 3518), 96; Canada, Sessional Papers, 1891, no. 8A, 211, 1892, no. 11, liii; U.S. Department of Commerce, Bureau of the Census, *Historical Statistics of the United States: Colonial Times to 1970,* Bicentennial ed., 93d Cong., 1st sess., 1973, H. Doc. 93-78, Part 1, 201.

Note: More than 95 percent of the Canadian catch went to American markets, so the American index was used for both Canadian and American figures. The indexed value is based on the Warren and Pearson index of wholesale prices, 1910–1914 = 100.

net fishermen as a group were men with "considerable capital" and able "to carry on a large business." Among the gill-net fishermen, given the broad spectrum of technology used, from the Mackinaw boat and a few nets to steam-powered tugboats setting miles of gill nets, great variations in income existed: "Participation in the gill-net fishery does not imply the possession of any considerable amount of capital, as in the pound fishery, and hence we find all classes of fishermen employed." Beyond those generalizations, Kumlien's findings were spotty and impressionistic. He referred to those who were poor, those in comfortable circumstances, those who were moderately wealthy, and so on.[1]

In a study of the Great Lakes fisheries conducted in 1885, the United States Commission of Fish and Fisheries cited specific examples of wages paid to hired fishermen. They ranged from $20 to $35 a month plus board, depending on location, with rates running as high as $50 a month with board for trained fishermen and $60 to $80 a month plus board for foremen and boat captains. On fishing tugs, captains earned $50 to $100 a month; engineers, $75 to $85; and fishing crewmen, $25 to $50. The common wage of $2 a day for fishermen in the more populous parts of the Great Lakes in 1885 was the same as that of industrial workers.[2]

Still another approach to the income question is through the prices that fishermen received for their catch, as found in official records. The average size and value of catch per fisherman shown in table 7.1 are low, for they are based on all fishers, full time and part time, and those who gathered the data believed that fishers tended to underreport. Different methods of enumeration and compiling data probably account for the wide gap in values for the years 1885 and 1890 for American and Canadian fishers.

Average income in 1880 helps explain the rush of fishermen and dealer-entrepreneurs to exploit the American waters of the Great Lakes over the next five years. So many fished that they drove down the average poundage and income per fisher cited in official American reports in 1885. In Canada's richest Great Lakes fishing ground, Georgian Bay, which was undergoing its first extensive development, one fisherman described the expansion that occurred between 1880 and 1885: in 1880, a fisherman "would make from $900 to $1,600 from the season's catch." After that year, "many young farmers" went into fishing using equipment provided by the dealers, profits grew, "and the number of fishermen also increased greatly. . . . In 1885 the fishing trade became very large, it was, it may be said, at its height in the Georgian Bay."[3] Production there accounts in large part for the increase in pounds harvested and in income per fisher reported for all Canadian Great Lakes waters in that year compared with 1880.

This great surge of fishing in the 1880s created special problems for the fishermen. To keep up in the competitive struggle for an overtaxed resource, larger investments in gear were essential if a fisher hoped to maintain harvests equal in size to those of the past. Actually, he needed larger harvests to cover additional costs. One "old and experienced" fisherman of the Great Lakes expressed the fisherman's problem well in 1885. Gone were the days when a sailboat with a crew of four fishing eight to twelve nets caught 2,000 or 3,000 pounds at one haul. According to him, "Now it takes a gang of sixty to eighty nets to catch as many pounds, and it takes a steam tug and seven men to tend the nets. We may catch more fish now, altogether, but we don't make as much money as we did a while ago."[4]

The average investment in apparatus made by American and Canadian fishermen based on the data collected by the two governments grew in the 1880s. Indexed with 1880 at 100 and 1890 at 82, the increase was significant—$52 for American and $71 for Canadian fishers—especially in light of the size of average investments in apparatus for all fishers, which ranged from $100 to $257 in 1880 to 1890.[5] These averages, spread over a total of fishermen, some of whom owned no equipment and others of whom owned a great deal, show the trend in capital costs. At the very time that fishermen in American waters experienced an average decline in income from the catch, their investments in apparatus grew. Small wonder that by 1890, after an all-time high in 1885, the number of American fishers had declined by approximately 620. In the Canadian Great Lakes, however, where the average value of the catch was growing noticeably, the number of fishers recorded in the 1885 and 1890 counts showed an increase of 200. Fish stocks in Canadian waters were in far better condition than those in American waters, given the later development of commercial fishing in Canada and the government's regulation of the industry. By comparison, American waters had been freely and more heavily exploited for a longer time.

In the face of the price and production-cost squeeze of the 1880s that eroded income, the fishermen who owned their boats and gear tried to make up the difference in a glutted market with uniformly low prices year after year by catching more fish. While many of them recognized the danger to the resource, market forces and the need for income or the desire for profits could and often did override those concerns and spurred on their efforts.

They blamed their troubles largely on the highly competitive dealer-entrepreneurs who dominated the industry. The middlemen who paid them less than the going wholesale price for the catch to compensate for processing and marketing services; who often furnished the fishermen with goods, supplies, and credit; and who often supplied the gear to fish on shares or by another arrangement exercised a powerful influence in their lives. The relationship between fishermen and dealers often became adversarial. Fishermen felt that they were underpaid for the catch and overcharged for goods. They bargained, sometimes withheld fish, sought rival dealers to compete for their catch, and tried to devise methods of direct marketing to circumvent the middlemen. To cite one example, fishermen in Erie, Pennsylvania, in effect went on strike in August 1894. H. F. Moore, a field investigator for the Joint Commission Relative to the Preservation of the Fisheries in Waters Contiguous to Canada and the United States, reported that fishermen had taken their nets out of the water because of a disagreement with the dealers over prices. Established longtime fishermen who hoped to continue the occupation believed that dealers greatly handicapped them by outfitting young men who had no permanent interest in fishing. Samuel Wilmot, the chairman of the Dominion Fishery Commission, agreed, criticizing "merchants, supply houses, and capitalists" for lending freely to supply new fishers with nets and other essentials on credit, a practice that led to "waste and destruction" of the fish resource and to illegal fishing as debtors struggled to pay their creditors. Unquestionably, the plentiful, almost limitless number of workers who were willing to enter the fishery free-for-all put the large producer-entrepreneur-dealer at an advantage over smaller longtime fishers who were quite generally short of both capital goods and working capital.[6]

American fishermen complained repeatedly that the expansion of large dealers into the Canadian waters of the Great Lakes tended to flood the market and keep wholesale prices down. They especially criticized the entrepreneurial push into Lake of the Woods, which straddles Ontario, Manitoba, and Minnesota, and Lake Winnipeg, in Manitoba, where lower labor and production costs resulted in millions of pounds of whitefish and sturgeon entering the market in competition with their Great Lakes catch. They found it very hard to compete.

THE WORK ON THE WATER

The nature of the fisherman's work deserves careful examination in order to assess the way fishers affected the resource. By any measure, fishing on the Great Lakes was often rough, hard work. Exposed to the elements, fishermen watched the weather very closely.[7] Work began early in the morning and varied somewhat in length with the type of fishing done and with the weather. In general, it was a long day involving heavy physical labor, under conditions varying from sunny, calm, and beautiful to almost beyond endurance. In 1893, the Wisconsin superintendent of fish hatcheries spoke of the physical rigors of fishing in November:

> The lives of the lake fishermen are not easy ones. . . . In all kinds of weather the nets must be looked after, and usually the catch is largest when the great gales sweep the lakes. In November the best run of fish occurs, as the herring, whitefish, lake trout, and blue fins leave deep water and seek the shallow spawning grounds. Oil-skins sheeted with ice, numb fingers cut and bleeding from drawing in freezing nets, and faces frost bitten by icy spray are common experiences.[8]

Fluctuating catches made fishermen apprehensive about earning a living in a dangerous occupation that often seemed like a game of chance. Why was the harvest so uneven? Many variables produced the fluctuations: life cycles of the fish, season-long temperatures, cyclical long-term weather patterns, lake levels, and human activity that disrupted and altered the lake habitat. October and November, the spawning time for whitefish, herring, and trout, were especially important months for harvesting the waters. As James Milner noted in 1872, spawning season was the one time of the year when fishermen could count on a good run of fish. The "run of the trout upon the reefs in October, and of the whitefish in the shallow waters in November" gave them a chance to make up for poor catches earlier in the year. "They look forward to this season with certainty of some success if it does not prove too stormy." Alfred Booth, the leading fish merchant in Chicago, remarked after forty years of experience with Great Lakes fishing: "No one can say what the year's business will be until it is over. The best prospects come far short, and the poorest opening may turn out remarkably well." Fishermen agreed wholeheartedly with Booth's assessment. Fishing, they commonly remarked, was a gamble.[9]

Yet experience made a great difference in how well fishermen fared. Those who had spent much of their lives on the lakes acquired a remarkable store of knowledge about the various species of fish: their habits, their movements, the places and ways they could be caught at different times of the year, and the most effective methods to harvest them for market. They developed work skills that gave them an advantage in a highly competitive industry.[10]

Considering the two most prevalent types of fishing on the Great Lakes, pound net and gill net, work routines did vary considerably. The pound-net fishermen lived less risky, more sedentary, routine lives than the gillnetters. On the southern shore of Lake Erie, the location of the largest pound-net fishery on the lakes—from Cleveland to the Detroit River, where 888 pounds were fished in 1885—they often worked for a wage (figure 7.1). Given the size of the capital investment required by pound-net fishing, frequently persons "who possess considerable capital" and business ability owned the equipment, but did not themselves fish. Their hired workers tended the nets and brought in the catch. At the beginning of the season, fishermen set the nets using a pile driver, operated either by steam or by manpower, to install the stakes (figure 7.2). "Driving stakes is considered the hardest work connected with the pound fishery," noted Ludwig Kumlien.[11]

In some locations, notably the western end of Lake Erie, fishers set and removed nets twice in a fishing season: set in March, removed in June; reset in September, removed in October when the weather turned stormy. At the height of the season, fishermen tended the nets daily, usually going out at daybreak, emptying the pot or bowl, and loading the fish into a pound-net boat or a collecting steamer (figure 7.3). In western Lake Erie, given its shallow waters, pound nets could extend far into the lake, an exceptional one being ten miles long. In Lakes Michigan and Superior, the pots occasionally were set as deep as eighty-six to ninety-seven feet. More often, pounds were set at forty to seventy feet, but most often in twenty to thirty feet of water. While procedures varied with the depth of the pots, a windlass being essential for those in deeper waters, generally the fishermen, several in a crew, took a pound-net boat inside the crib and lifted first the tunnel of the net and then the crib so that the fish were crowded together at the back of it—"shoaling up," as it was known. Then the fish were dipped or scooped out. The work demanded a great deal of heavy lifting, scooping, and pulling to retrieve the fish.[12]

Gill-net fishermen were a more varied group than pound netters. Some worked from steam tugs, handling many miles of net, while others fished

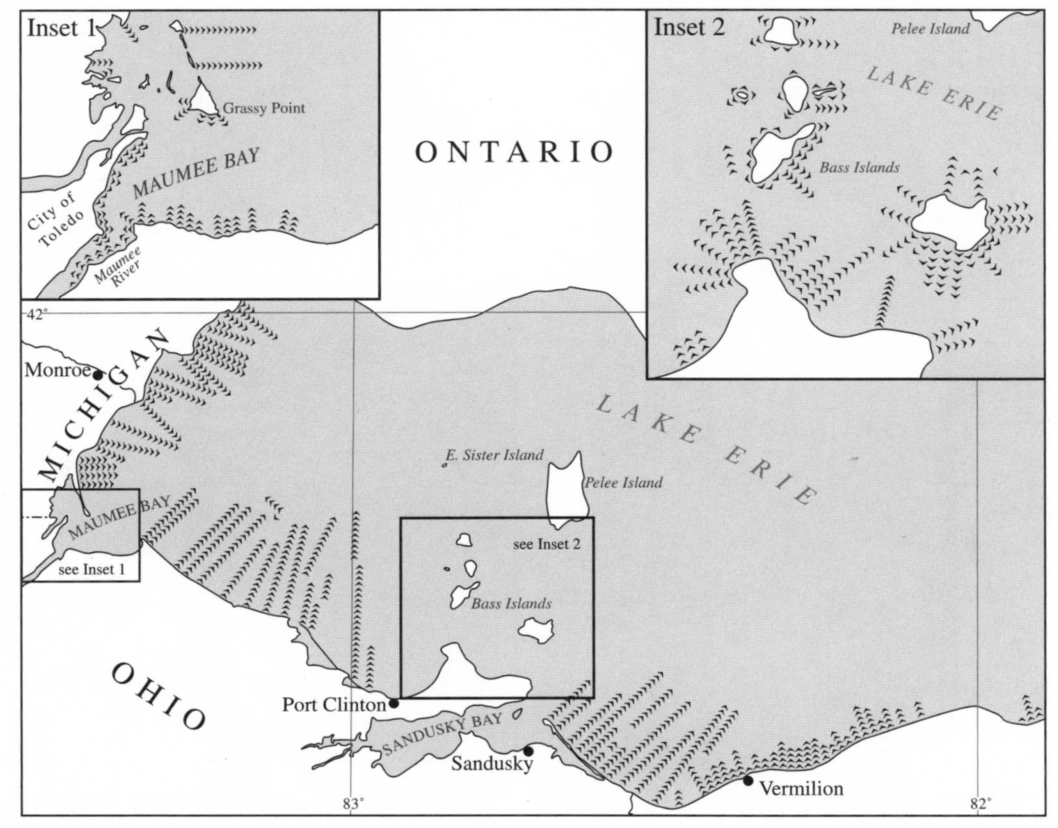

Figure 7.1. Concentration of pound nets in western Lake Erie, 1885. (Adapted from Hugh M. Smith and Merwin-Marie Snell, "Review of the Fisheries of the Great Lakes in 1885," U.S. Commission of Fish and Fisheries, *Report,* 1887, Appendix, 50th Cong., 2d sess., 1889, H. Misc. Doc. 133 [Serial 2661], facing 233; Cartographic Laboratory, University of Wisconsin–Madison)

Figure 7.2. Crew of a stake boat driving stakes for a pound net, Lake Erie. (Drawn by H. W. Elliott; from Hugh M. Smith and Merwin-Marie Snell, "Review of the Fisheries of the Great Lakes in 1885," U.S. Commission of Fish and Fisheries, *Report,* 1887, Appendix, 50th Cong., 2d sess., 1889, H. Misc. Doc. 133 [Serial 2661], facing 28)

Figure 7.3. Crew of a pound-net boat lifting the pot of a pound net, Lake Erie. (Drawn by H. W. Elliott; from Hugh M. Smith and Merwin-Marie Snell, "Review of the Fisheries of the Great Lakes in 1885," U.S. Commission of Fish and Fisheries, *Report,* 1887, Appendix, 50th Cong., 2d sess., 1889, H. Misc. Doc. 133 [Serial 2661], facing 250)

from sailing craft of different sizes with "light rigs" and "heavy rigs," depending on what the boat could accommodate. Kumlien characterized them as a class as "the most venturesome men, and at the same time the most skillful seamen, of the lakes. In certain regions they set their nets near the shore, but in other localities they invariably fish at a distance of 20 to 30 miles from land, and frequently encounter storms, which, were it not for their skill in managing their boats, would inevitably overwhelm them."[13] Successful gill-net fishing demanded hard work, skill, and experience. During the fishing season, which lasted from April through November on the upper lakes and from March into December on the lower, gill-net fishers set and tended nets, ideally raising and resetting them every few days.

Fishermen working on steam tugs set the nets from the stern of the boat as it moved forward slowly and took them in over the bow with the assistance of rollers. Lifting nets was especially heavy labor, performed by manpower before the 1890s when steam-powered gill-net lifters came into use. Fishing crews removed the fish from the nets, gutted them, and packed them in fish boxes, icing the catch either on the boat or at the dock.

Gill-net fishing procedures on sailboats varied from those on tugs, but the basic operations were the same. In 1885, the average Lake Michigan sailboat, noted a report by the Commission of Fish and Fisheries, carried 60 to 100 nets, while steamers fished "several times" as many nets. Nets varied considerably in length, generally between 200 and 300 feet, and as much as 600 feet. In 1885, fishermen on the Great Lakes used 97,000 gill nets, extending 5,300 miles in length.[14] All fishermen who used nets spent a great deal of time caring for them, and boats demanded constant, careful maintenance. Fishermen did most of the repair and maintenance work in the off-season.

For many years, wet nets retrieved into net boxes went ashore where shoresmen reeled them to dry (see figure 3.4). By the 1890s, fishermen had adopted a different system. Instead of drying nets frequently, according to John Noble, who was interviewed by a team from the Joint Commission, "now we lift a gang and set it right back into the water. It is a quicker way of working than the old way." Nets treated with lime and salt, tanning liquid, or lye and hemlock bark could remain wet for two months. Other fishermen preferred to treat their nets with coal tar.[15]

Successful commercial fishers relied heavily on their ability to size up weather conditions and their maritime savvy to survive on lake waters given to sudden violent storms and very high waves. Drownings seem few in comparison with the thousands of survivals. Fishermen in St. Joseph, Michigan, "have probably suffered more from disaster than any others on the whole of the lakes," noted Frederick W. True in 1879. Ten years earlier, two fishing boats had gone down, drowning nine fishermen. In April 1875, a sudden squall struck eleven St. Joseph fishing boats far from shore. Four went down, carrying eleven fishermen with them, and not one returned with all its nets, sails, apparatus, and rigging. Between 1860 and 1885, a total of twenty-seven fishermen from St. Joseph lost their lives.[16]

ATTITUDES TOWARD THE FISH

The hazards and rough, heavy nature of the fishermen's work shaped the way they thought about the fish and themselves. They regarded the fish they caught and prepared for market much as farmers viewed their market-bound livestock. Indeed, many a farmer-fisher in the fall months turned from lifting nets and gutting fish to butchering the winter's meat supply. Fishermen routinely took the catch live from the water and expeditiously prepared it for market without thinking very much about the fish as living for any other purpose than to provide food and to ensure a livelihood. Many did as their fathers and grandfathers had before them. Ingeborg Holte, a lifelong member of a fisher family on Isle Royale, made these observations about the fisherman's view of fish life: "My father was kind, sweet and very soft-hearted. He did not harm anyone or anything. He used to say he could not kill a fly, which was ironic to me, because every day for at least half of every year, he killed fish. This did not bother him in the least. I guess he did not think of them as living animals. To him they were cold-blooded vertebrates, in a class by themselves, and put there specifically for him to catch."[17]

Much of what fishermen observed about fish life contributed to their detached attitude. Fish cannibalized one another and ate their own eggs and fry. It was difficult for a fisher to develop much sentiment for a trout once he had witnessed its voracious eating habits, especially if he had taken one from the water with a whitefish its own size sticking out of its mouth. Fishermen shared the view of a Michigan state fish and game warden who remarked, "The lake trout is a Chicago man; he eats up everything that comes his way." One longtime tender of the nets on Georgian Bay characterized the trout as "one of the dirtiest fish in the lake." It ate anything.[18] Fishermen believed that they were using the resource as it should be used. They worked very hard out of doors in all kinds of weather, risking their lives on treacherous lake waters and applying their skills and capital to make a living for themselves and to supply the people of Canada and the United States with wholesome, high-quality inexpensive food.

Many fishermen who lived along the lakeshore and who planned to make a living by harvesting the waters over a long period of time wanted to use the resource with care. They developed a sense of what they believed the fish could tolerate—for example, the number that could safely be harvested, the level of maturity at which they should be caught, and the time of year they should be fished. Captain Larry King of Thessalon, Ontario, who fished in Georgian Bay, remarked, "I believe a man that is fishing and making a home here with an intention to live here will be likely to save his ground all he can, and if it is a man merely here for a year or two he will get all he can out of it. I live here and I will do all I can to save the fish." A fish dealer in Cleveland expressed similar sentiments. Permanently located fishermen in productive fishing areas wanted the resource preserved for future use, but "where a man goes into a region and merely puts his nets in for what he can get out of it at the time you can suppose him to be reckless." He cited the fishing on Lake of the Woods as a good example of the latter. A mining engineer who knew the fisheries of the Great Lakes well testified to the Dominion Fishery Commission in 1893: "I have been very much among the fishermen since 1865; watched their operations; in fact, could not help but do so. Some of the fishermen have evinced a desire to protect the fish, especially the resident fishermen. A portion have no other object than to catch all they can irrespective of consequences."[19]

Corollary to the resident fishermen's attitude toward the fish as a source of a living over the long term was their disdain for nonresident fishers, for migrant fishermen with no attachment to their fishing grounds, and for very large licensed entrepreneurs like Charles Gauthier, whom the fishermen of the North Channel of Lake Huron felt abused their special dominion leases, mined the resource, and left for untapped waters.[20] The resident fisherman felt about his fishing ground in some ways like the owner of a family farm felt about his land. He intended to use it and pass it along to the next generation, and there were those who did so. Attitudes varied widely, of course, and there is not enough data to give any idea of how many fishers were conservation minded and how many simply wanted to use nature's bounty as they found it in the very immediate future. It seems highly unlikely that even the most preservation minded among them could resist the threat of starvation in hard times and conduct their fishing for the long-term well-being of the resource.

DESTRUCTION AND WASTE

Whatever their views about the resource, fishermen utilized a technology of harvest that was extremely destructive of the fish. The documented record of tremendous waste stretched back to the 1830s, when fishers, who generally considered sturgeon to be worthless pests that got into the nets and tore them to pieces, pulled them out of the water and stacked them in piles on the beach to rot. Nets were the great destroyers. Seines took all fish from the waters, large and small, many of them unmarketable, useful only as fertilizer for the farmer's field. Gill nets roused very substantial controversy among fishermen and fishery experts because of their destructiveness. Aside from the arguments that raged over the appropriate mesh extension, the nets caught all species of a certain size, whether desired or not. Many of the fish drowned in the nets and began to decay before the fishermen could lift them. Stormy waters often set gill nets afloat, with entrapped fish. Irretrievable, the nets sank, and the rotting fish fouled the waters. Some fishery authorities and fishermen believed that the floating gill nets continued to trap fish and generate very considerable decayed matter. The destruction of a rich and much used fishing grounds at the entrance to Green Bay, according to Frederick True in 1879, stemmed in large measure from gill nets that had been lost between Washington Island and St. Martin's Island in several consecutive fall fishing seasons:

> As many as three thousand nets have been lost in one autumn, carrying down with them 500,000 to 600,000 whitefish. Although the loss of the nets was a great discouragement to the fishermen, it is the opinion of all that the presence of so large a mass of decaying fish on the spawning beds affected a much more serious injury in that it drove away the fish which were wont to congregate there. Many of the nets were grappled up in spring completely filled with fish, but the stench from them was so horrible that the fishermen could not take them into their boats.

One knowledgeable observer estimated in 1885 that the loss of whitefish due to rotting in gill nets on Lake Erie amounted to at least 400 to 500 tons.[21]

Fishermen used gill nets heavily in the spawning season throughout the lakes. Their use on Lake Erie drew especially strong criticism. Gill-net steamers followed herring and whitefish from the eastern end of the lake in the fall as they migrated to their spawning grounds in the western end, fishing as they went. Canadian fishery authorities deplored this pursuit, labeling it the "American system." At the spawning grounds, the gill nets again proved to be a very efficient mode of capture. Fishermen made great catches by covering the fine whitefish spawning beds with gill nets. In 1894, a fisher boasted of his luck during the spawning season on a small reef in Lake Superior, south of Split Rock and north of Duluth, "a favorite spawning place for trout." There he once took 1,000 pounds of trout from an 800-foot length of net after having clubbed the fish to death.[22]

The pound net, too, had its critics, for the pot of the pound trapped all comers large and small. If the size of the mesh were appropriately regulated, small, unmarketable fish could escape through larger mesh, argued many fishermen, and since the fish remained alive until the net was lifted, the pound net was far less wasteful than the gill net. Yet gillnetters insisted that pounds did trap many small fish—for example, immature whitefish that often were bruised or crushed when the pots were lifted. It was very difficult to handle them gently enough to ensure their survival after they were returned to the water. In 1894, a fish dealer in Cleveland told interviewers from the Joint Commission that in 1892 fishermen using pound nets had caught 3,000 tons of small blue pike, weighing from one-quarter to one-half a pound apiece, along the Ohio shore of Lake Erie.[23]

The argument between gillnetters and pound netters over who was doing the greater damage continued throughout the nineteenth century, each advocating restrictions on the net used by the other as the industry grew, the competition stiffened, and the technology increased harvest efficiency. Evidence collected by the Dominion Fishery Commission, which investigated the Ontario fisheries in 1892 and 1893, documented fully the massive destruction of young fish in both pound and gill nets as a result of the widespread use of small mesh.[24]

Most of those in government given the responsibility to protect the Great Lakes fish resource blamed the fishermen for the decline in the preferred commercial species. As a state fish and game warden in Petosky, Michigan, succinctly expressed the officials' viewpoint in 1894:

> Over-fishing, beyond all question, has caused the main destruction of the fish. When the poor fisherman used to go out in his Mackinaw boat and set a few gillnets, or go out in a rickety old pound boat, and perhaps attend to the fish from 2 pound nets, it was impossible, from the very nature of things, to destroy all the fish, but when a tug can take out 10 to 100 miles of gillnets and stretch nets enough to go twice the length of Lake Michigan, you cannot expect that thing to go on for years without wiping out the fish.[25]

This statement illustrates how the image of the Great Lakes fisherman changed among most government conservation personnel from the hard-working provider of human food in the 1870s to the destroyer of the resource in the early 1890s. While that image did have considerable validity, it was in some ways a hasty characterization, for, as the fishermen pointed out, forces other than fishing had long been at work to weaken the resource. From very early on, they spoke of the effects of spawning grounds ruined by development, of water polluted by contaminants from lumbering and other industrial operations, and of water quality reduced by less identifiable pollutants. While those responsible for protecting the resource did not give serious enough thought to these complaints, they had much validity. It is always easy to assign blame to the most obvious target, as did the fish and game authorities, and to shift blame from oneself, as did the fishermen. On balance and with careful investigation, it seems that both the officials and the fishers offered valid explanations for a declining resource. The fishermen identified the factors that, in the long run, have led North Americans to recognize the very serious problem of pollution in Great Lakes waters that makes the catch questionable as food.

FISHERS AND THE REGULATION DILEMMA

Fishermen expressed mixed feelings about regulation as a way of conserving the fish. They had a cultural bias against restricted use that was traceable to their experience of fishing and hunting freely in areas of new settlement and, in some cases, to their memory of European family homelands where lingering feudal privilege and restriction created hardships. The British tradition held that fish were the common property of the people and available for their use, but that government retained the authority to protect fish resources from misuse. The authority to protect had been so infrequently used since colonial times that when governments at the state, provincial, and national levels sought to implement it in the late nineteenth century, fishermen balked.

The evidence gathered by two investigating commissions working in the 1890s to identify problems and regulatory needs in the Great Lakes commercial-fishing industry includes a good deal about fishermen's attitudes toward both regulation and the fishery resource. One investigating body, the Dominion Fishery Commission, made an intensive survey of the fisheries of the province of Ontario in the fall of 1892 and of 1893. The other, the Joint Commission Relative to the Preservation of the Fisheries in Waters Contiguous to Canada and the United States, conducted its intensive survey of the Great Lakes mainly in the summer of 1894. Both sent investigators to commercial fisheries around the lakes to conduct interviews with fishermen and others closely associated with the industry. The Canadian investigators took sworn testimony; the Canadian and American investigators conducted interviews less formally and in more casual settings.

The study of the fisheries of Ontario by the Dominion Fishery Commission began when prosperity still generally prevailed and finished one year later, after the Panic of 1893 had deteriorated into depression. The Joint Commission gathered its testimony in the summer of 1894 as industrial and commercial stagnation in the Great Lakes region reached its depths and when memories of Jacob Coxey's march on Washington and the riotous demonstrations by unemployed workers in Cleveland on May

1 and 2 were still fresh in mind. Misery, hunger, family hardships, unemployment, strikes, unrest, and protest spread through the Great Lakes region as well as elsewhere. The great industrial areas along Lakes Michigan, Erie, and Ontario and the commercial fisheries of those lakes were adjacent to each other. Fishermen were keenly aware of urban labor and industrial distress. The deepening economic gloom accounts in some measure for the differences in tone between the two sets of interviews, conducted within eighteen months of each other.[26]

Both commissions proceeded from the premise that the Great Lakes fish resource was declining and in need of government policies to save the fish, hoping that their work would lead to constructive regulation. Therefore, the bulk of the evidence they sought related to fishermen's ideas about regulation: what, how, when, where, and by whom. The investigating teams collected evidence from a selective sample of fishermen. Some of those who gave evidence to the Dominion Fishery Commission volunteered; others apparently did so by official request. As a whole, these were established fishermen who had more than a decade, some even a lifetime, of experience on the lakes to draw on in forming their ideas. The same holds true for the fishermen interviewed by the Joint Commission. Its investigators talked to resident fishermen who had lived in the same communities for substantial periods of time and who had fished the Great Lakes for a decade or more. The two investigations quizzed fishermen who had witnessed the vast expansion of the commercial-fishing industry during the 1880s, and some who had watched fishing grow from the early nineteenth century to the early 1890s. In a few cases, the two investigating bodies interviewed the same people.

The Dominion Fishery Commission's interviews reveal that the great majority of the 102 fishermen who gave evidence said they favored regulation of some kind, that a few totally opposed regulation, and that all had excellent reasons for being wary about restrictions.[27] With but one or two exceptions, they agreed that fishing had declined seriously, that the industry was overcrowded, that fish needed protection during the spawning season, that far too many small immature fish had been harvested, that small meshes in pound and gill nets and in seines were responsible for the slaughter of small fish, and that the legal mesh size had to be revised by the Department of Marine and Fisheries.

Granted these conditions, the fishermen hesitated when it came to establishing rules and enforcing them. They had lived under a system of regulated fishing established by the dominion government first in 1868 and were aware of the problems of enforcement, which was a very difficult task given the physical characteristics of the fishing grounds, the speed required to catch lawbreakers in the act (especially gill-net fishermen), and the dominion's underfunded and poorly staffed enforcement arm. They knew that the laws were widely disregarded and that the administration of justice was unequal. Some were caught, and many others escaped. Reported Samuel Fraser, a fishery overseer for the dominion government in Midland, Ontario: "Every man here thinks the fishery laws are a fraud." While fishermen agreed widely about the need to protect spawning fish, they had very different ideas about the timing of the closed season. Some suggested that a closed season would not be necessary if fish hatcheries to stock the waters were established. Fishermen knew that mesh extensions were too small, but differed on the appropriate size for different species in different locations.[28]

Above all, these Canadian fishermen deeply resented the idea of having to comply with regulations to conserve the fish when their vigorous competitors, the Americans, had none. They felt that Canadian rules merely held down Canadian fishermen and that the Americans, in one way or another, got the catch. As one experienced Canadian fisherman in Port Arthur, Ontario, expressed his mixed feelings, the closed season is good for the fish "but not for my own interest. . . . It is hard when the Yankees fish alongside, but my idea is that close season should be established." Similarly, Captain Joseph King of Thessalon, Ontario, remarked: "They [the Americans] will come and put in their gill nets about half a mile from here during the close season, as we have to smoke our pipe and look at them raise the fish. If they had to have a close season all around the boundary line it would be fair, but us having a close season and those fellows [Americans] off there killing the fish, I do not think it is fair." Fishermen in Meaford, Ontario, echoed King's views.[29] Canadian fishing communities at the western end of Lake Erie became fonts of similar criticism.

After all, thought Canadian fishermen, the Americans had organized the market and furnished capital to Canadian fishers to supply markets in the United States at the expense of the resource in Canadian waters. United States tariff policy crippled Canadian fishermen in the American market and put them at the mercy of American dealers. Americans were also responsible for the atrocity of enormous log rafts moving from Georgian Bay across Lake Huron to supply sawmills in Michigan, leaving a trail of destroyed nets and fishing grounds in their wake. Worst of all, Americans fished illegally in Canadian waters. A few fishermen observed that uniform rules for all the Great Lakes waters would help, while some others called for the abandonment of all regulations and adoption of the "American plan." When testifying in Meaford in November 1892, John McCrae had the following exchange with the two commissioners, both advocates of regulated conservation:

Q. Who takes the most fish?
A. The smartest man.
Q. Which is the smarter, Canadian or American?
A. He is a Yankee.[30]

In the summer of 1894, the Joint Commission sent investigating teams to communities around the Great Lakes, with the exception of Lake Michigan, which lies entirely within the United States, in order to visit and talk with fishermen and others associated with the commercial-fishing industry and collect stenographically recorded interviews. The unpublished, original records of the teams' work provide another excellent source for the ideas of the Great Lakes fishermen, both Canadian and American, who revealed themselves as cognizant of the troubled industry and the declining resource, and desirous of saving it, but uncertain about how it should be done. Many were fearful and pessimistic about the future of commercial fishing. Some of the interviewees were very keen observers of the habits of the fish, of the great changes in the industry and the resource over many decades, of the growing problem of water pollution, of the damaged spawning grounds, and of the failure of laws in both Canada and the United States to protect the Great Lakes. The unpublished records add a broader dimension to the fishermen's ideas about how and why the fisheries had deteriorated in the four decades preceding 1894 than is found in the published reports of both the Joint Commission and the Dominion Fishery Commission. They highlight more fully the fishermen's frustrations with the political patchwork of Great Lakes waters and clearly show how the depression of the 1890s influenced the fishermen's attitudes about government intervention into the commercial-fishing industry. The fishermen emerge as people of far more intelligence and perception than either the commonly held negative stereotypes or the frequently pejorative assessments of government officials suggest.

Nowhere in the interviews does the impact of the depression show more clearly than in those conducted in communities around Lake Erie. Of the fisheries of the Great Lakes, those of Lake Erie employed the most people, operated with the heaviest capital investment, and produced the most valuable catch.[31] More Lake Erie fishermen lived amid industrial workers' misery than did fishermen elsewhere on the Great Lakes. Lake Erie received very intensive scrutiny by several teams of Joint Commission investigators.

The fishermen of Lake Erie reported real distress to the interviewers in the summer of 1894. They suffered from four successive years of poor harvests and from the tightening grip of the depression. They had vivid memories of the retrenchment in the pound-net fishery in 1890 in the area around Huron and Sandusky, Ohio, and along the Michigan shore when heavily indebted fishermen had to sell out to their dealer creditors. A Sandusky fisherman told an interviewer: "If the fish hadn't dropped off I would have my own twine as I used to. I kept getting behind so from year to year that I was glad to get out of it. We let the twine go and saved our homes."[32]

When investigators asked A. J. Stoll, a pound-net fisher and dealer in Sandusky, if many were giving up, he attributed the fallout largely to the indebtedness that fishermen had accumulated with dealers. Citing his own case, he noted that he furnished his fishermen with pound nets, "with the understanding, of course, that I would pay them a certain market price, and by that means they were to pay for their nets. In my experience of 13 years my fishermen owed me $46,000." In adjusting his business to depression market realities, he had the debtors give him a bill of sale for their possessions, and he, in turn, gave them a receipt in full. According to Stoll, "It cost me about $54,000 to clear up with the fishermen. Now a good many of them are out of employment and the best of them we have picked out and keep them now as fishermen for the Sandusky Fish Company." He noted that in the early 1880s, the fishermen sometimes had paid off their entire debts in one season, but as the number of fish declined, they fell farther and farther behind. The years 1890 to 1894 had been especially bad. Then the total of fishermen's indebtedness to him had doubled.[33]

The 100 fishermen who were formally interviewed commonly remarked that too many were in the business and that Lake Erie was overfished. "Most of them profess themselves in favor of a heavy reduction in the amount of apparatus," noted the investigators. To remedy the decline in the catch, most favored the idea of a closed season, generally in the fall, but many suggested summer and winter as well. Noted the investigators: "Each desire a closed season at such time as will leave him untrammelled and embarrass his competitors." In Dunkirk, New York, where fishermen harvested whitefish and trout in the spring, summer, and autumn well into November, "all close seasons are regarded as a delusion."[34]

Many of the American fishermen who worked on Lake Erie favored the idea of licensing, noting that Canada had such a system, which they regarded as stricter than they would like to see adopted. Yet they did see value in licensing, especially if it protected a fisherman's right to certain grounds. Others feared that licensing might simply help the sportfishermen who would siphon off all the funds collected for commercial licenses to serve their needs. Support for licensing came mainly from the pound-net fishermen of the western end of the lake, whereas at Erie, Pennsylvania, and Dunkirk, New York, the tug-fishing region, fishermen generally opposed a license system and, indeed, regulation in general. One very successful fisherman with almost four decades of experience on Lake Erie claimed that a license system was not in keeping with "American ideas."[35]

While very much aware of the destruction of small fish and the threats to the long-term health of the resource, the fishermen debated the issue of how to save small fish, but came to no general agreement. The gill-net fishermen argued that the pound-net fishermen of the western end of Lake Erie were the offenders, and if they enlarged the mesh of their pounds, the small fish could escape. The pound-net fishermen claimed that a larger mesh would lead to the gilling of larger fish, and it would be far better to sort the fish at the crib, returning the small ones to the water. Tug fishermen scoffed at the idea of being able to sort fish at the pound, given the often turbulent weather conditions on the lake. Others suggested that small fish would be either damaged in the pot of the pound net before liberation or injured in the effort to return them to the water. So the argument went, a seemingly unresolvable one, given the nature of the Lake Erie fishery, where both gill- and pound-net interests were very strong.[36]

Disagree as they did over licensing, instituting closed seasons, regulating the size of net mesh, and saving the small fish, Lake Erie fishermen—100 in formal interviews, and another 100 in conversations—told the investigators that they favored the hatchery program. Only four or five criticized it as useless in maintaining the fish population. Asked whether the lake's fish resources should be protected by the state or federal government (in Canada, the authority was vested in the dominion), the fishermen favored putting the fisheries under the control of national authorities. Of the forty who expressed opinions, thirty-seven favored federal control, two vehemently opposed it, and one was indifferent.[37] Plainly in 1894, the discouraged fishermen of Lake Erie were ready to try some form of government assistance to improve the depressed state of their industry. Would they still feel the same way once the economy improved?

In communities around Lake Huron, Georgian Bay, Lake Ontario, and Lake Superior, the investigating teams found support for the general idea of closed seasons to protect spawning fish and wide variation in when they should occur, findings that paralleled those documented by the Dominion Fishery Commission. Here and there came the suggestion that the only way to help the fish would be to suspend fishing for a few years, not that this would ever come to pass.[38] As had those interviewed by the Dominion Fishery Commission, the Canadian fishermen strongly urged the establishment of uniform Canadian and American closed seasons enforced at the national levels. Although many of them criticized the content of Canadian regulations and the failure of the authorities to enforce them fully, the majority supported the idea of some regulation.

Both Canadian and American fishermen who worked on Lake Superior favored minimal to no regulation more consistently than did those who fished on the other lakes surveyed in 1894, and they preferred that authority be in the hands of national officials. A majority turned thumbs down on licensing and on restricting the number of fishermen. They were very lukewarm about regulating mesh size and restricting the amount of apparatus that could be used by any one fisher. At the same time, they were concerned about the destruction of small fish. In the opinion of a merchant in Port Arthur, Ontario, for years associated with the fisheries, "There is always a war between the fishermen and the authorities, who are trying to keep them back. The fisherman thinks he should get them now and make a living out of them."[39]

Given the purpose for which the Joint Commission was created, its field-workers geared their questions to regulation, and thus the fishermen's ideas about it were those most fully expressed in the interviews. To conserve or not to conserve was the central question. Closely related to regulation were a better knowledge of the fish species and their habits, a determination of whether the different kinds of fish had increased or decreased in number over the years, and an exploration of the way changes in the fish habitat may have influenced fluctuations in number. Thus the investigators naturally chose to interview people with a knowledge of the fisheries that extended over time and in so doing interviewed a special sample. Their interview responses revealed the ideas of a body of experienced Great Lakes fishermen who had thought a lot about changes on the lakes and in the industry from as early as the first decade of the nineteenth century to the 1890s, fishermen who did care about the future of the resource. In observing the fish, some of them looked beyond the immediate practical questions of learning when and how to make the largest catch and tried to learn broadly about fish life cycles and habits. In observing their fellow fishers, they saw everything from opportunists with a short-term stake in the resource to those who planned to stay around a lifetime and wanted the fish population to maintain itself. They saw quite clearly the effects of population growth and economic development on the Great Lakes basin and on the lake waters, and they thought about the repercussions of those changes on the fish population. They remembered the time when the fish were bountiful and offered their explanations of why they had declined, stressing technological change and overfishing as major factors. They evaluated the successes and failures of attempts to regulate the fisheries. Their accounts offer posterity a view of Great Lakes fishermen with widely varied ideas about and expectations for the resource.

By the early 1890s, the commercial fishermen of the Inland Seas found themselves in an extremely difficult position. As part of a highly competitive, overexpanded industry that was largely created and controlled by

American dealers, caught in the sluggish market of depression times, and dependent on a declining resource, they struggled to survive. Could it have been only a decade earlier that they had flourished in expansive boom times? Many of the American fishermen seriously considered the wisdom of federal regulations, and some thought that international regulations written and administered by Canada and the United States would be the most desirable alternative.

In 1894, many saw the future as did Captain Donald McCauley, who had begun fishing at Southampton, Ontario, on Lake Huron in 1855: "I am near done out, and the fishery is near done out too. I am getting old and the fishing is getting slack and I guess we will both pull out together. I know the tugs can stand it a good deal better than the boats, but a good many of the tugs are going to quit soon."[40]

Probably no fisherman realized more clearly that the early 1890s represented the end of an era than Peter Calgiosgie, an Indian from Sault Sainte Marie, Ontario, who thought that so much dynamiting at the Sault for the construction of a canal had driven the fish away. He told the Dominion Fishery Commission in November 1893: "I am a Canadian. I was born at Sault Ste. Marie. I am 73 years of age. About 15 or 20 years ago [I] could catch plenty of whitefish here in the Sault Rapids. Could catch any number with scoop-nets and canoes. They are nearly all gone now. Only a few small ones left, hardly worth fishing for."[41]

Part II

Great Lakes Waters in a Developing Drainage Basin 1815–1900

When westward-moving people occupied the southern part of the Great Lakes region beginning in modest numbers in the late eighteenth century and growing to tens of thousands in the nineteenth, their use of land and water resources soon changed the fish habitat. The following three chapters examine the main components of nineteenth-century development and suggest how each influenced Great Lakes fish life.

8

Agriculture, Lumbering, Mining, and the Changing Fish Habitat

Just as Quick as They Began to Clear the Country Up the Fish Began to Disappear

The Great Lakes contain 94,250 square miles of water and act as the catch basin for drainage from a surrounding 201,460-square-mile land area. Given their physical characteristics, their midcontinental location, and their history of human use, particularly in the past 150 years, the lakes have shown greater short-term sensitivity to the development of adjacent land areas than have the North American coastal waters in the same time period, given their larger area and greater capacity to dilute pollutants. Particularly significant for the marine habitat of the Great Lakes then and now is the rate at which their waters can clear themselves of the diverse pollutants emptying into them. In 1967, Robert H. Rainey calculated that Lake Erie could rid itself of 90 percent of dissolved or suspended pollutants in 6 years if no more were added; Lake Ontario, in 20 years; Lake Michigan, in 100 years; and Lake Superior, in more than 500. But pollution is a continuing reality created by direct and indirect discharges from human activity on basin lands, from atmospheric emissions, and from "resuspension of sediment and cycling through biological food chains." The marine habitat and its life are ever changing.[1]

The lands surrounding the Great Lakes contained a rich variety of natural resources: agricultural land of varying quality, hardwood and deciduous forests, and such fossil fuels and minerals as coal, gas, oil, uranium, copper, zinc, gold, silver, iron ore, and nickel (figure 8.1). The basin also provided quantities of salt, gypsum, limestone, sandstone, sand, and gravel. Well endowed by nature and located in the midcontinent, with distinct transportation and market advantages, the region attracted a veritable flood of people bent on improving their well-being by using its natural wealth. They combined their skills, capital, and labor with those natural resources to make a significant contribution to the national development of the United States and Canada in the nineteenth century. By 1900, the Great Lakes region, greatly altered from what it had been fifty years earlier, emerged as a major North American urban and industrial area: supplier of timber, iron ore, copper, and agricultural products; producer of iron, steel, and a wide variety of producer and consumer goods; and home to 3,643,000 people.

Very obvious and probably most taken for granted of all the resources of the Great Lakes basin were the lakes themselves and their tributary waters, natural avenues of transportation that linked the Atlantic Ocean, vast parts of the North American midcontinent, and the Gulf of Mexico, and a magnificent source of seemingly unlimited amounts of high-quality water. No resource became so burdened with growing, changing human expectations as the waterways. People came to expect the lakes to satisfy their complex and growing needs. For the Native North Americans, the lakes provided natural paths for movement, food, and aesthetic and recreational pleasure. Euro-Americans saw them first as avenues for the fur trade, missionary activity, and empire building, and later as routes for settlers into undeveloped regions. Later in the nineteenth century, they provided an inexpensive way to carry logs, lumber, iron ore, and copper to mills and markets. Tons of grain and coal traversed their waters. Growing cities turned to the lakes to supply drinking water and to dispose of sewage and garbage. The region's people regarded the lakes, their wetlands, and their tributary rivers and streams as sources of food. Fish were used as table fare, as a means of earning a livelihood, and for recreational sport.

Change occurred at different times in different parts of the drainage basin. In general, Lakes Ontario and Erie and southern Lakes Huron and Michigan experienced notable change first. In Georgian Bay, the North Channel of Lake Huron, northern Lake Michigan, and Lake Superior, change came later, in the last three decades of the nineteenth century. It followed the influx of people: beginning on Lake Ontario at the end of the eighteenth century; then moving westward around the shores of Lake Erie, especially after 1815; and, from the 1830s to the 1860s, expanding

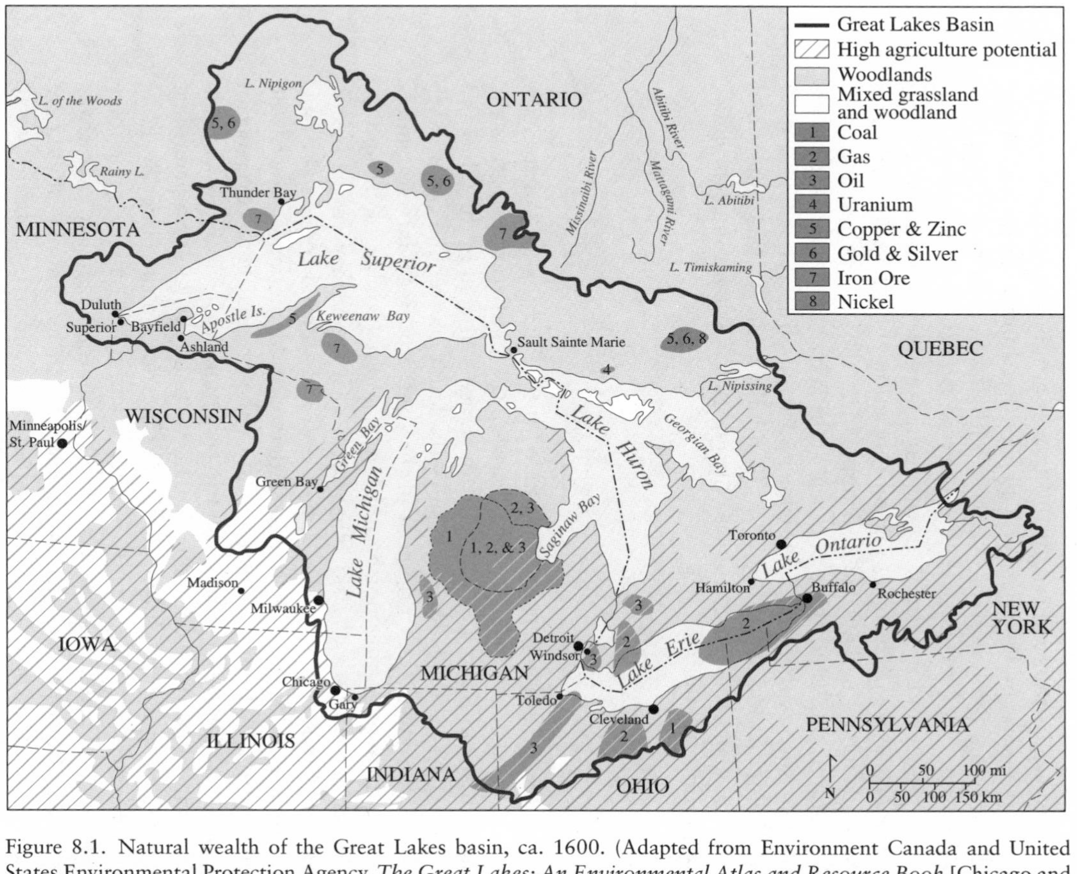

Figure 8.1. Natural wealth of the Great Lakes basin, ca. 1600. (Adapted from Environment Canada and United States Environmental Protection Agency, *The Great Lakes: An Environmental Atlas and Resource Book* [Chicago and Toronto: Environmental Protection Agency and Environment Canada, 1987], 2, 6, and Helen Hornbeck Tanner, ed., *Atlas of Great Lakes Indian History* [Norman: University of Oklahoma Press, 1987], 14–15, 20–21; Cartographic Laboratory, University of Wisconsin–Madison)

through Ohio, Indiana, the southern half of the Lower Peninsula of Michigan, Illinois, and Wisconsin along Lake Michigan to the southern portions of Green Bay. Because of differences in climate, in accessibility to national transportation networks and markets, and in the natural resource base, the northern region of the Great Lakes basin did not develop as intensively as the southern. In 1900, areas around northern Lake Superior and Georgian Bay were still defined as frontier according to the United States Bureau of the Census, with fewer than two people per square mile. Wherever development of land resources, population increase, urban and industrial growth, and commercial fishing occurred, and when the use of the lakes for transportation and waste disposal characterized human activity, the fish population showed early change and often decline. In the northern portions of the lakes, a fish population composed of species that had been widely distributed in the lakes in 1800 lasted longest, and around Isle Royale in Lake Superior, this remote and beautiful place, the best examples of trout species known since the era of exploration remain.

AGRICULTURE

Agricultural development greatly altered the habitat of the Great Lakes region. Except for a small grassland area in the southernmost part of the Lake Michigan basin and small oak openings scattered in the Ohio and Ontario parts of the Lake Erie basin, woodlands covered the Great Lakes region: deciduous trees primarily in the southern areas, mixed conifers and hardwoods farther north, and boreal forest (poplar, birch, spruce, and fir) to the north of Lake Superior and Georgian Bay. In the basin's deciduous woodlands, where climate and soils proved congenial to agricultural development, incoming settlers cleared the land, plowed the soil, and planted crops. This removal of the original land cover began modestly in parts of the Lake Ontario shoreline before 1800. As R. Cole Harris and John Warkentin have noted, the southern Ontario peninsula, surrounded by Lakes Huron, Erie, and Ontario and the upper St. Lawrence River, was "still a densely forested tract broken only here and there by beaver meadows, by Indian campsites or, on some light and excessively drained soils, by prairie dotted with oaks" as late as 1780. In 1860, more than 1.5 million people lived there, and "its forests had been largely cleared. . . . Fields, fences, barns, and villages comprised a new landscape that eradicated the landscape of 1780."[2] The same process had permanently changed the vegetation and the landscape on the southern shores of Lakes Ontario and Erie, in New York and Ohio, two decades earlier. It had produced a similar effect in the 1850s in southern Michigan and in the thin band of Great Lakes drainage basin in Illinois and Wisconsin between Chicago and Milwaukee on the western shore of Lake Michigan.

In the larger part of these areas, wheat farming with the wheat–fallow–wheat system of culture initially prevailed, laying bare the earth in a wasteful, soil-depleting system of agriculture that led to erosion and to soil-laden runoff into streams, rivers, and lakes. In a band three or four miles wide along the shores of Lakes Ontario and Erie—from the Bay of Quinte to the Essex Peninsula in the north, and from Oswego, New York, to the islands in western Lake Erie near Sandusky, Ohio, in the south—farmers found the lake-tempered lands well suited to growing fruit for commercial purposes in the 1840s and 1850s. By midcentury, pioneer settlers in the southwestern counties of Michigan, along the Lake Michigan shoreline, had experimented enough with fruit crops to know that the lakeshore climate and soils furnished an ideal combination for growing fruit. In the latter half of the century, grape vineyards and apple, peach, pear, plum, and cherry orchards along Lakes Ontario, Erie, and Michigan flourished under a regime that required careful cultivation and fertilization. Here orchardists introduced arsenicals, London Purple and Paris Green, to control the ravages of insect pests in the 1870s, followed at the end of the century with lead arsenate, which became the standard insecticide used in farming. While the fruit belts remained a significant feature of Great Lakes agriculture, wheat farming soon gave way to general farming and to dairy farming, which led to an increase in both the amount of runoff containing manure and pesticides and the volume of soil and plant material entering the lakes. Aside from manure, farmers most frequently applied lime and salt to stimulate plant growth. In areas of intensive fruit and vegetable cultivation for urban markets, farmers used phosphate fertilizers on a very small part of land under cultivation.[3]

Contemporaries commented again and again how in their lifetimes they had seen the forests disappear, the land transformed into prosperous farms, and the stream flow changed from relatively even in the warm months to more sudden rushes of water in rainy seasons, making erosion and flood damage very real.[4] Agricultural development accelerated erosion and introduced into stream, river, and lake waters nutrients that lowered oxygen levels essential to many fish species and created greater turbidity, which affected both marine plant and animal life whose nutritional and light requirements were harmonious with the conditions that had existed in the preagricultural ecosystems. As agricultural land use intensified during the nineteenth century, its impact on lake waters escalated. In reviewing that process, Thomas H. Langlois noted in 1954 that "once beautiful clear blue lakes have been fed by warm muddy streams until they also have become roily and yellow. Their plant life has been smothered out, and their once clean gravel bottoms have become covered with silt." With these changes came changes in the species composition and the abundance of fish.[5]

Clearing and cultivation produced a drying effect on soils generally and changes in the wetlands along lakes and rivers that spoiled them as a habitat for wildlife and fish. Wetlands served as spawning and feeding grounds for fish, but once loaded with sediments from increased soil erosion and their waters made turbid, they no longer provided the right conditions for many species. The wetlands protected lake waters by filtering pollutants, removing sediments, producing oxygen, recycling nutrients, and absorbing both chemicals and nutrients; but as the burden of foreign substances loaded on them increased, their protective impact diminished and they became less desirable places for fish and wildlife to inhabit.[6]

The ways that farmers and entrepreneurial developers altered wet and swampy lands lying in the drainage basin added yet other dimensions to agriculture's impact on the waters of the Great Lakes. Swamps and wetlands unsuitable for cultivation were widely regarded as useless. At first, farmers avoided them. But as land values rose, they seemed worth reclaiming, for in many cases the soil yielded excellent crops after it had been properly drained. This drain-and-cultivate mentality served in part as the rationale for members of Congress to advocate giving to the states enormous areas of wetlands identified as swamps on federal surveyors' plats. A law passed in 1849 gave federally owned swamplands to Louisiana, and legislation in 1850 gave federal wetlands to the balance of the public-land states in which they were located, on the understanding that the states would sell the lands and use the money to reclaim them. Millions of acres of wetlands lay in the states located partially within the Great Lakes drainage basin. In Michigan, the one state entirely within the basin, 7,374,000 acres of unsold federal land were selected as "swamp," an underestimate of the magnitude of such areas, made decades after the public domain had gone on the market. The midwestern states soon realized that the income from sales of the lands they had received from the federal government would not begin to pay for their reclamation. While the federal swampland grants in the Midwest failed to achieve the stated goals, the states created systems that they hoped would foster reclamation.[7]

The western basin of Lake Erie provides a vivid example of the way in which agricultural development changed wetlands. On the Essex Peninsula in Ontario, many thousands of acres with a potential for rich, level farmlands remained in brush and swamp in 1860, and farmers tilled only the higher locations. They long avoided the heavy, wet soils in much of present-day Essex and Kent Counties because the high reclamation costs did not justify bringing them into production. For the American side of the western Lake Erie basin, maps prepared in 1930 for a special census report, *Drainage of Agricultural Lands,* revealed a great concentration of formerly wet and swampy lands in the Lower Peninsula of Michigan and in portions of northern Ohio that drained into the lake. Before it was settled, most of the land lying between Detroit and Sandusky was very marshy, abounding in birds, animals, and wild rice. Lake Erie waters around the Bass Islands were so clear that black bass were visible twelve to fifteen feet below the surface.[8]

The Black Swamp of the Maumee, Tiffin, and Portage River valleys, 1,500 square miles in northwestern Ohio, long a roadblock to travel and settlement, is a prime example of an extensive wetland area reclaimed for agriculture by a slow process that extended over fifty years and was considered nearly completed at the end of the nineteenth century by resort to drainage districts and tiling. Martin R. Kaatz, historian of the process, concluded his account of the struggles of people in this swampy region with a tribute to their accomplishment: "A vigorous transformation of the natural landscape has taken place in northwestern Ohio. A vast swamp which formerly dominated the pattern of roads and villages has disappeared leaving it its wake a fertile and productive segment of the Corn Belt." But the Black Swamp could no longer perform the important function of reservoir for water storage capable of slow release as needed. In his study, Langlois explained the negative consequences of the drainage of Black Swamp and farming methods on aquatic plants, lesser organisms, and fish in western Lake Erie waters.[9]

For marine life, the impact of land drainage made itself clearly felt. In the marshes along the shore of Lake Erie around Port Clinton and Sandusky, the once very large population of turtles and frogs had diminished notably by 1885. A decade later, fishermen in the area remarked on the decline in the catfish population, caused, they believed, by the drainage and reclamation of marshy lands. In the altered habitat, many of the eggs and fry dried up in isolated pools. The report of the Joint Commission Relative to the Preservation of the Fisheries in Waters Contiguous to the United States and Canada, published in 1896, attributed the dying out of bullheads, grass pike, and largemouth bass in some locations along the southwestern shore of Lake Erie to the drainage of coastal marshlands.[10]

Farmers on the Essex Peninsula, across Lake Erie from Ohio, began draining their lands artificially in the late 1860s, embarking on ditching projects, a reclamation system facilitated by the Provincial Drainage Act of 1872. By 1880, great change was evident. Noted the Ontario Agricultural Commission, the law "has done wonders for Essex. Under this act thousands of acres have been brought into cultivation, and are today yielding a profitable return from land that was, till recently, all but worthless."[11] The search for ways to reclaim wet farmlands followed a similar course in the American Midwest. With the federal swampland grant an obvious failure, states turned to their own devices. As early as 1857 and 1859, legislators in Michigan and Ohio enacted laws to permit the formation of drainage districts. Farmers organized districts as the century progressed, and they tiled more and more of their lands, especially in the 1880s and 1890s. Entrepreneurial developers explored the feasibility of draining marshes, swamps, and even small lakes to turn rich earth into cropland.

Before 1900, agricultural development substantially altered the ability of cultivated land to absorb and hold water. Although drainage facilitated cultivation, it contributed very substantially to changing the water qualities of the Great Lakes and thus the habitat of the plants and animals that lived in them. Agricultural non-point pollution, a subtle, long-term change, did not greatly impress fishery experts charged with the task of explaining the decline of the Great Lakes fisheries until well into the twentieth century. In the 1940s, a dozen years before the publication of Kaatz's articles on the Black Swamp, Great Lakes fishery experts began a long-overdue debate on the impact of agricultural land drainage and cultivation on the fish population of Lake Erie. The adverse effects of siltation from the erosion of agricultural land and, specifically as a significant example, the drainage of the Black Swamp captured the attention of a growing number of scientists who believed that pollution and not just overfishing had seriously eroded the fisheries. By the 1970s, fishery experts were advocating a "no till" or "reduced tillage" program for lands that drained into Lake Erie. Agricultural development accelerated the pollution of the waters of Lakes Michigan, Huron, Erie, and Ontario to varying degrees. Around Lake Erie, 67 percent of the lake basin was in agricultural production; Lake Michigan, 44 percent; Lake Ontario, 39 percent; and Lake Huron, 27 percent. Climate and soils protected Lake Superior. Only 3 percent of its basin went into farms. While there is no measure of the amount of pollution from agricultural activity, before 1900 it was and it continues to be massive.[12]

LUMBERING

Second only to agriculture, commercial lumbering had a major impact on the Great Lakes marine habitat during the nineteenth century. Three separate processes contributed to change in Great Lakes waters: harvesting the timber, transporting the logs down streams and rivers and over the lakes, and milling the logs. A mere glance at a map of the original vegetation of the Great Lakes basin reveals the wealth of timber: from the deciduous tree cover around Lakes Erie and Ontario; northwest to the vast mixed deciduous and coniferous forests of the watersheds of Lake Huron, Georgian Bay, northern Lake Michigan, and southern Lake Superior; and finally to the boreal forests around northern Lake Superior (see Figure 8.1). White and red pines, the most coveted of these trees for commercial purposes, stood intermixed with hardwoods. Commercial lumbering made its greatest impact on the waters of Lakes Michigan and Huron, Georgian Bay, and southern Lake Superior.

The removal of forest cover to fill the needs of the lumber market began modestly in the 1830s, escalated in the 1850s, reached its height in the late nineteenth century, and declined in the early decades of the twentieth as lumbermen exhausted the Great Lakes pinelands. The magnificent stands of the pineries fell to ax and saw to fill the needs of expanding populations in Canada and the United States as settlers moved into undeveloped regions in search of economic opportunity in commerce, industry, and agriculture, and a better quality of life. In Michigan alone, by the end of the century, loggers had cut more than 160 billion board feet of pine, principally from the mixed forests in the Lower Peninsula, leaving devastated forestlands and hundreds of thousands of acres of cutover, burned-over, eroding lands. The fine stands of the Georgian Bay watershed and the pineries adjacent to Lake Superior remained important sources of lumber. At century's end, the age of lumbering, during which the streams tributary to Lakes Michigan and Huron were used as the major means of delivery, was over, and the railroads for at least a decade had carried most of the logs from the woods and most of the lumber to market.

Notoriously wasteful, the timber harvest would have made an even greater impact on land and water had clear-cutting been the practice in the nineteenth century, which it was not, given the preference for pine and the nature of the intermixed pine–deciduous forest. Lumbermen harvested pines first and hardwoods later. Still, the devastation was great. The system of cutting left behind a tangled mass of slash and brush that dried and served as a tinderbox for fires started by settlers clearing the land, construction crews laying railroad tracks, sparks flying from locomotives, and lightning. Fires followed the big cut especially during the decades from 1870 to 1920 in the Great Lakes drainage basin. Among the more notorious were those in 1871 in the Lower Peninsula, where fire cut a swath through 2.5 million acres from the eastern shore of Lake Michigan across the peninsula to Port Huron. On the western shore of the lake, fire swept the Fox River valley and swiftly moved north from Green Bay, Wisconsin, two-thirds of the way to Escanaba, Michigan. On the eastern side of Green Bay, the woods, farms, and villages of the Door Peninsula south of Sturgeon Bay suffered severely. A conservative estimate of damage to the western shore of Lake Michigan placed the destruction at a minimum of 1,280,000 acres. Between 1,000 and 1,500 people died in Michigan and Wisconsin, and the damage to land, water, fish, and wildlife was incalculable. The cutting of forests removed a kind of vegetation that was very effective in retaining soil moisture, and fire hastened and exacerbated the process.[13]

A discerning insight into the effects of the timber harvest on land, water, and vegetation comes from the pen of Filibert Roth, a special agent of the Department of Agriculture who in 1898 surveyed forestry conditions in northern Wisconsin at the behest of E. A. Birge for the Wisconsin Geological and Natural History Survey. Roth's elaborate, detailed, on-site investigation of the forestlands roughly west and north of the city of Green Bay left for posterity a graphic description of the immediate results of lumbering and a map of his labors. The area of the survey included four counties within the drainage basin of Lake Superior and six within that of Lake Michigan. He found that the pines had been cut in the forests adjacent to Lake Superior from the city of Superior to Ashland, in those next to rivers, and in those close to railroads. These had been mixed forests in which pine dominated. "Considerable" merchantable pine remained in other parts of the counties. The hardwoods and hemlock in Ashland County had been culled, but not those in Bayfield, Douglas, and Iron Counties. Fires in the pineries along the lake in Ashland County had taken their toll. In Bayfield County, according to Roth, "bare wastes of great extent occur in all localities where pine logging has been going on." Fire, he noted, had destroyed the unharvested hardwoods standing among pine slash.[14]

In Forest, Florence, Oconto, Shawano, Marinette, and part of Langlade Counties, whose rivers drained into Green Bay, Roth found the aftermath of lumbering more dramatic, considering that the cut had begun earlier (figure 8.2). Loggers had felled most of the pines, and fires had burned over much of the land. He pointed out that burned-over lands formed "a far greater proportion of the area than is usually supposed." Roth estimated that in Florence County, 20 percent of the land surface had been burned over. In Marinette County, where before lumbering "a heavy stand of pine mixed with hardwoods occupied the part next to Green Bay," lands ravaged by the Peshtigo fire twenty-seven years earlier were "now bare or brush land with some settlement." In Oconto and Shawano Counties, farmers had already drained and were in the process of further draining and cultivating large areas of burned-over swamps.[15] Farming in the cutover land, with its very mixed results for those who performed the heavy labor of removing stumps and planting crops, was well under way at the end of the century, an adaptation of the mixed pine–hardwood forest areas of the Great Lakes that took a heavy toll on land and water resources and people.

On the basis of his observations and the evidence he collected from people who lived in the forested areas of northern Wisconsin, Roth ar-

Figure 8.2. Cutover and burned-over forestland near Laona, Wisconsin, Forest County, in the headwaters of the Peshtigo River. This twentieth-century photograph suggests the kind of devastation that Filibert Roth found in Forest County in 1898. (Photograph courtesy State Historical Society of Wisconsin, Madison; photograph no. WHi [X3] 13338)

gued that the removal of forest cover had made "decided changes in drainage and soil moisture." The flow of all larger rivers had diminished, he maintained, and miles and miles of corduroy roads ceased to be used because the earth had dried to the point where they were not needed. Swamps had dried up and, without ditching, could be easily used for pasture and cultivated field. Hardwood thickets had replaced swamp timber.[16]

There is no way to measure the effects of the commercial-lumber harvest on Great Lakes waters. Yet given its magnitude and its disruption of complex balances involving tree cover, soil, and water, lumbering contributed to erosion, siltation, and fertilization, adding to those problems at the same time that agricultural development contributed greatly to the same processes of change.

While the removal of tree cover triggered one set of changes, the systems used to deliver logs to mill and market generated another that massively affected river and lake waters. Conducted in the spring, log drives down streams and rivers to mills located near the Great Lakes, where lumber schooners had easy access, disrupted and, in some cases, destroyed the fish population. They swept all before them, produced massive pileups, scoured streambeds, and altered the configuration of waterways. To facilitate the delivery of the logs to mills, lumbermen built systems of dams to control the flow of water, enabling them to create floods when necessary to keep the logs moving. But the dams blocked the passage of fish upstream to feed and spawn. The logging companies also constructed booms, sluices, scaling ponds, and sometimes small canals along rivers and as connectors to small lakes, to facilitate the movement of logs, as well as much larger canals, such as the Sturgeon Bay Ship Canal, to create shortcuts in the Great Lakes delivery system itself. Canal building had an impact on Great Lakes fish. Two examples show very different effects. The Sturgeon Bay Ship Canal in Wisconsin created new currents that carried "great quantities of fish" to the vicinity of Little Sturgeon, making pound netting possible, reported Hugh M. Smith and Merwin-Marie Snell in their study of the Great Lakes. The series of canals built at Sault Sainte Marie, ship traffic, and lumbering activity that utilized the St. Mary's River ultimately destroyed the famous whitefish grounds at the rapids, which the Indians had found so productive for centuries.[17] The Great Lakes also served as arteries for the transportation of logs, a notable example being the large log rafts that were pulled from Georgian Bay across Lake Huron to mill towns on the eastern shore of the Lower Peninsula of Michigan.

Sawmills produced enormous quantities of sawdust and wood scrap. Commonly dumped directly into the rivers and the lakes, this refuse floated on the surface until it became waterlogged and then sank to the bottom. Some of the larger mills loaded barges with sawdust for transport offshore and dumped it in deeper waters. Sawdust clogged harbors and river channels, necessitating dredging operations. The damage to spawning and feeding grounds cannot be calculated with precision, but contemporaries regarded it as very serious. So devastating were its effects in Canadian waters generally that in 1890 the Minister of Marine and Fisheries urged immediate action to curb the threat to "serious permanent injury to the navigation and fisheries." Gone were the days when Canada could any longer show "a very great deal of forbearance . . . towards mill-owners and manufacturers." He was not alone in his assessment. A group of persistent critics of sawdust dumping that included naturalists, scientists, public-health officials, and sportsmen joined with commercial fishermen and government officials appointed to protect the fish resource during the last four decades of the nineteenth century in condemning the ways in which the commercial-lumber industry was despoiling the environment.[18]

By all odds, complaints about the negative impact of lumbering on fish life were louder, longer, and more numerous than those about any other source of water pollution. Fishers told state, provincial, and national governments about the lumbermen's devastating influence on marine life, and officials charged with study and policy recommendations for the fisheries investigated and assessed the validity of these criticisms, usually concluding that they were quite justified. Beginning in the early 1870s and continuing for the balance of the century, they publicly denounced pollution damage from lumbering, often using forceful language, none more so than Samuel Wilmot, Superintendent of the Dominion Hatcheries and lifelong observer of Great Lakes fish life. In his report on fish-breeding operations, published in 1890, he devoted twelve pages to the problems of sawdust pollution, quoting widely from reports released by the fish commissions of American states and the United States Commission of Fish and Fisheries, from articles published in scientific journals, and from a study conducted by a select committee of the Canadian Senate on sawdust problems in the Ottawa River. Wilmot characterized sawdust as literally a poison on the spawning beds, a killer of marine insect and plant life on which fish depended for food. He noted, "It is an artificial product, alien to and engendering latent diseases of various kinds, with fatal results in all waters where fish life exists." Once settled along the shores in rivers, streams, inlets, and lakes, "it forms a compact mass of pollution," a "fixed imperishable foreign matter" that covers the bottoms with "a mantle of death," an "endless graveyard to the innumerable colonies of insect life which inhabited these former well adapted natural abodes for their existence." Dramatic and somewhat flowery in expression though he was, Wilmot knew his fish.[19]

Very extensive spoliation of the marine habitat in Lakes Michigan and Huron, in Georgian Bay, and along the southern shore of Lake Superior as a result of lumbering operations particularly drew fire from fishing interests. Lake Huron and Georgian Bay, which were the most damaged, merit attention given the widespread character of the devastation and the many ways in which lumber-related economic activities affected the marine habitat. Fishermen, dealer-fishers, and government field-workers clearly revealed their thoughts about these matters in the detailed testimony collected in 1893 by the Dominion Fishery Commission on the Fisheries of the Province of Ontario and that gathered a year later by the Joint Commission Relative to the Preservation of the Fisheries in Waters Contiguous to Canada and the United States. The original records of the Joint Commission, transcribed stenographic reports of the interviews, and observations of the officials involved, when consolidated, fill fifteen single-spaced typed pages. The abridged, printed reports collected by the Dominion Fishery Commission are less voluminous, but nevertheless carry the same forceful message. Both investigating bodies talked to fishermen and dealers whom they considered reliable sources of information given their fishing experience over periods ranging from one to several decades.

Lake Huron and Georgian Bay fishers and dealers complained about sawdust and mill refuse, citing spoiled navigation, dredging of harbors, ruined nets, and destruction of spawning and feeding grounds as major burdens on their efforts to make a livelihood. The impacts varied from place to place and over time. In 1892, for example, an observer reported that currents passing through the Straits of Mackinac into Lake Huron had left a massive trail of sawdust and mill refuse that covered the bottom for a mile out into the water at St. Ignace and along the shore for as much as five or six miles.[20] Until the mid-1880s, fisherman who worked on Georgian Bay and adjacent to the Bruce Peninsula found sawmill activities very troublesome. A member of the Canadian House of Commons with a Georgian Bay constituency told the House in 1883 that the accumulation of sawdust in river mouths and harbors seriously interfered with navigation.[21]

In the mid-1880s, when United States tariff regulations allowed saw logs to enter the country duty free, milling along the shores of Georgian Bay tapered off. Lumbermen then began to send log rafts, assembled principally at the mouths of the Whitefish, Spanish, and French Rivers and at Byng Inlet, to American mills, mainly in Bay City and Alpena, Michigan, where local log supplies had dwindled. The Georgian Bay fishermen's complaints shifted in emphasis to the devastation left by bark that was ground off the log rafts, seriously fouling the water and littering the lake bed. For example, William A. Clark of Collingwood, Ontario, a fisherman for three decades, confirmed the damage: "I have known a raft to lie for three or four days in sight right over the principal feeding grounds of the whitefish, and it is both destructive to the fish and also to the nets." The bottom of Georgian Bay, he lamented, "is becoming literally rotten with the bark of those large rafts."[22] On the American shores of Lake Huron, sawdust and mill refuse remained the menace to fishers that they had been for many years. Bark ground off log rafts, they believed, fouled the lake waters and bottom, destroying fish habitats and nets alike, and churned through the waters with every "big blow," but this problem took second place to mill waste as the primary pollutant in these fishermen's thoughts.

In 1894, interviewers for the Joint Commission heard many complaints about the lumber industry's pollution of Lake Huron other than the widespread condemnation of sawmill and log-raft wastes. The growth of lumber-related industries and population centers led to frequent dredging operations and to dumping of general and industrial sewage into the lake and its tributary rivers. Much of this kind of criticism originated from American fishermen who pinpointed as polluters the pulp mills in Alpena and Port Huron, a tannery in Cheboygan, and the saltworks scattered along the Saginaw River from Bay City to Saginaw. Very few of the Canadian fishers interviewed complained about discharges from the tannery and the several saltworks located on their side of Lake Huron.

Nor did they report trouble from dumping sewage and dredging. Specifically cited, the Alpena Sulphite Fiber Company, established in 1883 to produce pulp for the use of paper mills elsewhere, produced an acid waste in its four vats. It drained directly into the river. According to Casper Alpern, a local fish dealer, that sewage was "poison to the fish" and ruined the ice harvest in winter: "We dare not fill our boilers here in the river as it affects them to use that water."[23]

When Richard Rathbun of the Joint Commission visited Port Huron, Michigan, he reported that the Black River flowing into the St. Clair was "a dark river, foul smelling with sulphurated hydrogen coming from decay. It would seem impossible for anything to live in it." A pulp mill polluted the water with acids, according to one fish dealer, killing thousands of fish and creating an "intolerable" stench.[24]

These contemporary assessments of the paper industry's pollution of Lake Huron illustrated a growing problem for the waters of the Great Lakes. In general, paper mills utilizing wood pulp sprang up in communities whose peak as lumber producers had passed and in those with unusually fine sources of water power, such as Niagara Falls and Watertown, New York, and the cities in the Fox River valley, tributary to Green Bay, in Wisconsin, beginning in the latter 1870s. Paper manufacture was a growing industry in the Great Lakes drainage basin in the 1880s and 1890s. When the Ontario Agricultural Commission made its survey in 1880, it documented three large paper mills in the easternmost county bordering Lake Ontario and three in County York, in the Toronto area.[25]

The saltworks along the Saginaw River, another lumber-related industry utilizing mill wastes as fuel in the evaporation process, spoiled the fish habitat, complained two Bay Port fishers. A scientist on the Joint Commission investigating team agreed. The industry was a substantial one. In Saginaw County, the first well was sunk in 1859, and the expansive era began four years later. Production escalated from 4,000 barrels in 1860 to more than 1.1 million barrels twenty years later.[26]

Nor did the tanneries on Lake Huron escape the critical notice of the fishermen. Those in Cheboygan, Michigan, and Southampton, Ontario, are examples of secondary lumbering industries that utilized hemlock bark and hides. The Cheboygan location was in the midst of plentiful supplies of hemlock bark, but was farther from a source of hides. The Southampton tannery had the advantage of having a supply of hides closer at hand. Inexpensive transportation by Great Lakes ships enabled both tanneries to achieve a cost advantage that made their chosen locations profitable. In general, when access to a supply of hides justified it, entrepreneurs built tanneries in logging communities near sawmills. In 1864, for example, Guido Pfister, a very prominent Milwaukee tanner and leather-goods merchant, opened tanneries in Two Creeks, north of

Two Rivers, Wisconsin, on Lake Michigan, and other tanneries were established in the area between Manitowoc and Two Rivers. Labor and transportation costs sometimes made a location close to urban slaughterhouses more cost effective. Whether in rural or urban areas, tanneries spewed tan liquor and wastes from hide preparation into river and lake waters. Fishermen in Cheboygan denounced the tannery's waste products, tan liquor and the liquid from washing hides, dumped directly into the river as fish killers. Noted one, "You can see the stuff in the river. It is red." This is in contrast to the testimony from interviewees in Southampton, where more persons thought that the tannery wastes dumped into the river did not harm the fish than claimed that they did.[27]

The fishermen of Lake Huron who were interviewed by investigators from the Joint Commission in 1894 clearly identified a series of pollution problems that they believed contributed to the decline of the catch and threatened their livelihoods. In so doing, they told about a small part of a much larger reality that sooner or later came to be shared generally by all areas of the Great Lakes drainage basin where commercial lumbering had flourished. While to some extent self-serving, considering the severe criticism that government officials in the United States and Canada leveled at harvesters as the principal cause of the declining fish population, the fishermen's comments contained more than a grain of truth.

The interviews leave for posterity a rare record of fishermen's ideas about environmental change. One Georgian Bay fisher, John Barret Van Vlack, who initially worked the waters of Lake Ontario at a time when the salmon yet remained, made an especially acute judgment of environmental change. He told his interviewers, "Just as quick as they began to clear the country up the fish began to disappear."[28] He well understood the fate of the fish. Taken together, farming and commercial lumbering dramatically changed the nature of the lands and waters in the Great Lakes drainage basin.

MINING

In somewhat different ways, during the nineteenth century another group of industries based on natural resources, those utilizing the mineral and fossil-fuel wealth of the Great Lakes drainage basin—principally copper and iron and, to a lesser extent, lead, zinc, gold, silver, coal, and petroleum—directly and indirectly altered the nature of lake waters to the detriment of fish life.[29] The rearrangement of natural waterways to construct commerce-bearing canals that would connect the mines of the Upper Peninsula of Michigan with the industrial centers to the south began in earnest in the 1850s, decades before railroads reached southern Lake Superior. The canal at Sault Sainte Marie, built to provide Lake Superior shipping with an outlet around the rapids of the St. Mary's River, opened in 1855, the first major "improvement" to facilitate the shipment of ore.

On the Keweenaw Peninsula, copper mines in the newly opening Portage Lake district joined forces in 1859 to dredge the mouth of the Portage River at Lake Superior. In 1862, they embarked on a larger project, designed to deepen the river channel to the lake. Further disruptions of marine life followed when Calumet and Hecla, a major copper producer at Torch Lake, dredged a connecting channel between Torch and Portage Lakes through two miles of marshland to permit access for the largest steamships. This "improvement," completed in 1875, paled in comparison with the Portage Lake and Lake Superior Ship Canal, which cut completely through the Keweenaw Peninsula. A $2.5 million project that was constructed between 1868 and 1873 and was supported by a 450,000-acre federal land grant, the canal proved to be a boon to the copper producers of the Keweenaw and a very important shortcut for ship traffic moving to and from the head of the lakes (Duluth, Minnesota, and Superior, Wisconsin) and industrial centers on Lakes Michigan and Erie. What had been a quiet, shallow Portage River leading to two inland lakes became a heavily used ship canal far less supportive of fish life.[30]

Moreover, the system of copper mining and smelting seriously altered Torch and Portage Lakes, long before the introduction of chemical methods of retrieving copper came into use in the early twentieth century. The ore-refining process required huge amounts of water for the stamping mills, and it came from the lakes and was returned to them in far different condition, filled with particles of copper-bearing sands. As copper mining expanded and huge piles of tailings or stamp sands accumulated, mining companies loaded these wastes aboard scows and dumped them in the lakes. The Army Corps of Engineers in 1882 reported enormous tailing dumps in Portage Lake. Each of five major stamping mills had dumped 1 million tons of tailings into the lake in areas varying in size from 400 to 650 feet out from the shore and, in some cases, for as much as 1,000 feet along the shore. The Quincy Mine had begun loading tailings onto barges and dumping them in the middle of the channel. By 1882, the mills were adding about 500,000 tons of stamp sands to the waterway annually. These dumps created a navigational hazard, and once the federal government took over the operation of the waterway, as the Army Corps of Engineers recommended in 1886, dumping came under federal control. The Quincy Mine then built a new stamping mill on Torch Lake, and the lake became the dumping ground for stamp sands. Other mining companies followed suit. For a century, from the late 1860s to the 1960s, 20 percent of Torch Lake was filled with tailings.[31]

In 1860, successful local smelting of copper began in Hancock on Portage Lake. Before that, ore was shipped to Detroit, Cleveland, and

Pittsburgh. By 1866, about half of the ore still went to those cities for smelting. Ultimately, all smelting was done near the mines, the most cost-effective system. At first utilizing Keweenaw timber for fuel, but shortly after the opening of the canal at Sault Sainte Marie and well before the complete deforestation of the Keweenaw, mining companies experimented with coal and found it a cost-effective substitute for local timber. The shift to coal took place gradually from the 1860s through the 1880s.[32] Coal-fired boilers as well as steamboats produced clinkers, and lake waters became a dumping ground for them also. One of the highly visible effects of copper mining was a disrupted, scarred landscape, with much of the earth stripped of tree and plant cover and subject to erosion.

Copper mining destroyed forever parts of the fish habitat as it had been before the mining boom reorganized the natural waterways to make them serve the mining industry and added metals and millions of tons of tailings and sediments to lakes and rivers, in addition to the sewage, trash, and garbage generated by the mining communities during the first half century of expansion. The bird's-eye views of Hancock and Houghton in 1873 show the extensive industrial development at Portage Lake, with its stamp mills, smelters, and foundries spewing black smoke skyward and filling the air with coal soot and toxic fumes and with its houses and barren landscape extending up the steep hillsides to the Quincy Mine (figure 8.3). Larry D. Lankton has noted that the hills were deforested in the 1850s and remained bare for three-quarters of a century. A further negative impact on the marine environment came early in the twentieth century when mining companies introduced flotation processes for refining stamp sands.[33]

While it is not possible to assess the potential repercussions of copper mining on Lake Superior waters adjacent to the Keweenaw Peninsula, mining-related disruption of the movements of fish from Lake Superior into and out of the Portage River and Portage and Torch Lakes did have a negative impact on fish life, and the destructive effect on the marine habitat of the wastes generated by the mining operations and the mining communities generally should be pondered. Hard times fell on the small fishing village of Craig, at the mouth of the Portage River, where in 1885 thirty to forty families, including sixty-four fishermen, lived. Settled primarily by Finns, it was "the only settlement in the region where any considerable percentage of people are interested in fishing."[34] And the time when Ojibwes fished the waters of Torch Lake by torchlight and spear had long since passed in the wake of copper mining's triumph in the Keweenaw.

Copper-mining interests, some of them identical to those operating on the Keweenaw Peninsula, especially the Quincy Mine, exploited the copper deposits of Isle Royale. Small in comparison with development on the

Figure 8.3. Bird's-eye view of the Quincy, Pewabic, and Franklin mines, located on the hill; below, along Portage Lake, are the Lake Superior smelter and the Pewabic and Franklin stamp mills, Hancock, Michigan, 1873. (Photograph courtesy Houghton County Historical Society, Lake Linden, Michigan)

mainland, the mines on the island produced about 1 million pounds of refined copper between 1847 and 1883. Island mining utilized roasters, stamp mills, and deep mine shafts especially in the later period, destroying timber, scarring the earth's surface, and producing stamp-mill waste, piles of "poor rock," and toxic roaster fumes. Mining polluted Lake Superior, but given the limited period of production and transportation of much ore to Lake Erie's southern shore for refinement, the impact on Isle Royle, while very real, was far less than that on the Keweenaw Peninsula.[35]

At about the same time that unruly prospectors descended on the Keweenaw in search of copper in the mid-1840s, farther east on the southern shore of Lake Superior other wealth seekers made a rush for newly discovered iron-ore deposits, hoping to seize an early advantage in developing the Marquette Range, the first of the iron ranges in the Great Lakes drainage basin brought into production. The Menominee Range of Michigan and Wisconsin would follow, yielding its first ores to the market in 1877, and the Gogebic-Penokee in 1884. The ores of the Vermilion Range of Minnesota first came to the dock at Two Harbors in 1884, and the Merritt brothers dug test pits in the Mesabi Range in 1889 and 1890. Both the Vermilion and the Mesabi lay inland, beyond the Lake Superior watershed.

While the impact of nineteenth-century iron mining on Great Lakes waters was very real, it differed from that of Keweenaw copper mining, which relied on smelters that operated close to the mines and which dumped enormous quantities of stamp-mill tailings directly into waters close to and connecting with Lake Superior. The amount of smelting near the iron mines was much smaller, and the technology of iron mining differed from that of copper mining. The iron mines were located farther from lake waters than were the Keweenaw copper mines. Moreover, given the nontoxic character of most of the mine waste from the Marquette, Menominee, and Gogebic-Penokee Ranges, toxic runoff was slight during the nineteenth century, given the mining methods then in use. Nor, given the distance from lake waters, were the mining operations in the Vermilion and Mesabi directly productive of toxic waters. The beneficiation, or refining, process used in all the iron ranges of southern Lake Superior in the twentieth century did add to adjacent waters toxic substances that were detrimental to fish and other aquatic life.[36]

Removing the ore from the earth changed the fish habitat of the lakes in less obvious ways. The destruction of natural vegetation and the disruption of the earth's surface changed water-flow patterns. Open-pit methods prevailed in the Marquette Range during the first two decades of mining there, but in the 1870s shaft mining became common. Shafts came earlier in the mining history of both the Menominee and the Gogebic-Penokee. They quickly reached depths at which water had to be pumped out utilizing enormous Cornish pumps. Pumping lowered the water table, and mine water discharged on the surface added significantly to the volume of silt-bearing runoff. But precisely what impact this had on fish life in the lakes is not known. The destruction of wetlands and the draining of lakes to get at the ore bodies beneath them characterized iron mining around the Great Lakes throughout its history.

Possibly the greatest impact on hydrography came from the deforestation that accompanied the exploitation of the ore deposits of the Marquette, Menominee, and Gogebic-Penokee Ranges. Mining and timber cutting went hand in hand. Shaft mining required large amounts of timber to create safe tunnels and passages. Charcoal-fired iron furnaces of the Upper Peninsula, producers of iron with especially fine properties for certain uses and prized as an additive to iron smelted in other ways, while gradually declining in number in the late nineteenth century, continued to consume enormous quantities of hardwoods. Harlan Hatcher has well described their "formidable inroad on natural resources": "The furnaces . . . ate up charcoal by the thousands of bushels and the charcoal pits consumed the forests by the thousands of acres." By 1903, the furnaces of the Upper Peninsula used timber stands at "an average of 30 acres every day of the year." They were located at points where charcoal, ore, and limestone could be assembled economically and from where pig iron could be shipped to market, often at water's edge—for example, on the Garden Peninsula, east of Escanaba, on Lake Michigan, where the Jackson Mine ran the Fayette Furnace, or in Marquette on Lake Superior. Considering the timber needs of the mining industry, its engrossment of timberland, and its entrance into the commercial-lumber market, mining companies contributed to the erosion and siltation of lake waters as surely as did commercial-lumbering enterprises not associated with mining.[37]

Taken together, the iron ores of Michigan, Wisconsin, and Minnesota created a greater disruption of fish habitat near smelters than near mines. Given the geographic distribution of the raw materials essential for the production of iron and steel, entrepreneurial leaders in the developing midwestern iron and steel industry, by the time of the Civil War, had found it most cost effective to ship iron ore from the mines of the Lake Superior region southward over the Great Lakes, which furnished inexpensive water transportation, and coal from Pennsylvania on the newly created railroads, to the southern shores of Lakes Erie and Michigan for smelting. There a band of industrial communities grew from Erie, Pennsylvania, to Chicago where iron- and steelmaking and heavy manufacturing burgeoned in the late nineteenth century. They used lake water intensively, and they created and returned to the lakes vast amounts of human and industrial waste that degraded the marine habitat.

Moreover, transporting and delivering iron ore disrupted fish life. Harbors had to be built and rivers dredged, wetlands filled, large and small canals dug, and enormous docks constructed. Before 1900, enormous ore-loading docks came to dominate the harbors at Duluth and Two Harbors, Minnesota; Superior and Ashland, Wisconsin; and Marquette and Escanaba, Michigan. Vast unloading facilities rose in the ports of Detroit; Toledo, Huron, Lorain, Cleveland, Ashtabula, and Conneaut, Ohio; Erie, Pennsylvania; and Buffalo, New York. Massive disruption of lake waters accompanied these harbor-port developments to accommodate the ore fleets. The growth in size of carriers made dredging of the St. Clair Flats in 1872 and construction of larger locks at Sault Sainte Marie in 1896 essential. As ore-carrier technology changed, a whole series of ongoing port and waterway improvements followed to accommodate the larger craft. Ore carriers, like other ships and boats, dumped wastes directly into the Great Lakes while in transit.

While the copper and iron mines of Lake Superior were the largest mining operations adjacent to the Great Lakes in the nineteenth century, smaller extractive ventures abounded and should be added to the tally of environmental disrupters in the Great Lakes drainage basin. Among them was the mining activity along the lower edge of the Precambrian shield in Ontario where it dips southward to within twenty-five to thirty miles of the shore of the Bay of Quinte. Loyalists from the American colonies and others who settled in that area in the late eighteenth century found the bay to be a veritable cornucopia of fish life. Lake Ontario salmon ascended the Trent, Moira, and Salmon Rivers, which are tributary to the bay. The Trent and the Moira and their tributaries wind north from the Bay of Quinte into the Precambrian shield area, where incoming settlers began mining for iron ore at Marmora as early as 1821 and for gold at Madoc as early as 1866. Small-scale mining grew thereafter, producing silver, copper, lead, arsenic, and a sulfuric acid by-product as well as gold and iron for market.[38] Toxic waters from many of these operations went into the tributaries of the Bay of Quinte. While evidence of the direct or indirect impact of nineteenth-century mining on the bay's declining fish population and its contribution to the disappearance of the salmon remains elusive, the gold mining would surely have been detrimental to spawning salmon in the rivers. The by-products of mining generally were harbingers of current heavy-metal pollutants.

Another example of mining in Ontario, well known in the annals of Great Lakes history, is the Silver Islet Mine, located on a very small island about a mile from the tip of Thunder Cape in Lake Superior. There the construction and operation of the silver mine, which lasted from 1869 to 1884, unquestionably affected lake waters, which ultimately engulfed it and ended the multimillion-dollar ore yields.[39] Enormous tonnages of sandstone for construction and limestone for a multitude of purposes—including use in blast furnaces, for which it is an essential ingredient, as well as for harbor improvements, road construction, cement manufacture, and lime production—came from Michigan and from the Apostle Islands and Bayfield, Wisconsin. Gypsum mined in the Grand River valley of Ontario and in the Grand Rapids and Saginaw Bay areas of Michigan provided a main ingredient in fertilizer and plaster. At the end of the nineteenth century, coal production began in the Saginaw River valley.[40]

In addition to the salt wells on the Lower Peninsula of Michigan that were developed as an adjunct industry to lumbering, an entrepreneur in Goderich, Ontario, who was prospecting for oil discovered a rich vein of salt nearly 1,000 feet below the surface, and mining began in 1866. Others quickly followed his lead, and by 1872 ten wells were operating in the Maitland River valley. They served to stimulate lumbering because of the enormous quantities of wood needed for the evaporation process. The Ontario Agricultural Commission noted in 1880 that Goderich salt had also fostered both the fishing and pork-packing industries locally. Sixty miles farther north on the Lake Huron shore at Kincardine, "extensive salt wells" gave "employment to a large number of persons." In Marine City, Michigan, on the St. Clair River in 1882 a vein of rock salt came into production, and entrepreneurs developed a continuation of that vein in Detroit after 1900. Exploitation of rock salt in Sarnia, Ontario, also occurred in the early twentieth century.[41]

While the fishermen of Saginaw Bay complained about the impact of salt wells on fishing, fishermen interviewed in Goderich in 1894 did not complain about either local industry or dredging and harbor improvements being detrimental to fish life. However, harbor development created in part by the rise of the salt industry did adversely affect the fish. To make way for commerce, harbor remodeling changed the natural course of the Maitland River and involved dredging and deepening the water and constructing an extensive breakwater. The river's original entrance into Lake Huron, with its fine protected lagoon-like harbor, many islands, and minor channels, was moved. In the words of a local historian: "The river was lifted from its bed, cut off from the harbour and given its present course into the lake." From the construction begun in 1872 came a twenty-five-acre harbor. The bountiful fish that had so impressed Samuel Strickland in 1828 had long since vanished. Then he had noted that the harbor "appeared to swarm" with fish: "When the sun shone brightly, you could see hundreds lying near the surface."[42] To what extent nineteenth-century salt production in Goderich and Kincardine contaminated rivers and lakes remains undetermined. Unquestionably, the physical modifications to land and water in those communities emanating from the economic activity generated by salt production did have a detrimental effect on the fish life of Lake Huron.

The development of the petroleum industry in Ontario and northwestern Ohio, according to fishermen in the 1890s, adversely affected fish life. In Ontario, the fields in Petrolia, Oil Springs, and Oil City came into production in the late 1850s. By 1860, twenty-seven small refineries were operating around Oil Springs. The Ontario Agricultural Commission in 1880 called this field "the principal seat of the great petroleum industry in Canada." The field in Wood County, Ohio, opened in 1885 and 1886. By 1896, 5,500 wells were producing 30,000 barrels a day. Fishermen whom H. F. Moore and B. L. Hardin, investigators for the Joint Commission, interviewed in the Toledo and Port Clinton area in the summer of 1894 complained that oil overflow from refineries and from the wells downriver in Wood County entered the Maumee and Portage Rivers and killed the fish as it flowed toward Lake Erie.[43]

A fisherman in North Toledo complained about oil from a nearby refinery, noting that it was dumped at night, at times leaving a very smeared shore and waters so coated that "you could track a boat through it. . . . I think it is very injurious to the fish." Similarly, fishermen in the Petrolia and Oil Springs area in Ontario, located at the headwaters of the North Sydenham River, which flows into Lake St. Clair, complained in the early 1890s about refuse from oil refineries that got into the natural waters and killed fish.[44] Oil waste from the field in the Petrolia area, which was farther away from lake waters than the oil field in Ohio, probably had spent its most immediately apparent destruction of fish life before reaching Lake St. Clair. The extent to which, in the immediate vicinity of the wells and refineries, it influenced plant and animal life connected in the food chain with Great Lakes fish is another question.

Mining, like agriculture and lumbering, contributed to changing the habitat of Great Lakes fish from what it had been before the massive developmental expansion of the late nineteenth century. Its repercussions were far less obviously direct than those of the gold-mining operations in the Sacramento–San Joaquin watershed of California that so devastated the salmon population, but nevertheless very real.[45]

Of the three major components of rural development—agriculture, lumbering, and mining—mining probably made the lesser while agriculture and lumbering taken together the greater impact on the marine habitat of the Great Lakes before 1900. They resulted in extensive changes in hydrography and in the rate of soil erosion and the consequent siltation of Great Lakes waters. In contrast urban population growth and industrial development created more obvious localized changes in the quality of the waters of the Great Lakes.

9

Commerce, Community Growth, Industrial-Urban Development, and the Changing Fish Habitat

Gill Nets Filled with Filth

Accompanying and complementing the development of farming, lumbering, and mining in the rural landscape, the growth of commerce, transportation systems, manufacturing, and village, town, and city population centers introduced other kinds of physical changes in the Great Lakes drainage basin that altered lake waters and the kinds of fish life they supported. Nature's ready-made transportation system, the waterways, appealed to the first generation of developers as a way to move people and goods without the expense and delay of building roads. Moreover, the Great Lakes and the river systems radiating from them created the possibility of access to a very large part of the midcontinent, to the Atlantic Ocean by way of the St. Lawrence River, and to the Gulf of Mexico via the Mississippi.

The region's early entrepreneurs dreamed of creating a great interconnecting waterway system to stimulate trade and develop markets. Budding communities along the lakes soon aspired to becoming important ports for trade and business, and well before the mid-nineteenth century, city fathers sought to dominate the commerce of their hinterlands and hoped to expand into national and international markets. A boomer spirit permeated their thinking. Harbors had to be developed first. Then came canals to improve on nature's connections between lakes and rivers and, most elaborate of all, the grandest of waterway dreams, a series of canals to link the Great Lakes ports with the St. Lawrence River in a seaway, an all-water route to the North American midcontinent. That dream was very much a mid-nineteenth-century vision, as was that of railroad dominance of the North American land transportation system. Railroads quickly overtook waterways in importance, but never replaced them for certain kinds of traffic, particularly heavy, bulky cargoes. Instead, a kind of interdependent relationship developed between the two systems over time, and in this the Great Lakes and their canal systems continued to serve very important transportation functions. Ports became focal points linking railroads and waterways.

Initial port development in the nineteenth century seems simple compared with the complex of facilities that had arisen in such cities as Toronto, Hamilton, Buffalo, Cleveland, Detroit, Chicago, and Duluth by the end of the century. Early improvements usually involved dredging to enlarge harbor entrances and to deepen rivers that flowed into the Great Lakes and building breakwaters, piers, docks, and warehouses. Wet, swampy lands often disappeared as construction crews extended shorelines and dug short canals to improve ships' access. Such canals included the one that cut through Minnesota Point to improve the harbor in Duluth. Once railroads became a reality, land-filled shore areas permitted rail lines to run close to the water and onto loading docks, making it easier to transfer cargo to and from ships. As the major ports grew into urban-industrial centers between 1870 and 1900, the disruption and extensive alteration of the natural lakefront escalated.[1]

The most conspicuous example of massive physical change to accommodate industrial-urban development began before 1900 at the southern end of Lake Michigan, now Indiana's industrial duneland, with plans projected for East Chicago in 1887. Its promoters boosted it as a choice location for expansion of overcrowded Chicago industry. In Whiting, Indiana, Standard Oil began building a major refinery in 1889. Early in the twentieth century, U.S. Steel developed its mill in Gary, Indiana. Such industrial growth involved the extensive rearrangement of dunes, rivers, and wetlands and the construction of canals. The beneficial effects of vast areas of Lake Michigan's southernmost wetlands as water purifiers, water-flow control mechanisms, and feeding and breeding grounds for fish and other wildlife greatly diminished.[2] Developers, like the majority of their contemporaries, gave scant thought to the consequences of their actions for the well-being of the natural world in general and certainly not to the fate of natural spawning and feeding grounds for the fish population.

In yet other ways, growing port cities produced substantial changes in the habitats of the Great Lakes during the last four decades of the nineteenth century. The largest urban-industrial centers developed in the southern Great Lakes, with high concentrations of population and manufacturing activity. A combination of advantages—accessible means of transportation, bountiful natural resources, plentiful labor and capital, expanding domestic markets in both Canada and the United States, government policies designed to encourage development, and aggressive entrepreneurial leadership—spurred the growth of Toronto, Hamilton, and Rochester on Lake Ontario; Buffalo, Cleveland, and Toledo on Lake Erie; Detroit on the Detroit River; Chicago and Milwaukee on Lake Michigan (figure 9.1); and Duluth and Superior on Lake Superior. The combined population of these urban-industrial centers grew from 215,460 in 1850 to 3,643,000 in 1900. According to census data, their industrial output mushroomed, particularly during the last two decades of the century. The value of their manufactured products totaled $479,101,000 in 1880. In 1900, it stood at $1,581,000,000. With this growth came a pronounced increase in foundries and machine shops, iron smelting and steelmaking, other metal-producing and -fabricating industries, meatpacking, brewing, chemical production, paint and varnish making, printing and publishing, and oil refining. These industrial activities especially burdened water resources with pollutants that were highly destructive for fish life.[3]

The cities around the Great Lakes developed rapidly at a time when sizable American and Canadian urban centers were abandoning the privy vault-cesspool system of human-waste disposal, which broke down under the burden of increased use of domestic water and contamination of well water. Cities opted to build sewers designed to empty into adjacent streams, rivers, and lakes on the theory that their dilution in natural running water purified sewage and industrial wastes. Great Lakes city fathers were in step with national trends when they turned to the lakes and their tributary rivers as an enormous, perfect natural sink.[4]

Guardians of the fish and fishers recognized the relationship between pollution and the decline in the fisheries adjacent to the growing industrial cities of the Great Lakes. They left abundant evidence of that impact, vividly describing what they saw and expressing their fears for both public health and marine life.

Rapid growth in Chicago, especially during the 1860s, produced a crisis in sewage disposal and in the drinking-water supply. The city depended on Lake Michigan for both essential services. A filthy harbor at the mouth of the Chicago River led to illness and foul smells. One remedy was to move the water-intake pipe farther out into the lake. In 1871, the city took a major step in getting sewage away from its water supply by reversing the flow of the Chicago River into the Des Plaines, sending the filthy, polluted mass down into the Illinois River by diverting Lake Michi-

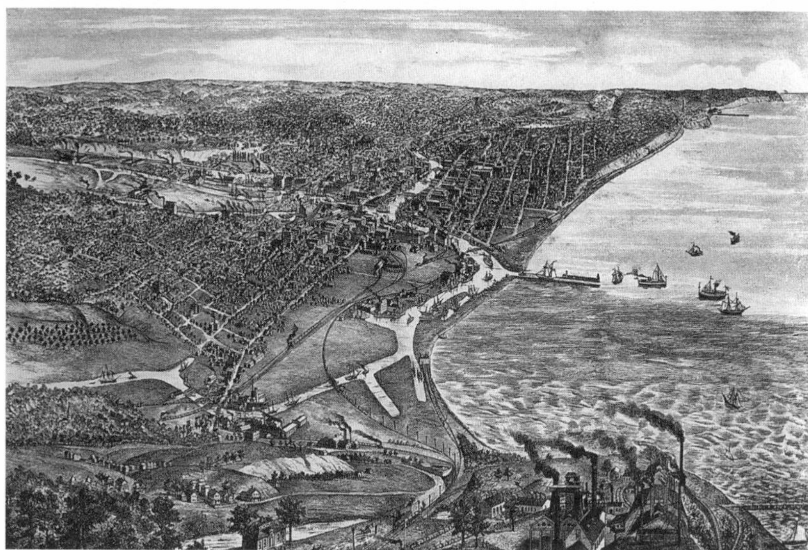

Figure 9.1. Growth of Milwaukee and its harbor: (*top*) Adolph Hoeffler made this pencil drawing in 1852, probably from the site of the future steel plant at Bay View, seen in 1881 in a bird's-eye view from the south along the shore of Lake Michigan (*bottom*). Note that in the thirty years between the recording of the two views, the harbor entrance, the "straight cut," replaced the very constricted Milwaukee River entrance, enabling steamboats and sailing ships to enter the inner harbor to unload their cargoes. (Photographs courtesy State Historical Society of Wisconsin, Madison; photograph nos. WHi [X31] 386 and WHi [X3] 22628)

gan waters to create the flush. In 1872, James W. Milner noted in his report for the United States Commission of Fish and Fisheries that fishing at the mouth of the Chicago River had been poor for years, but thought that "it is quite possible, now the filthy current of the river no longer flows into the lake, that there may be some success with nets." For a time, there seemed to be an improvement in fishing in Chicago, but when reassessed in 1885, it was rated as very minor.[5]

In Milwaukee—where producing iron and steel, engines, and heavy machinery took its place on the industrial roster along with milling, brewing, tanning, and meatpacking in the late nineteenth century—human and industrial wastes burdened the rivers that flowed into the harbor, threatening both human and fish life. In their special report on the Great Lakes for the Commission of Fish and Fisheries, Hugh M. Smith and Merwin-Marie Snell noted that fisheries in the marshes flanking the river for several miles "have ceased to be productive as the water has become so polluted that very few fish now enter it." Crayfish were the only catch in the Menominee River valley, where wastes from tanneries and other industry eliminated them well before the end of the century. The fishery at the mouth of the Milwaukee River, noted the report, "has of late deteriorated, chiefly on account of the polluted condition of water flowing from the river." The investigators pointed out that fishermen who worked off Milwaukee on Lake Michigan never left offal on the fishing grounds: "The spoiled fish are brought to the city and thrown into the river, after being pricked so that they will sink." Thus the different groups of fishermen worked at cross-purposes with one another, and the Milwaukee River assumed a pollution burden from the fishers of the lake, as well as from sources on the land, sending all of it into Lake Michigan. Early in Milwaukee's history, the city's fishermen ventured forth in Mackinaw boats to take large catches, roughly one half of which was whitefish. By 1870, whitefish "were growing scarce rapidly" and, by 1885, had dwindled to a very small part of the catch and had decreased in size as well. Through the years, the fishermen had to venture farther and farther from shore as well as farther north to make their catches.[6]

Similar deterioration of the fisheries in urban port areas developed around Toronto and in Burlington Bay, on which Hamilton is located. In Toronto, the sewage generated by a growing city with a very substantial manufacturing component in its economy went directly into the harbor. In 1897, O. B. Sheppard, the Inspector of Fisheries of the dominion government, noted that "the fish in the waters of Lake Ontario in the vicinity of Toronto are decreasing both in quantity and size year by year." When a few years later farmers living along the Humber River, which enters the lake at Toronto, petitioned the Department of Marine and Fisheries to compel dam owners on that river to construct fish passes, the condition of its waters became a matter of record. After an on-site investigation, Sheppard advised against requiring dam owners to build fishways. The amount of water coming down the river, he argued, had declined markedly, and in Lake Ontario, from where the fish ascended the Humber, their population was dwindling. Industrial pollution from water-powered mills along the river and at its mouth compromised the fish habitat. Fishing on the Humber was virtually "a thing of the past." In 1900, the Humber was a far cry from the river of rich salmon runs it had been sixty years earlier.[7]

Urban-industrial pollution posed problems at Hamilton as well. The whitefish population in Burlington Bay, especially in the waters close to Hamilton, noted a fisherman of thirty-five years, when quizzed by members of the Dominion Fishery Commission in 1892, had greatly deteriorated. Daniel McGwyn, a resident of Burlington Beach since 1857, noting that the nets had been laid up for five years, clearly described the change. In 1860, fishermen could take 200 to 300 whitefish and trout at a single haul of the seine: "What would you catch now?—None at all, at present time no whitefish are taken." This suggests excessive fishing using the seine, a very destructive type of net. But at the same time, Hamilton, a growing industrial city, sent its sewage directly into the bay, and wastes such as those from coal-distillation operations, for which Coal Oil Inlet in Burlington Bay had been named, were a long-standing and growing pollution problem. As justification for permission to spearfish in Burlington Bay, in February 1897, citizens of Hamilton, in a petition to the Minister of Marine and Fisheries, noted that Burlington Bay had become contaminated with sewage and filth from the city, driving out the higher grades of fish and "leaving a rougher class of fish in their place." During the summer, the fish in the shallow waters of the bay were not fit for food, but in winter they were in good condition and would help feed the poor of Hamilton, if spearing in winter were allowed.[8]

While the specter of pollution in the immediate vicinity of large cities drew attention, conditions in large waterways, such as Lake Ontario and the Detroit and Niagara Rivers, also aroused concern and even led to abrasive episodes between Canada and the United States. State senator Donald McNaughton of Rochester, New York, used his position as chair of a meeting of United States and Canadian fish and game officials, held in Hamilton in December 1891, to draw attention to the broader problem. The dumping of sewage into the streams of Canada, Michigan, and New York had to stop, he maintained. He had seen his home waters—Lake Ontario, the Genesee River, and Irondequoit Bay—despoiled in that way, wrongful acts tantamount, he believed, to poisoning stream or well water that was used for family consumption.[9]

McNaughton reported conditions well known to the fishermen of

Lake Ontario. Two years later, when the investigators for the Joint Commission did their fieldwork on Lake Ontario, those interviewed described two river currents as carriers of a great mass of rubbish and foreign matter: the current of the Niagara, at the eastern end of the lake, and the current of the Genesee, at midlake. From the growing city of Rochester, the Genesee, supplier of its industrial waterpower, carried sewage and refuse into the lake, according to fishermen, as far as eight miles out and along the shore for five. One fisherman complained about lifting "gill nets filled with filth . . . from Rochester." The catalog of rubbish found in nets included entrails of cattle, diapers, grapevines, logs, rags, old trousers, and other clothes. One fisherman observed, "At times the river current can be outlined in the lake, the discoloration being very noticeable." Another commented that in 1894 he had noticed "black, greasy streaks on the water." The river, complained the fishermen, drove away the fish. Two other New York rivers flowing into Lake Ontario carried industrial filth that fish could not tolerate. The Oswego River, reported B. E. Ingersoll in 1890, "is so filthy with sewage and refuse from manufactories" that it should not be considered for a salmon-restocking experiment. Another observer similarly reported that the Black River, the power source of Watertown, New York, would be a poor choice for such an effort because "the water is contaminated by refuse from paper mills situated not far from its mouth, and the acid used is said to kill pike, bass, and other fish, and would prove equally injurious to salmon."[10]

Because the Detroit and Niagara Rivers are shared by the United States and Canada, the ways in which urban sewage and garbage disposal fouled their waters led to friction between the two countries and brought the problem to public notice dramatically in 1895, with the seizure of a garbage barge by Canadian authorities. Lake pollution always attracted attention first as a public-health issue, and so it was in these cases. Threats to supplies of public drinking water produced the conflict. Yet the problem of polluted waters in the Niagara and Detroit Rivers was not new in 1895. For decades, pollution had increased steadily from the wastes of the adjacent growing urban-industrial communities. When field-workers for the Joint Commission interviewed Lake Ontario fishermen in 1894, they complained about the Niagara River current. From Youngstown, New York, at the mouth of the Niagara, the current carried all kinds of rubbish as well as scum and oil on the surface of the water. Discolored water spread as far as fifteen miles out into the lake and eastward along the shore for about eighteen miles. Fish disliked the dirty bottom and the sewage-laden water.[11]

In the Detroit River, conditions had grown steadily worse for fish life as the nineteenth century progressed. Early in the century, the waterway system connecting Lakes Erie and Huron, the St. Clair River, Lake St.

Clair, and the Detroit River supported a bounteous fish life, including many thousands of whitefish. That population dwindled under the impact of heavy fishing, increasing lake traffic, and physical alterations, such as the construction of a canal through the flats of northern Lake St. Clair, "a very deep canal lined with dikes," the frequent dredging and deepening of ship channels, and the improvement of harbors. In addition, Detroit, a fast-growing urban-industrial city, placed an ever larger burden of waste into the Detroit River and Lake Erie. Fishermen and fishery experts noted the pollution problem with increasing frequency in the 1890s. Hershel Whitaker, president of the Michigan Board of Fish Commissioners, observed in 1891: "The fisheries upon the Detroit twenty years ago were wonderfully profitable. . . . But the sewage from the City of Detroit has killed off the fish to a great extent." In light of the continued decline in yield since the good fishing of the early 1870s, a Detroit fisherman blamed the growth of the city and the volume of its sewage for destroying the fishery. A fellow fisher interviewed by H. F. Moore of the Joint Commission in 1894 painted a bleak picture. He blamed the canal built through the St. Clair Flats and gill nets fished at the mouth of the Detroit River. He added, "In the Detroit river there are two feet of pitch from the gas works and from the waste of coal. White fish will not go in a dirty bottom. . . . I caught white fish for the last time in the St. Clair river 19 years ago; that is the last we got." The herring had dropped off altogether, and the sturgeon had declined.[12] Thus the garbage-dumping problems that came to a head in the late spring of 1895 were but two more examples of the well-established practice of using the Detroit and Niagara Rivers as waste-disposal systems.

By early June 1895, the residents of Amherstburg, Ontario, were more than fed up with garbage-laden barges pulled from Detroit by tugs dumping their loads in Canadian waters. Rotten fruits and vegetables, dead animals (including rats), slaughterhouse offal, excreta, and other offensive materials drifted in and piled up on the Canadian side of the Detroit River very close to the intake pipe of the Amherstburg waterworks and along the riverbank in other locations. The stench was enormous, and a public-health officer of Malden Township condemned the foul-smelling mess as a health hazard. It would pollute the water and could cause typhoid fever and other diseases.

The customs officer at Amherstburg, George Gott, decided to do something to save the health of the town, especially since Detroit was experiencing an outbreak of smallpox. Failing to receive the kind of support he wanted from officials in Ottawa, Gott decided to proceed under authority of the customs laws. On the evening of June 6, he acted with the assistance of Captain Edward Dunn of the *Petrel,* a dominion cruiser that patrolled the Great Lakes to enforce both fishery and customs regulations, to seize a garbage scow and its attendant tug. Also instrumental in the seizure of the garbage boats were the local constable, the local health officer, and an American who lent his yacht to assist Amherstburg authorities in reconnaissance upriver to spot the approach of the garbage boats. The American was glad to help because he found the garbage a nuisance that interfered with his dredging operations at the mouth of the Detroit River.

One shot across the bow of the tug stopped both it and the garbage scow, which had partially dumped its load. Arrested, jailed, convicted, and fined on two counts—the custom's charge of breaking bulk in Canadian waters without first touching port, and the other charge of unloading garbage without a permit in the township of Malden and creating a health hazard—the captain and crew, in the employ of the Detroit Sanitary Company, rankled at Canadian justice. The customs fine and costs totaled $450. The fines for garbage dumping were set at $50 a person plus costs or fourteen days in jail. Only the tug captain paid. Meanwhile, Captain Dunn, acting under the directions of the Ontario Health Officer, supervised the removal of the "offensive and dangerous" garbage from the dock in Amherstburg to Middle Sister Island in Lake Erie, where it was unloaded and "disposed of." The incident led to an inquiry by the United States Department of State that concluded in 1897 with a vindication of Canadian actions.[13]

Shortly after Captain Dunn's crackdown on garbage dumping at Amherstburg, authorities in Fort Erie, Ontario, summoned him to arrest Americans who were dumping the filth and garbage generated in Buffalo, New York, in Canadian waters just above the international bridge. Again using a meticulous and well-cloaked game plan, Dunn, with the help of local authorities, succeeded in arresting the dumpers. They were convicted and fined.[14]

Pollution problems in large and growing urban-industrial areas attracted far more attention than did lake pollution generated by the smaller population centers that proliferated along the Great Lakes. All put raw human sewage into rivers, streams, and lakes. Gas companies were common in towns with a population of a few thousand and more, and they, too, contaminated nearby bodies of water. The distillation of coal to make gas for lighting produced ammoniated waters, tars, and oils as by-products. Methods of preventing these wastes from entering natural waters were imperfect at best, and companies often dumped them untreated into rivers, lakes, and streams.[15]

Many communities boasted industries of various sizes that utilized waterpower if it was available. That required damming rivers and streams that flowed into the lakes. The dams interfered with the natural movements of some lake fish that habitually went up the rivers to spawn and feed. Industries also added wastes to the waters, some of it very detrimental to fish life—for example, those from textile plants, pulp and paper mills, tanneries, meatpacking establishments, and breweries.

The Canadian shores of the Great Lakes were generally less densely populated and had less manufacturing activity than the American, yet there, too, community development and manufacturing contributed to change in the Great Lakes fish habitat. In 1880, the Ontario Agricultural Commission made a general survey of economic activity along with its detailed study of farming. For the counties with Great Lakes shoreline frontage, the survey reported a substantial array of cotton, woolen, grist, flour, paper, pulp, saw-, and shingle mills; cheese, canning, furniture, wheel, hub, carriage, wagon, railway car, agricultural implement, and machinery factories; meatpacking establishments and tanneries; breweries; brickyards and foundries; salt, cement, and paint works; and shipbuilding yards, quite aside from the concentrated multifaceted industry of Toronto and Hamilton. While the commission's survey was by no means exhaustive, it did identify hundreds of such businesses. They operated at locations scattered all along the shores of Lakes Ontario, Erie, and Huron and Georgian Bay, with the largest number found on the Lake Ontario shoreline, all of them casting their untreated wastes into the lake waters, under the assumption that they would be so diluted that they could do no harm.[16]

Fishers and others who were concerned about the well-being of the fish population believed that pollutants generated by development did real damage, and they recorded their views. Nineteenth-century reports of the United States Commission of Fish and Fisheries repeatedly called attention to the subject, as did those of the Canadian Department of Marine and Fisheries and the state and provincial fishery commissions. Antipollution laws had been part and parcel of the fishery codes in Canada and the United States from colonial times. Responding to the growth of water pollution, legislators expanded the perimeters of control somewhat in the late nineteenth century because of concern for human health, not the well-being of fish. Given the minor place in the economy of the Great Lakes region that the commercial-fishing industry occupied, a general antipathy for regulation, and a strong public preference for meat in the daily diet, legislation to preserve the fish habitat generated little popular support.

Learned observers also spoke of the impact of developmental change on natural waters and their fish populations. Many of them probably took their cues from George Perkins Marsh, who clearly stated his concept of the interrelationship between people and the other parts of the natural world around them. Asked to prepare a report for the Vermont legislature on the advisability of embarking on an artificial-propagation program to stem the decline in the fish population, he wrote in 1857 that the current wisdom blamed wasteful fishermen, dammed streams, and refuse from sawmills, factories, and other polluters emptied into the waters for spoiling aquatic life. But he maintained, "It is however probable that other and more obscure causes have had a very important influence in producing the same result. Much must doubtless be ascribed to the general physical changes produced by clearing and cultivation of the soil." As a result, he noted, "it is certain that while the spring and autumnal freshets are more violent, the volume of water in the dry season is less" than before and that "summer temperature of the brooks has been elevated." With the trees gone, land drained more rapidly, streams became "more *torrential,*" streambeds were altered, and floods swept away fish and eggs, spawning beds, and food sources. "Human improvements" had almost completely changed the physical conditions of fish life.

In 1864, in *Man and Nature,* he more fully developed his ideas about the decline in the fish population, elaborating his earlier positions in more forceful, persuasive language and placing greater emphasis on mills and industry. They severely damaged and destroyed fish that lived and spawned in freshwater. Declared Marsh, "Milldams impede their migrations, if they do not absolutely prevent them, the sawdust from lumber mills clogs their gills, and the thousand deleterious mineral substances, discharged into rivers from metallurgical, chemical, and manufacturing establishments, poison them by shoals."[17]

These are the lines of argument advanced again and again by those who attributed deterioration in the Great Lakes fish population in part to environmental change. Among them Samuel Wilmot, Canadian pioneer in the artificial propagation of fish; James W. Milner, author of the Commission of Fish and Fisheries report on the Great Lakes fisheries; Seth Green, former fish dealer, sportsman, and self-trained fish culturist in Rochester, New York, who was famous for successfully restocking Atlantic coastal rivers with shad; Ramsay Wright, professor at the University of Toronto who at the request of the Ontario government prepared a survey of the fish and fisheries of that province; and Edward E. Prince, Dominion Commissioner of Fisheries, to mention the most obvious. Probably most people who were familiar with fishery problems accepted the idea that the changing aquatic environment had serious consequences for fish life. Yet in official reports, thoughtless human greed, wastefulness, and uncontrolled harvesting of the resource were cited as the primary causes of the deterioration of the fisheries. Perhaps this was the case for the very reason that Wright suggested. They fell into the category of reasons for decline about which policy makers believed they could do something. They might be able to stem the tide of destruction by regulating the rate and methods of harvest. Thus nineteenth-century contemporaries, from the harvesters of the waters to the advocates of a utilitarian conservation policy, recognized the reality of pollution as a destroyer of the fish of the Great Lakes. But they, like their twentieth-century counterparts, found methods of control hard to identify and even harder to implement.

While this discussion of the agents of change acting on Great Lakes waters in the nineteenth century is in no sense complete, farming, lumbering, mining, urban-industrial and commercial growth, and the rise of smaller communities were the main segments of human activity that changed forever the lake waters from what they had been at the beginning of the nineteenth century. We do not know exactly the way in which and the degree to which they changed, but change they did.

10

The Fish React

Changing Species in Changing Waters

The Danger Line of Destruction . . . Is Being Approached

No one will ever know the number of fish species that vanished from the waters of the Great Lakes in the wake of growing population density, development, and commercial fishing. Undoubtedly, many did, some of them gone before anyone recorded their existence. An idea of the magnitude of loss may be inferred from M. B. Trautman's study of decline in the Sandusky River. Between 1850 and 1976, over half of eighty-eight species had either declined markedly or disappeared. In his report on the Great Lakes fishing industry, published in 1926, Walter Koelz assessed the losses since the mid-nineteenth century in leading commercial species: "We are faced with the extermination of the sturgeon in all the lakes, of the bluefin in Lake Superior, the blackfin in Lake Michigan, and the bloater in Lake Ontario, and with the reduction of the whitefish from first place in abundance in 1880 to fourth place in 1922." He should have added the *Salmo salar* of Lake Ontario, decimated sixty years earlier. Without doubt, great changes had occurred, and more came shortly. Here the discussion of changing fish populations in changing waters focuses on three main topics: change in the populations of the major commercial species, lake whitefish, trout, herring, and sturgeon; the impact of intruded species; and the interaction among the varied species during the nineteenth century. By the end of the 1920s, the close of the first phase in the history of the Great Lakes fisheries was imminent.[1]

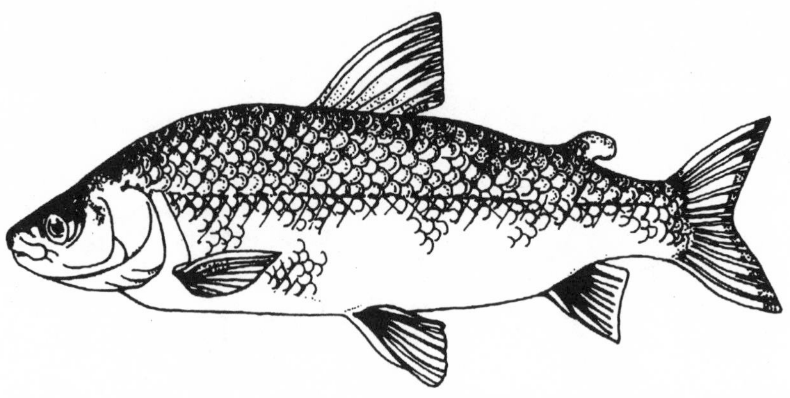

Figure 10.1. Lake whitefish (*Coregonus clupeaformis*). (Drawing by Christine Kohler; courtesy University of Wisconsin Sea Grant Institute)

THE BIG FOUR OF COMMERCIAL FISHING: LAKE WHITEFISH, TROUT, HERRING, AND STURGEON

Lake Whitefish: Gregarious and Delectable

When in 1820 Henry Schoolcraft led an exploring party through the Great Lakes searching for the source of the Mississippi River, he marveled at the variety and the delicacy of the fish at Mackinac Island. "Of these," he noted, "the white fish is most esteemed for the richness and delicacy of its flavour, and there is a universal acquiescence in the opinion formerly advanced by Charlevoix, 'that whether fresh or salted, nothing of the fish kind, can excel it'" (figure 10.1). This high praise expressed the sentiments of scores of Native Americans, explorers, fur traders, and missionaries of the wilderness era and of those who came into the Great Lakes region in succeeding centuries. Older Michigan settlers looked forward to the opening of the fishing season and a taste of whitefish, "dainty fare," according to Bella Hubbard, the state's pioneer geologist, in 1880. Marine biologist James W. Milner reported in 1872 that travelers from the eastern United States gave Lake Superior whitefish very high marks. They were best when taken fresh from the water and broiled. Few went as far as a Georgian Bay fisherman who under oath, in 1893, told investigators for the Dominion Fishery Commission: "I prefer whitefish as best. I eat them constantly."[2]

The excellence of whitefish as food made them the most sought after commercial species of the Great Lakes, a preference also noted among the fishers who harvested the freshwaters of northern Europe and Asia. Both Milner and Hubbard believed that these fish could not survive the

Table 10.1. Lake whitefish production from the Great Lakes, 1879–1899 (in thousands of pounds)

Year	Lake Ontario	Lake Erie	Lake St. Clair	Lake Huron	Lake Michigan	Lake Superior	Total
1879	1,851	3,537	273	4,289	12,030	2,356	24,336
1885	451	3,718	98	4,080	8,653	5,178	22,178
1889	470	3,630	295	7,605	5,524	4,795	22,319
1890	553	2,546	269	6,974	4,564	4,192	19,098
1893	415	1,549	50	5,449	2,446	3,068	12,977
1897	474	1,044	48	1,951	3,345	2,124	8,986
1899	422	2,584	9	2,461	1,770	1,756	9,002

Source: Compiled from Norman S. Baldwin, Robert W. Saalfeld, Margaret A. Ross, and Howard J. Buettner, *Commercial Fish Production in the Great Lakes, 1867–1977*, Technical Report no. 3 (Ann Arbor, Mich.: Great Lakes Fishery Commission, 1979).

Note: The figures for Lake St. Clair include those for the St. Clair and Detroit Rivers.

heavy catches. When Milner surveyed the Great Lakes commercial fisheries for the United States Commission of Fish and Fisheries in 1871 and 1872, whitefish had been aggressively harvested for two decades by an expanding commercial-fishing industry that operated in Canadian and American waters. While there were no systematic records of the catch for the years 1850 to 1870, Milner was convinced from what he learned in his fieldwork that the harvest had peaked and was already in decline. Eight years later, Hubbard expressed his pessimism about the future of whitefish. From his personal observation, he noted that a half century of change in commercial fishing had made the whitefish available year round, all over the United States and even in Liverpool, and at a very reasonable price. He feared that "the greed of trade outruns all sober precautions" and that the fish of the Great Lakes waters and the rivers of Michigan, once so abundant, would be "exterminated, and this great industry of Michigan will cease to be remunerative."[3]

The figures that remain showing production for the lakes as a whole confirm the realism and pessimism in Milner's and Hubbard's observations. Whitefish experienced a marked decline between 1879 and 1899, from 24,300,000 to 9,000,000 pounds (table 10.1).

Given the goal of the Commission of Fish and Fisheries of reversing the national decline in food fish, Milner, when assigned to make a survey of the Great Lakes, paid special attention to the whitefish. His was the first such detailed study and was long the widely cited authoritative statement on the species. He noted that the physical nature and behavior of the common whitefish made them an easy catch for fishermen, probably second only to the salmon in vulnerability. Gregarious and moving in schools, whitefish were bottom feeders, eating crustaceans, mollusks very widely distributed over the lake floor, and some kinds of insect larvae. They did not have teeth and did not eat other fish or aquatic vegetation, according to Milner's field observations. Later studies showed that they did sometimes eat small fish. "The mouth," wrote Milner, "is constructed for nibbling along the bottom." They moved slowly, eating as they went. Whitefish were found "in all depths in more or less abundance," he noted somewhat vaguely. In the twentieth century, marine biologists consider the common whitefish of the Great Lakes to be a shallow-water species that lives in depths ranging from 60 to 180 feet, but occasionally deeper.[4]

Milner observed the movement of these fish, concluding, contrary to popular belief, that they probably did not migrate along the lake coasts. In general, he believed, they moved toward the shore twice a year: in the summer for a brief time, probably seeking aerated waters, and in the autumn to spawn. They then went back into the deeper parts of the lakes, where they remained for most of the year. Contemporary accounts tell of spectacular summer runs of whole schools of whitefish close to shore and of catches by the thousands with seines.[5]

Spawning season presented the fisherman with the best opportunity to harvest whitefish. They followed the fish with their nets as they moved toward the shore from deeper waters from October to December, depending on the locality. The fishers took them either legally in the United States, for want of restrictions and enforcement, or illegally in Canada by evading fishery overseers and patrol boats on the lookout for poachers. Once in shallow water, the fish remained until they were ready to spawn. Milner noted that many whitefish ascended rivers to spawn, naming the Detroit, the St. Mary's, and, on Lake Superior, the Michipicoten and the Nipigon. He added that given the development of lumbering on Green Bay, many rivers in that area of Wisconsin had been ruined for spawning. He suggested, "There is a probability that there was a time when the white-fish ascended many of the clear rivers of the northern lakes, though that this was a universal habit is not probable, at any rate since the white man has been in the country." His findings indicate that the fish spawned in late afternoon and at night in shallow lake waters, six to sixty feet deep, often over gravel or honeycombed rock, splashing and jumping from the water.[6] Whether remaining in the lakes or ascending rivers to spawn, the whitefish were an easy catch. Most of the spawn perished, much of it wasted in netting and handling the fish, and a great deal fell victim to natural predators other than humans.

Lake trout, burbot (lawyers), and northern pike were, as Milner noted, predators of young and adult whitefish. It is possible that trout were partially responsible for the decline of whitefish in Lake Huron and Georgian Bay that was so obvious by the 1890s as well as in other parts of the Great Lakes region, a view endorsed by contemporary fishery experts,

Figure 10.2. Lake trout (*Salvelinus namaycush namaycush*). (Drawing by Christine Kohler; courtesy University of Wisconsin Sea Grant Institute)

while others felt that there was "no basis for the theory." But Milner was convinced that the combined pressures of the destructive and wasteful methods of commercial fishing and the disturbance, destruction, and pollution of the naturally preferred habitat of the species had already done severe damage to the whitefish population. He heard many comments to that effect from fishermen and others knowledgeable about the problem. He concluded,

> As everywhere civilized man disturbs the balance of nature, and becomes the great enemy of all forms of life that do not conform to his artificial methods for their protection. Not only by the hundreds of artifices for the capture of the white-fish, but in the foul drainage from the cities, smelting-works, and manufactories, and in the quantities of sawdust from the mills, they are driven from their favorite haunts and spawning-grounds, and their food destroyed by waters tainted with fatal chemical combinations.[7]

The forces that Milner identified in 1872 as destroyers of the whitefish escalated during the balance of the century.

Lake Trout and Herring: The Hunters and the Hunted

As whitefish declined in numbers, fishermen turned first to lake trout and then to herring as commercial mainstays. The trout are notorious predators (figure 10.2). Contemporary observers noted that their habits were very different from those of whitefish. Early fishers harvested a number of different subspecies and races of trout found in each of the Great Lakes, some of them living near shore, where they were easy to catch and therefore the first exploited. During his fieldwork, James Milner found that trout generally stayed at depths of 180 feet and more in Lake Michigan, moving into shallow water during the spawning season. He characterized the trout as a ravenous eater, consuming both small and large fish, at times so large that the major part of the prey protruded from the trout's mouth while the stomach digested the "forward part." Trout ate garbage thrown overboard by passing steamboats. They consumed both whitefish of various sizes and herring, the latter a very important food source. John Brice, writing for the Commission of Fish and Fisheries in 1897, characterized the lake trout as "an omnivorous feeder" with a "ravenous appetite. It greedily devours all fishes possessing fins of flexible character, and jackknives, corncobs, and other articles equally indigestible have been found in its stomach." An experienced Lake Erie fisherman and Detroit fish dealer noted that a trout weighing ten to fifteen pounds "will have half a peck of small fish in him." The fishermen of the early 1870s claimed that the trout "always bites best when he is fullest."[8]

Far less group-oriented than whitefish, trout did not move about in schools, but hunted independently. They came shoreward in October, selecting rock and clay bottoms, reefs, and honeycombed rock in waters ranging from very shallow to 100 or even 200 feet deep to cast their spawn before retreating into deeper water. They also spawned in rivers. The eggs hatched in January or early February. Fishermen counted on the spawning season to make the catch. Milner noted that five pounds was an average weight for trout caught in gill nets, but fifteen-pound fish were not unusual. He spoke of very large specimens, reminiscent of the giant trout described by the Jesuit missionaries. Fishing ports cherished the tales of the largest trout taken. These stories told of trout weighing from fifty to ninety pounds. About the authenticity of one such fish story Milner felt very confident, a catch made in 1870 at Mackinaw weighing eighty pounds, a report verified by a local priest. By 1897, they rarely exceeded eighteen to twenty pounds.[9]

The biological behavior of lake trout gave them far greater chance of survival than the whitefish had in the contest with commercial fishermen, and given the popularity of whitefish over trout for food, their Great Lakes population in general held up reasonably well during the nineteenth century, except in Lake Ontario. From 1879 into the twentieth century, Canadian waters, the larger part of that lake, produced most of the trout. American waters slipped from 100,000-pound levels to 41,000 pounds in 1890, the high recorded yield for the next eighty-seven years. Similarly on Lake Huron, the Canadian waters, by far the larger part of the lake including Georgian Bay, were the major producers of trout. In general, the American waters of Lake Superior, the greater part of the lake containing the most numerous spawning grounds, have produced the

Table 10.2. Lake trout production from the Great Lakes, 1879–1899 (in thousands of pounds)

Year	Lake Ontario	Lake Erie	Lake St. Clair	Lake Huron	Lake Michigan	Lake Superior	Total
1879	1,008			2,677	2,659	1,653	7,997
1885	328			6,514	6,431	4,400	17,673
1889	133			5,991	5,580	4,387	16,091
1890	146			6,657	8,364	3,306	18,473
1893	246			7,484	8,526	5,471	21,727
1897	156			4,086	7,823	5,337	17,402
1899	120			6,684	5,286	5,808	17,898

Source: Compiled from Norman S. Baldwin, Robert W. Saalfeld, Margaret A. Ross, and Howard J. Buettner, *Commercial Fish Production in the Great Lakes, 1867–1977,* Technical Report no. 3 (Ann Arbor, Mich.: Great Lakes Fishery Commission, 1979).

Note: The figures for Lake St. Clair include those for the St. Clair and Detroit Rivers.

most trout (table 10.2). Lake Superior, which is still the least polluted of the Great Lakes, has the most heterogeneous trout population. It sustains both whitefish and trout, due largely to the determination of United States and Canadian fishery biologists to concentrate the attack on the lamprey problem there with TFM (3-trifluormethyl-4-nitrophenol), the lamprecide developed in 1958.[10]

When Milner made his study of the Great Lakes fisheries, his investigations in Lake Michigan showed that herring, not whitefish, were the principal diet of lake trout, and young herring have continued to be a major trout food (figure 10.3). As W. B. Scott and E. J. Crossman pointed out a century later, "In many respects, the lake herring is to aquatic predators what the rabbit is to its terrestrial counterparts, and forms part of the diet of a large number of fishes." Mainly the lake trout, but also northern pike, burbot, yellow perch, and walleyes feed on herring.[11]

In Milner's time, herring were hunted by natural predators, but not by fishermen, because they were not a popular food fish. Milner reported that they appeared in the shallower waters of Lake Erie and Green Bay, where "they are found in vast schools, crowding into the pound-nets in masses until the 'cribs' are filled to the surface of the water." He noted that a method of lightly pickling and then smoking herring that recently had been used in Waukegan, Illinois, and Sandusky, Ohio, produced a delicious food. Improved handling and curing methods did make herring far more marketable as the century wore on, and for the fishermen their desirability as a catch changed dramatically as the whitefish population declined.[12]

In relatively shallow Lake Erie, particularly where, in the 1850s,

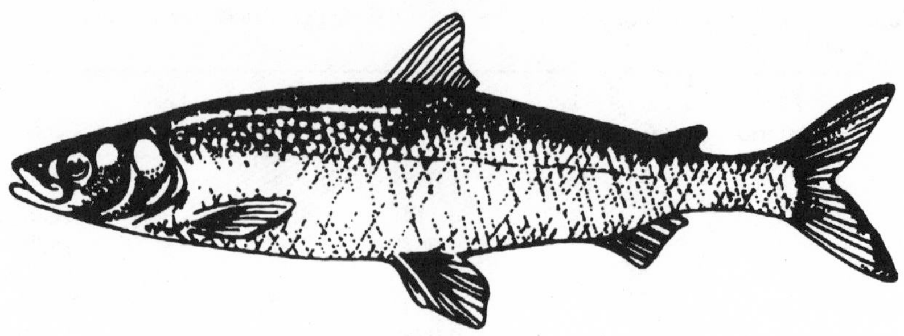

Figure 10.3. Lake herring (*Coregonus artedii*). (Drawing by Christine Kohler; courtesy University of Wisconsin Sea Grant Institute)

whitefish abounded and trout were found in the deeper parts of the eastern end of the lake, the vast catches of herring did not begin until late in the century. John W. Post of Sandusky, a very successful dealer in fresh fish, dated the commercial catch of herring on Lake Erie from "about 1876 or 1877, at the time of the big railroad strike." Also in Lake Huron's Saginaw Bay, another comparatively shallow-water area, the trout and whitefish that had been so bountiful until the mid-nineteenth century declined and a prolific herring population held up well, despite a large population of predatory yellow perch and walleye, large commercial catches, and the pollution in the bay from human and industrial sewage that was dumped into the Saginaw River.[13]

The herring sustained themselves during the nineteenth century partly because their commercial desirability came relatively late and because their principal food, plankton, abounded in the shallow lake waters they preferred from September through June. A very active fish in its food search, herring moved cyclically from shallow to deeper waters during the warmest parts of summer. There they stayed, far less accessible to fishermen. The main commercial catch came in the fall, coinciding with their movement into spawning grounds in waters as shallow as 10 to as deep as 210 feet. The fish spawned near the surface, and the eggs sank to the bottom, where many of them were devoured by herring, yellow perch, and other fish. They hatched in April and May. The huge number of herring in the Great Lakes before the beginning of aggressive commercial harvests probably helps explain how they continued to fill fishermen's nets so lavishly for so long (table 10.3). Their seemingly inexhaustible abundance led fishery experts in the 1890s to think that they needed no protection. The herring were the marvel of Lake Erie. Herring production fluctuated but did not show a sharp break until 1925, after forty-five years of aggressive commercial exploitation and increasing pollution.[14]

Table 10.3. Lake herring production from the Great Lakes, 1879–1899 (in thousands of pounds)

Year	Lake Ontario	Lake Erie	Lake St. Clair	Lake Huron	Lake Michigan	Lake Superior	Total
1879	924	12,349	369	1,314	3,050	34	18,040
1885	1,900	25,306	—	2,836	3,312	325	33,679
1889	5,016	44,103	884	5,251	9,569	387	65,210
1890	3,084	44,559	518	3,976	7,480	203	59,820
1893	1,963	27,105	161	5,000	20,085	1,309	55,623
1897	1,380	25,103	23	5,749	23,814	728	56,797
1899	1,408	39,705	—	5,548	24,745	1,317	72,723

Source: Compiled from Norman S. Baldwin, Robert W. Saalfeld, Margaret A. Ross, and Howard J. Buettner, *Commercial Fish Production in the Great Lakes, 1867–1977,* Technical Report no. 3 (Ann Arbor, Mich.: Great Lakes Fishery Commission, 1979).

Note: The figures for Lake St. Clair include those for the St. Clair and Detroit Rivers. The harvests for Lakes Ontario, Huron, and Michigan included chub as well as herring. For Lake Michigan, figures (in thousands of pounds) for chub are available for the 1890s: 1890, 1,398; 1893, 1476; 1897, 387; 1899, 2,462.

Lake Sturgeon

Said the Sturgeon to the Eel
Just imagine how I feel

In 1872, James Milner noted, "A parasite that troubles the sturgeon is the lamprey-eel . . . which is found very frequently attached to the skin." The freshwater lampreys or lamprey eels, as they were called in the nineteenth century, annoyed their sturgeon hosts,[15] which dispatched the unwelcome parasites by leaping from the water and landing with a splash. The lampreys were but a minor nuisance to the sturgeon, compared with the commercial fishermen. The harvesters' aggressive and wasteful ways in the last four decades of the nineteenth century, more than any other stress, produced the tremendous decline in the sturgeon population of the Great Lakes. Of the five major commercially harvested species of the Great Lakes, the sturgeon ranks second only to the salmon in decimation (figure 10.4).[16]

Scott and Crossman very appropriately called the sturgeon's relationship to humans during the nineteenth century "kaleidoscopic." Before the 1860s, fishermen considered them terrible nuisances that became entangled in nets, ripping and spoiling them, and spawn eaters of the worst kind. They sucked in whitefish eggs by the gallon. As a Lake Erie fisherman in 1894 expressed the general feeling of many: "A sturgeon is like a hog in a hen roost. They go around and suck up all the spawn there is. . . .

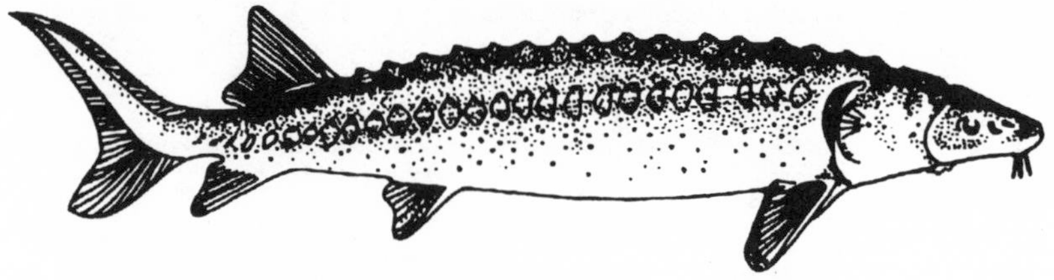

Figure 10.4. Lake sturgeon (*Acipenser fulvescens*). (Drawing by Christine Kohler; courtesy University of Wisconsin Sea Grant Institute)

You take a sturgeon weighing 50 lbs., what a lot of spawn he is going to lick up in 24 hours."[17] Before the 1860s, sturgeon were wounded and thrown back in the water to deter other sturgeon from coming into fishing grounds; killed and stacked up ashore; burned as fuel in steamboat boilers, where their oil made a good fire; fed to pigs; used as fertilizer on fields; and simply left to rot. In a word, these very ancient, majestic, and long-lived fish were wasted. But when a firm in Sandusky demonstrated their commercial worth in the mid-1860s, sturgeon began to be fished heavily for market, although they continued to be destroyed as nuisances in remote areas. Fishermen rationalized their aggressive onslaught as a way to make good money and to conserve the whitefish and other choice commercial species.

The Great Lakes sturgeon are the largest of the lake fish, growing to nearly eight feet long and weighing as much as 310 pounds, which was the recorded size of the largest caught in the twentieth century. It came from Batchawana Bay in Lake Superior in 1922. Such size has been very rare in the twentieth century, but it serves as a reminder of the days of the explorers and missionaries when some very large and aged sturgeons lived in the Great Lakes. Marine biologists have concluded that the lake sturgeon that escapes the fisherman can live for well over fifty years, and the age of that taken in Batchawana Bay was estimated at 100 years. One study of sturgeon in Lake Nipigon, in the Thunder Bay area of Ontario, published in 1923 recorded, among many, a forty-seven-year-old sturgeon that was sixty-three inches long and weighed sixty-four pounds.[18]

Over the years, fishermen have argued about the sturgeon's spawning time, but currently it is agreed that generally it comes in May and June, when the fish migrate in schools to their spawning grounds. As late as the last quarter of the nineteenth century, sturgeon in the southernmost parts of the Great Lakes spawned in rivers tributary to the lakes. For example, Milner observed in 1872 that sturgeon began to congregate near the shores of and at the mouths of rivers tributary to southern Lake Michigan, especially the Kalamazoo River, in early June. Schools of sturgeon crowded close to shore at Pier Cove, Michigan, every year and stayed for about two weeks.[19]

As development spoiled the waters and dams impeded the way, sturgeon chose rocky areas along the shores or sandy or hard clay bottoms well inshore, spawning in two to fifteen feet of water. They did have a homing sense, returning to the same location at spawning time. Sometimes they traveled very considerable distances, as did their anadromous relatives of the oceans. They made themselves very obvious in shallow lake waters and an easy prey for the fishermen. Observers repeatedly commented on the rolling, splashing, leaping movements of these big fish at spawning time. The glutinous eggs adhered to rocks or other surfaces and hatched in five to eight days. Thereafter, the fish grew slowly, reaching sexual maturity in twenty years.

Sturgeon frequented shallow lake waters, less than thirty feet deep. There these toothless bottom feeders found plentiful supplies of small organisms, especially thinner-shelled shellfish, sucking them in with their tubelike mouths. While they did ingest some fish eggs in the process, they were incidental. Contrary to the claims of fishermen, they did not seek fish eggs for food and were not the great destroyers of the whitefish. Given their habits and lengthy maturing period, they could not withstand intensive fishing and became increasingly scarce by the end of the nineteenth century. Marine biologists have concluded that once overexploited, the lake sturgeon population cannot be restored to its earlier size.[20]

The sturgeon of the Great Lakes especially interested James Milner, as they had Louis Agassiz, who had identified four species in Lake Superior in 1850. When he made his survey of the Great Lakes fisheries in 1871 and 1872, Milner reported a commercial catch of sturgeon in Lake Erie off Sandusky, Ohio, where 14,000 mature sturgeon, taken with eighty-five pound nets, weighed 700,000 pounds, a catch larger than that at any other location on the lakes except Green Bay, Wisconsin. What he found in Sandusky greatly impressed him, a thriving, growing business begun in 1865 by Siemon and John Schacht, brothers who earlier had fished on the Delaware River. In Sandusky, they specialized in the commercial preparation of sturgeon by producing smoked sturgeon, oil, caviar, and isinglass made from the bladders. The caviar went to markets in Germany. The firm processed 10,000 to 18,000 fish a year. Milner lauded the success of the Schacht brothers: "Out of a shameful waste of a large supply of food they have established a large and profitable industry." He hoped that similar ventures would make use of the sturgeon, for, as he observed, "excepting the vicinity of large cities, where they are generally marketable, the sturgeon are destroyed in the most wanton and useless manner." Particularly did he recommend that such a business be started in Green Bay, where sturgeon were being "uselessly destroyed or sold by

Table 10.4. Lake sturgeon production from the Great Lakes, 1879–1899 (in thousands of pounds)

Year	Lake Ontario	Lake Erie	Lake St. Clair	Lake Huron	Lake Michigan	Lake Superior	Total
1879	546	2,112	1,091	252	3,840	—	7,841
1885	441	5,187	278	1,041	1,407	224	8,578
1889	259	1,656	131	840	612	156	3,654
1890	581	2,660	151	723	947	145	5,207
1893	160	1,151	146	907	312	66*	2,742*
1897	144	549	55	452	138	41*	1,379*
1899	173	960	94	428	96	21	1,772

Source: Compiled from Norman S. Baldwin, Robert W. Saalfeld, Margaret A. Ross, and Howard J. Buettner, *Commercial Fish Production in the Great Lakes, 1867–1977*, Technical Report no. 3 (Ann Arbor, Mich.: Great Lakes Fishery Commission, 1979).

Note: The figures for Lake St. Clair include those for the St. Clair and Detroit Rivers.

*Figures are for only Michigan and Ontario.

the wagon-load for a trifle." He noted that a dealer in Chicago had more orders for smoked sturgeon than he could fill.[21]

His predictions about the sturgeon as a profitable venture for fishermen turned into reality in the following two decades. Sandusky remained the Great Lakes production center for caviar, smoked sturgeon, oil, and isinglass, but dealers in Toledo and Oconto, Wisconsin, on Green Bay, had entered the business by 1879. By 1885, sturgeon was also being processed by firms in South Chicago; Michigan City, Indiana; Michigan fishing ports from St. Joseph through Muskegon; the area around Port Clinton, Ohio; and Irving and Buffalo, New York. Buffalo boasted a caviar of "very superior quality" that served a worldwide market, while its smoked sturgeon went to the large eastern cities.[22]

In 1872, sturgeon seems to have been more or less abundant in "all localities" in American portions of the Great Lakes, reported Milner, especially around the islands in western Lake Erie, in Green Bay, in southern Lake Michigan, and in Chequamegon Bay, located in southern Lake Superior. In the Canadian parts of the lakes, they were very plentiful in Georgian Bay and the shallow waters of the North Channel of Lake Huron and in the western end of Lake Erie. By the time the investigators for the Joint Commission surveyed the fisheries of the waters of the United States and Canada in 1893 and 1894, the sturgeon had declined disastrously in the face of the aggressive commercial harvests (table 10.4). The fishermen and dealers who were interviewed spoke repeatedly about the drop in numbers. Great Lakes fishing enterprises in search of more sturgeon, the most valuable catch of the lakes, already had moved into the rich supplies of the Lake of the Woods, Rainy Lake, and the Rainy River, in western Ontario and eastern Manitoba, making the first extensive sturgeon harvest there in 1892. This market-driven onslaught ruined the sturgeon population in all American waters, where the sturgeon harvest rose to a high in about 1890 and reached a national total of 12 to 15 million pounds for several years thereafter. By 1912, it was below 1 million pounds. Hugh Smith, United States Commissioner of Fisheries, noted that "on the Great Lakes the yield declined more than 90 per cent in 18 years."[23]

Government experts reporting on Great Lakes matters tended to softpedal the rough and brutal aspects of commercial fishing, but in relation to the sturgeon, as to the salmon, they spoke out. For many years, harvesting techniques for sturgeon included the use of seines, gill nets, pound nets, and gaff hooks attached to poles, the last used from rowboats on the "rolling" ground at spawning time. Fishers trolled with three-pronged grappling hooks. By the 1890s, when dwindling catches and falling market prices led the fishers to make strenuous efforts to catch sturgeon, they turned to anchored set lines with hooks attached, particularly in the area around Buffalo and, at the other end of Lake Erie, in the St. Clair River, Lake St. Clair, and the Detroit River. In 1894, H. F. Moore, a marine biologist investigator for the Joint Commission, lashed out at the "barbarous" methods of grappling for sturgeon in these locations. They mutilated the fish, tearing away large patches of skin and flesh and ripping out eyes.[24]

Edward E. Prince, a British-trained biologist and the Dominion Commissioner of Fisheries, also condemned the grapnel, or hook, system of fishing for sturgeon as cruel, wasteful, and destructive. His American counterpart, Hugh Smith, United States Commissioner of Fisheries, wrote his lament on the "Passing of the Sturgeon" in his official report, calling the story of the sturgeon "one of the most distressing in the whole history of the American fisheries." He reminded Americans that within his generation, sturgeon had been pulled out of the Potomac River near Mount Vernon and left to rot, "witnesses to the cruelty, stupidity, and profligacy of man." Philip Neilson, a processor of sturgeon in Sandusky who predicted the extermination of these fish in the Great Lakes, made a less emotional and more fundamental assessment of their decimation when he told William Wakeham and Richard Rathbun in an interview in 1894: "The great trouble in the United States [is], when they go into a thing they go in head over heels, and just get all there is in it and do not consider the future at all, and the next generation will have to take care of themselves."[25]

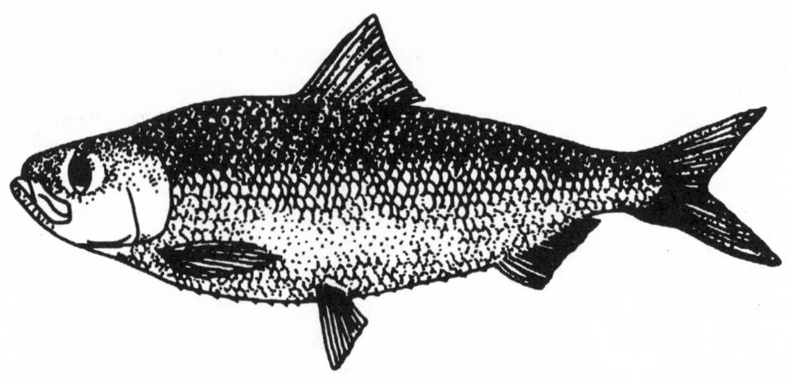

Figure 10.5. Alewife (*Alosa pseudoharengus*). (Drawing by Christine Kohler; courtesy University of Wisconsin Sea Grant Institute)

THE INTRUDERS

While the great commercial standbys—lake whitefish, trout, herring, and sturgeon—reacted to the stresses of overfishing, habitat destruction, and pollution, the fish population of the Great Lakes changed markedly as the result of both the expansion of certain species already present and the influx of fish not native to the lakes. A massive readjustment in the fish life of the Great Lakes characterized the latter half of the century, a highly complex process involving many agents of change, some identifiable and others quite possibly obscured forever.

Intruded species sometimes entered the Great Lakes by way of the canals built to connect them with rivers and the Atlantic Ocean, and fishery managers sometimes introduced them. In the 1870s, fish culturists experimenting with ways to increase species suitable for commercial use released two into Great Lakes waters: the alewife and the carp. They disrupted the native fish, an illustration of how good intentions could backfire without careful preliminary study of potential fish interaction.

Many believe that Seth Green introduced alewives into Lake Ontario in 1870 when he tried to plant East Coast American shad into that lake, the fry of the two fish having been intermixed accidentally (figure 10.5). Some think that they may have come on their own by way of the Hudson River and Erie Canal. Whichever way they arrived, they were identified in 1873 as present in Lake Ontario, where they multiplied. Fishermen came to regard them as a serious nuisance, and because of annual die-offs, residents in Lake Ontario communities complained loudly. On June 21, 1894, the furor over rotten fish reached the Canadian House of Commons, where it became a part of interparty repartee. Sir Richard Cartwright complained, "About this time every year a very large number of small dead fish are found floating about all over the lake. I think they call them shad." Replied Sir Charles Hibbert Tupper, Minister of Marine and Fisheries: "They call them Seth Green shad. He was a fishculturist." Cartwright asked, "Could you have him hanged?" Responded Tupper, "I am afraid our jurisdiction does not go through his country. He is dead now." Worse than the stench, alewives polluted the water, fouled the bottom, and were largely responsible for the decline in whitefish, according to Lake Ontario fishermen. One resident of a community on Lake Ontario who believed that they had decimated the whitefish went to Washington, D.C., and consulted a Dr. Bean, who identified them as "shad herring." He told the investigators for the Joint Commission: "They advised me to come home and make a fortune by putting them up for a Lake Ontario sardine."[26]

Walter G. Robbins, a fish dealer in Buffalo, New York, expounded his theories about alewives to the Joint Commission interviewers, telling how they had quickly filled Lake Ontario and fishing had immediately declined. He believed that the "avalanches" of alewives ate the little fish and "all the food." They "absolutely depopulated the waters except the bull-head and black bass." Alewives may have made their way into Lake Erie by the end of the nineteenth century. A fisherman in the area around Sandusky and Toledo told H. F. Moore, a field-worker for the Joint Commission, that he had loaded a boat full of alewives, or sawbellies, as he called them, and had taken as many as 600 or 700 pounds out of one net. Generally they are dated from the early 1930s in Lake Erie, but unless fisherman Alex Nielsen did not know his fish, they were present much earlier. Because alewives were so prolific and competed with young whitefish, herring, chub, and perch for plankton and ate the small fish as well, they had a great influence on the marine life of the lakes. Alewives must be counted as one factor in the dramatic change in the fish population of Lake Ontario by the 1890s.[27]

Another intruded species was the sea lamprey, an ancient predatory fish whose recorded presence in Lake Ontario dates to at least the 1830s. It may have been a native dating back for centuries, or it may have entered from the Atlantic Ocean by way of the Erie Canal or have been carried up the St. Lawrence River by overseas shipping bound for Lake Ontario ports. Sea lampreys were a well-established population in Lake Ontario in the 1890s and a menace to whitefish. In a list of causes for the declining fish population in the lake, the investigators for the Joint Commission noted, "Lampreys are often found on whitefish. They are not the same kind as those found in the creeks." Samuel Wilmot, chairman of the Dominion Fishery Commission, who was very knowledgeable about Great Lakes fish species, reported in 1894, "In Lake Huron and the Georgian

Bay there is evidence of the ravages of the lamprey eel, from their marks being found upon the bodies of the whitefish and other fish when caught. This eel inhabits Lake Ontario in vast numbers." Similarly, the Joint Commission field-workers heard again and again about the lamprey eel, but it is not clear, except for the evidence for Lake Ontario cited by Wilmot, whether those interviewed were referring to the freshwater silver lamprey or a species similar to the sea lamprey.[28]

The most authoritative statement about lampreys other than the silver lamprey comes from B. A. Bensley, a professor of zoology at the University of Toronto, who in 1915 wrote "The Fishes of Georgian Bay." He noted two species of lampreys present in the bay: the silver lamprey and a species he included "provisionally" and termed the lake lamprey. With an "average length about 15 inches," it was also found in the lakes of northern and central New York and in Lake Ontario, where it was abundant and was "commonly taken by fishermen on whitefish and lake trout." From the statements of fishermen, he believed that this lamprey was present in the upper Great Lakes "in small numbers." He referred to it as a "dwarfed fresh water representative of the marine lamprey." Perhaps the lampreys that Georgian Bay fishermen described to Bensley had entered those waters through the Trent–Severn Waterway, which in June 1907, after decades of starts and stops, linked the Trent River system, which empties into Lake Ontario, with the Severn River system, which drains into Georgian Bay.[29]

The presence of the lampreys in Great Lakes waters during the nineteenth century was far less of a threat to whitefish and trout than it came to be in the 1930s, when the lamprey population virtually exploded and seriously threatened the fisheries of Lakes Huron, Michigan, and Superior. Is the generally accepted proposition that the sea lamprey entered the upper lakes by way of the enlarged and improved Welland Canal the whole story?

The history of the introduction of German carp into American waters is relatively well known (figure 10.6). Regarded as a great panacea for the general decline of the fish population on the Atlantic coast and in the eastern half of the United States, carp, thought Spencer Baird, secretary of the Smithsonian Institution and Commissioner of Fish and Fisheries, could further his campaign to replenish the supplies of food fish. The commission's fish-rearing ponds for carp on the grounds of the Washington Monument and in Druid Hill Park in Baltimore produced great results in only a few years. In his report of 1879, Baird cited the beginning of distribution of young carp as among the "most noted features in the history of the Commission for the year."[30]

For a time, enthusiasm for carp ran high. In 1888, Seth Green wrote a small book in which he advocated that farmers raise carp and provided

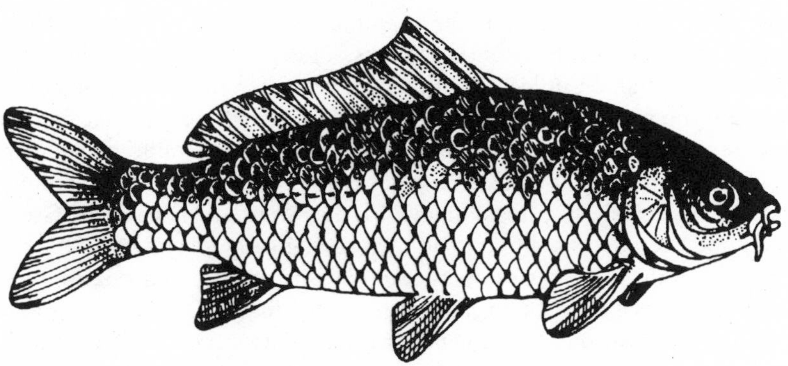

Figure 10.6. Common carp (*Cyprinus carpio*). (Drawing by Christine Kohler; courtesy University of Wisconsin Sea Grant Institute)

instructions on the construction of carp ponds. It contained no cautions or criticisms of the species. And four years later, the Ontario Fish and Game Commissioners were "delighted" to find carp in seines in the Grand River below a dam, surmising that they had come in from Lake Erie, having spread from the American side. Great Lakes waters did support a substantial carp population by the 1890s. Introduced into Sandusky Bay in 1888, carp soon became numerous in the shallow waters of western Lake Erie. In 1893, 631,000 pounds went to market; six years later, 3.6 million pounds. The harvest in 1908 approached 9 million. The carp also found their way, either by deliberate planting or by natural migration, into Lakes Michigan, St. Clair, and Huron before the end of the century.[31]

In the 1890s, fish culturists and the public began condemning the introduction of carp as a serious mistake. While opinions were far from unanimous, they were hotly expressed. John Brice, appointed as Commissioner of Fisheries in 1896, condemned the carp in the Potomac River for having cleaned out the black bass. "There will be no more carp distributed by the United States Fish Commission while I am in charge of it, and they will be cleaned out of all the ponds wherever they may be that come under the authority of this office," he declared. Edward E. Prince, the Dominion Commissioner of Fisheries, in the same year strongly discouraged the planting of carp in Canadian waters based on what he had learned about the way they were destroying the fish habitat in many places in the United States. The case against them, maintained Prince, was very clear. They made poor table fare compared with whitefish, trout, and other commercial species of the Great Lakes, and they were notorious for spoiling wetland areas, streams, and rivers because they uprooted vegetation and left muddy, murky water in their wake. They liked wild rice and most water plants and all manner of animal matter. Noted Prince, "Their natural food appears to be insects, frogs, and spawn of other fishes; but they devour offal, or, indeed, anything edible, either animal or vegetable." They ate the spawn and the young of the preferred commercial species and competed with them for food. They were very prolific and hardy, capable of surviving at a wide range of temperatures. They grew rapidly and ate voraciously, like hogs. In a word, they were a menace in the Great Lakes and the waters tributary to them, ecologically revolutionary.[32]

In 1899, the Deputy Commissioner of Fisheries of Ontario scathingly characterized the carp as an invading menace that roots like a hog and "multiplies like vermin," producing "nothing but evil results." He added, "It is believed to be the only fish which will drive that gamey fish, the black bass from its spawning beds." One fisherman of western Lake Erie waters complained in an interview with investigators for the Joint Commission about the way carp destroyed marsh vegetation. He had "seen them playing around in a few inches of water, their dorsal fins above the surface, rooting up the wild rice."[33] While it is impossible to calculate the extent of the damage the carp did to the preferred commercial-fish species in the western end of Lake Erie, these predatory transplants must have been among the stresses affecting them in the late nineteenth century and contributing to the complaints of enthusiasts of sportfishing about the scarcity of black bass.

A NEW FISH POPULATION PROFILE EVOLVES

While alewives, sea lampreys, and German carp exemplify the transplanted disrupters of the big four, the expansion in the population of what contemporaries called the "rough, coarse" fish, native to the lakes, provided yet another agent of change. The result of commercial fishing and alterations in lake habitat, their growing numbers further altered the composition of the fish population as new balances between predators and prey and readjustments between the varied species and food sources evolved. The trend had reached very noticeable proportions by the end of the nineteenth century. The label "rough, coarse" fish meant different things to different people. For the fishermen who saw their livelihood dwindle as the higher-paying catch declined, it meant those species that brought little income. To others, the term meant specific fish like the bowfin, popularly called dogfish. In Canada, they were "classed as one of the most voracious and worthless fish in our waters—fishermen call them lawyers."[34] Carp, sheepshead, bullhead, and suckers generally fell into the category of rough fish.

In 1894, Samuel Wilmot, Superintendent of Fish Culture for Canada, lamented the changes in the fish population of Lake Erie:

> Formerly Lake Erie was called "Whitefish Lake" by the fishermen, and Fish Dealers Everywhere: This was on account of the vast quantities of whitefish that were at one time taken in that Lake; —the Whitefish are now largely fished out, and Erie is now called by the Fishdealers the "Herring Lake"—with the same overfishing of Herring, and with no close season for their protection, it will soon lose its character as a "Herring Lake," and become a Blue Pickerel Lake: —Thus a once famous lake for the two better kinds of fish will soon become the resort only of the inferior kinds.

As chairman of the dominion-appointed Ontario Fishery Commission, which gathered evidence from fishermen during 1892 and 1893 with the object of recommending regulations to conserve the fisheries, Wilmot had learned a great deal about species shifts in the Canadian waters of Lake Erie. There, he believed, "voracious and coarse fish" had increased phenomenally, largely because of the comparatively warm waters and shallowness of the lake and the "weedy nature of many of the bays and shores." He expressed alarm about the data revealed in the 1892 returns of the Department of Marine and Fisheries, showing a very substantial increase in various species in the perch and pike families and in coarse fish during the preceding decade. The pickerel harvest in 1892 approached 1.5 million pounds, almost six times larger than it had been in 1882. The pike catch had grown fivefold from its 25,300 pounds in 1882, and the coarse fish harvest had more than doubled to over 1 million pounds. The voracious blue pickerel, noted Wilmot, ate the fry of the "more marketable fish." Add to that pike and "coarser fish," whose expanded population threatened all small fish with their "voracious and destructive" ways. These species contributed much to the decline of the whitefish in Lake Erie, he believed.[35]

While parallel information in those years for the American waters of Lake Erie is not available, fishermen there harvested 17,955,000 pounds of pike and perch family species in 1885 and 16,645,000 in 1890. Pike and perch species increased noticeably elsewhere. For example, northern pike, a very voracious fish, grew in numbers in Lake Ontario after 1880. Pike and pickerel harvests increased substantially between 1882 and 1892 in the Canadian waters of Lakes St. Clair and Huron. In the American portion of Lake Huron, they grew by well over 1 million pounds by conservative estimate between 1885 and 1890, and in the American waters of Lakes Michigan and Ontario, they also escalated.[36]

In many areas of the Great Lakes, the impact of environmental change—sometimes abrupt, often subtle, and slowly continuous—contributed to a much altered fish population profile. This was particularly noticeable in urban and industrial areas, where people and their economic activities affected the more shallow lake waters and where commercial fishing reached substantial proportions earlier than elsewhere. In southern Lake Michigan by 1885, for example, yellow perch, a fish adaptable to many conditions and capable of getting along on low levels of oxygen, had expanded very notably, occupying waters once abounding in whitefish but now degraded by urban-industrial population growth and heavy lake traffic. Noted the statistical agent of the Michigan Board of Fish Commissioners in 1885: "In the immediate vicinity of large towns around the entire lake coast the common yellow perch (*perca Americana*) is caught in large quantities. This is especially true of Lake St. Clair and the southerly end of Lake Michigan."[37]

In Green Bay in northern Lake Michigan, where lumbering and commercial fishing made a heavy impact, whitefish, trout, and sturgeon had declined notably by 1885. Perch and suckers found the waters congenial and, between 1885 and 1890, grew to a larger proportion of the fishermen's catch. The recorded 78,500 pounds of suckers caught in 1885 was small compared with the 1,249,000 pounds harvested in 1890 from the Green Bay waters of Michigan and Wisconsin. The 78,500-pound total probably was a partial figure. Wholesale fish dealers in Green Bay, Wisconsin, told investigators from the Commission of Fish and Fisheries in 1885 that of the nearly 3 million pounds of fish they handled, 1.3 million were trout, herring, and whitefish and the balance was largely suckers, yellow perch, pickerel, and pike. Of those, perch accounted for more than 500,000 pounds. The shallow, fertile waters of Green Bay still yielded large fish harvests, with species that were adaptable to many levels of turbidity and oxygen growing numerically in the production profile.

In Saginaw Bay in Lake Huron, another relatively shallow, fertile body of water that was being contaminated by refuse from lumbering and by a growing burden of human and industrial sewage principally from the Saginaw River, the whitefish and trout harvest declined between 1885 and 1890, and yellow perch, suckers, mullet, pike, pickerel, and herring flourished.[38] Canadian fishery overseers spoke of a similar change in Burlington Bay in Lake Ontario in the 1890s. Changes in the fish population of the water linkages among Lakes Ontario and Erie, Lake St. Clair, and the St. Clair and Detroit Rivers, in the 1880s and 1890s, were little short of revolutionary, as heavy fishing and degrading fish habitats seriously eroded once very valuable commercial fisheries. Whitefish and herring, long harvested by fishermen for the adjacent Detroit market and, in the late nineteenth century, seined and confined in ponds to provide fresh fish for winter consumption, declined sharply before 1900, while sturgeon, northern pike, carp, suckers, channel catfish, yellow perch, and walleye gradually dwindled after 1900. No catch of smallmouth bass was recorded for Michigan waters after 1898, and in 1901 commercial fishing for them was prohibited in Ontario waters.[39]

MEASURES OF CHANGE IN THE FISH PROFILE

Change was widespread in the Great Lakes. Dipping into the records of the harvest and following them over a period of time makes very evident the pervasive nature of changing species in changing waters. To explain the trend through the years in different localities with precision, relating it to the twenty ecoregions identified in the Great Lakes drainage basin,[40] is a monumental challenge that requires a host of research projects over an extended period of time. It is no mean task to identify relationships among species, production levels, changing water habitats, lake levels, weather, disease, food availability, and a host of other variables that contributed to the shifts in species profiles. However, a number of the main trends in the changing fish population in the nineteenth century can be identified: the extermination of the Lake Ontario salmon, the decline of the whitefish, the near destruction of the sturgeon, the inroads into herring and trout populations, the coming of the sea lamprey to Lake Ontario, the introduction of the alewife and carp, the rise of pike and perch family populations, and the general expansion of "rough fish."

The production data for the Great Lakes as a whole help bring into focus the way in which the "big four" of commercial fishing—whitefish, trout, herring, and sturgeon—lost ground in relation to other species in the total catch (table 10.5). Between 1880 and 1899, the big four declined from 74 percent of total production to 69 percent and dropped further in 1903 to 63 percent. Among those species that grew in numbers as the preferred four declined, the most prominent were fish that are tolerant of slightly turbid to turbid waters and are capable of surviving in waters with relatively little oxygen, or even no oxygen for a considerable period of time, and with relatively abundant phosphorus and chlorophyll. They included yellow perch, suckers, bullheads, catfish, muskellunge, northern pike, grass pike, blue pike, pickerel, mullet, saugers, walleye, carp, bowfin (lawyer, dogfish), freshwater drum (sheepshead), and burbot (ling).[41] Lake whitefish, trout, herring, and sturgeon, in contrast, needed less turbid waters with more oxygen and cleaner spawning grounds. As the area of such habitats declined, so did the big four of commercial fishing.

These production totals obscure wide variations, perhaps most readily illustrated in the cases of Lake Superior, the least changed lake, and Lake Ontario, the most changed. Lake Superior was remote from urban and industrial centers, supported very little farming around its shores, was affected by lumbering notably on its southern shore only, and was the last of the Great Lakes to be harvested intensively by commercial fishermen. Superior was a deep, cold lake with limited fishing grounds around its shores, containing about one-quarter of the total lake area. The commer-

Table 10.5. Great Lakes production by species groups, 1880–1903

Year	Total Catch	Whitefish, Trout, Herring, and Sturgeon (%)	All Other Fish (%)
1880	80,379,000	74	26
1885	121,290,000	68	32
1890	143,406,000	72	28
1893	134,211,000	69	31
1899	146,617,000	69	31
1903	114,050,000	63	37

Sources: The total production figures were compiled from A. B. Alexander, "Statistics of the Fisheries of the Great Lakes in 1903," in U.S. Commissioner of Fisheries, *Report,* 1904, Appendix, 58th Cong., 3d sess., 1904, H. Doc. 479 (Serial 4897), 651, and, with the exception of 1880, Norman S. Baldwin, Robert W. Saalfeld, Margaret A. Ross, and Howard J. Buettner, *Commercial Fish Production in the Great Lakes, 1867–1977,* Technical Report no. 3 (Ann Arbor, Mich.: Great Lakes Fishery Commission, 1979); the figure for 1880 was compiled from U.S. Commission of Fish and Fisheries, *Report,* 1895, 54th Cong., 2d sess., 1896, H. Doc. 104 (Serial 3518), 97, and Canada, *Sessional Papers,* 1881, no. 11, 291; information on the habitat requirements of various species was compiled from George C. Becker, *Fishes of Wisconsin* (Madison: University of Wisconsin Press, 1983).

Note: The years used for compiling the figures were governed by the data that were available. The United States did not systematically collect data on fisheries production until 1913.

cial big four made up 96 percent of the total catch in 1879 and 97 percent in 1903.[42]

Lake Ontario was the first of the Great Lakes to support urban and industrial centers and agricultural development, was the most accessible from the Atlantic Ocean and the St. Lawrence River and thus the earliest to host ships from overseas with whatever live fish species they may have carried in with them, and was deep with only about one-half its total area suitable to sustain a fish population. The commercial big four made up 63 percent of the total catch in 1879 and 41 percent in 1903. At the turn of the century, Lake Ontario received loads of pollutants from the Genesee and Niagara Rivers, from industry in Watertown, New York, via the Black River, from the urban-industrial areas around Toronto and Hamilton, from nutrient-laden runoffs produced by surrounding farmlands, and from lumbering refuse. According to witnesses, alewives and sea lampreys stressed the lake whitefish and trout populations. One longtime observer of Lake Ontario fishing at Sackets Harbor, New York, downriver from industrial Watertown, told William Wakeham and Richard Rathbun in 1894: "Our lake is in a peculiar condition during the summer. We say that the lake is in bloom twice a year." The bay at Sackets Harbor, recipient of the Black River's industrially polluted waters, for the first time had "tufts of green stuff" floating on it, and the "green stuff" also covered the rocks for miles around the bay. The scientists did not venture an explanation for Colonel W. B. Camp, who offered the information. Camp lamented that the conditions of his youth, when the lake had been "full of fish," had changed. He reviewed the shift in species. The salmon had disappeared. The whitefish and trout were long since gone from the bay. The pickerel had left the bay, and the bullheads died there: "The fish have become almost exterminated in our bay." But the prolific alewives endured, periodically dying and rotting on the bottom and the shore.[43]

THE CHALLENGE OF CHANGE

Among those who noticed the changing harvest, the commercial fishermen with alarm and those charged with managing the supply of commercial fish in the Great Lakes with grave misgivings about the future of the resource, the latter harped on the theme of overfishing and understandably so. Two Canadian authorities, in particular, wrote more broadly about the changing species profile in the Great Lakes. Both Edward E. Prince and Samuel Wilmot puzzled over the nature of the transformations, suggesting an upset in "natural balances." Prince observed that once natural balances between predators and prey are disturbed, "as in the great lakes, by fishing operations on a vast scale the results are frequently quite inexplicable." Why, he wondered, should the decline of whitefish in Lake Erie have been followed by an "enormous increase" in herring rather than a "great increase in such predaceous species as the blue and yellow pike-perch or pickerel"? In Lake Huron and Georgian Bay, however, the decline of whitefish "seems to have been accompanied by a very appreciable increase in the quantity of great lake trout," a predator. The changes in the fish population were hard to explain, but Prince was convinced that physical changes in the lakes and the lands around them had to be taken into consideration as well as overfishing with ever more efficient and destructive technology.

Wilmot also spoke of the significance of nature's balances. Once weakened by heavy fishing, commercial species could be destroyed by their natural enemies and parasites. From the vantage point of a lifetime of observation and fish propagation, he understood far better than many the magnitude and causes of what was happening to the fish population of the Great Lakes. Wilmot sounded the warning in 1893: "The danger line of destruction of the fisheries of the great lakes is being approached."[44] Many fishermen and fishery experts agreed: conditions called for serious thought and action to save the fish.

Part III

Policy Makers and the Great Lakes Fisheries 1801–1896

Scholars have tended to give nineteenth-century efforts to make and enforce fish and game laws in Canada and the United States short shrift because they did not achieve their stated goals. They deserve far more careful consideration. As conservers of natural wildlife, it is true, these measures failed for the most part to realize their ostensible objectives, but so have many twentieth-century efforts. A careful consideration of the forces that led to nineteenth-century regulatory laws, the attempts to enforce them, and the reasons for their failure reveal important milestones in the evolution of fish and wildlife conservation in North America. The system developed over time by trial and error, borrowing from the past and subject to the influence of commercial and sports-oriented pressure groups and politicians anxious to please their constituencies. Influential in the process also were concerned scholarly observers, including both biological scientists and humanists, self-taught naturalists, and policy makers who advocated long-term sustained yields of commercial and sport fish, by regulating catches to allow the remainder to reproduce and replenish their numbers.

11

The First Regulators

The Provinces and the States

American Fishermen Have the Whip-Hand of Their Legislatures

Desires of the early settler-developers in New York and Upper Canada to exploit the bountiful salmon population of Lake Ontario led to the first regulation of Great Lakes fishing. Never since have Canadian and American lawmakers been in such agreement about the need to manage the fisheries. In the first decade of the nineteenth century, the New York legislature and the legislative councils and assemblies of the province of Upper Canada devised controls "for the Preservation of the Fishery" that clearly showed the different ways of thinking in the two nations about the Great Lakes resource and the government's role in its regulation.

Consider first the actions of successive New York legislatures and the motives that shaped them. On April 3, 1801, New York lawmakers approved a measure prohibiting the use of seines, nets, weirs, or other obstructions in the Big Salmon, Little Salmon, Great Sandy, and Little Sandy Rivers or creeks flowing into Lake Ontario, or within 1,650 feet of the mouths of these streams, to divert the salmon from ascending to their spawning grounds. People could not build dams on the designated streams "below where salmon are found." By October 1, 1801, those who owned dams across steams flowing into Lakes Ontario, Erie, and Champlain had to build a slope or fishway to enable fish to pass upstream. Persons failing to comply would be fined.[1]

That law was just the beginning. Over the next forty-seven years, the

New York legislature passed twenty-three more laws relating to the salmon of Lake Ontario. An analysis of these regulations, considered in light of the area's early development, reveals various interests at work to appropriate the water and fishery resources of Lake Ontario's southern shore. Some of the incoming settlers regarded the salmon as the principal bounty of river and stream, an important source of food. Others viewed the rivers primarily as a source of power to run saw- and gristmills. They favored damming the rivers and creeks. The conflict between the two groups created a seesaw regulatory record, in which the power-manufacturing interests eventually emerged as the winners. On the Genesee River, the advocates of waterpower and commerce won the contest very early, with the founding and rapid growth of Rochester, New York. Advocates of fish for food could not compete with the economic clout of the mill-owner and merchant beneficiaries of the Erie Canal and the western development, which brought them fortunes and political influence.[2]

To think of the 1801 law as "an Act for the Preservation" of salmon for long-term human use distorts the intent of the framers. In reality, it was a law to ensure the continuation of the salmon runs to supply food for early pioneer settlers. Of all the twenty-four New York laws relating to Lake Ontario salmon, it most clearly expressed their wishes and those of the region's early fish merchants.

A similar law passed in 1813 introduced the idea of protection for salmon during the spawning season, a recurrent provision in legislation of the next few years until 1822, when a statewide law designed "for the preservation" of selected species made it illegal to fish for salmon between October 20 and February 1. Given its heavy emphasis on the protection of species prized for hook-and-line fishing, the law probably originated with the influential sportfishing interests of the state. Unenforced, largely because such power lay with local courts, which were sympathetic to the antiregulatory stance of local residents, it posed no barrier to the harvesting of spawning salmon in the rivers and streams of the southern shore of Lake Ontario. The local hold on the fisheries became even stronger when in 1826 the New York legislature gave the county courts of common pleas the authority to regulate fishing in county waters to prevent the destruction of the fish.[3]

Representing both the advocates of waterpowered mills and those trying to preserve the salmon runs, the New York legislature turned ever more frequently to the balancing act established in English law and applied earlier in Atlantic coastal areas from Connecticut north through New Brunswick to appease the competing factions: fishways in dams to allow fish to move up- and downstream. Why not ensure multiple use of the waters and satisfy all? As early as 1813, prohibitions of dam construction on the Salmon River disappeared when the legislature allowed persons owning mills or mill privileges there to build dams, "as many dams . . . as they . . . may think proper," as long as they provided a fishway or slope not exceeding forty-five degrees and wide enough to allow boats and rafts to pass. The fishways did not work well, according to local observers. Fish congregated at the base of dams as they struggled to ascend rivers, making them an easy catch. With good times spurring economic growth in 1836, the legislature repealed all acts relating to dams and other obstructions in the Salmon River. Thus ended the contest over the use of those river waters, with the milling interests victorious at a time when commercial salmon fishing was responding to boom times and the catches were still very large, according to the testimony of a fish dealer in Pulaksi, New York. New York laws relating to Lake Ontario salmon served the immediate interests of various groups and did not ensure a long-term sustained yield.[4]

Across Lake Ontario in Canada, similar concerns about protecting salmon emerged in the early nineteenth century. The legislatures of Upper Canada, the Province of Canada (created in 1841 with the unification of Upper and Lower Canada), and the Dominion of Canada (created in 1867) recognized the value of salmon as food consumed close to home and as part of a wider domestic and foreign commerce. As settler-developers moved in an ever-growing stream around the northern shore of Lake Ontario in the early nineteenth century, the first of seven pieces of legislation to protect salmon enacted by 1865 went on the statute books, the first Canadian regulation of Great Lakes fishing. "It is found necessary to make provision for the preservation of Salmon in the Rivers and Creeks of this Province," noted the Legislative Council and Assembly of Upper Canada in the preamble to a law passed on March 10, 1807. By its terms, fishers on the northern shore of Lake Ontario could use spears and hooks and lines, but were prohibited from setting nets, weirs, "or other engines" to take salmon and salmon fry in or at the mouths of any of the creeks or rivers draining into Lake Ontario. The law said nothing about dams as barriers. Somewhat simpler than New York's legislation of 1801, which included a ban on building dams, this law had the same intent: to facilitate the upstream passage of the fish during their annual spawning runs. Both spoke to the food needs of early settler-developers.[5]

Three years later, in 1810, the legislators of Upper Canada introduced the idea of a closed season, from October 25 to January 1, for the eastern Lake Ontario area, with a much more comprehensive and more strongly worded provision than the one enacted three years later in New York. Throughout the first six decades of the nineteenth century, as the bountiful salmon population declined, the Canadian legislators expanded the closed season until in 1865 the Province of Canada specified July 31 to May 1 as the period when salmon should not be taken. Rod and line fishermen, who could fish from May through the end of August, were exempt. These laws showed a recognized need for regulatory preservation and, seemingly, a stronger commitment to British precedents than that displayed in New York.[6]

As for the blockage of streams by mill dams, general provisions for fishways went on the statute books of Upper Canada on March 25, 1828, theoretically balancing the interests of both advocates of maintaining fish as a food source and those of using streams as a power source for mills. The legislature of Upper Canada wrote into law in 1810, 1821, 1823, and 1845 specific safeguards for mill owners against torch-bearing spear-fishers, prohibiting them from coming closer than 100 yards to any mill or dam. The New York statutes did not include such a provision.[7]

Unique also to the Canadian laws for Lake Ontario salmon were prohibitions against hiring Indians to circumvent the closed seasons. The law passed in 1823 stated the case clearly. The provision for a closed season for salmon "is in great measure defeated by persons employing Indians to catch salmon, after the expiration of the time" allowed by law. Hereafter, no one could employ Indians to fish out of season, buy fish from them, or receive "under any pretense whatever, from any Indian or Indians, any salmon" caught during the closed season. A law passed in 1858 included further protections by stipulating the size of mesh and prohibiting the taking of salmon at any "salmon-leap" or artificial pass or in spawning pools and ponds.[8]

Comparing the body of legislation enacted in Canada and in New York by the mid-nineteenth century, there are some very real differences. Most striking, the provisions in the Canadian laws that applied to the Lake Ontario salmon contain the ingredients of a utilitarian conservation policy. The increasing emphasis on a longer and more generalized closed season is one such component. The requirements for fishways and the restrictions on the use of weirs, seines, nets, and other harvesting gear to block the passage of the fish upstream could be so classified had they and the closed-season regulations been enforced, but they were not. The antiblockage laws, which theoretically would facilitate spawning, just resulted in massive destruction upstream. However, the increased emphasis on prohibiting the possession of salmon in the closed season and the elaborate statement, in the law of 1845, of fines, jail sentences, court procedures, and a bounty to constables for bringing in offenders, along with a mileage allowance for their efforts and a reward to the informer, represented broader and more elaborate safeguards for salmon than those established by New York.[9]

THE PROVINCIAL ROOTS OF THE FISHERY ACT OF 1868

What began in Upper Canada with the law passed in 1807, regulating methods of catching salmon, grew incrementally over the following decades into a full-scale fishery policy for the Atlantic Ocean and Great Lakes promulgated in 1868 by the Dominion of Canada. In 1857 and 1858, the Legislative Council and Assembly of the Province of Canada amalgamated bits and pieces of earlier laws into a single measure, "An Act respecting Fisheries and Fishing," a codification of fishing laws undertaken as the result of the consolidation of Lower Canada (Quebec) and Upper Canada (Ontario) into the Province of Canada in 1841. Over the years, one principle of protecting the fish population after another had gone on the statute books, until by 1857 and 1858, they added up to an impressive foundation on which the Dominion of Canada would base its fishery policy in 1868. As Alan B. McCullough, historian of the commercial fisheries in Canada's Great Lakes waters, has noted, protective legislation applied to the Great Lakes grew after 1807 to include regulation of the methods of fishing, closed seasons while fish were spawning, penalties for the sale of protected fish taken out of season, restrictions on where fishing was allowed, requirements for fishways at dams, protection of fish in especially sensitive areas (for example, the Niagara, St. Clair, and Detroit Rivers; Burlington Bay and the adjacent Dundas Marsh), restriction of the right to fish to residents, penalties for the sale of fish taken out of season, and safeguards for commercially significant species: salmon, whitefish, trout, and herring.

The laws of 1857 and 1858 went further, establishing the power of government to lease fishing grounds and thus modifying the general principle of the common of the fishery: fishing as a "public right." The laws of the 1850s encouraged fish-hatching experiments generally beyond those undertaken by Richard Nettle, who, as Superintendent of Fisheries for Canada East, received public funds to experiment with salmon hatching in Quebec City in 1857.[10] Legislators recognized the problems of pollution by prohibiting the dumping of fish wastes, lime, ballast, drugs, and chemicals into the waters of the Province of Canada.

Most significantly, as McCullough points out, the legislation of 1857 and 1858 completely revised the system of enforcement, removing it from municipal control. Thereafter, the province would enforce the laws under the direction of the Superintendent of Fisheries aided by fishery overseers. Licenses for fishermen became the principal control mechanism. The Province of Canada thus embarked on a policy of regulating, nurturing, and conserving the resource in all its waters, a plan very much in contrast to what Canadian fishermen came to call the "American system," or free and unlimited access to the fisheries, with few controls. The province placed the principles for regulating the use of the resource on the statute books, but enforcement remained difficult. Fishermen balked at the new licensing system, claiming that long use guaranteed to them their fishing rights, and at times forcibly resisted enforcement officers.[11]

One very experienced fisheries overseer, John W. Kerr—who knew the western end of Lake Ontario well at the time when the salmon crowded the beaches of the lake from Port Whitby, east of Toronto, to the mouth of the Niagara River before they ascended the rivers to spawn—told a House of Commons select committee on fisheries in 1869: "All the Salmon have been destroyed in consequence of Contraventions of the Fishery laws."[12] Fishermen in Canada resisted rules and regulations, as did those in the United States. With the creation of the dominion in 1867, the responsibility for administering the fisheries passed to the national government. It assumed the headache of enforcement, and Ontario (formerly Upper Canada and then, after 1841, Canada West) created as a province at the time of confederation, lost control over the experiment in fishery administration that it had created. Not until the turn of the century, after prolonged bickering between Toronto and Ottawa about which, the provincial or the dominion government, had jurisdiction over fishery management and after protracted legal action did Ontario again become significant.

EARLY REGULATION IN THE GREAT LAKES STATES

In contrast to the system established in the Province of Canada in 1857 and 1858, the state of New York, which began regulating the harvest of Lake Ontario salmon, as did Upper Canada, went a very different route in managing the waters of the Great Lakes. While its legislation in the 1850s and 1860s contained elements of protection—such as mandating the methods of fishing, establishing closed seasons, special protection such as restrictions on fishing gear used in designated areas of Lakes Erie and Ontario, banning the dumping of lime and poisons into the waters, and requiring the construction of fishways in dams—the laws were piecemeal, limited in application, and often exempted all or parts of Lake Ontario. They emphasized regulation where fishing seemed to one interest group or another to be depleting the fisheries, or they applied to a species that was greatly in demand and declining very noticeably, especially sport fish. Enforcement was handled at the local level. There were no state officials charged with the responsibility, and licenses were not required. Fishermen operated freely and with little restraint. This mid-nineteenth-century New York legislation characterized the general thrust of fishery policies in the Great Lakes states for some decades. When the favored commercial species noticeably diminished and fishermen, policy makers, and fishery experts believed that real trouble threatened, more restrictive state policies followed in the 1880s and 1890s.

The evolution of state regulation of the Great Lakes fisheries during the nineteenth century can be well illustrated in the policy-making record of three Great Lakes states: Ohio, Michigan, and Wisconsin. They collectively controlled the largest portion of American waters, 80 percent of the total 94,250 square miles, and produced the largest share of income from the fishing industry of the eight Great Lakes states. In 1892, for example, these three earned 79 percent of the value of the catch from all American Great Lakes waters.[13]

The three states developed similar policies, but they differed in specific content according to the locations and types of fisheries and the various kinds of influence that commercial-fishing interests exerted on the state legislatures—in all cases very real. None adopted a comprehensive policy for Great Lakes waters. None required licenses for Great Lakes commercial fishermen during the nineteenth century. The regulations of all three had a temporary, piecemeal, hit-and-miss quality, and none endured for more than a few years before a legislature changed it. Considering the period before 1865, all three states began by regulating the harvest in specific locations, limiting and specifying the kinds of nets permitted. Early legislation often contained antipollution clauses, such as a ban on the dumping of sawmill refuse, offal, lime, or other deleterious substances. Frequently there appeared in the laws the idea of making sure that fish had access to rivers and streams emptying into the lakes. Wisconsin and Michigan experimented with statutes requiring nets to be registered or pound-net-fishing locations to be plainly marked and registered with the county recorder of deeds.[14] All three states left the enforcement of their laws up to local authorities.

The character of legislation began to change in 1865, first in Michigan. Legislators passed a law that would apply to fish in all state waters, with very specific protections for whitefish, the principal commercial species, which had been fished heavily for about a quarter century, and for speckled trout, the sportsman's delight, which had declined notably in inland lakes, rivers, and streams. The law prescribed the mesh sizes of pound and trap nets that were used to catch whitefish and required fishermen to return spawn to lake waters, but said nothing about gill nets. To the county boards of supervisors went the enforcement and regulatory power for fishing with pound and trap nets and the responsibility for charging nonresidents a $50 fee for a fishing license. For all intents and purposes, the law was a dead letter. In 1873, the Michigan legislature passed the first fishing law that specifically mentioned the Great Lakes, exempting them from regulation and thus making laissez faire the official policy and allowing the expansion of the commercial-fishing interests operating in the lakes. The Wisconsin legislature passed its first law applying to all its Great Lakes waters in 1879, and Ohio did so in 1880.[15]

STATE AND FEDERAL COOPERATION

During the 1870s and 1880s, the issue of conserving the Great Lakes fisheries cut a much larger swath in the legislative and administrative records of Ohio, Michigan, and Wisconsin than it had earlier in the century. The national government helped focus the attention of state policy makers on the need to preserve the fisheries for long-term use, due in large measure to the influence of the United States Commission of Fish and Fisheries, which was established in 1871 and ably headed by Spencer F. Baird. In the years after 1871, Ohio, Michigan, Wisconsin, and the other Great Lakes states generally cooperated with the commission, following a whole range of ideas that Baird and his successors suggested, especially those relating to artificial propagation and stocking programs and the experimental introduction of nonnative species.[16]

In 1871, Baird assigned biologist James W. Milner of Waukegan, Illinois, "an earnest, patient, and able investigator," the task of studying the fisheries of the Great Lakes. Milner laid the foundation for the propagation and planting program and called for legislation to protect young fish, particularly the regulation of mesh size in pound nets, and to prevent fishermen from throwing fish offal and sawmills from dumping sawdust into fishing waters. When it came to closed seasons on the lakes, he was very guarded and even somewhat ambivalent. He considered the first priority, propagation and restocking, to be a positive, restorative program, whereas regulation at its best could do no more than maintain the status quo.[17]

In the course of his fieldwork and data collection in 1871 and 1872, Milner brought his findings and ideas about the measures the states could adopt to preserve the resource to the attention of state leaders, recommending the establishment of state fishery commissions to cooperate with the Commission of Fish and Fisheries and calling for state propagation and planting programs, a panacea for the decline in the Great Lakes fish population, which already had become apparent. He was very specific about the decline in the whitefish population, suggesting that it had been noticeable in the 1860s. The states followed Milner's advice and appointed fishery commissions.[18]

In the long run, the hatchery and stocking programs, funded from state coffers with minimal federal support, turned out to be the most successful part of the efforts of the state fishery commissions (figure 11.1). They relied on the Commission of Fish and Fisheries for technical

Figure 11.1. At the federal hatchery in Northville, Michigan, workers (*top*) select and strip ripe trout and (*bottom*) monitor hatching boxes and pick eggs, a task often done by women because of their small and nimble fingers. (From [*top*] U.S. Commission of Fish and Fisheries, *Report,* 1896, 55th Cong., 1st sess., 1897, H. Doc. 32 [Serial 3572], facing 55; [*bottom*] U.S. Commission of Fish and Fisheries, *Report,* 1897, 55th Cong., 2d sess., 1897, H. Doc. 299 [Serial 3687], facing 97)

information and free distribution of fish eggs of experimental species for the breeding programs. State legislatures, impressed with the success of similar programs elsewhere, appropriated larger and larger sums to build more hatcheries, employ more workers, and plant more fry. Through coordinated federal and state efforts, literally hundreds of millions of eggs were hatched and the fry planted in the Great Lakes before 1900. By the 1890s, the fishery commissions of Michigan and Wisconsin secured special railroad cars to carry fry from hatchery to planting sites. Because of the work with game fish, they convinced the railroads to give them special favors for the distribution program and their work generally. With no stretch of the truth, they argued that well-stocked streams for sportfishermen were lures to vacation and summer travel by rail.

The sport-fish component of the programs of state fishery commissions especially appealed to legislators. Many of them and their most influential constituents were devoted to rod and reel. Moreover, sportfishing brought enormous sums into the state economy, noted the Wisconsin Commissioners of Fisheries as early as 1881, and by 1888, they were touting Wisconsin as "A Summer Paradise" for sportsmen, due in no small measure to stream-stocking programs. Probably, argued the commissioners, these programs earned as much for the state as did its resident Great Lakes commercial fishermen. Similarly, the Michigan State Board of Fish Commissioners, in its biennial report of 1888, spoke of the growing importance of sportfishermen: "The summer pleasure seeker belongs to that portion of the community which has money and spends it freely, and as a consequence a large amount of money is left each summer by this class in our State." These visitors had exerted a great influence on the development of the Grand Traverse region and elsewhere.[19]

The establishment of the state fishery commissions in 1873 marked the beginning of a long and increasingly more complex relationship between the state and federal governments in matters relating to the fisheries of the Great Lakes. The states relied on the Commission of Fish and Fisheries for studies of the status of the fisheries, and three were undertaken: in 1879, 1885, and 1891 to 1892. In Detroit in 1883, at a meeting of fish commissioners of states bordering the Great Lakes held to consider better protection for lake fish, representatives from Michigan, Minnesota, and Ohio endorsed the group's resolution, which called for the Commission of Fish and Fisheries to make a careful study of the Great Lakes fishing industry. What they wanted was very specific. They asked the commission "to send one of its steamers with a sufficient force of scientific men to the Great Lakes, for the purpose of investigating the habits of the fish natural to those waters, the method of fishing pursued therein, and all other matters connected with the fishing industries." The states made similar requests for biological surveys in 1888 and 1891.[20] The Commission of Fish and Fisheries did not undertake these studies, but continued to concentrate on ocean fisheries.

The states succeeded to some degree in convincing Washington to establish hatcheries on their lakeshores. By June 1890, four federal stations were operating on the Great Lakes—one in Sandusky, Ohio; one each in Northville and Alpena, Michigan; and one in Duluth, Minnesota—producing tens of millions of fry for planting. Ohio was in the process of acquiring an additional station in Put-in-Bay. In the mid-1890s, construction began on the next Great Lakes federal station in Cape Vincent, New York, at the juncture of Lake Ontario and the St. Lawrence River.[21] Ever watchful for ways to get federal help, the state commissions promoted a whole series of ideas suitable for federal funding. For example, the Michigan State Board of Fish Commissioners, soon after the passage in 1887 of the Hatch Act, which established agricultural experiment stations at land-grant colleges, promoted the idea of state, university and college, and federal cooperation to address the problems of the Great Lakes fisheries. If agriculture merited federal assistance of that nature, why not the fishing industry? The Great Lakes states sought a subsidy to keep the commercial fishery viable, but at the same time their requests contained a clear message about the conservation of a natural resource, an appeal to help them achieve the goal of sustaining the fish population for long-term use. Occasionally, state legislatures or fish commissions suggested that the federal government establish and enforce regulations for the Great Lakes fisheries, but such ideas had no widespread support.[22] Rather, the states jealously guarded their rights to make the rules for their Great Lakes waters and enforce them. Their desire for federal assistance in no way sanctioned federal control.

In 1892, when the decline in yields from the Great Lakes had reached critical proportions according to fishermen, dealers, and fishery policy makers alike, an international conference on the state of fisheries held in Detroit, with representatives present from Canada, Ontario, Maine, New York, Ohio, Michigan, Minnesota, and the Commission of Fish and Fisheries, endorsed the competence of states to protect fish and game. In the same year, the American Fisheries Society, at its annual meeting, went on record in favor of state jurisdiction and regulation.[23]

BEYOND THE HATCHERY-STOCKING PROGRAM

The state fishery commissions gradually assumed many functions beyond the central hatchery-stocking program. In the face of an escalation in commercial fishing in the 1880s and perceived threats to the fish population, they drafted regulatory measures and worked with state legislative committees to secure their enactment. They felt that both regulation and stocking were essential to save the fish. Seemingly with little effect on public opinion, they warned repeatedly in strong language about the threats to the resource from overfishing, waste, and pollution, a theme that appears in the earliest reports and continues throughout the balance of the century. In the 1880s, they called for fish wardens with authority to enforce the laws and for penalties to deter lawbreakers. The commissions promoted the idea that interstate cooperation was necessary to protect the resource. They advocated involving the educational expertise of their state universities in the struggle to save the fish.

The Wisconsin Commissioners of Fisheries argued in their second report, released in 1875, that commercial fishing deserved a place in the curriculum of the University of Wisconsin as a branch of agriculture. They appealed to state pride: "Four of the universities of Virginia have added fish-culture as a branch of university-education, and other States, no doubt, will soon follow her example. Wisconsin, in this matter, ought not to be behind her sister States." Three years later, they returned to the subject, arguing more strongly for the scientific study of the habits of fish. Study could provide a "wonderful mine of useful information." In 1888, the commission began enlisting the help of Professor Edward A. Birge, an eminent zoologist, first to investigate a fish disease problem and then to study the fish of the lakes of northern Wisconsin. In 1895, he became an ex-officio member of the commission by legislative action.[24]

In May 1888, Herschel Whitaker, a member of the Michigan State Board of Fish Commissioners, strongly recommended cooperation with state educational institutions to improve the quality of the artificial-propagation program, and the commission received funds for biological research from 1889 to1896. The Ohio Fish and Game Commission reported in 1895 that Ohio State University had agreed to expand the state hatchery in Sandusky in order to study parasites and insect life in state waters and to foot the bill for improved facilities.[25] The members of these commissions—political appointees, most often lawyers and bankers by profession, and sportfishers by avocation—acted as protectors of the fish resource for the executive branch of government in a variety of ways. Their reports leave the reader with the impression that they were sincerely dedicated to saving the fish of the Great Lakes, but that they floundered and failed for a number of reasons. Hampered by the popular idea that the fish belonged to the people, free for the taking, they ventured into a difficult policy-making area: preservation of natural resources, then in its infancy. They had very limited knowledge about the distribution, eating habits, and life cycles of most Great Lakes species. They felt handicapped by the tremendous variations in the habitats of the lake fish and the physical configurations of the lakes, which made regulations hard to frame and even harder to enforce. They heartily endorsed hatchery and planting work to bolster the fish population, a program popular with fishermen, dealers, and sportsmen.

FISHERY COMMISSIONS AND THE FISHING INDUSTRY

State fishery commissioners found their advisory role for regulation difficult to carry out. Sportfishers generally supported restrictive fishing laws. The commercial-fishing industry opposed them or at least attempted to shape them to maximize marketable yields and income. The fishermen and dealers engaged in many a battle with the fish commissions over regulations designed to conserve the resource. They feared that restrictions on the harvest would make their investments in fishing gear worthless and ruin their occupations—and with good reason. Regulations could not be enforced equitably. Those who obeyed the law lost in the economic contest to those who broke it and reaped larger harvests. Regulations handicapped the fishers in an aggressive, highly competitive, and overcrowded business in which open fishing rewarded the most efficient with the biggest catch. Fishermen knew that this scramble to fill the nets depleted the resource, but a large group of them, part-time and temporary fishers, did not worry. Many long-term fishers did, but felt powerless to prevent destructive fishing. The pressures of low prices for fish and increasing costs for boats and fishing gear encouraged the taking of a maximum catch. Moreover, the dealer system of organization in the industry fostered overfishing. Thus organizing to oppose or to control regulation made more sense than organizing to ensure long-term yields.

Opposition to regulation came from many quarters in the industry, from large powerful dealers to associations of fishermen, including those with many levels of investment at stake, and individual fishermen whose stake in the business was very modest, but highly important because it meant a living for them and their families. Those engaged in the commercial-fishing industry knew the political process and used it to prevent the enactment of restrictions that they believed would hurt income. They contacted their representatives in state legislatures, wrote to governors, held public meetings to talk over their problems and adopt resolutions, testified before legislative committees, criticized state fish commissions, aired their views in the press, and generally made their wishes known in no uncertain terms. The commissions always worked in a partisan political environment, often finding their best judgment about how to maintain the fish population challenged and cast aside. Because they recommended legislation to conserve the fish and for some years had the responsibility for supervising the enforcement of fishery regulations, the commissions and the fishermen often assumed a sharply adversarial relationship. A paper trail of their conflicts runs through state statutes, fishery commission reports, newspaper articles and editorials, and unpublished state and federal archives, revealing many examples of commercial dominance over legislation.[26]

A careful study of the efforts of the commercial-fishing industry to shape policy in Wisconsin, Michigan, and Ohio revealed that the conflict followed distinctly different scenarios in the three states. In Wisconsin, it unfolded as a generally low-key, often subtle battle, somewhat obscured and occasionally erupting dramatically at the local level. The Commissioners of Fisheries tried to act with restraint and satisfy all participants. In Michigan, the commercial fishermen and dealers organized an association and took on the Board of Fish Commissioners in a noisy brawl in the legislature and the press, wielding sufficient influence to prevent restraints on their businesses. In their frustration, the fish commissioners warned, blamed, scolded, and bemoaned the devastation to the fish population, but admitted that they were powerless to stop it. In Ohio, two large and powerful groups of fishermen utterly opposed to each other in regulatory matters battled in and out of the legislature, while the Ohio Fish and Game Commission helplessly pleaded for the good sense of conserving the fish. In each of the three states, the advocates of regulation to conserve the resource lost the battle.

The experience in Ohio serves as an example. In Ohio, the battle of gill-net versus pound-net fishermen dominated the efforts of the Fish and Game Commission to promote protective measures. The two very powerful groups fought each other to a draw, producing a regulatory vacuum. Ohio possessed the most productive waters of the Great Lakes, along the southern shore of Lake Erie, a veritable cornucopia of whitefish, sturgeon, and herring, to mention only the most popular commercial fish. The western end of the lake, with its many islands and shallow fertile waters, was a nursery for numerous varieties of fish. It was also a physically perfect setting for pound nets. Fishermen set them in tentacle- and web-like patterns from the shores of Maumee Bay, around the islands, and east almost to Cleveland. In 1885, here was found the largest concentration of pounds in the Great Lakes (see figure 7.1). Some of them, reported the Chief Fish and Game Warden of Ohio in 1888, extended into the lake for as much as seven and eight miles and contained a series of pounds one after another. The eastern end of Lake Erie, though, was much deeper and less of a spawning and feeding area, dominated by gill-net fishermen who traveled for many miles in pursuit of the catch and who, in the 1880s, followed the migration of fish to the western spawning grounds each fall with their gill-net steamers. Cleveland was the market center for gill-net fishing in Ohio, the location of the largest dealers, who dominated fishing in the waters of eastern Lake Erie. Toledo and Sandusky were the market centers for pound-net fishing, where another group of well-to-do fish merchants dominated the lives of pound-net fishers.

The very geography of Lake Erie, its wide variety of fish species, and the richness of the harvests made it extremely difficult to regulate, as did its fish-dealer entrepreneurs. Fifty-three of them handled the $1.8 million worth of fishing products from the American waters of the lake in 1885. Forty of these were Ohio companies, accounting for $1,024,443 of the total. The eleven firms in Sandusky alone claimed $662,300 worth of fish products. In 1885, Sandusky was said to be "the largest market for fresh-water fish in the world."[27]

When in 1873 the Ohio legislature established the three-member Fish Commission and charged it with the task of studying the condition of the fish population in Ohio waters, discovering ways to make the state's waters more productive, and investigating the status of artificial propagation, the appointees promptly assessed the causes for the decline in the supply of fish, citing pound nets, which destroyed young fish, as one. They also blamed public attitudes that made any regulation very difficult: "It does not accord with the prevalent ideas of humanity to imprison a person for obtaining food from 'nature's preserve,' especially when that 'preserve' is not private property." They returned to the same theme in 1881, claiming that in general people "do not look upon a man who violates the game and fish laws, be he shooter, seiner, or dealer, as they would upon any other criminal."[28] The Ohio legislature did little to regulate fishing in Lake Erie until 1880, when the pound-net fishery, which had developed extensively in the preceding two decades, was well established as the most productive fishery on the lake. Then a regulatory law that was plainly advantageous to the pound-net interests and punitive for gill-net fishers went on the statute books.[29]

When the Fish Commission and the industry leaders revised the law in 1883, a compromise of sorts between gill-net and pound-net interests rid it of the ban on fishing in the autumn spawning season, prohibited fishing at any time near islands, in bays and shoals, and on reefs, but left the responsibility of enforcement with the commission but without a budget to do so. Initially endorsed by large Lake Erie fishing interests as essential to prevent their financial ruin, the statute quickly became a dead letter, a victim of competition among dealers. Complained the commissioners, "[S]ome of the richest of the dealers . . . sought to get the better of their brother-dealers by encouraging illegal fishing—*providing the fish were brought to them for sale*."[30]

During the next decade, the main components of regulation were a closed summer season, bans on fishing in parts of Lake Erie as defined in the law of 1883, a limitation on the use of gill nets to waters over thirty feet deep, and a requirement that gill nets be set a specific distance from shore and from pound nets. The legislature did not restrict mesh sizes for any nets, nor did it specify rules for pound netters. But it did respond to the continual call from the Fish Commission for better enforcement. In 1886, it established the Fish and Game Commission and put in place a system of county wardens who were dependent on the payment of fines for having violated the law to reward their enforcement efforts, which in effect meant that they received almost no compensation. In 1887, for example, the Fish and Game Commission reported eighty-six convictions and a total in fines of $862 in fifty-six counties. Two years later, it provided for a state warden and a special warden for Lake Erie, where fishermen's violations of the law created more than one-third of the commission's total expenses. When in December 1888 the chief warden reported on the first year of his activities, he described his problems with Lake Erie fishermen. Upon fishermen's complaints, he had been arrested for seizure of their nets, tried for "grand larceny," and acquitted, only to be rearrested for "malicious destruction of property" and again acquitted. According to the commission's report, "The fishermen then sued for the full value of the nets. The case is now pending." A similar incident occurred in Cleveland in 1895.[31]

Hamstrung in writing regulatory laws by pressure from the fishing industry and defied in enforcing them, the Fish and Game Commission in 1888 began advocating another system of control: surveying and platting the fishing grounds and then leasing them to the highest bidders for a period of years. The leaseholders would operate them under bond "for the careful observance of laws for the fullest protection of the fish." The commission proposed to tax pound and trap nets to pay for the survey. "Leading fishermen" reportedly liked the leasing idea, which they hoped would put an end to competitive overcrowding of pound-net locations. How they felt about the tax on nets remained to be seen. In the spring of 1889, the Ohio legislature provided funds for the survey of the Lake Erie fishing grounds and established a tax rate for using fishing nets of all types in the lake. Contested by fishermen, the law was declared unconstitutional and was repealed one year later.[32]

In its annual report of 1894, the Fish and Game Commission laid before Governor William McKinley a concise one-page summary of the very real fishery problem in Lake Erie. It noted that this most valuable of all Ohio fisheries languished after a period of annual growth from 1882 to 1890. Since 1891, the most valuable species in the commercial catch had been declining. The commission had tried to sustain the yields by advocating laws that would protect the fish during spawning seasons, noted the commissioners, "but as regularly as the General Assembly convened, the fishermen and dealers from one end of the lake to the other, tried to defeat any and all bills offered or recommended by the Commission." Why? They did it because the fishing seasons in the eastern and western ends of the lake differed. What suited the gill-net fishermen of the east was not acceptable to the pound netters of the west. The commissioners conceded that "a majority of those engaged in the industry have favored no law that would protect the fish." Pound-net and gill-net fishermen bitterly blamed each other for wasting the resource. The current law prohibiting all fishing on reefs, the favored spawning grounds, was unenforceable because "there is not a man in Ohio who could go before a jury and locate to a certainty a single reef in the lake." The commissioners reiterated their plea for an adequate survey of fishing grounds and a lease law. But their analysis and plea came in the depths of a depression, and no politician wanted to limit fishing in hard times with both fishermen and fishing enterprises struggling to survive.[33]

Once better times returned, though, the situation remained the same: hopeless disagreement among fishermen about regulation and strong resistance to enforcement of the laws that were on the books. In 1900, the Fish and Game Commission admitted its futile efforts over the years in words very similar to those sent to McKinley in 1894.[34]

Participants in the struggle in 1894 to revise fishery regulations confirmed the commission's assessment of the conflict between gillnetters and pound netters when they gave their testimony to field investigators for the Joint Commission Relative to the Preservation of the Fisheries in Waters Contiguous to Canada and the United States. The largest dealer on Lake Erie, A. J. Stoll, president of the Sandusky Fish Company, described the legislative process, noting that every time various dealers testified before the legislature, each favored a specific set of regulations. This system of testimony in itself was a mistake, according to Stoll. The Fish and Game Commission, not the legislature, should hear these presentations, and he inferred that the commissioners should weigh them and present a proposal to the legislature. In justifying his view, he noted that for ten years the same scenario had been repeated: "The ordinary legislator does not comprehend what is required, and you get them all mixed up and they do not know what they are talking about, and you get them worn out and wear yourself out trying to tell them something." The legislators had always ended up putting together a package that contained parts of the different proposals, hoping to give each faction something.[35]

A large fish dealer in Cleveland, E. R. Edson, made the most succinct statement of those interviewed by the investigators for the Joint Commission. He commented on the legislative impasse of the spring of 1894, characterizing it as part of a twenty-year battle: "It has been the west end against the east end." As a result, "the fish and the fishing industry have suffered through the quarrels of the large fishermen and the dealers, and there is no reason in trying to disguise it."[36]

Most caustic in its assessment of the squabble over a new fishing law in early 1894, the German-language *Demokrat,* published in Sandusky, brilliantly castigated the fishing industry for overfishing the resources of Lake Erie with a network of pounds at the western end and general sweeps of the lake with gill nets from east to west in the spawning season. While dealers and fishermen bickered over who was to blame, pound netters or gillnetters, the resource declined. Consumers were the greatest losers, "deprived of one of the cheapest and healthiest articles of food." As the editor acidly remarked, "[T]he trough is empty and the hogs are fighting. The sin which has been committed against nature is always revenged and so in this case." The factions were so contrary that regulation at the state level was hopeless, claimed the *Demokrat.* The national government should make the regulations.[37]

From across the lake in Canada came another reaction to the developments in Ohio in 1894. The Canadians were watching the fish dealers in Ohio squabble over the provisions of a new fishery law, and they had an eye on the legislators in Lansing, Michigan, as well. Deep concern about the fish population of Lake Erie and the disaffection of Canadian fishermen with dominion fishery policy compared with the "free system" across the water, during the depression years, were potential political dynamite. Government officials in Canada followed the developments in the newspapers, hoping for the enactment of fishery laws that would bring to Ohio waters regulations similar to Canadian rules and thus defuse Canadian fishermen's complaints about their unfair competitive position. They read and preserved in departmental files the reports in newspapers published in Sandusky and Cleveland and those in the *Fishing Gazette,* published in New York, relating to the struggle for a new law. Knowing full well the track record of the Great Lakes states in regulating fishing in the lakes, they never entertained high hopes for change. Thus when reform failed to materialize in early 1894, they were not surprised. In an editorial entitled "Too Much Freedom," the *Ottawa Citizen* reported the latest evidence of "shameful depletion of the Lake Erie fisheries on the American side," contrasting it with the "comparatively continued abundance of fish on the Canadian side of the lake, where close seasons are enforced, the fishing appliances regulated by law, and only fish of a certain size are permitted to be taken."[38]

During the late nineteenth century, the fishery commissions of Wisconsin, Michigan, and Ohio, in somewhat different ways, found their efforts to establish the principle of regulated harvests and sustained yields repeatedly thwarted by commercial fishers who discovered that organization and effective lobbying inside and outside state legislatures served their interests well. Experience at the state level put them in good stead to help defeat the implementation of the Treaty of 1908, which was designed to secure joint regulation of the Great Lakes fisheries by the United States and Canada. Soon they would arrive on Capitol Hill armed with fish and nets to demonstrate in congressional hearings just how right they were about proposed regulation.

Meanwhile, the antiregulatory stance of the commercial-fishing industry cast a strong negative influence over the state and provincial movement to achieve intergovernmental cooperation. State fish commissioners believed that truly effective control could come only from treating the Great Lakes as a geographic whole. Without the authority to do more than relate informally to Canada, they emphasized interstate cooperation to overcome part of the handicap of divided waters. The states could cooperate in promoting fish-hatching projects, exchanging information, undertaking scientific research, and developing uniform regulations for fishing. To accomplish this, the Great Lakes states and the province of Ontario called conference after conference to discuss their common needs. The record is remarkable and speaks to the dedication of those who took the trouble to attend the meetings and contribute their ideas to the deliberations. Such a conference convened in Detroit in October 1883, hosted by the Michigan Board of Fish Commissioners, and was followed the next year by a meeting in Milwaukee, hosted by the Wisconsin Commissioners of Fisheries, who regarded the meeting of commissioners from other states and fishermen as a forum for the discussion of Great Lakes fishing regulations. In 1891 and 1892, at the suggestion of the Ontario Board of Game and Fish Commissioners, concerned officials gathered first in New York City, then in Rochester, New York, and Hamilton, Ontario, and twice in Detroit over a period of fifteen months.[39] All these groups produced sets of recommendations that they hoped the delegates would take home and have their legislatures enact.

At that point, the reform effort hit the all-too-familiar obstacle, the inability to get legislative action because of the political pressure exerted by the commercial-fishing industry. Sir Charles Hibbert Tupper, the Canadian Minister of Marine and Fisheries from 1888 to 1895, put it succinctly when he told the House of Commons in 1896 that "the American fishermen have the whip-hand of their legislatures."[40] Thus interstate cooperation as a vehicle for saving the fish proved futile. The Great Lakes states, acting either unilaterally or collectively, could not implement the idea of sustained yield to ensure long-lasting benefit to more people.

It is easy to blame the commercial fishermen for the failure to consider the long-term well-being of the resource. But it should be remembered that when the commercial fishermen of the Great Lakes resisted regulation, they faced no opposition from the vast majority of Americans of the region in the late nineteenth century. Most people approved of the rapid exploitation of agricultural lands, the unregulated harvest of timber, and the uncontrolled scramble for iron and copper. The public endorsed the growth and development that massively transformed the landscape and revolutionized the habitat of the Great Lakes fish. That fish and game laws even went on the statute books is something of a tribute to the naturalists, formally and informally trained biologists, zoologists, sportsmen, and mixed band of early conservationists who recognized destruction at work and accurately predicted almost irreparable damage to the fish and wildlife populations. The fishery commissions of the Great Lakes states must be counted among them.

12

Changing Ideas

The United States and the Great Lakes Fishery

All Things Considered

The very nature of the federal system cast the American national government in an advisory, fact-finding, nonregulatory role for the fisheries of the American Great Lakes, but indirectly it influenced the thinking of regional fish conservationists on the issue of regulating commercial fishing and on the need for laws controlling the use of lakes, rivers, and streams in ways designed to protect the fish habitat. The federal government conducted extensive surveys of the status of the fisheries of the Great Lakes and scientific research projects that broadened the knowledge available to state policy makers. Federal influence began in 1871, when Congress established the Commission of Fish and Fisheries and Spencer F. Baird became head of the newly created agency.

Baird, an eminent zoologist and the secretary of the Smithsonian Institution, had more to do with the directions taken by the fishery policies of the Great Lakes states than did any other single individual. His growing interest in marine biology in the 1860s, sparked by his study of the work of European biologists and his observations of the fish and fisheries of the Atlantic coast, most particularly the decline of fish populations in the coastal waters frequented by Massachusetts fishermen, aroused his concern about the status of the fish resource generally. Baird was largely responsible for the creation of the Commission of Fish and Fisheries, which was charged with the responsibility of determining whether the fish of the coastal waters, rivers, and lakes had diminished and, if so, why and of recommending "what protective, prohibitory, or precautionary measures should be adopted."[1]

Baird tackled his duties with the deep dedication and intellectual curiosity characteristic of his career. From 1871 until his death in 1887, he directed the work of the commission, shaping its philosophy and policies and successfully appealing to Congress for appropriations. Among his wide-ranging interests, which were strongly oriented toward ocean research, his support for the idea of restoring dwindling fish populations by means of artificial propagation and stocking, popular among advocates for preserving marine life, greatly influenced the fishery policies of the Great Lakes states.

Under Baird's leadership, the commission's annual activity reports assumed broad dimensions, bringing to their readers articles on research done internationally, reports about the impact of water pollution on fish life, Baird's analysis of the causes for declines in the fish population of the United States, the thinking of fishery experts on regulation, statements about the importance of fish as a food source in various nations, along with much information on fish propagation. In 1881, the commission began its annual publication of the *Bulletin,* designed "largely for the benefit of commercial fishermen." It included observations and research findings, which, along with the annual reports and the results of special federal surveys of the Great Lakes commercial-fishing industry, went to state commissions.[2]

Between 1871 and 1892, the Commission of Fish and Fisheries modified its official position on management policy for the Great Lakes fish population, shifting from a heavy emphasis on restocking the waters to a more balanced approach recognizing an essential role for regulatory legislation and sponsorship of scientific research programs. Change came gradually and quite pragmatically as evidence mounted that propagation and stocking programs did not sustain the fish populations in the lakes. The state fishery commissions, hamstrung by commercial-fishing interests, contributed to the federal commission's changing position on the need for both regulation and scientific research. As the regional and national components of the partnership interacted, they educated each other.

Reports published by the commission reveal how its position on artificial stocking and regulation evolved from 1871 to 1892. James W. Milner and Spencer Baird clearly expressed the official position in the 1870s on the best ways to replenish declining fish populations. In preparing a report on the status of the Great Lakes fisheries for the newly created commission in 1871 and 1872, Milner observed, "The experience of the past, both in Europe and the older portions of our country, indicates the inadequacy of protective legislation in preventing the decrease and extermination of the food-fishes." He believed that certain kinds of laws could slow down destruction, but that the real restorative hope lay in artificial propagation. He disapproved thoroughly of Canadian policy for the Great Lakes: "The Canadian laws are sweeping and stringent in character. By exacting license-fees from the fishermen they control the extent of fishing in all localities, and limit the number of nets to each mile of the shore in accordance with the judgment of the fishery-officers. Their system of laws and policing the whole extent of shores is an expensive and cumbersome method of protecting the fishes." Canada would have done better to spend enforcement dollars on artificial culture and planting.[3]

In 1878, Baird made his position on regulation clear in a paper entitled "Human Agencies as Affecting the Fish Supply, and the Relation of Fish Culture to the American Fisheries." Following the thinking of his mentor, George Perkins Marsh, he noted the adverse impact of the western European development of North America on fish and game. Speaking largely in terms of the eastern seacoast, he advocated regulations as part of the formula for restoring fish populations to once productive rivers. Fish ladders to help spawning fish navigate around dam barriers should be legally required. The discharge into waterways of sawdust, gas refuse, chemicals, and other contaminants that adversely affect fish had to be stopped. "The pounds, number, and size of mesh of nets" should be regulated. Certain days of the week should be designated as nonfishing days. Legislatures had to place "an absolute prohibition" on fishing after a specified date.[4]

Yet Baird soon learned that laws such as these to bolster restocking efforts faced opposition in state legislatures, where political and economic considerations shaped policy. He hoped to influence state fishery commissions sufficiently to have them implement his ideas, thus securing uniform policy from state to state, but given their very limited influence he could not succeed. Nor did his advocacy of federal legislation to regulate both sea and inland fisheries produce results, except for the waters of the Potomac River within the District of Columbia and for the construction of a fishway on the Potomac at Great Falls, between Maryland and Virginia.[5]

Given the constitutional restraints on the federal government that prevented the enactment of uniform national fishery regulations, Baird saw the opportunity for leadership in the areas of fostering fish propagation and planting and of undertaking research to identify and broaden knowledge about the varied fish species. The research efforts were truly impressive, employing the most eminent and well-trained zoologists to be found in American academic institutions. The commission's research program initially was heavily oriented to the Atlantic coastal fisheries, with work headquartered at Wood's Hole, Massachusetts, and then broadened to include the deep-sea and Pacific coastal fisheries. Baird believed that it should encompass the Great Lakes and interior waters as well.[6] In part because of state pressures, the federal commission sanctioned some work on the Great Lakes before Baird's death in 1887, but it was a very minor part of its research effort. Not until the deterioration in the populations of commercial-fish species became unmistakable did the Great Lakes figure more prominently in the commission's basic scientific research programs, seeking to identify and catalog species; to analyze food sources, life cycles, and habits of the various species; and, at the turn of the century, to begin a biological survey.

Meanwhile, the Commission of Fish and Fisheries monitored the fisheries of the Great Lakes, reporting on their status from time to time. Conceived as profiles of the commercial-fishing industry, the studies concentrated on the technology and statistics of production as a gauge of how well the stocking programs sustained the fish population. Incidentally they included a substantial amount of information about the industry's economic structure, the ethnic backgrounds and social classes of fishermen and dealers, and the impact of pollution on fish life. The commission also followed with deep interest the hatchery and stocking work for the Great Lakes undertaken by Samuel Wilmot in Ontario and by the Great Lakes states, encouraging it and constructively cooperating with it. It gave the Great Lakes state fishery commissions 237 million whitefish and perch eggs between 1880 and 1890.[7] Their hatchery superintendents issued glowing reports of success inspired by Baird's leadership.

Yet the commission's reports repeatedly showed that all was not well with the Great Lakes fish population. Evidence suggests both real differences of opinion among the commission staff and a failure to report to the public and to evaluate the findings of its on-site surveys critically and systematically. Milner had sounded the first official alarm over extremely wasteful fishing practices, water pollution, and the declining whitefish population. The commission's next publication to reveal problems in the fisheries of the Great Lakes came in 1875, when E. W. Nelson recorded his findings on the fish populations in the Chicago area, calling attention to pollution of the waters. Anyone who carefully read the findings of Ludwig Kumlien, as elaborated by Frederick W. True, for the report co-published by the Commission of Fish and Fisheries and the Bureau of the Census on the status of Great Lakes fisheries in 1879 could spot the red warning flags about declining whitefish populations, pollution, wasteful fishing, and enhanced harvesting technology posted throughout.[8]

Spencer Baird responded to the documented whitefish decline and to pressure for help from the congressional delegations of the Great Lakes states by advocating federal control of the hatchery in Northville, Michigan. The plan became reality in August 1880, when Northville became the first federal hatchery on the Great Lakes. Originally a private business established by N. W. Clark, the hatchery had supplied the commission with whitefish eggs since 1874. Expanded production there and the creation in 1882 of a second hatchery in Alpena, Michigan, followed. Two years later, Baird succeeded in getting Congress to authorize the lease of War Department land at Sault Sainte Marie to the Michigan Board of Fish Commissioners for hatchery development.[9] The commission continued to press for more federal hatchery facilities in the following years.

In one of the commission's rare Jeremiah-like assessments, Charles W. Smiley, a member of its scientific staff, reviewed Milner's and Kumlien's findings for the newly created Fish Commission *Bulletin* in 1881. He concluded that—given the increased catch, the nearly 500 percent improvement in the effectiveness of "the apparatus of capture" during the 1870s, the decline in the average size of trout and whitefish, the exhaustion of a number of fishing grounds revealed by meticulous study of the evidence, and the fishermen's continued pressure to catch as many fish as possible—"it cannot be denied that a crisis has been reached such as seriously to alarm all who are interested in these lake fisheries." Smiley believed that "in the natural order of events, remarkable diminution, if not complete collapse is to be anticipated in the coming decade." He advocated regulation of mesh sizes and legislation to prevent water pollution in addition to artificial propagation.[10]

While this evaluation painted a grim picture, the annual reports for the next few years showed the commission still very enthusiastic about the success of hatchery and stocking programs. Positive results with Great Lakes whitefish, Pacific coast salmon, and East Coast shad, noted the report in 1884, seemed to indicate substantial progress in stemming the tide of decline.[11]

In 1885, the Commission of Fish and Fisheries embarked on a very extensive survey of the fisheries along the American shores of the Great Lakes, a grand sweep, to determine "more definitely the present condition of the fisheries" and to record "any important changes that have occurred in the locality of methods of the fisheries since the census of 1880." The Department of State needed the data for upcoming negotiations with Great Britain. The survey apparently was also the response to the request of Minnesota, Wisconsin, Michigan, and Ohio for a thoroughgoing scientific study of the habits of fish and methods of harvest. Investigators made the survey between August and early November, visiting each community, describing it, and gathering data from fishermen on the kinds and value of apparatus, boats, steamers, sailing vessels, the number of persons employed, the catch by species, the location of pound nets, and important fishing sites. By the time Baird wrote his annual report for 1885, the investigators could give a general impression of what they had found. They reported a very noticeable growth in the commercial-fishing industry. Those who tended the nets thought that the catch had markedly increased in locations where large numbers of fry had been planted.[12]

The detailed results, when compiled and published in 1887, differed from the first impressions in this most elaborate of all the reports on the Great Lakes fisheries released by the Commission of Fish and Fisheries in the nineteenth century. The report emphasized geographic, historical, commercial, and economic dimensions, with "less consideration . . . to natural history and the various scientific problems connected with the fisheries," noted the introduction.[13] There also Hugh M. Smith and Merwin-Marie Snell, the compilers, emphasized growth and large production totals. They did not bring up front for the readers' attention the troublesome findings, which were buried in the report. A careful sifting of the massive detail about fishing from station to station around the American shores leads to the conclusion that the combination of unregulated, aggressive fishing and water pollution had created serious inroads into the fish population in Lakes Michigan, Huron, and Ontario by 1885. The fishermen who reported declines, particularly in the whitefish population, far outnumbered those who gave rave reviews of the benefits of artificial stocking.

In the southern portion of Lake Michigan, the whitefish population was markedly down, and fishermen reported declines in the lumbering region of the north, attributing the trouble to sawdust and mill refuse. Fishermen who worked on Lake Huron cited overfishing and lumbering as the causes for the scarcity of whitefish. Investigators along the southern shore of Lake Ontario found many commercial fishermen who had turned to guiding the growing number of vacationing sportsmen and to farming as sources of income. For want of a harvest, commercial-fish shanties stood unused. Production totals for the lake were down in poundage and value compared with those in 1880. Lake Superior, a relatively new field for intensive commercial fishing, produced few complaints except for L'Anse Bay at the base of the Keweenaw Peninsula, on the Upper Peninsula of Michigan, from where whitefish apparently had fled because of pollution from lumbering.[14] Reports on Lake Erie abounded in superlatives about high production, with virtually no complaints about declines. They cited the very positive judgment of Frank N. Clark, superintendent of the hatchery in Northville, Michigan, about the effects of stocking the waters.

Whether the Commission of Fish and Fisheries should have presented a better balanced and more systematic analysis of the findings for public consumption is a question secondary in importance to the fact that with these findings at hand, it continued to endorse restocking as the way to sustain the fish population on the assumption that not enough artificial planting had been done in the Great Lakes and thus it was too early to make a judgment about the program's effectiveness.

Two studies by the commission, both indicative of fishery problems, preceded its announcement in 1892 calling for regulation to help maintain the resource: the surveys of Lake Erie by Seymour Bower and the report on Lake Ontario by Hugh M. Smith. Given the repeated appeals for federal assistance by the Ohio Fish and Game Commission, the Commission of Fish and Fisheries twice sent Seymour Bower to inspect the Lake Erie fisheries and report his findings, which were summarized in the annual report of 1892. He noted that he was not surprised to find that fishing had declined there because the lake was "so thoroughly, persistently, and exhaustively canvassed." It was within the power of humans to completely deplete the lake of fish, he noted gloomily. Wasteful fishing and the harvest of small fish defeated the efforts of hatcheries to restock the waters. Regulations were definitely needed, but the state of Ohio could not succeed in legislating given the divided local and sectional interests and the war between pound-net and gill-net fishermen. Bower despaired of improvement, concluding that the division of Lake Erie by "arbitrary and intangible lines" should be abolished: "Rational and effective measures must be based on the fact that in its water life the lake is a unit."[15]

Smith prepared the report on the fisheries of Lake Ontario before undertaking the general report for all the lakes. A high level of interest in the dismal fish yields there, he noted, had created an unusually vigorous agitation by fish and game clubs and by economic and trade organizations. The press widely reported their views. Conferences attended by Canadians and Americans pondered the problem. New York had revised its laws to protect the fish in its water more effectively, and Congress had appropriated funds for the establishment of a fish hatchery in Cape Vincent, New York.[16]

Obviously the political heat was on when Smith began to write the report in 1891. Rapidly compiled from the commission's material at hand, the report described the physical characteristics of Lake Ontario; cited employment, capital investment, and yields of the fisheries in 1890; compared yields in 1880 and 1890; and gave an account of the Canadian import trade. A lengthy description of the commercial-fish species followed, including an extended note on the disappearance of the Atlantic salmon from the lake and another on alewives, the intruders that were considered to be a serious nuisance. Smith advocated propagation and stocking to improve the fish population. The American waters of Lake Ontario had received the least help by means of artificial propagation, but had received a very strong dose of restrictive legislation designed primarily to aid sportfishing. He thought that rules and "prohibitory" measures had been in effect long enough to tell whether they would increase the catch. They had failed to do so. He cited with pride the past policy of the Commission of Fish and Fisheries of emphasizing artificial propagation, "positive methods," thus reducing the need for prohibitive laws. He believed that the Lake Ontario case proved the point. He did not consider the possible impact of pollution or question whether the food supply for the fish was adequate.[17]

When the report of the major survey of the Great Lakes conducted in 1891 and 1892 was released by the Commission of Fish and Fisheries, Smith had abandoned the emphasis on propagation and stocking so noticeable in his report on Lake Ontario. The tone of this report was in stark contrast to the general and unwarranted optimism of the survey of 1885, of which he was co-author. Stated Smith, "Up to within a comparatively short time no serious or apparently permanent diminution in the general supply had been observed. Even at the present time the output is wonderfully well maintained, all things considered."[18] While he did not mention it, yields from American waters had dropped by 3 million pounds between 1889 and 1890, and in 1892 stood very close to the 1890 total. Worse was yet to come, for in 1893 they declined by another 17 million pounds.

The production break was at hand. Sensing this, Smith cautioned that overfishing in the Great Lakes demanded attention: "In looking . . . for the continued increase and prosperity of the lakes fisheries, the necessity for rational regulations in certain lines must be recognized." He cited, in particular, conditions in Lakes Erie and Ontario. Total yields in Erie had been larger than ever in 1890, but a larger amount of apparatus and a larger proportion of cheaper species of fish in the catch accounted for that result: "Even a very marked increase in the quality of fishing apparatus has not been able to keep up the supply of the whitefish, sturgeon, and pike perches." As for Lake Ontario, the decline in commercial fishing there made its waters unimportant to the production figures for the Great Lakes. Whitefish and trout had diminished during the 1880s in a manner "unparalleled in the history of the lake fisheries."[19] Smith did not abandon the commission's dedication to artificial propagation. But he did acknowledge that the program had not sustained the Great Lakes fish population. Both regulation and propagation were absolutely necessary.

Whatever had happened to the 643 million whitefish, trout, and perch fry planted by the Commission of Fish and Fisheries in lake waters between 1876 and 1891?[20] Many believed that they had survived and grown, but that many had been caught in small-mesh nets before they had reached maturity. Others thought that the fry had been eaten by fish or had died from shock when planted. Some fishery experts felt that the plantings had not been large enough.

The United States Fish and Fisheries Commission in 1892 accepted as key elements in management policy what had been the Canadian formula since the 1860s: regulation, licensing, and enforcement, on the one hand, and propagation and stocking, on the other. Interstate cooperation, which Spencer Baird had fostered as a method to achieve uniform regulation, had failed. The reasonable solution seemed to be international cooperation between the United States and Canada. The United States had to use its treaty-making power to foster a joint regulatory role with its northern neighbor. The Canadians had long since been ready to cooperate, a goal of management set forth very early in the history of the Department of Marine and Fisheries.

13

Canada's Regulated Fishery 1868–1888

There Never Was a People under the Sun So Utterly Reckless and Careless

In marked contrast to the primary emphasis on stocking and minimal regulation in the American waters of the Great Lakes, the Dominion of Canada, under the leadership of the Conservative Party, adopted a watchful, protective policy for its Great Lakes fish resource. Canada adhered closely to British colonial models. The Americans opted for unfettered exploitation. The Canadian system of regulation and enforcement, adopted in 1868, drew more and more favorable comments from conservation-minded American observers in the two succeeding decades, but American fishermen found it irritating because it hampered their ability to fish in Canadian waters. In other areas of fishery policy—for example, the importance of artificial propagation and stocking as a way to sustain the fish population—the two nations agreed. They cooperated in that work, exchanging information and sharing experimental quantities of eggs and fry, and in broader research designed to expand the body of knowledge about fish species and their habitat, mirroring a larger general international exchange of information among fishery experts.

Until the end of the nineteenth century, the Canadian fishery policy for the Great Lakes operated at a distinct advantage over the American. The founders of the dominion placed the regulation of the fisheries under the control of the central government, a decision made in light of friction generated by American fishermen operating in the bountiful waters off the Maritime Provinces.[1] Thus one government took responsibility for Great Lakes waters instead of eight states and one federal commission.

THE FISHERY LAW OF 1868

The "Act for the regulation of Fishing and protection of Fisheries" passed in the first session of the first parliament of the Dominion of Canada. It was a general statement of policy for all the dominion's ocean and inland waters that established rules, regulations, and procedures for commercial fishing on the Great Lakes. With only minor modifications, it defined Canadian fishery policy for the balance of the nineteenth century. Modeled on the Province of Canada's fishery law of 1858, it clearly reflected the British formula developed over hundreds of years in common law and by parliamentary acts, which had been transferred to North America and adapted to New World conditions, as well as contemporary British views on fishery policy.[2]

The act of 1868 provided for the appointment of fishery officers to enforce the law and for a system of "fishery leases and licenses for fisheries and fishing." It extended very specific safeguards to the salmon of Lake Ontario, already in critical condition, specifying closed seasons, mesh sizes of nets, and distance between nets. It protected entrances to spawning streams and spawning grounds and prohibited the taking of roe, salmon fry, parrs and smolts, and fish less than three pounds in weight. Fishermen could not harvest young fish in general.

The specification of closed seasons and the regulation of mesh size protected whitefish and lake trout. Fish were not to be sold or bought during closed seasons. Owners of dams had to build fishways. Fishermen could not obstruct navigation with their equipment, set nets or any other device to prevent the passage of fish from one body of water to another, or obstruct access to spawning grounds. The law prohibited the use of spears and grapnels except under special circumstances. To prevent "injuries to fishing grounds and pollution of rivers," the law prohibited boats from dumping fish offal, ballast, coal ashes, stones, or "other deleterious substances." Sawdust and mill rubbish, lime, chemicals, drugs, poisonous matter, and dead fish could not be "drawn into, or allowed to pass into" waters used by the fish species named in the law. The Minister of Marine and Fisheries could create protected fish propagation areas, where intruders would be subject to a $200 fine or as much as four months in prison. Special provisions permitted the collection of fish eggs during the spawning season for propagation purposes. The law set fines for lawbreakers and described the powers given to fishery officers—for example, to make arrests and issue search warrants and to search boats and other property for illegally taken fish and illegally used materials when there was "cause to believe" that the law had been broken.

To the Governor in Council went the authority to alter or amend regulations when necessary to improve the management and regulation of the fisheries, a sweeping delegation of authority that guaranteed adaptability to changing circumstances and locational differences. In the following decades, the Privy Council frequently made such changes at the recommendation of the Department of Marine and Fisheries. The law of 1868, elaborate and thoughtfully constructed on the basis of past experience, stood in stark contrast to the hodgepodge of legislation enacted in the Great Lakes states because it addressed the needs of all the ocean, river, and lake fisheries of the dominion, where fishing was a more important part of the economy than in the United States.

The officials in both Canadian and Great Lakes state governments who were responsible for protecting the fish resource found enforcement to be their major problem. Given the vast area of the fisheries and their presence both near settled and developed parts of the drainage basin and in very remote regions of Lakes Superior and Huron and Georgian Bay, where comparatively few people lived, a sizable staff and generous sums had to be allocated to protect the resource. Would governments spend the dollars to do so? In the Great Lakes states, as already noted, the answer for many decades was no. The Department of Marine and Fisheries, however, developed a system for enforcing the fishery laws that curbed some of the worst excesses that resulted from the unlicensed open access to the fisheries that prevailed in American waters.

Canadian law encouraged a controlled development of the Great Lakes fish resources for home consumption and for Canadian commercial markets, which would ensure to the fishermen well-filled nets for decades to come. Responsible for implementing the law, the Department of Marine and Fisheries, created in 1868, was headed by a member of the cabinet, the Minister of Marine and Fisheries, and included an advisory staff knowledgeable about ocean and Great Lakes fish, a superintendent of fish culture, administrative assistants, clerks, and appointed overseers who were stationed at critical places around the lakes and who accepted applications for licenses from local fishermen, kept a watchful eye for illegal fishing, made arrests when necessary, and informed Ottawa about local conditions and problems. Fishery guardians assisted the overseers as necessary. The department officials in Ottawa reviewed applications for licenses and approved or denied them on the basis of the number considered safe for the fish population and an assessment of the applicant's worth. Overseers distributed the licenses.

The Department of Marine and Fisheries often did not license those who had abused fishing privileges in the past or who fronted for American interests. It preferred to license fishermen who were British subjects, especially resident independent fishermen who sold the catch in Canadian markets, and refused to license nonresidents, except visiting sportsmen. Canadian fish were for Canadians. Over years of experience, the department developed a resistance to leasing large fishing grounds to entrepreneurs who operated with hired workers because they tended to overexploit the resource. The preference for the small-scale operators in the Great Lakes fisheries mirrors the official partiality to the small farmer, settler-developers expressed in early policies for the granting of agricultural land in Upper Canada.[3]

But the parallel with farm tenure stops there. The Department of Marine and Fisheries did not recognize occupancy, use, and improvement of a fishing station as establishing a right to fish. A person who had long fished at a particular location was not automatically granted a license. In matters of land disposal in the Canadian Great Lakes region, law and practice repeatedly acknowledged the idea that one who improves and uses land deserves preferential treatment when the land is sold.[4] If a fisherman sold his fishing-station improvements and gear to another, he could not transfer his license to the new owner. For a modest fee, the dominion government granted the right to fish to a specific person for his use only. This position annoyed fishers who understood the principle of occupancy and demonstrated use as it applied to agricultural land. Why should it not apply in fishing as well as farming?

The licensing requirement not only irked many fishermen, but sometimes led to violent protest, which made thorough, effective enforcement of fishing regulations very difficult. Underfunded, understaffed, and underequipped, the enforcement officers had to protect thousands of miles of coastline, which included a complexity of islands and shores, especially in Georgian Bay. Some fishermen could and did find hiding places and fished as they pleased. The Department of Marine and Fisheries employed twelve overseers in 1869 and gradually appointed more, to bring the total to thirty-three in 1891. The number of all paid Great Lakes fishery officers grew from twenty-three to ninety between 1868 and 1896.[5] Poorly compensated, earning only $200 to $300 a year, overseers could not give a great deal of time to the task of enforcement and make a living. Moreover, members of the House of Commons regarded the position as a source of political patronage and insisted on naming their choices to fill it. The Minister of Marine and Fisheries could remove those who violated their oaths and sometimes did. Nor were all the political appointees poor choices. Some did their jobs extraordinarily well, and at very considerable hardship, sacrifice, and danger to themselves.

At the other extreme were overseers who took a very relaxed attitude toward their responsibility, winked at recommending licenses for persons whom they knew worked in collusion with dealers, and, at worst, accepted substantial favors from powerful fishing enterprises, especially American-owned and -operated ones, to look the other way while they broke the law. Nevertheless, overseers did make arrests for illegal activity, confiscate nets and boats, and testify in court. In addition, the very fact that they were there had a deterrent effect, and they were not alone. They could and did call on Ottawa for help. The Department of Marine and Fisheries sent officers of the Dominion Police, when needed, to back up local overseers. The overseers were short on enforcement equipment other than sailboats and rowboats until 1888, when the first steam-powered craft went into service.[6]

THE FIRST DECADE OF EXPERIENCE WITH THE FISHERY LAW OF 1868, 1868–1878

During the decade following its creation, the Department of Marine and Fisheries identified a series of objectives that remained high on its agenda for the balance of the century. These goals included creating an effective artificial-propagation and stocking program, developing and effectively enforcing fishery regulations, controlling pollution, preventing the blockage of streams, countering American exploitation of the Canadian Great Lakes fisheries, maintaining dominion supremacy over the fisheries in the face of provincial protests, and establishing unified Canadian–American control and management of the fish and water resources of the Great Lakes.

During the first decade, Samuel Wilmot initiated the propagation and stocking program. Dedicated to restoring the population of Lake Ontario salmon to the bountiful numbers of his youth on the family farm near Newcastle, Ontario, Wilmot in 1866 began to experiment with artificial propagation in the basement of his house on Wilmot's Creek. This location later evolved into the Newcastle Hatchery (figure 13.1). Here he conducted the first hatching and stocking experiments for the Great Lakes. His efforts showed real promise when the newly organized government of the Dominion of Canada sent representatives to observe his work. In June 1869, the chairman of the House of Commons Select Committee on Fisheries and Navigation reported enthusiastically on Wilmot's progress with both salmon and whitefish, "earnestly" recommending that the House encourage his work: "Mr. Wilmot is eminently deserving of commendation and remuneration." The House responded with a modest appropriation, continuing the policy of subsidizing artificial propagation that dated from 1857, when the Province of Canada supported Richard Nettle's work with salmon and speckled-trout eggs in a small hatchery in

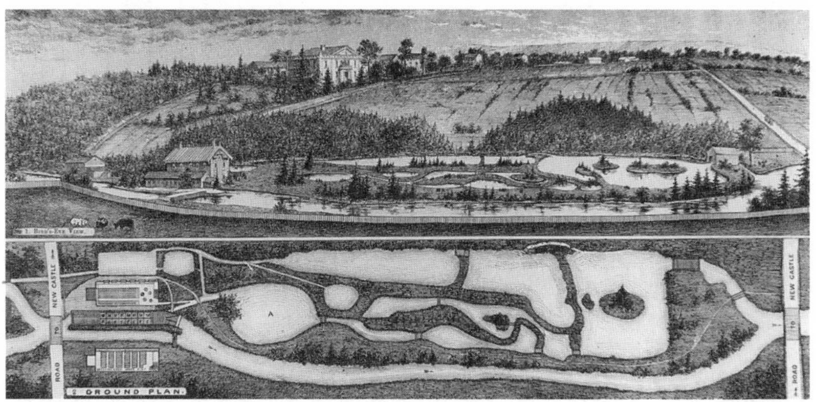

Figure 13.1. Bird's-eye view of the Newcastle Hatchery, Newcastle, Ontario. (From Commissioner of Fisheries, "Report," in Canada, *Sessional Papers,* 1878, no. 1, Appendix 1, frontispiece)

Quebec City. Thus began Wilmot's long and distinguished service to the Department of Marine and Fisheries. In 1876, he became the Superintendent of Fish Culture for Canada and continued this work until his retirement in 1895.[7]

Wilmot's experiences with salmon culture over fifteen years, from 1866 to1881, at the Newcastle Hatchery are well worth noting because they made a substantial contribution to knowledge about the physical nature and life cycle of Lake Ontario salmon, hatchery methods, and the relationship between people and the fish resource. So are his perceptive observations about the changing natural environment, which he believed would lead, more than anything else, to the extinction of the salmon. Local violence disrupted the hatchery experiments at Wilmot and Grafton Creeks as inland residents retaliated against the hatchery houses' blockage of the salmon's passage upstream into farming country. Residents there wanted to spear them for table fare or sale, but Wilmot believed that salmon allowed to migrate naturally were lost forever and so were their spawn. Night riders with blackened faces, brandishing spears and torches, descended on the hatchery houses at spawning time. Toughs who beat up Wilmot and destroyed the fish defeated the best efforts of law-enforcement officers to protect the project. Wilmot's reported experiences abounded in vigilante ruffians and ineffective judges and juries who either sympathized with or were afraid of the guilty.[8] Nevertheless, the artificial propagation and planting program continued.

Wilmot pushed for the creation of more hatcheries. In 1870, he won the endorsement of the Department of Marine and Fisheries for the idea of establishing salmon hatcheries in Nova Scotia and New Brunswick and, in 1871, in Quebec to regenerate the salmon population of the Gulf of St. Lawrence and its tributaries. The House of Commons had funded four salmon-breeding stations by 1873. Dominion hatcheries numbered seven by 1875, including a whitefish hatchery at Sandwich, Ontario, on the Detroit River.[9] By the end of the century, the number had grown to fifteen for the entire country, but only two, Wilmot's early creations, served the needs of the Great Lakes. Lake hatcheries grew in number after 1900.

Cognizant of the many pitfalls involved in enforcement, the House of Commons Select Committee on Fisheries and Navigation decided to conduct a dominion-wide survey in 1868 and 1869 of fishery overseers, fishermen, and other residents familiar with fishing in their regions. The committee hoped to determine price, production, and consumption patterns; to find out how well regulations to protect the fisheries were obeyed; and to learn how the respondents believed the laws and their administration could be improved. The results, printed in the House of Commons *Journal* in 1869, painted a dreary picture. In answer to a group of questions designed to determine if migratory spawning fish were endangered, the thirteen respondents in the Great Lakes region maintained that many different species of fish ascended the rivers or tried to do so annually, that many of the waterways were dammed and without workable fishways to allow passage up and downstream, and that fish ascending the streams were often killed illegally. Most particularly did the observers of Lake Ontario mention the destruction of the salmon as a prime example of waste by the unlawful use of spears and nets during spawning season. They observed that regulations were generally not observed. One Lake Erie respondent believed that "the law regarding fish slides is a dead letter."[10]

Especially critical of the sad state of enforcement and the widespread contempt for regulation, John W. Kerr, overseer for the district around Hamilton, blamed lawbreaking for much of the destruction of fish. The thirteen respondents believed that the dominion fishery overseers were well informed about the law and that they understood their duties. They preferred overseers appointed by the dominion government to those appointed by municipalities, but were ambivalent about having nonresidents fill the position as a possible way of minimizing personal conflict between the fishermen and law-enforcement officers. The conclusions from these responses were obvious. The Department of Marine and Fisheries needed a larger enforcement staff. Between 1869 and 1878, it added twenty-two Great Lakes overseers to its original group of twelve.[11]

While the problem of enforcement figured in only a minor way in parliamentary debates in the 1870s, one very revealing exchange between Peter Mitchell, the Minister of Marine and Fisheries, and members who represented counties around northeastern Lake Ontario highlighted the enforcement issue in 1872. "Foreigners who come from the other side of the line" had been taking hundreds of tons of salmon and other fish illegally, using spears and nets, in the spring and fall, and they had to be stopped, complained one member of Parliament. Mitchell responded that the government wanted to enforce the laws and protect the fish, "but it is very difficult for the Department, with the small sum of money and staff at their disposal, to protect effectually all the waters of so extensive an area as that watered by the St. Lawrence and great lakes." Moreover, it was not just poaching foreigners who caused the damage by breaking the law, but farmers and settlers did not cooperate, and "until they do their duty it is almost impossible for the small staff of public officers to give anything like effective protection to the waters of the Dominion."[12] Nowhere on the Great Lakes in the 1870s did local residents so clearly show their contempt for fishery regulation and hatchery policies than at Wilmot's hatchery sites.

Peter Mitchell, A. J. Smith, and James C. Pope, the first three Ministers of Marine and Fisheries who served in the years 1868 to 1878, agreed that the blockage of streams and the pollution of streams and rivers by sawdust and mill rubbish created by the large and powerful lumbering industry posed a serious menace to the fish populations of interior waters and a difficult policy-making problem. The provincial and dominion governments tended to be lenient with the more powerful and lucrative lumber industry and to sacrifice the fish. Efforts made by the dominion to impose fines on those violating the antidumping provisions of the fishery law of 1868 and of the law passed in 1872 that was designed to strengthen them proved very frustrating. Offenders promised to change their ways and respect the statutes, but failed repeatedly to do so. They believed that practices that were tolerated would become a "sort of recognized privilege, excused at least if not justified by the importance and wide-spread benefits of manufacturing industries." Periodically they would be criticized, but that would be all. They would not be compelled to comply or be fined for not doing so.[13]

The Department of Marine and Fisheries, however, urged its officers to crack down on operations that dumped sawdust and mill refuse and repeatedly instructed them to evaluate the adequacy of fishways. Mill owners were ordered to make amends, and the department encouraged the development of fishway designs to recommend as workable for migrating fish. Yet these efforts did not stem the tide of destruction in streams and rivers. A loophole in the law encouraged noncompliance, for it allowed exemptions from fishway and pollution standards for rivers and streams when applicants for exemption could make a convincing case that enforcement made very little sense. Requests for exemption proliferated, and, given the "persistent indifference and active antagonism of the manufacturing interest," enforcement seemed almost impossible. A. J. Smith noted in 1876 that the possibility of exemption encouraged mill owners to assert that the trouble and cost of changing their milling systems to comply with the law would be a serious financial burden.[14]

The first decade of the surveillance of the fisheries by the Department of Marine and Fisheries closed with the publication of an elaborate study entitled "Sawdust and Mill-offals on the Lower Ottawa River." The Ottawa was an exempted river in which lawmakers gazed upon masses of floating sawdust and sawmill debris that had turned a once beautiful waterway into a vast waste way for the lumbermen. In 1883, A. W. McLelan, the Minister of Marine and Fisheries, explained to a critical member of the House of Commons that the decision "some years ago" to exempt the Ottawa had been the result of the conviction that lumbering was more important on that river than fishing.[15] The eyesore before them as well as problems in their constituencies encouraged members of Parliament from the Lake Huron and Georgian Bay region to bring the issue of pollution from logging forward in debate again and again in the following decade.

The first Ministers of Marine and Fisheries shared the conviction that cooperation between Canada and the United States was essential to protect the fish resource of the Great Lakes. In 1872, citing the "rapid diminution of marketable fishes in those waters which border on the United States and Canada," especially in Lakes Erie and Huron, Peter Mitchell urged joint action to stop the decline. He hoped that New York, Ohio, and Michigan would consider, adopt, and enforce some form of "moderate restrictions." Canada, in turn, would try to modify its regulations to help create uniform rules for the waters of Lakes Erie and Huron. If this could be done, he predicted, a "marked improvement" in the fisheries would follow. Again the following year, the minister called for the implementation of uniform regulations, given the "manifest decline of the fisheries on the American shores of the Great Lakes." In 1874, pledging cooperation with the United States Commission of Fish and Fisheries and state fishery commissioners, A. J. Smith made the plea more forcefully: "At present the unrestricted and destructive manner in which fishing is carried on by United States citizens near our water boundary, compels us to allow greater privileges to Canadian fishermen than consist with the due preservation of fish."[16]

In 1875, frustrated by the failure to receive from the United States positive responses to these suggestions, W. F. Whitcher, the Commissioner of Fisheries, summarized the efforts to stimulate American action in a report, which he sent to the Governor General in Council. For the first time, the issue took the diplomatic route to the United States Department of State, with a request for official communications with state governors and an invitation for them to turn their attention to the problem. In February 1875, Spencer Baird invited A. J. Smith to attend a meeting in New York of federal and state fish commissioners. The agenda called for discussion of artificial propagation and the kinds of regulations needed to protect the fish. Clearly, the Commissioner of Fish and Fisheries and the Minister of the Department of Marine and Fisheries did achieve a degree of cooperation through corresponding, sharing official reports, considering the possibility of joint hatchery projects, and undertaking joint explorations of the Atlantic coastal waters. The Canadian fishery authorities praised the work of the newly founded American Fish Culturists' Association, one of Baird's many offspring. But cooperative management of the Great Lakes fisheries remained an elusive goal.[17] With the 1876 report of the Department of Marine and Fisheries, the issue dropped from the annual reports and did not reappear for fifteen years. Meanwhile, the staff of the Department of Marine and Fisheries closely monitored American efforts to achieve cooperation and uniform laws among the Great Lakes states and waited in vain for the enactment of state laws harmonious with those of Canada.

REGULATION IN A DECADE OF EXPANSION, 1879–1888

A vast expansion in fish production of the Canadian Great Lakes characterized the years from 1879 to 1888. From 10 million pounds in 1879, the harvests escalated to 26 million in 1888, responding primarily to market demand for fresh fish in the United States and to the expansion of American dealer-entrepreneurs into Canadian waters. Simultaneously, the lumbering industry in the Georgian Bay region grew remarkably, in large measure to supply American markets. Canadians reacted in various ways to the invasion. Many fishermen welcomed the aggressive American operations, which opened markets for the bountiful fish of their Great Lakes waters, not in strong demand in Canada. The development of the resource created jobs for them. Canadian fish dealers found themselves engulfed by large American enterprises that operated widely on the Great Lakes and often ended up working for them. The Department of Marine and Fisheries found both the escalation of fishing and the increase in American and Canadian poaching a great challenge. The growth of lumbering led to more problems with mill refuse and, particularly, sawdust pollution. The construction of dams to facilitate the delivery of logs to mills also added to the burdens of enforcement. For public consumption, the department spoke enthusiastically about the growth in fish harvests and, probably tongue in cheek, attributed the increase to "judicious protection and a strict observance of the fishery laws," but worries mounted within the department. Many overseers' reports repeatedly asserted that the laws were well observed or generally well observed and that the fishermen who produced for the American markets received "remunerative" prices for the catch.[18]

Accompanying these optimistic assessments was an undercurrent of deep concern about the changing fish populations in Lake Ontario, Georgian Bay, and Lake Huron: a decline in preferred market species and a rise in "coarser types." Georgian Bay overseers reported unlicensed fishing, flagrant violation of closed seasons, illegal setting of traps and pound nets, use of 2,000 to 3,000 more fathoms of net per license than authorized, inefficient fishways, illegal dumping of offal and sawdust, and disregard of the five-inch mesh requirements. They cited American disrespect for Canadian laws. They blamed Canadian magistrates for imposing very light penalties on owners of sawmills who dumped refuse into the water. They condemned fish dealers who encouraged Indians to disobey the closed season. They bemoaned a lack of steam-powered craft to apprehend lawbreakers as a real barrier to effective enforcement.[19]

Members of Parliament from constituencies around Lake Huron and Georgian Bay who opposed the Conservative Party, which was in power, made no bones about publicizing the growing fishery problems. During debates in the House of Commons, they challenged the Department of Marine and Fisheries to do a better job of enforcing the laws. In 1883, for example, William E. O'Brien of Muskoka County lashed out at the department, charging that the fisheries in Georgian Bay were virtually unprotected because of the ineffectual enforcement system. Only three overseers were assigned to the 200 miles of coast stretching from Collingwood to Killarney, and they did not go out on the water to visit the fishing grounds. As a result, unlicensed fishermen using nets with illegal mesh sizes and operating during closed seasons caught fish at will, he claimed. Surely the resource would be better served by officers in boats cruising the fishing grounds and enforcing the law. He condemned the growing problem of sawdust pollution and attacked the hatchery and planting program as a foolish waste of money. Scolded O'Brien, "It seems to me that there never was a people under the sun so utterly reckless and careless about their resources as are the people of Canada."[20]

Political opponents of the Conservatives had struck pay dirt in the Georgian Bay and Lake Huron constituencies with the fishing issue. O'Brien's attack on the Department of Marine and Fisheries inaugurated repeated criticisms during the next three years. They arose from the stresses on fish and fishermen created by prosperity and expansion during the 1880s and the failure of the department to address the resultant problems, especially those stemming from the reorganization and consolidation of the commercial-fishing industry, the expanded market demand, the presence of American operations in Canadian waters, the increasingly deadly technology of fishing (especially gill-net steamers), and the rise in pollution.

In 1886, with markets glutted in Canada and the United States and prices low, fishers and others from Georgian Bay communities directed nine petitions to the House of Commons, seeking the abolition of close seasons for trout and whitefish in Ontario and "thereby placing them on an equal footing with their American competitors."[21] This rising tide of complaint and condemnation of fishery policy set the stage for the reforms of Charles Hibbert Tupper.

14

Charles Hibbert Tupper and the New Broom 1888–1896

'Rah for the Gallant Petrel

With the Conservative victory in the election of 1887, the implementation of fishery laws on the Great Lakes stood on the brink of a thoroughgoing shake-up. Charles Hibbert Tupper, a vigorous thirty-five-year-old Harvard-trained lawyer from Nova Scotia who had grown up in a province where many made a living by commercial fishing and who had chosen to follow his prominent father into the political arena, accepted the appointment of Minister of Marine and Fisheries in 1888.[1] Elected to the House of Commons in 1882, he had become fully aware of the fishery problems of Lake Huron and Georgian Bay, specifically, and the Great Lakes generally.

A TIME FOR CHANGE

Charles Tupper acted both as a new, vigorous, and ambitious cabinet minister and as an official concerned about protecting the fishery resources by putting teeth into the established system of regulation and restocking, which he felt was notably superior to the policy of open entry and unregulated fishing in American waters. He swept vigorously with a new broom. As he later described the situation: "I found in the Dept. of Marine and Fisheries a great deal of laxity on the part of those holding offices, remuneration for which was sometimes nominal. . . . Consequently there were a great many dismissals." Removals brought constituents' complaints to members of the House of Commons and ultimately to Prime Minister Sir John Macdonald. In his efforts to tighten the enforcement of laws that prohibited the dumping of offal and sawdust into rivers, Tupper noted, "I began a vigorous enforcement prosecuting offenders right and left in the different provinces." Macdonald on one occasion told him to stop his officers from executing an injunction against the dumping of offal by large British Columbia canneries owned by politically influential Conservatives. Tupper refused.[2]

Tupper planned to rejuvenate the Canadian fishery policy for the Great Lakes as delineated at the time of confederation, a movement in which Conservative Sir Charles Tupper, his father, had played a leading role. The independent and venturesome fishermen and dealer-entrepreneurs of the Great Lakes faced a determined advocate of conservation by regulation and law enforcement, and one thoroughly loyal to country, Crown, and British traditions. Tupper descended from Loyalists who had left Cape Cod for Nova Scotia at the time of the American Revolution. Moreover, Tupper acted from the conviction that a major crisis loomed for the fish population of the Great Lakes. Macdonald once remarked of young Tupper: "His only fault, if it be a fault, is that he would like to carry all his reforms in a day."[3] Because his administration highlighted the differences between the American and Canadian systems, the ways they functioned, and the ways they interacted in flush and in depression times, it merits attention, all the more so because Tupper served during a critical juncture in the history of fisheries management, when Canadian and American fishery experts, after thirty years of differences, agreed on the implementation of policies necessary to save the fish.

Inaugurating Cruiser Patrols

As a newly appointed cabinet member, Tupper made the enforcement of fishery regulations a high priority. In 1888, a reasonably prosperous year, the Department of Marine and Fisheries sent the *Cruiser,* the first steam-powered enforcement vessel to patrol the Canadian Great Lakes waters, to inspect the fishing grounds on Lake Huron and Georgian Bay and to monitor fishermen's compliance with the regulations.

Captain Alfred F. Holmes, who kept a complete log of his enforcement work, followed the practice of having the overseers come aboard with him to tour their districts, inspecting fishing activity, examining applicants and issuing licenses, and seizing and removing illegal nets. He found precisely the kinds of violations that overseers had been reporting: the use of small-mesh nets and more yardage than authorized. Fishing without licenses was common, and large dealers based in Detroit and Buffalo bought much of the catch. Holmes noted other evidence of entrepreneurial control; at Squaw Island, for example, he found "over fifty boats and three tugs" operating hundreds of thousands of yards of small-mesh gill nets. James and Charles Noble of Killarney, Ontario, controlled these nets and illegal pound nets elsewhere. They sent the catch to the Buffalo Fish Company, with which they had a marketing agreement. During the last ten days of October, this Killarney firm as well as others, observed Captain Holmes, were preparing to launch fishing operations during the closed season. Receiving orders to lay up the *Cruiser* on October 31, he could not pursue violators of the closed season. Holmes concluded that the patrol vessel had exerted a very positive influence on law enforcement. Fishermen and dealers understood that the government intended to protect the resource. There was hope for preservation of the fisheries of the Great Lakes.[4]

The findings proved highly beneficial to the Department of Marine and Fisheries, which under Tupper's direction continued using the *Cruiser* on Georgian Bay from 1889 to 1891. Meanwhile, construction began on a new and more efficient steamer. By the time Tupper stepped down in 1894, two vessels built specifically for the surveillance of the Great Lakes fisheries were patrolling Lakes Erie, Huron, and Superior: the cruiser *Petrel* and the steamer *Dolphin*. The establishment of the patrol system was one part of the reinvigorated enforcement scheme. During the next seven years, the department proceeded to dismiss ineffective and corrupt overseers and appoint new ones, to designate strategically located lighthouse keepers as overseers, to authorize the use of guardians during the fishing and closed seasons, and to encourage all its personnel to step up enforcement. The department renewed efforts to stop pollution, especially to prevent the dumping of lumber wastes into the waters, to crack down on dam blockage, and to promote the use of the newest and most effective fish ladders.[5]

Aside from the enforcement program, other major reforms initiated by Tupper included establishing a special commission to study the Ontario fisheries, appointing a well-trained academic to make recommendations about fishery management and to engage in research and writing, and implementing the creation of a commission of investigators from Canada and the United States to study the question of joint regulation of their contiguous waters.

Charles Hibbert Tupper

Establishment of the Dominion Fishery Commission on the Fisheries of the Province of Ontario

To understand more fully the nature of the decline in the preferred commercial species so apparent by the early 1890s, both the United States and Canada undertook special studies of the Great Lakes. While Hugh Smith directed a survey of the American waters and prepared a report that was published in 1892, Charles Tupper in 1891 named the Dominion Fishery Commission on the Fisheries of the Province of Ontario to gather information to use in revising regulations, especially those for the Great Lakes. The commission's charge was to collect evidence on spawning seasons, gill-net and pound-net mesh sizes, "and other matters connected with the Fisheries." Samuel Wilmot, Superintendent of Fish Culture for Canada, served as chairman. He worked with Edward Harris, president of the Long Point Company of eastern Lake Erie, which had been incorporated by businessmen in Hamilton and St. Catherine's in 1866 when it made its first purchase of Crown lands to use primarily as a private hunting and sportfishing preserve.[6]

The commissioners collected data in 1892 and 1893 by traveling to various locations around the Great Lakes and taking sworn testimony from approximately 100 fishermen and others well acquainted with the commercial-fishing industry. The commission's extensive report, dated March 1, 1893, served as a guide for the regulation of closed seasons and of pound and gill nets. Evidence gathered reflected the condition of the Great Lakes fisheries, presenting a grim picture of exploitation, and the report included a call for much needed reform. Warned the commission: "Should the present very exhaustive methods not be prohibited in all matters, all the better qualities of fish must soon become only a present luxury for the rich, and ere long be exterminated."[7] The small-mesh gill net was the principal culprit in reducing the number of trout and whitefish to "below nature's balance." As the preferred commercial species declined, "voracious or coarse fish"—such as blue pickerel, pike, lamprey eels, and dogfish—had increased. The report singled out the destruction of huge quantities of young fish and the practice of wasteful fishing as major contributors to the decline in the size and vigor of the Great Lakes fish population.

Very significant also were extensive changes in the lands that surrounded and the streams and rivers that flowed into the lakes, reported the commission. These transformations had altered the fish habitat, ruining spawning grounds, blocking upstream migrations, and polluting the waters. Adding insult to injury, Americans fished in Canadian waters, principally Lake Erie and the southern end of Lake Huron, irritating the

Canadian fishermen, who questioned the restraints placed on them while the Americans had none. American dealers bought large quantities of the Canadian fishermen's catch, taking them into the United States by using various legal dodges to avoid paying the duty on Canadian fish, whereas Canadian dealers had not a chance of avoiding the duty of three-quarters of a cent per pound on Canadian fish destined for American markets.[8]

The commissioners concluded that the prime causes for the "depletion of the fisheries" were the illegal fishing during spawning seasons, destruction of small fish in seines and in both pound and gill nets, waste of large quantities of fish in "unlimited lengths of gill-nets," use of small-mesh nets, and dumping of sawmill and log-raft refuse in the water. These practices interfered with the natural order of things, depriving the fish of freedom to spawn and destroying them before they reached reproductive maturity.[9]

The commission's findings provided the evidence that Tupper needed to plan for changes in regulations. It is perhaps the most obvious example of a technique he used repeatedly when issues arose: conducting an investigation to gather factual knowledge on which to act. A lawyer by training, he liked to have plenty of evidence. But the report came with a political price tag. In a series of press releases that embarrassed the administration, Commissioner Edward Harris accused Tupper of having suppressed the most devastating evidence of waste.

Appointment of Edward E. Prince

In 1892, the Department of Marine and Fisheries took a further step to improve the quality of its protective system with the appointment of an academically trained marine biologist, Edward E. Prince. Up to that point, the department had relied on industrious, able men schooled in fishery matters by hands-on experience, observation, and wide reading, but not by academic study. Tupper wanted an adviser with the standing of the recently deceased Spencer Baird. As he told Parliament, Canada, with its fine fisheries, lacked what the United States at the national and state levels and European countries large and small had: scientifically trained persons as part of their advisory systems. They contributed greatly to constructive policy decisions, he believed. Failing to attract a trained Canadian to the position, the search spread to England, where "splendid men" applied, so many that it was difficult to make a choice, Tupper told Parliament. The department selected Professor Edward E. Prince, trained at the Universities of St. Andrews, Cambridge, and Edinburgh and with a good record of professional service to both Conservative and Liberal governments in England, Ireland, and Scotland.[10]

The appointment of Prince as Commissioner and General Inspector of Fisheries aroused critics of the administration. Allegedly speaking for their fisher constituents, they complained that this man, who had spent so much time studying the fisheries of the British Isles, did not understand those of Canada. Also because he was a man of book learning and theories, his ideas about regulation of the fisheries were impractical and should not be imposed on hardworking fishermen who were struggling to make a living.[11]

The downturn in the economy in 1893 and the ensuing three-year depression created rough waters for the reform program and the commercial-fishing industry. It marked a turning point in Tupper's seven-year efforts as Minister of Marine and Fisheries. The appointment of Prince was the last of his notable reforms, preceded by the reinvigoration of enforcement, the survey of the fisheries of Ontario, and, most important of all, the establishment of the Joint Commission Relative to the Preservation of the Fisheries in Waters Contiguous to Canada and the United States.

REFORM UNDER FIRE

In the best of times, attempts to tighten enforcement has created friction with fishermen regardless of century and country. Given the depression and a hungry Liberal Party watching for issues to help it into office in the early 1890s, efforts to regulate and sustain an already overexploited fish population in the Great Lakes brought down an avalanche of criticism in the House of Commons about Charles Tupper's administration of the Department of Marine and Fisheries. With hard times went an escalation in both domestic and American poaching in Canadian waters that taxed the ingenuity of enforcement officers and increased the fiscal burden of protection. The very fabric of conservation by regulation and stocking came under heavy fire from fishermen, especially those who operated in waters near the American shores of the Great Lakes and observed Yankee fishermen following the open, unregulated system of exploitation. Tupper found himself dueling with his Liberal opponents in the House of Commons while his department staff dealt with an ever heavier load of enforcement problems. Both the attempts at enforcement and the fight in Parliament that contributed to the Liberal victory in 1896 helped to cripple the reform program. Illuminating the way the system worked in the latter years of Tupper's ministry, the original records of the Department of Marine and Fisheries provide insights into the interaction of fishermen, government officials, and the fish resources of the Great Lakes during the depression years of 1893 to 1896.

Better enforcement was in many ways the most crucial, difficult, and vulnerable part of the reform effort. Tupper spoke cogently about the matter and the immediate opportunities it presented for political opponents to champion aggrieved fishermen instead of thinking about the good sense of protecting the resource.[12] He fought to retain and tighten the regulatory system despite heavy criticism and hard times.

While the Department of Marine and Fisheries, using the expertise of Edward Prince and the data gathered by the Dominion Fishery Commission, worked to adjust regulations on closed seasons, the sizes of net mesh allowed, and the length of nets permitted, complaints escalated. Canadian fishermen understood how to make their voices heard by writing directly to the department and by petitioning Parliament. They asked their members of Parliament to intercede for them individually. They knew that letters from the clergy and from lawyers had a potent influence on government. Canadians sometimes claimed that American fishermen had the advantage in exercising political clout, stating that "every [American] fisherman is a politician" or, as a Canadian fish dealer noted in 1893, that Americans are situated differently from Canadians: "A man can go up to Congress and boodle these statesmen." In reality, both Canadians and Americans used their elected officials to achieve their goals.[13] Moreover, members of the House of Commons who opposed the Conservative government understood fully how to investigate on their own, solicit complaints from their constituents, and level charges of lax and corrupt enforcement against the Department of Marine and Fisheries. They combed official records for evidence of malfeasance and had no trouble finding it, for the department had been seeking just such proof to use in improving its staff of overseers and its level of enforcement generally. Reform ammunition created cannon fodder for the opposition.

Discrimination

Fishermen charged that the Department of Marine and Fisheries showed varied gradations of political, personal, religious, racial, ethnic, and economic discrimination in issuing licenses and enforcing laws. A few examples will illustrate. One fisher claimed that he did not get the licenses he wanted, whereas two "well to do farmers" with more influence received some of his improved locations: "All i want is whats fair and honest between man and man for it is pretty hard when you see wealthy farmers beating fishermen out of their hard work." A protest about the department's refusal to transfer a license from one fisherman to another provoked a writer to note that "the Long Point Co. can get licenses for 7 nets with no truble[.] it looks bad[.] gives the rich the benefit and the poor no shoe."[14] The theme of discrimination against small hardworking fishermen and favoritism shown to larger operators runs throughout complaints to the department and in oral testimony as well.

Over the years, the Department of Marine and Fisheries did unquestionably give advantages to some sizable fishing operations, on the assumption that they would harvest the fish in a way that protected the resource. A case in point was Charles Gauthier of Windsor, who first appeared in the official records as the successful bidder to build the Sandwich Hatchery in 1875. At that time, he had been fishing commercially in the Detroit River for a decade. In 1879, he received extensive rights to fish in the waters off the Duck Islands in Lake Huron. Thereafter, his business expanded to include a freight steamer, four tugs, thirty sailboats, and "a large outfit of pound nets and gill nets" by 1884. Nurtured by the Department of Marine and Fisheries with low-cost permission to fish, Gauthier's enterprise provoked devastating criticism in the report of the Dominion Fishery Commission. The testimony of Lake Huron and North Channel fishermen on lawbreaking and wasteful spoliation of the resource promoted the Tupper administration to deny Gauthier and Company any more licenses.[15] Similarly, S. T. Reeves, another large-scale entrepreneur in the area of Detroit and Windsor, bought the Duck Islands, took up fishing where Gauthier left off, and quickly incurred the disapproval of the Department of Marine and Fisheries because of his connection with the American-owned Buffalo Fish Company, his failure to pay fishermen, and his wasteful fishing practices, particularly the slaughter of small, immature fish, cited by local fishermen. Cases like these led the department to prefer applicants who were bona fide fishermen, residents of Canada, British subjects, and owners of their equipment. One license per person was ideal.[16] But it was hardly the ideal of many fishermen, and it was not the actual practice.

In an age of friction between Catholics and Protestants in both Canada and the United States, the Department of Marine and Fisheries was occasionally accused of an anti-Catholic bias. James and Charles Noble of Killarney, very substantial fishermen and a target of a departmental crackdown for illegal fishing, claimed that anti-Catholicism in part motivated the action. In a prepared statement made in the spring of 1894, Nelson Couture, a Georgian Bay fishermen, reported that the overseer "has stated that he has no use for Frenchmen and that he will soon drive them out of the fishing business on the north shore." The Reverend J. Paquin, resident priest at Wikwemikong on Manitoulin Island in Georgian Bay, who ministered to reservation Ojibwes, complained to the Department of Marine and Fisheries that the overseer sometimes refused the Indians' applications for fishing licenses.[17] Indians living on reservations charged that the Department of Marine and Fisheries under Conservative management violated their treaty rights and either did not allow them to fish or circumscribed those rights by limiting the times and types of fishing. The allegations that the department displayed anti-Catholic and anti-

French biases cannot be documented. Indeed, the record of licenses issued in the areas of Manitoulin Island, northern Georgian Bay, and North Channel includes those for many fishermen of part French, part Indian background. Catholic priests, such as Paquin, frequently interceded on their behalf. The Indians, though, were correct in their charges against the Department of Marine and Fisheries, which did exhibit a prejudicial attitude toward and legal unfairness in administering the law when Native North Americans were concerned.

Political considerations also affected the chances of an applicant getting a license or receiving special treatment. Particularly common were cases where fishermen appealed to their members of Parliament for favors. A good example among the many is that of two fishermen who operated illegally in 1892. The department destroyed their nets and suspended their licenses. They then asked their member of Parliament to intercede with Tupper to waive the rule against giving licenses to those who had broken the law. The member, Colonel D. Tisdale, wrote very aggressively on behalf of his two constituents and succeeded in getting permission for them to use seines, which had been banned in general in Great Lakes waters.[18]

Political affiliation and the vote sometimes entered the discussion when fishermen's licensing problems were at issue, especially in the election year of 1896. Conservative candidates urged the Minister of Marine and Fisheries to give special favors to their fisher constituents. It is impossible to determine with any precision the extent of political favoritism, but fishermen believed that it was very real. Tupper, though, repeatedly denied such requests.[19]

During the depression of the 1890s, fishermen and many of their overseers wrote of the poverty and hardships created by the economic downturn and asked for special concessions. Officials often sympathized with their plight and made exceptions, such as lending confiscated nets to fishermen in Port Stanley who had worked for a fisherman who had failed and left them without wages due and in debt for food and clothing.[20] Moreover, in poor times and good, officials repeatedly displayed a sympathy for the poor in administering the laws.

Regulation, Fair or Foul?

Discrimination was one thing; allegedly unfair and poorly conceived restrictions were another. Many fishermen protested that fishing regulations made it very hard to earn a living and that proposed changes promised to make a difficult struggle worse in hard times. Popular attitudes notwithstanding, the Department of Marine and Fisheries under Charles Tupper's administration revised the restrictions on fishing, tightening those that seemed from all available evidence to need changing, and then proceeded to enforce the laws. The major changes applying to the Great Lakes included a more careful definition of closed seasons, an increase in mesh sizes of pound and gill nets, a general prohibition of seining and trap netting, a stricter application of the anti-spearfishing provisions of the existing law, and more restrictions on the use of both pound nets and hoop nets, the latter favored particularly by fishermen in certain parts of Georgian Bay. A stronger penalty for pollution went on the record.

Tupper's efforts to save the fish stirred up a hornet's nest of protest. Angry fishermen wrote to the Minister of Marine and Fisheries, and officials responded, vigorously defending their policies. One case in which the issues and arguments were especially well expressed deserves notice because it reveals the nature of the conflicts. It arose in February 1895, when nine citizens of Southampton, Ontario, signed a petition and sent it to the fishery overseer, requesting a license for six trap nets for William Hazzard to use in Georgian Bay adjacent to the Bustard Islands. The overseer recommended that the department not issue the license because the Bustards had been badly depleted by illegal fishing with trap nets in back channels where they were almost impossible to detect. Two years earlier in that area, though, the overseer had come upon a fisherman with a boatload of illegal trap nets, the very person, he believed, who was the subject of the petition. Soon afterward, H. M. Smith, a fisherman-dealer's agent in Southampton, wrote to the Minister of Marine and Fisheries complaining that the department favored gill nets too much. Trap nets had the advantage of helping to clear out undesirable rough fish, he argued. They should be legalized out of consideration for commercial fishers. Smith implied that regulations favored "the whims of a few inexperienced sportsmen."[21]

The department responded in a clear, forceful, and reasoned defense of its policies. In his reply to Smith, the deputy minister said flatly that the mass of evidence at hand on the harmful effects of trap nets justified the ban on their use. Moreover, "the fisheries should be regarded as a permanent and valuable source of food and wealth for the whole country." It would be wrong to allow a few fishing firms to endanger and destroy them. The department's job was to "take steps (1) to permit only a legitimate amount of fishing, enabling fishermen to do well without permanent danger to the industry, (2) To prohibit nets and methods of fishing which are unreasonably destructive and impossible to control." Given the "present depressed and glutted state of the fish market," increased fishing and sanctioning of trap nets would not benefit fishermen, but would harm the resource. The trap net was particularly bad because it was very hard to detect and thus allowed "certain men to take unfair advantage of law abiding fishermen." Trap nets had been known to capture "entire shoals of valuable fish." Therefore, they were banned from use and, when discovered, destroyed.[22]

Fishers in all the waters of the Canadian Great Lakes protested the ban on seining. In April 1894, the *Canadian,* published in Sarnia, Ontario, challenged the department's position that seining disturbed spawning grounds and destroyed small unusable fish, arguing that the Lake Huron beach is a "shifting shingle, not a natural spawning ground." Asked the editors: Why not just regulate mesh size and not ban seines?[23]

At Toronto Island, three licensed seine fishers protested, using the Toronto Island Association to support them. Among them was one of the very few licensed women fishers of record, Annie Ramsey, a widow whose sons fished for her. Toronto Island was "a small island, so called fishermans island situated east of the eastern outlet of Toronto Bay, built upon which are some 12 shanties used as summer residences and also the fishermans shanties of which there are two." Noted W. H. Lockhart Gordon, president of the Toronto Island Association, in writing to Tupper: "These people are all deserving, hardworking persons who are dependent on fishing for their living . . . they cannot make sufficient to live on by fishing with the gill net alone." Furthermore, some of those involved in seine fishing were essential and irreplaceable members of the Toronto lifeboat crew. Gordon obviously pulled out all the stops in his appeal, but Tupper refused to lift the prohibition on seining. In May 1894, twenty-six citizens of Toronto petitioned in favor of granting the licenses, specifically pointing out the distress that would come to Annie Ramsey if the request were denied, an interesting example of invoking Victorian chivalry to get the desired result. Again Tupper refused. Georgian Bay fishermen added their protest by petition to the Minister of Marine and Fisheries, and dozens of letters from Lake St. Clair fishermen denouncing the ban on seines poured into the Department of Marine and Fisheries in 1894 and 1895.[24]

Complaints about control ranged far beyond the ban on trap nets and seines, citing the unfairness of regulations for gill nets and pound nets, the licensing system itself, the favoritism shown to special interests by fishery overseers, the practice of departmental blacklisting of fishermen who had violated regulations, and the failure of the department to allow fishermen to assign license "rights" to others. Fishermen seasoned most of their complaints liberally with anti-American feeling, which ran especially strong in areas around the western end of Lake Erie, the Detroit and St. Clair Rivers, and Lake St. Clair, where the fishers of Canada and the United States operated in close proximity.

INTO THE NATIONAL POLITICAL ARENA

What the correspondence of the Department of Marine and Fisheries revealed in a one-on-one dimension, the debates in the House of Commons debates, from 1890 to1896, mirrored in broader perspective. The discussion of troubles in the Canadian Great Lakes commercial-fishing industry surfaced in the House of Commons in 1890 and 1891, but the real escalation came in 1893 when the Department of Marine and Fisheries began to implement changes in fishery regulations based on the findings of the Dominion Fishery Commission. Criticism of the policies initiated by Charles Tupper resulted from the multifaceted consequences of American dominance in the Great Lakes fishing industry. Aggressive American entrepreneurial activity fed Canadian patriotic and nationalistic feelings. It was easy to blame the Conservatives, who had long cherished notions of reciprocity and in 1887 had engaged in a campaign for commercial union, a method of boosting the Canadian economy advocated by Sir Charles Tupper, father of the Minister of Marine and Fisheries.[25] Fishery interests long in favor of reciprocity had soured in their feelings toward the United States, given the protective tariff policy in 1890 that in effect closed the American market to Canadian fish dealers.

Critics in the House of Commons cited the differences between the huge catch reported from the American and the small harvest from the Canadian waters of Lake Erie and between the two countries' fishery policies. They bemoaned the folly of the dominion government's outlays for law enforcement and stocking. The Americans made huge hauls from the lake, spent little or nothing on stocking, and virtually ignored efforts at regulation and enforcement. The expenditure of public funds by the dominion government had not helped Canadian fishermen, and controls on fishing had hurt them and given the Americans the competitive advantage. This was unfair. Even worse, overseers appointed by the Department of Marine and Fisheries actually worked in collusion with large American enterprises, such as Post and Company of Sandusky. The evidence of this, brought up during debates in the House of Commons, came from a special investigation of suspected wrongdoing initiated by the Department of Marine and Fisheries, using one of its better overseers, Fred Kerr of Hamilton.[26]

Critics of Tupper strengthened their case by presenting petitions that allegedly were initiated by the angry fishermen who operated on the Detroit and St. Clair Rivers and Lake St. Clair, charging departmental favoritism and condemning fishery regulations as "unreasonable and vexatious" and "calculated" to injure fishermen and the industry as a whole. For a long time, the fishermen had been promised uniform regulations in American and Canadian waters, but it had failed to materialize. According to a member of the House of Commons, "What our fishermen want is either uniformity of laws or uniformity of privileges."[27] These were the central arguments repeated over and over during the depression years in condemnation of the dominion's fishery policy.

Members of Parliament from the areas around western Lake Erie and the Detroit and St. Clair Rivers fueled their lengthy blasts at Tupper's administration of the Department of Marine and Fisheries with emotional tirades centered on alleged capricious, tyrannical, and misinformed regulations devised by bureaucrats and experts like Edward Prince, who had no appreciation of the fisherman's lifelong work harvesting the waters, his investments in equipment, and his responsibility to support his family. McGregor, a member of Parliament from North Essex, likened Tupper to the czar of Russia, claiming that his fishermen constituents believed that the Canadian fishing laws treated them as harshly as the czar treated the Jewish population of Russia.[28] That the stereotype of the poor, industrious, misunderstood, abused fisherman did not fit the reality of the varied income and investment patterns among the body of fishers mattered not. For political purposes, it was powerful, fully as potent as the argument that officials of the Department of Marine and Fisheries were dupes who allowed Americans to circumvent the law to suit their purposes.

Without question, Tupper's administration of the day-to-day business of the enforcement of fishery laws on the Great Lakes waters suffered from his heavy responsibilities in the Bering Sea seal arbitration between Canada and the United States, a diplomatic effort to control seal hunting on land and at sea, which occupied much of his time from 1890 to 1893. He closely supervised the preparation of data while in Ottawa, and he spent a good deal of time away from the capital. From late February through mid-May 1890, he was in Washington assisting in negotiations with the United States that led to a formal convention,[29] and then, from mid-June through mid-August and for most of November and December 1892, in London helping to prepare the British case. He was away from Ottawa again from January to August 1893, this time in London and Paris working strenuously as the British agent in the Bering Sea arbitration.

The opponents of regulation made an extended case for themselves in debates in the House of Commons in Tupper's absence in 1893, with very little defense on the part of the Acting Minister of Marine and Fisheries.[30] They took up the cudgel again in 1894, this time with Tupper present. Under heavy attack, he answered with a strong defense of his policies, one response consuming two hours and twenty minutes on June 13, 1894, in which he made a classic statement of the fishery policy of the Conservatives since confederation; pointedly answered the critics of Edward Prince, who derided him as a scholar from the British Isles who knew little about the Great Lakes; and defended Samuel Wilmot, who had spent most of his life dealing with the problems of the Great Lakes fisheries. Tupper spoke from experience about the almost universally negative reaction of independent-minded fishermen to regulation and pointed out that "every time you punish a man you excite an enormous amount of sympathy in the district for that man." This offered the perfect seedbed for manipulation of the vote. Tupper noted that when fishermen are punished for having violated regulations, "the man who has only a smattering of knowledge of these questions, who uses what he calls horse sense, and refuses to look into any of the authorities on the subject" organizes discontented fishers against a "tyrannical" Department of Marine and Fisheries.[31]

He showed the results of American fishery policy and explained why regulation had done a far better job of preserving the fisheries in Canadian waters and thus should be retained for the well-being of the fishermen and the public alike. In the United States, the fisheries were in a state of collapse: "Ruin all round meets them and stares them in the face." Official reports showed the loss of hundreds of thousands of dollars and bankrupt companies, and "those remaining in the business were endeavoring to save themselves from absolute ruin by moving on to Lake Superior, and, even further west, to the Lake of the Woods, moving westward as so many of our own fishermen have had to do. . . . We have not yet reached anything like the condition of our neighbours."[32]

He decried the proposition that Canada stocked the lakes and the fish promptly swam off into American waters to be caught there. When he cited the study of fish movements and the results of similar scientific observations and work, the representatives of fishing constituencies replied with their habitual contempt for investigation, observation, and regulatory recommendation, claiming, as always, that the fishermen were the only persons with reliable knowledge based on practical experience. Tupper boasted that the use of the cruiser patrols on the Great Lakes had effectively checked American poaching. Neither his scornful characterization of the "demagogue" nor his reasoned defense of the Conservative Party's fishery policy since 1868 quieted the clamor.

In 1895, after Tupper had been appointed as Minister of Justice and attorney general in one of the Conservative Party's cabinet reshuffles, critics in the Liberal Party continued to pound away at the Department of Marine and Fisheries, concentrating their attack on what they characterized as the department's shameful prosecution of James and Charles Noble of Killarney, Ontario.[33]

While the political battle over fishery policies for the Great Lakes raged in the House of Commons, the Department of Marine and Fisheries worked strenuously to ensure better enforcement of regulations. Most of the effort went forward as part of overseers' work routines. Two notable exceptions that reveal many of the more common enforcement problems in widely different settings, the Pelee Island incident and the Noble brothers' case, would not have been so well documented had it not been for their political overtones in the waning years of Conservative ascendancy in 1894 and 1895. One involved wealthy American sportfishermen and illustrates the challenges to law enforcement created by fisheries adjacent to urban-industrialized areas on Lake Erie, while the other involved a large Canadian commercial fishery and offers some insights into the obstacles to law enforcement in the remote fisheries of Georgian Bay.

The Pelee Island incident originated in carefully laid plans to crack down on American poaching, utilizing the cruiser *Petrel* and the steam launch *Dolphin* to apprehend lawbreakers. Plans for the project emphasized that "both *cruisers should be well armed* and prepared for any emergency that may arise in seizing any American Fishing Tug found fishing in our waters with good and sufficient men on Board" to make a successful seizure. The *Petrel* already had a cannon on deck when in March 1894 the Fisheries Protection Service furnished Captain Edward Dunn with ten Spencer rifles, ten Colt revolvers, and ten cutlasses considered essential in the war on poachers noted for their daring and their penchant for armed resistance.[34]

In April 1894, the *Petrel,* well manned and well armed, set sail for Lake Erie under the command of Dunn, an experienced Georgian Bay mariner and dedicated officer. Much of the work that he and other patrol captains performed was routine and uneventful: visiting overseer stations and supervising license problems; transporting government officials; grappling for, lifting, and destroying illegal nets; gathering information on the nature of the fishing season and the catch; inspecting sawmills; and searching for evidence to use in prosecuting lawbreakers. But the seizure of fishing boats and vessels also played a central role in patrol activities. Summarizing the enforcement actions in Dunn's log for 1894, he reported five seizures, four of them tugs and steam craft on Lake Erie, and one a skiff on Lake Superior. In addition, between July and November 26, the *Petrel* seized two miles of set lines, 127 gill nets, and 25 trap nets, the last 20 being American whitefish gill nets set in the western end of Lake Erie during the closed season.[35]

Captain Dunn's first two seizures of the season on Lake Erie were American sportsmen's yachts in the waters off Pelee Island, carrying wealthy, important people bound for a fishing holiday. They were among hundreds of vacationing American fishermen attracted to the island's fine fishing waters over the past two decades. Beginning in the 1870s, sportsmen sang Pelee's praises, making it well known among the wealthy of Boston, New York, Cincinnati, Chicago, and the cities along the southern shore of Lake Erie. In 1886, the magazine *American Field* considered it such an attractive and well-known fisherman's retreat that it ran a feature story on the Pelee Club, organized in 1884 with twenty-five shares worth $1,000 apiece subscribed largely by "aristocrats" from Chicago and New York. They came to fish for black bass during the legally specified fishing seasons in spring and fall, no wives and children allowed, but each member could bring a guest to enjoy the very well appointed clubhouse and beauty of the place.[36]

In a comedy of errors and misunderstandings, on May 8, 1894, Dunn apprehended approximately fifty wealthy American businessmen and professionals primarily from Cincinnati, Dayton, and Springfield, members of the Dayton Pelee Club, fishing with hook and line from rowboats off Pelee Island in Canadian waters without licenses, arrested them, and towed their yachts, the *Visitor* and the *Leroy Brooks,* to Amherstburg, Ontario. All those apprehended were detained, the fishermen for only a few hours, the captains for longer. Rufus H. King, president of the club, wrote an extended letter to the Minister of Marine and Fisheries explaining the events as he understood them. The Canadian Privy Council, convinced that there had been no intent to break the law, decided in July 1894 to fine each vessel $40 and costs connected with the seizure.[37] By way of contrast, Captain Peterson, in command of the *Dolphin* later that summer, seized the American tug *Grace* while it was fishing illegally in the vicinity of Port Colborne, an action that led to prolonged litigation, involved the United States Department of State and the British Foreign Office, and ended with damages being paid to the owners of the vessel.

While the Pelee Island incident involved a minor offense in the view of most Canadians, including Dunn, the American press in cities around Lake Erie registered considerable local excitement. Reactions varied, with some editors taking the view that American boats could stay out of trouble by staying out of Canadian waters. Others tended to fault the Canadians, claiming that Dunn had been officious in taking an armed party aboard the yachts to alter their machinery so they could not sail away. A Detroit newspaper considered the Canadians discourteous for having arrested American sportfishermen out on a holiday. After all, Canadians had always been welcome at Belle Isle! Another editor opined that the action was a kind of retaliation for American hostility to British and Canadian sealing infractions in the Pacific. Some bristled at the arrest procedures. A cruiser armed with a cannon sent to arrest sportfishermen in rowboats was very heavy handed! The Canadians insisted that the cannon was purely a deterrent for lawbreakers and not intended for offensive use. Captain Dunn fired it to salute the queen's birthday and to commemorate other national occasions.

The *Detroit News* saw the humor in the incident and printed a front-

Figure 14.1. "Battle of Lake Erie (1894)," *Detroit News*, 11 May 1894. (Photograph courtesy the Burton Historical Collection, Detroit Public Library)

page cartoon lampooning the affair entitled "Battle of Lake Erie (1894)" and captioned "We have met the enemy and we are theirs" (figure 14.1). A poem followed, praising the Canadian action and showing popular distaste for the wealthy in depression times:

> 'Rah for the gallant Petrel; 'Rah for the Petrel's men;
> Here's to their red hot visit; Here's may they come again!
> It's rather a butt-end visit; but who in hades cares,
> Since the big guns frowned from the portholes on a bunch of millionaires!
> Go for 'em Johnny Crapaud; go for 'em Bob Canuck;
> Truss 'em up Johnny Thompson, swinge 'em just for luck.[38]

The Department of State considered the arrest inevitable, given the circumstances, and, to the ire of locals, did not undertake an investigation. Tupper felt that the seizure had made its point and would serve as a warning to American sportsmen in the future to obey Canadian regulations and, most particularly, to refrain from fishing for black bass in Pelee Island waters where, he believed, they had contributed greatly to the decline of the species.

Many Canadians applauded the *Petrel*'s action, especially those long irritated by bumptious, belligerent talk about annexing Canada; by a careless, casual disregard for the border; and by Yankee expressions of arrogance and superiority. But not all Canadians approved of the seizures. Those who made money on wealthy American sportfishers at Pelee Island thought that the government was very shortsighted. These Americans generated a good deal of business and provided income for those who catered to their needs. And the commercial fishermen of Pelee Island depended "on American Fishing Companies who get them into their powers by selling them nets and provisions to be paid for by their catch." They were in such trouble trying to clear their debts that they did not favor the enforcement of Canadian regulations. Frivolous and insignificant as the incident seems, take it apart a thread at a time and many of the elements of the relationship between people and Great Lakes fish in 1894 are there.[39]

The case of James and Charles Noble illustrates a very different enforcement environment, presenting virtually insurmountable challenges to fishery overseers. Beautiful Georgian Bay—with its many islands, coves, inlets, and tributary rivers—provided an exceptionally fine spawning ground for whitefish, trout, and pickerel, and a cornucopia for commercial and sportfishers. It also offered numerous places where fishing craft could evade enforcement patrols. Killarney, opposite the easternmost shore of Manitoulin Island, was the setting for the Noble case. An isolated village accessible in the 1890s by boat or by an overland trek of fifty miles from the nearest railroad station, Killarney was home to English Canadians, French Canadians, Native North Americans, and métis who depended mainly on the fish resource for food and income.

The Noble brothers developed the location as the headquarters for their fishing operations. In Killarney, in Collingwood, and at various island locations in Georgian Bay, they operated a large fishing business in the 1890s, an enterprise that had begun modestly two decades earlier. According to their statements, in 1893 their operations included catching fish, buying fish, and running a general merchandise business that dealt particularly in nets and a variety of vessel and sailor supplies. In 1892 and 1893, the company claimed assets of $81,000 and employed 100 to 120 workers. It operated one large boat, four fishing tugs, and numerous sailing craft and sold the catch to the Buffalo Fish Company under contract. The Nobles offered credit to fishermen, who purchased boats and supplies at the beginning of the season and paid for them with the catch, surrendering the boat and equipment at the end of the season if their debts had not been cleared. The Nobles secured licenses for the fishermen working for them from the Department of Marine and Fisheries.[40] Killarney was the Noble brothers' company village. Those who lived there depended on them for a livelihood, since few employment alternatives existed. They were virtually trapped in Killarney during the winter season with little work to do. There the word of the Nobles was, in effect, the law.

When in 1888 Charles Tupper initiated the patrols of the *Cruiser* on Georgian Bay, where fishery regulations were often ignored, Captain Alfred Holmes identified the Nobles as lawbreakers. This is the first time they so appear in existing official records. They were fishing with illegal pound nets and small-mesh gill nets using literally hundreds of thousands of yards, far beyond specified limits.[41]

Thereafter, the Department of Marine and Fisheries kept a watchful eye on the Nobles' enterprise and compiled a list of ways it broke the law. In 1890, 1891, and 1892, according to department records, the Nobles furnished boats and illegal nets to fishermen to use without licenses.[42] With the appointment in 1892 of Thomas H. Elliott as the new overseer in Sault Sainte Marie, charged with cleaning out illegal activity in his division, and with the decision in 1893 to have all lighthouse keepers watch for and report violations of the fishery laws, matters with the Nobles soon came to a head. While some lighthouse keepers ignored the instructions, Pierre de Lamorandier, the keeper in Killarney, tried to comply.

By the summer of 1893, he found himself in serious trouble in the community. On June 19, his driving mare was shot in a way that made her virtually useless. Troubles escalated in the fall, when seven tons of hay were "maliciously set afire," forcing Lamorandier to sell five steers before they were ready for market. A milk cow also had to be sold for want of food to carry her through the winter. Fishermen twice stole the underwear of his wife and daughter and wore them for dancing to make fun of the family. Sticks of stove wood were hurled at the house at night. The bellows in Lamorandier's blacksmith shop was destroyed, and his business was boycotted. His brother's fishnet was cut. Fishermen insulted his son. Neighbors and former friends no longer spoke to him. His children lost their friends. By late December 1893, he feared injury to himself. The priest in Killarney warned him of "hard talk" against him among the fishermen. Lamorandier believed that Charles Noble intended to give him "all the trouble he can." "We are always uneasy," he wrote to Tupper. He had asked for a detective in the fall of 1893. The Dominion Police sent an officer who traveled by rail to the nearest station, fifty miles away. He could not get to Killarney by either boat or horse. Again in February 1894, Lamorandier asked for a "good sharp detective" to come right away while the fishermen were still together in Killarney, infiltrate their ranks dressed as "a shanty man," and collect the evidence of illegal activity.[43] He repeated the request in March. Finally, H. Giroux, a detective with the Dominion Police, arrived and went undercover posing as a shanty man who was working temporarily until the mills opened. He gathered evidence for a report that showed that the hostilities directed at the frightened lighthouse keeper were very real. The Nobles encouraged drunken fishermen without licenses to intimidate Lamorandier, and they possibly planned to have his barn burned.[44]

Meanwhile, Elliott, the overseer for the district who had vouched for the veracity of Lamorandier's reported difficulties, continued his crackdown on illegal fishing generally. When in the spring of 1894 the Nobles applied for licenses, he refused to send their applications to Ottawa, acting on the instructions of the Department of Marine and Fisheries. The Nobles proceeded to fish without licenses. In May, the department seized four of their tugs and impounded them in Sault Sainte Marie while the Noble brothers were in Ottawa pleading their case for licenses before the department. Tupper made his position on the Nobles very clear. They had persistently and defiantly broken the regulations. Their violations were "the most flagrant which have come before the Department for a long period." There were no extenuating circumstances. They must pay the penalties.[45]

Detective Giroux feared that the Nobles would return from Ottawa and set their men on Lamorandier, but the lighthouse keeper believed that the seizure of the Nobles' tug, "a terrible blow to them," might be the end of his troubles. There was a lull, but harassment resumed in the fall, with damage to his crops and livestock, an assault on his son, threats of a storekeepers' boycott on sales to him, and further threats to have him, Elliott, and a constable removed from their positions. Intimidation continued in the summer and fall of 1895.[46]

Lamorandier was a very valuable fishery officer, given his tribal connections to the Ojibwes and his willingness to take a hard line on enforcement, even though it meant alienating the community and placing him and his family in jeopardy. Hard times, continuing in 1896, exacerbated the enforcement problems in the area of Killarney and Manitoulin Island, where fishermen were hard-pressed to make a living and to keep food on the table. In the winter of 1894/1895, the department bent the rules and allowed 100 yards of gill net per family to fish for home consumption.[47]

At the same time, enforcement continued, with officers in the Georgian Bay district making arrests at risk of life and limb. The fishermen, desperate to continue fishing, wanted to avoid apprehension, fines, and placement on the department's blacklist, never again to be licensed. One example illustrates their fears. In May 1894, Elliott caught four fishermen illegally taking pickerel. They resisted arrest, and Elliott got warrants for them. Three of the four fled in a boat during a heavy gale and were believed drowned. A constable found the fourth, who resisted arrest and had to pay fines for assault and illegal fishing.[48]

Far away from the action on Georgian Bay, meanwhile, the Nobles vented their anger against Charles Tupper and the Department of Marine and Fisheries in the press and with the business community. They succeeded in having their creditors in Montreal, Toronto, and Hamilton bring pressure on Tupper to go easy with them. They hired a lawyer who prepared a pamphlet stating that the Nobles had been the targets of a conspiracy instigated by the Department of Marine and Fisheries and distributed it widely to the press and to members of the House of Commons. The Nobles pictured themselves as struggling entrepreneurs who had worked hard all their lives to build a business in the wilderness, only to see it threatened by bureaucrats in Ottawa who were motivated by anti-Catholicism and a personal prejudice against them. They claimed that they were victims of entrapment and that Elliott had set the trap. Long known as Conservatives, the Nobles sought favor with the office-hungry Liberals. They succeeded in getting Sir Wilfrid Laurier, the leader of the Liberal opposition, to come to their assistance in a full-scale debate in the House of Commons on June 3, 1895, that filled forty-three pages of fine print. The Liberal press took up their cause, drawing copy from the pamphlet that had been prepared by their lawyer. As a result of their efforts, the Nobles managed to forestall the sale of their tugs at auction, get them released on bond, and, in 1895, secure licenses to fish. They sued for damages and were to get repeated delays in hearings before a special commission appointed to investigate the grievances of the Nobles.[49]

The Noble case turned into a political asset for the Liberals, who seized on it as evidence of the misuse of governmental power in their campaign in 1895 and 1896 to bring down the Conservatives. It took the spotlight in the House of Commons debates, along with the complaining fishermen of western Lake Eire, the Detroit River, and Lake St. Clair. From 1894 to 1896, conservation of the fisheries became so confused with political one-upmanship that the idea of saving the fish for long-term use got shoved into the background. The Nobles' legal battle for compensation from the Department of Marine and Fisheries dragged on and on. Twice, in 1899 and 1902, it surfaced in a very lengthy debate in the House of Commons, where it was rehashed in great detail. It finally came to a conclusion in 1902, when the Privy Council sanctioned an award of $18,563 in payment of damages to the Nobles.[50]

But the influence of the Noble brothers' case lived on in the minds of fishermen. According to W. H. Bennett, the Conservative member of Parliament from East Simcoe, the small fishermen of his constituency repeatedly asked him if the Nobles had paid their fines. They saw Noble boats out fishing regularly, breaking the laws, as in the past, and getting away with it. C. and J. Noble was for its day a large and powerful enterprise, believed to be worth at least $200,000. Why, the small fishermen wanted to know, should it escape paying fines and having its equipment confiscated when they, often in the face of hunger, felt the lash of the law? They believed that the powerful and influential did as they pleased while the powerless paid. What was he supposed to tell his constituents, Bennett asked the House of Commons, when they find out that the government has awarded the Nobles more than $18,000 in damages? Contempt for regulations and even more difficult problems with enforcement were sure to follow.[51]

While both the Pelee Island incident and the Noble brothers imbroglio became very newsworthy stories, most cases of enforcement on the northern shore of Lake Erie and in Georgian Bay, which were legion, escaped publicity. Had his campaign to conserve the fisheries been launched in prosperous times, Tupper might have had greater success in convincing the fishermen and the general public that the very valuable fisheries of the Great Lakes needed protection as a long-term source of livelihood and food. Then Canadians might have reacted more intensely to American dominance of the resource. Moreover, Tupper worked in an unfavorable political climate, as a leading Conservative at a time when the Conservatives, long in control of the government, were loosing their unity and vigor. With the victory of the Liberal Party in the election of 1896, fishery policy for the Great Lakes stood on the threshold of changes that diluted the Conservative formula for saving the resource and gave Ontario a large share in administration, regulation, and enforcement. In very significant ways, nevertheless, the Conservative formula lived on. The hatchery and stocking program continued to grow and the interest in and encouragement of scientific study of fish species and natural habitats increased, while the most fundamental of Sir Charles Hibbert Tupper's attempted reforms, cooperative management of the fish population and the waters of the Great Lakes by the United States and Canada, remained a very significant, difficult, and elusive goal.

15

To Save the Fish

The Crisis of the 1890s and the Canadian–American Joint Commission of 1892

Concert and Harmony of Action Is Necessary

By the 1890s, most of the developed regions in the United States and Canada showed clear evidence of environmental problems. In most of these areas, an articulate minority spoke out about what they perceived to be a threat to natural resources from the careless, thoughtless, wasteful ways in which people used them, and the Great Lakes region was no exception. There the consequences of massive deforestation and the excesses of the lumbering industry drew the fire of conservation-minded critics. Suggestions of concern about the practices of farmers crept into the agricultural press in the columns of advice on how to both farm and preserve land for long-term use. Apprehension about water quality, public health, and the pollution of natural waters produced a public outcry and demand for safe water. Sportsmen bemoaned the slaughter of wildlife. Fishers and those responsible for protecting the fish resources of lakes, rivers, and streams warned that stocks had dwindled and some species had disappeared. While concerns about the state of marine life largely fell on deaf ears, they were one aspect of the larger misgivings about the inroads that nineteenth-century development had made into nature's bounty.

From the 1870s, the midcontinent had had its share of Jeremiahs warning of a bleak future. Their numbers grew as the end of the century approached. A good example of their thoughts found in the press and popular literature concerned specifically with the decline in natural resources in the Great Lakes states appeared in the *Chicago Times* in 1881. Noted the writer:

> Possessed as they are of a soil of excessive fertility, with far more than ordinary volume and richness, a climate that favors the sowing and reaping of harvests which are the envy of the older nations; of boundless lakes and rivers, once teeming with fish of the choicest descriptions and swarming with an endless variety of game for the food of her people—yet these dependent, short-sighted and shiftless dwellers of this modern paradise seem to study the more practical methods of total and rapid exhaustion rather than the retention and increase of those means upon which their sole hope and reliance rests for their future welfare and prosperity. Where is the noble buffalo which once darkened the vast feeding-grounds of this fertile country? Mercilessly swept from existence. Slaughtered for their hides! What has become of the long lines of waterfowl which but a few years since made their home with us, and, in their migrations through the Illinois valley, made their annual pilgrimages to the vast swamps of northern Indiana, the Calumet and the lakes of Fox river? Ask the inventors and dealers in improved fire-arms. . . . What of the great lakes? . . . And where are the fish?

The article went on to cite the writings of Seth Green, a pioneer in the artificial propagation of fish and a Commissioner of Fisheries of the state of New York who had analyzed the reasons for the decline in the population of Great Lakes fish, especially the whitefish.[1]

Between 1850 and 1893, commercial fishing on the Great Lakes evolved into a wasteful, exploitative, profit-oriented, and market-driven industry, influenced by ongoing environmental changes that made the fish habitat less adapted to the principal market species of the day. At the same time, the government policy makers responsible for devising ways to conserve the resource for long-term use—hamstrung by lack of funds and public interest, by divided political jurisdiction over lake waters, by insufficient scientific knowledge, and by the opposition of the fishermen—failed to develop an effective management policy. These three major elements—the pollution of the waters, the nature of commercial fishing, and the unsuccessful efforts of policy makers—converged to create the crisis of the 1890s, a nineteenth-century example of failure to sustain a fish resource created by the same factors that have led to crises in many parts of the world in the twentieth century.

By 1890, those responsible for making Great Lakes fishery policy, after two decades of trying, had concluded that interstate compacts or other forms of binding agreements between the states or between the states and the province of Ontario to achieve a uniform policy for the fisheries were not possible. The British and American political systems, which had done such a thorough job of dividing the waters, seemed incapable of uniting them for the purpose of conservation management. Policy makers concluded that the national level seemed to be the last best hope, yet the United States government lacked the constitutionally enumerated power to regulate the fisheries. Perhaps it might do so using its treaty-making power. The Canadian and American national governments needed to develop and enforce uniform, joint regulation. This goal led to the creation in 1892 of the Joint Commission Relative to the Preservation of the Fisheries in Waters Contiguous to Canada and the United States, an investigative body charged with collecting information and making recommendations to Canadian and American lawmakers. Its labors, recommendations, and cool official reception in both countries mark the beginning of repeated efforts over the past century to establish cooperative management of the waters and fish resources of the Great Lakes.

ESTABLISHING THE JOINT COMMISSION

The Canadians, long advocates of a system of unified regulation for the Great Lakes fisheries, suggested forming a joint commission to study needs and make recommendations in 1891. Under the leadership of the Conservatives, the Department of Marine and Fisheries had called repeatedly for intergovernmental cooperation to achieve uniform regulation, and in 1874, Canada had proposed a reciprocity treaty with the United States that included the appointment of joint commissions to deal with a number of Great Lakes issues, including ways to "promote the propagation and protection of fish in the common inland water."[2] The idea languished until the early 1890s. Then, with Charles Hibbert Tupper holding the post of Minister of Marine and Fisheries, the idea came to the fore again. The Canadians and Americans had been embroiled in controversy over the northeastern Atlantic fisheries, finally reaching an impasse in the late 1880s. At the same time, the Bering Sea seal-hunting controversy moved slowly toward settlement. Tupper inherited these problems when he assumed his cabinet post in 1888.

In 1891, Tupper went to Washington to work with the British ambassador on a resolution of the Bering Sea controversy. Although deeply involved with this negotiation, he did not lose sight of the Great Lakes fishery problems. In his annual report of 1891, he noted that the declining fish population in the Great Lakes needed "protection and multiplication; and to make these effective, concert and harmony of action is necessary between all the Government authorities interested." In support of the idea, he cited examples of international agreements to protect fish in shared rivers. He noted that on June 30, 1885, Germany, the Netherlands, and Switzerland had signed a ten-year convention to protect the salmon population of the Rhine River. Luxembourg soon became a signatory. He also pointed out that in September 1890, France, Belgium, and the Netherlands had proposed a similar five-year experiment to protect the salmon of the Meuse. Shared waters called for cooperation. Had he chosen to cite an American example of efforts to cooperate to manage fish in a shared internal waterway, Tupper might have mentioned the attempts of New England states in the eighteenth century to protect fish in rivers that were state boundaries.[3]

Quite aside from the conflict over fur seals in the Bering Sea, in 1891 Great Britain, acting on behalf of Canada, requested an informal conference with the United States to discuss unsolved issues between them. Among the many considerations, a reciprocity treaty and tariff adjustments may have been Canada's top priorities, but canal tolls, rights of transit, boundaries, and other matters needed discussion. The United States stalled and finally consented to meet. Representatives of the countries met in February 1892 in Washington. The conferees agreed on February 15 to appoint a joint commission of two experts, one American and one Canadian, to study and report on restrictions and regulations to prohibit destructive fishing practices in territorial and contiguous waters, to prevent pollution and obstruction detrimental to fish in contiguous waters, to establish and enforce closed seasons in both countries, and to restock and replenish contiguous waters with fish eggs.

Article 5 of the document called for the two countries to consider and discuss the findings as soon as the reports came to them, with the goal of reaching an agreement to carry them into effect, "by treaty or concurrent legislation" of the national governments "or the legislatures of the several States and Provinces, or both, as may be found most advisable." Nothing in the reports "shall be deemed to commit either Government to the results of the investigation." Thus the commission's findings would be purely advisory. Adopted by both Great Britain and the United States on December 6, 1892, the agreement took the form of an exchange of notes at the suggestion of the United States, "a simpler and more expeditious" method than a convention.[4]

THE JOINT COMMISSION AT WORK

Charged with the responsibility of investigating and reporting on ways to prevent destructive fishing, water pollution, and obstruction, the Joint Commission had a formidable task before it. It had to suggest a way to control an aggressive, exploitative, profit-driven industry, taking into account the decline in choice commercial-fish species and the deteriorating fish habitat. Working amid complaints about poaching American fishermen and bullying Canadian cruiser captains, it had to function even-handedly with regard to all the policy- and rule-making arms of government in the United States and Canada—not only at the national level, but also the governments of the eight Great Lakes states and of an increasingly critical, assertive Ontario trying to establish its authority over the fisheries of the Great Lakes.

The United States named Richard Rathbun, a member of the scientific staff of the United States Commission of Fish and Fisheries, as its commissioner, and Great Britain appointed William Wakeham, a fisheries expert, medical doctor, and commander of *La Canadienne,* a cruiser assigned to the protection of the fisheries in the Gulf of St. Lawrence.[5] They met in early March 1893 in Washington to agree on the definition of waters included in their investigation and to develop a plan for collecting data. They opted for very extensive fieldwork to supplement the body of information already compiled by both governments.

So began a remarkable and very extensive survey conducted by on-site visits and observations and by oral interviews. Starting on the Atlantic seacoast in the early spring of 1893 and concluding on the Pacific three years later, teams of two investigators made the visits and interviewed fishermen, fish dealers, game wardens, hatchery superintendents, and local officials using a set of common questions and taking notes in pocket-size notebooks. They also gathered scientific information on various fish species, observed fishing operations, conducted some experiments with different types of nets and mesh sizes, and examined fishery establishments ranging from rather humble shanties to large packing plants and hatcheries.

By the end of the 1893 season, the teams had worked their way westward along the northern shores of Lakes Ontario and Erie. During the 1894 season, they completed their investigation of the Great Lakes, except Lake Michigan, which was excluded from the study because it lies entirely within American jurisdiction, finally suspending work in late November. They were about a year behind schedule, according to the original completion deadline for the entire project: June 1895. Another year would be needed to take the investigators from the Great Lakes to the Pacific coast. The commissioners were wallowing in data. As Rathbun explained in requesting additional time: "These inquiries have been conducted on a scale far exceeding any of a similar nature heretofore undertaken, and the amount of material secured in the way of field notes and stenographic testimony is much greater than had been anticipated."[6] No wonder Rathbun was overwhelmed. The original records of this remarkable project, preserved at the National Archives, fill two standard reading-room trucks. He made a further plea in April 1896 for time to digest and analyze the data. The commissioners had spent a full month working on the materials and condensing the testimony and notes into 15,000 typewritten pages. They requested and received a final deadline of December 30, 1896.[7]

THE FINDINGS AND RECOMMENDATIONS OF THE JOINT COMMISSION

The field notes of the investigators and the testimony of the witnesses are prime sources of detailed information about the human impact on the fish resources of the Great Lakes. Preserving the thoughts of many people associated with the fisheries in the 1890s, they constitute an invaluable record for social, economic, and environmental history and for marine biology. If the Joint Commission had done nothing but assemble these field notes, it would have made a substantive contribution to society by recording the devastating influence of a half century of development on the marine life of the Great Lakes. For William Wakeham and Richard Rathbun, the notes provided the evidence to build a case for the joint regulation of the fisheries of the Great Lakes and other contiguous waters.

In contrast, the published report is far less meaty. For each lake, it includes a description of the body of water; a statement about the biological behavior of each commercially important fish species; records of yields by species comparing years and changing methods of harvest over time; a summary of current conditions; and a set of rules and regulations recommended to conserve the fish. The rich and insightful details found in the original documents do not appear in print. Wakeham and Rathbun literally fulfilled the tasks with which they were charged, primarily to investigate "exhaustive or destructive methods of taking fish or shellfish" in territorial and contiguous waters of Canada and the United States and to suggest ways of preventing or limiting the waste of fish food. In general, they steered clear of criticizing the economic and cultural environment that was largely responsible for the destruction. But they acknowledged the negative impact of certain political realities. Divided jurisdiction over naturally unified waters created vast problems. The commissioners advocated uniform regulations that extended across political boundaries. Moreover, the general misunderstanding prevalent about the location of the boundary between the United States and Canada through the Great Lakes, they argued, generated much of the anger about fishermen operating outside their national waters. Many believed that the area of the lakes three miles beyond each shore was a neutral "high seas" that fishers from both nations could use in common. The location of the boundary had to be settled, and fishermen had to be provided with charts to prevent further abrasive international incidents created by Americans poaching in Canadian waters.[8]

Above all, the report called for a joint management program based on an analysis of the physical evidence gathered about methods of fishing, pollution of waters, and knowledge of the behavior of the various species of fish. Because of diverse and constantly changing conditions, the regulations had to be flexible. A rigid set of rules would not work. If the two governments decided to act jointly, Wakeham and Rathbun urged the creation of a "permanent joint commission, to be composed of competent experts . . . which shall be charged with the direct supervision of these fisheries, and shall be empowered to conduct the necessary investigations and to institute such modifications in the regulations as the circumstances may call for from time to time." This proposal went far beyond the formulas that had been suggested at the state and provincial levels of government. It resembled the Canadian system, by which Parliament passed fishery laws and the Governor in Council had very broad power to change them.[9] In practice, the Minister of Marine and Fisheries usually made the suggestions for change.

In an elaborate set of recommendations for Lakes Ontario, Erie, Huron, and Superior, the Detroit and St. Clair Rivers, Lake St. Clair, and Georgian Bay, Wakeham and Rathbun spelled out exactly what they believed would be essential to save the fish. The commissioners based their ideas on data that had been collected by the two national governments over a considerable period of years—Canadian records dating from 1868 and American records beginning in 1871—and on the very substantial body of information that the investigators for the Joint Commission had gathered during their fieldwork.

The report portrayed a once-bounteous natural resource seriously eroded and, Wakeham and Rathbun believed, urgently in need of constructive regulation to save the fish. In the case of every lake and river examined, data collected by the field-workers was cross-checked against official records obtained in other ways and verified the decline of one or more of the preferred commercial species. The commissioners attributed the sorry state of affairs to overfishing and to vastly improved fishing technology used by ever-larger numbers of fishermen in pursuit of the wealth of Great Lakes waters. They downplayed the effects of pollution as a major factor in declining harvests.[10] Probably they did so because they did not believe that it was as serious as it really was. Their definition of pollution did not take into account the extensive changes wrought by the erosion and siltation of lake waters following agricultural development and deforestation, but only well-documented point pollution. Moreover, they had no way to measure the influence of changes in the physical nature of lake water over time.

But Wakeham and Rathbun were sufficiently impressed with testimony about pollution to develop general guidelines for its prevention.

They included them in the recommendations for each lake with appropriate variations. The Great Lakes should not be used as a dump and sewer for fish offal and dead fish, city garbage, sawdust, waste from gasworks and oil refineries, and other substances deleterious to fish life. Dredging spoil should be handled carefully to prevent injury to fishing grounds. Interestingly, the commissioners said little about sewage discharged into lake and river waters, already a serious problem in urban areas. One of the rivers into which massive amounts of sewage were dumped, the Detroit River, got short shrift. Wakeham and Rathbun spoke of the great decline of herring and whitefish in that river, but emphasized the influence of very heavy fishing as the paramount cause.[11]

In their discussion of Lake Ontario, the commissioners concluded that the real damage to the fish population had occurred early in the history of commercial fishing because of the widespread use of seines. They believed that the whitefish and trout populations had started to decline before fishermen began using either gill or pound nets. While the pollution in the Bay of Quinte and elsewhere from lumber mills had contributed to the spoliation of spawning grounds, that contamination was secondary in explaining the decline. As for the claims of the fishermen that dying and decaying alewives polluted the waters and spoiled spawning areas, thus killing the whitefish, Wakeham and Rathbun pointed out that the trout and whitefish populations had fallen long before the alewives were introduced.[12] While willing to cite the general guidelines for curbing pollution in their recommendations for Lake Ontario, they gave far greater weight to the need for stringent regulations on commercial fishing to protect whitefish, trout, herring, and other species. They seemingly ignored some of the evidence gathered about pollution.

Wakeham and Rathbun cited overfishing and the destruction of young fish as the "principal causes of decrease among the important food-fishes" in Lake Erie. They doubted that pollution had played an important role in the decline of the whitefish. The recent sharp drop in the number of herring, they were convinced, came from the system of tugs following the fish from east to west, gillnetting all the way as the fish proceeded toward their spawning ground. The decline and the new method of pursuit coincided, argued the commissioners, and followed a long period of aggressive fishing.

In their summary of conditions for Lake Erie, however, Wakeham and Rathbun did allot a half page to problems of pollution and spoliation of spawning grounds, more space than they gave to these threats in any other lake summary. They called for a halt to dumping large quantities of fish offal and unwanted fish found intermixed with the fishermen's catch into Lake Erie waters. In addition, they noted, "large quantities of city garbage are also dumped into the lake." They continued, "We have not been able to ascertain what influence other kinds of pollution may exert in the lake proper, but some of its tributary streams and bays have been seriously affected by the drainage from large communities and manufacturing establishments situated thereon, and especially by the overflow of petroleum and waste products derived from the use of oil." These contaminants had greatly damaged spawning grounds in some places. Dredged materials from harbor-improvement projects had ruined some fishing grounds. They added, "The draining of marsh lands has caused the extensive dying out in some places of grass pike, the large mouthed black bass, and bullheads." This was the strongest statement in the printed report of the effects of point pollution and shoreline alterations, which was to be expected, given the extensive development along the southwestern shore of Lake Erie, where the waters were the most shallow, the most contaminated, and the most desired by spawning fish.[13]

Wakeham and Rathbun considered the reasons for the marked decline in the whitefish population of Lake Huron a mixed bag. In their discussion of this lake, they made their strongest statement about the effects of pollution on fish life, citing sawdust dumping and log rafting as the destroyers of whitefish spawning grounds and food sources. Lumbering activity undoubtedly had a negative impact on the species. The commissioners recommended that steps be taken to protect spawning grounds from the wastes of lumbering and all kinds of manufacturing. This suggestion faithfully reflected what the teams of investigators had learned from the fishermen they interviewed. The commissioners assigned very little importance to the effects of pollution on the declining fish harvests in Lake Superior and Georgian Bay. While the testimony of those interviewed and the observations of the investigators indicated the presence of lumbering activity and contamination of the waters by bark, mill refuse, and sawdust, Wakeham and Rathbun did not consider them of sufficient magnitude to merit serious consideration. Overfishing, they concluded, was the real culprit in both bodies of water.[14]

In extensive detail, species by species and location by location, Wakeham and Rathbun suggested the regulations necessary to check the continued depletion of the resource. Fishermen should be licensed. Commercial fishermen had been licensed in Canada since 1869. The American states had either no license requirements or occasional requirements for limited categories of Great Lakes fishermen. The commissioners relied primarily on regulation of mesh size, limits on the number of nets fished, prohibition of certain types of fishing gear, protection of spawning grounds, closed seasons for overharvested species, establishment of a minimum legal size for fish caught (for example, four feet for sturgeon), specified dates for lifting pound nets at season's end, rules for the placement of nets, special regulations flexibly applied to prevent the netting of immature fish, and even restrictions on the number of fish caught. The use of explosives for fishing should be outlawed. They strongly advocated continued artificial propagation of fish and stocking programs.[15] They did not recommend specific ways to curb pollution.

The portion of the report devoted to the four Great Lakes surveyed, the Detroit and St. Clair Rivers, Lake St. Clair, and Georgian Bay filled 107 pages of very fine print, 65 percent of the total on the fisheries in contiguous American and Canadian waters. Rathbun and Wakeham rendered their findings in the matter-of-fact, low-key, descriptive, and dispassionate prose characteristic of scientific writing in the late nineteenth century, avoiding gross examples of waste and useless slaughter of immature fish. They could easily have written a sickening exposé had they chosen to do so. Probably they wrote as they did hoping that a judicious tone would attract more support.

The report had a number of strikes against it. Its proposed system of regulation could be construed as an invasion of the powers of the Great Lakes states. Suppose that the United States and Canada agreed to the recommendations and all the Great Lakes states adopted them. They would be administered by an international regulatory commission, which would have authority to modify the rules as necessary. Would the states not be surrendering their sovereign power to make regulations for their fisheries? What authority did the federal government have under its powers to make treaties and conduct foreign affairs to infringe on states' rights? The regulation of fishing was not an enumerated power. It belonged to the states. The agreement took cognizance of that, suggesting that the findings of the commission might be implemented by concurrent state legislation, developed at the initiative of the states, even though that had become a forlorn hope.

In addition, the timing of the publication of the report was wrong. The investigations had begun during the economic downturn in 1893 and had proceeded slower than anticipated, and the recommendations came to the Canadian and American governments for consideration in early 1897, when the economy had improved and the political climate in both countries had changed in the elections of 1896. Those fishermen and dealers who had testified in 1894 that they favored regulation spoke from a sense of despair in depression times. They considered regulation as inherently unfair because it was almost impossible to enforce. At the same time, their ideas on the subject were complex, as were their views on conserving the resource for the benefit of future generations of fishermen. The declining resource and the depression made them pause and reflect, yet the industry as a whole did not favor regulation. Without the solid support of American commercial fishermen, an agreement to regulate commercial fishing between the United States and Great Britain, acting for Canada, stood little chance of being implemented by the United States. The likelihood of success seemingly would be better in Canada because its fishermen already worked within a regulated system. They complained of its unfairness largely because the rules for all Great Lakes fishermen were not the same. Yet political developments in the years 1894 to 1896 militated against the acceptance of the recommendations of the Joint Commission, for the rising Liberals allied themselves with the Canadian fishermen who wanted no regulation at all.

Thus the fate of the report of the Joint Commission comes as no surprise. It went to Congress with a statement by lame-duck president Grover Cleveland on February 24, 1897, a mere one-sentence transmittal, devoid of presidential commentary on its merit, and with a letter from Secretary of State Richard Olney to Cleveland dated February 23, 1897. Olney characterized the report as "valuable, interesting, and exhaustive." Referred to the House Committee on the Merchant Marine and Fisheries and ordered printed, there it remained, as unpopular in the salmon-fishing regions of far northwestern Washington State as in the Great Lakes states.[16] President William McKinley, an advocate of business interests from Ohio, could hardly be expected to champion its recommendations.

The principal reaction in Canada to the report of the Joint Commission came from the officials of the Department of Marine and Fisheries. For them, the Joint Commission represented a positive step toward a regulatory reform that they had espoused as early as 1872. "It is not unreasonable to look for results of great importance," the department's annual report of 1892 noted optimistically. Ensuing annual reports tracked the commission's progress year by year and stressed the critical importance of joint regulation, finally noting in 1897 that the report of the Joint Commission would be printed. Even before the completed document went to the Department of Marine and Fisheries, it became a tangential part of debates in the House of Commons when members from the Maritime Provinces attacked Sir Wilfrid Laurier's ideas about free trade in fish and freedom for all to fish in Canadian coastal waters. The report did not come forward to the Liberal Party–dominated House of Commons for further discussion. Advocates of international reform in the Department of Marine and Fisheries voiced their disappointment over the fate of Wakeham and Rathbun's effort by their continued strong criticism of the ways in which the neighbor south of the border had wasted the fish resources of the Great Lakes. They took sheer delight in reporting stories from American newspapers that commended the Canadian system of fisheries management.[17]

Thus Charles Hibbert Tupper's attempt to establish uniform policies for the management of the natural resources and marine life of the Great Lakes as a whole failed for political reasons, the victim of the American federal system and the political power of commercial-fishing interests that argued that regulation would ruin profits, jobs, and families. Nevertheless, it remains a milestone in the history of attempts to manage and conserve shared contiguous natural resources by international cooperation, and the goal of the agreement of 1892 remained alive to be reconsidered at the turn of the century and to come forward a second time as a formal treaty in 1908.

Part IV

Toward Lamprey Eve

The Great Lakes Fisheries, 1896–1933

From 1896 to 1933, the problems of the Great Lakes fish population worsened as overfishing continued, pollution of the marine habitat increased, and policy makers at all levels of government struggled in vain to make regulatory conservation a reality. The failure of the attempt in 1908 to secure international joint regulation of Great Lakes commercial fishing, pressures during World War I to produce ever-larger tonnages of lake fish, and strong government support of business in the postwar years, accompanied by a withering in dedication to the conservation ideals of the progressives, combined to hasten the end of an era. The age when lake whitefish, trout, herring, and sturgeon dominated the Great Lakes harvest faded into the past, its passing marked dramatically by the herring crash on Lake Erie in 1925 and by the invasion of the sea lamprey.

16

Commercial Fishing

From Prosperity to Recession

Eat More Fish—They Feed Themselves

Market forces that drove the commercial-fishing industry from 1896 to 1929 go far in explaining the continued downward spiral of the most valuable fish species of the Great Lakes. Like many segments of the Canadian and American economies in the years between 1896 and 1914, the Great Lakes fishing industry enjoyed a period of recovery from depression doldrums followed by better times. Given the declining harvests of most of the choice commercial species, expanded markets, and improved marketing systems and facilities, demand sent prices upward to levels unheard of during the decades of a very flat, oversupplied market in the late nineteenth century, when the best fish, year after year, brought to those who tended the nets five or six cents a pound and the less salable species earned one to three cents. Well might fishermen rejoice that the depression of the early 1890s had given way to good times. World War I produced an unusually heavy demand for Great Lakes fish, and after a brief period of economic downturn following the war, demand sent prices to levels attractive enough to encourage fishermen to strive for ever larger harvests. The general downturn came with the onset of the Great Depression.

Nowhere else on the Great Lakes did the improvement in fishermen's fortunes have such a marked effect on the industry's organization as on the northern shore of Lake Erie. Canadian entrepreneurs and fishermen seized the initiative to develop the commercial fishery on a scale beyond

Figure 16.1. W. F. Colby and Company gill-net steamer (*left*) and the Kolbe fishing docks, Port Dover, Ontario, 1915. (Photograph courtesy National Archives of Canada, Ottawa; negative no. PA71644)

anything it had been before. Utilizing a well-developed railroad system for easy marketing and the telephone, which permitted daily contact with dealers in Toronto, Buffalo, and New York, and with high hopes for profits, Canadian entrepreneurs put money into tugs, processing plants, and icehouses in Port Maitland, Port Dover, Port Burwell, Port Stanley, and Erieau (figure 16.1). The catch of herring escalated from 2.6 million pounds in 1904 to 14.2 million pounds in 1917, inspiring increased investments and expectations for the future that proved to be overly optimistic. During the "great herring years," the major fish houses that would dominate the commercial-fishing industry in Ontario until the mid-twentieth century began business, as Frank Prothero has explained in detail in *The Good Years.*[1]

Entrepreneurs in cities and towns around the American waters of the Great Lakes responded by expanding existing businesses and founding new ones. Data gathered during special studies of the American Great Lakes fisheries showed an escalation in dealerships from 121 in 1899 to 183 in 1917 and a falling off to 159 in 1922 in the wake of price fluctuations at the end of the war.[2] The highly competitive and volatile character of the commercial-fishing industry, with its rapid adjustments to markets, remained as obvious a characteristic as it had been in earlier decades.

When in 1923, Walter Koelz, an aquatic biologist for the United States Bureau of Fisheries, the successor of the United States Commission of Fish and Fisheries, undertook a study of commercial fishing on the Great Lakes, he added economic dimensions to his work that had not been present in earlier surveys. They were in keeping with the ideas of Herbert Hoover, the Secretary of Commerce and thus head of the executive department of which the Bureau of Fisheries was a part. With Lake Erie, producer of the largest volume of the Great Lakes catch, as its focus, the study reported average price levels of the various species between 1890 and 1922, the years when the commission or the bureau had collected special data and indexed the price per pound of the principal commercial fishes using 1899 as the base. The result showed that the indexed prices rose far beyond the 1899 levels, with a very marked increase from 1908 to 1917. Whitefish, for example, rose from 7.36 cents a pound in 1899 to 13.26 cents in 1917 and stood at 18.8 cents in 1922. Most species sold for much more in 1922 than they had in 1899, and most of the commercial fish, except trout and blue pike, made larger indexed price gains than did general indexed wholesale prices in the same period.[3]

Responding to the market, the realities of a deteriorating resource, less rigorous regulation, spotty enforcement of fishing codes, and the availability of new technology, the Great Lakes commercial fishermen and fisher-dealers increased the intensity of the harvest. They invested more in capital equipment and experimented with new ways of harvesting, processing, storing, and marketing. Based on data gathered for the American and Canadian industries for 1899, 1903, 1917, and 1922, in indexed dollars, investment peaked in 1917, with World War I prices and government encouragement to expand production, and had declined by 1922. In current dollars, the records showed a continuous rise of $7,139,000, from $5,648,000 in 1899 to $12,787,000 in 1922. In indexed dollars, capital invested grew by $9,598,446 between 1899 and 1922, from $2,987,064 to $12,585,510.[4]

CHANGING PRODUCTION PROFILE

The harvest of commercial fish from Great Lakes waters between 1896 and 1929 totaled well over 100 million pounds year after year, except in 1926, 1928, and 1929, in the wake of the devastating decline in herring, a major species in the catch for decades. At first glance, these generalized figures by themselves might seem to suggest that the fish held their own in the face of aggressive fishing for most of the period, but in reality they testify to the need for more intensive harvests to maintain the same levels of production.

Generalized totals of production do not show the size of fish and the profile of species in the catch. When segregated into species, the figures

Table 16.1. Total major commercial species production: whitefish, trout, herring, and sturgeon, 1879–1930, from the Great Lakes of Canada and the United States (in thousands of pounds)

Year	Whitefish	Trout	Herring	Sturgeon
1879	24,336	7,997	18,040	7,841
1885	22,178	17,673	33,679	8,578
1890	19,098	18,473	59,820	5,207
1893	12,977	21,727	55,623	2,742
1899	9,002	17,898	72,723	1,772
1903	7,653	22,656	40,523	687
1908	10,931	19,123	56,089	375
1913	4,329	16,989	47,653	138
1918	9,802	17,218	76,712	161
1923	9,358	16,073	43,179	136
1924	8,472	17,668	46,757	128
1925	8,721	17,962	25,874	106
1926	9,544	17,973	22,322	124
1927	9,940	17,546	30,264	107
1928	10,547	15,823	20,922	107
1929	11,857	16,561	25,571	70
1930	13,567	14,512	28,904	115

Source: Compiled from Norman S. Baldwin, Robert W. Saalfeld, Margaret A. Ross, and Howard J. Buettner, *Commercial Fish Production in the Great Lakes, 1867–1977,* Technical Report no. 3 (Ann Arbor, Mich.: Great Lakes Fishery Commission, 1979).

indicate something about the nature of the catch. Table 16.1 gives the historical perspective of the harvest totals for the four species considered the most important to the industry from 1879, the first year for which data are available for both Canadian and American waters, at three- to five-year intervals to 1923, and annually thereafter through 1930. The whitefish and the sturgeon clearly were in decline. The trout seemingly were holding their own through 1929, although the general perception among fishermen and biologists was that they were becoming more scarce. The herring fishery of Lake Erie, which showed marked problems and decline in the mid-1920s, explains the dip in herring production in 1925.

Comparing the catch of the four preferred species with the balance of the marketed harvest, frequently referred to as "rough fish," including a wide variety from perch to sheepshead to carp, and expressing the latter as a percentage of the total, the volume of the balance rose markedly, from a low of 26 percent in 1879 to 51 percent in 1930. Stated another way, the four preferred species made up 74 percent of the total catch in 1879 and only 49 percent in 1930 (table 16.2). The fishermen kept the total catch at a reasonably uniform level during the twentieth century by

Table 16.2. Production of all Great Lakes fisheries by species groups, 1879–1930, in Canada and the United States, all lakes (in thousands of pounds)

Year	All Species	Major Commercial Species	All Other Species	Major Commercial Species as % of Total Catch
1879	79,057	58,244	20,813	74
1885	121,290	82,108	39,182	68
1890	143,406	102,598	40,808	72
1893	134,211	193,069	41,142	69
1899	146,617	101,395	45,222	69
1903	114,050	71,519	42,531	63
1908	139,266	86,518	52,748	63
1913	107,854	69,109	38,745	64
1918	146,347	103,893	42,454	71
1923	113,313	68,746	44,567	61
1924	113,412	73,025	40,387	65
1925	100,671	52,663	48,008	52
1926	98,530	49,963	48,567	51
1927	107,869	57,857	50,012	54
1928	89,557	47,399	42,158	52
1929	98,712	54,059	44,653	54
1930	116,246	57,098	59,148	49

Sources: Compiled, with the exception of 1913, from Norman S. Baldwin, Robert W. Saalfeld, Margaret A. Ross, and Howard J. Buettner, *Commercial Fish Production in the Great Lakes, 1867–1977,* Technical Report no. 3 (Ann Arbor, Mich.: Great Lakes Fishery Commission, 1979); the figure for all species for 1913 is from International Board of Inquiry for the Great Lakes of Canada and the United States, *Report and Supplement* (Washington, D.C.: Government Printing Office, 1943), 7.

marketing more and more "rough fish," most of which adapted readily to changing conditions in the Great Lakes.

Carp, which had graduated from a despised species to a commercially viable one for Lake Erie fishermen in the 1890s, increasingly came into its own as a marketable variety in the early twentieth century. Much of it went to New York in refrigerator railroad cars for sale as fresh fish, and a market for smoked carp developed. In 1919, the Bureau of Fisheries, acting on the request of commercial fishermen working on Lake Erie, resumed the artificial propagation of carp, a program that it had abandoned in the face of severe criticism. Of the "rough fish" in the commercial catch in Lake Erie, carp, suckers, yellow perch, walleye, blue pike, sauger, and sheepshead made up 39 million pounds in 1914 and 36 million pounds in 1930.[5] A half century earlier, many of these species could not have been marketed, but with commercial uses developed for them, such as fish meal, oil, and fertilizer, they helped keep the commercial-fishing industry viable.

CHANGING HARVEST TECHNOLOGY

The newer fishing technology—which allowed the harvesting of fish at greater depths, the use of larger amounts of nets, faster transit to and from fishing grounds, and more effective ways of setting nets and utilizing hooks—also helped the fishermen stay in business. They could literally comb the waters from top to near bottom. The fish found fewer and fewer areas congenial to life where they could escape capture. Two innovations that came into general use at the turn of the century greatly enhanced the fisherman's catch: the mechanical net lifter and the motor-powered fishing vessel. The steam-powered net lifter had been introduced around 1891. By 1899, nearly all gill-net steamers were using patented net lifters, enabling a crew to use more nets and to fish at greater depths.

In the summer of 1899, a fishing firm in Marquette, Michigan, introduced naphtha engines as an auxiliary means to propel sailboats, allowing them to travel farther and to fish more than double the number of nets. One year later, a number of boats were using naphtha. With the advent of the gasoline engine, fishermen turned to its use. By 1903, 101 gasoline-powered launches were operating in the American waters of the Great Lakes, and by 1917, gasoline-fueled boats made up 60 percent of the engine-powered "vessels fishing" and 91 percent of the boats transporting the catch. Walter Koelz noted that in 1924 gasoline-powered launches from twenty-five to fifty feet in length used for inshore fishing dominated, having replaced sailboats in that size category early in the century, and a few large tugs had shifted from steam to gasoline engines (figures 16.2 and 16.3).[6]

A larger number of sailboats and rowboats continued to be used in the Canadian than in the American pound-net fishery. While fishermen began using diesel engines in the 1920s and at the end of the decade made a pronounced shift from wooden to steel tugs, both the diesel engine and steel hulls became common only after the Great Depression. The pioneer in using diesel power was Captain P. C. Robinson, the former commander of the Canadian patrol cruiser *Vigilant* and a partner in the Port Dover Fish Company, founded in 1918.[7]

Fishermen experimented with the apparatus of capture. The use of hooks took on new importance in the early twentieth century, especially in trout fishing. Using a somewhat different setting system than in the past, fishermen tied hooks to four-foot fine lines. The lines were then fastened to a heavy cord that was as much as several miles long. Commonly, 2,500 to 3,000 hooks were used in hook gangs, either fastened to the bottom or floated, according to Koelz. In the first decade of the twentieth century, fishermen also found that they could enhance their catch by using

Figure 16.2. Bay of Quinte fishermen with sailboats and catch, ca. 1910. (From Ontario Game and Fisheries Commission, "Fifth Annual Report," 1911, in Ontario, *Sessional Papers,* 1912, no. 10, facing 10)

the bull net, an adaptation of the gill net, generally with a three-inch mesh, designed to permit fishing from very near the bottom upward to twenty-five feet, whereas the ordinary gill net took fish within only about five feet of the bottom. Another technique used with gill nets, floating or canned nets, gained popularity. Fishermen attached air-filled tin cans to nets, making it possible to adjust the depth of set readily rather than using the traditional method of placing the nets in one position, anchored to the bottom of the lake. In the summer of 1929, as fishermen continued to experience difficulty in maintaining their harvest levels, they turned to the deep trap net. Introduced in Port Hope, Michigan, on Lake Huron to take whitefish, the use of the deep trap net spread rapidly in that lake and into northern Lake Michigan and Green Bay. It was like a submerged pound net with a covered top that was fished at a depth of 60 to 125 feet. After an investigation in cooperation with the departments of conservation of Wisconsin and Michigan, the Bureau of Fisheries reported that deep trap nets took too many adult whitefish, glutting the market and depleting the breeding stock, and that they destroyed too many small fish.

Figure 16.3. Examples of expensive, effective technology of the harvest in the 1920s: (*top*) two gill-net steamers, one with an open deck and the other with a housed fore, returning to port, Lake Erie; (*bottom*) fishermen clearing gill nets with the help of a power-driven gill-net lifter, whose drum is evident. (From Walter Koelz, "Fishing Industry of the Great Lakes," in U.S. Commissioner of Fisheries, *Report,* 1925 [Washington, D.C.: Government Printing Office, 1926], Appendix 11, facing 588, 595)

They were illegal in Ontario, but very hard to detect. Fishermen continued to use them, especially in Georgian Bay, despite the efforts of enforcement officers. Bull nets remained legal in the Canadian waters of Lake Erie "as long as they were allowed in any one of the states that bordered on Lake Erie."[8]

The response of Great Lakes fishermen in the early twentieth century to declining fish stocks and rising prices was not unique. Under similar conditions in many different places and times, fishers turned to more effective harvesting methods and expanded operations to keep their occupation viable.[9]

FISHERMEN: MEASURES OF WORK FORCE, CAPITAL, PRODUCTIVITY, AND INCOME

During the period from 1899 through 1922, the total number of persons employed in commercial fishing on the Great Lakes declined. The combined American and Canadian counts dropped from 10,335 in 1899 to 9,782 in 1922. These figures represent the number of harvesters at work on the water, but not the number of shoresmen employed in packing houses. The combined figures obscure a very real difference in developments in the two nations, for the number of Canadian fishermen grew with each of the counts taken. It increased by 1,000 during this time period, whereas the number of American fishermen fluctuated from census to census. Comparing the figures in 1899 and 1922, the number of American fishermen fell by 1,611.[10] The Canadian figures reflect a growth in production, especially on Lake Erie and on Lakes Ontario and Superior, where the fish resource was more plentiful than in the other Great Lakes and where Ontario followed a more relaxed licensing and enforcement policy than had the dominion. A decision by the British Privy Council in 1898 assigned the right to license to Ontario, and the dominion subsequently gave up enforcement. With the growth in Canadian production went a threefold expansion in the use of gill-net yardage in the herring fishery on Lake Erie alone, largely between 1910 and 1918, with the initial increase in gill nets among fishers in the Port Stanley area.[11]

Beyond a census of fishermen at work on the water, the data gathered by the governments of the Dominion of Canada, the province of Ontario, and the United States provide some insights into the economic performance of fishermen from 1899 to 1922. The average catch in pounds per fisherman, derived by dividing the catch by the number employed on the water, was larger, on average, in American than in Canadian waters (table 16.3). But the averages are flawed and should be viewed with reservations, since Canadian harvesters caught many of the fish reported in American production totals. In addition, the Canadian averages are lower possibly

Table 16.3. Canadian and U.S. fisherman's average size and value of catch and average capital investment, with combined averages (CGL) for all Great Lakes fishermen, 1899–1922

	Pounds			Indexed Value			Indexed Investment in Capital		
Year	Canada	U.S.	CGL	Canada	U.S.	CGL	Canada	U.S.	CGL
1899	11,033	15,157	14,176	271	158	184	223	309	289
1903	7,713	12,378	11,215	330	187	223	189	418	361
1908	9,025	13,918	12,570	479	271	324	253	371	340
1917	12,000	13,547	13,080	811	929	892	773	1,552	1,309
1922	9,463	13,826	11,945	641	931	828	900	1,504	1,278

Sources: Compiled from Norman S. Baldwin, Robert W. Saalfeld, Margaret A. Ross, and Howard J. Buettner, *Commercial Fish Production in the Great Lakes, 1867–1977,* Technical Report no. 3 (Ann Arbor, Mich.: Great Lakes Fishery Commission, 1979); Canada, *Sessional Papers,* 1901, no. 22, 181; 1905, no. 22, 198–199; 1910, no. 22, 228–229; Ontario, *Sessional Papers,* 1919, no. 14, 30–31; 1923, no. 14, 46–47; U.S. Commission of Fish and Fisheries, *Report,* 1901, Appendix, 57th Cong., 1st Sess., 1901, H. Doc. 705 (Serial 4391), 579; A. B. Alexander, "Statistics of the Fisheries of the Great Lakes in 1903," in U.S. Commissioner of Fisheries, *Report,* 1904, Appendix, 58th Cong., 3d sess., 1904, H. Doc. 479 (Serial 4897), 647–649; Bureau of the Census, *Fisheries of the United States: 1908* (Washington, D.C.: Government Printing Office, 1911); and U.S. Commissioner of Fisheries, *Report,* 1919 (Washington, D.C.: Government Printing Office, 1921), Appendix 10, 53–56, and *Report,* 1924 (Washington, D.C.: Government Printing Office, 1925), Appendix 4, 278; the price index is from Walter Koelz, "Fishing Industry of the Great Lakes," in U.S. Commissioner of Fisheries, *Report,* 1925 (Washington, D.C.: Government Printing Office, 1926), Appendix 11, 591.

because Canadian fishermen did not invest as heavily in boats and apparatus of capture as did American fishermen. There is no way to explain precisely the reasons for the differences.

The value of the catch per fisher based on the value of the Great Lakes harvest indexed for each nation, with 1926 used as the base year, shows that American fishermen averaged a smaller gross income for their catch in 1899, 1903, and 1908 than did their Canadian counterparts. In 1917 and 1922, Americans averaged a larger gross income for the catch. The differences reflected in these national averages, too, should be regarded as questionable, given reporting flaws and the keenly competitive nature of the fishermen, who could and often did transfer their operations from place to place. Moreover, the average values per pound of the catch in the waters of both nations derived from the official records are very low compared with the actual values shown in Walter Koelz's report. Looking at the indexed average values of the catch for all Great Lakes fishermen, all rose markedly between 1903 and 1917 and declined in 1922 to 93 percent of the 1917 levels. The Ontario Game and Fisheries Commission reported in 1911 that the Canadian Great Lakes fisherman made an "average annual profit" of between $400 and $800. Fishing took place during six or seven months of the year, and, as in the past, fishermen often combined fishing with other occupations, even during the fishing season.[12]

The reported values of capital investments by fishers in Canada and the United States, although an underestimate, are a reflection of relative differences, with the Americans having far more invested in boats and equipment than the Canadians. While data for both countries show that the average size of the catch per fisher did not increase in proportion to the larger amount of capital invested, many felt that fish prices justified buying new and more efficient gear, boats, and equipment and that strong competition for a declining resource made these investments essential. Others, especially older fishermen, retired from the labor force, and still others found employment off the water. Some very strongly committed fishers changed locations. For example, a second generation of Washington Islanders, in order to overcome the sharp decline in once-bountiful home waters, left the Green Bay area for better fishing in southern Lake Michigan, where they operated boats out of Racine and Kenosha, Wisconsin, and Waukegan, Illinois. The last port had real merit, some claimed, because the laws of Illinois were less rigorous and more easily evaded than those of either Wisconsin or Michigan. Moreover, alternative employment in the off-season or in poor fishing seasons was close at hand. The strong bond between fishers and life on the water should never be discounted in the decision-making process.[13]

The data compiled by the Great Lakes states, the province of Ontario, and the national governments of the United States and Canada reveal a troubled industry with basically stagnant production levels and ever-larger capital investments to maintain them. The investment in physical plants for handling the harvest ashore as well as that in apparatus of capture had grown since the 1880s, with a marked escalation in the twentieth century. Fishermen and dealers wanted to make maximum profitable use of those investments and, in order to do so, had to maintain and increase the harvest or at least improve the marketability of all the harvest, "trash" fish included. Their efforts bore heavily and destructively on the fish resource and taxed the ingenuity of those developing more effective ways of harvesting the fish and more creative ways of marketing the catch. Organizational changes in the industry also greatly influenced production and thus pressure on the fish population.

STRUCTURE AND STRATEGIES OF THE INDUSTRY

Several main currents run through the changing organizational structure and strategies of the Great Lakes commercial-fishing industry in the first three decades of the twentieth century. Among them, the continued but weakening influence of American dealer-entrepreneurs merits careful consideration, including the rise of A. Booth and Company to multimillion-dollar corporate status before World War I, followed by its notable decline in the late 1920s. A related factor was the rise of Canadian-owned and -operated fishery businesses. In addition, throughout the industry, labor and capital moved more and more to collective ways of organization and operation to achieve their goals. A well-pronounced tendency in the late nineteenth century, the principle of cooperation spread in the twentieth to include smaller units of production and a labor union movement. Finally, industry leaders engaged in campaigns to improve the market quality of their products and to encourage greater consumption of fish, goals for which they succeeded in winning government assistance.

The Rise and Decline of A. Booth and Company

To some degree, the catalyst for these currents of change emanated from the expansive plans of the A. Booth Packing Company, which was headquartered in Chicago. At the close of the nineteenth century, the Booth company initiated a campaign to consolidate and dominate the entire fishing industry of the Great Lakes by controlling the majority of fish dealers. Long building strength in the Great Lakes commercial fisheries and heir to a number of dealerships that had failed during the depression of the 1890s, the Booth company orchestrated a merger designed to consolidate the "principal fisheries of the Great Lakes." Incorporated under Illinois law on July 20, 1898, as A. Booth and Company, with a capital of $5.5 million, the firm was commonly referred to as the "fish trust," one among the many consolidations in the American business world in an age of corporate growth. The combination of enterprises, argued the Booth interests, would eliminate wasteful competition, make the market far steadier with few losses from oversupply, and help prevent the harvest of small, immature fish. The corporation also contemplated the propagation of species native to the Great Lakes to stock the waters. The combination made good business sense and good conservation policy, claimed the corporation. In July 1899, the Booth interests incorporated, under Canadian law, the Dominion Fish Company, a consolidation of its operations on the Great Lakes, in Manitoba, and in "the sea or inland waters in Canada or adjacent thereto," with a stated capital stock of $200,000.[14] Dominion was a subsidiary of the Chicago-based business. Neither A. Booth and Company nor the Dominion Fish Company was a small operation, and both engaged in packing, processing, and marketing a wide variety of products other than Great Lakes fish.

Key and dominant in the commercial-fishing industry of the Great

Lakes through the 1920s, A. Booth and Company, renamed the Booth Fisheries Company in 1909, and the Dominion Fish Company adopted business strategies designed to maximize profits in a period of very favorable markets. They are significant for the opposition they generated among fishers, the more generalized anti-American feeling they created among Canadians, the influence they wielded in dealing with governing authorities, and the negative consequences they had for the fish populations of the Great Lakes and elsewhere.

As already noted, the Booth company's operations on Lake Superior in the late nineteenth century had aroused the hostility of fishermen in Port Arthur, Ontario, and the ire of the Department of Marine and Fisheries and, given company policies, had tended to erode the fish resource during the last quarter of the nineteenth century. American fishermen as well often found themselves in an adversarial position with the company, a common state of affairs in relations between dealers and fishers. Whether north or south of the international border, Great Lakes fishers complained about the kinds of contracts that Booth offered for their catch. Prices were the sore point. After 1899, Booth and Dominion paid fishermen too little and then resold at substantially higher prices, the fishermen felt, taking an unfair share of the income that they generated by their rough, strenuous work on the water at the mercy of nature.

The administrators in the Department of Marine and Fisheries were especially alert for irregularities in the Booth company's operations. Deserved or not, the American firm had gained a reputation for intimidating overseers, breaking the laws, and fleecing the fishermen. Charles Hibbert Tupper and his able policy adviser, the marine biologist Edward E. Prince, had blown the whistle on the A. Booth Packing Company in the 1890s. Tupper was gone, but a vigilant Prince remained, hampered in his efforts to save the fish by the transfer of the licensing of fishermen and the enforcement of fishery policy to the province of Ontario after 1898. Prince remained alert for reports of infractions, which came to him from the Dominion's inspectors and fisheries patrol service. Moreover, individual fishermen and proprietors of small fishing and related businesses did not hesitate to protest about the business practices of the Booth company to members of the House of Commons. Much criticism of the American "fish trust" went into Canadian official records from 1898 to 1914.

In the spring of 1898, four months before the organization of A. Booth and Company under Illinois law, Matthews, the president of the Reform Association of Port Arthur, called on Prince in Ottawa to discuss the Port Arthur Fish Company and to urge the Department of Marine and Fisheries to grant ten new pound-net licenses to Canadians who would, in effect, fish for the company. The firm, operating for the A. Booth Packing Company, bought the fish under contract, provided the transportation to market, and sold the fish. As Matthews saw the matter, "[T]o curtail or injure the Co. would be a *serious matter* for *Port Arthur*, this being the main industry and the only available outlet for the fish. The local fishermen are poor and could not carry on the fisheries. The Co paid out *$27,000* last year." Thus he stated the rationale that was cited time and again in support of the itinerant merchant fish dealer: performance of a valuable service for isolated communities and enhancement of local economies. Prince, who had long been disgusted with the ways of American companies and with poaching American fishermen, warned the Minister of Marine and Fisheries to beware and, given the Booth company's business record, to exercise extreme caution in issuing licenses.[15]

Prince soon received reports from department officers that confirmed his fears about the Booth company's plans for Lake Superior. During the final months of his service in 1898, Thomas Elliott, one of the most able and energetic of the overseers on the Great Lakes who was stationed in Sault Sainte Marie, Ontario, reported the views of dealers and fishermen in the area of the North Channel and Manitoulin Island. They feared a "powerful syndicate" of two-thirds of the Great Lakes fish firms that were already under Booth's control and already lowering fish prices "below living rates," in an effort to drive them out of business. Fishermen from other locations on the lakes reported similar fears.[16]

Canadian fishermen's complaints about the operations of A. Booth and Company in the first decade of the twentieth century came from three areas: Georgian Bay, Lake Erie, and, in Manitoba, the whitefish-rich waters of Lakes Winnipeg, Winnipegosis, and Manitoba. The first salvo in the House of Commons came on June 14, 1899, when Charles Tupper, former Minister of Marine and Fisheries during the Conservative government of the 1880s and 1890s and strong critic of American exploitation of Canadian resources, asked searching questions about Booth-owned companies that were operating in Manitoba and Georgian Bay. He lamented the company's policy of paying low prices to Canadian fishermen and then reselling the catch for double the amount. Less than a year later, A. W. Puttee, the member of Parliament representing Winnipeg, made an extended attack on the behavior of "the combine" in Manitoba waters, alleging illegal and very extensive overfishing, to the detriment of both Indian and non-Indian residents and of the resource as a whole. This was a mere prelude to the very extended protest about the operations of the Booth company's interests in Manitoba waters led by W. H. Bradbury of Selkirk in 1909. On May 13, Bradbury conducted a veritable tirade against the Booth interests, calling the company a "great vampire which has sucked the heart's blood out of our fishery." Responding to the heavy criticism, the Department of Marine and Fisheries undertook an investigation of the Manitoba fisheries and made a report in January 1910.[17]

Meanwhile, the push of A. Booth and Company to control the commercial-fishing industry of the Great Lakes led to friction on Lake Erie. Activities there provide an excellent example of the ways in which the Booth company's interests wielded political influence in Canada. On August 23, 1900, the *Petrel,* the patrol cruiser of the Department of Marine and Fisheries assigned to Lake Erie, seized and retained the *Kate Wilson,* a tug owned by William Wilson and operated out of Erie, Pennsylvania, for A. Booth and Company. E. A. Carter, the secretary of the Booth company, contacted Leighton McCarthy, a lawyer in Toronto and member of the House of Commons, for help in getting the tug released. Writing to Sir Louis Davies, the Minister of Marine and Fisheries, McCarthy sought mercy using Carter's words: "This William Wilson is a representative gentleman, but poor. All that he has in the world is his fishing tug and I ask you for our Company and humanity's sake to do everything you possibly can to have the Canadian Government release this boat to Mr. Wilson." Wilson had not intentionally fished in Canadian waters. Neither he nor other Lake Erie fishermen knew the location of the boundary line, argued Carter.[18]

In his letter to Davies, McCarthy went on to cite the political advantages for the Liberals of releasing the tug. A. Booth and Company carried on large operations in his own constituency and elsewhere, and the firm was powerful. A company officer had told him that the fate of the *Kate Wilson* would determine how the company wielded its very considerable influence in the coming elections. Thereafter, the Minister of Marine and Fisheries made a convincing argument to his superiors for clemency, and by order of the Privy Council on April 4, 1901, the tug was released, with Wilson assuming legal costs incurred by the government in enforcing the law.[19]

Whether the release of the *Kate Wilson* encouraged officials of the Booth company to think that the Canadian cruiser *Petrel* was a paper tiger is unknown, but it did show that political clout was a potent weapon, and they continued to use it. One of the Booth company's affiliates, the M. Doyle Fish Company of Toronto, urged the Department of Marine and Fisheries not to extend the fishing season in the fall of 1901 and again in 1905, both times citing the depletion of the fish population as the reason for halting the harvest. The company considered the market oversupplied and the glut a threat to prices. Complaints about "this grasping corporation," as one Ontario district fishery overseer put it; evidence of Booth company tugs poaching on Lake Erie; and the seizure, confiscation, and sale of a Booth-owned tug by Canadian authorities appeared in departmental records through 1905. Captain Edward Dunn learned in the same year that the captains of tugs fishing for the Booth company received daily instructions about the location of the *Vigilant,* which had been added to the Canadian fishery enforcement fleet for service on Lake Erie in November 1904.[20] The tugs were faster and more maneuverable than the *Vigilant.*

Among the many critics of A. Booth and Company, the Ontario Game and Fisheries Commission castigated the firm's operations as the principal menace to the fisheries of the Great Lakes, recommending as a remedy the prohibition of the export of fish taken from Ontario waters. Anti-Booth feelings surfaced in cartoons published in Detroit newspapers. One depicts the animosity of American fishing companies that competed with Booth. The president of the Wolverine Fish Company sits in a small boat owned by the "Anti Trust Fish Co." and holds up on the point of a spear a large, vicious, predatory fish with a big mouth lined with sharp teeth and labeled Trust. A. Booth and Company is represented in the same cartoon series by a caricature of the manager of its Detroit office, neatly dressed with high starched collar and bow tie, levering a barrel labeled A. Booth & Co. Fish & Oysters over a terror-stricken live fish (figure 16.4).[21]

For the Department of Marine and Fisheries, problems related to the Booth company's operations on Lake Erie, created by the firm's aggressive pursuit of dominance on the Great Lakes, paled into insignificance compared with the Squaw Island controversy on Georgian Bay. The dispute dramatically illustrates the highly competitive and intense pursuit of commercial fishing in the Georgian Bay area and its consequences for the lives of fishermen and the natural world, of which they were one part. Squaw Island, with its fine natural harbor, a safe haven in rough weather, is located to the east of Manitoulin Island in extremely well stocked fishing waters. It had long served the needs of Georgian Bay fishermen. For countless decades, Ojibwe fishers had fully understood the advantages of Squaw Island for protection and as a place to dry nets and cure fish.

The Dominion Fish Company, the Canadian subsidiary of A. Booth and Company, purchased a lease to operate on Squaw Island in 1902. It acquired not only a fine location, but also a legacy of opposition by fishermen who operated on the island to earlier large-scale fisher-leaseholders, dating from 1885. In 1902, the animosity was further sharpened by the decline in the whitefish and sturgeon populations and the heightened spirit of competition among fishers for those that were left.

According to official findings, the Dominion Fish Company controlled "practically all of the fishing plant of the Georgian Bay." It used Squaw Island heavily. The employees lived there and fished from there. Rival fishing companies challenged the Booth company in 1902, offering fishermen a better price for their catch than Dominion offered. Those who still lived on Squaw Island and made it a base for their fishing operations but sold to Booth's rivals found themselves the defendants in a suit brought on May 3, 1902, by the Booth interests to eject them and to force them to pay damages for causing the Dominion Fish Company to forgo the use of the island for its fishing operations. This case never went to trial, but in a settlement out of court, the plaintiffs assumed all costs and the defendants received permission to stay on the island and agreed to sell their fish to Dominion at a specified price. In essence, Booth held on and determined the prices that fishermen received for their catch.

Dissatisfaction lingered, and the fishermen still wanted to sell their catch to other companies for better prices. They feared that if they did so, they would be forced from the island, from where they had fished for decades. The Department of Marine and Fisheries—weary of petitions, letters from members of Parliament, arguments over who owned what (uncertain about whether the Dominion of Canada or the province of Ontario held jurisdiction over the island), and pressures from the Booth interests—decided to refer the Squaw Island controversy to the Georgian Bay Fisheries Commission. On April 18, 1906, by Order in Council, it assumed the task of wading through the hot and angry testimony and made its recommendations one year later. The commission argued that the Dominion Fish Company should have confirmed its rights to the exclusive use of the fishing properties that it had purchased. "Any lease or right of exclusive occupancy" of the island should be canceled, and none should be issued in the future. Finally, Squaw Island should be opened to any "duly licensed" fisherman and any fish dealer for the business of fishing, and permission should be granted "to erect wharves, ice-house, cabins, on any part of the island not already occupied on the payment of a small ground rent to the department." Simply put, the Dominion Fish Company's claims to monopoly use of Squaw Island should be nullified.[22]

These are examples of the ways in which the largest dealer on the Great Lakes, A. Booth and Company, tried to maintain control in the Georgian Bay fishing grounds, the richest in the Canadian waters of the Great Lakes. Its activities on Lake Erie illustrate the ways in which the corporation tried to make inroads into the most productive of the Great Lakes. On Lake Erie, it never dominated fish producers as it did on Georgian Bay and on Lakes Superior, Huron, Michigan, and Ontario. It was virtually impossible to do so, given the easy access to national markets by means of the railroads connecting the fishermen and dealers who operated on Lake Erie with the market in New York, where so much of the fish from Lake Erie went. On Lake Erie, the Booth company ran fishing tugs from Erie, Pennsylvania, and Ashtabula, Ohio. Its monopoly or

Figure 16.4. Jabs at the powerful A. Booth and Company: (*above*) Edgar A. Davis, of the Wolverine Fish Company of Detroit, spears the TRUST, a vicious species that symbolizes the Booth interests; (*facing*) Angus G. McDonald, manager of the Detroit office of the Booth company, casually rolls a barrel over a live fish. (From Newspaper Cartoonists Association of Michigan, *Our Michigan Friends "As We See 'Em": A Gallery of Pen Sketches in Black and White* [Detroit: Press of William Graham Printing, 1905], 130, 215; photographs courtesy State Library of Michigan, Lansing)

near monopoly of marketing the fishermen's catch gave Booth the best chance of setting prices for fish directly from the nets. This was the preferred tool for all dealers and the reason that they usually found themselves in an adversarial position with fishers.

The operations of A. Booth and Company rose to their heights before World War I, experienced many challenges from rivals, earned the ill will of many fishermen and of the Department of Marine and Fisheries and the Ontario Game and Fisheries Commission, and went through one bankruptcy in 1908. Reincorporated as the Booth Fisheries Company in

1909, it held on as a major force in the Great Lakes commercial-fishing industry until the Great Depression, and then greatly reduced its operations on the Great Lakes in the wake of a second bankruptcy. After being reorganized, it maintained its operations in the Wisconsin waters of Lake Superior until the mid-1960s. When in the 1920s, the firm developed a slick publicity piece for shareholder and public consumption, the Great Lakes fishery received short shrift. It was listed as the focus of one department, "Freight and Transportation on Great Lakes," and at the end of the text there appeared a small illustration of a fishing tug entitled "One of Fleet of Eleven Steel Tugs Operating on Great Lakes," a fitting symbol of the company's origins.[23] The major operations of the Booth company had long since been elsewhere, primarily in the fisheries of the Atlantic and Pacific Oceans, with a number of salmon and sardine canneries among its principal assets.

The Weakening of the American Dealer System

The American dealer system on the Canadian Great Lakes had weakened by World War I, challenged by the rise of Canadian companies at the western end of Lake Erie that developed business relationships with local fishermen who cast their lot with Canadian enterprises rather than the established and much criticized Yankee dealers.[24] In addition to high prices, greatly relaxed regulations in Canadian waters, and a bountiful fish population, changes in American tariff policy assisted the growth of Canadian-owned fishing businesses and their ability to compete in the American market. In the past, Canadian dealers had no way of circumventing the duty of three-quarters of a cent per pound imposed on fresh fish imported from Canada in 1890. The reduction to one-quarter of a cent per pound in 1897 helped and even more so did the abolition of the duty in 1913. From then to 1922, when new legislation imposed a duty of one cent per pound, Canadian companies had greater access to American markets, where most of their catch went.[25]

As transportation and communications improved in Great Lakes fishing communities, making them increasingly accessible to the economic mainstream, fishers found ways to compete with and bypass established dealers. Many used the telephone to decide when it was advantageous to sell and forwarded the catch to market independently of local dealers using refrigerated railroad cars. For example, a report prepared in 1903 by direction of the United States Commissioner of Fisheries noted that many fishermen who operated on the Saginaw River shipped their fish directly to the New York market when the prices made it profitable to do so, having in the meantime kept their fish alive in live cars or large box enclosures.[26] In the 1920s, the construction of new and better roads made truck transportation another viable link to markets, providing additional opportunities for fishermen to act independently of local dealers.

Cooperation, Association, and Collective Action

In the early twentieth century, the growth of many forms of collective action characterized change in the organization of the commercial-fishing industry as individual fishermen and small fishing businesses responded to intensified competition and to higher prices for the catch and as they sought to offset the power wielded by larger dealers and the massive, well-organized A. Booth and Company. The idea of several fishermen joining forces to operate in the fishery in the Canadian waters of Lake Erie led to the formation of small cooperatives. A cooperative established in Rossport, Ontario, on Lake Superior, to resist the Booth company's control in 1900 lasted until 1919.[27]

Similarly, fishermen who worked on the American waters of Lake Superior turned to the cooperative model. In Cornucopia, Wisconsin, southwest of the Apostle Islands, fishermen grappling with isolation and the need for market access other than through fisheries controlled by Booth or through other firms in Bayfield found workable alternatives. After trying to send fish by rail and often loosing money because of train delays and questionably honest consignees, one took his troubles to the local general merchant in 1925. The proprietor of the store, Herman Ehlers, and all the fishermen in Cornucopia organized a cooperative to ship the catch to Chicago. Ehlers received a 3 percent commission. The system worked well, and it is said that the number of boats fishing out of Cornucopia grew from three to twenty. The Scandinavian fishermen of the Minnesota portion of the Lake Superior North Shore organized the Duluth Fisherman's Union, a cooperative business arrangement that also lobbied the state legislature.[28] The cooperative idea appealed to Great Lakes fishermen who found themselves in a situation analogous to that of Canadian and American farmers. They wanted to reduce expenses for equipment, shipment, and storage by eliminating the middleman.

At the same time, Lake Erie fishermen who worked off the Ohio shore and out of Erie, Pennsylvania, cooperated to bargain with dealers and to strike for more equitable prices for their catch, as they did in 1906. In 1908, fisherman in Erie were again on strike for seven weeks. According to the findings of the United States Tariff Commission in 1924, organized Lake Erie coastal buyers who owned the vessels and the Fishermen's Union fixed the prices paid to gillnetters for herring and blue pike by negotiation. Bargaining often failed. In 1924, the American fishermen went on strike from July 27 to August 19.[29] Noted the commission: "a year without a strike has come to be abnormal, for in at least six years of the last decade strikes have occurred in the United States industry."[30]

Fishermen's efforts to work in groups in Ontario found very substantial expression during World War I, with the formation of such trade associations as the Lake Erie Fishermen's Association, the Canadian Fishermen's Association on Lake Superior, and the Lake Huron and Georgian Bay Fishermen's Association. More followed in succeeding years.[31]

What did the escalation of cooperative activities mean for the fish resource of the Great Lakes? Often it strengthened and focused the groups contending for the catch at a time when its quality was declining, and it heightened the aggressive pursuit of the most valuable species. But in the case of fishers organized into unions to bargain with dealers, it may have slowed the harvest of herring in Lake Erie.

Market and Distribution Strategies

Another very notable change in the industry's organizational emphasis that affected the fish population related to markets and distribution. Both government and industry placed more and more emphasis on plans to make fish products more widely available, to improve their quality and variety, to create uses for fish formerly considered unmarketable, and to encourage the consumption of fish in Canada and the United States.

In the twentieth century, marketing innovations related less to expanding markets to larger geographic areas than to improving the quality of the product for the consumer. The findings of the Joint Commission concerning Lake Erie revealed a serious need for fishermen and dealer-packers to clean up their acts. The commissioners concluded that "considerable quantities of fish in more or less advanced states of decomposition are put upon the market usually salted, sometimes frozen or fresh." The issue of public health needed serious attention and strong legislation that was carefully enforced to correct the conditions in the fish-packing industry.[32]

With these realities in mind, moderate- to large-size packers and wholesale dealers supported and engaged directly in the development of improved freezing and storage methods that would produce a healthy, superior product and be cost effective. A good example is W. F. Kolbe and Company of Port Dover, Ontario. Robert Kolbe, son of the company founder and a mechanical engineer by profession, developed a brine-based freezing process in 1925 that was much more rapid than the common ice and salt method. The fish retained a better color and firmer flesh, making them more readily marketable. A number of other fish processors adopted the new freezing process, including some that were owned by the Booth Fisheries Company. Kolbe and Company also introduced filleting to the Canadian Great Lakes commercial-fishing industry. In 1926, only small quantities of a few species were filleted for market in Canada and the United States. Yet the technique held promise for the future, for it saved freezing and transportation costs and reduced spoilage.[33]

The largest and most far-flung fish enterprise in North America, the Booth Fisheries Company—organized to fish on its own account and to buy from fishermen, to process the catch, and to distribute and market the products of North American ocean and freshwater fisheries—vigorously pushed marketing and distribution in the twentieth century. In the mid-1920s, it boasted, "Few corporations have so extensive a distributing organization as the Booth Fisheries Company." It operated ten retail stores as well as branch wholesale businesses in every major city in the United States and Canada. Nearly $6 million of its $23 million of capital assets were allocated to distribution. It ventured into manufacturing such fish products as "fish cakes ready to fry, boneless herring, finnan haddie, fish flakes and smoked fish of all kinds" beyond its long-standing line of canned salmon and oysters.[34] Booth became known in the industry for aggressive, experimental marketing. It challenged competitors that expected to find niches in the market.

With growing investments in harvesting and processing equipment, fishers, processors, and wholesale dealers searched for ways to maintain and increase the supply of fish. More intensive fishing and more efficient modes of capture seemed to offer part of the answer for the Great Lakes commercial-fishing industry. In addition, supplies of fish from sources other than the Great Lakes could be transported to packing and processing plants that were well connected by rail with both markets and alternative areas of supply. Competition with the harvesters and dealers of freshwater fish from Canadian lakes to the north and west of the Great Lakes put all producers of fish from the Great Lakes under very real pressure. American fishermen faced the further reality that Canadian fishermen could market freshwater whitefish, trout, Lake Erie herring, and pike in Chicago and New York at a lower cost than they could. Surely these findings of the Tariff Commission in 1925 justified a duty on Canadian fish high enough to protect American fishermen of the Great Lakes and elsewhere.

WORLD WAR I AND THE GREAT LAKES FISHERIES

World War I had a devastating impact on the Great Lakes fish resource. As the Canadian and American governments worked strenuously to bolster the Allied cause, they targeted fish as well as agricultural products for increased production. Both governments urged the public to eat more fish. Both offered technical information to improve packing and marketing methods. Both developed and disseminated printed information for homemakers on fish cuisine. The Bureau of Fisheries sponsored public lectures and demonstrations on seafood cookery. Canada used the National Expo in Toronto to educate the public on the virtues of fish in the diet, even opening a restaurant to serve fish dinners. A poster designed for the United States Food Administration reminded Americans of their patriotic duty by picturing fish swimming in deep-green waters: "Save the Products of the Land—Eat more fish—they feed themselves" (figure 16.5). In its efforts to improve the market quality of fish, the Canadian government offered transportation subsidies to ensure more rapid delivery to market.[35]

The government of Ontario took advantage of wartime conditions to address the frequently heard criticism that it was difficult to buy fresh Great Lakes fish in local markets. In 1917, it embarked on a program to buy fish and distribute them. At first, it utilized the rarely tapped resources in Lakes Nipigon and Nipissing, where fishermen operated on provincial contract. Thereafter, the program targeted 20 percent of commercial fishermen's catch for government purchase at a price per pound that was based on an average of the prices of the preceding five years. The promise to sell 20 percent of the catch to the government if asked became a condition for a fishing license. The fish were marketed at set government prices, which authorities hoped would encourage the consumption of and control the runaway prices for fish, thus reducing consumer demand for meat. The fishermen cooperated, and the Ontario government reported 3 million pounds sold by 600 fish dealers in 1918 at a cost of 5 cents a pound less than the uncontrolled going market rates.[36] The following year, the number of dealers handling government fish declined by almost one-third, due to the wider availability of meat, officials thought.

In both Canada and the United States, authorities eased regulations for fishing on the Great Lakes, and, in the face of high prices for fresh fish and government encouragement to expand harvests, concerns about conservation went on hold for the duration of the war.[37] The superintendent of the Ontario Department of Game and Fisheries argued against conservation in wartime: "When this barbarous world wide war ends . . . when the despicable barbarians are relegated to restricted confines of their despised country," then Ontario should institute stringent conservation of fish and game. Meanwhile, ease restrictions on licenses for gill-net tugs, open reserves heretofore unused, and win the war.[38]

The war deeply affected the Great Lakes commercial-fishing industry. Governmental encouragement and high fish prices contributed to average harvests from 1914 to 1918 greater than those during any other five-year period in the twentieth century.[39] The war encouraged expansion in the industry, with the entry of new firms and the investment of additional

Figure 16.5. Charles Livingston Bull, poster to support the wartime programs of the United States Food Administration, ca. 1918. (Photograph courtesy National Archives, Washington, D.C.)

capital by those already established. Retrenchment followed, particularly in the doldrums of 1921.

Wartime pressure for expanded fisheries focused official and public attention on the need for better sanitary conditions and pure-food standards in the marketplace, the importance of government inspection of fish and processing plants, and the nutritional value of fish. At the same time, the push to harvest greater quantities of fish broadened governmental research on the fisheries from the scientific to expanded market analysis, human nutrition, and modern consumerism. These policy directions accentuated by the war carried over into the 1920s, to the benefit of the commercial-fishing industry. Officials of the national, state, and provincial governments did not talk about the impact of wartime industrial and agricultural production on the Great Lakes or about the burden that officially sanctioned overfishing placed on the fish population.

Considering the developments in the commercial-fishing industry of the Great Lakes from 1896 to 1929, it is difficult to find expressions of deep concern for conservation and the long-term productivity of declining commercial species. Caught up in the competitive pressures and encouraged by wartime demands, fishers and dealer-entrepreneurs both large and small fished and marketed aggressively, hastening the decline of the commercial resource as nineteenth-century fishermen knew it. They realized that both overfishing and pollution were ruining the fish population, but feared for their livelihoods and profits. They distrusted regulations and those who enforced them.

17

Policy Makers and the Ever-Widening Stain

We Have Very Largely Fouled Ourselves

While harvests eroded the strength of key Great Lakes commercial-fish species in the early twentieth century, continued deterioration in the marine habitat hastened their decline. Ever larger portions of those lake waters, once rich in dissolved oxygen that had supported a cornucopia of salmon, whitefish, trout, herring, and sturgeon, changed to more turbid, fertile, warmer waters that were polluted in varying degrees and acceptable to perch, pike, pickerel, carp, suckers, and other species. A tremendous growth in human activity in the Great Lakes basin created these changes, many of which evolved from the major sources of pollution significant in the late nineteenth century. The spoliation of waters also escalated in the twentieth century in different and often more lethal ways, largely from changed patterns of production and consumption, adding to the residuals of earlier decades, creating immediate problems, and laying the groundwork for future troubles.

CREATORS OF GROWING POLLUTION

Population growth, especially in the urban areas of the southern Great Lakes basin, ranks high as a cause for the increasing pollution of the lakes. For ten major lakeshore urban-industrial centers—Rochester, Toronto, and Hamilton on Lake Ontario; Buffalo, Cleveland, and Toledo on Lake Erie; Detroit on the Detroit River; Chicago and Milwaukee on Lake Michigan; and Duluth–Superior on Lake Superior—the Canadian and American census counts showed a combined total growth of residents from 3,643,000 in 1900 to 8,500,000 in 1930.[1]

Industrial growth fostered this expansive urban development. Considering the same ten cities, the value of their industrial products in current dollars escalated from $1,581,000,000 in 1900 to $12,126,000,000 in 1931. Indexed with 1926 as the base year, that growth totaled almost $8 billion.[2] Industrial expansion changed the character of the southern shores of Lakes Erie and Michigan and the nature of the economies of Detroit and Windsor. Industry developed and flourished on the western shore of Lake Michigan from Chicago through Kenosha, Racine, Milwaukee, Sheboygan, Manitowoc, and Green Bay. Rochester, Buffalo, London, Hamilton, Toronto, and Kingston in the eastern Great Lakes basin, long-established industrial centers, experienced a similar pattern of growth. The potential of the Niagara River to generate electric power made it a focus for industrial development. In 1929, for the first time, the United States census delineated two "industrial areas" in the Great Lakes basin: Chicago and Milwaukee.

Urban-industrial expansion created heavy burdens of human and industrial waste dumped into lakes, rivers, and streams, usually untreated, given the public perception that the really significant pollution issue was the human health requirement for drinking water that was safe from bacterial diseases. The most cost-effective way to obtain clean water was to filter and treat water for human use and to rely on the natural waters to dilute sewage. The system, as Joel Tarr has explained, neglected the chemical pollution from industry and overestimated the finite ability of natural waters to dilute. Upton Sinclair vividly portrayed the results of urban-industrial spoliation of natural waters in his description of Bubbly Creek, an arm of the Chicago River, used by Chicago meatpackers to dispose of wastes. On the creek's surface, some areas of grease and solid filth supported foraging chickens, and chemicals formed a lethal effervescent mixture that produced bubbles of carbonic acid gas, hence the name.[3]

Among the major sources of industrial pollution were iron- and steelmaking, metal refining, forging, foundry and machine shop and other metalworking, electroplating, electrical machinery production, and petroleum refining. They all grew enormously and, in the process, sent wastes into the lake systems that damaged the marine habitat. Similarly, the growing chemical industry produced immediate and long-term pollution. The dislocations and demands created by World War I deeply affected both the chemical and metalworking industries. The war years transformed the American chemical industry in size, in diversity and complexity of inorganic products, in production methods, and in research and development of organic chemicals. Before the Great Depression, the industry did not create as great an environmental impact as it would in the following decades, primarily because of the production and use of organic chemicals, but its negative influence was real. Urban-industrial centers around the Great Lakes—especially Rochester, Cleveland, Detroit, and Chicago—and Niagara Falls had sizable, growing chemical industries, and, in Ontario, the chemical valley near Sarnia began to take shape, nurtured by its salt deposits and Petrolia's oil wells. Chemical production based on the bountiful salt deposits in Michigan played a major role in transforming that state's economy after 1900. In their study of the management of industrial wastes before the creation of the Environmental Protection Agency, Craig E. Colten and Peter N. Skinner have concluded that pressures generated by World War I to innovate and to produce diverted the attention of chemical manufacturers away from concern about their toxic wastes for years.[4]

Yet another notable change in the industrial profile of the southern Great Lakes basin was the rise of automobile manufacturing and its ancillary suppliers. It cut a wide swath of industrial change in Detroit, the dominant city of production, and in Milwaukee, Racine, Kenosha, Toledo, Cleveland, and Buffalo.[5] Both the manufacture of and the widespread operation of gasoline-powered vehicles triggered a whole set of environmental changes most often associated with air and land pollution, but they also had real significance for the Great Lakes waters.

The long-term impact on the Great Lakes of industrial growth during the World War I years and the 1920s came from the massive dumping and discharge of wastes directly into the waters, which led to the gradual buildup of concentrated toxins. Industrial expansion also laid the basis for future troubles generated by the disposal of industrial wastes on land, from where inadequately contained toxins made their way either by runoff or by groundwater into wells and natural water bodies. The contamination of Love Canal, near Niagara Falls, New York, by industrial toxins is only one notorious example of waste-dumping problems that originated before 1930, when the partially built canal began to be used as a dump site for chemical wastes.[6]

With industrial growth adjacent to the Great Lakes came new demands for plant locations that consumed wetlands and created landfills that projected into the lakes. Deeper harbors to accommodate bulk carriers, more canals to facilitate direct delivery to plants, and reorganization of natural waters to suit industrial convenience were all part of manufacturing expansion that impinged on the marine habitat. The dredging and disruption of lake and shore were widespread. Industrial growth created larger and larger amounts of air polluted with all manner of contami-

Figure 17.1. Industrial wastes discharged into the Fox River at Neenah, Wisconsin, an example of a common practice in the Great Lakes basin. (Photograph courtesy State Historical Society of Wisconsin, Madison; photograph no. WHi [X3] 48600)

nants, ranging from emissions of coal smoke to toxins from metal and petroleum refining and chemical production, a prelude to the more severe air pollution to come in the second half of the twentieth century. Airborne wastes settled into lake waters directly, descended into them with precipitation, or entered them in the runoff from land.

In the northern parts of the Great Lakes basin, industries based on timber and mineral resources accounted for much of the industrial activity immediately adjacent to extractive locations and in port cities. Logging and milling continued in the basins of Lakes Superior, Huron, and Ontario, decades after the big cut of timber in Michigan and Wisconsin. Pulp- and papermaking grew in importance, as did chemical industries based on the by-products of lumbering. The combination of refuse from sawmills, toxic residues from chemical plants, and waste fluids from pulp and paper mills further destroyed the quality of Great Lakes waters for fish life (figure 17.1).

Mining in the northern arc of the Great Lakes basin added another load of pollutants to lake waters. In the early twentieth century, the copper-mining industry on the Keweenaw Peninsula in Michigan turned to the refinement of tailings, which contained significant amounts of copper. Hydraulic dredges scooped them from Torch Lake. In 1915, a leaching process that used cupric ammonium carbonate was introduced, followed a year later with the addition of a flotation process that used coal tar creosotes and pyridine oil. All the mills were using salts of xanthic acid for flotation at the end of the 1920s. Tailings, chemicals, and the residuals from gravity concentration and leaching and flotation went into Torch Lake. According to the Michigan Department of Natural Resources, "This resulted in a very turbid lake with a changing shoreline configuration." A monitoring and managing agency of the Canadian and American governments, the International Joint Commission, designated Torch Lake as one of forty-two areas of pollution concern in the Great Lakes region in the 1980s. In 1984, in an effort to correct the Torch Lake pollution, the Michigan Department of Natural Resources suggested a remedial plan that makes it clear that at different times and in different degrees the chemical-refining processes did have an adverse impact on fish life, possibly including the formation of tumors. The report further stated, "The aquatic animal communities living in or on sediments with high copper concentrations, are reduced in diversity, density, and biomass."[7]

After 1900, mining operations grew in the Great Lakes basin in Canada, where the extremely rich Sudbury ores—bearing nickel, copper, iron, cobalt, gold, and platinum—came into production. The smelting and concentration of complex copper–nickel sulfide ores produced toxins that were highly detrimental to all forms of life. Animals, vegetation, humans, and marine life alike suffered. Much of the damage came from smelter emissions that spread devastation by air across the landscape.

In 1904, the Geological Survey of Canada reported vegetation killed for miles around Sudbury: "A more desolate scene can hardly be imagined than the fine white clay or silt of the flats, through which protrude, at intervals, rough rocky hills, with no trees or even a blade of grass to break the monotony." A half century later, a critic spoke of the Sudbury area as a region of "Scorched Earth." A study undertaken in 1994 estimated that smelter emissions had biologically damaged a 6.56-square-mile area around Sudbury.[8]

Sudbury lies in the headwaters of the Spanish River, which empties into the North Channel of Lake Huron. The extent to which air- and waterborne toxic pollutants generated there affected fish life in the North Channel cannot be measured with precision, but they did affect it. In 1985, the International Joint Commission designated the Spanish River harbor as an area of pollution concern. The remedial action plan for it, published in 1993, reported that sediments in the "nearshore zone adjacent to the river exceeded provincial Openwater Disposal Guidelines for

PCBs, nickel, copper and zinc. The source(s) of these metals are the historic and ongoing mining/milling/smelting activities in the Sudbury Basin. The source(s) of the PCBs remains unknown." Pollution from the operation of pulp and paper mills has also been a major problem, adversely affecting drinking water, marine life, and water for livestock. While progress has been made in controlling pollutants since 1985, the mouth of the Spanish River remains a carefully monitored area.[9] Without doubt, the refinery that International Nickel located in 1918 in Port Colborne, a response to wartime emergency conditions, contributed immediately to the pollution problems at the eastern end of Lake Erie.

Farmers and orchardists located in those parts of the Great Lakes basin where soil and climate were congenial to agriculture contributed heavily to the ongoing changes in lake waters in the early twentieth century as they responded to the favorable prices for their products before World War I and then to government pressures and price incentives to produce during wartime. The lands of the Great Lakes basin located south of a line running roughly from the tip of the Door Peninsula in eastern Wisconsin through the base of the Bruce Peninsula in southeastern Ontario and arching over the northern shore of Lake Ontario to its eastern end produced a wealth of agricultural products. Lying primarily in the hay and dairy regions of the United States and Canada, they included the Great Lakes fruit and specialty-crop belt and substantial areas of more intensive field-crop production. Compared with the traditional agriculture of the last quarter of the nineteenth century, the more intensive agriculture of the early twentieth century involved the use of more efficient tools and machinery, the application of more commercial fertilizers and pesticides, and expanded efforts to drain wetlands. In the 1920s, despite the onset of hard times for farmers, they purchased tractors and more efficient tilling and harvesting equipment in an effort to compensate for lower prices by farming more effectively and intensively to produce larger yields. Agricultural practices in the early twentieth century increased siltation from erosion and generated a greater nutrient load and more toxins from pesticides, principally arsenicals, in the runoff that emptied into Great Lakes waters than they had in the past. Agricultural production, a primary source of changes for marine life in the nineteenth century, has continued in various ways to make a devastating impact throughout the twentieth century.[10]

Petroleum stood high on the roster of additional burdens on Great Lakes waters in the early twentieth century. The production and refinement of oil became serious concerns to health authorities and all those worried about the fishery resources of Lake Erie, in particular, before 1900. The negative impacts of petroleum pollution escalated in importance for both the Great Lakes and the Atlantic coastal fisheries in the years before the Great Depression. With the beginning of transportation of oil by tankers, the advent of gasoline- and diesel-powered vessels, the growing use of petroleum and its products in industry, and the increasing number of gasoline-powered vehicles and the extensive construction of roads to accommodate them, petroleum generated wastes that ended up in the waters of the Great Lakes.

The advent of electricity for industrial, commercial, and domestic use led to massive efforts to harness waterpower to generate electrical energy. In the early twentieth century, the potential of Niagara Falls triggered the construction of generating stations nearby and made the Niagara River area a further lodestone to industrial development. Engineers exploited many lesser sites, utilizing the waters of the Great Lakes basin to produce electrical energy for industrial and home use. Coal-powered plants also made a very substantial impact on the environment of the region, discharging warm toxic water into lakes and streams and polluting them with coal-smoke emissions.

The volume of ship traffic on the Great Lakes, very substantial at the turn of the century and growing both in tonnage and in size in the case of bulk carriers, produced a significantly negative impact on the fish population. Fishery experts tended to disagree, yet none could deny that vessels churned up waters, which, in turn, eroded shorelines and increased siltation; that they left substantial quantities of waste, coal clinkers, garbage, and sewage to sink to the bottom; and that increasingly they were discharging petroleum products to foul the waters. Walter Koelz, a leading authority on the Great Lakes fisheries in the 1920s who believed that ship traffic harmed fish life, noted that more tonnage went through the canal at Sault Sainte Marie, given its importance for shipments of iron ore, than traveled through the Panama Canal. The International Joint Commission reported in 1918 that sewage discharged by passing vessels heavily polluted the St. Mary's River, creating a health hazard for residents of both the Canadian and American towns of Sault Sainte Marie. It noted further that more than 37,850 ships, with a registered tonnage of 76,677,264 and carrying a freight of more than 100,000,000 tons, had moved up and down the Detroit River in 1916. The study maintained that pollution created by boat traffic on the Great Lakes harmed the waters to a far greater degree than was generally believed, creating a "menace to public health in both countries."[11] Moreover, as in the past, extensive canal construction to facilitate the movement of vessels on the Great Lakes and to create better linkages with the Atlantic Ocean and the Gulf of Mexico changed the fish habitat. The improvements made to the Welland Canal, which linked Lake Ontario and Lake Erie, bypassing the Niagara River and Niagara Falls, many marine biologists believe, provided an entrée for the sea lamprey into Lake Erie, with devastating consequences for the native fish population. The greater the number of connections and the larger the connectors, the greater the chance for intruded species.

The agents of change on the Great Lakes—including the manufacturing and chemical industries, logging and mining operations, farming, the petroleum and electrical industries, and shipping—suggest major causes for the increasing deterioration of the Great Lakes marine habitat from 1896 to1929. But they are in no sense a complete catalog, and their impact is not quantifiable.

A SCIENTIST DEFINES THE PROBLEM

At the end of the nineteenth century, Edward E. Prince, the Dominion Commissioner of Fisheries, wrote an extended essay, "Water Pollutions as Affecting Fisheries," in an effort to bring a scientific perspective to the rising tide of concern apparent in the press and the official records of all the governments with jurisdiction over the Great Lakes and responsibility for fisheries. He drew on the published writings of scientists; the observations of fishermen, sportsmen, and lawmakers; and his own extensive scientific experience with the fisheries of the British Isles and Canada. Thoughtfully weighing and balancing this body of information, he wrote broadly and critically about the problem of pollution, questioning popular assumptions and calling for scientific experiments to collect the data essential to demonstrate whether foreign substances added to the water harmed fish life. The materials he gathered from many sources clearly indicated "how little is actually known of the effects upon fishlife of these various pollutions from accurate and thoroughly scientific experiment. Common opinion and popular ideas more largely prevail than reliable and demonstrated knowledge." Considering the waters of the Great Lakes, how right he was. Before 1926, when scientists began a limnological survey of Lake Erie in response to the decline of herring in the lake, only three such surveys had been undertaken: in Lake St. Clair, in Grand Traverse Bay, and in Lake Nipigon.[12]

Prince challenged those who jumped to the conclusion that water pollution explained the decline and disappearance of fish when very often other factors were at work and, in some degree, were responsible for the damage. Ever a believer that overfishing and poaching during spawning seasons played the most prominent role in the general decline in the Great Lakes fish populations, he also stressed decimation from disease and "a poisonous or noxious condition of the water at particular seasons of the year." He cited the annual die-off of the alewives in Lake Ontario as a case in point. Moreover, he noted, deforestation and cultivation of the land often so completely changed the quality of lake waters that they could not support fish life.

Yet despite all his cautions about careful observation and experimentation before reaching conclusions, Prince listed a vast array of pollutants responsible for actual and potential damage, citing specific examples of where, when, and how they wreaked their devastation. About the widely accepted view that sawdust floating on the water killed fish, he had reservations, and concluded that the blanket condemnation of its poisonous effects on fish had not been proved. He did agree, though, that sawdust lying on the bottom had damaged feeding and spawning grounds. Floating sawmill rubbish was not a hazard, he suggested. Sunken rubbish was another matter. He believed that fishermen had correctly assessed the problems created for fish life by the great rafts of pulp wood carried from Georgian Bay across Lake Huron to Michigan, leaving in their wake a mass of ground-off bark and wood fiber to sink and foul the bottom. About the impact of the fluid wastes from pulp mills, he was less certain and stressed the importance of testing case by case.[13]

Prince spoke assuredly, however, about the chemical pollution created by industry as a whole, citing manufacturing districts in England and the United States that once abounded in fish, but where waters had been so poisoned by industrial wastes that "all fish life has practically disappeared." He singled out for special mention paper and textile mills (especially those that ret flax), chemical works, and tanneries as major producers of poisonous wastes. Water pollution and destruction of fish life that resulted from the mining and refining of iron, coal, gold, lead, copper, and tin and from the production of wood alcohol, carbolic acid, and coal gas, with its tarry and oily wastes, came in for scrutiny, as did the waste products from distilleries and beet-sugar factories. Prince cited the devastating impacts on fish life from these kinds of pollution. He wrote cautiously about the effects of human sewage on fish life, suggesting that while the public believed almost unanimously that it was as injurious to fish as it was to humans, only careful scientific study could lead to a valid assessment.[14]

Prince's twenty-six-page essay expresses the ideas of a university-trained and experienced zoologist at the turn of the century, one very knowledgeable about the pollution problems of the Great Lakes, after having observed and tried to alleviate them during the preceding eight years. He wrote in a judicious tone, recognizing the very real influence of economic interests far larger and more powerful than those of sport- and commercial fishers. Yet he remained optimistic that those who created pollution could and should neutralize waste materials before releasing them into the waterways. Above all, he advocated scientific research to produce a body of reliable information that policy makers and fishery managers could refer to as they worked to solve the problems already apparent and that would continue to grow and change in the future.

POLICY MAKERS AND WATER POLLUTION

The pollution of natural waters vitally affected public health in many areas along the East Coast, in the St. Lawrence and Mississippi River valleys, and in the Great Lakes region in the late nineteenth and early twentieth centuries. Raw sewage emptied into waterways that served as public water supplies carried the scourge of typhoid fever in epidemic proportions. With widespread public support, progressives adopted the cause for safe, clean drinking water as one of the objectives of public-health reform in Canada and the United States. Chicago was notorious for outbreaks of typhoid. There, according to Nelson Manfred Blake, almost 2,000 people died from the disease in 1891. Using a somewhat different time frame, April 1891 to April 1892, Stuart Galishoff found that 2,400 had died from typhoid fever. The death rate per 100,000 ran as high as 330 from 1910 to 1912 in Sault Sainte Marie, Ontario, and in all the Great Lakes communities studied by the International Joint Commission in 1914, it far exceeded that of 5 per 100,000 in northern European cities "with safe water supplies."[15]

A select special committee of the Canadian House of Commons took up the typhoid problem in 1913 in the wake of an epidemic in Ottawa, gathering evidence and taking testimony preparatory to Parliament's passing a law to curb pollution from sewage in navigable waters. Health authorities in Ontario, searching for an uncontaminated water supply for the city of Toronto, already had tested the waters in Lake Ontario opposite Toronto and had found that all the samples collected from shore to midlake were contaminated with sewage bacteria. The committee's reports containing the testimony of experts, including medical doctors, bacteriologists, and civil engineers, laid out the problem. Every municipality on the Great Lakes was discharging sewage into lake waters, which were used for the drinking water supply. "We have very largely fouled ourselves," a professor of bacteriology and hygiene at Queens University told the select committee.[16] Theodore Roosevelt, speaking in Buffalo in 1910, called for the protection of Great Lakes waters from pollution, with the admonition that "civilized people should be able to dispose of sewage in a better way than by putting it into drinking water."[17]

The United States and Canada advocated reform legislation at the state or provincial and national levels. Progressive national leadership in both countries favored the control of pollution, which threatened health and property in transboundary waters, and this became one objective of the International Joint Commission, created by treaty in 1909, along with the larger goal of managing the contiguous waters for the benefit of agriculture, industry, and power generation by facilitating navigation, regulating water levels, and controlling water diversions. The enormous volume of sewage and industrial wastes dumped into the St. Mary's, Detroit, and Niagara Rivers particularly needed regulation. In the areas adjacent to these rivers, public health was definitely at risk from "gross" pollution. The commission's investigation of the extent of pollution of these rivers, begun in 1913, documented the seriousness of the problems, and its final report, published in 1918, recommended ways to rectify them. The recommendations were never adopted. Not charged with studying the effects of pollution on fish, the International Joint Commission did mention the negative impact of contaminated water for fish life in its final report.[18]

While the issue of increasing water pollution as a menace to fish and wildlife was of far less importance to the general public than that of contamination as a threat to human health, it did seriously concern a small but growing segment of Great Lakes fishery experts, including academically trained natural scientists, fish culturists, officials charged with formulating conservation policies, commercial fishermen, sportsmen, and sportsmen's organizations. They claimed that pollution ruined many a spawning ground, destroyed sources of food, and, in extreme cases, produced mass poisoning and/or asphyxiation. Their thinking focused on point pollution. They did not say very much about the siltation created by soil erosion generated by lumbering, agriculture, and shoreline alterations, and they did not think about air pollution as a cause of deterioration of natural waters. Government fisheries reports did not express concern about the possibility of polluted groundwater working its way into natural waterways. In the early twentieth century, studies of groundwater contamination focused on threats to supplies of well and public drinking water.[19] The advocates of reform to save the fish from polluted waters were neither numerous nor influential enough to secure reform legislation and appropriations to conduct scientific experiments at an effective level. The United States Commissioner of Fisheries and the Bureau of Fisheries received a growing number of requests for help to fight pollution of the fisheries, especially during the first three decades of the twentieth century, but lacked the funds to investigate them.

The threats posed by water pollution were nothing new to protectors of the fisheries in the twentieth century. They had carried enough weight in the minds of legislators in Canada and the United States in the nineteenth century that the lawmakers had included antipollution provisions in fishery laws. This concern was a long-standing one in North American history, having been written into law in the Massachusetts Bay Colony as early as 1668. The fishery regulations of Canada, patterned on the fishery codes of England, included an antipollution provision. An adaptation of the law passed by the Parliament of the Province of Canada in 1858, it was essentially the same in the legislation of 1906 and 1932 as it had been in the initial statute of 1868: a ban on putting or knowingly permitting to be put "lime, chemical substances or drugs, poisonous matter, dead of decaying fish, or remnants thereof, mill rubbish or sawdust or any other deleterious substance" into waters supporting commercial or game fish, as the statute of 1906 put it.[20]

Similarly, the Great Lakes states included antipollution clauses in their nineteenth-century laws and from time to time added to the list of forbidden categories. Sometimes incorporated into fishery laws, as in Michigan and Wisconsin, and other times separate and distinct from them, as in Ohio, antipollution regulations mirrored the public's concern for human health. Two laws enacted in Ohio in 1888 spelled out in detail the penalties for putting dead animals or offal from meat- and fish-packing houses or waste from privies into the waters of the state, requiring them to be buried. A separate law forbade dumping any refuse from coal mines, from oil wells, tanks, and refineries, and from gasworks, as well as whey and filth from cheese making, into Ohio's waters, but did not mention manufacturing as a broad category. None of the other fishery commissions of the Great Lakes states as clearly identified and reported the nature of pollution problems as did that of Ohio. The annual reports of the Ohio Fish Commission beginning in 1873 noted that the state waters were "fast becoming great sewers." The commissioners called for stronger legislation in 1893, 1895, and 1900. The annual report of 1895 noted that the "best and most experienced fishermen" all along the Great Lakes had expressed alarm about pollution and wanted controls to protect the fish. Warned the commissioners, "In the very important matter of our lake fisheries, unless some well defined protection is afforded, this great source of food supply will be ruined." The state legislature in 1908 passed a law to require the "purification of sewage and public water supplies."[21] This category of legislation, common to all the Great Lakes states, while basically designed to protect humans, did ban many forms of pollution that were very destructive to fish. But at the same time, the quest for safe drinking water involved the use of some substances, such as chlorine, that destroyed fish life.

THE ENFORCEMENT DILEMMA

In the Great Lakes states, antipollution laws that aimed to conserve marine life went largely unenforced; in Canada, enforcement was sporadic, coming in response either to reports by fishery overseers and inspectors or to complaints directed to Ottawa and Toronto by fishermen and residents of lakeshore communities, with one very notable exception. It related to the problem of sawdust pollution, an issue that produced a forty-year struggle between a determined conservation-minded faction made up of "sportsmen, public health advocates, individuals concerned with recreation, naturalists, scientists, and proponents of water navigation improvements," on the one hand, and the lumbermen and their business associates, on the other.[22] R. Peter Gillis has ably analyzed the struggle and victory of the forces of conservation in 1903, when the government of Prime Minister Sir Wilfrid Laurier came down firmly against dumping. Inspectors for the Department of Marine and Fisheries and overseers for the Ontario Department of Fisheries watched for violations of the prohibition on dumping sawdust and confronted offending mill owners with orders to cease. Environmentally, the victory may well have been a mixed bag because many of the lumbermen turned to burning their refuse, and others utilized it to make chemicals or pulp and paper, all of which produced other forms of pollution.

Examples of Canadian efforts to enforce bans on the kinds of pollution destructive to fish life other than refuse from lumbering illuminate the kinds of existing problems and the attitudes that enforcement officials encountered. The records of both the Department of Marine and Fisheries and the Ontario Department of Fisheries, or, beginning in 1907, the Department of Game and Fisheries, abound in pollution horror stories. Comments fall into two categories: generalized laments about the growth of pollution and its impact on the fish population, and descriptions of the deterioration of fish life in specific locations. Prominent among them were Burlington Bay (at the western end of Lake Ontario), Toronto Bay, Detroit area waters, the Niagara River, and the communities of the Grand River.[23]

Repeatedly a target for fishermen's and overseers' complaints in the 1890s, pollution in Toronto Bay and harbor worsened through the early decades of the twentieth century, they felt.[24] An overseer in the Toronto region noted in 1907 that the problem with fishing in Toronto Bay was the "large amount of poisonous matter poured into the bay through the city sewers," especially toxic among those he noted were refuse from gasworks and poisonous wastes from tanneries, the paint works, and the wallpaper factory.[25] The program for the cleanup and improvement of Toronto harbor undertaken in the early twentieth century included dredging as well as building a new trunk sewer to carry away the wastes of this city's commerce and industry. A fishery overseer in Toronto noted in 1912 that the scarcity of fish was due in part to the dredging of sewage and dirt out of Toronto Bay. They were taken into Lake Ontario and dumped. "The trout grounds have become practically destroyed . . . and there is practically no herring to be had," according to the overseer.[26] In 1914, another overseer in the Toronto district commented on the scarcity of fish in Lake Ontario opposite the lakeshores of Durham, Ontario, York, and Peel Counties. The catch there "in the last ten years, all put together, would not amount to a good catch for one season."[27] The water quality in Toronto Bay improved in 1917, but the fish remained scarce.[28]

Wastes generated in the Detroit area continued to spoil the fisheries of the Detroit River in Canada and those at the western end of Lake Erie, as they had in the mid-1890s, while the Niagara River, as in the past, spewed sewage and rubbish into Lake Ontario. Lamented the Ontario Superintendent of Game and Fisheries: "There is no doubt that pollution of public waters is increasing at an alarming rate in the lakes, bays and rivers in both countries."[29] Clearly this problem called in part for joint action by Canada and the United States.

The degradation of the Grand River, a major tributary on the northern shore of Lake Erie, illustrates the changes that moderate-size urban centers wrought in the fish habitat and the ways that economic pressures thwarted conservation goals. The discharges from manufacturing operations in Waterloo and Brantford killed fish in the Grand River, arousing the ire of residents who complained to overseers of the Department of Marine and Fisheries in the mid-1890s. The fishery overseer investigated and confirmed multiple sources of pollution at Brantford, both industrial and municipal.

In 1896, the Brant County Rod and Gun Club appealed to the Minister of Marine and Fisheries for help in cracking down on the local board of health and city council. The club members wanted to stop the construction of a sewer for another major manufacturing plant within city limits. The Massey Harris agricultural-machinery factory discharged more than enough wastes. The new Waterous Engine Works would double the amount of sewerage going into the river. An investigation followed, but nothing was done because the new sewer was part of future construction. The following year, the local overseer heard complaints about petroleum pollution emanating from the Brantford Gas Works. When a member of Parliament interceded for the company, the Minister of Marine and Fisheries decided to take no action. But the communities along the Grand River continued to protest, and the province of Ontario responded to the complaints about pollution generated by a starch factory in 1905 by claiming that it solved the problem when it discharged the alkaline wastes into a nearby lake instead of into the river! Noted the report of the Ontario Department of Fisheries, when local governments tried to crack down, companies threatened to leave unless they were allowed to continue polluting the waters. Locals could not expect provincial help with stocking their waters if they could not enforce their municipal antipollution regulations, admonished the Superintendent of Game and Fisheries in his annual report in 1909.[30]

More reports of pollution of the Grand River came to the Department of Marine and Fisheries in 1911 and 1912, one involving overflow from the sewerage farm in Waterloo, and the other concerning waste from mills in Paris, Ontario, and both resulting in fish kills. The kind of evidence found in the Waterloo case is dramatically instructive. An overseer for the Ontario Department of Game and Fisheries went to Bridgeport, a town south of Waterloo from where the appeal for help had come. Reported David Jolly, Jr.:

> I went up there yesterday and found things worse than reported. Hundreds of fish were lying dead on the shore and the town claim they have buried over two tons. A small spring creek empties in the pond and hundreds of fish were struggling to get up to it. All over the pond the fish could be seen with their heads partly out of the water. The pond looked almost like ink.

After tracing the problem to its source, Jolly and the local board of health official found the cause, an overflow of raw sewage from the Waterloo sewerage farm into a swamp, then into the creek, and finally into the Grand River, a distance of almost one and a half miles lined with dead fish all along the way. At the river, Jolly found still more dead fish. He reported that "the one side of the river is quite dark and the other quite clear." The Department of Marine and Fisheries notified the mayor of Waterloo to correct the problem, which was both a menace to fish life and a violation of the Fishery Act. The investigation in Paris in 1912 revealed intermittent pollution from mill waste and led to an evaluation of the water in the Grand River to determine whether it harmed fish life.[31]

Another example of pollution came from a region remote from the busy, populous northern shores of Lakes Erie and Ontario: the vicinity of Thornbury and Clarksburg on the Beaver River near its entrance into Notawasaga Bay, an arm of southern Georgian Bay. When in 1912 the inspector for the Department of Marine and Fisheries visited these communities, he heard laments that the game fish in the river were almost extinct and that the only fish that inhabited the bay were suckers and carp. An investigation revealed a discharge of fluid, a "dark and very poisonous liquid," from a plant that made wood alcohol. About 1,200 gallons a day went into the river from the Standard Chemical Iron and Lumber Company's newly acquired plant. This was no small local firm. Its letterhead identified it as a manufacturer of wood chemicals, charcoal, iron, and lumber; it had five factories, one refinery, and one blast furnace; and it was headquartered in Toronto. The Department of Marine and Fisheries sent the company a copy of the Fisheries Act, indicating that the discharge was illegal. The company replied by expressing innocence of wrongdoing and apparently had a member of the Senate intercede on its behalf.

Meanwhile, the local fishery overseer for the Ontario Department of Game and Fisheries proceeded to collect samples of the refuse dumped into the Beaver River by Standard Chemical. Persistence was essential. He could not find out when the company would dump, but finally succeed in getting samples on his sixth trip. Analyzed by the chief chemist of the Inland Revenue Department, the samples showed "very extensive contamination of the stream with acrid matters, certain to be inimical to fishlife." The plant manager promised to divert washings and waste into a specially constructed well that was located sixty-five feet from the riverbank and did so by late August 1913. The plant remained under the fishery overseer's surveillance. Sanitary engineers considered the containing well a safe and workable toxic-waste disposal system. They also recommended using containment ponds and waste dumps on designated land sites.[32]

The dominion and provincial governments in 1913 and 1914 investigated complaints about discharges of "sulphurous acid" from paper mills into streams and lakes, to the detriment of fish life. The Ontario Board of Health had its chief officer study the problem. He argued that the damage was minimal and cited the industry's argument that to prohibit the discharge of wastes would put one of the largest new industries in Ontario out of business.[33]

These episodes offer a glimpse into a large and complex panorama of lake pollution and the perennial conflict between business and industrial interests, opposed to regulation and resource conservation, and policy makers and conservationists who advocated antipollution measures. Many other examples might be cited. Continuing small discharges of waste materials over time created larger problems.

THE GROWING IMPORTANCE OF THE POLLUTION ISSUE, 1900–1930

Overshadowed by the public-health dimensions of water pollution and then by the influence of World War I, evidence of the growing spoliation of natural waters for fish life drew ever more critical comment from commercial fishermen, sportsmen, the public, and government conservers of the resource in the 1920s. Oil, tar, and petroleum products particularly aroused alarm, leading the Bureau of Fisheries to publish an explanatory booklet for general use and a more extensive and technical publication on the effects of oil pollution on marine and wildlife.[34]

Three research projects on the Great Lakes fisheries documented the damage done to fish populations by industrial pollution. John Van Oosten's studies of herring in Saginaw Bay in Lake Huron revealed that Dow Chemical's discharge of dichlorbenzol, between 1915 and 1918, retarded their growth. In 1922, the Bureau of Fisheries cited an example of the way in which pollution in the extreme western part of Lake Erie hampered the work of the hatchery and stocking program. "Trade wastes from the Raisin, Maumee, and Detroit Rivers" had created a decline in the run of whitefish, making it useless to try to collect whitefish eggs there. The report also spoke of cooperative research involving the Bureau of Fisheries, the University of Michigan, and the Michigan Department of Health that documented pollution from sugar-beet factories and sewage in the Saginaw River system. It noted the devastating effects on fish life resulting from the oxygen-consuming bacteria that these wastes carried.[35] These three investigations of the effects of pollution on Lake Huron and Lake Erie waters paled by comparison with the large cooperative limnological study of Lake Erie done in the latter 1920s, discussed in chapter 20.

The participation of the Bureau of Fisheries in this cooperative research mirrored a broader interest in the impact of industrial toxins on fish life in the 1920s. A critical survey of the literature of that kind of pollution, centering on the effects of specific chemicals, done in 1950 listed 126 published studies, 61 of which had been done before 1930. Two-thirds of those appeared in print in the 1920s.[36]

On the eve of the Great Depression, most fishery experts believed that pollution generated by human activity was localized and caused by waste products of human activity. Among the marine biologists, a minority thought that the problem went beyond local, point pollution. Walter Koelz expressed their forebodings when he reviewed the possible impact of pollution on the fisheries of the Great Lakes. The contamination of areas that serve as feeding and spawning grounds, he observed, has "contributed in no small degree to the reduction of the fish supply." He believed that the debris from early lumbering operations still smothered lake bottoms. Industrial pollution of rivers and bays "has made barren some of the most productive fishing grounds, and the continuation of the evil is not only preventing the recovery of these grounds but is spreading its effects." He thought that the dumping of ashes from steamboats, given the great volume of this material, must have an adverse effect, as did throwing fish offal into the waters. He feared that pollutants not only killed fish, but probably did widespread damage to their food supply.[37]

In 1929, Carl L. Hubbs, a zoologist at the University of Michigan who had investigated the pollution of the steams of the Saginaw River system, in commenting on the pollution of the western end of Lake Erie, suggested that soil erosion and silting were "even more important" than sewage in harming fish life. Those concerned about nonpoint pollution were heard, but they were a minority with a small voice. In succeeding decades, the advocates of farming as the spoiler in western Lake Erie would grow in number and stature.[38]

Clearly in 1930, marine biologists were uncertain and divided in their views about the impact of pollution in the Great Lakes and about the relative importance of its sources. Fishermen were sure that pollution was ruining the fish population. Lawmakers focused on public health and the needs of the more productive and influential industrial and agricultural sectors, and they gave the ailing Great Lakes fisheries little attention, except when spectacular developments demanded a response. The majority of people in both Canada and the United States much preferred meat in their diet and, as a majority, remained indifferent to the issue of the contamination of the fisheries. Those who lived in areas where water pollution threatened the health of humans as well as that of fish and other wildlife—such as the lower Fox River valley and the southern parts of Green Bay in Wisconsin or the sewage-laden beaches around Lake Erie—voiced their alarm. We do not know in any measurable way how significantly pollution affected fish life by the end of the 1920s, but we do know that it influenced the quality of the marine habitat, ruined spawning grounds, killed fish, and cast an ever-widening stain in the waters.

18

Public Policy and the Declining Fish Resource

Return to the Faith of the Fathers

During the first thirty years of the twentieth century, the governments empowered to regulate fishing on the Great Lakes struggled in vain to stem the decline of whitefish, trout, herring, and sturgeon. In a strongly nationalistic era permeated with progressive advocacy of internationalism and conservation, they worked to shape fishery policies that would ensure the long-term use of the resource, laboring under pressures from a variety of interests. Emerging early in the century and influential in policy making by midcentury, biological scientists in academic institutions and governments sought to influence lawmakers. They argued that a combination of pure and applied scientific research could lead to effective regulation in Great Lakes waters and that their efforts deserved government funding.

Very successful among the groups that sought to shape policy, the commercial-fishing industry continued to exert great influence. Generally opposed to regulation, commercial harvesters regarded sportfishers as adversaries and deeply distrusted scientific "experts." Both sportsmen and scientists advocated the regulation of commercial fishing; both blamed it in large measure for ruining the resource. Sportfishers in the Great Lakes region, a stronger interest group than ever, had developed real clout with local governments in the late nineteenth century. They included many prominent politicians, professionals, and businessmen who knew how to use the political system to their advantage. They organized into fish and game conservation clubs and lobbied for what they wanted. They faced off with the commercial fishermen's associations, which were well organized to lobby for regulations favorable to their short-term interests. Least influential and unable to make their rights respected in the policy-making process were the Native North American fishers of the Great Lakes, who voiced their grievances to the United States Bureau of Indian Affairs and the Canadian Department of Indian Affairs, reporting infractions of their treaty rights by sport- and commercial fishermen and governments. Neither sport nor commercial fishers respected the Indians' fishing rights, until forced to do so decades later.[1] Diverse and often conflicting, these groups shaped policy for the highly competitive Great Lakes fishing industry, which, spurred on by favorable markets, continued to aggressively harvest a weakened and declining resource.

THE RISE OF SCIENTIFIC INVESTIGATION

Most of the groups that tried to influence fishery policy in the twentieth century had a lobbying track record that dated from the late nineteenth century. The academic biologists interested in both pure and applied science come closest to being newcomers to the political process. Those concerned with propagating and planting fish were old hands at the game. Most of the experimental work relating to Great Lakes fish that had been funded by the governments of Canada, the United States, and the Great Lakes states during the last three decades of the nineteenth century had grown from the propagation and stocking programs, the panacea for maintaining fish populations so widely and enthusiastically endorsed by leading fishery-resource managers in Europe and North America. Hatchery staff invented and patented new equipment and new ways of handling fish eggs to ensure greater success with hatching the eggs, better methods of handling the fry, and improved systems of planting them. Experimentation with fish ladders challenged the imaginations of others, principally those involved in administering fishery regulations, as they searched for ways to overcome the obstacles that dams posed for migrating fish.

While the work of fish culturists, despite its failure to arrest the declines in commercially preferred species, still received widespread approval, academic biologists studying fish in Canada and the United States, as elsewhere in the Western world, began to pursue avenues of investigation other than identifying and cataloging species. Newer directions apparent in the 1890s, while not immediately embraced, were ultimately recognized as productive of information essential to the design and implementation of constructive fishery policy. The newer approach came to be known as aquatic ecology, the study of biological life-forms in water in relation to their environment. Herschel Whitaker, the Fish Commissioner of Michigan, who fought long and hard with the commercial interests, employed Jacob Reighard, a morphologist at the University of Michigan and a pioneer of aquatic ecology in the Great Lakes region, in an effort to rehabilitate the dwindling population of whitefish. The uncomfortable partnership was short lived, lasting from 1889 to 1896. Reighard established a temporary mobile field station on Lake St. Clair in 1893. His objective was to create a "complete picture of life in the lake." His work showed that Lake St. Clair was short on plankton. In 1896, the field station moved to Traverse Bay for a study of whitefish. The investigation concluded that they had enough food, but that overfishing had led to their decline. The final report on the investigations at Traverse Bay pleaded for the establishment of a year-round biological station to ensure progress in research, a venture that the state of Michigan would not support. The Michigan Board of Fish Commissioners lost research funds, and Reighard turned to the United States Commission of Fish and Fisheries as a possible source of money.[2]

The federal commission was not oblivious to the need for research on the Great Lakes to save the fish, but it was slow to act. Meanwhile, the fishery commissions of Wisconsin, Ohio, and Michigan sought liaisons with the state universities to achieve the same goal, and, beginning in the 1880s, they asked the Commission of Fish and Fisheries for "scientific" help. The Joint Commission Relative to the Preservation of the Fisheries in Waters Contiguous to Canada and the United States, whose American representative, Richard Rathbun, was a staff member of the federal commission, identified subjects for future study that could contribute to the conservation of fish, emphasizing the need for knowledge of the life histories of the various species. An early effort dates from 1897, when A. J. Woolman began a study of the food of the principal fishes of Lake Superior. His findings, it was hoped, would make the work of fish culture more effective, and, more broadly, they would document food supplies in relation to the movements and numbers of commercial fish.[3]

The following year, the Commission of Fish and Fisheries took a tentative step in new directions. Well aware of the threats to Lake Erie, it responded to Reighard's proposal for a biological study of the lake and a permanent research station at Put-in-Bay, in Ohio, where there was heavy commercial fishing and the federal government operated a large herring, pike, and whitefish hatchery (figure 18.1). The grant was small, intended for a trial period. The commissioner's official report for public and, especially, congressional consumption enthusiastically described the summer work of 1898 as having been "of such value," so important to the future of fish culturing, that it should be continued and enlarged. Under Reighard's direction, the work at Put-in-Bay continued in part through 1902.

Figure 18.1. Hatchery and steamer *Shearwater,* Put-in-Bay, Ohio. (From U.S. Commission of Fish and Fisheries, *Report,* 1896, 55th Cong., 1st sess., 1897, H. Doc. 32 [Serial 3572], facing 49)

The researchers tried to devise methods to measure levels of plankton and studied rotifers and protozoa, parasites, nutrition of algae, nutrient supply of aquatic plants, spawning habits of fish, and specific species, such as sturgeon and carp. But the Commission of Fish and Fisheries always cast a critical eye and harbored the feeling that the work was not closely enough related to conserving the commercial species of fish. The commission, short of funds for scientific work and required to justify practical application of its work, could not support the building of a large and accurate body of scientific information on which meaningful policy could be formulated. In 1903, after it became part of the Department of Commerce and Labor, the commission ceased to support Reighard's experiments.[4] In 1902, the last year of its funding, the biological survey embarked on a study of the various species of whitefish in the Great Lakes and the locations in which they were found. The work at Put-in-Bay highlighted the need for a permanent, well-equipped, and federally funded research station on the Great Lakes, but the effort in 1902 to secure the concurrence of the House of Representatives with a bill passed by the Senate to create it failed, and despite later attempts to get federal appropriations, the matter lapsed until the 1920s. The commission's early, brief venture into the study of fish life related to the natural environment of the Great Lakes was part of a more general shift in its research program that led it to support elaborate studies of the life histories of commercially important species.[5] While World War I diminished scientific research, in other ways wartime pressure to produce food stimulated new thrusts in research by the Bureau of Fisheries as it embarked on projects to maximize the use of the nation's "aquatic resources," furthering this goal by building a laboratory to test fishery products in Washington, D.C. Argued the commissioner in his report in 1919, the fishing industry really needed experiment stations analogous to the agricultural experiment stations, where applied science to assist the industry would be undertaken.[6]

The idea of broadened research programs to give economic help to commercial fishing carried over into the 1920s, when the Bureau of Fisheries hosted conferences with industry representatives to discuss problems and needs, ranging from the pollution of coastal waters to high transportation costs and the need to improve the quality of marketed products. It conducted experiments in fish preservation and improved merchandising and made market surveys of large distribution centers, such as New York, Pittsburgh, Louisville, Chicago, Minneapolis, St. Paul, and Seattle, in an effort to understand more fully market structure and commodity movements. The bureau's economic bulletin series indicated the new dimension of research once it had become part of the Department of Commerce and Labor. When Walter Koelz wrote a report, "The Fishing Industry of the Great Lakes," in the mid-1920s, he included carefully prepared economic analyses of the industry, a first in the federal government's studies of the commercial-fishing industry of the Great Lakes, which dated from 1872.[7]

Along with the new emphasis on economic research by the Bureau of Fisheries, the directions of scientific work on the Great Lakes fish population changed. Research reports published beginning in 1924 notably downplayed the significance of fish culture and subscribed to a broad kind of scientific work to achieve fishery conservation goals. In 1923, the bureau outlined priorities for its biological inquiries, calling for research based on three components: the study of the biology of fishes, crustaceans, and mollusks, "their life histories and *ecological* relationships"; of plankton, the food source; of the "physical and chemical factors that determine the abundance of planktonic forms." Thus in the early 1920s, ecology took its place as a stated objective for the bureau's scientific work. Its research emphasized life histories and was designed to reveal rate of growth, age of maturity, spawning, food, feeding habits, patterns of migration, enemies, and "other elements in the environment" that tended to reduce numbers, which it regarded as having "prime" importance in conserving the fisheries.[8] A research focus on pollution in the Great Lakes was forced on the bureau in the late 1920s.

During the next few years, much of the extended research on whitefish done by Koelz and the special work on Lake Huron herring undertaken by John Van Oosten at the University of Michigan appeared, providing an array of evidence that helped explain the decline in these species as it related to pollution and to their life histories. For example, the studies of Lake Huron revealed that the spring catch of whitefish did not spawn until the fifth and, mostly, the sixth year of their lives, a finding that revealed as useless much of past regulation that was predicated on the assumption of earlier maturity. In the summer of 1923, 70 percent of the whitefish caught in Lake Huron off Alpena, Michigan, were in their fifth year, and only 45 percent of the females were sexually mature, even though they were of legal size limit. By 1925, both Van Oosten and Koelz had completed major studies on herring and whitefish.[9] In 1926, following the precipitous decline in Lake Erie herring, Congress appropriated enough money to provide a modest beginning for a Great Lakes fisheries laboratory. The University of Michigan, which had played such a key role in investigations on the Great Lakes during the preceding two decades, became its headquarters, "a temporary laboratory," in 1927. And Congress funded further research to address critical problems of Lake Erie.[10]

Investigations of the fisheries of the Great Lakes in Canada displayed the same general evolution as those in the United States, but suffered a setback when they became entangled in the controversy between the Dominion of Canada and the province of Ontario over control of the fisheries. The parallels between fishery investigations in the two countries were many. In both Canada and the United States, scientists interested in the marine biological study of the Atlantic Ocean had pursued research without government support for decades before the 1870s.[11] Fishery-resource managers in both nations agreed that hatchery and planting programs could contribute greatly to maintaining the fish population, and much of the private and public experimentation related directly to these efforts.

Both Canadian and American biologists in academia engaged in research on the fish populations of the Great Lakes region, concentrating on identifying and describing species. Louis Agassiz had done the earliest well-known study of this kind, which was published in 1850. The governments at the state or provincial and national levels in both countries looked to biological scientists in academia for technical knowledge and, especially after 1900, for assistance with government-funded fishery research projects. The Department of Marine and Fisheries however, did not foster scientific experiments with ocean fish before 1900 as extensively as did the Commission of Fish and Fisheries under the leadership of Spencer Baird, first at Woods Hole, Massachusetts, and later on the West Coast. But the Canadian government did pioneer in fish culture and led the way at the Newcastle Hatchery before Baird and the Commission of Fish and Fisheries embarked on it in 1872.[12]

The Canadian government's fishery work at the end of the nineteenth century broadened beyond artificial propagation and planting programs.

Edward E. Prince, a professor of zoology and anatomy at St. Mungo's College, in Glasgow, before his appointment in 1892 as Commissioner of Fisheries to advise and assist the Department of Marine and Fisheries, charted the new directions. He provided scientific information to make the implementation of the fishery law more effective. He wrote papers relating to fishery problems in a style suited to a broad reading audience, headed special investigations, and served as Canada's representative expert on international fishery questions. Prince strongly advocated scientific research designed to build a base of knowledge about the life histories of fish species and about water pollution. This could lead to intelligent regulation to save the fish, he believed. He advocated establishing marine biological stations, pressing his agenda on the Minister of Marine and Fisheries. Prince began his advocacy in his first formal report, in which he called for the establishment of marine biological stations on the Atlantic coast and along inland waters to study fish life in "these vast inland seas," in the belief that better knowledge of ocean and inland fisheries could "alone lead to their prosperity and growth in the future." In 1898, he established a management board for the first marine biological station. It became the Biological Board of Canada in 1912 and later the Fisheries Research Board.[13]

The call for government assistance with marine biological work had begun two full decades before Prince's appointment, when in 1871 the Natural History Society of Montreal requested and received permission to have research workers aboard government vessels in the Gulf of St. Lawrence. In 1872, the Minister of Marine and Fisheries took note of American experimental work on the Atlantic coast and James Milner's investigation of the Great Lakes fisheries, suggesting that Canada should make similar efforts. But it was not until 1899, at the prodding of the British Association for the Advancement of Science and with pressure from the Canadian universities, in large measure orchestrated by Prince, that a marine biological station was established at Passamaquoddy Bay, an inlet of the Bay of Fundy in New Brunswick. Seven Canadian university scientists served as trustees on its first board of managers.[14]

In 1901, the House of Commons appropriated $1,500 toward the establishment of a biological laboratory on Georgian Bay, to be organized and directed by university faculty. The choice of location on the Great Lakes reflected both the desires of a science club at the University of Toronto and, more important, the ideas of Prince, A. P. Knight, professor of biology and physiology at Queen's University, and Ramsay Wright, professor of zoology at the University of Toronto, all dedicated to a better understanding of fish life and, for some years, advocates of such biological stations. Since the 1880s, the fisheries of Georgian Bay had been a concern for the Department of Marine and Fisheries and an important part of the dominion's investigation of the fisheries of Ontario in 1892 and 1893, and they were surveyed again in 1905 by a special commission. The Minister of Marine and Fisheries reported the decision to establish the Georgian Bay station with enthusiasm, citing the "great success" and "excellent work" of the laboratory in the Maritime Provinces. Each summer from 1902 through 1913, a group of Canadian academic marine biologists, with University of Toronto scientists most heavily represented, gathered at the Georgian Bay Biological Station to collect data for a systematic survey of plant and fish life in the bay, with some attention given to the flora and fauna of the region more generally. Working on the widely accepted proposition that a full understanding of fish life was essential for the intelligent regulation of the fisheries, the scientists completed thirteen investigations of fish species and their life histories for publication. Work plans included studying problems identified by the Georgian Bay Fishery Commission. In 1904 and 1905, for example, the scientific staff undertook systematic surveys of spawning grounds to collect evidence to be used in determining closed seasons and studied the effects of different types of nets on captured fish. In 1915, the Biological Board of Canada published the results of the research done at the Georgian Bay Biological Station, 222 pages in length, primarily about the fish species and the animal and plant life on which they depended, with an analysis of their environment and distribution.[15]

In November 1910, the Biological Board had considered whether to move the Georgian Bay laboratory, and in 1914 the board closed it, probably in large measure because of Ontario's persistent campaign to expand its control over fish resources. Clearly, the experimental work on the Great Lakes fisheries markedly diminished, and the dominion focused scientific work on the ocean fisheries. The province had long looked to the University of Toronto for assistance in biological matters. For example, Ramsay Wright had written a report on the fish and fisheries of Ontario for the Ontario Fish and Game Commission, published in 1892. The province established the Biological and Fish Culture Branch in 1925. Its work initially involved investigating the suitability of waters for fish plantings; but by 1928 its inquiries had broadened, and Ontario participated in the limnological survey of eastern Lake Erie.[16]

The thinking and work of the marine biologists in Canada and the United States during the early decades of the twentieth century represented a turning point, a retreat from the early faith in artificial propagation and planting. By the mid-1920s, the Marine Biological Board questioned whether the expenses of the artificial propagation program could be justified.[17] The Canadian government gave the responsibility for all its hatcheries in Ontario to the province in the 1920s, but retained federal hatcheries elsewhere. In the United States, artificial propagation and planting also came under strong criticism. Condemned by some critics in both nations for producing weak fish unable to hold their own in natural settings, by others for indiscriminately dumping fry and fingerlings without carefully considering their chances for survival, and by still others for ill-considered mixing of species that cannibalized one another, artificial propagation programs had to adopt much more sophisticated procedures. In both Canada and the United States, they continued to play a role in the maintenance of fish populations.

Elmer Higgins of the Division of Scientific Inquiry in the Bureau of Fisheries explained his views on the tasks of the future at the "Symposium on Fisheries and Fishery Investigations," a conference sponsored by the bureau, in January 1927. The bureau's duty, he maintained, was "to return to the faith of the fathers" and find out how much the ocean and inland fisheries had diminished and why. The bureau should suggest ways to remedy "the evil." Scientists had to know the composition of the commercial catch and the ways it varied as a result of natural fluctuations and human actions. A body of knowledge about life histories, migration patterns, and ecological relations had to be gathered. Research must give these objectives first priority, lest the decline of the fisheries, already "a reproach upon the American democratic system of government," continue, to the detriment of future generations.[18]

The relationship between Canadian and American scientific investigators was a positive one. They shared their findings as they worked within the larger community of marine biologists, whose interests in knowledge were international and whose work depended in large measure on political processes and the forces that shaped them. In both nations, the government agencies that funded scientific research that was designed to help ensure a long-term use of the fish resource also financed projects that encouraged the fishing industry to improve the quality of its product and to expand marketing possibilities and fish consumption. This kind of assistance fostered larger harvests, precisely what the Great Lakes fish population could not stand. The balancing act spelled out hundreds of years before in British objectives for fishery policy—use and conservation—still had not achieved balance.

ONTARIO CHALLENGES FEDERAL GREAT LAKES FISHERY MANAGEMENT

After the victory of the Liberal Party, led by Sir Wilfrid Laurier, in 1896, the dominion government, an advocate of the regulated long-term use of fish resources since 1868, gradually lost its primary role in the management of the Great Lakes fisheries. In large measure because the fish resource became enmeshed in a power struggle between the Dominion of

Canada and the province of Ontario and because of the persistent and aggressive American exploitation of Canada's Great Lakes waters, fishery policy for the lakes drifted away from the regulated careful use of resources with future generations in mind. This happened at the very time when many progressive conservationists advocated just such a policy for natural resources.

The struggle between the governments of Ontario and the dominion grew from the definition in the British North America Act of spheres of authority within the federal system. The provinces generally wanted a stronger role. During the late nineteenth century, Ontario became more and more determined to control and direct the development of its natural wealth, engaging in struggles with the dominion government over the provincial boundary and over the export of saw logs and the refined nickel ores of the Sudbury area. Ontario wanted to develop a manufacturing sector in its economy and to curtail the influence of American capital investments, which cast the province in the colonial role of supplier of raw materials for American industries. The question of which government controlled the Great Lakes fisheries was part of this larger issue, a dimension of the federal contest given little attention by historians. None expressed the provincial point of view more clearly than Kelly Evans, a commissioner of the Ontario Game and Fisheries Commission: "The vital necessity for Ontario to secure for her present and future population the economic benefits from a magnificent commercial fishery must be apparent to every thinking citizen of Canada."[19]

Which government had the right to issue fishing licenses? This was the question that Ontario and the dominion debated in the courts from the mid-1880s to 1898. The British North American Act clearly had given the authority to make fishery regulations to the dominion, which, since 1868, had regulated, licensed, and enforced the fishery laws. In 1898, the Privy Council in London finally settled the question. The dominion retained the authority to make the regulations, and Ontario won the right to issue licenses and collect the fees. Temporary chaos ensued as the two governments tried to make the transition and to develop new administrative procedures. Enforcement as well as licensing became the responsibility of the province, which soon began to claim the right to make regulations. There followed, from 1900 to 1911, a period of bickering, friction, resentment, acerbic exchanges, and provincial conferences over the power to regulate.[20]

This struggle marked the beginning of the virtually complete withdrawal of the dominion government from policy making for the fisheries of the Great Lakes. By the early 1920s, regulations concerning Ontario fisheries became law after the Canadian government consulted the Ontario Department of Game and Fisheries of its desires and accepted them.

Similarly, the sport- and commercial-fish hatchery programs, so long developed and maintained by the dominion, gradually became the responsibility of the province between 1913 and 1926.[21] The biological research facility run by the federal government on Georgian Bay closed in 1914. While the strengthening of provincial power at the expense of Ottawa did not bring a halt to scientific research on the Great Lakes, it dampened the thrust. By the late 1920s, the authority wielded by Ontario, the loosening of regulations, and the rise of a Canadian-owned and -operated Great Lakes fishery organized to lobby for favorable rules of the harvest had emerged simultaneously to create a pattern of resource exploitation similar to that in American waters.

AMERICAN DOMINANCE DRAWS FIRE

"The Yankees to the south of us must south of us remain," wrote E. Pauline Johnson, a Canadian poet, in one verse of "Canadian Born," published in 1903.[22] No one better expressed the growing anti-American feeling that escalated among Canadian fishermen and officials charged with protecting the fish resources of the lakes. The issues were the same as in the preceding two decades: American dealers' dominance of the commercial-fishing industry, inequitable rules and therefore unfair competition between Canadian and American fishers, unequal access to the American market, and American poaching. The increasing scarcity of whitefish, in particular, and the greater competition among fishermen for the catch fueled this kind of thinking. Many nonfishers rankled at their inability to buy Great Lakes fish delivered directly from fishermen's nets to local markets rather than through American distributors. Politicians took heed of the discord and used it to their advantage.

Members of the Georgian Bay Fisheries Commission, appointed by the dominion government in 1905, having taken fishermen's testimony at almost all stations on Georgian Bay and the North Channel, could not ignore the issue of American dominance over the fishermen and the fish resource. The commission's final report proposed a solution. Well aware of the heavy demand in the United States for Canadian fish supplied by American companies, the limited demand for fish in Canadian markets, the organized harvest and distribution system developed by the Americans and the absence of a Canadian counterpart, and the duty in the United States on fish caught by Canadians (one-quarter of a cent per pound at the time of the report), the commission recommended establishing a government agency in two or three locations. It would buy fish from Canadian fishermen "at current remunerative rates," either sell them immediately or refrigerate them, and fill orders from both Canadian and American buyers. The agency would become the middleman, cutting out the "large monopolies who seek to crush out all smaller enterprises and fair competition. . . . [T]hese unscrupulous combines who try . . . to monopolize the whole fish business on both sides of the line, keep the fishermen in their clutches, dictate the price of fish in the wholesale and retail markets, and, from a Canadian point of view, work ruin to the fishing population and the fishing industries." The commission went further, suggesting a ban on the exportation of whitefish, the species that was declining so seriously in Georgian Bay. Neither recommendation was implemented.[23]

The ink was hardly dry on the Georgian Bay study when, in 1909, the Ontario Game and Fisheries Commission began an inquiry into all matters relating to fish and game animals, certainly in some measure a response to the negative assessment in the report of the Georgian Bay Fisheries Commission of Ontario's performance as an issuer of licenses and an enforcer of the dominion's fishery laws. The study severely criticized American commercial-fishing operations in Canadian waters, pointedly referring again and again to the "trust" and the "alien corporation," meaning A. Booth and Company, and describing it as an outstanding evil and a major problem. The company's dominance must be broken for the sake of Canadian fishermen and the preservation of the resource. The report concurred in the proposal by the Georgian Bay Fisheries Commission for a government-controlled fish agency, but, of course, Ontario, not the dominion, should administer it. The plan of the Ontario Game and Fisheries Commission for marketing reform floundered, as did the commission's call for a five-year ban on exports of whitefish and trout.[24]

While the two commissions deliberated and bemoaned the problems stemming from American exploitation of the Canadian Great Lakes fish resource, the Department of Marine and Fisheries stepped up its surveillance of the Great Lakes to stop American poaching, especially in Lake Erie. The ensuing struggle on the lake between Canadian patrol cruisers and American fishermen belied the official image of the peaceful, unguarded border between good neighbors. Present to some extent in past decades, interloping, aggressive American fishermen set their nets in Canadian waters more conspicuously and in larger numbers than ever before in the early years of the twentieth century. Driven by market demand, favorable prices, and declining resources, tugs fishing for dealers and operating out of Buffalo, Erie, Ashtabula, Cleveland, and Sandusky particularly worked the mid–Lake Erie waters with careless disregard for or in deliberate violation of the international boundary. They often did not know where the boundary was and did not carry the appropriate navigational tools to determine their positions accurately. They simply followed the fish.

Captain Edward Dunn of the cruiser *Petrel* bore the brunt of the crackdown by the Department of Marine and Fisheries. During the 1898 season, he seized American gill nets by the hundreds and, in 1900, a poaching tug, the *Kate Wilson.* For the next five years, the problem escalated. In 1902, Edward Prince, the Commissioner of Fisheries, reported that poaching in Lake Erie was "*assuming* a *serious* aspect." He recounted Captain Dunn's observation that whole fleets of tugs regularly crossed into Canadian waters and fished a mile or so inside the boundary, using their whistles to warn fellow poachers of the approach of the *Petrel.* After hastily retreating across the boundary, they tooted their whistles at the Canadian patrol vessel. Dunn seized 998 nets in 1902, more than in any year since 1895, most of them off Long Point and around Point Pelee, where fine fishing grounds lay close to the boundary. He enumerated some of the obstacles he faced. Paid agents of American fishing companies kept tug captains informed of the whereabouts of the *Petrel* as they left port for the fishing grounds. Ninety-seven tugs were registered and fished from the port of Erie, Pennsylvania, alone, many of them far faster than the *Petrel.* He told his superiors that he needed a faster and less conspicuous vessel to rout the poachers.[25]

The Canadians decided to step up enforcement and, during the 1903 season, seized three tugs, fired with rifles on another, the *Silver Spray,* as it escaped into American waters, and confiscated 1,007 nets. Captain Dunn believed that the extensive poaching resulted from the generally light season on Lake Erie. In dismay, he wrote to Prince in September 1903: "I am a loss to know what to do, there are so many nets in our waters, that all I can take out would be only a drop in the bucket; the American fishermen were never so persistent as at the present time." Moreover, fishermen from Erie, Pennsylvania, and Dunkirk, New York, were said to be arming to defy the *Petrel.* Dunn claimed that he was unable to hire a tug to help him apprehend poachers because American fishermen threatened to blow up or burn Canadian tugs whose captains cooperated in enforcing the law.[26]

One of the seizures in 1903 led to the most protracted dispute in the history of Canadian efforts to protect the fish resources of Lake Erie. The tug *Kitty D,* owned by a fishing company in Buffalo and valued at $4,000 to $5,000, was seized on July 3, 1903. In 1908, the Privy Council in London decided in favor of the owners of the *Kitty D.*[27]

While the Department of Marine and Fisheries lost the *Kitty D* case on the basis of flawed evidence about the location of the seizure, it continued its vigorous enforcement campaign of seizing and selling tugs and nets. It reached a tragic climax with the sinking of the *Grace M.* In June 1905, using the *Vigilant,* a faster boat that in November 1904 had replaced the *Petrel,* Captain Dunn accidentally collided with the *Grace M* while pursuing it for fishing illegally in Canadian waters (figure 18.2). The tug rolled and sank, and Dunn rescued the captain, the engineer, and

Figure 18.2. Patrol cruiser *Vigilant.* (Photograph courtesy National Archives of Canada, Ottawa; negative no. PA159651)

one fisherman. The other two fishermen drowned. This time, the evidence was very clear cut, and the captain of the *Grace M* volunteered that he had been at fault for having left the wheel during the evasive maneuvers. Yet it was the kind of accident that no one wanted to happen, and it had a chastening effect on American poachers who had made fun of the conspicuous and slow *Petrel* and had scoffed at rifle fire from enforcement vessels. The United States added to the efforts by sending a revenue cutter to help stop American poaching in Canadian waters. In 1907, the dominion issued an Order in Council that authorized Ontario law-enforcement officers to arrest poaching Americans, further strengthening the anti-poaching forces on Lake Erie.[28]

Although troubles continued, they seem to have leveled off from 1906 to the outbreak of World War I. But during the first decade of the twentieth century, illegal American fishing strengthened the case for uniform regulations and enforcement. In 1902, Captain Dunn ventured the opinion in his report that unless some arrangement were made with New York, Pennsylvania, Ohio, and Michigan for well-enforced, uniform regulations on Lake Erie, "the time is not far distant when the fisheries will not be worth protecting."[29]

FLAWED FEDERALISM AND FISHERY CONSERVATION

Captain Edward Dunn's observation echoed the general line of thinking among many fishery experts in Canada and the United States who held to the position they had taken in 1892: the Great Lakes and their drainage basin had to be treated as a geographic unit where a uniform policy prevailed. They placed great emphasis on well-conceived and well-enforced rules for fishing as being essential, along with artificial propagation and stocking, and, to a lesser degree, pollution control. That was the formula to save the fish.

Again they confronted the thorny issue of federalism in the United States. Nothing had changed. Each of eight Great Lakes states still made its own rules. While the states pressed the federal government for more and more assistance with hatching programs and research, they remained adamant about retaining the power to regulate their fisheries and to set conditions for federal cooperation. Michigan, which had by far the largest segment of lake waters (equal in size to the Canadian waters), even took a feisty stance with the federal hatchery program, prohibiting federal officials from collecting spawn and insisting that its licensed fishermen do it. State law-enforcement officers arrested federal personnel, and state attorneys challenged federal law in the courts. The Commissioner of Fisheries complained that Michigan, so long involved in artificial propagation and planting programs, and long the beneficiary of federal hatchery efforts, had severely hampered the work.[30]

At the same time, many state fish and game administrators recognized the need for uniform regulation, none more so than the members of the Ohio Fish and Game Commission as they witnessed growing problems in Lake Erie. The states clung to the idea that they could handle the matter by interstate compacts, but, as in the past, their efforts floundered. For example, a committee of representations of Great Lakes states met in Chicago in the summer of 1897 to draw up recommendations for uniform state fishery regulations, but its work failed to produce results. In 1905, a conference of fishery commissioners, fishery committees of state legislatures, fish wardens, superintendents of hatcheries, and others from the Great Lakes states recommended that state legislatures adopt the conference's proposed uniform regulations for the Great Lakes. It also urged that the state legislatures ask Congress to assume jurisdiction over the Great Lakes waters "for the purpose of propagating and protecting fish in said waters" and that the states indicate their willingness to cede their jurisdiction to the federal government. Wisconsin and Minnesota did so, but no state agreed to the proposed uniform rules. As a member of the Michigan Board of Fish Commissioners lamented, "So that we are just where we started—nothing accomplished."[31] The American federal system remained the obstacle it had been.

Federalism in Canada posed a new stumbling block to the implementation of uniform regulation as Toronto struggled to wrest complete control of the Great Lakes fisheries away from Ottawa. In 1911, the Ontario Game and Fisheries Commission, while acknowledging that uniform regulation could have "very considerable" advantages for both Canada and the United States, feared that the United States would use consent to a joint code as a lever in dealing with the Canadian government to have it throttle Ontario's anti-American policies.[32]

More so than ever before, a solution at national levels by international agreement seemed to offer the best possibility for uniform management of the fisheries of the Great Lakes. The rising number of incidents between American poachers and Canadian patrols gave the matter additional urgency. Once uniform rules and enforcement prevailed, the poaching would stop, many argued.

JOINT REGULATION AND THE TREATY OF 1908

In the first decade of the twentieth century, when the conservation of natural resources figured in popular and political thinking, Canada and the United States picked up the unfinished business of the 1892 Joint Commission Relative to the Preservation of the Fisheries in Waters Contiguous to the United States and Canada, and of the Joint High Commission, created in 1898 to resolve troublesome issues between the two countries, including the need for joint regulation of the fisheries in their contiguous waters. In 1905, the administrations of Sir Wilfrid Laurier and Theodore Roosevelt, aware of a broad range of mounting water-use problems in the lakes and rivers shared by the two nations, approved the establishment of the Waterways Commission, a temporary committee to study the issues, as a step on the way to the creation, in 1909, of the permanent International Joint Commission. As for the issue of uniform regulations for the fisheries of the Great Lakes, Secretary of State Elihu Root in the spring of 1906 initiated the effort to try again when he wrote to Sir H. M. Durand, the British ambassador to the United States: "The present is now regarded by this Government as a favourable time to carry into effect the unfulfilled stipulation of 1892, and it is hoped that the same view will be entertained by His Majesty's Government."[33]

Picking up where the Joint High Commission had left off with a drafted article for a treaty, Great Britain, acting on behalf of Canada, and the United States, using that draft with minor alterations, developed a treaty for joint regulation of the fisheries in shared boundary waters that both nations ratified in 1908. It called for the creation of the International Fisheries Commission, consisting of one representative of each nation, whose task it would be, "within six months after being named, to prepare a system of uniform and common international regulations for the protection and preservation of the food fishes" in designated waters. Canada and the United States agreed to put these regulations into operation and to enforce them by legislative and executive action "with as little delay as possible." The treaty enumerated specific categories of rules for the commissioners to develop: closed seasons and definitions of the kind, size, and ways of using nets, "engines, gear, apparatus, and other appliances." Also they were to plan a "uniform system or registry" and a program for concurrent propagation of fish. The rules adopted were to stay in force for four years "from the date of their executive promulgation," and then could be amended with the agreement of both nations. The commission would continue for the life of the treaty.[34] It was not assigned regulatory powers, but it would perform a "draft and recommend" function, in distinct contrast to what the members of the Joint Commission of 1892 had had in mind when they had recommended the establishment of an independent international commission of experts with rule-making powers.

The treaty never went into effect, and the British finally withdrew it in 1914. Between the treaty's ratification in 1908 and its withdrawal after the Canadian and American governments had struggled to achieve its implementation, the reasons for its demise grew in number and complexity.[35] Part of the reason for its failure lay in the terms of the treaty. Six months did not allow enough time for the two fishery experts and their staffs to gather the necessary information and draft reasonable regulations for the Great Lakes and the other boundary waters, a huge and tremendously varied area. The short time frame may have related in part to Roosevelt's wish to have the international arrangement in place before he left office in March 1909. It may also have been designed to avoid a repetition of the long delay between fieldwork and report experienced with the effort in 1892.

David Starr Jordan, an eminent American zoologist and the president of Stanford University, who had been named to represent the United States on the International Fisheries Commission, plunged into the fieldwork promptly. The Canadians named Samuel Torel Bastedo, the former Ontario Deputy Commissioner of Fisheries, who joined Jordan and worked with him intermittently from June to December 1908, when he resigned as commissioner to accept a different appointment in the Canadian government. Edward Prince replaced Bastedo (figure 18.3). By then, Jordan and Bastedo had drawn up a draft of regulations, but in fairness to Prince the deadline was extended to June 1, 1909. Jordan and Prince

Figure 18.3. Commissioners named in 1908 by the United States and Canada to develop joint regulations for Great Lakes fishing: (*above*) David Starr Jordan in later years (Photograph courtesy Stanford University Archives, Stanford, California); (*facing*) Edward Ernest Prince. (Photograph courtesy Royal Society of Canada, Ottawa)

did additional fieldwork, made revisions, and met the deadline, but they continued to visit locations where fishermen who had been consulted throughout the process expressed dissatisfaction. A real difference developed between the two governments about how to deal with revisions based on these later investigations. Jordan wanted to modify the report of June 1, 1909, and Prince wanted to leave it alone until after its adoption and then make changes. The Canadian view prevailed. Both governments withheld announcing the regulations to the general public until they went to the Canadian Parliament and to the United States Senate in early February 1910. By then, the recommendations had become a matter of common knowledge and had fostered discord among fishermen, state fishery commissioners, and provincial fishery authorities. Resistance and criticism ran high.

For the next four years, the recommendations swirled about in a whirlwind of protests alleging that they would be unfair to fish dealers and fishermen and a threat to their livelihoods if implemented. Critics in state and provincial governments perceived them as putting at risk their proprietary interests in the federal systems of government. In Canada, they became an issue as the provinces and the dominion government engaged in a struggle over control of the fisheries. In the United States, champions of states' rights denounced the federal government for using its treaty-making authority to encroach on powers that the Constitution clearly left to the states.

The provision for federal enforcement of fishing regulations developed according to the terms of the treaty horrified them further. Canadian authorities, long skeptical about the ability of the United States government to win support for the idea of a treaty in the face of state opposition, lamented in Parliament and in departmental correspondence that their fears were all too real. Jordan believed that the fishing interests were genuinely divided on the merits of most of the proposed regulations and that there never could be a set of rules that pleased everyone. Clearly, those who contacted their senators and representatives in Washington were opposed to some part of the rules that would curtail their earnings. They often put it more bluntly. The regulations would put dealers out of business and create great hardships for fishermen, their families, and whole communities.

The groundswell of American protest surfaced in the fall of 1908, after the initial fieldwork of the summer months, and the Department of State hastened to invite state fishery commissioners to a conference on November 23 to discuss the proposed regulations and, after learning of fishermen's protests, expanded the invitation to include some in the commercial-fishing industry, specifically those who had contacted their senators. On January 1, 1909, Jordan informed Root about locations of friction and resistance: the Bay of Quinte in Lake Ontario, the western end of Lake Erie, Saginaw Bay, the bays north of Isle Royale, and the Lake of the Woods.[36] Prince felt that the lobster fishers of Passamaquoddy Bay and, above all, the salmon fishermen of the Frazer River, Puget Sound, and the Strait of Juan de Fuca presented real trouble.

The Canadian government tried to control the inevitable criticism that erupted by emphasizing that once uniform regulations were in place, most of the fishermen's troubles would vanish. The American fishermen, the real troublemakers, would be under control at last. The Minister of Marine and Fisheries often repeated this reassurance, but the argument failed to silence those opposed to the treaty. In early 1909, members of the House of Commons complained at length that they had not been informed about the content of the proposed recommendations, and they feared that the regulations would be proclaimed without their input. When pushed, the Minister of Marine and Fisheries noted that there would have to be laws to carry out the regulations and they could serve as a control. Presumably he was referring to appropriation of funds for enforcement. The answer did not satisfy members of the House of Commons who charged that the treaty had usurped their power to regulate Canadian fisheries and had transferred it to members of an international commission without providing for parliamentary approval of the regulations they had developed. They attacked the right of the British government to negotiate such a treaty with the United States, relating almost solely to the control of Canada's natural resources, without at least including a clause that clearly called for Canadian parliamentary approval of regulations developed pursuant to the treaty, and they made much of what some members of the House of Commons chose to call secrecy in keeping the regulations under wraps until after they were proclaimed.

In 1910, the House of Commons did vote to accept and implement the regulations, but complaints continued as time went by without the concurrence of the United States. Criticism of the regulations surfaced in New Brunswick, Quebec, Ontario, and British Columbia. The regulations drew fire from two Great Lakes locations, the Detroit and Niagara River areas, which long had been sources of friction between American and Canadian fishers. The Canadian government tried to secure provincial support by holding an explanatory conference in Ottawa, analogous to the meeting that the Department of State had held in November 1908 with state fishery commissioners and commercial-fishing interests. Visits to the provinces followed.[37]

To the consternation of advocates of the treaty in Canada, legislative scrutiny in the United States began early and went on and on. The Department of State's legal counsel ruled that the treaty required both legislative and executive approval to implement the regulations. Presidential proclamation, as the Canadians hoped, was not enough. Once the Senate Committee on Foreign Relations began hearings on the regulations in February 1910, Great Lakes fishing interests continued the protest that they had started in the fall of 1908. They found champions in Senator Henry Cabot Lodge of Massachusetts, egged on by Representative George Loud of Michigan. Senator T. E. Burton of Ohio voiced the opposition of trapnet fishermen in Sandusky and Toledo. Fishermen who operated on Saginaw Bay descended on Washington armed with nets and herring to show the members of the Foreign Relations Committee just why the mesh size for pound nets allowed by Michigan state law was good and should not be changed to the larger size that the treaty stipulated. Effectively led by the Robert Beutel Company, which dealt in fresh, salt, and frozen fish and in coal and ice and had offices in half a dozen fishing ports, the fishermen from Saginaw demanded that their complaints be satisfied. They knew well how to hold legislative bodies hostage to their interests, for the commercial fishermen of Michigan had decades of experience in shaping state legislation by pressure tactics.[38]

Given Canada's opposition to changing the drafted regulations, Jordan believed that it would be easiest to remove Saginaw Bay from the area covered by the treaty and, to make things fair, allow Canada to exempt the North Channel, which is what it had wanted at the time of drafting the treaty. He could argue that there was good precedent for doing this.[39] Both Lake Michigan and Georgian Bay had been excluded as a quid pro quo in the negotiations because they did not really fit the definition of contiguous waters. Then, in 1910, once the impasse over regulations loomed, those trying to settle differences became obsessed with the long and very troublesome tradition of territoriality. They seem to have ignored the relation of the fish to the Great Lakes as a geographic whole. How did Georgian Bay and Saginaw Bay relate to the whole of Lake Huron? Were they nurseries for its fish, as some contended? Or were they independent subhabitats with their own ecological structures?

Moreover, the experience of the two nations in commercial fishing on the Great Lakes during the past quarter century colored the thinking of those involved in trying to achieve joint regulation. The Department of Marine and Fisheries had long perceived the Americans as a very negative influence on the fish resources, harvesting without control and greatly overfishing the waters. They felt that the Canadian system of controlled exploitation was vastly superior to the American tradition of free entry and would have liked to see it adopted. As it was, the regulations were a watered-down version of Canadian rules; when American commercial-fishing interests called for further dilution, the Canadians were galled, and they resisted. The more amendments the Americans asked to have considered, the more annoyed the Canadians became. Fishery conservationists believed that the Canadians were right in trying to hold the line to the original draft. But the Americans needed congressional approval in order to achieve any of the goals of the treaty. Responding to the virtually unregulated tradition of the common of the Great Lakes fishery, American fishery experts could only hope to find some formula for acceptance of the general principle of joint regulation, which they supported. Thus Jordan and the scientific staff of the Bureau of Fisheries advocated compromise and change of the regulations as originally reported in June 1909.

The formula devised by Jordan and Prince for conserving the fisheries arrived at a stalemate, with the House of Commons refusing to make changes until after implementation, and the United States Senate, in deference to the commercial fishermen, refusing to vote to implement until their criticisms were either rectified or in some manner eliminated. The first bill to adopt the regulations, introduced in 1910, failed to pass. It was reintroduced in the Senate on April 6, 1911, with the regulations that caused controversy having been eliminated. It passed the Senate but not the House. In the spring of 1911, the administration of William Howard Taft replaced Jordan on the International Fisheries Commission with a political appointee who had no fisheries expertise.[40]

The problem of surmounting the opposition of American commercial-fishing interests to the treaty passed to Woodrow Wilson and his Secretary of State, William Jennings Bryan, in March 1913. Anxious to have the treaty implemented, they first tried through the British ambassador to get the Canadians to alter their position. When that effort failed, they worked seriously to save the treaty by exerting pressure on Congress from both the White House and the State Department. They succeeded in getting the Senate to approve the unaltered regulations, but efforts to force the House of Representatives to act in February and March 1914 failed. The Ohio delegation was united in opposition to the treaty because of Canada's refusal to do away with the ban on trap nets. The West Coast salmon-fishing interests supported the representatives from Ohio, and they could not be budged. In disgust, the Canadians drew up new fishery regulations for their waters, and the British withdrew the treaty.[41]

The Department of Marine and Fisheries regarded the failure of the treaty of 1908 as the end of the era when the formula for saving the fish that had been implemented after 1868—regulation, licensing, enforcement, and stocking the waters—had been their best hope. The divided waters, with virtually unregulated American fishermen competing with regulated Canadian fishermen, given its inherent unfairness, could not continue, opined Edward Prince. With the failure of the treaty, "a calamity ruinous to the great Boundary Fisheries of both countries," Canada might well have to abandon its fifty-year policy of regulation. That did not happen. Instead, a form of gradual regulatory equalization followed the failure to adopt the treaty. At the prodding of Ontario, the dominion regulations became more lax, and the American states, each on its own and without uniformity, moved closer to a licensing and enforcement policy. By the mid-twentieth century, with the lamprey onslaught well under way, the process of change had left the Canadian Great Lakes "relatively unregulated."[42]

After the failure to adopt the treaty of 1908, attempts to implement uniform regulations by international agreement would be made again in 1940, urged by marine biologists in both Canada and the United States as the most workable way to conserve the fish stocks of the Great Lakes. They, too, would founder on the rock of commercial-fishing interests. A major disaster, the devastation that followed the sea lamprey's invasion of the Great Lakes, finally produced a limited form of cooperation by treaty between the two nations in 1954. Its purpose, though, was not joint regulation, but cooperation to stem the tide of a disaster.

THE POLICY-MAKING BALANCE SHEET

For those involved in devising policies and enforcing laws for the fisheries of the Great Lakes in the early twentieth century, the successes and failures in their efforts to save the fish during the years must have led to somber reflection. On the positive side, the Great Lakes states could note that they had initiated commercial-licensing policies, had begun the surveillance of their lake waters, and had made arrests. Ontario could boast that it had virtually gained control of its fish resources, had improved the enforcement of its regulations, had developed a hatchery and stocking program, and had established a research division to contribute to better conservation. The Department of Marine and Fisheries could point to the experimental work of its Georgian Bay Biological Station, its careful survey of the Georgian Bay fisheries, its crackdown on American poaching, and its second effort to achieve joint regulation of the fisheries in shared waters under the terms of the treaty of 1908. The Bureau of Fisheries could cite its record of work in the hatchery and stocking programs, its broadened scientific research program that emphasized ecological concepts, its greater attention to Great Lakes problems, and its efforts to help the commercial-fishing industry by conducting fish-processing experiments, market research, and reporting services. Yet they all knew that the preferred commercial fish were declining, that species were disappearing, and that their goals were eluding them. They had done a far better job of serving the commercial interests than of saving the fish. The chastening lesson of the dramatic drop in the herring population in Lake Erie made that realization painfully and dramatically apparent.

19

The End of an Era

The Impossible, the Incredible Happened

In two locations on the Great Lakes, Georgian Bay and Lake Erie, the consequences of aggressive and competitive fishing, the changing marine habitat, and the inability of policy makers to protect the resource converged to signal the coming of the end of an era in the history of the fish population. The years when salmon, whitefish, trout, herring, and sturgeon were the mainstays of the most bountiful commercial fishing on the Great Lakes stretched from the colonial period to the late 1920s. Too many people, too many fishermen, too many changes in the marine habitat, too many technical refinements in ways of fishing, not enough public concern, and not enough knowledge about how to protect and conserve the resource spelled decline. Unmistakable trouble signs became evident in the highly productive fisheries of Georgian Bay in 1908, and the bountiful Lake Erie herring population suffered irreparable loss in 1925.

The fisheries of Georgian Bay, often the subject of debate in the House of Commons from the mid-1880s, drew more and more attention. Especially in the decade after 1895, complaints escalated in a flood of letters and petitions to the House of Commons and the Department of Marine and Fisheries calling for changes in fishing regulations. Simultaneously, more and more requests for licenses poured into the department and, after 1898, the Ontario Department of Fisheries. Better times, higher prices, and strong competition between smaller fishing enterprises and larger operators like James and Charles Noble of Killarney and the Dominion Fish Company, the Canadian subsidiary of A. Booth and Company, produced the groundswell of discontent. To calm criticism, the government of Sir Wilfrid Laurier opted to appoint a study commission in 1905 under the direction of Edward E. Prince to investigate the causes for complaint and to recommend remedies. Conducted in the midst of the heated controversy between the dominion and Ontario over the administration of fisheries law, this exploration of the threats to Georgian Bay, which expanded to include those to Lake Erie as well, was the last major study of the problems in regulating the fisheries of the Great Lakes conducted unilaterally by the national government.[1]

Based on extended interviews with fishermen and dealers and on experimental fieldwork, the findings of the Georgian Bay Fisheries Commission portrayed a fishery with major problems created principally by waste and overfishing. It reported a marked decline in the whitefish harvests from a high of 2,347,000 pounds in 1875 to 1,259,000 in 1906, and the size of the marketed fish had decreased. The number of gill-net tugs had grown steadily from 6 in 1875 to 43 in 1906, and the miles of gill net fished had increased from 490 to 2,114 in the same time period. The immense slaughter had destroyed the balance of nature, "and the extinction of the whitefish will inevitably follow, . . . unless effective protective measures are immediately adopted," the report stated. Production figures showed that trout, "better adapted by nature for self-protection and reproduction" than whitefish, seemed to be holding their own, but considering both the quantity of nets and the smaller size of mesh, they also were declining and needed regulatory protection. Yellow pickerel, however, seemed to be increasing and gaining market popularity. The sturgeon had reached a "critical state," requiring a three-year harvest moratorium beginning in 1908. The herring population seemed satisfactory, but had to be protected because of its importance as food for trout and pickerel. "Coarse fish," such as sucker, carp, and mullet, were "undoubtedly" increasing in numbers, particularly in the North Channel, and should be discouraged by requiring fishermen to remove unwanted rough fish from their nets and to dispose of them on land.[2]

To conserve the commercial fisheries for long-term productivity, the commission proposed a new set of regulations based on the testimony gathered from fishermen, the observations of the commissioners, and the results of a number of experiments done by the staff of the Georgian Bay Biological Station at the commission's request. The recommendations included the use of larger mesh sizes to avoid taking small, immature fish; the closer regulation of the allowable yardage of gill nets per boat; and the restriction of gill- and pound netting to specified locations. They suggested that the number of licensed fishermen be reduced and that the closed season be determined according to geographic location. They called for the complete reorganization of the enforcement system, the hiring of better qualified personnel, and the imposition of much higher fines for illegal fishing. They advocated the creation of a Georgian Bay Game Fish Preserve, extending from Killarney southward along the shore of Georgian Bay to Cedar Point, located in the vicinity of Christian Island, a vast natural spawning area for game fish that were rarely harvested by commercial fishermen. To counteract American entrepreneurial influence in sapping the fishery resources of Georgian Bay, the commissioners recommended the suspension of exports of whitefish and the development of government marketing agencies to serve Canadian producers and consumers alike.[3]

Keenly and painfully aware of the ways in which the political system had utterly failed the conservation effort, the members of the Georgian Bay Fisheries Commission added an extended critique of what they believed to be the shortcomings of Canadian federalism. They considered the division of authority over the Great Lakes fisheries between the national and provincial governments a disaster for the resource because both were uncertain about which one had the authority to act. The report charged that the province attached conditions to licenses that negated the primary authority of the dominion to make fishery regulations. Enforcement rested in limbo, with both Ottawa and Toronto assuming part of the task and neither performing it adequately. As a consequence, the fish resource suffered. Lamented the commissioners, "Indeed, we have come to the conclusion that the system as administered by both governments is inadequate, inefficient and almost wholly useless."[4]

Prince argued that given the "gravity of the situation," the report's "somewhat drastic" recommendations were essential to save the fish. Yes, the government of Canada operated along well-established party lines. Yes, fishermen and political officeholders would complain and press their cases upon the Minister of Marine and Fisheries and the House of Commons. "But," continued Prince, "we believe that the fisheries of the Georgian Bay are in such a state, and are so badly in need of the regulations which we have recommended to be adopted, that no considerations, however important from the narrow point of view of expediency or otherwise, should interfere with proper administrative measures."[5]

The report of the Georgian Bay Fisheries Commission was the most elaborate and the final statement made by the dominion about what Great Lakes fishery management should be in the period before 1930, a clear and forceful expression of the components of policy from 1868 to 1908: protection of spawning grounds, artificial propagation and stocking of the waters, fishing by license as a way to limit entry, and regulation of closed seasons, fishing methods, and harvesting locations.

For Prince, an academically trained marine biologist who had come to Canada in 1892 to advise the Department of Marine and Fisheries on fishery problems, the report was a distillation of his insights about those fisheries gained from sixteen years of study and observation and his assessment of the obstacles that the political systems of Canada and the United States presented to those who would save the fish. A strong conservative, he feared the ways that socioeconomic forces influenced policy, and while he might advise the Minister of Marine and Fisheries to ignore the flack and follow the "scientifically sound" recommendations of the report of the Georgian Bay Fisheries Commission, he must have known that this would not happen. The commission's work had little impact on regulations for commercial fishermen, with perhaps one exception. In 1910, the upper limit of the fine for fishing with illegal equipment was raised to $1,000. Given the impending joint regulation of the fisheries under the terms of the treaty of 1908 between Great Britain, acting on behalf of Canada, and the United States, the stricter rules for fishing on Georgian Bay temporarily went on hold and ultimately went by the board. World War I intervened, and in succeeding years, relaxation was the trend, including the abandonment of the closed season for whitefish and trout in Great Lakes waters. Prince lost his influence, and, in its place, the developmental bent of Ontario gained ascendancy. Fishermen continued to overharvest the waters, pollution grew, and yields from Georgian Bay and the North Channel continued to falter and experienced a long-term decline.[6]

For Lake Erie, the signals that the end of an era was at hand were more obvious and dramatic than for Georgian Bay. Beginning in the 1880s, repeated Jeremiah-like assessments foretold disaster from overfishing, and, as predicted, harvests of preferred commercial species became smaller decade by decade. Walter Koelz summarized the process of deterioration in 1924, lamenting the attrition in the premier commercial species as a result, primarily, of overfishing. Lake Erie's main harvest, he noted, was "'rough fish'; that is species other than whitefish, herring, and trout." In American waters in 1922, the most abundant catch included herring, blue pike, sauger, carp, perch, sheepshead, yellow pike, and suckers; in Canadian waters, blue pike, herring, perch, whitefish, and yellow pike. Whitefish, once abundant in the western end of the lake where they spawned, had disappeared from the overfished, polluted waters. The herring population of Lake Erie was down generally, compared with that in the recent past (figure 19.1). Koelz noted that herring had been "practically exterminated" on the western flat. He spoke positively about the fishermen's unions because their actions forced an increase in fish prices. He believed that had the prices "asked for them [herring] by the organized producers" not risen, thus curtailing demand, they "would have been far more seriously depleted." The sturgeon were almost gone. Trout, never abundant in Lake Erie, continued to be caught in small numbers

Figure 19.1. Gill-net steamer *Earl Bess* with a load of herring caught in spawning season, part of a thirty-ton catch, Lake Erie, November 1918. (From Walter Koelz, "Fishing Industry of the Great Lakes," in U.S. Commissioner of Fisheries, *Report,* 1925 [Washington, D.C.: Government Printing Office, 1926], Appendix 11, facing 553)

at the eastern end. Walleyed pike (also called pickerel, blue pickerel, and yellow pickerel), sauger, yellow perch, sheepshead, suckers, and carp made up a large part of the catch in the western end of the lake, all of them species that seemingly could better tolerate the changed environment, living as they did in lake waters surrounded by agriculture and urban-industrial development. But these species, too, yielded uneven harvests and showed signs of decline in American waters. In Canadian waters, where the fishery had developed notably after 1908, the whitefish harvest fell off after 1920, while blue pike, yellow perch, and herring remained commercially important. These were the essential features of the fish population in Lake Erie fish as Koelz noted them in 1924.[7]

Koelz's study of the Great Lakes commercial fisheries was still at the printer when the fishermen of Lake Erie experienced a debacle of major proportions: the sudden, dramatic decline in the herring population in 1925. The decline that had been proceeding for some years from west to east culminated in a sharp drop in production, from 32,200,000 pounds in 1924 to 5,700,000 in 1925, a blow from which the herring of Lake Erie have never recovered. As Koelz described it, "In 1925 . . . the impossible, the incredible happened. The herring of Lake Erie, suddenly and without warning, gave out." Fishermen caught only stray individuals, even though "dozens of boats, with miles of nets, set virtually from top to bottom in the lake, undertook the search." The story was the same the next year: "A fishery that annually yielded as many high-class fish as could be sold (around 25,000,000 pounds, almost one-sixth of the Great Lakes total yield) was no more."[8]

With the most productive of the Great Lakes plainly in trouble, the commercial-fishing industry and the public demanded action. It involved finding out why the population of herring had collapsed. Inevitably, the United States Bureau of Fisheries and its collaborating investigators had to address the issue of the pollution of Lake Erie, long a source of public outcry, as a possible cause. The ensuing limnological investigation, undertaken in 1928, drew together in a cooperative effort the Ontario Department of Game and Fisheries, the New York Department of Conservation, the Buffalo Society of Natural Sciences, the city of Buffalo, New York, and the Bureau of Fisheries. They supported a team to study the eastern part of the lake, while another team investigated limnological conditions in the western end under the auspices of the Ohio Division of Fish and Game with the assistance of the Bureau of Fisheries. Both teams studied the physical, biological, and chemical conditions in Lake Erie, paying particular attention to pollution, in an attempt to settle the debate about whether pollution or overfishing had created the sharp drop in the fish population.[9]

A report published in 1932 about the results of the study showed that pollution in western Lake Erie involved ninety-five square miles of water. Using the count of tubificid worms as a criterion, the investigators found heavy pollution at the mouths of the Maumee and Raisin Rivers, in Ohio and Michigan, respectively, in an area of ten square miles. Moderate pollution at the mouth of the Detroit River extended for ten square miles. The total area of light pollution was about seventy-five square miles. Waters with light pollution probably would be suitable for spawning, but those with heavy and moderate pollution would not. The investigators noted that conditions in the open lake were "apparently normal." In conclusion, they suggested that the main damage done to commercial fishing by contamination from sewage and reduction of spawning areas had "no doubt been offset, at least in part if not entirely, by the increase in plankton, which serves as food for young fish and for the adults of plankton-feeding species." Thus, according to many scientists, the principal culprit in despoiling Lake Erie remained overfishing. The fishermen saw things differently and remarked at times that "the fish are bound to be poisoned, anyway, and they might as well catch them as soon as possible."[10]

Marine biologists had been long convinced that research and an accumulation of more knowledge could lead to positive regulation to save the fish population. They knew that they needed a far broader base of scientific data than they had to make reasonable recommendations about the regulation of the fisheries. But they had experienced real difficulty in securing financial support for their work. In the wake of the herring crisis in Lake Erie, Congress and the state legislatures became more generous in providing appropriations for scientific research. In 1927, the Great Lakes got its first permanent biological research laboratory, located in Ann Arbor, Michigan, and staffed by fisheries biologists. Marine biologists in Canada and the United States launched a whole series of investigations. With Lake Erie as a catalyst, the Bureau of Fisheries took the lead in working out the cooperative arrangement for the limnological investigation of Lake Erie. It worked with state officials and fishermen to codify and revise state fishery laws and to begin a series of studies of "the effect of gear on the fish population," the causes for fluctuations in harvests, and the "life histories of nine important market species."[11]

Similarly, the crash of the herring population in Lake Erie spurred policy makers into renewed action to achieve cooperation among the Great Lakes states and the province of Ontario as a way to implement uniform regulations. In 1927, the governors of Ohio and Michigan invited representatives from the other Great Lakes states and Ontario to discuss ways to conserve the lake's fish population. The conference held in Ohio in February 1927 dealt specifically with Lake Erie, and the meeting held in Michigan in March considered measures for conservation that would apply to all the Great Lakes. A second conference met in Lansing, Michigan, in February 1928 to discuss in detail the content of proposed joint regulations; it reconvened in December to complete and approve a set of recommendations for "the use of gill nets, size limits of fish, the taking of spawn, the control of pollution, and the collection of fisheries statistics."[12]

As the decade ended, those responsible for formulating fishery policies remained strongly convinced that intergovernmental cooperation could save the fisheries not only of Lake Erie, but of the other Great Lakes and that they were not far from achieving that goal. In the depths of the Great Depression of the early 1930s, conservation officials of Ontario, New York, Pennsylvania, Ohio, and Michigan, organized as the Lake Erie Advisory Committee, actually came to a meeting of the minds about joint regulations based on the pooled survey evidence gathered by all of them, the Toronto Agreement, and the governing bodies concerned adopted four out of five of them in 1933. New York very shortly opted out because it could not enforce the closed season, and the other members followed suit. The effort came so close and yet remained so far from success. Disillusionment with cooperation spread in the general gloom of the depression.[13]

In the 1920s, the same decade in which the herring population of Lake

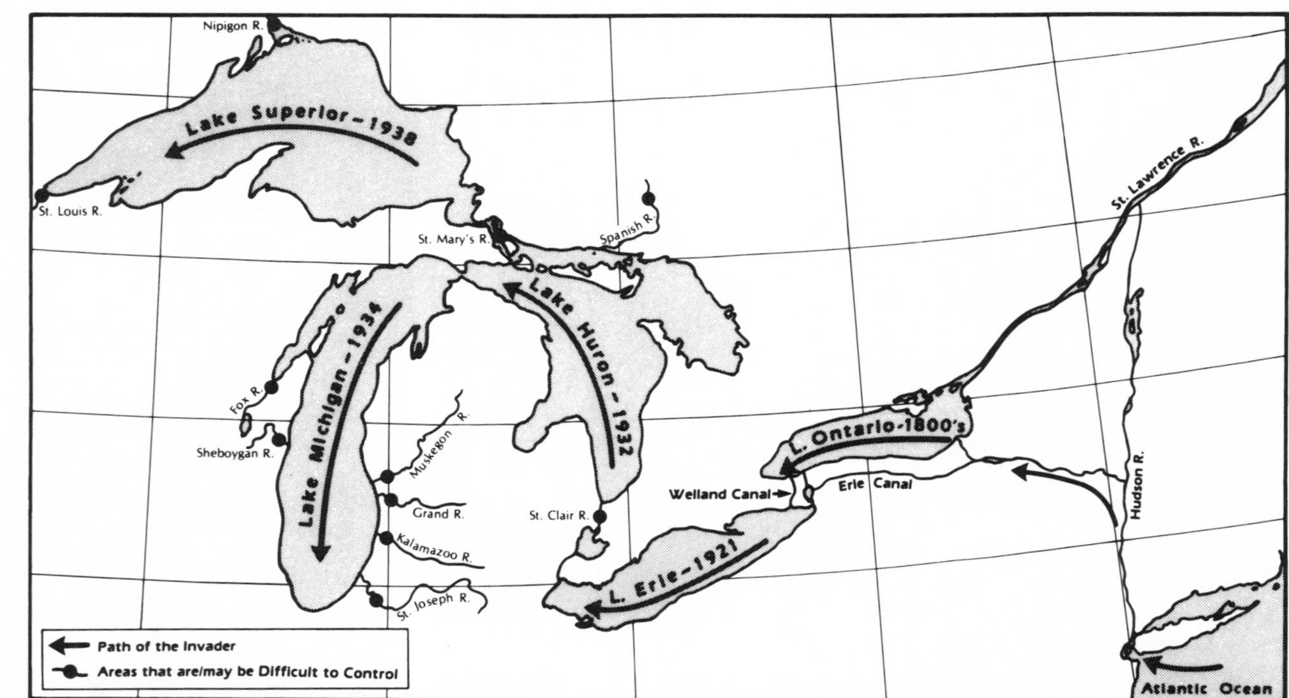

Figure 19.2. Sea lamprey invasion of the Great Lakes. (Map by Jana Fothergill; from University of Wisconsin Sea Grant Institute, *The Fisheries of the Great Lakes: 1984–1986* [Madison: University of Wisconsin Sea Grant Institute, 1986], 8)

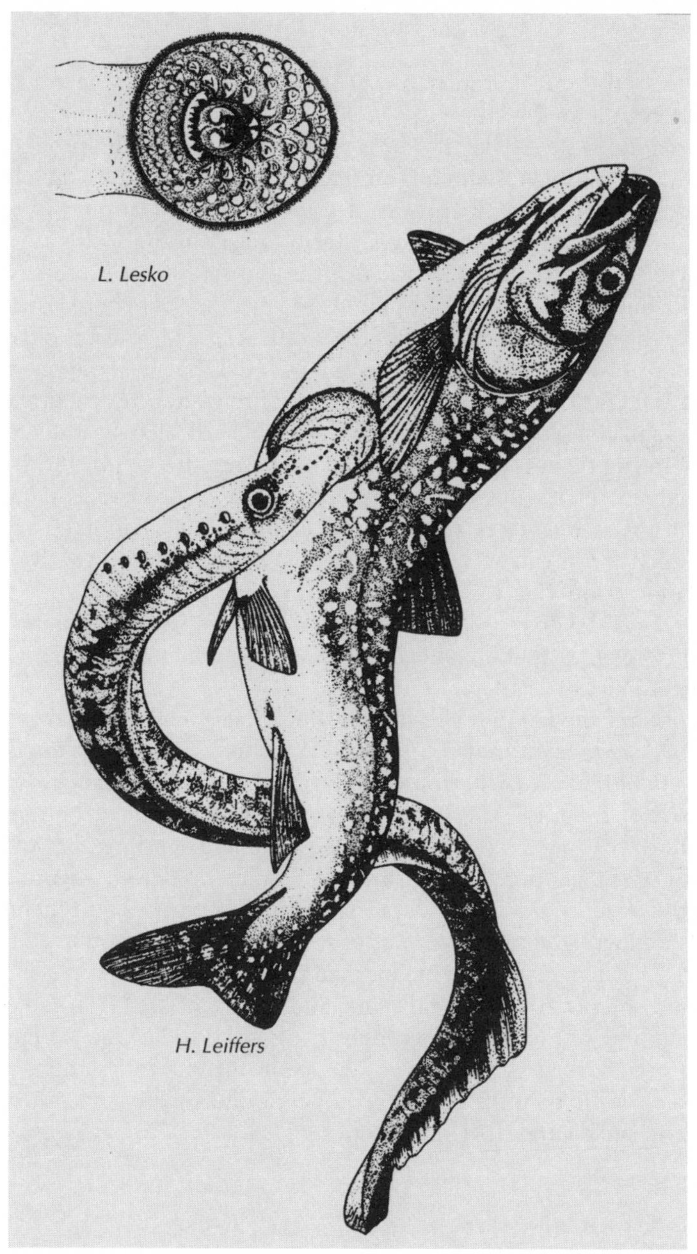

Figure 19.3. Sea lamprey attached to a lake trout and feeding. The mouth has rows of teeth, and the tongue has one tooth that is used to puncture fish and feed on blood. (From Thomas A. Edsall and John E. Gannon, *A Profile of the St. Mary's River* [Ann Arbor: Michigan Sea Grant College Program, 1993], 13; courtesy Michigan Sea Grant College Program, University of Michigan, Ann Arbor)

Erie dropped so precipitously, an intruded species soon to have a revolutionary impact on the fish of the Great Lakes quietly and with little notice appeared in the same lake. In 1921, a fisherman caught and brought into the Royal Ontario Museum in Toronto an "eel," the like of which he had never seen in Lake Erie. Biologists identified it as a sea lamprey like those found for many decades in Lake Ontario, where in the 1920s it was on the increase. Whether a landlocked form that had been introduced into the lake during the postglacial period or a sea lamprey that had entered the lake through the Erie Canal, in the 1920s it spread devastation among the fish in Lake Ontario. It is generally believed that the lamprey moved from Lake Ontario into Lake Erie by way of the newly restructured Welland Canal, completed in 1919, which redirected the flow of water, downstream from Erie into Ontario, making it an attractive avenue for the lamprey, which moves upstream when in search of spawning areas. For reasons not entirely clear, the lamprey did little damage in Lake Erie and thus was not recognized as a menace to its floundering fishery. By 1930, it had moved into the St. Clair River and by 1932 into Lake Huron, where it did very real damage, devastating the trout and whitefish (figure 19.2). Evidence suggests that it had been present in Georgian Bay earlier, during the years 1901 to 1914.[14]

Whatever the lamprey's route into the upper Great Lakes, once there a veritable explosion in its population acted as a catalyst for the demise of the era of the whitefish, trout, herring, and sturgeon in the Great Lakes commercial fisheries. The trout population had proved to be the most resilient of that big four so important to commercial fishing, but with the coming of the lamprey, it also suffered a dramatic decline (figure 19.3). With the onset of the Great Depression, the fishermen found themselves confronted with the twin problems of seriously eroding resources and falling prices. These developments marked the close of the first phase in the environmental history of fish, fishers, and people of the Great Lakes and the beginning of the second, wrought by the invasion of the sea lamprey, which was marked by a complex change in the fish population, by the need for drastic revision in fishery policies, and by greater cooperation between Canada and the United States.

20

Reflections

What of the Great Lakes? . . . and Where Are the Fish?

Authors often conclude their books with a review of historical literature showing how their interpretations differ from those of other authors and shed new meaning on the subject at hand. This book is the first that deals with the fish resources of the Great Lakes considered as a geographic whole, tracing environmental, economic, and policy-making themes from the colonial era of exploration to the Great Depression. It cannot claim to correct earlier authors' errors of fact and judgment, but awaits the work of others to receive the kind of assessment and critical scrutiny that further intensive research can provide. This conclusion examines some of the characteristics and the broader significance of the decline of the Great Lakes fisheries for the Canadian and American experience and for international marine conservation.

Considering the amount of time it takes to damage a natural resource critically, decades can pass between the beginning of use and a recognized crisis. This is surely true in the case of the fish resource of the Great Lakes. The problems that eventually came to threaten the fish population of the lakes originated in the wilderness period when Great Britain and the newly created United States divided the waters and the fishes in 1783, when both nations adopted a policy of Indian removal that led to a sharp decline in the subsistence-fishery pattern of use, and when, shortly thereafter, they fostered agricultural and commercial development in the Great Lakes basin. These policy decisions set the stage for intensive use of the Great Lakes region, but their consequences for the fish population did not become clear for more than a century, when roughly fifty years of commercial fishing had seriously weakened the whitefish, trout, herring, and sturgeon populations and had exterminated the Atlantic salmon of Lake Ontario.

The rapid decline of the choice commercial species of the Great Lakes is a special case in the exploitation of the region's natural wealth because, unlike farmlands, forests, and mineral resources, fish were common property. They were free for the taking in American waters and in Canadian waters until 1857, when they became subject to a modest license fee and loosely enforced regulations. The Great Lakes were an open invitation to commercial fishing once markets developed, as they did in the second half of the nineteenth century with the rapid growth of the national population, the development of the West, and the spread of the railroad net in all directions from the lakes. The common of the fishery made entry into commercial ventures very attractive and easy because it required little capital—an invitation to a young in-migrating population in search of better livelihoods. Under this particular set of circumstances, the rapid, competitive, and destructive exploitation of the resource followed. Thoughtful contemporaries saw what was happening. As early as 1881, a writer in the *Chicago Times* sounded the alarm by asking, "What of the great lakes? . . . And where are the fish?"[1]

The divided jurisdiction over the fisheries of the Great Lakes led to almost insurmountable obstacles to conservation efforts. While partition does not always mean stalemate, in this case the division of the waters hamstrung the state or provincial and national efforts to control the exploitation of the fish resource, a constraint recognized as increasingly important beginning in the 1870s as the parts of the whole failed to find ways to control aggressive overfishing. Thus at the end of the nineteenth century, conservationists looked to international coöperation as the way to save the fish, an objective that became a component of the progressive conservation agenda in Canada and the United States.

Leaders in both countries knew that joint regulation presented a challenge. In both Canada and the United States, the democratic process required the approval of voters for the successful implementation of policies; in both, a sizable number of people depended on the Great Lakes fish resource for their livelihoods and business profits; in both, commercial-fishing interests opposed regulation; and in both, the vast majority of people preferred to eat meat rather than fish. Fish occupied a minor place in diets, which goes far in explaining why the efforts to preserve the Great Lakes fisheries failed to gain widespread public support. Both nations had to undertake research in order to understand the nature of the resource. The Canadians had a stronger tradition of regulation, inherited from the British colonial system. The Americans, having experienced a century of laissez-faire economic policies and entrepreneurial development, were entering an era of more regulation that, they believed, would restore economic and political democracy, which had been lost along the way. Canadians and Americans nurtured both nationalistic feelings and a low-key antagonism toward each other.

In the 1890s, despite these challenges, Great Britain, Canada, and the United States proposed to save the Great Lakes fish population by joint regulation, the beginning of a fifty-year effort and a prime example of how difficult it is to arrive at international agreements on environmental and conservation problems. The first attempt to address the control of commercial fishing and the threat of pollution in the Great Lakes, undertaken in the early 1890s by the Joint Commission Relative to the Preservation of the Fisheries in Waters Contiguous to Canada and the United States, produced a carefully researched report that recommended a system of dual regulation of fisheries and water pollution, but it was never implemented. The failure of this effort, followed by unsuccessful attempts at international regulation of the Great Lakes fisheries in 1908 and 1946, spelled the defeat of collaborative regulation. A spectacular crisis, the sea lamprey onslaught, finally led to joint action in 1954, not regulation, by then considered passé by many, but an effort to save the fish through cooperative research under the guidance of the Great Lakes Fishery Commission.

In a dozen or more other cases, Canada and the United States have agreed to establish joint regulatory commissions on fish, migratory birds, and water pollution. Why, then, could the two nations not establish a joint arrangement to manage the Great Lakes fish population? Anthony Scott suggests that the absence of pressure from an outside third power may explain, at least in part, the failure. Kurkpatrick Dorsey argues that a combination if uninspired leadership for reform, the unappealing physical character of fish, the political pressure of commercial-fishing interests, and the concept of fisheries as common property contributed to failure in 1908.[2] Given the repeated agreements of the United States and Canada on so many Great Lakes legal issues, the proprietary rights of the eight Great Lakes states to regulate their lake waters proved to be critical in the failure of joint regulation of the fisheries. The commercial-fishing industry appropriated states'-rights arguments to protect its economic interests, and the states, then and now, jealously guard their constitutional right to regulate their Great Lakes waters. They still resort to the familiar argument that those closest to the problems involved understand them best, far better than a distant central government.

The cooperative efforts to control pollution, an objective of joint agreements to save the fish of the Great Lakes since 1892, survived over time, leading to the creation of Canadian–American agencies without direct regulatory power. The International Joint Commission, established by treaty in 1909, was the first. It has the authority to investigate, to offer recommendations, and, under certain circumstances, to make binding decisions about questions related to water levels, obstructions, and pollution in the boundary waters if they pose a threat to human health and property. It undertook three major projects in 1912 and in the 1940s on Great Lakes pollution. In 1964, at the request of Canada and the United States, the commission began an extensive survey of water-quality problems in the lakes. Its findings led to the Great Lakes Water Quality Agreements of 1972 and 1978. They confer no power to regulate, but authority to work through the commission in making studies, publishing findings, and recommending appropriate action to governmental agencies for implementation.[3]

Aside from what the late-nineteenth- and early-twentieth-century history of the Great Lakes fisheries tells us about joint efforts to conserve the marine resources, that history broadens our understanding of the development of the Great Lakes region, highlighting the key role of its water resources. As Canada and the United States tried to overcome the problems that arose as a result of divided contiguous waters, they had to take into account many conflicting ideas and satisfy many interest groups. Early experiments in compromise brought to light the kinds of discord that would arise repeatedly in the future. For example, consider the hostile feelings between fishery experts and fishermen. Fishermen liked government stocking programs that were planned and implemented by fishery managers. But when the experts talked about regulation, fishers denounced their advice as impractical and uninformed.[4] Thus when those in government responsible for fishery conservation again and again blamed overfishing for the depletion of the resource, commercial fishers flexed their political muscle. Their message was clear and now very familiar in arguments about the protection of resources and the environment in Canada and the United States. Don't spoil profits, don't eliminate jobs, and don't hurt family income. The two national governments could not reconcile the basic conflict between advocates of long-term conservative use of Great Lakes fish and proponents of immediate use for short-term economic gain, a seemingly eternal disagreement that plagues efforts to maintain environmental quality.

The effort to save the fish of the Great Lakes by regulating harvests and controlling pollution shares some characteristics with other episodes in Canadian–American cooperative attempts to conserve marine resources. Repeated negotiations over long periods is one, evident in the cases of the cod fisheries of the North Atlantic, the fur seals of the Bering Sea, the sockeye salmon of the Pacific Northwest, and the halibut of the northern Pacific as well as the fish of the Great Lakes.[5] Deep concern about resource depletion among policy makers, inequitable exploitation by an aggressive, expansive industry, and squabbles tainted with violence between opposing nationals triggered decisions to try cooperation in all these cases. The goals of the governments were the same in all the negotiations: to ensure long-term yields for commercial fishers and to provide products for human consumption.

Long before talks about any of those fisheries began, many advocated saving the fish, including people with a love of nature, organizations devoted to preserving wildlife, biological scientists, naturalists, self-made fishery experts, and frustrated policy makers who could not get their governing agencies to do the job unilaterally. Canadian and American historians have yet to give these kinds of conservationists sufficient attention. They were legion in the Great Lakes area in the late nineteenth and early twentieth centuries and very evident in the reports of the fish and game commissions of Ontario and the Great Lakes states, which recognized sportsmen's organizations as their allies. They appealed to hunters and fishers to organize local clubs, to exert leadership in the enforcement of fish and game laws, and to set an example in their communities by educating people to appreciate wildlife and advocating its conservation for future generations. From such grassroots efforts developed some of the support for national conservation movements in the early twentieth century.

Why did the fishermen of the Great Lakes fail to unite to support ways to ensure long-term harvests? They were well aware of the decline of the fish populations and worried about it. For a number of reasons, most, but not all, opposed regulation. They argued that rules could not be evenly enforced. There were too many ways to evade them and not enough enforcement personnel to do the job. Those who did as they pleased got the largest portion of the harvest, and those who obeyed the law suffered. Thus regulations were inherently unfair. The fishermen also argued that conditions in the lakes were extremely varied, making it impossible to draw up regulations that allowed for those differences. Moreover, a traditional hostility between regulating agencies and fishermen existed, in large measure based on the proposition that the fish belonged to the people, that, indeed, they were God-given. Working against cooperation among fishermen was the wide variety in their working conditions, including those who fished full time or part time, those for whom fishing was casual seasonal labor, and those who planned on staying in the industry for life and then passing the business along in the family. By nature hardy and independent and in business for themselves, their attitude made them very hard to organize. The reality was that some fishermen, generally those with the most at stake, did organize into associations, but their major purpose was to oppose regulation at the state or provincial and national levels, not to encourage policies designed to ensure long-term harvests, which many believed to be a hopeless goal, especially given the increasing pollution of the Great Lakes.

The history of fishery policies from 1801 to 1933 reveals how the American and Canadian federal systems worked at cross-purposes to efforts to conserve marine life. In the United States, the eight states that fell heir to fishery regulation by virtue of Article 10 of the Constitution and the acquisition of lake waters adjacent to their shores at the time of their admission to the union repeatedly refused to give regulatory authority to the federal government but, at the same time, expected all kinds of federal help with the fishing industry. Put bluntly, it was and is a familiar attitude: let the federal government subsidize, but the states will regulate and enforce. In Canada from 1868 to 1898, the dominion government made and enforced uniform regulations for the fisheries of the Great Lakes and assumed responsibility for artificial propagation, planting, and experimentation. In 1898, by order of the Privy Council in London, control of the fisheries was divided between the province of Ontario and the Dominion of Canada, which led to a twenty-year battle between Toronto and Ottawa over regulation and administration that eroded the management of an already weakened resource that was in need of protection from an aggressive commercial-fishing industry. The federal systems in both Canada and the United States created complications for the unified management of the Great Lakes fish resources.

The forces of nationalism and displays of abrasive feelings among and between the Canadian and American people accompanied the rise and decline of the Great Lakes fishing industry from 1850 to 1933. Poaching American fishermen and large fish-packing companies emerged as the illegal exploiters of Canadian resources, and the United States government proved to be a weak restraint on an aggressive commercial-fishing industry that effectively exercised political clout. With much justification, the Canadians claimed that their fishery management policies were superior to state efforts and complained that the way in which American fishers harvested the waters corrupted their Canadian counterparts and encouraged them to defy the laws designed to save the fish.[6]

While the decline of the Great Lakes fishery resources by 1933 was the result of many circumstances unique to a specific location and time period, it is not unique in the environmental history of aquatic resources in the larger framework of human experience. It stands as one example of the way in which waters and marine life change with population growth, economic development, commercial fishing, increasingly efficient technologies of harvest, and, especially, the rise of economic interests far more powerful than fishing that compete for the use of water resources. The depletion of the fish population also illuminates the need for a body of accurate scientific information on which to base policies and the very difficult task of realistically assessing the size of fish populations and their ability to sustain themselves in an environment so affected by intruded species and habitat changes associated with economic growth. With rapidly changing conditions, was it possible to devise policies to sustain the fish resource for long-term use?

In the 1990s, a century after the first joint effort of Canada and the United States to control the problems of overfishing and pollution in the Great Lakes, the world is confronted with the reality of seriously declining marine populations in the oceans. For more than a decade, the press has frequently reported trouble signs, and within the space of a few months in 1995, *National Geographic,* the *Ecologist,* and *Scientific American* made the plight of the ocean fisheries a primary focus.[7] The general causes of the degradation are frequently cited as overfishing by a subsidized, aggressive industry that uses the advanced technology introduced in the 1950s and 1960s, pollution from heavily populated and extensively developed land areas, and the failure of regulatory conservation—the same general circumstances cited a century ago as causes of the fishery problems in the Great Lakes. The parallels are striking, and the geographic differences are very real. The Great Lakes are far smaller than the oceans and are surrounded by land that was rapidly settled and developed. Their waters and marine life reacted much more quickly to changing conditions than did those of the vast oceans separating the continents. The fishing industry of both oceans and lakes exerted a dominant influence on policy makers and justified its actions by using the oft-repeated argument that the waters are so vast and the fish so fecund that depletion is impossible. The historical record of commercial fishing in both the Great Lakes and the oceans, however, shows that depletion is possible. It also demonstrates the frustrations and failures of regulatory policy. Current efforts by the United Nations to harmonize, control, and conserve the ocean fisheries are akin to those undertaken by Canadian and American policy makers to regulate and preserve the Great Lakes fisheries beginning in 1892. One of the major challenges facing all the peoples of the world today remains as it was a century ago: to save the fish.

Notes
Glossary of Fish Species
Bibliography
Index

Notes

PREFACE

1. Margaret Beattie Bogue and Virginia A. Palmer, *Around the Shores of Lake Superior: A Guide to Historic Sites* (Madison: University of Wisconsin Sea Grant College Program, 1979); Margaret Beattie Bogue, *Around the Shores of Lake Michigan: A Guide to Historic Sites* (Madison: University of Wisconsin Press, 1985).

2. Harlan Hatcher, *Lake Erie,* American Lakes Series, ed. Milo M. Quaife (Indianapolis: Bobbs-Merrill, 1945); Fred Landon, *Lake Huron,* American Lakes Series, ed. Milo M. Quaife (Indianapolis: Bobbs-Merrill, 1944); Grace Lee Nute, *Lake Superior,* American Lakes Series, ed. Milo M. Quaife (Indianapolis: Bobbs-Merrill, 1944); Arthur Pound, *Lake Ontario,* American Lakes Series, ed. Milo M. Quaife (Indianapolis: Bobbs-Merrill, 1945); Milo M. Quaife, *Lake Michigan,* American Lakes Series, ed. Milo M. Quaife (Indianapolis: Bobbs-Merrill, 1944).

3. Nute, *Lake Superior,* 171–194.

4. Frank Prothero, *The Good Years: A History of the Commercial Fishing Industry on Lake Erie* (Belleville, Ont.: Mika, 1973).

5. George Vukelich, *Fisherman's Beach* (New York: St. Martin's Press, 1962).

6. Thomas C. Kuchenberg and Jim Legault, *Reflections in a Tarnished Mirror: The Use and Abuse of the Great Lakes* (Sturgeon Bay, Wis.: Golden Glow, 1978).

7. William Ashworth, *The Late, Great Lakes: An Environmental History* (New York: Knopf, 1986).

8. Alan B. McCullough, *The Commercial Fishery of the Canadian Great Lakes* (Ottawa: Environment Canada, 1989).

9. Timothy C. Lloyd and Patrick B. Mullen, *Lake Erie Fishermen: Work, Identity, and Tradition* (Urbana: University of Illinois Press, 1990).

10. Robert Doherty, *Disputed Waters: Native Americans and the Great Lakes Fishery* (Lexington: University of Kentucky Press, 1990).

11. Grace Lee Nute, "The American Fur Company's Fishing Enterprises on

Lake Superior," *Mississippi Valley Historical Review* 12 (March 1926): 483–503; Stephen Bocking, "Fishing the Inland Seas: Great Lakes Research, Fisheries Management, and Environmental Policy in Ontario," *Environmental History* 2 (January 1997): 52–73; Neil S. Forkey, "Maintaining a Great Lakes Fishery: The State, Science, and the Case of Ontario's Bay of Quinte, 1870–1920," *Ontario History* 87 (spring 1995): 45–64; Lynn H. Halverson, "The Commercial Fisheries of the Michigan Waters of Lake Superior," *Michigan History* 39 (March 1955): 1–17; June Drenning Holmquist, "Commercial Fishing on Lake Superior in the 1890s," *Minnesota History* 34 (summer 1955): 243–249; John Van Oosten, "Michigan's Commercial Fisheries of the Great Lakes," *Michigan History Magazine* 22 (winter 1938): 107–145; Thomas F. Waters, *The Superior North Shore* (Minneapolis: University of Minnesota Press, 1987), 136–194; Bogue, *Around the Shores of Lake Michigan,* 76–84; Bogue and Palmer, *Around the Shores of Lake Superior,* 149–153; Frank N. Egerton, *Overfishing or Pollution? Case History of a Controversy on the Great Lakes,* Technical Report no. 41 (Ann Arbor, Mich.: Great Lakes Fishery Commission, 1985). For other examples of treatments of parts of Great Lakes fishery history, see McCullough, *Commercial Fishery,* 137–153.

12. Environment Canada and the United States Environmental Protection Agency, *The Great Lakes: An Environmental Atlas and Resource Book* (Chicago and Toronto: Environmental Protection Agency and Environment Canada, 1987), 36.

13. Harold C. Jordahl, Jr., telephone conversation with author, 6 September 1996.

14. Richard C. Hoffmann, "Economic Development and Aquatic Ecosystems in Medieval Europe," *American Historical Review* 101 (June 1996): 631–669.

CHAPTER 1: LEGACIES FROM THE WILDERNESS

1. Claude Dablon, in *Jesuit Relations and Allied Documents,* ed. Reuben G. Thwaites, 73 vols. (Cleveland: Burrows, 1899), 42:71.

2. Measures of physical features are from Environment Canada and United States Environmental Protection Agency, *The Great Lakes: An Environmental Atlas and Resource Book* (Chicago and Toronto: Environmental Protection Agency and Environment Canada, 1987), 3–4.

3. Quoted in W. Vernon Kinietz, *The Indians of the Western Great Lakes, 1615–1760* (Ann Arbor: University of Michigan Press, 1940), 27–28.

4. Quoted in Kinietz, *Indians of the Western Great Lakes,* 239–240.

5. See, for example, Dablon, in *Jesuit Relations,* ed. Thwaites, 42:71, 73, and Joseph Chaumont, in *Jesuit Relations,* ed. Thwaites, 43:261.

6. Charles E. Cleland, "The Inland Shore Fishery of the Northern Great Lakes: Its Development and Importance in Prehistory," *American Antiquity* 47 (October 1982): 761, 768.

7. Harold Hickerson, *The Chippewa and Their Neighbors: A Study in Ethnohistory* (New York: Holt, Rinehart and Winston, 1970), 13–16.

8. Cleland, "Inland Shore Fishery," 762.

9. Quoted in Otto Fowl, *Sault Ste. Marie and Its Great Waterway* (New York: Putnam, 1925), 100.

10. Robert E. Ritzenthaler and Pat Ritzenthaler, *The Woodland Indians of the Western Great Lakes,* 2d ed. (Milwaukee: Milwaukee Public Museum, 1983), 65.

11. Chaumont, in *Jesuit Relations,* ed. Thwaites, 43:261; Paul Kane, *Wanderings of an Artist among the Indians of North America* (London: Longman, Brown, Green, Longmans and Roberts, 1859), 31.

12. Cleland, "Inland Shore Fishery," 762–763.

13. Gary A. Wright, "Some Aspects of Early and Mid-Seventeenth Century Exchange Networks in the Western Great Lakes," *Michigan Archaeologist* 13 (December 1967): 181–197; Graham Alexander MacDonald, "The Saulteur-Ojibwa Fishery at Sault Ste. Marie, 1640–1920" (master's thesis, University of Waterloo, 1978), 33–34.

14. Helen Hornbeck Tanner, ed., *Atlas of Great Lakes Indian History* (Norman: University of Oklahoma Press, 1987), 18–23.

15. Richard White, *The Middle Ground: Indians, Empires and Republics in the Great Lakes Region, 1650–1815* (New York: Cambridge University Press, 1991), 40–49, 128–141.

16. James M. McClurken, "Wage Labor in Two Michigan Ottawa Communities," in *Native Americans and Wage Labor: Ethnohistorical Perspectives,* ed. Alice Littlefield and Martha C. Knack (Norman: University of Oklahoma Press, 1996), 69; Charles E. Cleland, "Indians in a Changing Environment," in *The Great Lakes Forest: An Environmental and Social History,* ed. Susan L. Flader (Minneapolis: University of Minnesota Press, 1983), 83–95.

17. Christopher Vecsey, *Traditional Ojibwa Religion and Its Historical Changes,* American Philosophical Society Memoirs (Philadelphia: American Philosophical Society, 1983), 152:6–8, 59–63, 72–80, 96–98, 109, 145–149, quote on 72. Examples of legends and traditions are in William Jones, *Ojibwa Texts Collected by William Jones,* parts 1 and 2 (Leyden: Brill, 1917–1919), and in Victor Barnouw, *Wisconsin Chippewa Myths and Tales and Their Relation to Chippewa Life* (Madison: University of Wisconsin Press, 1977). Thomas Vennum, Jr., discusses legends about wild rice in *Wild Rice and the Ojibway People* (St. Paul: Minnesota Historical Society Press, 1988), 58–80.

18. Calvin Martin, *Keepers of the Game: Indian–Animal Relationships and the Fur Trade* (Berkeley: University of California Press, 1978), 71–74; Shepard Krech III, ed., *Indians, Animals, and the Fur Trade: A Critique of Keepers of the Game* (Athens: University of Georgia Press, 1981); Vecsey, *Traditional Ojibwa Religion,* 19–22, 57–58, 71, 82–83, 100, 118–120, 141–143, 158–159, 198–205.

19. Gerald M. Craig, *Upper Canada in the Formative Years, 1784–1841* (Toronto: McClelland and Stewart, 1963), 20–41.

20. The legal framework for Great Lakes waters and fishery regulation following is taken in part from Margaret Beattie Bogue, "In the Shadow of the Union Jack: British Legacies and Great Lakes Fishery Policy," *Environmental Review* 11 (spring 1987): 19–34.

21. Don Courtney Piper, *International Law of the Great Lakes: A Study of*

Canadian–United States Cooperation (Durham, N.C.: Duke University Press, 1967), 8–17; John Bassett Moore, *History and Digest of International Arbitrations to Which the United States Has Been a Party,* 6 vols. (Washington, D.C.: Government Printing Office, 1898), 1:1–2, 162–195.

22. Francis N. Thorpe, *The Federal and State Constitutions, Colonial Charters . . . ,* 7 vols. (Washington, D.C.: Government Printing Office, 1909), 2:967, 4:1927, 5:2897, 7:4072.

23. Order in Council, Court at Windsor Castle, 18 July 1898, file 164, part 2, frames 240–248, Microfilm Reel T-2736, Records of the Department of Marine and Fisheries, Record Group 23, National Archives of Canada, Ottawa.

24. Bogue, "In the Shadow of the Union Jack," 20–28.

25. Alice Outwater, *Water: A Natural History* (New York: Basic Books, 1996), 3–33.

CHAPTER 2: LAKE ONTARIO SALMON IN AN EARLY AGRICULTURAL-COMMERCIAL ECONOMY

1. Canada, House of Commons, "Seventh Report of the Select Committee on Fisheries, Navigation, etc.," in *Journals,* 1869, Appendix 3, 68, 80; Paul Kane, *Wanderings of an Artist among the Indians of North America* (London: Longman, Brown, Green, Longmans and Roberts, 1859), 30–32; William Sherwood Fox, "The Literature of *Salmo Salar* in Lake Ontario and Tributary Streams," *Proceedings and Transactions of the Royal Society of Canada* 24 (May 1930): 45–55; Anthony Netboy, *The Atlantic Salmon: A Vanishing Species?* (Boston: Houghton Mifflin, 1968), 331–334.

2. Quoted in Canada, *Sessional Papers,* 1899, no. 11A, lxii, and George Brown Goode, "The Salmon—*Salmo salar,*" in George Brown Goode, *The Fisheries and Fishery Industries of the United States,* Section 1, 47th Cong., 1st sess., 1881, S. Misc. Doc. 124 (Serial 1998), 473–474.

3. Elizabeth M. Simpson, *Mexico, Mother of Towns: Fragments of Local History* (Buffalo, N.Y.: Clement, 1949), 176; B. E. Ingersoll, interview with William Wakeham and Richard Rathbun, Oswego, New York, 4 October 1894, Lake Ontario Interviews, Records of the Joint Commission Relative to the Preservation of the Fisheries in Waters Contiguous to Canada and the United States, Record Group 22, National Archives, College Park, Maryland; Canada, *Sessional Papers,* 1869, no. 12, 85; 1882, no. 5, Supplement 2, "Report on Fish Breeding," 37.

4. John Barret Van Vlack, interview with William Wakeham and Richard Rathbun, Collingwood, Ontario, 11 September 1894, 1 Georgian Bay Interviews, Records of the Joint Commission.

5. Goode, "Salmon," 473–474. Testimony about the size of the salmon is also found in Simpson, *Mexico,* 176; C. H. Strowger, interview with William Wakeham and Richard Rathbun, Webster, New York, 3 October 1894, Lake Ontario Interviews, Records of the Joint Commission; Canada, *Sessional Papers,* 1869, no. 12, 87; 1871, no. 5, 275; 1876, no. 5, 239.

6. Quoted in Goode, "Salmon," 474.

7. Ingersoll interview; quoted in Canada, *Sessional Papers,* 1872, no. 5, 79.

8. Canada, *Sessional Papers,* 1869, no. 12, 87; 1879, no. 3, 366; 1891, no.

8A, 77; Canada, House of Commons, "Seventh Report," 2; U.S. Commission of Fish and Fisheries, *Report,* 1878, 45th Cong., 3d sess., 1878, S. Misc. Doc. 31 (Serial 1834), xxxii; Goode, "Salmon," 470; Ramsay Wright, "Natural History of Ontario Fish," in Ontario, *Sessional Papers,* 1892, no. 79, 449; "Statement of Differences between Salmon and Salmon Trout in Great Lakes," 14 January 1898, file 2035, part 1, frame 33, Microfilm Reel T-3197, Records of the Department of Marine and Fisheries, Record Group 23, National Archives of Canada, Ottawa; Fox, "Literature of *Salmo Salar,*" 52; A. A. Blair, "Scales of Lake Ontario Salmon Indicate a Land-Locked Form," *Copeia,* 10 December 1938, 206; Hugh MacCrimmon "The Beginnings of Salmon Culture in Canada," *Canadian Geographical Journal* 71 (September 1965): 98.

9. Joseph Chaumont, in *Jesuit Relations and Allied Documents,* ed. Ruben G. Thwaites, 73 vols. (Cleveland: Burrows, 1899), 43:261.

10. Quoted in Fox, "Literature of *Salmo Salar,*" 49; Claude Dablon, in *Jesuit Relations,* ed. Thwaites, 52:79.

11. Simpson, *Mexico,* 39; quoted in Fox, "Literature of *Salmo Salar,*" 48.

12. Simpson, *Mexico,* 175.

13. Ingersoll interview; *Laws of New York, 1816–1818* (Albany: Websters and Skinners, 1815), 4:74; Hugh M. Smith, "Report on an Investigation of the Fisheries of Lake Ontario," U.S. Fish Commission, *Bulletin* 10 (1890): 197; Canada, House of Commons, "Seventh Report," 2.

14. Canada, *Statutes of the Province of Upper Canada* (Kingston: Thompson and McFarlane, 1831), 328–329.

15. Canada, *Sessional Papers,* 1869, no. 12, 85; 1899, no. 11A, lxii; quoted in Canada, House of Commons, "Seventh Report," 80; Canada, Senate, *Parliamentary Debates,* 26 April 1872, 168.

16. Canada, House of Commons, "Seventh Report," 2; Simpson, *Mexico,* 177, 254; Richard Follett, "'Salmo salar' of the St. Lawrence River," *Transactions of the American Fisheries Society* 62 (1932): 367.

17. M. Smith and Merwin-Marie Snell, "Review of the Fisheries of the Great Lakes in 1885," in U.S. Commission of Fish and Fisheries, *Report,* 1887, Appendix, 50th Cong., 2d sess., 1889, H. Misc. Doc. 133 (Serial 2661), 297; Smith, "Fisheries of Lake Ontario," 198; *American Field: The Sportsman's Journal,* 2 January 1886, 8.

18. *Laws of New York* (Albany: Charles R. and George Webster, 1802), 1:422–423; *Provincial Statutes of Upper Canada* (York: Lt. Gov., 1818), 221; MacCrimmon, "Beginning of Salmon Culture," 96–97; Richard Nettle, *The Salmon Fisheries of the St. Lawrence and Its Tributaries* (Montreal: Lovell, 1857), 5, 8; James Edward Alexander, ed., *Salmon-Fishing in Canada by a Resident* (London: Longman, 1860), 20; U.S. Congress, House, *Report of the Joint Commission Relative to the Preservation of the Fisheries in Waters Contiguous to Canada and the United States,* 54th Cong., 2d sess., 1896, H. Doc. 315 (Serial 3534), 22–24.

19. W. B. Scott and E. J. Crossman, *Freshwater Fishes of Canada* (Ottawa: Fisheries Research Board of Canada, 1973), 196.

20. MacCrimmon, "Beginning of Salmon Culture," 97. Biographical sketches of Wilmot are in John Squair, *The Townships of Darlington and Clarke Including*

Bowmanville and Newcastle Province of Ontario Canada (Toronto: University of Toronto Press, 1927), 64–69, and Alan B. McCullough, "Samuel Wilmot," in *Dictionary of Canadian Biography* (Toronto: University of Toronto Press, 1990), 12:1106–1107.

21. "Report on Fish Breeding in the Dominion of Canada, 1881," in Department of Marine and Fisheries, *Report,* 1881, in Canada, *Sessional Papers,* 1882, no. 5, Supplement 2, 39–40.

CHAPTER 3: PATTERNS OF GROWTH THROUGH 1872

1. Alan B. McCullough, *The Commercial Fishery of the Canadian Great Lakes* (Ottawa: Environment Canada, 1989), 15; Hugh M. Smith and Merwin-Marie Snell, "Review of the Fisheries of the Great Lakes in 1885," in U.S. Commission of Fish and Fisheries, *Report,* 1887, Appendix, 50th Cong., 2d sess., 1889, H. Misc. Doc. 133 (Serial 2661), 266.

2. Louis Falge, ed., *History of Manitowoc County, Wisconsin,* 2 vols. (Chicago: Goodspeed Historical Association, 1911, 1912), 1:35, 349, 412.

3. U.S. Congress, House, *Report of the Joint Commission Relative to the Preservation of the Fisheries in Waters Contiguous to Canada and the United States,* 54th Cong., 2d sess., 1896, H. Doc. 315 (Serial 3534), 143; William Wakeham and Richard Rathbun, "History of Fishing," A Georgian Bay, Subjects; Captain Joseph King, interview with William Wakeham and Richard Rathbun, Thessalon, Ontario, 17 September 1894, 2 Georgian Bay Interviews, Records of the Joint Commission Relative to the Preservation of the Fisheries in Waters Contiguous to Canada and the United States, Record Group 22, National Archives, College Park, Maryland.

4. William Sherwood Fox, *The Bruce Beckons: The Story of Lake Huron's Great Peninsula* (Toronto: University of Toronto Press, 1952), 109–115; Dorothy Wallace, ed., *Memories of Goderich: The Romance of the Prettiest Town in Canada,* 2d ed. (Goderich, Ont.: Jubilee 3 Committee, 1979), 19.

5. Norman Robertson, *The History of the County of Bruce and of the Minor Municipalities Therein, Province of Ontario, Canada* (Toronto: Briggs, 1906), 22. Other accounts of the MacGregor fishery are in Fred Landon, *Lake Huron,* American Lakes Series, ed. Milo M. Quaife (Indianapolis: Bobbs-Merrill, 1944), 133–135, and Fox, *The Bruce Beckons,* 108–116. They seem to stem primarily from the information collected by Norman Robertson, treasurer of Bruce County and secretary of the Bruce County Historical Society.

6. Graham Alexander MacDonald, "The Salteur-Ojibwa Fishery at Sault Ste. Marie, 1640–1920" (master's thesis, University of Waterloo, 1978), 73–86; McCullough, *Commercial Fishery,* 16; Grace Lee Nute, "The American Fur Company's Fishing Enterprises on Lake Superior," *Mississippi Valley Historical Review* 12 (March 1926): 483–503.

7. McCullough, *Commercial Fishery,* 15.

8. McCullough, *Commercial Fishery,* 15.

9. Norman S. Baldwin, Robert W. Saalfeld, Margaret A. Ross, and Howard J. Buettner, *Commercial Fish Production in the Great Lakes, 1867–1977,* Technical

Report no. 3 (Ann Arbor, Mich.: Great Lakes Fishery Commission, 1979), 186; table 4.1.

10. *Bayfield County Press,* 15 November 1879; Bela Hubbard, *Memorials of a Half-Century in Michigan and the Lake Region* (New York: Putnam, 1888), 276.

11. Canada, *Sessional Papers,* 1874, no. 4, lxxvi.

12. Frederick W. True, "The Fisheries of the Great Lakes," in George Brown Goode, *The Fisheries and Fishery Industries of the United States,* Section 2, 47th Cong., 1st sess., 1881, S. Misc. Doc. 124 (Serial 1999), 669.

13. Hubbard, *Memorials,* 276.

14. James W. Milner, "Report on the Fisheries of the Great Lakes: The Result of Inquiries Prosecuted in 1871 and 1872," in U.S. Commission of Fish and Fisheries, *Report,* 1872–1873, Appendix A, 42d Cong., 3d sess., 1872, S. Misc. Doc. 74 (Serial 1547), 7; Canada, *Sessional Papers,* 1873, no. 8, 134–141.

15. Milner, "Report on the Fisheries of the Great Lakes," 3–4.

16. Milner, "Report on the Fisheries of the Great Lakes," 3–4; Smith and Snell, "Review of the Fisheries of the Great Lakes," 266.

17. Milner, "Report on the Fisheries of the Great Lakes," 6–7.

18. For a succinct statement of Buffalo's transportation advantages, see Smith and Snell, "Review of the Fisheries of the Great Lakes," 288, and Milner, "Report on the Fisheries of the Great Lakes," 5.

19. Preliminary Draft, "Georgian Bay Fisheries Commission Report, 1908," file 1168, part 1, frame 716, Microfilm Reel T-3135, Records of the Department of Marine and Fisheries, Record Group 23, National Archives of Canada, Ottawa; True, "Fisheries of the Great Lakes," 643, 661; Ludwig Kumlien, "The Fisheries of the Great Lakes," in George Brown Goode, *The Fisheries and Fishery Industries of the United States,* Section 5, 47th Cong., 1st sess., 1881, S. Misc. Doc. 124 (Serial 2001), 766; Smith and Snell, "Review of the Fisheries of the Great Lakes," illustrations opposite 220, 227, 235; McCullough, *Commercial Fishery,* 26.

20. McCullough, *Commercial Fishery,* 27; True, "Fisheries of the Great Lakes," 673; Smith and Snell, "Review of the Fisheries of the Great Lakes," 234; Kumlien, "Fisheries of the Great Lakes," 757–758; Milner, "Report on the Fisheries of the Great Lakes," 3–4; Canada, *Sessional Papers,* 1873, no. 8, 140.

The pound net was first used on Lakes Erie and Ontario in 1850; Lake Huron, between 1850 and 1860; Lake Michigan, in 1856; and Lake Superior, in 1864, according to Smith and Snell, "Review of the Fisheries of the Great Lakes," 33, 72–73, 87, 149, 202, 213–215, 218, 222, 255, 258, 297, 322.

21. Nute, "American Fur Company's Fishing Enterprises," 483–503; Preliminary Draft, "Georgian Bay Fisheries Commission Report"; Milner, "Report on the Fisheries of the Great Lakes," 3–4.

22. Milner, "Report on the Fisheries of the Great Lakes," 13, 14; True, "Fisheries of the Great Lakes," 652; Kumlien, "Fisheries of the Great Lakes," 763; Smith and Snell, "Review of the Fisheries of the Great Lakes," 24.

23. Smith and Snell, "Review of the Fisheries of the Great Lakes," 76.

24. J. W. Slavin, "Freezing and Cold Storage," in Maurice E. Stansby, *Industrial Fishery Technology: A Survey of Methods for Domestic Harvesting, Preser-*

vation, and Processing of Fish Used for Food and for Industrial Products (1963; reprint, Huntington, N.Y.: Krieger, 1976), 283; Milner, "Report on the Fisheries of the Great Lakes," 5; Smith and Snell, "Review of the Fisheries of the Great Lakes," 99–101, 103, 211, 217. The great importance of two freezing methods and their adaptation to railroad cars are noted in Canada, *Sessional Papers,* 1874, no. 4, lxxxi.

25. Milner, "Report on the Fisheries of the Great Lakes," 14.

CHAPTER 4: THE EXPANSIVE HEYDAY, 1875–1893

1. Norman S. Baldwin, Robert W. Saalfeld, Margaret A. Ross, and Howard J. Buettner, *Commercial Fish Production in the Great Lakes, 1867–1977,* Technical Report no. 3 (Ann Arbor, Mich.: Great Lakes Fishery Commission, 1979), 186; A. Booth, "The Fisheries of the Great Lakes.—No. 1" *American Field: The Sportsman's Journal,* 7 November 1885, 438.

2. James W. Milner, "Report on the Fisheries of the Great Lakes: The Result of Inquiries Prosecuted in 1871 and 1872," in U.S. Commission of Fish and Fisheries, *Report,* 1872–1873, Appendix A, 42d Cong., 2d sess., 1872, S. Misc. Doc. 74 (Serial 1547), 3–4; A. B. Alexander, comp., "Statistics of the Fisheries of the Great Lakes in 1903," in U.S. Commissioner of Fish and Fisheries, *Report,* 1904, Appendix, 58th Cong., 3d sess., 1904, H. Doc. 479 (Serial 4897), 650; Canada, *Sessional Papers,* 1872, no. 5, 102–106; 1881, no. 11, 290; 1886, no. 11, 312; 1891, no. 8A, 210.

3. Canadian and American price indexes have been constructed using different formulas, which makes it impossible to express accurately indexed values for the two countries. Here the index for the United States is applied to the combined total values for capital investments of both. Warren and Pearson Wholesale Price Index, in U.S. Department of Commerce, Bureau of the Census, *Historical Statistics of the United States: Colonial Times to 1970,* Bicentennial ed., 93d Cong., 1st sess., 1973, H. Doc. 93–78, Part 1, 201. This price index is used throughout the chapter. Exchange rates from 1880 to 1890, when both countries were on the gold standard, were very stable. The *Detroit Free Press* quoted the Canadian dollar at 99½ cents throughout 1880 and 1885, and at 98 cents throughout 1890.

4. Milner, "Report on the Fisheries of the Great Lakes," 5; Canada, *Sessional Papers,* 1872, no. 5, 102–106; 1891, no. 8A, 210–211; 1892, no. 11, lii, liv; Frederick W. True, "The Fisheries of the Great Lakes," in George Brown Goode, *The Fisheries and Fishing Industries of the United States,* Section 2, 47th Cong., 1st sess., 1881, S. Misc. Doc. 124 (Serial 1999), 633; Hugh M. Smith and Merwin-Marie Snell, "Review of the Fisheries of the Great Lakes in 1885," in U.S. Commission of Fish and Fisheries, *Report,* 1887, Appendix, 50th Cong., 2d sess., 1889, H. Misc. Doc.133 (Serial 2661), 15; Hugh M. Smith, "The Fisheries of the Great Lakes," in U.S. Commission of Fish and Fisheries, *Report,* 1892, Appendix, 53d Cong., 2d sess., 1893, H. Misc. Doc. 209 (Serial 3264), 368.

5. Milner, "Report on the Fisheries of the Great Lakes," 7; Canadian production figures compiled from Baldwin, Saalfeld, Ross, and Buettner, *Commercial Fish Production,* 28, 66, 81, 121, 184. The value is estimated on the basis of per pound value derived from Milner's report times the combined American and

Canadian production figures, 39,330,000 pounds. Most of the Canadian catch was marketed in the United States.

6. J. W. Slavin, "Freezing and Cold Storage," in Maurice E. Stansby, *Industrial Fishery Technology: A Survey of Methods for Domestic Harvesting, Preservation, and Processing of Fish Used for Food and for Industrial Products* (1963; reprint, Huntington, N.Y.: Krieger, 1976), 283.

7. Georgian Bay Fisheries Commission, *Report and Recommendations* (Ottawa: Government Printing Bureau, 1908), 7; Smith and Snell, "Review of the Fisheries of the Great Lakes," 73.

8. Smith and Snell, "Review of the Fisheries of the Great Lakes," 13; Smith, "Fisheries of the Great Lakes," 387; Georgian Bay Fisheries Commission, *Report,* 16; Canada, *Sessional Papers,* 1891, no. 8A, 210.

9. Smith and Snell, "Review of the Fisheries of the Great Lakes," 235, 280–281; Smith, "Fisheries of the Great Lakes," 429, 454; Georgian Bay Fisheries Commission, *Report,* 16; Canada, *Sessional Papers,* 1891, no. 8A, 200.

10. Smith and Snell, "Review of the Fisheries of the Great Lakes," 99; Ludwig Kumlien, "The Fisheries of the Great Lakes," in George Brown Goode, *The Fisheries and Fishery Industries of the United States,* Section 5, 47th Cong., 1st sess., 1881, S. Misc. Doc. 124 (Serial 2001), 762.

11. Smith and Snell, "Review of the Fisheries of the Great Lakes," 265, 272.

12. Georgian Bay Fisheries Commission, *Report,* Appendix B, 43–44.

13. Based on a compilation of information in Smith and Snell, "Review of the Fisheries of the Great Lakes": Lake Erie, 237; Chicago, 78, 84–85, 167–168; Detroit, 231–232; Buffalo, 294.

14. True, "Fisheries of the Great Lakes," 655.

15. Booth, "Fisheries of the Great Lakes," 438.

16. Canada, *Sessional Papers,* 1873, no. 8, 62.

17. Captain E. Dunn, report, 23 January 1897, file 141, part 2, frames 81–82, Microfilm Reel (hereafter cited as MReel) T-2734; T. H. Elliott, fishery overseer, Sault Sainte Marie, Ontario, to Deputy Minister of Marine and Fisheries, 10 and 22 January 1898, file 120, part 3, frames 23, 25, MReel T-2727, Records of the Department of Marine and Fisheries, Record Group 23, National Archives of Canada, Ottawa.

18. U.S. Commission of Fish and Fisheries, *Report,* 1892, 53d Cong., 2d sess., 1893, H. Misc. Doc. 209 (Serial 3264), cxxxix, cxli.

19. Quoted in Canada, House of Commons, *Debates,* 13 June 1894, 4231.

20. U.S. Tariff Commission, *Lake Fish: A Study of the Trade between the United States and Canada in Fresh-Water Fish with Cost of Production Data,* Tariff Information Series, no. 36 (Washington, D.C.: Government Printing Office, 1927), 18; "Special Report on the Fisheries Protection Service of Canada," 1886, in Canada, *Sessional Papers,* 1887, no. 16, xvi–xxii; Hugh M. Smith, "Report on an Investigation of the Fisheries of Lake Ontario," U.S. Fish Commission, *Bulletin* 10 (1890): 183–184.

21. Canada, House of Commons, *Debates,* 5 April 1889, 1076–1078; 30 June 1891, 1533.

22. Canada, House of Commons, *Debates,* 30 June 1891, 1517–1518; Dominion Fishery Commission on the Fisheries of the Province of Ontario, "Re-

port," in Canada, *Sessional Papers,* 1893, no. 10C*, Part 1, "Evidence," 97–146, 232; Part 2, "Evidence," 37–123.

23. Smith, "Fisheries of the Great Lakes," 437–438; Canada, House of Commons, *Debates,* 27 March 1893, 3182–3192; 13 June 1894, 4226–4227.

24. Smith and Snell, "Review of the Fisheries of the Great Lakes," 153, 237, 242, 275; True, "Fisheries of the Great Lakes," 665; Edward H. Gruger, Jr., "Uses of Industrial Fish Oils," in Stansby, *Industrial Fishery Technology,* 260–262.

25. Smith and Snell, "Review of the Fisheries of the Great Lakes," 156, 158; R. Connable, Jr., general manager of the Connable Fishing Company of Chicago, Illinois, interview with A. J. Woolman, Bay of Bete Grise, Michigan, 18 July 1894, 3 Lake Superior Interviews and Field Notes, Records of the Joint Commission Relative to the Preservation of the Fisheries in Waters Contiguous to Canada and the United States, Record Group 22, National Archives, College Park, Maryland.

26. U.S. Commission of Fish and Fisheries, *Report,* 1895, 54th Cong., 2d sess., 1896, H. Doc. 104 (Serial 3518), 96. Derived from figures cited therein as indexed using Warren and Pearson Wholesale Price Index, in Bureau of the Census, *Historical Statistics of the United States: Colonial Times to 1970,* 201.

27. Gilbert Smith, interview with H. F. Moore and B. L. Hardin, Irving, New York, 9 August 1894, 4 Moore and Hardin Lake Erie Interviews; Samuel Corson, interview with William Wakeham and Richard Rathbun, Collingwood, Ontario, 12 September 1894, 1 Georgian Bay Interviews, Records of the Joint Commission.

28. Captain J. W. Post, interview with William Wakeham and Richard Rathbun, Sandusky, Ohio, 24 September 1894, 2 Wakeham and Rathbun Lake Erie Interviews; Louis Streuber, interview with William Wakeham and Richard Rathbun, Erie, Pennsylvania, 29 September 1894, 2 Wakeham and Rathbun Lake Erie Interviews; C. M. Clark, interview with William Wakeham and Richard Rathbun, Detroit, Michigan, 19 September 1894, 1 Wakeham and Rathbun Lake Erie Interviews; W. C. Heyman, interview with H. F. Moore and B. L. Hardin, Huron, Ohio, 21 July 1894, 3 Moore and Hardin Lake Erie Interviews, Records of the Joint Commission.

CHAPTER 5: A. BOOTH AND COMPANY BIDS FOR GREAT LAKES DOMINANCE

1. "The New Fishery Trust," *New York Times,* 2 October 1898, 5.

2. Henry Hall, ed., *America's Successful Men of Affairs: An Encyclopedia of Contemporaneous Biography* (New York: New York Tribune, 1896), 2:100; *Famous Booth Sea Foods: A Review of the Relation of the Booth Fisheries Company to the Fishing Industry* [promotional brochure] (1920s); quoted phrase and 1862 capital estimate from Illinois, vol.1, p. 333, R. G. Dun & Co. Collection, Baker Library, Harvard University Graduate School of Business Administration, Boston; E. Russell & Co., Dun, Barlow & Co., and R. G. Dun & Co., *The Mercantile Agency Reference Book and Key,* July 1871; R. G. Dun & Co., *The Mercantile Agency and Reference Book,* July 1883; July 1897. The company name changed over the years: A. Booth (1850–1880); A. Booth and Sons (1880–1885);

A. Booth Packing Company (1885–1898); A. Booth and Company (1898–1909); and, thereafter, Booth Fisheries Company.

3. *Famous Booth Sea Foods; Chicago Tribune,* 5 March 1902; Alfred T. Andreas, *History of Chicago from the Earliest Period to the Present Time,* 3 vols. (1884–1886; reprint, New York: Arno Press, 1975), 3:295; *Booth Forum* 2 [newsletter], June–October 1935, 4.

4. *Social Register, Chicago, 1900* (New York: Social Register Association, 1899), 13; *The Chicago Blue Book of Selected Names* (Chicago: Chicago Directory, 1897), 173, 495; Sidney Ratner, *New Light on the History of Great American Fortunes* (New York: Kelley, 1953), 12; Andreas, *History of Chicago,* 3:613.

5. Hugh M. Smith and Merwin-Marie Snell, "Review of the Fisheries of the Great Lakes in 1885," in U.S. Commission of Fish and Fisheries, *Report,* 1887, Appendix, 50th Cong., 2d sess., 1889, H. Misc. Doc. 133 (Serial 2661), 158; "Fishery Interests Combine," *New York Times,* 22 June 1898, 10; *Booth Forum,* June–October 1935, 4.

6. A. Booth, "The Fisheries of the Great Lakes.—No. 1," *American Field: The Sportsman's Journal,* 7 November 1885, 438; Smith and Snell, "Review of the Fisheries of the Great Lakes," 78, 91, 98–103, 200–201.

7. "Fresh and Salt Fish," *Bayfield County Press,* 9 January 1886, 1.

8. M. B. Johnson, agent for the A. Booth Packing Company, interview with Richard Rathbun, Bayfield, Wisconsin, 10 July 1894; Joseph La Belle, interview with Richard Rathbun, Bayfield, Wisconsin, 10 July 1894, 3 Lake Superior Interviews and Field Notes, Records of the Joint Commission Relative to the Preservation of the Fisheries in Waters Contiguous to Canada and the United States, Record Group 22, National Archives, College Park, Maryland.

9. Dominion Fishery Commission on the Fisheries of the Province of Ontario, "Report," in Canada, *Sessional Paper,* 1893, no. 10C*, Part 2, "Evidence," 114–117.

10. "General Account of Fishing," A Lake Superior, Notes by Subjects; Joseph Ganley, interview with Richard Rathbun, Sault Sainte Marie, Michigan, 20 July 1894, 4 Lake Superior Interviews and Field Notes; Richard Rathbun, notes, 20 July 1894, 5 Lake Superior and Lake Huron Interviews and Field Notes, Records of the Joint Commission.

11. Quoted in Dominion Fishery Commission, "Report," Part 2, 114, 116. [Italics added]

12. Johnson interview; "General Account of Fishing," A Lake Superior, Notes by Subjects, "Whitefish Point, Michigan, Notes"; D. H. Pratt, captain of pound-net crew of the A. Booth Packing Company, interview with Richard Rathbun, Whitefish Point, Michigan, 27 July 1894, 4 Lake Superior Interviews and Field Notes; quotation from D Lake Superior, Notes by Subjects, 158, Records of the Joint Commission.

13. "General Account of Fishing," A Lake Superior, Notes by Subjects; R. Connable, Jr., general manager of the Connable Fishing Company of Chicago, Illinois, interview with A. J. Woolman, Bay of Bete Grise, Michigan, 18 July 1894, 3 Lake Superior Interviews and Field Notes, Records of the Joint Commission; Smith and Snell, "Review of the Fisheries of the Great Lakes," 60, 286.

14. The account of the Booth business in Duluth and Isle Royale is based on

"List of Witnesses" and "General Account of Fishing," A Lake Superior, Notes by Subjects; 3 Lake Superior Subject Categories, 184; John Coventry, assistant manager of the A. Booth Packing Company, interview with Richard Rathbun, Duluth, Minnesota, 6 July 1894; S. P. Wires, superintendent of the U.S. Commission of Fish and Fisheries Station, interview with Richard Rathbun, Duluth, Minnesota, 2 July 1894, 2 Lake Superior Interviews, Records of the Joint Commission; Light Station journal, Menagerie Islet Light Station, 18 October 1875–15 November 1893, Museum Collection, Archives, National Park Service, Isle Royale National Park.

15. Ingeborg Holte, *Ingeborg's Isle Royale* (Grand Marais, Minn.: Women's Times, 1984), 10.

16. Coventry interview; "General Account of Fishing," "List of Witnesses," and "North Canadian Shore," A Lake Superior, Notes by Subjects; Peter Trombley, interview with William Wakeham and Richard Rathbun, Port Arthur, Ontario, 13 August 1894; J. Brunson, interview with A. J. Woolman, Port Arthur, Ontario, 27 July 1894, 1 Lake of the Woods and Port Arthur Interviews and Field Notes, Records of the Joint Commission.

17. Dominion Fishery Commission, "Report," Part 2, 67–68, 71–72.

18. Joseph Brunson, Port Arthur Fish Company, to D. F. Macdonell, 6 June 1895; D. F. Macdonell, fishery overseer, Port Arthur, Ontario, to Deputy Minister of Marine and Fisheries, 19 June 1895; E. Dunn, captain of *Petrel,* to John Hardie, Acting Deputy Minister of Marine and Fisheries, 22 June 1895, file 1594, part 1, frames 46, 53–55, Microfilm Reel (hereafter cited as MReel) T-3169, Records of the Department of Marine and Fisheries, Record Group 23, National Archives of Canada, Ottawa.

19. W. A. Beebe to Major Elliot, fishery overseer, Sault Sainte Marie, Ontario, 26 June 1895; W. A. Beebe to Captain Dunn, Port Stanley, Ontario, 29 June, 10 July 1895, file 1594, part 1, frames 56–61, 63–65, MReel T-3169; Edward E. Prince, "Memorandum: re Port Arthur Fish Company," 17 March 1898, file 471, part 1, frames 370–372, MReel T-2846, Records of the Department of Marine and Fisheries.

20. Extract from C. W. Turner, manager of the A. Booth Packing Company, to J. Brunson, 17 September 1894; Captain E. Dunn to William Smith, Deputy Minister of Marine and Fisheries, 25 September 1895, file 1594, part 1, frames 81, 83–85, MReel T-3169, Records of the Department of Marine and Fisheries.

21. "New Fishery Trust," 5; Articles of Incorporation, A. Booth and Company, 20 July 1898, Illinois Corporation Records, Illinois Secretary of State, Springfield; Dominion Fish Company, Records of the Corporation Branch, vol. 387, Record Group 95, National Archives of Canada, Ottawa.

CHAPTER 6: FISHERS OF THE GREAT LAKES, 1850–1893

1. For similar self-assessments in the 1980s, see Timothy C. Lloyd and Patrick B. Mullen, *Lake Erie Fishermen: Work, Identity, and Tradition* (Urbana: University of Illinois Press, 1990).

2. *Ashland Press,* 30 November 1872.

3. Hugh M. Smith and Merwin-Marie Snell, "Review of the Fisheries of the

Great Lakes in 1885," in U.S. Commission of Fish and Fisheries, *Report,* 1887, Appendix, 50th Cong., 2d sess., 1889, H. Misc. Doc. 133 (Serial 2661), 77, 144–145, 210; Ludwig Kumlien, "The Fisheries of the Great Lakes," in George Brown Goode, *The Fisheries and Fishery Industries of the United States,* Section 5, 47th Cong., 1st sess., 1881, S. Misc. Doc. 124 (Serial 2001), 764; Ruth Kriehn, *The Fisherfolk of Jones Island* (Milwaukee: Milwaukee County Historical Society, 1988), 38–39, 42–43; Ray McDonald, interview, 28 April 1978, Transcript, 3; Larry Ceskowski, interview, 29 March 1978, Transcript, 5, Sea Grant Commercial Fishing Oral History Project, Interviews, 1978–1979, Archives, State Historical Society of Wisconsin, Madison.

4. *Special History Study: Family-Managed Commercial Fishing in the Apostle Islands during the 20th Century* (Bayfield, Wis.: Apostle Islands National Lakeshore, U.S. Department of the Interior, n.d.), 61.

5. Roy and Irene Hokenson, interview, 9 December 1981, Transcript, Apostle Islands National Lakeshore, Bayfield, Wisconsin; "Scrapbook of a Fisherman's Wife; Mrs. Hokenson's Album Records Fishing Life on Lake Superior," *Wisconsin REA News,* October 1953, 12, quoted in *Special History Study,* 82–84.

6. Wisconsin Maritime Museum, *Harvesting the Inland Seas: Great Lakes Commercial Fishing* [traveling exhibition, introductory videotape] (Manitowoc: Wisconsin Maritime Museum, 1996).

7. Robert Doherty, *Disputed Waters: Native Americans and the Great Lakes Fishery* (Lexington: University of Kentucky Press, 1990), 25–29; James M. McClurken, "Wage Labor in Two Michigan Ottawa Communities," in *Native Americans and Wage Labor: Ethnohistorical Perspectives,* ed. Alice Littlefield and Martha C. Knack (Norman: University of Oklahoma Press, 1996), 91.

8. Doherty, *Disputed Waters,* 28–30; Dominion Fishery Commission on the Fisheries of the Province of Ontario, "Report," in Canada *Sessional Papers,* 1893, no. 10C*, Part 2, "Evidence," 116; T. H. Elliott to Deputy Minister of Marine and Fisheries, 4 July 1898, file 140, part 1, frames 57–58, Microfilm Reel (hereafter cited as MReel) 2734, Records of the Department of Marine and Fisheries, Record Group 23, National Archives of Canada, Ottawa.

9. T. H. Elliott to Deputy Minister of Marine and Fisheries, 15 January 1895; P. R. de Lamorandiere to Deputy Minister of Maine and Fisheries, 7 February 1895, file 1196, part 1, frames 340, 358, MReel T-3139, Records of the Department of Marine and Fisheries.

10. Fred Kerr, overseer, to Deputy Minister of Marine and Fisheries, 8 February 1894, file 180, part 1, frames 3–8, MReel 2741, Records of the Department of Marine and Fisheries.

11. J. C. Pollock to William Smith, Deputy Minister of Marine and Fisheries, 17 May 1894; J. C. Pollock to William D. McGee, 22 June 1894, file 807, part 1, frames, 23–25, 84–87, 90, MReel T-2953; Memorandum, E. E. Prince, Dominion Commissioner of Fisheries, May 1898, file 43, part 2, frame 224, MReel T-2670, Records of the Department of Marine and Fisheries.

12. Deputy Minister of Marine and Fisheries to Deputy Superintendent General of Indian Affairs, 10 August 1896, file 120, part 2, frames 363–364, MReel T-2727, Records of the Department of Marine and Fisheries.

13. Waldron Elias, interpreter, Saugeen Reserve, to Alexander McNeill, M.P.,

26 April 1895; A. McNeill to Minister of Marine and Fisheries, 4 May 1895; Minister of Marine and Fisheries to A. McNeill, 10 May 1895; C. W. Briggs to Department of Marine and Fisheries, 11 and 14 May 1895; memorandum, Edward E. Prince, 16 May 1895, file 727, part 1, frames 117–118, 121, 125–130, MReel T-2948, Record of the Department of Marine and Fisheries.

14. Ronald N. Satz, *Chippewa Treaty Rights: The Reserved Rights of Wisconsin's Chippewa Indians in Historical Perspective* (Madison: Wisconsin Academy of Sciences, Arts and Letters, 1991); on the Native Americans in Michigan, see Doherty, *Disputed Waters.*

15. See, for example, Gilbert P. McIntosh, president of the Fishery Association, Meaford, Ontario, 30 November 1892, in Dominion Fishery Commission, "Report," Part 1, "Evidence," 183–184.

16. George Brown Goode and Joseph W. Collins, "The Fishermen of the United States," in George Brown Goode, *The Fisheries and Fishery Industries of the United States,* Section 4, 47th Cong., 1st sess., 1881, S. Misc. Doc. 124 (Serial 2000), 45.

17. Smith and Snell, "Review of the Fisheries of the Great Lakes," 72.

18. Dominion Fishery Commission, "Report," Parts 1 and 2, "Evidence."

19. For examples of the latter locations, see Smith and Snell, "Review of the Fisheries of the Great Lakes," 195–197.

20. Kumlien, "Fisheries of the Great Lakes," 764; Frederick W. True, "The Fisheries of the Great Lakes," in George Brown Goode, *The Fisheries and Fishery Industries of the United States,* Section 2, 47th Cong., 1st sess., 1881, S. Misc. Doc. 124 (Serial 1999), 646. For a fascinating portrait of a Two Rivers patriarchal fisher family of French Canadian descent, headed by Old Man LeMere, as they lived in fear of the lamprey devastation of the 1950s, see George Vukelich, *Fisherman's Beach* (New York: St. Martin's Press, 1962)

21. Fred Landon, *Lake Huron,* American Lakes Series, ed. Milo M. Quaife (Indianapolis: Bobbs-Merrill, 1944), 133–135; William Sherwood Fox, *The Bruce Beckons: The Story of Lake Huron's Great Peninsula* (Toronto: University of Toronto Press, 1952), 117; Norman Robertson, *The History of the County of Bruce and the Minor Municipalities Therein, Province of Ontario, Canada* (Toronto: Briggs, 1906), 463; True, "Fisheries of the Great Lakes," 645, 661–662; Smith and Snell, "Review of the Fisheries of the Great Lakes," 171, 174, 199, 230–231, 246; the Finnish fishers in Portage Entry are documented in "General Account of Fishing," A Lake Superior, Notes by Subjects, Records of the Joint Commission Relative to the Preservation of the Fisheries in Waters Contiguous to Canada and the United States, Record Group 22, National Archives, College Park, Maryland; Kriehn, *Fisherfolk,* 12–30; Ceskowski interview, Transcript, 1.

22. Howard Sivertson, *Once upon an Isle: The Story of Fishing Families on Isle Royale* (Mount Horeb: Wisconsin Folk Museum, 1992), 104; Smith and Snell, "Review of the Fisheries of the Great Lakes," 156, 158.

23. James W. Milner, "Report on the Fisheries of the Great Lakes: The Result of Inquiries Prosecuted in 1871 and 1872," in U.S. Commission of Fish and Fisheries, *Report,* 1872–1873, Appendix A, 42d Cong., 3d sess., 1872, S. Misc. Doc. 74 (Serial 1547), 72–73; Lewis Cass Aldrich, *History of Erie County Ohio* (Syracuse, N.Y.: Mason, 1889), 407.

24. Quoted in Sivertson, *Once upon an Isle,* 107.

25. Smith and Snell, "Review of the Fisheries of the Great Lakes," 15.

26. Arnold R. Alanen and William H. Tishler, "Farming the Lake Superior Shore: Agriculture and Horticulture on the Apostle Islands, 1840–1940," *Wisconsin Magazine of History* 79 (spring 1996): 163–203; Smith and Snell, "Review of the Fisheries of the Great Lakes," 125–129, 273–274, 298; True, "Fisheries of the Great Lakes," 642–645; A. Booth, "The Fisheries of the Great Lakes.—No. 1," *American Field: The Sportsmen's Journal,* 7 November 1885, 438; Gilbert Smith, interview with H. F. Moore, Irving, New York, 9 August 1894, 4 Moore and Hardin Lake Erie Interviews, Records of the Joint Commission.

27. Captain Larry King, interview with William Wakeham and Richard Rathbun, Thessalon, Ontario, 17 September 1894, 2 Georgian Bay Interviews, Records of the Joint Commission.

28. "Fishermen: Occupation &c," A Georgian Bay, Notes by Subjects, Records of the Joint Commission.

29. Smith and Snell, "Review of the Fisheries of the Great Lakes," 289–291.

30. Smith and Snell, "Review of the Fisheries of the Great Lakes," 77, 132, 137, 191; Dominion Fishery Commission, "Report," Part 1, "Evidence," 313.

31. Smith and Snell, "Review of the Fisheries of the Great Lakes," 166–168, 274–275; Minister of Marine and Fisheries to William McGregor, 8 January 1898, file 2033, part 1, frame 47, MReel T-3197, Records of the Department of Marine and Fisheries.

CHAPTER 7: THE FISHERS AND THE FISH

1. George Brown Goode and Joseph W. Collins, "The Fishermen of the United States," in George Brown Goode, *The Fisheries and Fishery Industries of the United States,* Section 4, 47th Cong., 1st sess., 1881, S. Misc. Doc. 124 (Serial 2000), 47; Ludwig Kumlien, "The Fisheries of the Great Lakes," in George Brown Goode, *The Fisheries and Fishery Industries of the United States,* Section 5, 47th Cong., 1st sess., 1881, S. Misc. Doc. 124 (Serial 2001), 758, 762.

2. Hugh M. Smith and Merwin-Marie Snell, "Review of the Fisheries of the Great Lakes in 1885," in U.S. Commission of Fish and Fisheries, *Report,* 1887, Appendix, 50th Cong., 2d sess., 1889 H. Misc. Doc. 113 (Serial 2661), 88, 109, 174, 185, 187, 190, 194, 212, 220, 243, 247.

3. Nelson Harman, November 1893, quoted in Dominion Fishery Commission on the Fisheries of the Province of Ontario, "Report," in Canada, *Sessional Papers,* 1893, no. 10C*, Part 2, "Evidence," 101.

4. Quoted in A. Booth, "The Fisheries of the Great Lakes.—No. 1," *American Field: The Sportsman's Journal,* 7 November 1885, 438.

5. Investment in apparatus per fisher were calculated from Canada, *Sessional Papers,* 1881, no. 11, 274–284, 291; 1891, no. 8A, 210; 1892, no. 11, lii–lv; U.S. Commissioner of Fish and Fisheries, *Report,* 1895, 54th Cong., 2d sess., 1896, H. Doc. 104 (Serial 3518), 96; Hugh M. Smith, "The Fisheries of the Great Lakes," in U.S. Commission of Fish and Fisheries, *Report,* 1892, Appendix, 53d Cong., 2d sess., 1893, H. Misc. Doc. 209 (Serial 3264), 368–369.

6. "Notes of H. F. Moore," 27 August 1894, Erie, Pennsylvania, 4 Moore

and Hardin Lake Erie Interviews; Captain Alexander Clark, interview with William Wakeham and Richard Rathbun, Collingwood Ontario, 11 September 1894, 1 Georgian Bay Interviews, Records of the Joint Commission Relative to the Preservation of the Fisheries in Waters Contiguous to Canada and the United States, Record Group 22, National Archives, College Park, Maryland; Dominion Fishery Commission, "Report," Part 1, xi.

7. See, for example, Frederick A. Hansen, *Diary of a Norwegian Fisherman: The Collected Dairies of Frederick A. Hansen, April 1913 through December 1938, Sand Island, Wisconsin,* ed. Frederick H. Dahl (Jacksonville, Fla.: Paramount Press, 1989).

8. Wisconsin, Commissioners of Fisheries and State Fish and Game Warden, *Fifteenth Biennial Report,* 1893–1894 (Madison, Wis.: State Printer, 1895), 21.

9. James W. Milner, "Report on the Fisheries of the Great Lakes: The Result of Inquiries Prosecuted in 1871 and 1872," in U.S. Commission of Fish and Fisheries, *Report,* 1872–1873, Appendix A, 42d Cong., 3d sess., 1872, S. Misc. Doc. 74 (Serial 1547), 23; Smith, "Fisheries of the Great Lakes," 370.

10. John Noble, interview with William Wakeham and Richard Rathbun, Killarney, Ontario, 14 September 1894, 2 Georgian Bay Interviews; Captain Alexander Clark and Charles Duffey, interview with William Wakeham and Richard Rathbun, Collingwood, Ontario, 11 September 1894, 1 Georgian Bay Interviews, Records of the Joint Commission.

11. The pound-net count is in Smith and Snell, "Review of the Fisheries of the Great Lakes," 234; Kumlien, "Fisheries of the Great Lakes," 760–761.

12. Georgian Bay Fisheries Commission, *Report and Recommendations* (Ottawa: Government Printing Bureau, 1908), 8, file 1168, part 2, frames 29–59, Microfilm Reel T-3135, Records of the Department of Marine and Fisheries, Record Group 23, National Archives of Canada, Ottawa; Kumlien, "Fisheries of the Great Lakes," 757–761; Smith, "Fisheries of the Great Lakes," 372; Smith and Snell, "Review of the Fisheries of the Great Lakes," 25–28, 234–235.

13. Kumlien, "Fisheries of the Great Lakes," 762.

14. Smith and Snell, "Review of the Fisheries of the Great Lakes," 16, 76; Kumlien, "Fisheries of the Great Lakes," 763.

15. Noble interview; Captain Larry King, interview with William Wakeham and Richard Rathbun, Thessalon, Ontario, 17 September 1894, 2 Georgian Bay Interviews, Records of the Joint Commission.

16. Frederick W. True, "The Fisheries of the Great Lakes," in George Brown Goode, *The Fisheries and Fishery Industries of the United States,* Section 2, 47th Cong., 1st Sess., 1881, S. Misc. Doc. 124 (Serial 1999), 652; Smith and Snell, "Review of the Fisheries of the Great Lakes," 171.

17. Ingeborg Holte, *Ingeborg's Isle Royale* (Grand Marais, Minn.: Women's Times, 1984), 46.

18. Thomas Marks, interview with William Wakeham and Richard Rathbun, Port Arthur, Ontario, 13 August 1894, 1 Lake of the Woods and Port Arthur Interviews; C. S. Hampton, State Fish and Game Warden, interview with William Wakeham and Richard Rathbun, Petosky, Michigan, 21 August 1894, 5 Lake Superior and Lake Huron Interviews and Field Notes; Larry King interview, Records of the Joint Commission.

19. Larry King interview; E. R. Edson, interview with William Wakeham and Richard Rathbun, Cleveland, Ohio, 17 September 1894, 2 Wakeham and Rathbun Lake Erie Interviews, Records of the Joint Commission; Thomas H. Trethe-way, Sault Sainte Marie, Ontario, 10 November 1893, quoted in Dominion Fishery Commission, "Report," Part 2, "Evidence," 124.

20. Nelson Couture, Sault Sainte Marie, Ontario, 10 November 1893, in Dominion Fishery Commission, "Report," Part 2, "Testimony," 110–112; Captain Joseph King, interview with William Wakeham and Richard Rathbun, Thessalon, Ontario, 17 September 1894, 2 Georgian Bay Interviews; A. J. Woolman to Richard Rathbun, 30 November1894, D Lake Superior, Notes by Subjects, Records of the Joint Commission.

21. True, "Fisheries of the Great Lakes," 645; Smith and Snell, "Review of the Fisheries of the Great Lakes," 281.

22. Smith and Snell, "Review of the Fisheries of the Great Lakes," 260; "General Account of Fishing," A Lake Superior, Notes by Subjects, Records of the Joint Commission.

23. Edson interview.

24. Dominion Fishery Commission, "Report," Part 1, "Review," O–X.

25. Hampton interview.

26. Charles Hoffmann, *The Depression of the Nineties: An Economic History* (Westport, Conn.: Greenwood, 1970), 71–72; "Mob in Ugly Mood," *Detroit Free Press,* 2 May 1894, 1; "In the Hands of a Mob," *Detroit Free Press,* 3 May 1894, 1.

27. The published results of the two investigations are in Dominion Fishery Commission, "Report," and U.S. Congress, House, *Report of the Joint Commission Relative to the Preservation of the Fisheries in Waters Contiguous to Canada and the United States,* 54th Cong., 2d sess., 1896, H. Doc. 315 (Serial 3534).

28. Dominion Fishery Commission, "Report," Part 1, "Evidence," 156, 161, 234–235.

29. Dominion Fishery Commission, "Report": Port Arthur fisherman, Part 2, "Evidence," 64; Meaford fisherman, Part 1, "Evidence," 182–183; Joseph King interview.

30. Quoted in Dominion Fishery Commission, "Report," Part 1, "Evidence," 189.

31. U.S. Commissioner of Fish and Fisheries, *Report,* 1892, 53d Cong., 2d sess., 1893, H. Misc. Doc. 209 (Serial 3264), cxxxviii.

32. House, *Report of the Joint Commission,* 83; Walter Ladd, interview with H. F. Moore and B. L. Hardin, Put-in-Bay, Ohio, 20 June 1894, 2 Moore and Hardin Lake Erie Interviews; Thomas White, interview with H. F. Moore and B. L. Hardin, Sandusky, Ohio, 20 June 1894, 3 Moore and Hardin Lake Erie Interviews, Records of the Joint Commission.

33. A. J. Stoll, president of the Sandusky Fish Company, interview with William Wakeham and Richard Rathbun, Sandusky, Ohio, 24 September 1894, 1 Wakeham and Rathbun Lake Erie Interviews, Records of the Joint Commission.

34. "Lake Erie" [handwritten manuscript], 85, 125–126, Records of the Joint Commission.

35. "Lake Erie," 117–119; W. C. Heyman, interview with H. F. Moore and

B. L. Hardin, Huron, Ohio, 21 July 1894, 3 Moore and Hardin Lake Erie Interviews, Records of the Joint Commission.

36. "Lake Erie," 98–116.

37. "Lake Erie": views on hatchery program, 130; sample opinions, 153–156; summary figures, 156.

38. Samuel Corson, interview with William Wakeham and Richard Rathbun, Collingwood, Ontario, 12 September 1894, 1 Georgian Bay Interviews, Records of the Joint Commission.

39. "Regulations Suggested," D Lake Superior, Notes by Subjects; Marks interview, Records of the Joint Commission.

40. "Fishes, General; Decrease and Cause," D Lake Huron, Notes by Subjects, Records of the Joint Commission.

41. Quoted in Dominion Fishery Commission, "Report," Part 2, "Evidence," 129.

CHAPTER 8: AGRICULTURE, LUMBERING, MINING, AND THE CHANGING FISH HABITAT

1. Robert H. Rainey, "Natural Displacement of Pollution from the Great Lakes," *Science,* 10 March 1967, 1242–1243; Environment Canada and United States Environmental Protection Agency, *The Great Lakes: An Environmental Atlas and Resource Book* (Chicago and Toronto: Environmental Protection Agency and Environment Canada, 1987), 3.

2. R. Cole Harris and John Warkentin, *Canada before Confederation: A Study in Historical Geography* (New York: Oxford University Press, 1974), 110–111.

3. Robert Leslie Jones, *History of Agriculture in Ontario, 1613–1880* (Toronto: University of Toronto Press, 1946), 85–108, 210–212, 318–322; Harris and Warkentin, *Canada before Confederation,* 110–142; Paul W. Gates, *The Farmer's Age: Agriculture, 1815–1860* (New York: Harper & Row, 1960), 163–169; Fred Landon, *Western Ontario and the American Frontier* (Toronto: Ryerson Press, 1941), 246–260; Robert Leslie Jones, *History of Agriculture in Ohio to 1880* (Kent, Ohio: Kent State University Press, 1983), 213–230; Margaret Beattie Bogue, "The Lake and the Fruit: The Making of Three Farm-Type Areas," *Agricultural History* 59 (October 1985): 492–522, and "Liberty Hyde Bailey, Jr. and the Family Farm," *Agricultural History* 63 (winter 1989): 26–48; James Whorton, *Before Silent Spring: Pesticides and Public Health in Pre-DDT America* (Princeton, N.J.: Princeton University Press, 1974), 20–25; Ontario Agricultural Commission, *Report of the Commissioners and Appendices A to S,* 5 vols. (Toronto: Province of Ontario, 1881), vol. 2, *Appendix B,* 65–660.

4. See, for example, the comments of George Perkins Marsh, *Report Made under Authority of the Legislature of Vermont on the Artificial Propagation of Fish* (Burlington, Vt.: Free Press Print, 1857), 13–14.

5. Thomas H. Langlois, *The Western End of Lake Erie and Its Ecology* (Ann Arbor, Mich.: Edwards, 1954), 368–369.

6. Ralph W. Tiner, Jr., *Wetlands of the United States: Current Status and Recent Trends* (Washington, D.C.: Government Printing Office, 1984), 13.

7. Margaret Beattie Bogue, "The Swamp Land Act and Wet Land Utilization in Illinois, 1850–1890," *Agricultural History* 25 (October 1951): 169–180; Thomas Donaldson, *The Public Domain,* 47th Cong., 2d sess., 1882, H. Misc. Doc. 45, Part 4 (Serial 2158), 222.

8. Noel M. Burns, *Erie: The Lake that Survived* (Totowa, N.J.: Rowman and Allanheld, 1985) 7; Jones, *History of Agriculture in Ontario,* 314–315; Harris and Warkentin, *Canada before Confederation,* 121; U.S. Department of Commerce, Bureau of the Census, *Drainage of Agricultural Lands* (Washington, D.C.: Government Printing Office, 1932), 169, 255.

9. Martin R. Kaatz, "The Settlement of the Black Swamp of Northwestern Ohio: Early Days," *Northwest Ohio Quarterly* 25 (winter 1952–1953): 23–36; "The Settlement of the Black Swamp of Northwestern Ohio: Pioneer Days," *Northwest Ohio Quarterly* 25 (summer 1953): 134–156; and "The Settlement of the Black Swamp of Northwestern Ohio: Later Days," *Northwest Ohio Quarterly* 25 (autumn 1953): 215; Robert Thomas Allen, *The Illustrated Natural History of Canada: The Great Lakes* (Toronto: McClelland, 1970), 124; Langlois, *Western End of Lake Erie,* 22–25.

10. Hugh M. Smith and Merwin-Marie Snell, "Review of the Fisheries of the Great Lakes in 1885," in U.S. Commission of Fish and Fisheries, *Report,* 1887, Appendix, 50th Cong., 2d sess., 1889, H. Misc. Doc. 133 (Serial 2661), 254; "Lake Erie" [handwritten manuscript], 70, Records of the Joint Commission Relative to the Preservation of the Fisheries in Waters Contiguous to Canada and the United States, Record Group 22, National Archives, College Park, Maryland; U.S. Congress, House, *Report of the Joint Commission Relative to the Preservation of the Fisheries in Waters Contiguous to Canada and the United States,* 54th Cong., 2d sess., 1896, H. Doc. 315 (Serial 3534), 112.

11. Quoted in Jones, *Agriculture in Ontario,* 315.

12. Frank N. Edgerton, "Pollution and Aquatic Life in Lake Erie: Early Scientific Studies," *Environmental Review* 11 (fall 1987): 189–205; Environment Canada and Environmental Protection Agency, *Great Lakes,* 18.

13. Robert W. Wells, *Fire at Peshtigo* (Englewood Cliffs, N.J.: Prentice-Hall, 1968); Peter Pernin, "The Great Peshtigo Fire: An Eyewitness Account," *Wisconsin Magazine of History* 54 (summer 1971): 246–272; Rolland H. Maybee, *Michigan's White Pine Era, 1840–1900* (Lansing: Michigan Historical Commission, 1960); Robert F. Fries, *Empire in Pine: The Story of Lumbering in Wisconsin, 1830–1900* (Madison: State Historical Society of Wisconsin, 1951); Susan L. Flader, ed., *The Great Lakes Forest: An Environmental and Social History* (Minneapolis: University of Minnesota Press, 1983).

14. Filibert Roth, *On the Forestry Conditions of Northern Wisconsin,* Wisconsin Geological and Natural History Survey, Bulletin 1 (Madison: State of Wisconsin, 1898), 56–57.

15. Roth, *Forestry Conditions of Northern Wisconsin,* 59, 62, 64.

16. Roth, *Forestry Conditions of Northern Wisconsin,* 41–42.

17. Smith and Snell, "Review of the Fisheries of the Great Lakes," 128–129; Graham Alexander MacDonald, "The Saulteur-Ojibwa Fishery at Sault Ste. Marie, 1640–1920" (master's thesis, University of Waterloo, 1978), 171–180.

18. Quoted in Canada, *Sessional Papers,* 1890, no. 17, xxxiii–xxxiv; R. Peter

Gillis, "Rivers of Sawdust: The Battle over Industrial Pollution in Canada, 1865–1903," *Journal of Canadian Studies* 21 (spring 1986): 84–103.

19. Samuel Wilmot, "Report for the Year 1889," in Canada, *Sessional Papers,* 1890, no. 17, Part 2, 12–23. Complaints about the impact of lumbering on fishing are legion in Canada, Department of Marine and Fisheries, *Reports,* 1871–1900, and Manuscript Correspondence, Records of the Department of Marine and Fisheries, Record Group 23, National Archives of Canada, Ottawa; Ontario Fish and Game Commission, *Reports,* and Department of Fisheries, *Reports,* 1892–1910; special studies of the Great Lakes fishing industry done by the U.S. Commission of Fish and Fisheries: James W. Milner, "Report on the Fisheries of the Great Lakes: The Result of Inquiries Prosecuted in 1871 and 1872," in U.S. Commission of Fish and Fisheries, *Report,* 1872–1873, Appendix A, 42d Cong., 3d sess., 1872, S. Misc. Doc. 74 (Serial 1547); Smith and Snell, "Review of the Fisheries of the Great Lakes"; and Hugh M. Smith, "The Fisheries of the Great Lakes," in U.S. Commission of Fish and Fisheries, *Report,* 1892, Appendix, 53d Cong., 2d sess., 1893, H. Misc. Doc. 209 (Serial 3264); annual reports of the fish commissions of Michigan, Wisconsin, and Minnesota; House, *Report of the Joint Commission;* and Dominion Fishery Commission on the Fisheries of the Province of Ontario, "Report," in Canada, *Sessional Papers,* 1893, no. 10C*.

20. Smith, "Fisheries of the Great Lakes," 402–403.

21. Canada, House of Commons, *Debates,* 16 April 1883, 658.

22. Quoted in Dominion Fishery Commission, "Report," Part 1, "Review of the Report," Y–CC, "Evidence," 220. See especially Captain Alexander Clark, interview with William Wakeham and Richard Rathbun, Collingwood, Ontario, 11 September 1894; Samuel Corson, interview with William Wakeham and Richard Rathbun, Collingwood, Ontario, 12 September 1894, 1 Georgian Bay Interviews; John Noble, interview with William Wakeham and Richard Rathbun, Killarney, Ontario, 14 September 1894; Captain Joseph King, interview with William Wakeham and Richard Rathbun, Thessalon, Ontario, 17 September 1894, 2 Georgian Bay Interviews, Records of the Joint Commission.

23. 5 Lake Huron Interviews: First Arrangement of Notes, 318–319, 349–354; "Bark, Rafts, Logs" and "Pulp Mills," D Lake Huron, Notes by Subjects, Records of the Joint Commission.

24. 4 Lake Huron Interviews: First Arrangement of Notes, 63; 5 Lake Huron Interviews: First Arrangement of Notes, 318–319, Records of the Joint Commission; Michigan Board of Fish Commissioners, *Ninth Biennial Report,* 1888–1890, in Michigan, *Joint Documents,* 1890, 2:13.

25. Ontario Agricultural Commission, *Report,* vol. 2, *Appendix B,* 310–312, 650.

26. "Salt Works," D Lake Huron, Notes by Subjects; 5 Lake Huron Interviews: First Arrangement of Notes, 333, 337–338; D. C. Ridgley, "Notes on Saginaw River," Lake Huron, Scovell and Ridgley Interviews and Notes, 263–264, Records of the Joint Commission. The saltworks on the Saginaw River were only one part of the salt industry on the Lower Peninsula of Michigan that originated with lumbering. So did the salt wells at Frankfort, Manistee, and Ludington, Michigan. Dow Chemical's beginnings in Midland, Michigan, dating from Herbert H. Dow's test drilling in 1890 on the Salt River, tributary to the Saginaw,

related to the bromine found in local salt brines. See *History of Saginaw County Michigan . . .* (Chicago: Chapman, 1881), 412–416, and Willis F. Dunbar, *Michigan: A History of the Wolverine State,* rev. ed. George S. May (Grand Rapids, Mich.: Eerdmans, 1980), 473.

27. Margaret Beattie Bogue, *Around the Shores of Lake Michigan: A Guide to Historic Sites* (Madison: University of Wisconsin Press, 1985), 207; quoted in "Tanneries—Lake Huron," D Lake Huron, Notes by Subjects; 5 Lake Huron Interviews: First Arrangement of Notes, 302, 305–306, 352–357, Records of the Joint Commission.

28. John Barret Van Vlack, interview with William Wakeham and Richard Rathbun, Collingwood, Ontario, 11 September 1894, 1 Georgian Bay Interviews, Records of the Joint Commission.

29. Mining here is defined as the industry associated with the processes of ore removal, concentration, transportation, and smelting.

30. William B. Gates, Jr., *Michigan Copper and Boston Dollars* (Cambridge, Mass.: Harvard University Press, 1951), 18–22, 61–62.

31. Army Corps of Engineers, *Deposits of Sand in Portage Lake, Michigan,* 47th Cong., 2d sess., 1882, H. Ex. Doc. 85 (Serial 2110), 2–3, and *Portage Lake Canal,* 49th Cong., 2d sess., 1886, H. Ex. Doc. 105 (Serial 2482), 14–15; Larry D. Lankton and Charles K. Hyde, *Old Reliable: An Illustrated History of the Quincy Mining Company* (Hancock, Mich.: Quincy Mine Hoist Association: 1982), 77–79; Michigan Department of Natural Resources, "Remedial Action Plan for TORCH LAKE Area of Concern" (Typescript, Department of Natural Resources, Lansing, Mich., 27 October 1987), 1.

32. Gates, *Michigan Copper,* 27–29.

33. Lankton and Hyde, *Old Reliable,* 90–91, 141, 144, 146; C. Harry Benedict, *Red Metal: The Calumet and Hecla Story* (Ann Arbor: University of Michigan Press, 1952), 174–193; Larry Lankton, *Cradle to Grave: Life, Work, and Death at the Lake Superior Copper Mines* (New York: Oxford University Press, 1991), 248–250, 266; Gates, *Michigan Copper,* 28–29, 126–127.

34. "Portage Entry," A Lake Superior, Notes by Subjects, 42–44, Records of the Joint Commission; Smith and Snell, "Review of the Fisheries of the Great Lakes," 56–57.

35. Lawrence Rakestraw, *Historic Mining on Isle Royale* (Houghton, Mich.: Isle Royale Natural History Association and National Park Service, 1965), 1–21.

36. Larry Lynch, Solid and Hazardous Waste Division, Wisconsin Department of Natural Resources, and Thomas J. Evans, Wisconsin Geological and Natural History Survey, telephone conversations with author, December 21, 1993; Allan M. Johnson, Institute of Mineral Research, Michigan Technological University, Houghton, Michigan, telephone conversation with author, January 6, 1994; A. M. Johnson and D. M. Cregger, "Groundwater Contamination Problems in the Iron River Mining District of Michigan," in *International Symposium on Environmental Geotechnology, April 21–23, 1986,* ed. Hsai-Yung Fang (Allentown, Pa.: Envo, 1986), 1:184–196; Allan M. Johnson, "The Development of Guidelines for Closing Underground Mines: Michigan Case Histories," Report for the U.S. Department of the Interior, Bureau of Mines, 1983, 58, 62–63.

37. Harland Hatcher, *A Century of Men and Iron* (Indianapolis: Bobbs-

Merrill, 1950), 102; Bogue, *Around the Shores of Lake Michigan,* 71–72, 272–273.

38. Gerald E. Boyce, *Historic Hastings* (Belleville, Ont.: Hastings County Council, 1967), 60, 145–151, 293–295, 298–300, 310–312.

39. Grace Lee Nute, *Lake Superior,* American Lakes Series, ed. Milo M. Quaife (Indianapolis: Bobbs-Merrill, 1944), 167–170.

40. George N. Fuller, ed., *Michigan: A Centennial History of the State and Its People,* 2 vols. (Chicago: Lewis, 1939), 2:44.

41. Ontario Agricultural Commission, *Report,* vol. 2, *Appendix B,* 15, 211; Dorothy Wallace, ed., *Memories of Goderich: The Romance of the Prettiest Town in Canada,* 2d ed. (Goderich, Ont.: Jubilee 3 Committee, 1979), 50, 56–58, 218, 219, 234, 240; Jones, *History of Agriculture in Ontario,* 307; Victor Lauriston, *Lambton's Hundred Years, 1849–1949* (Sarnia, Ont.: Haines Frontier Printing, 1949), 295; Dunbar, *Michigan,* 413–414.

42. Wallace, ed., *Memories of Goderich,* 4, 12, 50, 100–101.

43. Wallace, ed., *Memories of Goderich,* 50; Ontario Agricultural Commission, *Report,* vol. 2, *Appendix B,* 251; *Commemorative Historical and Biographical Record of Wood County, Ohio: Its Past and Present . . .,* 2 vols. (Chicago: Beers, 1897), 1:201, 208; Edward O'Hara, interview with H. L. Moore and B. F. Hardin, Port Clinton, Ohio, 13 July 1894; C. M. Lamb, interview with H. L. Moore and B. F. Hardin, Toledo, Ohio, 7 July 1894; Lee Refsnider, interview with H. L. Moore and B. F. Hardin, Marengo Park, Michigan, 6 July 1894, 1 Moore and Hardin Lake Erie Interviews; L. O. Webster, interview with H. L. Moore and B. F. Hardin, Middle Bass Island, Ohio, 16 June 1894; George Gilbert, interview with H. L. Moore and B. F. Hardin, Put-in-Bay, Ohio, 19 June 1894, 2 Moore and Hardin Lake Erie Interviews; C. K. Martin and Charles Martin, interview with H. L. Moore and B. F. Hardin, Venice, Ohio, 19 July 1894, 3 Moore and Hardin Lake Erie Interviews; A. J. Stoll, president of the Sandusky Fish Company, interview with William Wakeham and Richard Rathbun, Sandusky, Ohio, 24 September 1894, 1 Wakeham and Rathbun Lake Erie Interviews, Records of the Joint Commission.

44. R. Cowdrey, interview with H. L. Moore and B. F. Hardin, North Toledo, Ohio, 5 July 1894, 1 Moore and Hardin Lake Erie Interviews, Records of the Joint Commission; Canada, *Sessional Papers,* 1893, no. 10A, Part 1, 263.

45. Arthur F. McEvoy, *The Fisherman's Problem: Ecology and Law in the California Fisheries, 1850–1980* (New York: Cambridge University Press, 1986), 47–62.

CHAPTER 9: COMMERCE, COMMUNITY GROWTH, INDUSTRIAL-URBAN DEVELOPMENT, AND THE CHANGING FISH HABITAT

1. Chicago is the prime example. See Harold M. Mayer and Richard C. Wade, *Chicago: Growth of a Metropolis* (Chicago: University of Chicago Press, 1969).

2. Powell A. Moore, *The Calumet Region: Indiana's Last Frontier,* Indiana

Historical Collections (Indianapolis: Indiana Historical Bureau, 1959), 39: 114–256.

3. Population and manufacturing data were compiled from *Census of the United States,* 1850–1900 (Washington, D.C.: Government Printing Office, 1853–1902); *Census of the Canadas,* 1851–1852 (Quebec: Lovell, 1853–1855), 1860–1861 (Quebec: Foote, 1863); *Census of Canada,* 1870–1871 (Ottawa: Taylor, 1873–1875), 1880–1881 (Ottawa: McLean, Roger, 1882–1883), 1901 (Ottawa: Dawson, 1901–1905).

4. Joel A. Tarr, *The Search for the Ultimate Sink: Urban Pollution in Historical Perspective* (Akron, Ohio: University of Akron Press, 1996), 9–14, 103–163.

5. Louis P. Cain, *Sanitation Strategy for a Lakefront Metropolis: The Case of Chicago* (De Kalb: Northern Illinois University Press, 1978); James W. Milner, "Report on the Fisheries of the Great Lakes: The Result of Inquiries Prosecuted in 1871 and 1872," in U.S. Commission of Fish and Fisheries, *Report,* 1872–1873, Appendix A, 42d Cong., 3d sess., 1872, S. Misc. Doc. 74 (Serial 1547), 8; E. W. Nelson, "Fisheries of Chicago and Vicinity," in U.S. Commission of Fish and Fisheries, *Report,* 1875–1876, Appendix, 44th Cong., 1st sess., 1875, S. Misc. Doc. 107 (Serial 1666), 785–786; Hugh M. Smith and Merwin-Marie Snell, "Review of the Fisheries of the Great Lakes in 1885," in U.S. Commission of Fish and Fisheries, *Report,* 1887, Appendix, 50th Cong., 2d sess., 1889, H. Misc. Doc. 133 (Serial 2661), 166–167.

6. Smith and Snell, "Review of the Fisheries of the Great Lakes," 152, 155, 157.

7. O. B. Sheppard, Inspector of Fisheries, to William R. Venning, Commissioner of Fisheries, Ottawa, Ontario, 18 October 1897, file 294, part 1, frame 245, Microfilm Reel (hereafter cited as MReel) T-2826; O. B. Sheppard to Edward E. Prince, Dominion Commissioner of Fisheries, 8 April 1901; memorandum, E. E. Prince, 17 April 1901; S. T. Bastedo, Deputy Commissioner, Ontario Department of Fisheries, to F. Gourdeau, Department of Marine and Fisheries, 25 April 1901, file 501, part 1, frames 250–252, 253, 259, MReel T-2847, Records of the Department of Marine and Fisheries, Record Group 23, National Archives of Canada, Ottawa.

8. Dominion Fishery Commission on the Fisheries of the Province of Ontario, "Report," in Canada, *Sessional Papers,* 1893, no. 10C*, Part 1, "Evidence," 305; Ontario, *Sessional Papers,* 1900, no. 27, 51; 1911, no. 13, 43–44; petition, Citizens of the City of Hamilton to Honorable John Costigan, Minister of Marine and Fisheries, February 1897, file 812, frames 17–18, MReel T-2953, Records of the Department of Marine and Fisheries.

9. Ontario, *Sessional Papers,* 1892, no. 79, 269.

10. Quoted in "Pollution," unlabeled binder, Lake Ontario, 59–60, Records of the Joint Commission Relative to the Preservation of the Fisheries in Waters Contiguous to Canada and the United States, Record Group 22, National Archives, College Park, Maryland; Hugh M. Smith, "Report on an Investigation of the Fisheries of Lake Ontario," U.S. Fish Commission, *Bulletin* 10 (1890): 198, 201.

11. "Pollution," 60–62.

12. Smith and Snell, "Review of the Fisheries of the Great Lakes," 227; On-

tario, *Sessional Papers,* 1892, no. 79, 291; Hugh M. Smith, "The Fisheries of the Great Lakes," in U.S. Commission of Fish and Fisheries, *Report,* 1892, Appendix, 53d Cong., 2d sess., 1893, H. Misc. Doc. 209 (Serial 3264), 416; George Clark, interview with H. F. Moore and B. L. Hardin, Ecorse, Michigan, 4 September 1894; A. Solomon, interview with H. F. Moore and B. L. Hardin, Detroit, Michigan, 24 August 1894, 1 Moore and Hardin Lake Erie Interviews, Records of the Joint Commission.

13. William D. Balfour to Commander E. Dunn, 17 July 1895, frame 20; "The Garbage Dumpers," *Echo* [Amherstburg, Ontario], 9? June 1895, frame 21; Captain Edward Dunn, statement under oath, 9 November 1896, frames 241–245; memorandum for Minister of Marine and Fisheries re "Grace A. Ruelle," 23 January 1897, frames 256–258, file 2247, part 1, MReel T-3217; Captain Edward Dunn to Edward E. Prince, Dominion Commissioner of Fisheries, 21 July 1896, frames 266–269; L. H. Davies, Minister of Marine and Fisheries, to Governor General in Council, 30 January 1897, frames 311–337, file 2247, part 1, MReel T-3218, Records of the Department of Marine and Fisheries.

14. Petition, Fort Erie Municipal Council to Privy Council of Canada, 26 November 1894; Fred Kerr, fishery overseer, to Deputy Minister of Marine and Fisheries, 15 December 1894; Privy Council Committee Report, 14 January 1895; L. Clarke Raymond, Welland, Ontario, to W. H. Montague, M.P., Secretary of State, 8 June 1895; Thomas D. Cowper, Welland, Ontario, to W. H. Montague, 8 June 1895; Telegrams, 15 June 1895; Commander E. Dunn to John Hardie, Acting Deputy Minister of Marine and Fisheries, Ottawa, Ontario, 15 June 1895, file 1923, part l, frames 2–41, MReel T-3194, Records of the Department of Marine and Fisheries; Canada, *Sessional Papers,* 1897, no. 11A, 192.

15. U.S. Commissioner of Fish and Fisheries, *Report,* 1875–1876, 847–849.

16. Data for counties bordering Great Lakes were compiled from Ontario Agricultural Commission, *Report of the Commissioners and Appendices A to S,* 5 vols. (Toronto: Province of Ontario, 1881), vol. 2, *Appendix B.*

17. George Perkins Marsh, *Report Made under Authority of the Legislature of Vermont on the Artificial Propagation of Fish* (Burlington, Vt.: Free Press Print, 1857), 12–15, and *Man and Nature,* ed. David Lowenthal (Cambridge, Mass.: Harvard University Press, 1965), 107–108.

CHAPTER 10: THE FISH REACT: CHANGING SPECIES IN CHANGING WATERS

1. Noel M. Burns, *Erie: The Lake That Survived* (Totowa, N.J.: Rowman and Allanheld, 1985), 140; Walter Koelz, "Fishing Industry of the Great Lakes," in U.S. Commissioner of Fisheries, *Report,* 1925 (Washington, D.C.: Government Printing Office, 1926), 609; Donald M. Gates, C. H. D. Clarke, and James T. Harris, "Wildlife in a Changing Environment," in *The Great Lakes Forest: An Environmental and Social History,* ed. Susan L. Flader (Minneapolis: University of Minnesota Press, 1983), 52–80.

2. Henry R. Schoolcraft, *Narrative Journal of Travels through the Northwestern Regions of the United States Extending from Detroit through the Great Chain of American Lakes, to the Sources of the Mississippi River in the Year 1820*

(1821; reprint, New York: Arno Press, 1970), 118; Bela Hubbard, *Memorials of a Half-Century in Michigan and the Lake Region* (New York: Putnam, 1888), 268, 275, 276–277; James W. Milner, "Report on the Fisheries of the Great Lakes: The Result of Inquiries Prosecuted in 1871 and 1872," in U.S. Commission of Fish and Fisheries, *Report,* 1872–1873, Appendix A, 42d Cong., 3d sess., 1872, S. Misc. Doc. 74 (Serial 1547), 43; Dominion Fishery Commission on the Fisheries of the Province of Ontario, "Report," in Canada, *Sessional Papers,* 1893, no. 10C*, Part 2, "Evidence," 95.

3. Barton W. Evermann and Hugh M. Smith, "The Whitefishes of North America," in U.S. Commission of Fish and Fisheries, *Report,* 1894, 54th Cong., 1st sess., 1895, H. Doc. 424 (Serial 3447), 283–324; Milner, "Report on the Fisheries of the Great Lakes," 14–17; Hubbard, *Memorials,* 276–277.

4. Milner, "Report on the Fisheries of the Great Lakes," 36, 45–46; George C. Becker, *Fishes of Wisconsin* (Madison: University of Wisconsin Press, 1983), 336.

5. Milner, "Report on the Fisheries of the Great Lakes," 46; Norman Robertson, *The History of the County of Bruce and of the Minor Municipalities Therein, Province of Ontario, Canada* (Toronto: Briggs, 1906), 22.

6. Milner, "Report on the Fisheries of the Great Lakes," 48–52; Becker, *Fishes of Wisconsin,* 336.

7. E. E. Prince, "The Propagation and Planting of Predaceous Fish," in Canada, *Sessional Papers,* 1902, no. 22b, 10; U.S. Congress, House, *Report of the Joint Commission Relative to the Preservation of the Fisheries in Waters Contiguous to Canada and the United States,* 54th Cong., 2d sess., 1896, H. Doc. 315 (Serial 3534), 136; Milner, "Report on the Fisheries of the Great Lakes," 64.

8. Milner, "Report on the Fisheries of the Great Lakes," 38–39; S. H. Davis, interview with William Wakeham and Richard Rathbun, Detroit, Michigan, 19 September 1894, 1 Wakeham and Rathbun Lake Erie Interviews, Records of the Joint Commission Relative to the Preservation of the Fisheries in Waters Contiguous to Canada and the United States, Record Group 22, National Archives, College Park, Maryland; John J. Brice, "A Manual of Fish Culture," in U.S. Commission of Fish and Fisheries, *Report,* 1897, Appendix, 55th Cong., 2d sess., 1897, H. Doc. 299 (Serial 3687), 104.

9. Milner, "Report on the Fisheries of the Great Lakes," 41; Brice, "Manual of Fish Culture," 103.

10. Norman S. Baldwin, Robert W. Saalfeld, Margaret A. Ross, and Howard J. Buettner, *Commercial Fish Production in the Great Lakes, 1867–1977,* Technical Report no. 3 (Ann Arbor, Mich.: Great Lakes Fishery Commission, 1979), 158–185; Becker, *Fishes of Wisconsin,* 323–329.

11. Milner, "Report on the Fisheries of the Great Lakes," 38; W. B. Scott and E. J. Crossman, *Freshwater Fishes of Canada* (Ottawa: Fisheries Research Board of Canada, 1973), 241.

12. Milner, "Report on the Fisheries of the Great Lakes," 65.

13. John W. Post, interview with William Wakeham and Richard Rathbun, Sandusky, Ohio, 24 September 1894, 2 Wakeham and Rathbun Lake Erie Interviews; "Fishes, General, Decrease—Lake Huron," 3, D Wakeham and Rathbun, Lake Huron Investigations, Records of the Joint Commission; *History of Bay*

County Michigan, with Illustrations and Biographical Sketches (Chicago: Page, 1883), 227.

14. Memorandum, Dr. William Wakeham, investigator for the Joint Commission, 2 December 1894, file 94, part 1, frame 136, Microfilm Reel (hereafter cited as MReel) T-2718, Records of the Department of Marine and Fisheries, Record Group 23, National Archives of Canada, Ottawa; Frank N. Egerton, "Pollution and Aquatic Life in Lake Erie: Early Scientific Studies," *Environmental Review* 11 (fall 1987): 189–205; Burns, *Erie,* 149–173; Baldwin, Saalfeld, Ross, and Buettner, *Commercial Fish Production,* 32–33; Becker, *Fishes of Wisconsin,* 341–345.

15. For the full text of the epigraph beginning this section see Laura E. Richards, *Tirra Lirra, Rhymes Old and New* (Toronto: Little, Brown, 1902), 22.

16. Milner, "Report on the Fisheries of the Great Lakes," 74–75. It was identified in the 1890s as the silvery lamprey. See Ramsay Wright, "Preliminary Report on the Fish and Fisheries of Ontario," in Ontario, *Sessional Papers,* 1892, no. 79, 439–440; Becker, *Fishes of Wisconsin,* 224.

17. Scott and Crossman, *Freshwater Fishes,* 88; J. Hutchinson, interview with H. F. Moore and B. L. Hardin, Dunkirk, New York, August 1894, 4 Moore and Hardin Lake Erie Interviews, Records of the Joint Commission.

18. Scott and Crossman, *Freshwater Fishes,* 85–86; Becker, *Fishes of Wisconsin,* 223.

19. Milner, "Report on the Fisheries of the Great Lakes," 73–74.

20. Scott and Crossman, *Freshwater Fishes,* 82–89; Becker, *Fishes of Wisconsin,* 221–226; Louis Agassiz, *Lake Superior: Its Physical Character, Vegetation, and Animals, Compared with Those of Other and Similar Regions* (1850; reprint, New York: Arno Press, 1970), 263–278; Seth Green, *Home Fishing and Home Waters: A Practical Treatise on Fish Culture* (New York: Judd, 1888), 68–70; E. E. Prince, "The Canadian Sturgeon and Caviar Industries," Special Appended Report, in Department of Marine and Fisheries, *Report,* 1904, in Canada, *Sessional Papers,* 1905, no. 22, liii–lxx; Wright, "Preliminary Report," 440–441; Brice, "Manual of Fish Culture," 189–191; George Brown Goode, "Notes on the Lampreys—Petromyzonidae," U.S. Fish Commission, *Bulletin* 2 (1882): 349–354.

21. Agassiz, *Lake Superior,* 263–278; A. J. Stoll, interview with William Wakeham and Richard Rathbun, Sandusky, Ohio, 24 September 1894, 1 Wakeham and Rathbun Lake Erie Interviews, Records of the Joint Commission; Lewis Cass Aldrich, *History of Erie County, Ohio* (Syracuse, N.Y.: Mason, 1889), 407, Milner, "Report on the Fisheries of the Great Lakes," 72–73.

22. Frederick W. True, "The Fisheries of the Great Lakes," in George Brown Goode, *The Fisheries and Fishing Industries of the United States,* Section 2, 47th Cong., 1st sess., 1881, S. Misc. Doc. 124 (Serial 1999), 642, 663, 665; Hugh M. Smith and Merwin-Marie Snell, "Review of the Fisheries of the Great Lakes in 1885," in U.S. Commission of Fish and Fisheries, *Report,* 1887, Appendix, 50th Cong., 2d sess., 1889, H. Misc. Doc. 133 (Serial 2661), 116–117, 160, 169–170, 172, 173, 177, 249, 254, 266–267, 287–288, 292–294.

23. Milner, "Report on the Fisheries of the Great Lakes," 73; House, *Report*

of the Joint Commission, 104, 126, 136, 140, 148; U.S. Commissioner of Fisheries, *Report,* 1913 (Washington, D.C.: Government Printing Office,1914), 67.

24. H. F. Moore, notes, Detroit, Michigan, 26 August 1894, 1–3, 1 Moore and Hardin Lake Erie Interviews, Records of the Joint Commission.

25. Prince, "Canadian Sturgeon and Caviar Industries," lviii–lix; U.S. Commissioner of Fisheries, *Report,* 1913, 66; Philip Neilson, interview with William Wakeham and Richard Rathbun, Sandusky, Ohio, 25 September 1894, 2 Wakeham and Rathbun Lake Erie Interviews, Records of the Joint Commission. Neilson was a member of the partnership of Fruechtnicht & Neilson, which in 1888 reportedly handled 225 tons of sturgeon, exporting large quantities to the German market. See Aldrich, *History of Erie County, Ohio,* 405.

26. House, *Report of the Joint Commission,* 56; Canada, House of Commons, *Debates,* 21 June 1894, 4737–4738; Colonel W. B. Camp, interview with William Wakeham and Richard Rathbun, Sackets Harbor, New York, 5 October 1894, Lake Ontario Interviews, Records of the Joint Commission.

27. Walter G. Robbins, interview with William Wakeham and Richard Rathbun, Buffalo, New York, 1 October 1894, 2 Wakeham and Rathbun Lake Erie Interviews; Alex Nielsen, interview with H. F. Moore and B. L. Hardin, Venice, Ohio, 18 July 1894, 3 Moore and Hardin Lake Erie Interviews, Records of the Joint Commission; House, *Report of the Joint Commission,* 56.

28. "Causes, Decrease of Fish," unlabeled binder, Lake Ontario, 40; Donald McCauley, statement, 1894, C Lake Huron, Notes by Subjects; Cloud Rutter, "Report on Lake Erie Investigation," in Lake Erie, 1894, 130; Lake Ontario, Notes by Subjects, 40; "Lampreys, St. Mary's River," 3 Lake Superior Subject Categories, 85, Records of the Joint Commission; Dominion Fishery Commission, "Report," Part 1, ix.

29. B. A. Bensley, "The Fishes of Georgian Bay," in Canada, *Sessional Papers,* 1915, no. 39b, 10; James T. Angus, *A Respectable Ditch: A History of the Trent–Severn Waterway, 1833–1920* (Kingston, Ont.: McGill–Queens University Press, 1988), 236, 240, 253.

30. U.S. Commission of Fish and Fisheries, *Report,* 1879, 46th Cong., 2d sess., 1879, S. Misc. Doc. 59 (Serial 1892), xi.

31. Green, *Home Fishing and Home Waters,* 59–61; Ontario, *Sessional Papers,* 1893, no. 76, 6; Prince, "Propagation and Planting of Predaceous Fish," 9; U.S. Commission of Fish and Fisheries, *Report,* 1894, 171, and *Report,* 1900, 56th Cong., 2d sess., 1900, H. Doc. 541 (Serial 4196), 179; Baldwin, Saalfeld, Ross, and Buettner, *Commercial Fish Production,* 40.

32. Prince, "Propagation and Planting of Predaceous Fish," 9; E. E. Prince, "The Place of Carp in Fish-Culture," in Canada, *Sessional Papers,* 1897, no. 11B, 33.

33. Ontario, *Sessional Papers,* 1900, no. 27, 39; Henry Herbst, interview with H. F. Moore and B. L. Hardin, Niedermeier, Michigan, 27 June 1894, 1 Moore and Hardin Lake Erie Interviews, Records of the Joint Commission.

34. Dominion Fishery Commission, "Report," Part 1, ix.

35. Memorandum, Samuel Wilmot, 23 January 1894, file 31, frames 22–28, MReel T-2669, Records of the Department of Marine and Fisheries; Canada,

Sessional Papers, 1883, no. 7, 217; 1893, no. 10A, 187; Dominion Fishery Commission, "Report," Part 1, ix.

36. Baldwin, Saalfeld, Ross, and Buettner, *Commercial Fish Production,* 73, 99; Smith and Snell, "Review of the Fisheries of the Great Lakes," 84–85, 208, 240–241, 303; Hugh M. Smith, "The Fisheries of the Great Lakes," in U.S. Commission of Fish and Fisheries, *Report,* 1892, Appendix, 53d Cong., 2d sess., 1893, H. Misc. Doc. 209 (Serial 3264), 393–394, 413, 432–433, 445.

37. Becker, *Fishes of Wisconsin,* 886–891; Smith and Snell, "Review of the Fisheries of the Great Lakes," 168–170; Michigan Board of Fish Commissioners, *Seventh Biennial Report,* 1884–1886, in Michigan, *Joint Documents,* 1886, 1:21.

38. Smith and Snell, "Review of the Fisheries of the Great Lakes," 85, 121, 122, 208; Smith, "Fisheries of the Great Lakes," 393–394, 413. For a long-term study of Green Bay fisheries, see Gerard Bertrand, Jean Lang, and John Ross, *The Green Bay Watershed: Past, Present, and Future,* Technical Report no. 229 (Madison: University of Wisconsin Sea Grant College Program, 1976).

39. Milner, "Report on the Fisheries of the Great Lakes," 12–13; Smith and Snell, "Review of the Fisheries of the Great Lakes," 227–232, illustration facing 220; Ludwig Kumlien, "The Fisheries of the Great Lakes," in George Brown Goode, *The Fisheries and Fishing Industries of the United States,* Section 5, 47th Cong., 1st sess., 1881, S. Misc. Doc. 124 (Serial 2001), 765–766; Baldwin, Saalfeld, Ross, and Buettner, *Commercial Fish Production,* 69–81.

40. Environment Canada and the United States Environmental Protection Agency, *The Great Lakes: An Environmental Atlas and Resource Book* (Chicago and Toronto: Environment Canada and United States Environmental Protection Agency, 1987), 36.

41. For an explanation in scientific terms of the changes in Great Lakes water and fish species between 1950 and 1972, see Stanford H. Smith, "Factors in Ecologic Succession in Oligotrophic Fish Communities of the Laurentian Great Lakes," *Journal of the Fisheries Research Board of Canada* 29 (June 1972): 717–730.

42. Figures were calculated from production data in Baldwin, Saalfeld, Ross, and Buettner, *Commercial Fish Production,* 158–183.

43. Figures were calculated from production data in Baldwin, Saalfeld, Ross, and Buettner, *Commercial Fish Production,* 6–27; Camp interview.

44. Prince, "Propagation and Planting of Predaceous Fish," 10–11; Wilmot statements in Dominion Fishery Commission, "Report," Part 1, vii–viii.

CHAPTER 11: THE FIRST REGULATORS: THE PROVINCES AND THE STATES

1. *Laws of New York* (Albany: Charles R. and George Webster, 1802), 1:422–423.

2. For a lucid account of the history of Rochester, New York, see Blake McKelvey, *Rochester on the Genesee: The Growth of a City* (Syracuse, N.Y.: Syracuse University Press, 1973). The conflict between the early use of waterpower and the preservation of fish life is discussed in Oscar and Mary Handlin, *Commonwealth: A Study of the Role of Government in the American Economy: Mas-*

sachusetts, 1774–1861 (Cambridge, Mass.: Harvard University Press, 1969), 71–73.

3. New York, *Laws,* 1813, 2:238–241; 1822, 6:224; 1826, 245–246.

4. New York, *Laws,* 1813, 2:287; 1835, 251; 1836, 169–170; George Brown Goode, "The Salmon—Salmo salar," in George Brown Goode, *The Fisheries and Fishery Industries of the United States,* Section 1, 47th Cong., 1st sess., 1881, S. Misc. Doc. 124 (Serial 1998), 473–474.

5. *Provincial Statutes of Upper Canada* (York: Lt. Gov., 1818), 221.

6. *Provincial Statutes of Upper Canada,* 275; *Statutes of the Province of Canada* (Quebec: Governor General, 1865), 52.

7. *Statutes of the Province of Upper Canada* (Kingston: Thompson and McFarlane, 1831), 275, 279–280, 328–329, 466–467; *Statutes of the Province of Canada* (Kingston: Province of Canada, 1845), 272

8. *Statutes of the Province of Upper Canada,* 329; *Consolidated Statutes of Canada* (Toronto: Parliament of the Province of Canada, 1859), 707.

9. *Statutes of the Province of Canada,* 1845, 272–274.

10. Hugh MacCrimmon, "The Beginnings of Salmon Culture in Canada," *Canadian Geographical Journal* 71 (September 1965): 96.

11. Alan B. McCullough, *The Commercial Fishery of the Canadian Great Lakes* (Ottawa: Environment Canada, 1989), 19–21.

12. Canada, House of Commons, *Journals,* 1869, Appendix 3, 80.

13. Hugh M. Smith, "The Fisheries of the Great Lakes," in U.S. Commission of Fish and Fisheries, *Report,* 1892, Appendix, 53d Cong., 2d sess., 1893, H. Misc. Doc. 209 (Serial 3264), 450.

14. Michigan, *Territorial Laws* (Lansing: State Printer, 1874), 2:748; Wisconsin, *General Acts,* 1864, 233–237.

15. Michigan, *Laws,* 1865, 717–719; 1873, 49; Wisconsin, *Laws,* 1879, 280–282; Ohio, *Laws,* 1880, 135–136.

16. Dean Conrad Allard, Jr., *Spencer Fullerton Baird and the U.S. Fish Commission* (New York: Arno Press, 1978); "Spencer Fullerton Baird and the Foundations of American Marine Science," *Marine Fisheries Review* 50 (1988): 124–129; and "The Fish Commission Laboratory and Its Influence on the Founding of the Marine Biological Laboratory," *Journal of the History of Biology* 23 (summer 1990): 251–270.

17. U.S. Commission of Fish and Fisheries, *Report,* 1879, 46th Cong., 2d sess., 1879, S. Misc. Doc. 59 (Serial 1892), xi–xii; James W. Milner, "Report on the Fisheries of the Great Lakes: The Result of Inquiries Prosecuted in 1871 and 1872," in U.S. Commission of Fish and Fisheries, *Report,* 1872–1873, Appendix A, 42d Cong., 3d sess., 1872, S. Misc. Doc. 74 (Serial 1547), 20–34.

18. James W. Milner to Governor of Michigan, 27 January 1873, C II Correspondence, National Affairs, Fish and Fisheries Commission, Records of the Executive Office, Box 7, Record Group 44, Michigan State Archives, Lansing; Milner, "Report on the Fisheries of the Great Lakes," 16; Michigan, *Laws,* 1873, 171–172; Ohio, *Laws,* 1873, 274–275; Wisconsin, *Laws,* 1873, 462; 1874, 579; *Wisconsin Statutes* (Revised), 1878, 454–455.

19. Wisconsin Commissioners of Fisheries, *Eighth Annual Report,* 1881 (Madison: State Printer, 1881), 8, and *Twelfth Biennial Report,* 1887–1888

(Madison: State Printer, 1888), 11–14; Michigan Board of Fish Commissioners, *Ninth Biennial Report,* 1888–1890, in Michigan, *Joint Documents,* 1890, 2:2.

20. U.S. Commission of Fish and Fisheries, *Report,* 1883, 48th Cong., 1st sess., 1883, H. Misc. Doc. 67 (Serial 2244), lxxi–lxxii; Michigan Board of Fish Commissioners, *Sixth Biennial Report,* 1883–1884, in Michigan, *Joint Documents,* 1884, 1:32, and *Eighth Biennial Report,* 1886–1888, in Michigan, *Joint Documents,* 1888, 1:80–82; Ontario Fish and Game Commission, "Report," in *Sessional Papers,* 1892, no. 79, 263.

21. U.S. Commission of Fish and Fisheries, *Report,* 1886, 49th Cong., 2d sess., 1886, S. Misc. Doc. 90 (Serial 2453), xliii–xliv; Minnesota Fish Commissioners, *Twelfth and Thirteenth Annual Reports,* 1884–1886 (St. Paul: Pioneer Press, 1887), 194–202; "A New United States Fish Hatchery," *American Field: The Sportsman's Journal,* 4 September 1886, 223; U.S. Commission of Fish and Fisheries, *Report,* 1889–1891, 52d Cong., 2d sess., 1892, H. Misc. Doc. 113 (Serial 3130), 10–11, 37–44, and *Report,* 1897, 55th Cong., 2d sess., 1897, H. Doc. 229 (Serial 3687), xxix.

22. Superintendent of Michigan State Fisheries, *Third Biennial Report,* 1877–1878, in Michigan, *Joint Documents,* 1878, 1:55–56; Michigan Board of Fish Commissioners, *Sixth Biennial Report,* 1883–1884, 30–31; Wisconsin, *Laws,* 1878, 705. See also Donald McNaughton, state senator of New York, quoted in Ontario, *Sessional Papers,* 1892, no. 79, 250; Hoyt Post, Michigan Fish Commission, to Governor John T. Rich, 28 November 1894, G II Correspondence, Records of the Executive Office, Box 56, Record Group 44, Michigan State Archives.

23. Michigan Board of Fish Commissioners, *Tenth Biennial Report,* 1890–1892, in Michigan, *Joint Documents,* 1892, 5:21–23, 26–27.

24. Wisconsin Commissioners of Fisheries, *Second Annual Report* (Madison: State Printer, 1875), 4; *Fifth Annual Report,* 1878 (Madison: State Printer, 1879), 21; *Third Biennial Report, 1887–1888* (Madison: State Printer, 1889), 15; and *Fifth Biennial Report, 1891–1892* (Madison: State Printer, 1893), 29–31; Wisconsin, *Laws,* 1895, 368.

25. Michigan Board of Fish Commissioners, *Eighth Biennial Report,* 1886–1888, 84–85; Ohio Fish and Game Commission, *Annual Report,* 1895, in Ohio, *Executive Documents,* 1895, Part 2, 350.

26. The discussion of the influence of the commercial-fishing industry on legislation is based largely on the same bodies of documents for the three states: fish commission reports, legislative journals, and session laws; Hugh M. Smith and Merwin-Marie Snell, "Review of the Fisheries of the Great Lakes in 1885," in U.S. Commission of Fish and Fisheries, *Report,* 1887, Appendix, 50th Cong., 2d sess., 1889, H. Misc. Doc. 133 (Serial 2661); Records of the Joint Commission Relative to the Preservation of the Fisheries in Waters Contiguous to Canada and the United States, Record Group 22, National Archives, College Park, Maryland; and Records of the Department of Marine and Fisheries, Record Group 23, National Archives of Canada, Ottawa. For Michigan, the governors' original incoming correspondence was also available: G II Correspondence, History Division, Records of the Executive Office, Record Group 44, Michigan State Archives.

27. Ohio Fish and Game Commission, *Thirteenth Annual Report,* 1888, in Ohio, *Executive Documents,* 1888, Part 1, 655; Smith and Snell, "Review of the

Fisheries of the Great Lakes," 242, 265, 268. The number of fish dealers was compiled from Smith and Snell, "Review of the Fisheries of the Great Lakes," 233–295.

28. Ohio Commissioners of Fisheries, *Report,* 1873 (Columbus: State Printer, 1874), 9; Ohio Fish Commission, *Sixth Annual Report,* 1881, in Ohio, *Executive Documents,* 1881, Part 2, 431.

29. Ohio, *Laws,* 1873, 274–275; 1880, 136; Ohio Commissioners of Fisheries, *Report,* 1873, 9; Smith and Snell, "Review of the Fisheries of the Great Lakes," 250.

30. Ohio, *Laws,* 1883, 110; Ohio Fish Commission, *Eighth Annual Report,* 1883, in Ohio, *Executive Documents,* 1883, Part 1, 1492.

31. Ohio Fish Commission, *Twelfth Annual Report,* 1887, in Ohio, *Executive Documents,* 1887, Part 2, 189–190; Ohio Fish and Game Commission, *Thirteenth Annual Report,* 1888, in Ohio, *Executive Documents,* 1888, Part 1, 648–649, 655–656; Ohio, *Laws,* 1886, 186–187; 1888, 172.

32. Ohio Fish and Game Commission, *Thirteenth Annual Report,* 1888, 647–648; "Fishermen Are Hot under the Gills," *Cleveland World,* 11 August 1895, in file 1593, part 1, frames 62–63, Microfilm Reel (hereafter cited as MReel) T-3168, Records of the Department of Marine and Fisheries; Ohio Fish and Game Commission, *Fourteenth Annual Report,* 1889, in Ohio, *Executive Documents,* 1889, Part 1, 506–507, 547–548; Ohio, *Laws,* 1889, 303, 316, 352; 1890, 78.

33. Ohio Fish and Game Commission, *Nineteenth Annual Report,* 1894, in Ohio, *Executive Documents,* 1894, Part 2, 333–334.

34. Ohio Fish and Game Commission, *Twentieth Annual Report,* 1895, in Ohio, *Executive Documents,* 1895, Part 2, 349, and *Annual Report,* 1900 (Columbus: State Printer, 1900), 4.

35. A. J. Stoll, interview with William Wakeham and Richard Rathbun, Sandusky, Ohio, 24 September 1894, 1 Wakeham and Rathbun Lake Erie Interviews, Records of the Joint Commission.

36. E. R. Edson, interview with William Wakeham and Richard Rathbun, Cleveland, Ohio, 17 September 1894, 2 Wakeham and Rathbun Lake Erie Interviews, Records of the Joint Commission.

37. *Daily Register* [Sandusky, Ohio], 1 March 1894, translation from German of "Destruction of Our Lake Erie Fisheries," *Demokrat,* 24 January 1894, file 1241, part 1, frame 13, MReel T-3142, Records of the Department of Marine and Fisheries.

38. "Too Much Freedom," *Ottawa Citizen,* 2 February 1894, file 1241, part 1, frame 16, MReel T-3142, Records of the Department of Marine and Fisheries.

39. Michigan Board of Fish Commissioners, *Sixth Biennial Report,* 1883–1884, 30–33, and *Tenth Biennial Report,* 1890–1892, 21–24; Wisconsin Commissioners of Fisheries, *First Biennial Report,* 1883–1884, 8–9; Ledger, Minutes of Wisconsin Fish Commission, 55, 57, Wisconsin State Archives, Madison; U.S. Commission of Fish and Fisheries, *Report,* 1892, 53d Cong., 2d sess., 1893, H. Misc. Doc. 209 (Serial 3264), clxxxiv–clxxxv; G. A. MacCallum, "The Assimilation of the Fishery Laws of the Great Lakes," U.S. Fish Commission, *Bulletin* 13 (1893): 17–20.

40. Canada, House of Commons, *Debates,* 14 September 1896, 1158.

CHAPTER 12: CHANGING IDEAS: THE UNITED STATES AND THE GREAT LAKES FISHERY

1. U.S. Commission of Fish and Fisheries, *Report,* 1880, 46th Cong., 3d sess., 1880, S. Misc. Doc. 29 (Serial 1947), 53–54.

2. Dean Conrad Allard, Jr., *Spencer Fullerton Baird and the U.S. Fish Commission* (New York: Arno Press, 1978), 307.

3. James W. Milner, "Report on the Fisheries of the Great Lakes: The Result of Inquiries Prosecuted in 1871 and 1872," in U.S. Commission of Fish and Fisheries, *Report,* 1872–1873, Appendix A, 42d Cong., 3d sess., 1872, S. Misc. Doc. 74 (Serial 1547), 20–24.

4. U.S. Commission of Fish and Fisheries, *Report,* 1878, 45th Cong., 3d sess., 1878 (Serial 1834), xlv–li.

5. Allard, *Spencer Fullerton Baird,* 152–157, 284–290.

6. Allard, *Spencer Fullerton Baird,* 164–180, 317–346.

7. Hugh M. Smith, "The Fisheries of the Great Lakes," in U.S. Commission of Fish and Fisheries, *Report,* 1892, Appendix, 53d Cong., 2d sess., 1893, H. Misc. Doc. 209 (Serial 3264), 457.

8. E. W. Nelson, "Fisheries of Chicago and Vicinity," in U.S. Commission of Fish and Fisheries, *Report,* 1875–1876, Appendix, 44th Cong., 1st sess., 1875, S. Misc. Doc. 107 (Serial 1666), 783–800; Frederick W. True, "The Fisheries of the Great Lakes," in George Brown Goode, *The Fisheries and Fishery Industries of the United States,* Section 2, 47th Cong., 1st sess., 1881, S. Misc. Doc. 124 (Serial 1999), 636–637, 641, 646–658, 666, 673.

9. Frank N. Clark, "Account of Operations at the Northville Fish-Hatching Station of the United States Fish Commission, from 1874 to 1882, Inclusive," U.S. Fish Commission, *Bulletin* 2 (1882): 355–372; U.S. Commission of Fish and Fisheries, *Report,* 1880, xxviii, and *Report,* 1884, 48th Cong., 1st sess., 1883, H. Misc. Doc. 68 (Serial 2245), XIX.

10. Charles W. Smiley, "Changes in the Fisheries of the Great Lakes during the Decade, 1870–1880," U.S. Fish Commission, *Bulletin* 1 (1881): 252–258. Parts of his report were quoted in Michigan Board of Fish Commissioners, *Sixth Biennial Report,* 1883–1884, in Michigan, *Joint Documents,* 1884, 1:10–11.

11. U.S. Commission of Fish and Fisheries, *Report,* 1884, 1152, and *Report,* 1885, 48th Cong., 2d sess., 1884, S. Misc. Doc. 70 (Serial 2270), lx.

12. U.S. Commission of Fish and Fisheries, *Report,* 1883, 48th Cong., 1st sess., 1883, H. Misc. Doc. 67 (Serial 2244), lxxii, and *Report,* 1885, lxi–lxii.

13. Hugh M. Smith and Merwin-Marie Snell, "Review of the Fisheries of the Great Lakes in 1885," in U.S. Commission of Fish and Fisheries, *Report,* 1887, Appendix, 50th Cong., 2d sess., 1889, H. Misc. Doc. 133 (Serial 2661), 8.

14. Smith and Snell, "Review of the Fisheries of the Great Lakes," 59, 73, 103, 109, 110, 116, 134, 138–139, 142, 146, 150, 152, 159, 161, 169, 171, 177, 179, 181–182, 215, 216, 225–226, 305, 322–324.

15. Smith, "Fisheries of the Great Lakes," 426–428.

16. Hugh M. Smith, "Report on an Investigation of the Fisheries of Lake Ontario," U.S. Fish Commission, *Bulletin* 10 (1890): 177.

17. Smith, "Report on an Investigation," 212–213.

18. Smith, "Fisheries of the Great Lakes," 363.
19. Smith, "Fisheries of the Great Lakes," 364, 420, 440.
20. Smith, "Fisheries of the Great Lakes," 457.

CHAPTER 13: CANADA'S REGULATED FISHERY, 1868–1888

1. Harold A. Innis, *The Cod Fisheries: The History of an International Economy* (New Haven, Conn.: Yale University Press, 1940), 364. The three provinces that joined the confederation in 1867 were Canada (Ontario and Quebec combined), Nova Scotia, and New Brunswick.

2. Canada, *Statutes,* 1st Parl., 1st sess., 1868, Part 2, 177–192; Alan B. McCullough, *The Commercial Fishery of the Canadian Great Lakes* (Ottawa: Environment Canada, 1989), 19–21, 83.

3. Both the 1 million acres of the Huron Tract acquired by the Canada Company and the 5,000 acres given to Colonel Thomas Talbot were granted on the premise that settlement by small-scale farmer-developers would be facilitated. See Lillian Gates, *Land Policies of Upper Canada* (Toronto: University of Toronto Press, 1968), 124–125.

4. Gates, *Land Policies,* 53, 161, 192, 211, 214, 245, 247, 268.

5. Canada, *Sessional Papers,* 1870, no. 11, 72–74; 1892, no. 11, 3–5; McCullough, *Commercial Fishery,* 21, 83.

6. Canada, *Sessional Papers,* 1891, no. 8A, viii. For an example of the Dominion Police in action, see pp. 234–235.

7. Hugh MacCrimmon, "The Beginning of Salmon Culture in Canada," *Canadian Geographical Journal* 71 (September 1965): 96; Edward E. Prince, "The Progress of Fish Culture in Canada," in Canada, *Sessional Papers,* 1906, no. 22, 89–108; Select Committee on Fisheries, Navigation, etc., *Seventh Report,* 16 June 1869, in Canada, House of Commons, *Journals,* 1869, Appendix 3, 1; Alan B. McCullough, "Samuel Wilmot," in *Dictionary of Canadian Biography* (Toronto: University of Toronto Press, 1990), 12:1106–1107.

8. Canada, *Sessional Papers,* 1869, no. 12, 86–89; 1870, no. 11, 61–62; 1873, no. 8, Appendix H, 103; 1877, no. 5, 367.

9. Canada, *Sessional Papers,* 1871, no. 5, 69; 1872, no. 5, 66; 1874, no. 4, lxxvi; 1876, no. 5, xxvi.

10. Canada, House of Commons, *Journals,* 1869, Appendix 3, Questionnaire Responses, 65–81.

11. Canada, House of Commons, *Journals,* 1869, Appendix 3, 80; Canada, *Sessional Papers,* 1869, no. 12, 14; 1879, no. 3, 323–332.

12. Canada, Senate, *Debates,* 26 April 1872, 168–169.

13. Canada, *Sessional Papers,* 1871, no. 5, 67–68; 1872, no. 5, 65.

14. Canada, *Sessional Papers,* 1875, no. 5, lxix; 1877, no. 5, xli.

15. Canada, *Sessional Papers,* 1877, no. 5, xli; 1878, no. 1, Appendix 3; Canada, House of Commons, *Debates,* 16 April 1883, 659.

16. Canada, *Sessional Papers,* 1873, no. 8, 67; 1874, no. 4, lxxvii; 1875, no. 5, lxix.

17. Canada, *Sessional Papers,* 1876, no. 5, xxiv–xxvi.

18. Canada, *Sessional Papers,* 1888, no. 6, v; 1883, no. 7, 221; 1884, no. 7, 227.

19. Canada, *Sessional Papers,* 1884, no. 7, 227; 1885, no. 9, 283–285; 1886, no. 11, 318; 1888, no. 6, 270–271; 1889, no. 8, 188.

20. Canada, House of Commons, *Debates,* 16 April 1883, 657–659.

21. Canada, House of Commons, *Debates,* 31 March 1884, 1236; 30 June 1885, 2954; 19 April 1886, 784; Canada, House of Commons, *Journals,* 1886, 17, 32, 51, 58, 60, 69, 75, 95, 211.

CHAPTER 14: CHARLES HIBBERT TUPPER AND THE NEW BROOM, 1888–1896

1. Vincent Durant, *War Horse of Cumberland: The Life and Times of Sir Charles Tupper* (Hantsport, Nova Scotia: Lancelot Press, 1985), 22; *A Standard Dictionary of Canadian Biography* (Toronto: Trans-Canada Press, 1934), 509–513.

2. Charles Hibbert Tupper, reminiscences on service as Minister of Marine and Fisheries, frames 3589–3591, Microfilm Reel (hereafter cited as MReel) M109, Sir Charles H. Tupper Correspondence, National Archives of Canada, Ottawa.

3. Sir Charles Tupper to Charles Hibbert Tupper, 23 June 1890, frame 443, MReel M106, Tupper Correspondence; Dominion Fishery Commission on the Fisheries of the Province of Ontario, "Report," in Canada, *Sessional Papers,* 1893, no. 10C*, Part 1, vii.

4. Canada, *Sessional Papers,* 1889, no. 8, 197–201.

5. Canada, *Sessional Papers,* 1890, no. 17, xxxv–xxxvi, xxxvii, Superintendent of Fish Culture, "Report," 12–23; 1891, no. 8A, viii, Superintendent of Fish Culture, "Report," 39–41; 1892, no. 11, xx; 1893, no. 10A, Appendix H, 189–194; 1896, no. 11A, 65–68. Dam and fishway problems in 1893 and 1894 are well illustrated in file 394, part 1, frames 4–139, MReel T-2833, and file 502, part 1, frames 3–196, MReel T-2847, Records of the Department of Marine and Fisheries, Record Group 23, National Archives of Canada.

6. Dominion Fishery Commission, "Report," Part 1, v; Harry B. Barrett, *Lore and Legends of Long Point* (Don Mills, Ont.: Burns and MacEachern, 1977), 143–147.

7. Dominion Fishery Commission, "Report," Part 1, vii.

8. Dominion Fishery Commission, "Report," Part 1, v–xi.

9. Dominion Fishery Commission, "Report," Part 1, DD.

10. Canada, House of Commons, *Debates,* 13 June 1894, 4240, 4260–4261; Kenneth Johnstone, *The Aquatic Explorers: A History of the Fisheries Research Board of Canada* (Toronto: University of Toronto Press, 1977), 43–44; obituary [Edward Ernest Prince], *Proceedings and Transactions of the Royal Society of Canada* 32 (May 1938): xx–xxiii.

11. Canada, House of Commons, *Debates,* 18 April 1894, 1589, 1593.

12. Canada, House of Commons, *Debates,* 12 June 1894, 4241–4242.

13. Ontario, *Sessional Papers,* 1892, no. 79, 275; Dominion Fishery Commission, "Report," Part 1, 50.

14. S. Joyce to Deputy Minister of Fisheries, 13 December 1895, file 43, part 1, frame 305, MReel T-2670; R. F. Cunningham to W. H. Montague, House of Commons, 24 March 1894, file 63, part 1, frames 47–48, MReel T-2675, Records of the Department of Marine and Fisheries.

15. Canada, *Sessional Papers,* 1876, no. 5, 228; Charles Gauthier to John Costigan, Minister of Marine and Fisheries, 15 April 1895, file 43, part 1, frames 203–205, MReel T-2670, Records of the Department of Marine and Fisheries.

16. Policy on licensing is found in file 120, part 1, frames 12–13, 22–35, 77, MReel T-2726; Minister of Marine and Fisheries to Mr. Killackey, 3 May 1894, file 31, part 1, frames 118–120, MReel T-2669, Records of the Department of Marine and Fisheries.

17. Nelson Couture, Spanish Station, Ontario, April 1894, file 120, part 3, frame 106; Reverend J. Paquin to Department of Marine and Fisheries, 9 April 1895, file 120, part 2, frame 35, MReel T-2727, Records of the Department of Marine and Fisheries.

18. Charles Hibbert Tupper to D. Tisdale, M.P., House of Commons, 24 March 1894, file 57, part 1, frame 67, MReel T-2673, Records of the Department of Marine and Fisheries.

19. Reverend C. W. Watch to Minister of Marine and Fisheries, 20 July 1896; W. D. Bates and Brother to William Ball, 15 May 1896; A. N. Stammers to William Ball, 14 May 1896; William Ball to Minister of Marine and Fisheries, 21 May 1896; Deputy Minister of Marine and Fisheries to William Ball, 27 May 1896, file 31, part 1, frames 219–239, 244–245, 252–253, 254, 257–259, MReel T-2669; R. Jackson, Port Coldwell, Ontario, to John Costigan, Minister of Marine and Fisheries, 28 April 1896, file 471, part 1, frames 161–163, MReel T-2846, Records of the Department of Marine and Fisheries.

20. A. B. Ingram, M.P., to John Costigan, Minister of Marine and Fisheries, 7 November 1895; Deputy Minister of Marine and Fisheries to A. B. Ingram, 1 December 1895, file 63, part 1, frames 106–107, 118, MReel T-2675, Records of the Department of Marine and Fisheries.

21. Petition, citizens of Southampton, Ontario, February 1895; T. H. Elliott, fishery overseer, to Deputy Minister of Marine and Fisheries, 22 February 1895; H. M. Smith, Southampton, Ontario, to John Costigan, Minister of Marine and Fisheries, 4 March 1895, file 120, part 1, frames 320–322, 345–347, MReel T-2727, Records of the Department of Marine and Fisheries.

22. Deputy Minister of Marine and Fisheries to H. M. Smith, 13 March 1895, file 120, part 1, frames 348–350, MReel T-2727, Records of the Department of Marine and Fisheries.

23. Clipping, *Canadian* [Sarnia, Ont.], 11 April 1894, file 43, part 1, frame 135, MReel T-2670, Records of the Department of Marine and Fisheries.

24. License list, 1894; W. H. Lockhart Gordon to Sir Charles Hibbert Tupper, 13 April 1894; petition on behalf of Toronto Island fishermen, April 1894; petition, citizens of Toronto, May 1894; Minister of Marine and Fisheries to J. C. Swart and other petition signers, 14 May 1894, file 294, part 1, frames 2, 31–32,

45–46, 58, 59–60, MReel T-2826; Petition, 4 May 1894, file 330, part 1, frames 32–33, MReel T-2829; Charles Northwood to John Costigan, 21 January 1895; Minister of Marine and Fisheries to Charles Northwood, January 1895, file 43, part 1, frames 163–174, MReel T-2670.

25. Edgar McInnis, *Canada, a Political and Social History* (Toronto: Rinehart, 1947), 355–361.

26. Canada, House of Commons, *Debates,* 27 March 1893, 3183–3196.

27. Canada, House of Commons, *Debates,* 27 March 1893, 3196, 3198.

28. Canada, House of Commons, *Debates,* 27 March 1893, 3204.

29. Charles H. Tupper to Sir John Macdonald, 6 February 1890; Charles H. Tupper to Sir Julian, 7 May 1890, frames 186–189, 393–394, MReel M-106, Tupper Correspondence.

30. Charles H. Tupper to the Honorable Mr. Mackenzie Bowell, 20 June 1893; Tupper to Bowell, 10 July 1893; Marquis of Ripon to Administrator, 5 September 1893, frames 1109–1110, 1116–1117, 1153, MReel M-107, Tupper Correspondence.

31. Canada, House of Commons, *Debates,* 13 June 1894, 4241.

32. Canada, House of Commons, *Debates,* 13 June 1894, 4238–4239.

33. Canada, House of Commons, *Debates,* 3 June 1895, 1979–2021; 5 July 1895, 3948–3979.

34. "Instructions for Lake Erie Fisheries Service," 11 October 1893; Fred Kerr, report, 1894; Edward E. Prince, notes on overseer Kerr's Report of Protection Cruise on Lake Erie, 9 January 1894, file 466, part 1, frames 2–5, 12–34, 35–42; Fred Kerr to Deputy Minister of Marine and Fisheries, 5 March 1894, file 467, part 1, frames 18–21, MReel T-2845; O. V. Spain to H. W. Johnson, 27 March 1894, file 467, part 1, frame 40, MReel T-2846, Records of the Department of Marine and Fisheries.

35. Dominion Fishery Commission, "Report," Part 1, Captain Edward Dunn, interview, 161–162; Captain Edward Dunn, interview with William Wakeham and Richard Rathbun, 13 September 1894, 2 Georgian Bay Interviews, Records of the Joint Commission Relative to the Preservation of the Fisheries in Waters Contiguous to Canada and the United States, Record Group 22, National Archives, College Park, Maryland; Canada, *Sessional Papers,* 1894, no. 11*, "Report of Capt. E. Dunn, on the Work Performed by the Cruiser 'Petrel' under His Command, during the Season of 1894," 73–76.

36. Bloodgood, "A Visit to Pelee," *American Field: The Sportsman's Journal,* 2 October 1886, 317–318.

37. Rufus J. King to Minister of Marine and Fisheries, 8 May 1894; extract from Report of the Privy Council, 16 July 1894, file 1262, part 1, frames 15–20, 91–95, MReel T-3144, Records of the Department of Marine and Fisheries.

38. Cartoon, "Battle of Lake Erie (1894)," *Detroit News,* 11 May 1894, 1.

39. Press coverage of the Pelee Island incident is found in "Seized by Canadians," *Detroit Free Press,* 10 May 1894, 1; "The Petrel Affair," *Detroit Free Press,* 13 May 1894, 4; and clippings from the *Detroit Tribune, Toledo Blade, Toledo Commercial, Daily Register* [Sandusky, Ohio], *Buffalo Courier,* and *Buffalo Express,* May 10–12, 1894, file 1262, part 1, frames 7–13, 26–28; A. Power, Dominion Department of Justice, to Acting Minister of Marine and Fisheries, 9 July

1894, file 1262, part 1, frames 67–68, MReel T-3144, Records of the Department of Marine and Fisheries.

40. For exhibits and documents, see file 1196, part 1, frames 9–48, MReel T-3139, Records of the Department of Marine and Fisheries.

41. Canada, *Sessional Papers,* 1889, no. 8, 197–198.

42. For charges against the Nobles, see file 1196, part 1, frames 363–364, MReel T-3139, Records of the Department of Marine and Fisheries.

43. P. R. de Lamorandier to Minister of Marine and Fisheries, 27 December 1893, file 90, part 1, frames 6–8; Lamorandier to Minister of Marine and Fisheries, 6 February 1894, file 89, part 1, frames 12–13, MReel T-2681, Records of the Department of Marine and Fisheries.

44. Extracts from reports of H. Giroux, officer of the Dominion Police, 21 May 1894, file 1196, part 1, frame 78, MReel T-3139, Records of the Department of Marine and Fisheries.

45. Sir Charles H. Tupper to Sir John Thompson, Minister of Justice, 9 June 1894, file 1196, part 1, frames 69–71, MReel T-3139, Records of the Department of Marine and Fisheries.

46. P. R. de Lamorandier to Minister of Marine and Fisheries, 2 July 1894; Lamorandier to Deputy Minister of Marine and Fisheries, 10 November 1894, file 90, part 1, frames 40–41, MReel T-2681; Lamorandier to Deputy Minister of Marine and Fisheries, 8 September 1894; Lamorandier to Minister of Marine and Fisheries, 22 and 24 July 1895; 2 September 1895, file 1194, part 1, frames 126, 310–312, 341, MReel T-3138, Records of the Department of Marine and Fisheries.

47. Canada, *Sessional Papers,* 1898, no. 11A, 187; petition, 2 January 1895; Acting Deputy Minister of Marine and Fisheries to T. H. Elliott and P. R. de Lamorandier, 11 February 1895, file 120, part 1, frames 280, 292, MReel T-2727, Records of the Department of Marine and Fisheries..

48. Memorandum, J. S. Webster, 26 May 1894, file 1194, part 1, frame 5, MReel T-3138, Records of the Department of Marine and Fisheries.

49. Canada, House of Commons, *Debates,* 3 June 1895, 1979–2022; key correspondence on the Noble case from 1894 to 1896 is in file 1196, part 1, frames 10–12, 107–109, 349–353, 378–379; part 2, frames 2–3, 198–201, 228–231, MReel T-3139; and file 1196, part 2, frames 2–3, 41–47, MReel T-3138, Records of the Department of Marine and Fisheries.

50. Memorandum of findings and award of damages, 24 May 1902, file 1196, part 3, frames 252–259, MReel T-3139, Records of the Department of Marine and Fisheries.

51. Canada, House of Commons, *Debates,* 2 June 1899, 4244–4255; 5 May 1902, 4228–4239, 4957–4958.

CHAPTER 15: TO SAVE THE FISH: THE CRISIS OF THE 1890S AND THE CANADIAN-AMERICAN JOINT COMMISSION OF 1892

Some of the material in this chapter appeared in Margaret Beattie Bogue, "To Save the Fish: Canada, the United States, the Great Lakes, and the Joint Commission of

1892," *Journal of American History* 79 (March 1993): 1429–1454. It is used with the permission of the Organization of American Historians.

1. Howell, "Food Supply of Fresh Waters," *Chicago Times*, 20 August 1881, 10.

2. Statement of William Wakeham and Richard Rathbun, in Louis Streuber, interview with Wakeham and Rathbun, Erie, Pennsylvania, 29 September 1894, 2 Wakeham and Rathbun Lake Erie Interviews, Records of the Joint Commission Relative to the Preservation of the Fisheries in Waters Contiguous to Canada and the United States, Record Group 22, National Archives, College Park, Maryland; James Morton Callahan, *American Foreign Policy in Canadian Relations* (New York: Cooper Square, 1967), 355.

3. Canada, *Sessional Papers*, 1892, no. 11, xliii–xliv, xlviii–xlix; Margaret Beattie Bogue, "In the Shadow of the Union Jack: British Legacies and Great Lakes Fishery Policy," *Environmental Review* 11 (spring 1987): 25.

4. U.S. Congress, House, *Report of the Joint Commission Relative to the Preservation of the Fisheries in Waters Contiguous to Canada and the United States*, 54th Cong., 2d sess., 1896, H. Doc. 315 (Serial 3534), 4–7. The report is also found in Canada, *Sessional Papers*, 1897, no. 11D. See also Callahan, *American Foreign Policy*, 423–424.

5. William Smith, Deputy Minister of Marine and Fisheries, to J. L. McDougall, Auditor General, 7 April 1894, file 1047, part 1, frames 15–16, Microfilm Reel (hereafter cited as MReel) T-3120, Records of the Department of Marine and Fisheries, Record Group 23, National Archives of Canada, Ottawa; Canada, House of Commons, *Debates*, 28 March 1893, 3342; House, *Report of the Joint Commission*, 7–9.

6. House, *Report of the Joint Commission*, 8–9.

7. House, *Report of the Joint Commission*, 11.

8. House, *Report of the Joint Commission*, 16.

9. House, *Report of the Joint Commission*, 15; Canada, *Statutes*, 1st Parl., 1st sess., 1868, Part 2, 189–190; *Revised Statutes of Canada*, 1906, 1:727–728.

10. House, *Report of the Joint Commission*, 59–62, 99–112, 115–116, 135–136, 139–142, 150–155.

11. House, *Report of the Joint Commission*, 63, 115, 116–117, 138, 142, 156.

12. House, *Report of the Joint Commission*, 60–61.

13. House, *Report of the Joint Commission*, 102–103, 112.

14. House, *Report of the Joint Commission*, 138, 142, 150.

15. House, *Report of the Joint Commission*, 63, 113–117, 137, 145, 155–156.

16. House, *Report of the Joint Commission*, 1. The *Congressional Record* reveals only that the *Report of the Joint Commission* was not reported out of committee. A search of the following record groups in the National Archives revealed nothing about the *Report* after it was referred to the Committee on Merchant Marine and Fisheries: Record Group 113, Records of the United States House of Representatives, Committee Papers of the Committee on Merchant Marine and Fisheries, 1897–1907; Record Group 59, General Records of the Depart-

ment of State, Reports of the Secretary of State to the President and Congress; M179, Miscellaneous Letters of the Secretary of State to the President and Congress; and M179, Miscellaneous Letters of the Secretary of State; and Record Group 22, Fish and Wildlife Service, including Records of the Commissioner of Fish and Fisheries.

17. Canada, *Sessional Papers,* 1892, no. 11, lxiii–lxiv; 1893, no. 10, 86; 1894, no. 11*, xxxiv, lxiii; 1896, no. 11A, xiii–xv; 1897, no. 11A, xxi–xxii. For the optimistic statement of 1892, Canada, *Sessional Papers,* 1893, no. 10, 86. Canada, House of Commons, *Debates,* 14 September 1896, 1144–1170. For sharp criticism by the Michigan Board of Fish Commissioners of the way the Great Lakes states managed fish resources, see Department of Marine and Fisheries, "Annual Report," 1897, in Canada, *Sessional Papers,* 1898, no. 11A, x–xi.

CHAPTER 16: COMMERCIAL FISHING: FROM PROSPERITY TO RECESSION

1. Norman S. Baldwin, Robert W. Saalfeld, Margaret A. Ross, and Howard J. Buettner, *Commercial Fish Production in the Great Lakes, 1867–1977,* Technical Report no. 3 (Ann Arbor, Mich.: Great Lakes Fishery Commission, 1979), 32; Alan B. McCullough, *The Commercial Fishery of the Canadian Great Lakes* (Ottawa: Environment Canada, 1989), 58, 62–63; Frank Prothero, *The Good Years: A History of the Commercial Fishing Industry on Lake Erie* (Belleville, Ont.: Mika, 1973), 16–30, 41.

2. U.S. Commission of Fish and Fisheries, *Report,* 1901, Appendix, 57th Cong., 1st sess., 1901, H. Doc. 705 (Serial 4391), 575–657; U.S. Commissioner of Fisheries, *Report,* 1904, Appendix, 58th Cong., 3d sess., H. Doc. 479 (Serial 4897), 643–731; *Report,* 1919 (Washington, D.C.: Government Printing Office, 1920), Appendix 10, 52–126; and *Report,* 1924 (Washington, D.C., Government Printing Office, 1925), Appendix 4, 275–357.

3. Walter Koelz, "Fishing Industry of the Great Lakes," in U.S. Commissioner of Fisheries, *Report,* 1925 (Washington, D.C.: Government Printing Office, 1926), Appendix 11, 591–592.

4. Capital invested was compiled from Canada, *Sessional Papers,* 1901, no. 22, 181; 1905, no. 22, 198–199; 1910, no. 22, 228–229; Ontario, *Sessional Papers,* 1919, no. 14, 30–31; 1923, no. 14, 46–47; U.S. Commission of Fish and Fisheries, *Report,* 1901, Appendix, 579; U.S. Commissioner of Fisheries, *Report,* 1904, Appendix, 647–649; *Report,* 1919, Appendix 10, 55–56; *Report,* 1924, Appendix 4, 278; and U.S. Department of Commerce, Bureau of the Census, *Fisheries of the United States: 1908,* Special Report (Washington, D.C.: Government Printing Office, 1911), 12. Price index used for Canadian data is M. C. Urquhart and K. A. H. Buckley, *Historical Statistics of Canada* (Toronto: Macmillan, 1965), 295, "Wholesale Price Indexes" (1926 = 100), and for United States data is U.S. Bureau of the Census, *Historical Statistics of the United States: Colonial Times to 1970,* Bicentennial ed., 93d Cong., 1st sess., 1973, H. Doc. 93–78 , part 1, "Wholesale Price Indexes (BLS)" (1926 = 100), 200.

5. U.S. Commission of Fish and Fisheries, *Report,* 1900, 56th Cong., 2d sess., 1900, H. Doc. 541 (Serial 4196), 178, and *Report,* 1902, 57th Cong., 2d sess.,

1902, H. Doc. 485 (Serial 4550), 128–130, 153; U.S. Commissioner of Fisheries, *Report,* 1904, 4, and *Report,* 1919, 36; Canada, *Sessional Papers,* 1914, no. 22, 255; Baldwin, Saalfeld, Ross, and Buettner, *Commercial Fish Production,* 40–64.

6. U.S. Commission of Fish and Fisheries, *Report,* 1901, Appendix, 588–589; U.S. Commissioner of Fisheries, *Report,* 1904, Appendix, 647, and *Report,* 1919, Appendix 10, 121; Koelz, "Fishing Industry of the Great Lakes," 555–556.

7. Prothero, *Good Years,* 33, 96–98.

8. Koeltz, "Fishing Industry of the Great Lakes," 556, 558–559; U.S. Commissioner of Fisheries, *Report,* 1932 (Washington, D.C.: Government Printing Office, 1932), Appendix 3, 467; McCullough, *Commercial Fishery,* 30, 32.

9. Simon Fairlie, Mike Hagler, and Brian O'Riordan, "The Politics of Overfishing," *Ecologist* 25 (March–June 1995): 46–73.

10. U.S. Commission of Fish and Fisheries, *Report,* 1901, Appendix, 579; U.S. Commissioner of Fisheries, *Report,* 1904, Appendix, 647; *Report,* 1919, Appendix X, 53; and *Report,* 1924, Appendix 4, 278; Bureau of the Census, *Fisheries of the United States: 1908,* 14; Canada, *Sessional Papers,* 1901, no. 22, 181; 1905, no. 22, 198–199; 1910, no. 22, 228–229; Ontario, *Sessional Papers,* 1919, no. 14, 30–31; 1923, no. 14, 46–47.

11. Koelz, "Fishing Industry of the Great Lakes," 589.

12. Ontario Game and Fisheries Commission, "Final Report, 1909–1911," in Ontario, *Sessional Papers,* 1912, no. 52, 36–37.

13. Julian Ellefson, interview, 30 June 1978; George Ellefson, interview, 22 May 1978; Ray McDonald, interview, 28 April 1978; Harold Johnson, interview, 31 May 1978, Sea Grant Commercial Fishing Oral History Project, Interviews, 1978–1979. Archives, State Historical Society of Wisconsin, Madison.

14. "The New Fishery Trust," *New York Times,* 2 October 1898, 5; Articles of Incorporation, A. Booth and Company, 20 July 1898, Illinois Corporation Records, Illinois Secretary of State, Springfield; Charter, Dominion Fish Company, 27 July 1899, vol. 387, Records of the Corporation Branch, Record Group 95, National Archives of Canada, Ottawa.

15. Memorandum, E. E. Prince to Minister of Marine and Fisheries, 17 March 1898, file 471, part 1, frames 370–372, Microfilm Reel (hereafter cited as MReel) T-2846, Records of the Department of Marine and Fisheries, Record Group 23, National Archives of Canada.

16. Prince memorandum, 17 August 1898; newspaper clipping and letters, E. E. Prince and J. W. Cross, fishery overseer, Port Arthur, Ontario, 17 August and 14 September 1898, file 2753, part 1, frames 1–4, MReel T-4008, Records of the Department of Marine and Fisheries; Canada, *Sessional Papers,* 1900, no. 11a, 205; 1902, no. 22, 145.

17. Canada, House of Commons, *Debates,* 14 June 1899, 4993–4994; 23 May 1900, 5939–5943; 13 May 1909, 6475–6500; 28 January 1910, 2667.

18. Leighton McCarthy to Sir Louis Davies, 8 September 1900, file 1593, part 1, frames 294–295, MReel T-3168, Records of the Department of Marine and Fisheries.

19. McCarthy to Davies, 8 September 1900; extract from Privy Council report, 4 April 1901, file 1593, part 1, frames 361–364, MReel T-3168, Records of the Department of Marine and Fisheries.

20. M. Doyle Fish Company to Minister of Marine and Fisheries, 22 October 1901 and 30 October 1905, file 1241, part 1, frames 296, 481, MReel T- 3143; Captain Edward Dunn to Lieutenant Colonel F. Gourdeau, 12 September 1905, file 1593, part 2, frames 326–327, MReel T-3168, Records of the Department of Marine and Fisheries; Ontario Department of Fisheries, "Report," 1904, in *Sessional Papers,* 1905, no. 31, 30; Canada, *Sessional Papers,* 1905, no. 22, 299.

21. Ontario Game and Fisheries Commission, "Final Report," 34–38; Newspaper Cartoonists Association of Michigan, *Our Michigan Friends "As We See 'Em": A Gallery of Pen Sketches in Black and White* (Detroit: Press of William Graham Printing, 1905), 130, 215.

22. Petition, Collingwood Fishermen to the Minister of Marine and Fisheries, March 1906, file 1168, part 1, frames 325–327, MReel T-3134; Georgian Bay Fisheries Commission, *Report and Recommendations* (Ottawa: Government Printing Bureau, 1908), Appendix B, "Report on the Squaw Island Fishery Grievances," 42–50, file 1168, part 2, frames 52–56, MReel T-3135, Records of the Department of Marine and Fisheries.

23. U.S. District Court, Northern Illinois and Chicago, Bankruptcy Court Dockets, vol. 28, Case Files, Case 15846, National Archives Records Center, Great Lakes Region, Chicago; *Famous Booth Sea Foods: A Review of the Relation of the Booth Fisheries Company to the Fishing Industry* [publicity brochure] (1920s), Baker Library, Harvard University Graduate School of Business Administration, Boston. Although the publication is not dated, one of the contemporary photographs shows 1920s-model Booth company trucks.

24. McCullough, *Commercial Fishery,* 57–63.

25. U.S. Tariff Commission, *Lake Fish: A Study of the Trade between the United States and Canada in Fresh-Water Fish with Cost of Production Data,* Tariff Information Series, no. 36 (Washington, D.C.: Government Printing Office, 1927), 18.

26. U.S. Commissioner of Fisheries, *Report,* 1904, Appendix, 689.

27. McCullough, *Commercial Fishery,* 58.

28. Norman W. Larson, "History of Ehlers Store and Jones Marina Cornucopia, Wis.," *Historical Happenings,* Bayfield County Historical Society, vols. 10–11 (summer 1989 and 1990); Roy and Irene Hokenson, interview, 9 December 1981, Transcript, Apostle Islands National Lakeshore, Bayfield, Wisconsin; Grace Lee Nute, *Lake Superior,* American Lakes Series, ed. Milo M. Quaife (Indianapolis: Bobbs-Merrill, 1944), 194.

29. Bureau of the Census, *Fisheries of the United States: 1908,* 225; U.S. Tariff Commission, *Lake Fish,* 37–38, 42, 46.

30. U.S. Tariff Commission, *Lake Fish,* 42.

31. McCullough, *Commercial Fishery,* 59.

32. "Lake Erie" [handwritten manuscript], 136–145, Records of the Joint Commission Relative to the Preservation of the Fisheries in Waters Contiguous to Canada and the United States, Record Group 22, National Archives, College Park, Maryland.

33. McCullough, *Commercial Fishery,* 62–63; Prothero, *Good Years,* 128; U.S. Tariff Commission, *Lake Fish,* 130–131.

34. *Famous Booth Sea Foods.*

35. Charles Livingston Bull for the U.S. Food Administration, ca. 1918, reprint, National Archives; U.S. Commissioner of Fisheries, *Report,* 1917, 45–51; *Report,* 1918 (Washington, D.C.: Government Printing Office, 1919), 18–21, 29–38; and *Report,* 1919, 5–15; Canada, *Sessional Papers,* 1911, no. 22, lxxvi–lxxvii; 1915, no. 39, xv–xvi, 219–220; 1916, no. 39, xvi; 1917, no. 39, xvii; 1918, no. 39, xiv; Canada, House of Commons, *Debates,* 3 February 1916, 558–578, 582; Select Standing Committee on Marine and Fisheries, "Final Report," 4 May 1916, in Canada, House of Commons, *Journals,* 1916, Appendix 3, 1–3.

36. Ontario, *Sessional Papers,* 1918, no. 14, 6–7; 1919, no. 14, 8–9; 1920, no. 14, 8.

37. Ontario, *Sessional Papers,* 1916, no. 14, 5; 1917, no. 14, 5–7.

38. Quoted in Ontario, *Sessional Papers,* 1917, no. 14, 6.

39. Calculated from Baldwin, Saalfeld, Ross, and Buettner, *Commercial Fish Production,* 186–187.

CHAPTER 17: POLICY MAKERS AND THE EVER-WIDENING STAIN

1. U.S. Census Office, *Twelfth Census of the United States Taken in the Year 1900,* part 1, *Population* (Washington, D.C.: Government Printing Office, 1902); U.S. Department of Commerce, Bureau of the Census, *Thirteenth Census of the United States: 1910,* vol. 3, *Population* (Washington, D.C.: Government Printing Office, 1912); *Fourteenth Census of the United States: 1920,* vol. 2, *Population* (Washington, D.C.: Government Printing Office, 1922); and *Fifteenth Census of the United States: 1930,* vol. 3, *Population* (Washington, D.C.: Government Printing Office, 1932); *Census of Canada,* 1901, vol. 1, *Population* (Ottawa: Dawson, 1901); *Census of Canada,* 1911, vol. 1, *Areas and Population by Provinces* (Ottawa: King's Printer,1912); Dominion Bureau of Statistics, *Seventh Census of Canada,* 1931, vol. 2, *Population by Areas* (Ottawa: King's Printer, 1933).

2. U.S. Census Office, *Twelfth Census of the United States Taken in the Year 1900,* part 2, *Manufactures* (Washington, D.C.: Government Printing Office, 1902); U.S. Department of Commerce, Bureau of the Census, *Thirteenth Census of the United States: 1910,* vol. 9, *Manufactures* (Washington, D.C.: Government Printing Office, 1912); *Fourteenth Census of the United States: 1920,* vol. 9, *Manufactures, 1919* (Washington, D.C.: Government Printing Office, 1923); and *Fifteenth Census of the United States: 1930,* vol. 3, *Manufactures, 1929* (Washington, D.C.: Government Printing Office, 1933); *Census of Canada,* 1901, vol. 3, *Manufactures* (Ottawa: Dawson, 1905); *Census of Canada,* 1911, vol. 3, *Manufactures for 1910 as Enumerated in June 1911* (Ottawa: King's Printer, 1913); Dominion Bureau of Statistics, *The Manufacturing Industries of Canada, 1931, Summary Report* (Ottawa: King's Printer, 1933); U.S. Department of Commerce, Bureau of the Census, *Historical Statistics of the United States: Colonial Times to 1970,* Bicentennial ed., 93d Cong., 1st sess., 1973, H. Doc. 93–78, Part 1, 200; M. C. Urquhart and K. A. H. Buckley, *Historical Statistics of Canada* (Toronto: Macmillan, 1965), 295.

3. Joel Tarr, *The Search for the Ultimate Sink: Urban Pollution in Historical Perspective* (Akron, Ohio: University of Akron Press, 1996), 111–129; Upton Sinclair, *The Jungle* (1906; reprint, New York: New American Library, 1960), 97.

4. William Haynes, *American Chemical Industry,* vol. 3, *The World War I Period: 1912–1922* (New York: Van Nostrand, 1945), xiv; Edmund P. Russell III, "'Speaking of Annihilation': Mobilizing for War against Human and Insect Enemies, 1914–1945," *Journal of American History* 82 (March 1996): 1505–1529; Craig E. Colten and Peter N. Skinner, *The Road to Love Canal: Managing Industrial Waste before EPA* (Austin: University of Texas Press, 1996), 145–146.

5. Census Office, *Twelfth Census,* part 2, *Manufactures;* Bureau of the Census, *Thirteenth Census,* vol. 9, *Manufactures; Fourteenth Census,* vol. 9, *Manufactures; Fifteenth Census,* vol. 3, *Manufactures.*

6. Colten and Skinner, *Road to Love Canal;* Lois Marie Gibbs, *Love Canal: My Story* (Albany: State University of New York Press, 1981).

7. Department of Natural Resources, "Remedial Action Plan for TORCH LAKE Area of Concern" (Typescript, Department of Natural Resources, Lansing, Mich., 27 October 1987), 1–3, 44–49.

8. Quoted in O. W. Main, *The Canadian Nickel Industry: A Study in Market Control and Public Policy* (Toronto: University of Toronto Press, 1955), 24; Jamie Swift, *The Big Nickel: Inco at Home and Abroad* (Kitchener, Ont.: Between the Lines, 1977), 113; W. Keller and J. M. Gunn, *Effects of Sudbury Smelter Emissions on Lakes in Ontario: A Review and Update* (Sudbury: Ontario Cooperative Freshwater Ecology Unit, 1994), 1–2.

9. Ministry of the Environment, Spanish Harbour RAP Team, *The Spanish Harbour Area of Concern, Environmental Conditions and Problem Definition, Remedial Action Plan, Stage One* (Toronto: Ontario Ministry of the Environment, 1993), iv, 11; Peter George, "Ontario's Mining Industry, 1870–1940," in Ian M. Drummond, with contributions by Peter George, Kris Inwood, Peter W. Sinclair, and Tom Traves, *Progress without Planning: The Economic History of Ontario from Confederation to the Second World War* (Toronto: University of Toronto Press, 1987), 56–58; Swift, *Big Nickel,* 113–120; Donat Marc LeBourdais, *Sudbury Basin: The Story of Nickel* (Toronto: Ryerson Press, 1953); Christopher Armstrong, *The Politics of Federalism: Ontario's Relations with the Federal Government, 1867–1942* (Toronto: University of Toronto Press, 1981), 42–48. For a conclusive demonstration of the long-term effects of metallic mine wastes in the environment, see Mats Eklund, *Reconstructions of Historical Metal Emissions and Their Dispersion in the Environment,* Linkoping Studies in Arts and Science, no. 127 (Linkoping, Sweden: Linkoping University, 1995).

10. Thomas H. Langlois, *The Western End of Lake Erie and Its Ecology* (Ann Arbor, Mich.: Edwards, 1954), 409–421.

11. Walter Koelz, "Fishing Industry of the Great Lakes," in U.S. Commissioner of Fisheries, *Report,* 1925 (Washington, D.C.: Government Printing Office, 1926), Appendix 11, 610; International Joint Commission, *Final Report on the Pollution of Boundary Waters Reference* (Washington, D.C.: Government Printing Office, 1918), 7, 19, 45.

12. Edward E. Prince, "Water Pollutions as Affecting Fisheries," in Canada, *Sessional Papers,* 1900, no. 11a, "Special Appended Reports," lxix; U.S. Commissioner of Fisheries, *Report,* 1929 (Washington, D.C.: Government Printing Office, 1929), Appendix 10, 712.

13. Prince, "Water Pollutions," lix, liii–lviii, lxiii–lxvii. For Prince's further

investigations and ideas on sawdust pollution, see Canada, *Sessional Papers,* 1907, no. 22a, 37–54, 111–119.

14. Prince, "Water Pollutions," lvii–lix, lxiv, lxvii.

15. Nelson Manfred Blake, *Water for the Cities: A History of the Urban Water Supply Problem in the United States* (Syracuse, N.Y.: Syracuse University Press, 1956), 260–263; Stuart Galishoff, "Triumph and Failure: The American Response to the Urban Water Supply Problem, 1860–1923," in *Pollution and Reform in American Cities, 1870–1930,* ed. Martin V. Melosi (Austin: University of Texas Press, 1980), 35–57; International Joint Commission, *Progress Report of the International Joint Commission on the Reference by the United States and Canada in Re the Pollution of Boundary Waters, Jan. 16, 1914* (Washington, D.C.: Government Printing Office, 1914), 14.

16. Canada, House of Commons, *Journals,* 1915, Appendix 1, 18–21, 28–29, 40–41, 46–47, 61, 173, 188–189, 207–209.

17. Quoted in Tarr, *Search for the Ultimate Sink,* 166.

18. *United States Statues at Large, 1919,* 36:2448–2455; International Joint Commission, *Progress Report,* 1, 3–15; *Final Report* 41, 46, 52; and *Activities Report, 1986* (Washington, D.C.: International Joint Commission, 1986), 19.

19. Blake, *Water for the Cities,* 260–263; Colten and Skinner, *Road to Love Canal,* 31–36.

20. *Colonial Laws of Massachusetts* (1672; reprint, Boston: City Council of Boston, 1887), 53; Canada, *Statutes,* 1st Parl., 1st sess., 1868, Part 2, 185; Canada, *Statutes,* 17th Parl., 3d sess., 1932, 1:181; *Revised Statutes of Canada* (Ottawa: King's Printer, 1906), 1:727.

21. Ohio, *Laws,* 1888, 268–269, 286–287; 1908, 74–77; Ohio Fish and Game Commission, *Fourteenth Annual Report,* 1889, in Ohio, *Executive Documents,* 1889, Part 2, 506, and *Twentieth Annual Report,* 1895, in Ohio, *Executive Documents,* 1895, Part 2, 351.

22. R. Peter Gillis, "Rivers of Sawdust: The Battle over Industrial Pollution in Canada, 1865–1903," *Journal of Canadian Studies* 21 (spring 1986): 86.

23. Gillis, "Rivers of Sawdust," 84–103; "Sawdust Pollution, Sault Ste. Marie District, 1894–1910," file 1324, part 1, Microfilm Reel (hereafter cited as MReel) T-3149; Thessalon River sawdust pollution, file 502, part 1, frames 518–525, MReel T-2848; Grand River sawdust pollution, file 1472, part 1, MReel T-3160; mill owner protests sawdust regulations, file 1669, parts 1 and 2, MReel T-3179, Records of the Department of Marine and Fisheries, Record Group 23, National Archives of Canada, Ottawa.

24. O. B. Sheppard, fishery inspector, to William R. Venning, Commissioner of Fisheries, 18 October 1897, file 294, part 1, frame 245, MReel T-2826, Records of the Department of Marine and Fisheries; Ontario, *Sessional Papers,* 1905, no. 31, 46; 1909, no. 32, 20; 1911, no. 13, 48; 1912, no. 13, 19; 1913, no. 13, 20; 1914, no. 14, 22.

25. Quoted in Ontario, *Sessional Papers,* 1908, no. 32, 21.

26. Quoted in Ontario, *Sessional Papers,* 1912, no. 13, 48.

27. Quoted in Ontario, *Sessional Papers,* 1915, no. 14, 23.

28. Ontario, *Sessional Papers,* 1917, no. 14, 13; 1918, no. 14, 8–9.

29. Quoted in Ontario, *Sessional Papers,* 1912, no. 13, 6.

30. For Grand River pollution, see file 1625, part 1, frames 3–48, MReel T-3171, Records of the Department of Marine and Fisheries; Ontario Department of Fisheries, "Report," 1905, in Ontario, *Sessional Papers,* 1906, no. 31, 14–15, and "Report," 1906, in Ontario, *Sessional Papers,* 1907, no. 33, 9–10; Ontario Department of Game and Fisheries, "Report," 1909, in Ontario, *Sessional Papers,* 1910, no. 13, 8–9.

31. David Jolly, Jr., to O. B. Sheppard, 24 August 1911; William A. Found to O. B. Sheppard, 25 August 1911; O. B. Sheppard to the Mayor of Waterloo, 29 August 1911, file 2394, part 1, frames 93–95, 99, MReel T-3988; A. Johnson to E. Tinsley, 10 January 1912; E. Tinsley to A. Johnson, 2 February 1912, file 319, part 1, frames 318, 323–324, MReel T-2827, Records of the Department of Marine and Fisheries.

32. T. J. Foster to William A. Found, 9 November 1912, file 502, part 2, frames 374–375, MReel T-2848; extract from report of T. J. Foster, 9 November 1912; A. Johnson, Deputy Minister of Marine and Fisheries, to Standard Chemical Company, 20 November 1912; T. J. Foster to William A. Found, 25 November 1912; George Grosbeley [?], Standard Chemical Iron and Lumber Company, to Deputy Minister of Marine and Fisheries, 27 November 1912; J. D. Hazen, Department of Marine and Fisheries, to R. H. Pope, the Senate, 18 December 1912; T. McKenney, game and fishery overseer, Thornbury, Ontario, to T. J. Foster, inspector of fisheries, Sault Sainte Marie, Ontario, [November or December] 1912; A. McGill to William Hamsworth, 1 January 1913; T. McKenney to T. J. Foster, 28 July 1913; T. McKenney to T. J. Foster, 27 August 1913, file 4237, part 1, frames 2–3, 5–7, 11–12, 17, 31, 33, MReel T-3392, Records of the Department of Marine and Fisheries; Colten and Skinner, *Road to Love Canal,* 7.

33. E. Tinsley, Superintendent, Ontario Department of Game and Fisheries, to C. Stranton, Acting Deputy Minister of Marine and Fisheries, 12 January 1914, file 3387, part 1, frame 43, MReel T-3371, Records of the Department of Marine and Fisheries.

34. U.S. Commissioner of Fisheries, *Report,* 1921 (Washington, D.C.: Government Printing Office, 1921), Appendix 7, 1–7, and *Report,* 1925 (Washington, D.C.: Government Printing Office, 1925), Appendix 5, 171–181.

35. U.S. Commissioner of Fisheries, *Report,* 1927 (Washington, D.C.: Government Printing Office, 1927), 1927, Appendix 7, 665, and *Report,* 1922 (Washington, D.C.: Government Printing Office, 1922), Appendix 13, 23–24.

36. Peter Doudoroff and Max Katz, "Critical Review of Literature on the Toxicity of Industrial Wastes and Their Components to Fish," *Sewage and Industrial Wastes* 22 (November 1950): 1432–1458.

37. Koelz, "Fishing Industry of the Great Lakes," 609–610.

38. U.S. Commissioner of Fisheries, *Report,* 1922, Appendix 13, 23; Frank N. Edgerton, "Pollution and Aquatic Life in Lake Erie: Early Scientific Studies," *Environmental Review* 11 (fall 1987): 189–205.

CHAPTER 18: PUBLIC POLICY AND THE DECLINING FISH RESOURCE

1. For a broad treatment of sportsmen and the conservation movement, see John F. Reiger, *American Sportsmen and the Origins of Conservation* (New York:

Winchester Press, 1975); Robert Doherty, *Disputed Waters: Native Americans and the Great Lakes Fishery* (Lexington: University of Kentucky Press, 1990).

2. Stephen Bocking, "Stephen Forbes, Jacob Reighard, and the Emergence of Aquatic Ecology in the Great Lakes Region," *Journal of the History of Biology* 23 (fall 1990): 478–485.

3. U.S. Commission of Fish and Fisheries, *Report,* 1897, 55th Cong., 2d sess., 1897, H. Doc. 299 (Serial 3687), xcix–c, and *Report,* 1898, 55th Cong., 3d sess., 1898, H. Doc. 221 (Serial 3816), cxlii–cxliii.

4. Bocking, "Stephen Forbes, Jacob Reighard," 484–494.

5. U.S. Commission of Fish and Fisheries, *Report,* 1899, 56th Cong., 1st sess., 1899, H. Doc. 692 (Serial 4001), xxi, cxix–cxxi; *Report,* 1900, 56th Cong., 2d sess., 1900, H. Doc. 541 (Serial 4196), 131–132; *Report,* 1901, 57th Cong., 1st sess., 1901, H. Doc. 705 (Serial 4391), 113–116; and *Report,* 1902, 57th Cong., 2d sess., 1902, H. Doc. 485 (Serial 4550), 127–128; Canada, *Sessional Papers,* 1914, no. 22, xiv; Elmer Higgins, "The Policy of the Bureau of Fisheries with Regard to Biological Investigations," in U.S. Commissioner of Fisheries, *Report,* 1927 (Washington, D.C.: Government Printing Office, 1928), Appendix 7, Part 2, 590.

6. U.S. Commissioner of Fisheries, *Report,* 1919 (Washington, D.C.: Government Printing Office, 1921), 5–15.

7. U.S. Commissioner of Fisheries, *Report,* 1921 (Washington, D.C.: Government Printing Office, 1921), 30, and *Report,* 1922 (Washington, D.C.: Government Printing Office, 1922), 6–7; Walter Koelz, "Fishing Industry of the Great Lakes," in U.S. Commissioner of Fisheries, *Report,* 1925 (Washington, D.C.: Government Printing Office, 1926), Appendix 9, 590–592.

8. Willis R. Rich, "Progress in Biological Inquiries Fiscal Year 1924," in U.S. Commissioner of Fisheries, *Report,* 1924 (Washington, D.C.: Government Printing Office, 1925), Appendix 2, 14–16. [Italics added]

9. Rich, "Progress in Biological Inquiries," 24; U.S. Commissioner of Fisheries, *Report,* 1925, xx, Appendix 3, 38, 49, and *Report,* 1926 (Washington, D.C.: Government Printing Office, 1926), Appendix 1, 15.

10. Elmer Higgins, "Progress in Biological Inquiries, 1927," in U.S. Commissioner of Fisheries, *Report,* 1928 (Washington, D.C.: Government Printing Office, 1928), Appendix 6, 245, 247; U.S. Commissioner of Fisheries, *Report,* 1927, xxv.

11. For a review of the work in Canada, see Edward E. Prince, "Marine Biological Station of Canada," in Canada, *Sessional Papers,* 1902, no. 22a, 1–8.

12. Louis Agassiz, *Lake Superior: Its Physical Character, Vegetation, and Animals, Compared with Those of Other and Similar Regions* (1850; reprint, New York: Arno Press, 1970), 246–377; Dean Conrad Allard, Jr., *Spencer Fullerton Baird and the U.S. Fish Commission* (New York: Arno Press, 1978), 111–163.

13. Alan B. McCullough, *The Commercial Fishery of the Canadian Great Lakes* (Ottawa: Environment Canada, 1989), 90–91; Canada, *Sessional Papers,* 1902, no. 22a, 1; Kenneth Johnstone, *The Aquatic Explorers: A History of the Fisheries Research Board of Canada* (Toronto: University of Toronto Press, 1977), 25–26.

14. Canada, *Sessional Papers,* 1872, no. 5, 68; 1901, no. 22, xi–xii; Canada, House of Commons, *Debates,* 10 June 1898, 7733.

15. Canada, House of Commons, *Debates,* 15 May 1901, 5197–5198; *Canadian Government Publications, 1953 Consolidated Annual Catalogue* (Ottawa: Queen's Printer, 1953), 181–182; Canada, *Sessional Papers,* 1903, no. 22, xvi–xvii; 1904, no. 22, vi; 1905, no. 22, xv; 1906, no. 22, xviii–xix; 1907, no. 22, xv–xvi; 1908, no. 22, xxi–xxii; 1909, no. 22, xx–xxi; 1910, no. 22, xxiv–xxvi; 1911, no. 22, xiv; Biological Board of Canada, *Contributions to Canadian Biology Being Studies from the Biological Stations of Canada, 1911–1914, Fasciculus II—Fresh Water Fish and Lake Biology,* in Canada, *Sessional Papers,* 1915, no. 39b.

16. Canada, *Sessional Papers,* 1912, no. 22, xv; McCullough, *Commercial Fishery,* 91; Ontario, *Sessional Papers,* 1927, no. 9, 4–5; 1928, no. 9, 4–6; 1929, no. 9, 5–12.

17. Department of Marine and Fisheries, "Report," in *Annual Departmental Reports,* 1925–1926, vol. 3, Appendix 2, 80–81.

18. Higgins, "Policy of the Bureau of Fisheries," 593–594.

19. Christopher Armstrong, *The Politics of Federalism: Ontario's Relations with the Federal Government, 1867–1942* (Toronto: University of Toronto Press, 1981), 8–53; Ontario Game and Fisheries Commission, "Final Report, 1909–1911," in Ontario, *Sessional Papers,* 1912, no. 52, 51.

20. For a detailed statement of the legal maneuvering between the governments of Ontario and Canada from 1885 to 1898, see McCullough, *Commercial Fishery,* 94–95. Documents relating to the details of the struggle are in file 94, part 1, Microfilm Reel (hereafter cited as MReel) T- 2718; file 120, part 3, MReel T-2727; file 164, parts 1–5, MReels T-2736 and T-2737; file 1241, part 2, MReel T-3134; and file 2787, part 1, MReel T-4012, Records of the Department of Marine and Fisheries, Record Group 23, National Archives of Canada, Ottawa.

21. John Beck, provincial fishery overseer, Selkirk, Ontario, to O. B. Sheppard, Dominion inspector, 17 July, 11 and 25 October 1911; E. Tinsley, Ontario Superintendent of Fisheries, to A. Johnston, Deputy Minister of Marine and Fisheries, 25 June 1912, file 319, part 1, frames 303, 306, 310, 330–332, MReel T-2827; A. Johnston to E. Tinsley, 3 July 1912, file 319, part 1, frame 334, MReel T-2828; E. Tinsley, Ontario Superintendent of Fisheries, to A. Johnston, Deputy Minister of Marine and Fisheries, 15 January, 26 November 1912; Order in Council, 27 December 1912; A. Johnson to E. Tinsley, 10 January 1913, file 565, part 1, frames 568, 573–575, 578–579, MReel T-2852; J. D. Hazen to R. J. Ball, 4 June 1913, file 165, part 5, frame 2122, MReel T-2739, Records of the Department of Marine and Fisheries; Canada, *Sessional Papers,* 1909, no. 22, 246; 1914, no. 22, 254–256, 358, 362–363, 376–380; 1916, no. 14, 5; *Statutes of Canada,* 1921, xiv; Canada, House of Commons, *Debates,* 1914, 1916; Ontario, *Sessional Papers,* 1915, no. 14, 7; 1917, no. 14, 5; 1919, no. 14, 7; 1920, no. 14, 7; 1927, no. 9, 4–5; 1928, no. 9, 4–6; 1930, no. 36, 14–16.

22. E. Pauline Johnson, "Canadian Born," in *Flint and Feather: The Complete Poems of E. Pauline Johnson (Tekahionwake)* (1912; reprint, Toronto: Hodder and Stoughton, 1969), 84.

23. Georgian Bay Fisheries Commission, *Report and Recommendations* (Ottawa: Government Printing Bureau, 1908), 20–23, file 1168, part 2, frames 28–59, MReel T-3135, Records of the Department of Marine and Fisheries.

24. Ontario Game and Fisheries Commission, "Final Report," 30, 34–35, 39, 46–48, 50, 52, 54.

25. The very detailed correspondence, memoranda, and news clippings on American poaching are in file 1593, parts 1–3, MReel T-3168, and file 1594, part 1, MReel T-3169; E. E. Prince to Minister of Marine and Fisheries, 14 October 1902, file 1593, part 1, frame 413, MReel T-3168, Records of the Department of Marine and Fisheries; Canada, *Sessional Papers,* 1903, no. 22, 280–281.

26. Canada, *Sessional Papers,* 1904, no. 22, 296–297; correspondence, memoranda, and news clippings on the *Silver Spray* incident in August 1903: Captain E. Dunn to Colonel F. Gourdeau, 20 August 1903; Captain E. Dunn to E. E. Prince, 24 September 1903; Captain E. Dunn to Captain O. G. V. Spain, 30 September 1903, file 1593, part 2, frames 104–114, 169, 174, MReel, T-3168, Records of the Department of Marine and Fisheries.

27. Extended documentation on the *Kitty D* incident is in file 1593, part 2, MReel T-3168, Records of the Department of Marine and Fisheries.

28. Canada, *Sessional Papers,* 1905, no. 22, 299; Captain Edward Dunn to Lieutenant Colonel F. Gourdeau, Deputy Minister of Marine and Fisheries, 7 June 1905; Memorandum, R. W. Venning, "Re Sunken United States Fishing Tug 'Grace M,'" 20 February 1906; correspondence, statements, and memoranda on the *Grace M* incident, file 1593, part 2, frames 295–296, 362–363, 297–361, MReel T-3168; Ontario Superintendent of Game and Fisheries to Deputy Minister of Marine and Fisheries, 5 May 1911, file 1593, part 3, frame 137, MReel T-3169, Records of the Department of Marine and Fisheries.

29. Quoted in Canada, *Sessional Papers,* 1903, no. 22, 281.

30. U.S. Commissioner of Fisheries, *Report,* 1904, 58th Cong., 3d sess., 1904, H. Doc. 479 (Serial 4897), 8–13, and *Report,* 1911 (Washington, D.C.: Government Printing Office, 1912), 18.

31. Ohio Commissioners of Fish and Game, *Annual Report,* 1904 (Columbus: State Printer, 1905), 3–5; quoted in John Van Oosten, "Michigan's Commercial Fisheries of the Great Lakes," *Michigan History Magazine* 22 (winter 1938): 136; U.S. Commissioner of Fisheries, *Report,* 1905, 59th Cong., 1st sess., 1905, H. Doc. 717 (Serial 4989), 11–12.

32. Ontario Game and Fisheries Commission, "Final Report," 50–51.

33. Elihu Root, Secretary of State, to Sir H. M. Durand, British ambassador to the United States, 15 March 1906, file 3214, part 1, frames 11–12, MReel T-4054, Records of the Department of Marine and Fisheries.

34. James Morton Callahan, *American Foreign Policy in Canadian Relations* (New York: Cooper Square, 1967), 457–459, 510–512; text of treaty, 11 April 1908, box 1, Records Concerning Relations with Canada International Fisheries Commission, Record Group 22, National Archives, College Park, Maryland.

35. The Canadian documents on the struggle are found primarily in file 3214, parts 1–3, MReels T-4054 and T-4055, Records of the Department of Marine and Fisheries; Canada, House of Commons, *Debates,* 1909–1912; and Department of Marine and Fisheries, "Reports," in Canada, *Sessional Papers,* 1910–1915. The American documents are in boxes 1–3, Records Concerning Relations with Canada; General Records of the Department of State, Record Group 59, Numerical File [microfilmed], M862, reel 602; Decimal File, 711.428, boxes

6635–6637, National Archives; U.S. Commissioner of Fisheries, *Reports,* 1908–1911, 1914–1915.

36. David Starr Jordan to Elihu Root, 1 January 1909, Numerical File, M862, reel 602, frames 535–536, General Records of the Department of State.

37. *Statutes of Canada,* 1910, 182; Canada, House of Commons, *Debates,* 1 February 1909, 379–384; 26 and 31 March 1909, 3445–3450, 3687–3702; 13 and 18 May 1909, 6501–6510, 6961–6979; 14 March 1911, 5218–5233; Deputy Minister of Marine and Fisheries to Under Secretary of State for External Affairs, 13 June 1914, file 3214, part 3, frames 132–137, MReel T-4055, Records of the Department of Marine and Fisheries.

38. David Starr Jordan to Huntington Wilson, Department of State, 16 June 1910; David Starr Jordan to Philander C. Knox, Secretary of State, 9 July, 16 December 1910; correspondence of protest, 18 February–5 April 1910, Decimal File, 711.428, box 6635, General Records of the Department of State; Robert Beutel and Company to David Starr Jordan, president of Stanford University, 15 February 1910; Barton W. Evermann, Bureau of Fisheries, to David Starr Jordan, 23 February 1910, file 3214, part 2, frames 50–51, 61–65, MReel T-4054, Records of the Department of Marine and Fisheries.

39. The Saginaw Bay issue is spelled out in detail in correspondence among Edward E. Prince, David Starr Jordan, and the British ambassador to the United States, February–March 1910, file 3214, part 2, frames 14–49, MReel T-4054, Records of the Department of Marine and Fisheries.

40. Memorandum re International Fisheries Treaty, 1911, box 2, Records Concerning Relations with Canada, International Fisheries Commission, Record Group 22; Senate Bill 6119, box 6635; Memorandum, Office of Counsellor to Diplomatic Bureau, 18 April, 1911, box 6636, Decimal File 711.428, General Records of the Department of State, Record Group 59, National Archives.

41. U.S. Senate and House bill, 5 February 1914; telegram, C. W. Wilson to James Hazen, Minister of Marine and Fisheries, 25 February 1914; clippings, "Snag for Fishery Treaty," *New York Times,* 14 March 1914, and "Canada to Draft New Fishery Regulations," *Halifax Morning Chronicle,* 1 October 1914, file 3214, part 3, frames 22–29, 36–43, 73, 113, 151, MReel T-4055, Records of the Department of Marine and Fisheries.

42. Memorandum, Edward E. Prince, 23 February 1914, file 3214, part 3, frames 99–105, MReel T-4055, Records of the Department of Marine and Fisheries; McCullough, *Commercial Fishery,* 96.

CHAPTER 19: THE END OF AN ERA

1. These problems are spelled out in great detail in petitions and correspondence in file 120, part 3, frames 314–515, and part 4, frames 9–18, Microfilm Reel (hereafter cited as MReel) T-2727; request for Order in Council, 6 August 1904, file 1168, part 1, frames 181–182, MReel T-3134, Records of the Department of Marine and Fisheries, Record Group 23, National Archives of Canada, Ottawa; Canada, *Sessional Papers,* 1909, no. 22, xiv.

2. Georgian Bay Fisheries Commission, *Report and Recommendations* (Ot-

tawa: Government Printing Bureau, 1908), 3–11: gill-net mileage, 16; whitefish, trout, and sturgeon, 9–11.

3. Georgian Bay Fisheries Commission, *Report and Recommendations,* 12–32.

4. Georgian Bay Fisheries Commission, *Report and Recommendations,* 28.

5. Quoted in Georgian Bay Fisheries Commission, *Report and Recommendations,* 33.

6. *Laws of Canada,* 1910, 181; *Statutes of Canada,* 1919, 1:clii; 1921, xiv; 1922, cxxii.

7. Walter Koelz, "Fishing Industry of the Great Lakes," in U.S. Commissioner of Fisheries, *Report,* 1925 (Washington, D.C.: Government Printing Office, 1926), Appendix 11, 586–601.

8. Norman S. Baldwin, Robert W. Saalfeld, Margaret A. Ross, and Howard J. Buettner, *Commercial Fish Production in the Great Lakes, 1867–1977,* Technical Report no. 3 (Ann Arbor, Mich.: Great Lakes Fishery Commission, 1979), 32; Walter Koelz, "Fisheries of the Great Lakes, General Review," in U.S. Commissioner of Fisheries, *Report,* 1927 (Washington, D.C.: Government Printing Office, 1927), Appendix 7, 661.

9. U.S. Commissioner of Fisheries, *Report,* 1929 (Washington, D.C.: Government Printing Office, 1929), Appendix 10, 712.

10. Elmer Higgins, "Progress in Biological Inquiries, 1931," in U.S. Commissioner of Fisheries, *Report,* 1932 (Washington, D.C.: Government Printing Office, 1932), Appendix 3, 468–469; Stillman Wright and Wilbur M. Tidd, "Summary of Limnological Investigations in Western Lake Erie in 1929 and 1930," *Transactions of the American Fisheries Society* 63 (1933): 27–285; Elmer Higgins, "Progress in Biological Inquiries, 1926," in U.S. Commissioner of Fisheries, *Report,* 1927, Appendix 7, 662.

11. U.S. Commissioner of Fisheries, *Report,* 1928 (Washington, D.C.: Government Printing Office, 1928), v, xi, Appendix 6, 219–220, and *Report,* 1929, v, Appendix 10, 642, 712.

12. U.S. Commissioner of Fisheries, *Report,* 1927, vii; "Second Great Lakes Fisheries Conference, Lansing, Michigan, Feb. 8, 1928," Commercial Fishing Materials, Box 15, Department of Natural Resources, Record Group 75–34, Michigan State Archives, Lansing; John Van Oosten, "Michigan's Commercial Fisheries of the Great Lakes," *Michigan History Magazine* 22 (winter 1938): 137.

13. The formation of the advisory committee and the Toronto Agreement are discussed in Van Oosten, "Michigan's Commercial Fisheries," 137–138.

14. Tom Kuchenberg and Jim Legault, *Reflections in a Tarnished Mirror: The Use and Abuse of the Great Lakes* (Sturgeon Bay, Wis.: Golden Glow, 1978), 52–54; Robert Thomas Allen, *The Illustrated Natural History of Canada: The Great Lakes* (Toronto: McClelland, 1970), 131; B. A. Bensley, "The Fishes of Georgian Bay," in Canada, *Sessional Papers,* 1915, no. 39b, 10.

CHAPTER 20: REFLECTIONS

Some of the material in this chapter appeared in Margaret Beattie Bogue, "To Save the Fish: Canada, the United States, the Great Lakes, and the Joint Commission of

1892," *Journal of American History* 79 (March 1993): 1429–1454. It is used with the permission of the Organization of American Historians.

1. Howell, "Food Supply of Fresh Waters," *Chicago Times,* 20 August 1881, 10.

2. U.S. Congress, Senate, Committee on Science, Commerce, and Transportation, *Treaties and Other International Agreements on Fisheries, Oceanographic Resources, and Wildlife Involving the United States,* Committee Print, 95th Cong., 1st sess., 1977, 729–822; Anthony Scott, "Fisheries, Pollution, and Canadian–American Transnational Relations," in *Canada and the United States: Transnational and Transgovernmental Relations,* ed. Annette Baker Fox, Alfred O. Hero, Jr., and Joseph S. Nye, Jr. (New York: Columbia University Press, 1976), 250–251; Kurkpatrick Dorsey, *The Dawn of Conservation Diplomacy: U.S.–Canadian Wildlife Protection Treaties in the Progressive Era* (Seattle: University of Washington Press, 1998), 103–104.

3. For the text of the treaty of 1909, see *United States Statutes at Large, 1909,* 36:2448–2455. For the Great Lakes Water Quality Agreement, see Senate, Committee on Commerce, Science, and Transportation, *Treaties and Other International Agreements,* 789–812. For the agreement of 1978, see Great Lakes Water Quality Agreement, 22 November 1978, in *United States Treaties and Other International Agreements* (Washington, D.C.: Government Printing Office, 1980), 30:Part 2, 1383–1397. The International Joint Commission's international projects, undertaken from 1912 to 1986, are found in International Joint Commission, *Activities Report* (Washington, D.C.: International Joint Commission, 1986), 19–24. See also Robert Spencer, John Kirton, and Kim Richard Nossal, eds., *The International Joint Commission Seventy Years On* (Toronto: Center for International Studies, 1981).

4. Canada, House of Commons, *Debates,* 13 June 1894, 4232–4233, 4240–4241, 4254, 4259–4261.

5. Harold A. Innis, *The Cod Fisheries: The History of an International Economy* (New Haven, Conn.: Yale University Press, 1940); James A. Crutchfield and Giulio Pontecorvo, *The Pacific Salmon Fisheries: A Study of Irrational Conservation* (Baltimore: Johns Hopkins University Press, 1969); Richard A. Cooley, *Politics and Conservation: The Decline of the Alaska Salmon* (New York: Harper & Row, 1963); Anthony Netboy, *The Salmon: Their Fight for Survival* (Boston: Houghton Mifflin, 1974), and *The Columbia River Salmon and Steelhead Trout: Their Fight for Survival* (Seattle: University of Washington Press, 1980); Briton Cooper Busch, *The War against the Seals: A History of the North American Seal Fishery* (Montreal: McGill–Queens University Press, 1985); Arthur F. McEvoy, *The Fisherman's Problem: Ecology and Law in the California Fisheries, 1850–1980* (New York: Cambridge University Press, 1986), 227–257; Dorsey, *Dawn of Conservation Diplomacy;* Harry N. Scheiber, "Pacific Ocean Resources, Science, and Law of the Sea: Wilbert M. Chapman and the Pacific Fisheries, 1945–70," *Ecology Law Quarterly* 13 (1986): 381–534.

6. Carl C. Berger, "Internationalism, Continentalism, and the Writing of History: Comments on the Carnegie Series on the Relations of Canada and the United States," in *The Influence of the United States on Canadian Development:*

Eleven Case Studies, ed. Richard A. Preston (Durham, N.C.: Duke University Press, 1972), 32–54. For expressions of Canada's pride in its regulated fishery policy, see Department of Marine and Fisheries, "Annual Reports," in Canada, *Sessional Papers,* 1876, no. 5, xxiv; 1892, no. 11, l–li; 1894, no. 11*, lxx; 1896, no. 11A, xiii–xv; 1898, no. 11A, x–xi.

7. Michael Parfit, "Diminishing Returns: Exploiting the Ocean's Bounty," *National Geographic,* November 1995, 2–37; "Overfishing: Its Causes and Consequences" [special issue] *Ecologist,* March–June 1995; Carl Safina "The World's Imperiled Fish," *Scientific American,* November 1995, 46–53.

Glossary of Fish Species

Alewife (*Alosa pseudoharengus*). Member of the herring family (pp. 162–163).

Black bass. Common name for largemouth bass (*Micropterus salmoides*), a member of the sunfish family and a very popular game fish.

Blackfin cisco (*Coregonus nigripinnis*). Commonly called blackfin, blackfin chub, and blackfin tullibee, a member of the trout family and a kind of lake herring, as it is popularly called.

Bluefin. *See* **Shortjaw cisco.**

Blue pickerel. *See* **Sauger.**

Blue pike. *See* **Sauger.**

Bowfin (*Amia calva*). Commonly called dogfish and lawyer, a member of the bowfin family.

Bullhead. Common name for black bullhead (*Ictalurus melas*) and brown bullhead (*I. nebulosus*), members of the bullhead catfish family.

Burbot (*Lota lota*). Commonly called lake lawyer, lawyer, and ling, a member of the cod family.

Carp. *See* **Common carp.**

Catfish. *See* **Channel catfish.**

Channel catfish (*Ictalurus punctatus*). Commonly called catfish, channel cat, Great Lakes catfish, and lake catfish, a member of the bullhead catfish family.

Chub. *See* **Blackfin cisco** and **Shortjaw cisco.**

Common carp (*Cyprinus carpio*). Commonly called carp, European carp, and German carp, a member of the minnow and carp family (pp. 164–166).

Dogfish. *See* **Bowfin.**

Drum. Common name for freshwater drum (*Aplodinotus grunniens*) and commonly called sheepshead, a member of the drum family.

German carp. *See* **Common carp.**

Grass pike. Common name for grass pickerel (*Esox americanus vermiculatus*), a member of the pike family.

Information for this glossary was derived from George C. Becker, *Fishes of Wisconsin* (Madison: University of Wisconsin Press, 1983).

Lake herring. Common name for cisco (*Coregonus artedii*), a freshwater member of the trout family (pp. 155–157).

Lake Ontario salmon (*Salmo salar*). Form of Atlantic salmon found in Lake Ontario in plentiful numbers as late as the 1840s, a member of the trout family (pp. 19–27, 175–178).

Lake sturgeon (*Acipenser fluvescens*). Member of the sturgeon family (pp. 157–161).

Lake trout (*Salvelinus namaycush namaycush*). Member of the trout family (pp. 153–155).

Lake whitefish (*Coregonus clupeaformis*). Member of the trout family, long popular as table fare (pp. 150–153).

Lamprey eel. *See* **Sea lamprey** and **Silver lamprey.**

Lawyer. *See* **Bowfin** and **Burbot.**

Ling. *See* **Burbot.**

Mullet. Common name for longnose sucker (*Catostomus catostomus*), quillback (*Carpiodes cyprinus*), and white sucker (*Catostomus commersoni*), members of the sucker family.

Muskellunge (*Esox masquinongy*). Member of the pike family, a popular game fish.

Northern pike (*Esox lucius*). Member of the pike family.

Pickerel. Common name for grass pickerel (*Esox americanus vermiculatus*), for members of the pike family, and for walleye, which is not a pike.

Pike. General designation for the pike family.

Sauger (*Stizostedion canadense*). Commonly called blue perchpike, blue pickerel, and blue pike, a member of the perch family.

Sea lamprey (*Petromyzon marinus*). Commonly called great sea lamprey, lake lamprey, lamprey eel, and landlocked sea lamprey, a member of the lamprey family (pp. 163–164, 328–330).

Sheepshead. *See* **Drum.**

Shortjaw cisco (*Coregonus zenithicus*). Commonly called bluefin, bluefin cisco, and shortjaw chub, a member of the trout family and a kind of lake herring, as it is popularly called.

Silver lamprey (*Ichthyomyzon unicuspis*). Commonly called bloodsucker, hitchhiker, lamprey eel, northern lamprey, and northern silver lamprey, a member of the lamprey family.

Smallmouth bass (*Micropterus dolomieui*). Commonly called smallmouth and smallmouth black bass, a member of the sunfish family.

Walleye (*Stizostedion vitreum vitreum*). Commonly called perchpike, pickerel, walleyed perchpike, and walleye pike, a member of the perch family.

Yellow perch (*Perca flavescens*). Commonly called lake perch, perch, and river perch, a member of the perch family.

Bibliography

MANUSCRIPTS

National Archives

National Archives of Canada, Ottawa

Records of the Department of Marine and Fisheries. Record Group 23. Microfilm Reels T-2665–T-4069. Great Lakes materials, 1884–1914.

Records of the Secretary of State. Record Group 95. Documents of Incorporation of the Dominion Fish Company.

Tupper, Sir Charles Hibbert. Correspondence, 1878–1926. Microfilm Reels M106–M109.

National Archives of the United States, Chicago, Illinois, Records Center

U.S. District Court of Northern Illinois and Chicago. Bankruptcy Case Files. Act of 1898.

National Archives of the United States, College Park, Maryland

General Records of the Department of State. Record Group 59. Decimal File, boxes 6635–6640. Numerical File, Microfilmed, M862, Reel 602, materials relative to treaty of 1908; Reports of the Secretary of State to the president and Congress, Report Books 19 and 20.

Records Concerning Relations with Canada, International Fisheries Commission. Record Group 22. Materials relative to treaty of 1908 between Great Britain and the United States, for "the protection, preservation, and propagation of the food fishes in the waters contiguous to the United States and the Dominion of Canada."

Records of the Joint Commission Relative to the Preservation of Fisheries in Waters Contiguous to Canada and the United States. Record Group 22. Great Lakes materials, 1893–1895. Fifty-eight volumes and eleven boxes, primarily field notes and transcribed interviews.

U.S. Congress. House of Representatives. Committee on Merchant Marine and Fisheries. Record Group 233. Records, 1896–1906.

State Archives

Archives of the Great Lakes states contain relatively few records relating to the fisheries before the 1920s, yet the few records, especially those of Michigan, add important information to the printed primary materials.

Illinois

Department of State. Articles of Incorporation of A. Booth and Company. Department of State, Springfield.

Michigan

Records of executive office, Board of Fish Commissioners, Department of Conservation, and Department of Natural Resources. Record Groups 44, 56–1, 60–12, 66–76A, 70–92, 75–34. Michigan State Archives, Lansing.

Minnesota

Game and Fish Commission. Game Warden's Reports and Letters, 1901–1906. Minnesota Historical Society, St. Paul.

Wisconsin

Miscellaneous unsorted correspondence, beginning 1909. State Documents. State Historical Society of Wisconsin, Madison.

Nevin, James [superintendent of Fitchburg Hatchery]. Diary, 1898. State Documents. State Historical Society of Wisconsin, Madison.

Wisconsin Fish Commission. Original Ledger, 1876–1900. State Documents. State Historical Society of Wisconsin, Madison.

Manuscript Collections

Kalmbach Family Papers. Green Bay Area Research Center, State Historical Society of Wisconsin, Green Bay.

R. G. Dun & Co. Collection, Baker Library, Harvard University Graduate School of Business Administration, Boston.

U.S. Department of the Interior. National Park Service. Menagerie Islet Light Station. Journal, 18 October 1875–15 November 1893. Isle Royale National Park, Museum Collection—Archives.

Interviews and Other Unpublished Materials

Hokenson, Roy and Irene. Interview, 9 December 1981. Apostle Islands National Lakeshore Library, Bayfield, Wisconsin.

LeClaire, Nelson J. Interview, 1960. Archives, State Historical Society of Wisconsin, Madison.

MacDonald, Graham Alexander. "The Saulteur-Ojibwa Fishery at Sault Ste. Marie, 1640–1920." Master's thesis, University of Waterloo, 1978.

University of Wisconsin College Sea Grant Program. Sea Grant Commercial Fishing Oral History Project. Interviews, 1978–1979. Archives, State Historical Society of Wisconsin, Madison.

Walstad, Justin. Interview, 16 July 1979. Apostle Islands National Lakeshore Library, Bayfield, Wisconsin.

PUBLISHED GOVERNMENT DOCUMENTS

Canada

Bensley, B. A. "The Fishes of Georgian Bay." In Canada, *Sessional Papers,* 1915, no. 39b, 1–51.

Biological Board. *Contributions to Canadian Biology Being Studies from the Biological Stations of Canada, 1911–1914, Fasciculus II—Fresh Water Fish and Lake Biology.* In Canada, *Sessional Papers,* 1915, no. 39b.

Canadian Government Publications, 1953 Consolidated Annual Catalogue. Ottawa: Queen's Printer, 1953.

Census of the Canadas, 1851–1852. Vols. 1–2. Quebec: Lovell, 1853, 1855.

Census of the Canadas, 1860–1861. Vols. 1–2. Quebec: Foote, 1863.

Census of Canada, 1870–1871. Vols. 1, 3. Ottawa: Taylor, 1873, 1875.

Census of Canada, 1880–1881. Vols. 1, 3. Ottawa: Maclean, Roger, 1882, 1883.

Census of Canada, 1901. Vols. 1, 3. Ottawa: Dawson, 1901, 1905.

Census of Canada, 1911. Vol. 1, *Areas and Population by Provinces.* Ottawa: King's Printer, 1912.

Census of Canada, 1911. Vol. 3, *Manufactures for 1910 as Enumerated in June 1911.* Ottawa: King's Printer, 1913.

Department of Marine and Fisheries. "Annual Reports." 1868–1929.

Dominion Bureau of Statistics. *The Manufacturing Industries of Canada, 1931, Summary Report.* Ottawa: King's Printer, 1933.

Dominion Bureau of Statistics. *Seventh Census of Canada,* 1931. Vol. 2, *Population by Areas.* Ottawa: King's Printer, 1933.

Dominion Fishery Commission on the Fisheries of the Province of Ontario. "Report." In Canada, *Sessional Papers,* 1893, no. 10C*.

Georgian Bay Fisheries Commission. *Report and Recommendations.* Ottawa: Government Printing Bureau, 1908.

House of Commons. *Debates,* 1869–1929.

House of Commons. *Journals,* 1867–1930.

House of Commons. Select Committee on Fisheries, Navigation, etc. "Seventh Report," 16 June 1869. In Canada, House of Commons, *Journal,* 1869, Appendix 3.

House of Commons. Select Standing Committee on Marine and Fisheries. "Final Report," 4 May 1916. In Canada, House of Commons, *Journal,* 1916, Appendix 3.

McCullough, Alan B. *The Commercial Fishery of the Canadian Great Lakes.* Ottawa: Environment Canada, 1989.

Prince, Edward E. "The Progress of Fish Culture in Canada." In Canada, *Sessional Papers,* 1906, no. 22, 89–108.
Prince, Edward E. "The Propagation and Planting of Predaceous Fish." In Canada, *Sessional Papers,* 1902, no. 22b, 7–19.
Prince, Edward E.. "Water Pollutions as Affecting Fisheries." In Canada, *Sessional Papers,* 1900, no. 11a, "Special Appended Reports," 1–26.
Provincial Statutes of Upper Canada. York: Lt. Gov., 1818.
Report of the Joint Commission Relative to the Preservation of the Fisheries in Waters Contiguous to Canada and the United States. In Canada, *Sessional Papers,* 1897, no. 11D.
Scott, W. B., and E. J. Crossman. *Freshwater Fishes of Canada.* Ottawa: Fisheries Research Board of Canada, 1973.
Sessional Papers, 1867–1929.
Statutes of Canada, 1867–1932.
Statutes of the Province of Canada, 1841–1866.

United States

Alexander, A. B. "Statistics of the Fisheries of the Great Lakes in 1903." In U.S. Commissioner of Fisheries. *Report,* 1904, Appendix. 58th Cong., 3d sess., 1904. H. Doc. 479 (Serial 4897).
Army Corps of Engineers. *Deposits of Sand in Portage Lake, Michigan.* 47th Cong., 2d sess., 1882. H. Doc. 85 (Serial 2110).
Army Corps of Engineers. *Portage Lake Canal.* 49th Cong., 2d sess., 1886. H. Ex. Doc. 105 (Serial 2482).
Bureau of the Census. *Fifteenth Census of the United States: 1930. Drainage of Agricultural Lands.* Washington, D.C.: Government Printing Office, 1932.
Bureau of the Census. *Fifteenth Census of the United States: 1930.* Vol. 3, *Manufactures, 1929.* Washington, D.C.: Government Printing Office, 1933.
Bureau of the Census. *Fifteenth Census of the United States: 1930.* Vol. 3, *Population.* Washington, D.C.: Government Printing Office, 1932.
Bureau of the Census. *Fisheries of the United States: 1908.* Special Report. Washington, D.C.: Government Printing Office, 1911.
Bureau of the Census. *Fourteenth Census of the United States: 1920.* Vol. 9, *Manufactures, 1919.* Washington, D.C.: Government Printing Office, 1923.
Bureau of the Census. *Fourteenth Census of the United States: 1920.* Vol. 2, *Population.* Washington, D.C.: Government Printing Office, 1922.
Bureau of the Census. *Thirteenth Census of the United States: 1910.* Vol. 9, *Manufactures.* Washington, D.C.: Government Printing Office, 1912.
Bureau of the Census. *Thirteenth Census of the United States: 1910.* Vol. 3, *Population.* Washington, D.C.: Government Printing Office, 1912.
Census Office. *Eighth Census. Manufactures of the United States in 1860.* Washington, D.C.: Government Printing Office, 1865.
Census Office. *Eighth Census. Population of the United States in 1860.* Washington, D.C.: Government Printing Office, 1864.
Census Office. *Report of the Statistics of Fisheries of the Great Lakes, 1879.* Washington, D.C.: Government Printing Office, 1881.

Census Office. *Report of the Statistics of Fisheries of the United States, 1890.* Washington, D.C.: Government Printing Office, 1894.

Census Office. *Report on the Manufactures of the United States at the Tenth Census, 1880.* Washington, D.C.: Government Printing Office, 1883.

Census Office. *Seventh Census of the United States, 1850.* Parts 1–2. Washington, D.C.: Government Printing Office, 1853.

Census Office. *Statistics of the Population of the United States at the Tenth Census, 1880.* Washington, D.C.: Government Printing Office, 1883.

Census Office. *Twelfth Census of the United States Taken in the Year 1900. Manufactures,* part 2, *States and Territories.* Washington, D.C.: Census Office, 1902.

Commission/Commissioner of (Fish and) Fisheries. *Annual Reports,* 1872–1933. 1872–1905 in U.S. Senate and House Docs.; 1906–1933 in Department of Commerce, Bureau of Fisheries, *Annual Reports.*

Congress. House of Representatives. *Report of the Joint Commission Relative to the Preservation of the Fisheries in Waters Contiguous to Canada and the United States.* 54th Cong., 2d sess., 1896. H. Doc. 315 (Serial 3534).

Congress. Senate. Committee on Commerce, Science, and Transportation. *Treaties and Other International Agreements on Fisheries, Oceanographic Resources, and Wildlife Involving the United States.* Committee Print. 95th Cong., 1st sess., 1977. Washington, D.C.: Government Printing Office, 1977.

Congressional Record. 1897–1915.

Department of Commerce. Bureau of the Census. *Historical Statistics of the United States: Colonial Times to 1970.* Bicentennial ed. 93d Cong., 1st sess., 1973. H. Doc. 93- 78, Part 1.

Department of the Interior. National Park Service. Apostle Islands National Lake Shore. *Special History Study: Family-Managed Commercial Fishing in the Apostle Islands during the 20th Century.* Bayfield, Wis.: U.S. Department of the Interior/National Park Service, n.d.

Donaldson, Thomas. *The Public Domain.* 47th Cong., 2d sess., 1882. H. Misc. Doc. 45, Part 4 (Serial 2158).

Fish Commission. *Bulletins.* Vols. 1–16.

Goode, George Brown. *The Fisheries and Fishery Industries of the United States.* 47th Cong., 1st sess., 1881 (Serials 1998–2003).

Higgins, Elmer. "The Policy of the Bureau of Fisheries with Regard to Biological Investigations." In U.S. Commissioner of Fisheries. *Report,* 1927, Appendix 7, 588–594. Washington, D.C.: Government Printing Office, 1928.

International Board of Inquiry for the Great Lakes Fisheries. *Report and Supplement.* Washington, D.C.: Government Printing Office, 1943.

Koelz, Walter. "Fishing Industry of the Great Lakes." In U.S. Commissioner of Fisheries. *Report,* 1925, Appendix 11. Washington, D.C.: Government Printing Office, 1926.

Kumlien, Ludwig. "The Fisheries of the Great Lakes." In G. Brown Goode. *The Fisheries and Fishing Industries of the United States.* Section 5. 47th Cong., 1st sess., 1881. S. Misc. Doc. 124 (Serial 2001), 757–769.

Milner, James W. "Report on the Fisheries of the Great Lakes: The Result of Inquiries Prosecuted in 1871 and 1872." In U.S. Commission of Fish and Fisheries. *Report,* 1872–1873, Appendix A. 42d Cong., 3d sess., 1872. S. Misc. Doc. 74 (Serial 1547).

Moore, John Bassett. *History and Digest of International Arbitrations to Which the United States Has Been a Party.* 6 vols. Washington, D.C.: Government Printing Office, 1898.

Smith, Hugh M. "The Fisheries of the Great Lakes." In U.S. Commission of Fish and Fisheries. *Report,* 1892, Appendix. 53d Cong., 2d sess., 1893. H. Misc. Doc. 209 (Serial 3264).

Smith, Hugh M. "Report on an Investigation of the Fisheries of Lake Ontario." U.S. Fish Commission, *Bulletin* 10 (1890): 177–213.

Smith, Hugh M. and Merwin-Marie Snell. "Review of the Fisheries of the Great Lakes in 1885." In U.S. Commission of Fish and Fisheries, *Report,* 1887, Appendix. 50th Cong., 2d sess., 1889. H. Misc. Doc. 133 (Serial 2661).

Tariff Commission. *Lake Fish: A Study of the Trade between the United States and Canada in Fresh-Water Fish with Cost of Production Data.* Tariff Information Series, no. 36. Washington, D.C.: Government Printing Office, 1927.

Thorpe, Francis N. *The Federal and State Constitutions, Colonial Charters. . .* 7 vols. Washington, D.C.: Government Printing Office, 1909.

Tiner, Ralph W., Jr. *Wetlands of the United States: Current Status and Recent Trends.* Washington, D.C.: Government Printing Office, 1984.

Treaties and Other International Agreements. Vol. 30, Part 2, *1978–1979.* Washington, D.C.: Government Printing Office, 1980.

True, Frederick W. "The Fisheries of the Great Lakes." In George Brown Goode. *The Fisheries and Fishing Industries of the United States.* Section 2. 47th Cong., 1st sess., 1881. S. Misc. Doc. 124 (Serial 1999), 631–673.

United States Statutes at Large. Vol. 36. 1909.

Canada and the United States

Baldwin, Norman S., Robert W. Saalfeld, Margaret A. Ross, and Howard J. Buettner. *Commercial Fish Production in the Great Lakes, 1867–1977.* Technical Report no. 3. Ann Arbor, Mich.: Great Lakes Fishery Commission, 1979.

Egerton, Frank N. *Overfishing or Pollution? Case History of a Controversy on the Great Lakes.* Technical Report no. 41. Ann Arbor, Mich.: Great Lakes Fishery Commission, 1985.

Emery, Lee. *Review of Fish Species Introduced into the Great Lakes, 1818–1974.* Technical Report no. 45. Ann Arbor, Mich.: Great Lakes Fishery Commission, 1985.

Environment Canada and the United States Environmental Protection Agency. *The Great Lakes: An Environmental Atlas and Resource Book.* Chicago and Toronto: Environmental Protection Agency and Environment Canada, 1987.

International Joint Commission. *Activities Report.* Washington, D.C.: International Joint Commission, 1986.

International Joint Commission. *Final Report on the Pollution of Boundary Waters Reference.* Washington, D.C.: Government Printing Office, 1918.

International Joint Commission. *Progress Report of the International Joint Commission on the Reference by the United States and Canada in Re the Pollution of Boundary Waters, Jan.16, 1914.* Washington, D.C.: Government Printing Office, 1914.

Ontario

Agricultural Commission. *Report of the Commissioners and Appendices A to S.* Vol. 2, *Appendix B.* Toronto: Province of Ontario, 1881.

Game and Fisheries Commission. "Final Report, 1910–1911." In Ontario, *Sessional Papers,* 1912, no. 52.

Keller, W., and J. M. Gunn. *Effects of Sudbury Smelter Emissions on Lakes in Ontario: A Review and Update.* Sudbury: Ontario Cooperative Freshwater Ecology Unit, 1994.

Legislative Assembly. *Journals,* 1884–1930.

Ministry of the Environment. Spanish Harbour RAP Team. *The Spanish Harbour Area of Concern, Environmental Conditions and Problem Definition, Remedial Action Plan, Stage One.* Toronto: Ontario Ministry of the Environment, 1993.

Ministry of the Environment, Ministry of Natural Resources, and Environment Canada. *Status Report Spanish River—Harbour Area Remedial Action Plan (RAP).* Toronto: Queen's Printer for Ontario, 1988.

Sessional Papers, 1867–1931.

Statutes, 1867–1932.

Wright, Ramsay. "Preliminary Report on the Fish and Fisheries of Ontario." In Ontario, *Sessional Papers,* 1892, no. 79, 420–476.

Massachusetts

Colonial Laws of Massachusetts. 1672. Reprint. Boston: City Council of Boston, 1887.

Michigan

Board of Fish Commissioners. *Biennial Reports,* 1873–1898 (some years located in Michigan, *Joint Documents* and some years printed as separate reports).

Department of Natural Resources. "Remedial Action Plan for TORCH LAKE Area of Concern." Typescript. Department of Natural Resources, Lansing, Michigan, 27 October 1987.

Johnson, Allan M. *The Development of Guidelines for Closing Underground Mines: Michigan Case Studies.* Houghton: Michigan Technological University, Institute of Mineral Research, 1983.

Laws and *Public Acts,* 1817–1933.

Minnesota

Board of Game and Fish Commissioners. *Annual Reports,* 1894–1906.

Board of Game and Fish Commissioners. *Biennial Reports,* 1908–1916.

Fish Commission. *Annual Reports,* 1881–1890.

Fish Commissioners. *Annual Reports,* 1875–1880.
Game and Fish Commission. *Annual Reports,* 1890–1893.
General Laws, 1857–1933.

New York

Commissioners of Fisheries. *Reports,* 1868–1874.
Laws. 1802–1933.

Ohio

Fish and Game Commission or Commissioners of Fish and Game. *Annual Reports,* 1888–1907.
Fish Commission or Commissioners of Fisheries. *Annual Reports,* 1876–1883.
General and Local Laws and Acts, 1857–1933.

Vermont

Marsh, George Perkins. *Report Made under Authority of the Legislature of Vermont on the Artificial Propagation of Fish.* Burlington: Free Press Print, 1857.

Wisconsin

Bertrand, Gerard, Jean Lang, and John Ross. *The Green Bay Watershed: Past, Present, and Future.* Technical Report no. 229. Madison: University of Wisconsin Sea Grant College Program. 1976.
Commissioners of Fisheries. *Annual and Biennial Reports,* 1874–1904.
Laws, General Acts, Statutes, 1838–1933.
Roth, Filbert. *On the Forestry Conditions of Northern Wisconsin.* Madison: State of Wisconsin, Geological and Natural History Survey, 1898.
Senate and Assembly. *Journals of Proceedings,* 1873–1905, 1907, 1917.

ARTICLES

Alanen, Arnold R., and William H. Tishler. "Farming the Lake Superior Shore: Agriculture and Horticulture on the Apostle Islands, 1840–1940." *Wisconsin Magazine of History* 79 (spring 1996): 163–203.
Allard, Dean C. "The Fish Commission Laboratory and Its Influence on the Founding of the Marine Biological Laboratory." *Journal of the History of Biology* 23 (summer 1990): 251–270.
Allard, Dean C. "Spencer Fullerton Baird and the Foundations of American Marine Science." *Marine Fisheries Review* 50 (1988): 124–129.
Blair, A. A. "Scales of Lake Ontario Salmon Indicate a Land-Locked Form." *Copeia,* 10 December 1938, 206.
Bocking, Stephen. "Fishing the Inland Seas: Great Lakes Research, Fisheries Man-

agement, and Environmental Policy in Ontario." *Environmental History* 2 (January 1997): 52–73.

Bocking, Stephen. "Stephen Forbes, Jacob Reighard, and the Emergence of Aquatic Ecology in the Great Lakes Region." *Journal of the History of Biology* 23 (fall 1990): 461–498.

Bogue, Margaret Beattie. "In the Shadow of the Union Jack: British Legacies and Great Lakes Fishery Policy." *Environmental Review* 11 (spring 1987): 19–34.

Bogue Margaret Beattie. "The Lake and the Fruit: The Making of Three Farm-Type Areas." *Agricultural History* 59 (October 1985): 492–522.

Bogue, Margaret Beattie. "Liberty Hyde Bailey, Jr., and the Family Farm." *Agricultural History* 63 (winter 1989): 26–48.

Bogue, Margaret Beattie. "The Swamp Land Act and Wet Land Utilization in Illinois, 1850–1890." *Agricultural History* 25 (October 1951): 169–180.

Bogue, Margaret Beattie. "To Save the Fish: Canada, the United States, the Great Lakes, and the Joint Commission of 1892." *Journal of American History* 79 (March 1993): 1429–1454.

Booth, A[lfred]. "The Fisheries of the Great Lakes.—No. 1." *American Field: The Sportsman's Journal,* 7 November 1885, 438–439.

Cleland, Charles E. "The Inland Shore Fishery of the Northern Great Lakes: Its Development and Importance in Prehistory." *American Antiquity* 47 (1982): 761–784.

Coggins, George Cameron. "Wildlife and the Constitution: The Walls Come Tumbling Down." *Washington Law Review* 55 (April 1980): 285–358.

Doudoroff, Peter, and Max Katz. "Critical Review of Literature on the Toxicity of Industrial Wastes and Their Components to Fish." *Sewage and Industrial Wastes* 22 (November 1950): 1432–1458.

Egerton, Frank N. "Pollution and Aquatic Life in Lake Erie: Early Scientific Studies." *Environmental Review* 2 (fall 1987): 189–201.

Fairlie, Simon, Mike Hagler, and Brian O'Riordan, "The Politics of Overfishing." *Ecologist,* March–April, May–June 1995, 46–73.

Follett, Richard. "*Salmo salar* of the St. Lawrence River." *Transactions of the American Fisheries Society* 62 (1932): 367.

Forkey, Neil S. "Maintaining a Great Lakes Fishery: The State, Science, and the Case of Ontario's Bay of Quinte, 1870–1920." *Ontario History* 87 (spring 1995): 45–64.

Fox, William Sherwood. "The Literature of *Salmo Salar* in Lake Ontario and Tributary Streams." *Proceedings and Transactions of the Royal Society of Canada* 24 (May 1930): 45–55.

Gillis, Peter. "Rivers of Sawdust: The Battle over Industrial Pollution in Canada, 1865–1903." *Journal of Canadian Studies* 21 (spring 1986): 84–103.

Halverson, Lynn H. "The Commercial Fisheries of the Michigan Waters of Lake Superior." *Michigan History* 39 (March 1955): 1–17.

Hoffmann, Richard C. "Economic Development and Aquatic Ecosystems in Medieval Europe." *American Historical Review* 101 (June 1996): 631–669.

Holmquist, June Drenning. "Commercial Fishing on Lake Superior in the 1890s." *Minnesota History* 34 (summer 1955): 243–249.

Kaatz, Martin R. "The Settlement of the Black Swamp of Northwestern Ohio: Early Days." *Northwest Ohio Quarterly* 25 (winter 1952–1953): 23–36.

Kaatz, Martin, R. "The Settlement of the Black Swamp of Northwestern Ohio: Later Days." *Northwest Ohio Quarterly* 25 (autumn 1953): 201–217.

Kaatz, Martin R. "The Settlement of the Black Swamp of Northwestern Ohio: Pioneer Days." *Northwest Ohio Quarterly* 25 (summer 1953): 134–156.

Larson, Norman W. "History of Ehlers Store and Jones Marina Cornucopia, Wis." *Historical Happenings*. Bayfield County Historical Society, vols. 10–11 (summer 1989 and 1990).

MacCrimmon, Hugh. "The Beginnings of Salmon Culture in Canada." *Canadian Geographical Journal* 71 (September 1965): 96–103.

Nute, Grace Lee. "The American Fur Company's Fishing Enterprises on Lake Superior." *Mississippi Valley Historical Review* 12 (March 1926): 483–503.

"Overfishing: Its Causes and Consequences" [Special issue]. *Ecologist,* March–June 1995.

Parfait, Michael. "Diminishing Returns: Exploiting the Ocean's Bounty." *National Geographic,* November 1995, 2–37.

Pernin, Peter. "The Great Pestigo Fire: An Eyewitness Account." *Wisconsin Magazine of History* 54 (summer 1971): 246–272.

Pisani, Donald J. "Fish Culture and the Dawn of Concern over Water Pollution in the United States." *Environmental Review* 8 (summer 1984): 117–131.

Rainey, Robert H. "Natural Displacement of Pollution from the Great Lakes." *Science,* 10 March 1967, 1242–1243.

Russell, Edmund P., III. "'Speaking of Annihilation': Mobilizing for War against Human and Insect Enemies, 1914–1945." *Journal of American History* 82 (March 1996): 1505–1529.

Safina, Carl. "The World's Imperiled Fish." *Scientific American,* November 1995, 46–53.

Scheiber, Harry N. "Pacific Ocean Resources, Science, and Law of the Sea: Wilbert M. Chapman and the Pacific Fisheries, 1945–70." *Ecology Law Quarterly* 13 (1986): 381–534.

Smith, Stanford H. "Factors in Ecologic Succession in Oligotrophic Fish Communities of the Laurentian Great Lakes." *Journal of the Fisheries Research Board of Canada* 29 (June 1972): 717–730.

Van Oosten, John. "Michigan's Commercial Fisheries of the Great Lakes." *Michigan History Magazine* 22 (winter 1938): 107–145.

Wright, Gary A. "Some Aspects of Early and Mid-Seventeenth Century Exchange Networks in the Western Great Lakes." *Michigan Archaeologist* 13 (December 1967): 181–197.

Wright, Stillman, and Wilbur M. Tidd. "Summary of Limnological Investigations in Western Lake Erie in 1929 and 1930." *Transactions of the American Fisheries Society* 63 (1933): 271–285.

Bibliography

BOOKS

Agassiz, Louis. *Lake Superior: Its Physical Character, Vegetation, and Animals, Compared with Those of Other and Similar Regions.* 1850. Reprint. New York: Arno Press, 1970.

Aldrich, Lewis Cass. *History of Erie County, Ohio.* Syracuse, N.Y.: Mason, 1889.

Alexander, James Edward, ed. *Salmon Fishing in Canada by a Resident.* London: Lovell, 1857.

Allard, Dean C. *Spencer Fullerton Baird and the U.S. Fish Commission.* New York: Arno Press, 1978.

Allen, Robert Thomas. *The Illustrated Natural History of Canada: The Great Lakes.* Toronto: McClelland, 1970.

Andreas, Alfred T. *History of Chicago from the Earliest Period to the Present Time.* 3 vols. 1884–1886. Reprint. New York: Arno Press, 1975.

Angus, James T. *A Respectable Ditch: A History of the Trent–Severn Waterway, 1833–1920.* Kingston: McGill–Queens University Press, 1988.

Armstrong, Christopher. *The Politics of Federalism: Ontario's Relations with the Federal Government, 1867–1942.* Toronto: University of Toronto Press, 1981.

Ashworth, William. *The Late, Great Lakes: An Environmental History.* New York: Knopf, 1986.

Barnouw, Victor. *Wisconsin Chippewa Myths and Tales and Their Relation to Chippewa Life.* Madison: University of Wisconsin Press, 1977.

Barrett, Harry B. *Lore and Legends of Long Point.* Don Mills, Ont.: Burns and MacEachern, 1977.

Becker, George C. *Fishes of Wisconsin.* Madison: University of Wisconsin Press, 1983.

Benedict, C. Harry. *Red Metal: The Calumet and Hecla Story.* Ann Arbor: University of Michigan Press, 1952.

Berger, Carl C. "Internationalism, Continentalism, and the Writing of History: Comments on the Carnegie Series on the Relations of Canada and the United States." In *The Influence of the United States on Canadian Development: Eleven Case Studies,* edited by Richard A. Preston, 32–54. Durham, N.C.: Duke University Press, 1972.

Blake, Nelson Manfred. *Water for the Cities: A History of the Urban Water Supply Problem in the United States.* Syracuse, N.Y.: Syracuse University Press, 1956.

Bogue, Margaret Beattie. *Around the Shores of Lake Michigan: A Guide to Historic Sites.* Madison: University of Wisconsin Press, 1985.

Bogue, Margaret Beattie, and Virginia A. Palmer. *Around the Shores of Lake Superior: A Guide to Historic Sites.* Madison: University of Wisconsin Sea Grant College Program, 1979.

Boyce, Gerald E. *Historic Hastings.* Belleville, Ont.: Hastings County Council, 1967.

Burns, Noel M. *Erie: The Lake That Survived.* Totowa, N.J.: Rowman and Allanheld, 1985.

Busch, Briton Cooper. *The War against the Seals: A History of the North American Seal Fishery.* Montreal: McGill–Queens University Press, 1985.

Cain, Louis P. *Sanitation Strategy for a Lakefront Metropolis: The Case of Chicago.* De Kalb: Northern Illinois University Press, 1978.

Callahan, James Morton. *American Foreign Policy in Canadian Relations.* New York: Cooper Square, 1967.

The Chicago Blue Book of Selected Names. Chicago: Chicago Directory, 1897.

Cleland, Charles E. "Indians in a Changing Environment." In *The Great Lakes Forest: An Environmental and Social History,* edited by Susan L. Flader, 83–95. Minneapolis: University of Minnesota Press, 1983.

Colten, Craig E., and Peter N. Skinner. *The Road to Love Canal: Managing Industrial Waste before EPA.* Austin: University of Texas Press, 1996.

Commemorative Historical and Biographical Record of Wood County, Ohio, Its Past and Present . . . 2 vols. Chicago: Beers, 1897.

Cooley, Richard A. *Politics and Conservation: The Decline of the Alaska Salmon.* New York: Harper & Row, 1963.

Craig, Gerald M. *Upper Canada in the Formative Years, 1784–1841.* Toronto: McClelland and Stewart, 1963.

Cronon, William. *Changes in the Land: Indians, Colonists, and the Ecology of New England.* New York: Hill and Wang, 1983.

Crutchfield, James A., and Guilio Pontecorvo. *The Pacific Salmon Fisheries: A Study of Irrational Conservation.* Baltimore: Johns Hopkins University Press, 1969.

Doherty, Robert. *Disputed Waters: Native Americans and the Great Lakes Fishery.* Lexington: University of Kentucky Press, 1990.

Dorsey, Kurkpatrick. *The Dawn of Conservation Diplomacy: U.S.–Canadian Wildlife Protection Treaties in the Progressive Era.* Seattle: University of Washington Press, 1998.

Drummond, Ian M., with contributions by Peter George, Kris Inwood, Peter W. Sinclair, and Tom Traves. *Progress without Planning: The Economic History of Ontario from Confederation to the Second World War.* Toronto: University of Toronto Press, 1987.

Dunbar, Willis F. *Michigan: A History of the Wolverine State.* Rev. ed. by George S. May. Grand Rapids, Mich.: Eerdmans, 1980.

Durant, Vincent. *War Horse of Cumberland: The Life and Times of Sir Charles Tupper.* Hantsport, Nova Scotia: Lancelot Press, 1985.

Eklund, Mats. *Reconstructions of Historical Metal Emissions and Their Dispersion in the Environment.* Linkoping Studies in Arts and Science, no 127. Linkoping, Sweden: Linkoping University, 1995.

Falge, Louis, ed. *History of Manitowoc County, Wisconsin.* 2 vols. Chicago: Goodspeed Historical Association, 1911, 1912.

Flader, Susan L., ed. *The Great Lakes Forest: An Environmental and Social History.* Minneapolis: University of Minnesota Press, 1983.

Fowl, Otto. *Sault Ste. Marie and Its Great Waterway.* New York: Putnam, 1925.

Fox, William Sherwood. *The Bruce Beckons: The Story of Lake Huron's Great Peninsula.* Toronto: University of Toronto Press, 1952.

Fries, Robert F. *Empire in Pine: The Story of Lumbering in Wisconsin, 1830–1900.* Madison: State Historical Society of Wisconsin, 1951.

Fuller, George N., ed. *Michigan: A Centennial History of the State and Its People.* 2 vols. Chicago: Lewis, 1939.

Gates, Donald M., C. H. D. Clarke, and James T. Harris. "Wildlife in a Changing Environment." In *The Great Lakes Forest: An Environmental and Social History,* edited by Susan L. Flader, 52–80. Minneapolis: University of Minnesota Press, 1983.

Gates, Lillian. *Land Policies of Upper Canada.* Toronto: University of Toronto Press, 1968.

Gates, Paul W. *The Farmer's Age: Agriculture, 1815–1860.* New York: Harper & Row, 1960.

Gates, William B., Jr. *Michigan Copper and Boston Dollars.* Cambridge, Mass.: Harvard University Press, 1951.

Gibbs, Lois Marie. *Love Canal: My Story.* Albany: State University of New York Press, 1981.

Green, Seth. *Home Fishing and Home Waters: A Practical Treatise on Fish Culture.* New York: Judd, 1888.

Hall, Henry, ed. *America's Successful Men of Affairs: An Encyclopedia of Contemporaneous Biography.* Vol. 2. New York: New York Tribune, 1896.

Handlin, Oscar, and Mary Handlin. *Commonwealth: A Study of the Role of Government in the American Economy: Massachusetts, 1774–1861.* Cambridge, Mass.: Harvard University Press, 1969.

Hansen, Frederick A. *Diary of a Norwegian Fisherman: The Collected Dairies of Frederick A. Hansen, April 1913 through December 1938, Sand Island, Wisconsin.* Edited by Frederick H. Dahl. Jacksonville, Fla.: Paramount Press, 1989.

Harris, R. Cole, and John Warkentin. *Canada before Confederation: A Study in Historical Geography.* New York: Oxford University Press, 1974.

Hatcher, Harlan. *A Century of Men and Iron.* Indianapolis: Bobbs-Merrill, 1950.

Hatcher, Harlan. *Lake Erie.* American Lakes Series. Edited by Milo M. Quaife. Indianapolis: Bobbs-Merrill, 1945.

Haynes, William. *American Chemical Industry.* Vol. 3, *The World War I Period: 1912–1922.* New York: Van Nostrand, 1945.

Hickerson, Harold. *The Chippewa and Their Neighbors: A Study in Ethnohistory.* New York: Holt, Rinehart and Winston, 1970.

History of Bay County Michigan, with Illustrations and Biographical Sketches. Chicago: Page, 1883.

Hoffmann, Charles. *The Depression of the Nineties: An Economic History.* Westport, Conn.: Greenwood, 1970.

Holte, Ingeborg. *Ingeborg's Isle Royale.* Grand Marais, Minn.: Women's Times, 1984.

Hubbard, Bela. *Memorials of a Half-Century in Michigan and the Lake Region.* New York: Putnam, 1888.

Innis, Harold A. *The Cod Fisheries: The History of an International Economy.* New Haven, Conn.: Yale University Press, 1940.

Johnson, A. M., and D. M. Cregger. "Groundwater Contamination Problems in the Iron River Mining District of Michigan." In *International Symposium on Environmental Geotechnology, April 21–23, 1986,* edited by Hsai-Yung Fang, 1:184–196. Allentown, Pa.: Envo, 1986.

Johnson, E. Pauline. *Flint and Feather: The Complete Poems of E. Pauline Johnson (Tekahionwake).* 1912. Reprint. Toronto: Hodder and Stoughton, 1969.

Johnstone, Kenneth. *The Aquatic Explorers: A History of the Fisheries Research Board of Canada.* Toronto: University of Toronto Press, 1977.

Jones, Robert Leslie. *History of Agriculture in Ohio to 1880.* Kent, Ohio: Kent State University Press, 1983.

Jones, Robert Leslie. *History of Agriculture in Ontario, 1613–1880.* Toronto: University of Toronto Press, 1946.

Jones, William. *Ojibwa Texts Collected by William Jones.* Parts 1–2. Leyden: Brill, 1917–1919.

Kane, Paul. *Wanderings of an Artist among the Indians of North America.* London: Longman, Brown, Green, Longmans and Roberts, 1859.

Kehoe, Terence. *Cleaning up the Great Lakes: From Cooperation to Confrontation.* De Kalb: Northern Illinois University Press, 1997.

Kinietz, W. Vernon. *The Indians of the Western Great Lakes, 1615–1760.* Ann Arbor: University of Michigan Press, 1940.

Krech, Shepard, III, ed. *Indians, Animals, and the Fur Trade: A Critique of Keepers of the Game.* Athens: University of Georgia Press, 1981.

Kriehn, Ruth. *The Fisherfolk of Jones Island.* Milwaukee: Milwaukee County Historical Society, 1988.

Kuchenberg, Tom, and Jim Legault. *Reflections in a Tarnished Mirror: The Use and Abuse of the Great Lakes.* Sturgeon Bay, Wis.: Golden Glow, 1978.

Landon, Fred. *Lake Huron.* American Lakes Series. Edited by Milo M. Quaife. Indianapolis: Bobbs-Merrill, 1944.

Landon, Fred. *Western Ontario and the American Frontier.* Toronto: Ryerson, 1941.

Langlois, Thomas H. *The Western End of Lake Erie and Its Ecology.* Ann Arbor: Edwards, 1954.

Lankton, Larry. *Cradle to Grave: Life, Work, and Death at the Lake Superior Copper Mines.* New York: Oxford University Press, 1991.

Lankton, Larry D., and Charles K. Hyde. *Old Reliable: An Illustrated History of the Quincy Mining Company.* Hancock, Mich.: Quincy Mine Hoist Association, 1982.

Lauriston, Victor. *Lambton's Hundred Years, 1849–1949.* Sarnia, Ont.: Haines Frontier, 1949.

LeBourdais, Donat Marc. *Sudbury Basin: The Story of Nickel.* Toronto: Ryerson, 1953.

Lloyd, Timothy C., and Patrick B. Mullen. *Lake Erie Fishermen: Work, Identity, and Tradition.* Urbana: University of Illinois Press, 1990.

Main, O. W. *The Canadian Nickel Industry: A Study in Market Control and Public Policy.* Toronto: University of Toronto Press, 1955.

Marsh, George Perkins. *Man and Nature.* Edited by David Lowenthal. Cambridge, Mass.: Harvard University Press, 1965.

Martin, Calvin. *Keepers of the Game: Indian–Animal Relationships and the Fur Trade.* Berkeley: University of California Press, 1978.

Maybee, Roland H. *Michigan's White Pine Era, 1840–1900.* Lansing: Michigan Historical Commission, 1960.

Mayer, Harold M., and Richard C. Wade. *Chicago: Growth of a Metropolis.* Chicago: University of Chicago Press, 1969.

McClurken, James M. "Wage Labor in Two Michigan Ottawa Communities." In *Native American Wage Labor: Ethnohistorical Perspectives,* edited by Alice Littlefield and Martha C. Knack, 66–99. Norman: University of Oklahoma Press, 1996.

McCullough, Alan B. "Samuel Wilmot." In *Dictionary of Canadian Biography,* 12: 1106–1107. Toronto: University of Toronto Press, 1990.

McEvoy, Arthur F. *The Fisherman's Problem: Ecology and Law in the California Fishery.* New York: Cambridge University Press, 1986.

McInnis, Edgar. *Canada: A Political and Social History.* Toronto: Rinehart, 1947.

McKelvey, Blake. *Rochester on the Genesee: The Growth of a City.* Syracuse, N.Y.: Syracuse University Press, 1973.

Melosi, Martin V., ed. *Pollution and Reform in American Cities, 1870–1930.* Austin: University of Texas Press, 1980.

Moore, Powell A. *The Calumet Region: Indiana's Last Frontier.* Indiana Historical Collections, vol. 39. Indianapolis: Indiana Historical Bureau, 1959.

Netboy, Anthony. *The Atlantic Salmon: A Vanishing Species?* Boston: Houghton Mifflin, 1968.

Netboy, Anthony. *The Columbia River Salmon and Steelhead Trout: Their Fight for Survival.* Seattle: University of Washington Press, 1980.

Netboy, Anthony. *The Salmon: Their Fight for Survival.* Boston: Houghton Mifflin, 1974.

Nettle, Richard. *The Salmon Fisheries of the St. Lawrence and Its Tributaries.* Montreal: Lovell, 1857.

Newspaper Cartoonists Association of Michigan. *Our Michigan Friends "As We See 'Em": A Gallery of Pen Sketches in Black and White.* Detroit: Press of William Graham Printing, 1905.

Nute, Grace Lee. *Lake Superior.* American Lakes Series. Edited by Milo M. Quaife. Indianapolis: Bobbs- Merrill, 1944.

Oliver, David D. *Centennial History of Alpena County, Michigan.* Alpena, Mich.: Argus, 1903.

Piper, Don Courtney. *International Law of the Great Lakes: A Study of Canadian–United States Cooperation.* Durham, N.C.: Duke University Press, 1967.

Pound, Arthur, *Lake Ontario.* American Lakes Series. Edited by Milo M. Quaife. Indianapolis: Bobbs-Merrill, 1945.

Prothero, Frank. *The Good Years: A History of the Commercial Fishing Industry on Lake Erie.* Belleville, Ont.: Mika, 1973.

Quaife, Milo M. *Lake Michigan.* American Lakes Series. Edited by Milo M. Quaife. Indianapolis: Bobbs-Merrill, 1944.

Rakestraw, Lawrence. *Historic Mining on Isle Royale.* Houghton, Mich.: Isle Royale Natural History Association and National Park Service, 1965.

Ratner, Sidney. *New Light on the History of Great American Fortunes.* New York: Kelley, 1953.

Reiger, John F. *American Sportsmen and the Origins of Conservation.* New York: Winchester Press, 1975.

Richards, Laura E. *Tirra Lirra, Rhymes Old and New.* Toronto: Little, Brown, 1902.

Ritzenthaler, Robert E., and Pat Ritzenthaler. *The Woodland Indians of the Western Great Lakes.* 2d ed. Milwaukee: Milwaukee Public Museum, 1983.

Robertson, Norman. *The History of the County of Bruce and of the Minor Municipalities Therein, Province of Ontario, Canada.* Toronto: Briggs, 1906.

Satz, Ronald N. *Chippewa Treaty Rights: The Reserved Rights of Wisconsin's Chippewa Indians in Historical Perspective.* Madison: Wisconsin Academy of Sciences, Arts and Letters, 1991.

Schoolcraft, Henry R. *Narrative Journal of Travels through the Northwestern Regions of the United States Extending from Detroit through the Great Chain of American Lakes, to the Sources of the Mississippi River in the Year 1820–1821.* 1821. Reprint. New York: Arno Press, 1970.

Scott, Anthony. "Fisheries, Pollution, and Canadian-American Transnational Relations." In *Canada and the United States: Transnational and Transgovernmental Relations,* edited by Annette Baker Fox, Alfred O. Hero, Jr., and Joseph S. Nye, Jr., 234–255. New York: Columbia University Press, 1976.

Simpson, Elizabeth M. *Mexico, Mother of Towns: Fragments of Local History.* Buffalo, N.Y.: Clement, 1949.

Sinclair, Upton. *The Jungle.* 1906. Reprint. New York: New American Library, 1960.

Sivertson, Howard. *Once upon an Isle: The Story of Fishing Families on Isle Royale.* Mount Horeb, Wis.: Wisconsin Folk Museum, 1992.

Social Register, Chicago, 1900. New York: Social Register Association, 1899.

Spencer, Robert, John Kirton, and Kim Richard Nossal, eds. *The International Joint Commission Seventy Years On.* Toronto: Center for International Studies, 1981.

Squair, John. *The Townships of Darlington and Clarke Including Bowmansville and Newcastle Province of Ontario Canada.* Toronto: University of Toronto Press, 1927.

A Standard Dictionary of Canadian Biography. Toronto: Trans-Canada Press, 1934.

Stansby, Maurice E. *Industrial Fishery Technology: A Survey of Methods for Domestic Harvesting, Preservation, and Processing of Fish Used for Food and for Industrial Products.* 1963. Reprint. Huntington, N.Y.: Krieger, 1976.

Swift, Jamie. *The Big Nickel: Inco at Home and Abroad.* Kitchener, Ont.: Between the Lines, 1977.

Tanner, Helen Hornbeck, ed. *Atlas of Great Lakes Indian History.* Norman: University of Oklahoma Press, 1987.

Tarr, Joel A. *The Search for the Ultimate Sink: Urban Pollution in Historical Perspective.* Akron, Ohio: University of Akron Press, 1996.

Taylor, Joseph E., III. *Making Salmon: An Environmental History of the Northwest Fisheries Crisis.* Seattle: University of Washington Press, 1999.

Taylor, William W., and C. Paola Ferreri, eds. *Great Lakes Fisheries Policy and Management: A Binational Perspective.* East Lansing: Michigan State University Press, 1999.

Thwaites, Reuben G., ed. *Jesuit Relations and Allied Documents.* 73 vols. Cleveland: Burrows, 1899.

Urquhart, M. C., and K. A. H. Buckley. *Historical Statistics of Canada.* Toronto: Macmillan, 1965.

Vecsey, Christopher. *Traditional Ojibwa Religion and Its Historical Changes.* Memoirs of the American Philosophical Society, vol. 152. Philadelphia: American Philosophical Society, 1983.

Vecsey, Christopher, and Robert W. Venables, eds. *American Indian Environments: Ecological Issues in Native American History.* Syracuse, N.Y.: Syracuse University Press, 1980.

Vennum, Thomas, Jr. *Wild Rice and the Ojibway People.* St. Paul: Minnesota Historical Society Press, 1988.

Vukelich, George. *Fisherman's Beach.* New York: St. Martin's Press, 1962.

Wallace, Dorothy, ed. *Memories of Goderich: The Romance of the Prettiest Town in Canada.* 2d ed. Goderich, Ont.: Jubilee 3 Committee, 1979.

Waters, Thomas F. *The Superior North Shore.* Minneapolis: University of Minnesota Press, 1987.

Wells, Robert W. *Fire at Peshtigo.* Englewood Cliffs, N.J.: Prentice-Hall, 1968.

White, Richard. *The Middle Ground: Indians, Empires and Republics in the Great Lakes Region, 1650–1815.* New York: Cambridge University Press, 1991.

Whorton, James. *Before Silent Spring: Pesticides and Public Health in Pre-DDT America.* Princeton, N.J.: Princeton University Press, 1974.

NEWSPAPERS AND PERIODICALS

American Field: The Sportsman's Journal. 1885–1886.

Ashland [Wisconsin] *Press,* 30 November 1872.

Bayfield [Wisconsin] *County Press,* 1879–March 1880, January 1886, December 1890–January 1891.

Chicago Tribune, 5 March 1902.

The Department of Marine and Fisheries, well aware of the power of public opinion, kept files of news stories on reactions to its policies and its administration of the laws. Hundreds of labeled clippings were preserved, reports from the press in a wide range of towns and cities, including Amherstburg, Collingwood, Goderich, Kingston, London, Ottawa, Owen Sound, Sarnia, Toronto, and Windsor, Ontario; Detroit, Sandusky, Toledo, Cleveland, and Buffalo on the southern shore of Lake Erie; and New York City. Major examples of such material are found in file 445, part 1, MReel T-2844; file 1241, part 1, MReel T-3142; file1262, part 1, MReel T-3144; file 1593, parts 1–2, MReel T-3168; file 2247, part 1, MReel T-3217, Records of the Department of Marine and Fisheries.

Detroit Free Press, 1880, 1885, 1890, 1 January–4 June 1894.

E. Russell & Co., Dun, Barlow & Co., and R. G. Dun & Co. *The Mercantile Agency Reference Book and Key,* July 1871.
"Fishery Interests Combine." *New York Times,* 22 June 1898, 10.
"Fresh and Salt Fish." *Bayfield County Press,* 9 January 1886, 1.
Green Bay State Gazette, January 1887.
Howell, "Food Supply of Fresh Waters." *Chicago Times,* 20 August 188l, 10.
"In the Hands of a Mob." *Detroit Free Press,* 3 May 1894, 1.
"Mob in Ugly Mood." *Detroit Free Press,* 2 May 1894, 1.
"The New Fishery Trust." *New York Times,* 2 October 1898, 5.
R. G. Dun & Co. *The Mercantile Agency and Reference Book,* July 1883, July 1897.

MISCELLANEOUS

Booth Forum [newsletter]. February–October 1935.
Famous Booth Sea Foods: A Review of the Relation of the Booth Fisheries Company to the Fishing Industry [promotional brochure].1920s.
Wisconsin Maritime Museum. *Harvesting the Inland Seas: Great Lakes Commercial Fishing* [traveling exhibition, introductory videotape]. Manitowoc: Wisconsin Maritime Museum, 1996.

Index

A. Booth and Company: activities of, 60–61; and anti-Americanism, 265, 268, 271, 308; awards for, 61; bankruptcies of, 271–72; cartoons depicting, 270 (fig.), 271 (fig.); and competition, 65, 66, 67, 68, 69, 71, 264, 268–69; control by, 56, 72; and cooperation in commercial fishing industry, 273; early years of, 60–62; between 1896 and 1933, 264–72, 273, 274, 275; expansion and dominance of, 61, 62–73, 88, 264–65, 267, 268, 269, 272; expansion into Canadian waters by, 57, 59, 65, 69–72; financing of, 61; fishermen's relationship with, 64–65, 67–69, 70–72, 265, 266, 268–69, 271; impact on commercial fishing of, 58; and Indians, 79; locations of, 61, 63 (fig.); and market and distribution strategies, 274, 275; after 1933, 272; rise and decline of, 264–72. *See also* Ainsworth and Ganley; Dominion Fish Company; Port Arthur Fish Company

A. Booth Fisheries Company. *See* A. Booth and Company

A. Booth Packing Company. *See* A. Booth and Company

Agassiz, Louis, 159, 302

agricultural-commercial economy, 14, 15, 19–27

agriculture: and changing species in Great Lakes, 169, 170; and Crisis of 1890s, 238; and developing drainage basins, 113–14, 116–20, 123, 128, 136, 141–42, 148, 325; and Lake Erie, 116, 117, 118–19, 120, 325; and Lake Huron, 116, 120; and Lake Michigan, 116, 117, 120; and Lake Ontario, 116, 117, 120; and Lake Superior, 116, 120; legacy of development of, 325, 331; and lumbering, 123; and pollution, 284, 286, 287, 289, 295; and regulation of fisheries, 193; in Upper Canada, 207; and World War I, 284. *See also* farmers

Ainsworth and Ganley, 65–66, 72, 77

air pollution, 281–82, 289

alewives, 162–63, 166, 169, 170, 171, 201, 245, 286–87

Alpena, Michigan, 126, 185, 199, 302

American Fur Company, 31, 39, 77

American Revolution, 9–10

"American system," 100, 179–80, 192, 217, 239–40, 248–49

Amherstburg, Ontario, 144, 145, 231

anti-Americanism: and Booth company operations, 265, 268, 271, 308; and boundaries, 308; and Canadian Department of Marine and Fisheries, 226, 227–28, 229, 230–33, 237, 308–9, 318; and commercial fishing industry, 266, 308; and competition, 227, 307; and destruction and waste of fish, 248; and enforcement, 227, 230–33, 308–11, 312; and fishermen, 307–8; and illegal fishing,

anti-Americanism (*continued*) 308–11; and International Fisheries Commission, 318; and Joint Commission study, 241–42, 248; and Lake Erie, 308–11; and licensing, 308; and markets, 307, 308; and Ontario–dominion controversy, 312; and Pelee Island incident, 230–33; and politics, 307; and price, 308; and Prince's 1905 study, 323; and public policy, 307–11; and regulation, 307, 310–11; and tariffs, 307; and Tupper administration, 226, 227–28, 229, 230–33, 237; and World War I, 310. *See also* Canada–U.S. relations, and American expansion into Canadian waters; poaching; tariffs
Apostle Islands, 62, 67, 85, 134, 273
aquatic ecology, 298–99
artificial propagation: and Booth company operations, 264; and Canadian policies, 204, 208–9, 336; of carp, 256; and conservation, 311; criticisms of, 214, 304–5; between 1879 and 1888, 214; and federalism, 311; in Georgian Bay, 323; and intergovernmental cooperation, 182–83, 204, 213; and International Fisheries Commission study, 313; and Joint Commission study, 247; in Michigan, 311; need for, 203; and Prince's 1905 study, 323; and public policy, 298; and research, 302, 304–5; and state fishery commissions–fishermen relationship, 189; and state universities' curricula, 186; U.S. Bureau of Fisheries program of, 256; U.S. Commission's support for, 182–83, 196–97, 199, 201–2, 203; Wilmot's program for, 208–9. *See also* hatcheries; stocking programs
Ashland, Wisconsin, 122, 133
Ashtabula, Ohio, 133, 269, 308
Atlantic Ocean: Booth company operations in, 272; and Canada–U.S. relations, 240; cod in, 334; and cooperation between Canada and U.S., 213; early regulation for, 176; and Fishery Act of 1868, 179; fishing policy for, 179; and Joint Commission study, 242; pollution along, 285; research about, 197–98, 302, 303
Atlantic salmon, 4, 5, 14, 19–27, 149, 201, 332
Baird, Spencer F., 35, 45–46, 164, 182, 195–200, 203, 213, 220, 302
bark: as pollutant, 126, 127, 246, 287
bass: black, 119, 163, 166, 231, 233, 246; and changing species in Great Lakes, 163, 165, 166, 168; decline of, 233; and developing drainage basins, 119, 143; ice fishing for, 87; and Joint Commission study, 246; and Lake Erie, 246; largemouth, 119, 246; and Pelee Island incident, 231, 233; smallmouth, 168; spawning of, 166; spearing of, 87; sportfishing for, 231
"Battle of Lake Erie (1894)" (cartoon), 232
Bayfield, Wisconsin: Booth company operations in, 62, 64–65, 67, 72, 79, 273; Boutin family from, 74–75; and developing drainage basins, 122, 134; fishermen in, 74–75, 76; and Indians, 79; and lumbering, 122; mining around, 134
Bay of Quinte, 10, 20, 24, 117, 134, 245, 259 (fig.), 316
beam-trawl, 56, 61, 84
Beaver River, 293–94
beavers: and wetlands, 15
Belgians: as fishermen, 81, 83
Bennett, W. H., 236–37
Bensley, B. A., 164
Bering Sea, 228, 240, 241, 334
Biological Board of Canada, 303, 304
biological research laboratory (Ann Arbor, Michigan), 327
Birge, Edward A., 122, 186
Black River, 127, 143, 170–71
Black Swamp, 119, 120
bloaters, 149
blue fins, 93, 149
boats: and changing technology, 258; and commercial fishing between 1896 and 1933, 258; and expansion of commercial fishing industry, 47, 49; and growth patterns of commercial fishing industry, 39; and harvesting technology, 39, 49; on Lake Michigan, 97; seizure of, 230. *See also type of boat*
Booth, Alfred: *American Field* articles by, 60; beam-trawl of, 56, 61, 84; on changes in commercial fishing industry, 53; contribution to fishing industry of,

85; early years of, 60–62; and expansion of commercial fishing industry, 44, 53; as immigrant, 85; and work of fishermen, 93–94. *See also* A. Booth and Company
Booth Fisheries Company, 265, 271–72. *See also* A. Booth and Company
boundaries: political division of Great Lakes and rivers, 9–13
Boutin family, 74–75
bowfin, 166, 169, 219
British North America Act (1867), 12, 306
Bruce Peninsula (Ontario), 30, 126, 284
Bryan, William Jennings, 319
Buffalo, New York: and American expansion into Canadian waters, 55, 56; and anti-Americanism, 308, 309; and changing species in Great Lakes, 160, 161, 163; dealers in, 53, 56, 163, 218, 254; and decline of mainstays of commercial fishing in Lake Erie, 326; and developing drainage basins, 133, 138, 139, 145; and expansion of commercial fishing industry, 53, 55, 56; fishermen from, 86; fishing company in, 309; and growth patterns of commercial fishing industry, 34, 37; harbor of, 138; ice fishing around, 86; and industrial-urban development, 139, 145; and mining, 133; pollution around, 280, 281; Roosevelt's (Theodore) speech about pollution in, 288
Buffalo Fish Company, 56, 218, 223, 233
bullheads, 119, 163, 166, 169, 171, 246
bull nets, 259, 261
burbot, 152, 155, 169
Burlington Bay, 20, 87, 141, 142, 168, 179, 291
Burton, T. E., 317–18

Canada–U.S. relations: and American expansion into Canadian waters, 33, 213; and Atlantic fisheries, 240; and Bering Sea controversy, 228, 240, 241, 334; and Canadian seizure of American garbage barge, 143; and data about commercial fishing industry, 46; and decline of mainstays of commercial fishing industry, 326; and developing drainage basins, 142–43; and division of Great Lakes and rivers, 9–12; and dumping, 144–45; and growth patterns of commercial fishing, 33; and industrial-urban development, 142–43; and need for cooperation, 203, 212–13; and Pelee Island incident, 230–33; and regulation in Canada between 1879 and 1888, 213, 214; and research, 305. *See also* joint management/regulation; *specific commission*
Canadian Department of Marine and Fisheries: and American expansion into Canadian waters, 54, 55; annual reports of, 248; and anti-Americanism, 226, 227–28, 229, 230–33, 237, 308–9, 318; and Booth company operations, 70–72, 265, 266, 267, 268, 269, 271; and changing species in Great Lakes, 167; and cooperation between Canada and U.S., 213; corruption in, 222; creation of, 206; criticisms of, 214–15, 221–37; and decline of commercial fishing mainstays, 321; and developing drainage basins, 124, 142, 146; discrimination by, 222–24, 227, 236–37; and Dominion Police, 208; enforcement by, 77–78, 206, 207–8, 210–11, 214, 217–18, 221–22, 225–26, 227, 228, 229–30, 233–37; and expansion of commercial fishing industry, 54, 55; and Fishery Law of 1868, 206, 208–13; functions/goals of, 206–7, 208; and growth patterns of commercial fishing industry, 34; and hatcheries, 209–10; and Indians, 77–79; and industrial-urban development, 141–42, 146; and International Fisheries Commission study, 318; and joint Canadian–U.S. regulation, 203, 208, 240, 248; labor force statistics of, 47; licensing by, 81; and lumbering industry, 124, 211–12; and Noble brothers operations, 233–37; and overseers, 207; and Pelee Island incident, 230–33; and policy balance sheet, 320; and pollution, 291, 292, 293; Prince appointed to, 220–21, 303, 323–24; and regulation, 103, 213–15, 224–26; research program of, 302, 303–4; and salmon in Lake Ontario, 24; special investigations by, 227; Tupper as head of, 216–37; and Wilmot, 209–10. *See also* Minister of Marine and Fisheries

canals: and changing species in Great Lakes, 162; and decline of fishing, 109; and developing drainage basins, 124, 128–29, 130, 133, 138, 144; and growth patterns of commercial fishing industry, 29; and industrial-urban development, 138, 144; and interconnecting waterway system, 138; and mining, 128–29, 130, 133; and pollution, 281, 285; at Sault Sainte Marie, 128–29
canoes, 6–7, 21, 22, 30, 39, 76, 109
Cape Vincent, New York, 20, 65, 185, 201
capital investment: and American expansion into Canadian waters, 54; and Canadian development of commercial fishing, 254; comparison of American and Canadian, 263; and competition, 263; and decline of mainstays of commercial fishing industry, 332; in early twentieth century, 254, 255, 262, 263; and expansion of commercial fishing industry, 45, 47, 54, 57; and income of fishermen, 91–92; and markets and distribution strategies, 275; and Ontario–dominion controversy, 306; and pound nets, 94; and productivity, 262; and regulation, 105; and work of fishermen, 94; and World War I, 276, 278
carp: artificial propagation of, 256; and changing species in Great Lakes, 162, 164–66, 168, 169, 257, 279; in Georgian Bay, 322; in Lake Erie, 256, 324, 325; and pollution, 279, 293; and Prince's 1905 study, 322; production of, 255, 256; research about, 300; smoked, 256
catfish, 119, 168, 169
caviar, 56, 85, 159, 160
Chaumont Bay, 20, 29, 31
Cheboygan, Michigan, 126, 127, 128
chemical pollution, 280–81, 282, 283, 286, 287, 293, 294
Chicago, Illinois: and American expansion into Canadian waters, 56; and changing species in Great Lakes, 160; commercial growth of, 60; and cooperation in commercial fishing industry, 273; dealers in, 53, 160; and developing drainage basins, 133, 138, 139, 141; as distribution center, 301; and expansion of commercial fishing industry, 53, 56; and growth patterns of commercial fishing industry, 34, 37; harbor of, 138; and industrial-urban development, 139, 141; interstate cooperation meetings in, 311; as market, 62, 65–66, 275; and mining, 133; pollution around, 280, 281, 288; poor people as fishermen in, 88; trout as analogy with man from, 98; U.S. Commission study of fishing in area of, 198. *See also* A. Booth and Company
Chicago River, 139, 141, 280
chub, 163
Civil War, U.S., 34, 60, 80, 89, 133
Clark, John P., 29–30
Cleveland, Ohio: and American expansion into Canadian waters, 56; and anti-Americanism, 308; dealers in, 51, 53, 56, 101, 188–90, 191; and developing drainage basins, 129–30, 133, 138, 139; and expansion of commercial fishing industry, 51, 53, 56; fishermen from, 88; and fishermen's attitudes toward fish, 99; and growth patterns of commercial fishing industry, 34, 37, 42; harbor of, 138; and industrial-urban development, 139; labor unrest in, 102–3; and mining, 129–30, 133; packing facilities in, 76; pollution around, 280, 281; and state fishery commissions–fishermen relationship, 188–90, 191, 192; and technological development, 56
closed season: Baird's views about, 197; and decline of mainstays of commercial fishing industry, 322, 323, 324, 327; and Dominion Fishery Commission report, 219; and early regulation, 177–78, 179, 180, 182, 189; and enforcement, 214, 218, 230; and Fishery Law of 1868, 205; in Georgian Bay, 322, 323, 324; and International Fisheries Commission study, 313; and Joint Commission study, 241, 246; need for uniform Canadian and American, 107; and Prince's 1905 study, 322, 323; regulation of, 104, 106, 107, 214, 215, 225; and state fishery commissions–fishermen relationship, 189, 192; and Tupper administration, 218, 222, 225
coal, 130, 133, 134, 285, 287, 290
collective action, 273–74, 335–36. *See also* cooperation

Collingwood, Ontario, 57, 65, 86, 126, 214, 233
commercial fishing industry: American dominance in, 307; and American expansion into Canadian waters, 53–56, 59, 65, 69–72, 93, 104–5, 208, 213, 214, 219–20, 222, 227, 306, 308–9, 323; and British colonial policy, 12, 14; Canadian, 92, 246, 264, 307; and changing species in Great Lakes, 150–62, 166, 167–68, 169–70, 171; characteristics of, 32–33, 254–55; cooperation/consolidations in, 264, 273–74, 335–36; decline of, 202; end of era of, 109; expansion of, 44–58, 182, 185, 200, 239, 276, 278; and Indians, 298; influence of, 247–48, 249, 297, 318, 332, 333, 334, 336; and International Fisheries Commission study, 316, 318, 319; and Joint Commission study, 245, 247–48, 333; mainstay species of, 3, 42–43, 150–62, 321–30, 332; measurements of change in, 45–49; patterns of growth through 1872 of, 28–43; and policy balance sheet, 320; and Prince's 1905 study, 324; and public policy, 297; roving, 66–67, 99; and sportfishing, 297–98; and state fishery commissions, 187–94, 196; in state universities' curricula, 186; and states, 333; structure and strategies of, 263–75; and Tupper administration, 227, 233; U.S. Commission reports about, 202; as use pattern, 15; in wilderness era, 15. *See also specific person, company, or topic*
competition: and anti-Americanism, 227, 307; and Booth company operations, 65, 66, 67, 68, 69, 71, 264, 268–69; and Canadian views about states' regulation debates, 192; and capital investment, 263; as characteristic of commercial fishing industry, 254; and collective action, 273; and dealer system, 51, 72, 272; and decline of commercial fishing mainstays, 278, 321–22; and expansion of commercial fishing industry, 51, 58; and fishermen–dealer relationships, 72; and fishermen–state fishery commissions relationship, 189; and income of fishermen, 89–93; and markets and distribution strategies, 275; and regulation, 108–9, 187, 189, 215; and state fishery commissions, 189, 190; and Treaty of 1908, 319; and Tupper administration, 227
Connable Fishing Company, 56–57, 66
conservation: and artificial propagation, 311; British policies for, 12, 14, 102; and developing drainage basins, 146; and division of Great Lakes and rivers, 12, 332; in early agricultural-commercial economy, 14, 15; and economic issues, 334; and enforcement, 291, 335; and ethnicity of fishermen, 85; and expansion of commercial fishing industry, 49; failure of nineteenth century, 186–87, 192, 193–94; and federalism, 336; and fishermen's attitudes toward fish, 99; grassroots efforts at, 335; and growth patterns of commercial fishing industry, 35, 37, 42; and harvesting technology, 49; and industrial-urban development, 146; innovations in methods of, 35, 37; and International Fisheries Commission study, 318; lack of support for, 146, 278, 335; and legacy of wilderness era, 8–9, 12, 14; and politics, 323; and pollution, 291, 294, 311; popularity of, 312; and Prince's 1905 study, 323; and public policy, 311–12; and salmon in Lake Ontario, 25–26, 27; sportsmen as allies of, 335; and stocking programs, 311; and Treaty of 1908, 312–20; and Tupper administration, 221; and World War I, 276. *See also* progressives; regulation
consumption of fish, 85–86, 264, 274, 276, 278, 279, 305, 335
cooperation: Canada–U.S., in commercial fishing industry, 264, 273–74, 335–36. *See also* joint management/regulation
copper mining, 129–31, 132, 133, 194, 282–83, 284, 287
Coventry, John, 67–68
crayfish, 141
Crisis of 1890s, 238–49
Cruiser (patrol vessel), 217–18, 234

Dablon, Claude, 3–4, 6, 23
dams: Baird's views about, 197; and beaver devastation, 15; and changing species in Great Lakes, 159; and developing drainage basins, 123–24, 141–42, 145–46, 147; and enforcement, 218; and Fishery

dams (*continued*)
Law of 1868, 205, 210; and industrial-urban development, 141–42, 145–46, 147; and lumbering, 123–24; and regulation, 175, 176–77, 178, 179, 180, 213; and research, 298; and salmon fishing, 22, 25, 26; and Tupper administration, 218
destruction and waste of fish: and anti-Americanism, 248; and changing species in Great Lakes, 152, 153, 157–58, 159–60, 161, 162; and developing drainage basins, 147–48; and Dominion Fishery Commission report, 219, 220; and dominion survey of 1868–69, 210; between 1830 and 1890s, 99–102; and Fishery Law of 1868, 211; and industrial-urban development, 141, 147–48, 211; and Joint Commission study, 245, 248; from Lake Erie, 100, 101, 245; from Lake Michigan, 101, 141; from Lake Superior, 100; and licensing discrimination, 223; and Milner report, 198; and pollution, 101, 102, 290, 293, 295; and Tupper administration, 219, 220, 223; U.S. Commission reports about, 198, 201
Detroit, Michigan: and American expansion into Canadian waters, 55; automobile manufacturing in, 281; cartoons about Booth company in newspapers of, 268; and changing species in Great Lakes, 168; dealers in, 53, 154, 218; and developing drainage basins, 119, 129–30, 133, 135, 138, 139, 144; entrepreneurs around, 223; and expansion of commercial fishing industry, 53, 55; and growth patterns of commercial fishing industry, 28, 29–30, 31, 33, 34, 37, 39; harbor of, 138; and harvesting technology, 39; health issues in, 144; and industrial-urban development, 139, 144; international conference in, 185, 193; and Pelee Island incident, 231–32; pollution around, 280, 281, 291, 292; state fishery commissioners meet in, 184; in wilderness era, 8
Detroit River: and changing species in Great Lakes, 152, 161, 168; and decline of mainstays of commercial fishing industry, 326; and developing drainage basins, 139, 142, 143–44, 145; fishermen of, 83; and growth patterns of commercial fishing industry, 29, 30, 31, 36; and industrial-urban development, 142, 143–44, 145; and International Fisheries Commission study, 316, 317; and Joint Commission study, 244, 245, 247; licensing for fishing in, 223; pollution in, 280, 285, 289, 292, 295, 326; pound nets in, 94; and regulation, 179; and Tupper administration, 223, 226, 227, 228, 236; whitefish hatchery on, 210. *See also specific topic*
diesel engines, 258, 285
discrimination: by Canadian Department of Marine and Fisheries, 222–24, 227, 236–37
distribution strategies, 274–75
Dixon (steamer), 68, 69, 70
docks/harbors, 133, 134, 135, 138, 144, 246, 281
dogfish. *See* bowfin
Dolphin (patrol boat), 218, 230, 231
Dominion Fish Company: as Booth company, 73, 264, 265, 268–69, 321
Dominion Fishery Commission on the Fisheries of the Province of Ontario: and American expansion into Canadian waters, 55, 219–20; and Booth company operations, 65–66, 70; creation of/charge to, 218, 219–20; and decline of fishing, 103, 109; and destruction and waste of fish, 101; and developing drainage basins, 125–26, 142; and discrimination in licensing, 223; and expansion of commercial fishing industry, 55; and fishermen–dealer relationships, 92; and fishermen's attitudes toward fish, 99; and industrial-urban development, 142; and interviews of fishermen, 81; and lumbering, 125–26; and regulation dilemma, 102–5, 107; report of, 219, 222, 227. *See also* Prince, Edward E.; Wilmot, Samuel
Dominion of Canada: and Booth company operations, 269; conservation by, 14, 336; creation of, 177, 180; and decline of mainstays of commercial fishing industry, 323; and expansion of commercial fishing industry, 45–47; licensing by, 54; Ontario's controversy with, 269, 302, 304, 305–7, 312, 316, 319, 322, 323,

324, 336; and pollution, 294; and Prince's 1905 study, 323; and regulation, 177, 179–80, 204–15, 336; and research/studies, 261, 302, 304; and title to waters and beds of Great Lakes, 12. *See also* Dominion Fishery Commission on the Fisheries of the Province of Ontario
Dominion Police, 208, 234, 235
Door Peninsula (Wisconsin), 81, 83, 87, 121, 284
drainage basins: and agricultural development, 113–14, 116–20, 128, 136, 148; and changing species in Great Lakes, 149–71; and commerce, 137–38; and Dominion Fishery Commission report, 219–20; effects on fish population of, 27, 113–14, 116, 128, 136, 331; and industrial-urban development, 136, 137–48; and Joint Commission study, 244, 246; and lumbering, 113–14, 116, 120–28, 132–33, 136, 148; and mining, 113–14, 116, 128–36, 148; and salmon in Lake Ontario, 27. *See also specific basin*
dredging: and developing drainage basins, 126, 127, 129, 133, 135, 138, 144, 145; and docks/harbor development, 138; and industrial-urban development, 144, 145; and Joint Commission study, 245, 246; and Lake Erie, 246; and lumbering, 126, 127; and mining, 129, 133, 135; and pollution, 281, 283, 291
drinking water, 114, 143, 280, 284, 288, 289, 290
Duluth, Minnesota: and American expansion into Canadian waters, 54; Booth's activities in, 65, 67–69, 70, 72; and developing drainage basins, 129, 133, 138, 139; and expansion of commercial fishing industry, 54; fishermen from, 72; harbor of, 138; hatchery at, 64, 69, 185; and industrial-urban development, 139; and mining, 129, 133; pollution around, 280
dumping: and changing species in Great Lakes, 156; and developing drainage basins, 129, 130, 132, 133, 142, 144–45; and Dominion Fishery Commission report, 220; and enforcement, 218; federal control of, 129; and Fishery Law of 1868, 205, 211; and industrial-urban development, 142, 144–45; and Joint Commission study, 245, 246; in Lake Erie, 245; in Lake Huron, 246; and mining, 129, 130, 132, 133; and pollution, 280, 281, 289, 290, 291, 294, 295; and regulation, 179, 180, 181, 182, 214; and Tupper administration, 217, 218, 220
Dunkirk, New York, 106, 309
Dunn, Edward, 70–71, 144–45, 230, 231, 267–68, 308–11
Dutch: as fishermen, 81, 83

ecology, 298–99, 301, 320
electrical industry, 285, 286, 289
Elliott, Thomas H., 234, 235–36, 266
enforcement: and anti-Americanism, 227, 230–33, 308–11, 312; Baird's views about, 197; boats for, 208, 214, 217–18; and Booth company operations, 267–68; in Canada, 77–78, 179–80, 197, 203, 237, 261, 290–92; commercial fishing industry's distrust of, 278; and conservation, 335; criticisms of, 308; and decline of mainstays of commercial fishing industry, 332; and dominion survey of 1868–69, 210; and dominion–Ontario controversy, 306, 323; of early regulations, 178, 181, 189; and expansion of commercial fishing industry, 255; and failure of nineteenth century reform, 173, 186; as fair or foul, 225–26; and federalism, 311; and Fishery Law of 1868, 205, 206, 207–8, 210–11; on Georgian Bay, 206, 207, 214, 217, 218, 230, 322–23; and industrial-urban development, 144–45, 148; and intergovernmental cooperation, 185; and International Fisheries Commission study, 313, 316; and Joint Commission study, 247; on Lake Erie, 218, 230–33, 308–11; on Lake Huron, 206, 217, 218; on Lake Ontario, 210–11, 291–92; on Lake Superior, 206, 218, 230; and marketing, 274; in New York, 176; and Noble brothers operations, 233–37; Ontario as responsible for Canadian, 265, 308; and poaching, 153, 211, 213, 229, 312; as political issue, 214, 227–37; and pollution, 290–94; and Prince's 1905 study, 322–23; problems of, 103–4, 148, 206, 210–11, 214, 291,

enforcement (*continued*)
335; and public policy balance sheet, 320; and regulation between 1879 and 1888, 213, 214; and regulation dilemma, 105, 107; state fisheries commissions' concerns about, 186, 191; and state fishery commissions–fishermen relationship, 187, 189, 190, 191, 192; and states, 206, 319–20; and technology, 261; and Treaty of 1908, 319; by Tupper administration, 217–18, 221–22, 225–26, 227, 228, 229–30, 233–37; U.S. Commission's concerns about, 203. *See also* overseers; patrol boats
entrepreneurs: and agricultural development, 120; and American expansion into Canadian waters, 53–56; Canadian, 253–54; characteristics of, 51; and developing drainage basins, 120, 127, 139; and expansion of commercial fishing industry, 53–56, 253–54; fishermen's attitudes toward, 99; and growth patterns of commercial fishing industry, 43; and industrial-urban development, 139; and interconnecting waterway systems, 137–38; late nineteenth century business, 51; and structure and strategies of commercial fishing industry, 264; and tanneries, 127. *See also* Canada–U.S. relations, and American expansion into Canadian waters; dealers; *specific person or company*
environment, 147, 167–68, 238–39
Erie, Pennsylvania: and anti-Americanism, 308, 309; and Booth company operations, 267, 269; and cooperation in commercial fishing industry, 273–74; dealers in, 53, 58; and developing drainage basins, 133; and expansion of commercial fishing industry, 50, 53, 58; fishermen from, 92, 106; and growth patterns of commercial fishing industry, 34; and harvesting technology, 50; and regulation, 106; tugs from, 267, 269, 309
Erie Canal, 24, 29, 37, 162, 163, 176, 330
erosion, 117, 130, 133, 244, 284, 295
Escanaba, Michigan, 61, 62, 121, 133
Essex Peninsula (Ontario), 117, 118, 119
ethnicity: of fishermen, 76, 80–81, 83–84
experimentation, 56–58, 255, 336. *See also* technology
explorers, 4–5, 8, 15, 150, 158
family fishing, 75–76, 83, 87
farmers: fishermen as, 67–68, 81, 85–86, 87, 98, 200; illegal fishing by, 211; mobile pattern characteristics of, 57. *See also* agriculture
federalism, 249, 305–7, 311–12, 316, 323, 336
fertilizers, 117, 134, 158, 256, 284
filleting, 274–75
Finns, 83, 130
fish: and changing species in Great Lakes, 149–71, 214, 257, 279, 330; as cheap food source, 34, 88; as common property, 179, 332, 333, 335; evolution of new profile of Great Lakes, 166–71; fishermen's attitudes toward, 84–85, 98–99; introduction of new species of, 162–66; measures of change in profile of, 169–71; quality of, 52, 92. *See also* "rough, coarse fish"; *specific species of fish*
fish dealers: and American expansion into Canadian waters, 54, 55, 213, 220; Canadian, 55, 213, 272; Canadians as partners of American, 54; and changing species in Great Lakes, 154, 160, 168; characteristics of, 51; control by, 52–53, 56, 57–58, 108–9; cooperation among, 274; and destruction and waste of fish, 101; and developing drainage basins, 125–26; dominance of, 43, 45, 53, 57–58, 187; and economies of scale, 51; and expansion of commercial fishing industry, 45, 48, 49, 50–53, 54, 55, 56, 57–58; fishermen's relationships with, 52, 67–69, 72, 76, 80, 85, 88, 91, 92, 93, 106, 265, 271, 272–73, 274; and Georgian Bay, 52; and growth patterns of commercial fishing industry, 32, 33, 36–38, 43; and hatchery programs, 187; increase in number of, 254; Indians used by, 214; and International Fisheries Commission study, 316; and Lake Erie, 51, 52–53, 272; and Lake Huron, 51; and Lake Michigan, 51, 53; and Lake Superior, 51, 52; and lumbering, 125; and market and distribution strategies, 274, 275; and Panic of 1893, 58; and patrol boats, 218; and pecking order among fishermen, 88; and regulation, 180, 187, 214; and size of dealerships, 37; and

state fishery commissions, 187; and tariffs, 55; and technological development, 56, 57–58; and Tupper administration, 217, 218; and U.S. Commission, 52; weakening of American system of, 264, 272–73; wholesale, 50–53; and World War I, 276. *See also specific city or company*
Fisheries Protection Service (Dominion of Canada), 71, 230
fishermen: attitudes toward fish of, 84–85, 98–99; blacklisting of, 226; blamed for destruction and waste of fish, 101–2; and Booth company operations, 64–65, 67–69, 70–72, 265, 266, 268–69, 271; and changing species in Great Lakes, 150, 153, 154, 163, 171; and conservation, 85; and Crisis of 1890s, 239; dealers' relationships with, 52, 67–69, 72, 76, 80, 85, 88, 91, 92, 93, 106, 265, 271, 272–73, 274; debts of, 52, 92, 106, 233–34, 236; dependency on steamers of, 69; and destruction and waste of fish, 99–102; and developing drainage basins, 125–26, 128, 135–36, 141, 143, 144; discrimination charges by, 222–24; and dominion survey of 1868–69, 210; between 1850 and 1893, 74–88; ethnicity and race of, 76, 80–85; and expansion of commercial fishing industry, 48, 49, 51, 253–54; as farmers, 67–68, 81, 85–86, 87, 98, 200; first, 5–9; and fish as common property, 335; fishery experts' relationships with, 334; and fishing as family effort, 75–76, 83, 87; and fishing as gamble, 94; as guides, 200; harrowing escapes and disasters faced by, 67, 74–75, 97–98; and hatchery program, 187; image of, 101–2; immigrants as, 80, 81, 84–85; income of, 89–93, 200; and industrial-urban development, 143, 144, 147; and International Fisheries Commission study, 316; knowledge of, 94, 108; and lumbering, 125, 126, 128; as lumber workers, 81, 86, 87; as miners, 86; and Noble brothers operations, 233–37; ownership of gear by, 88, 91–92; part-time, 32–33, 67–69, 85–86, 88, 187, 263, 335; pecking order among, 88; personal qualities of, 74, 75; and petroleum industry, 135–36; physical rigors of, 93–98; and pollution, 291, 296; poor people as, 88, 228; and price, 69, 85, 93; and Prince's 1905 study, 322; and regulation, 102–9, 180, 187, 224–26, 227–37, 334, 335–36; rivalry between Canadian and American, 104–5; and role of government, 105; self-image of, 74; and state fishery commissions, 187; and stocking programs, 334; trade associations of, 335–36; and Tupper administration, 217, 222–26, 227–37; urban dwellers as, 87–88; women as, 226; work of, 93–98, 335. *See also* capital investment; production; *specific topic*
Fishery Law (Canada, 1868), 179–80, 205–13, 290, 293, 306
fishing gear, 80, 86, 88, 91–92, 180, 246, 313, 327. *See also* capital investment; *type of gear*
Fishing Islands, 30, 32
fish inspectors/wardens, 24, 186, 190, 278, 290–91, 293. *See also* overseers
fish ladders, 197, 218, 298. *See also* fishways
fish oil, 56, 85, 160, 256
fishways, 177, 178, 179, 180, 197, 205, 210, 211, 214. *See also* fish ladders
Foreign Relations Committee, U.S. Senate, 317, 318
forest fires, 121–22, 123
Fox River, 7, 121, 127, 296
freezing techniques, 49, 51, 62, 274, 275
French Canadians, 80, 81, 83, 223–24, 233
freshwater lamprey/lamprey eel, 157, 219
fruit farming, 86, 116
fur trading/traders, 4–5, 15, 29, 31, 44, 57, 114, 150

gaff hooks, 5, 78, 161
Ganley, Joseph, 65, 72, 77
garbage, 143, 144–45, 245, 285. *See also* pollution; sewage; waste
Gary, Indiana, 4, 138
gasoline engines, 258, 281, 285
Gauthier, Charles, 99, 223
Genesee River, 20, 25, 142, 143, 170, 176
Georgian Bay: American expansion into, 55, 56, 323; and Booth company operations, 266, 268–69; changing species in,

Georgian Bay (*continued*) 150, 152, 154, 160, 163–64, 171, 214; decline of commercial fishing in, 321–24; effects of federalism on, 323; enforcement on, 322–23; and expansion of commercial fishing industry, 49–50, 52, 55, 56; fishermen on, 81, 83, 86, 91, 98, 99, 261, 322; and fishermen's attitudes toward fish, 99; and growth patterns of commercial fishing industry, 30, 39; and industrial-urban development, 146; and International Fisheries Commission study, 318; and Joint Commission study, 244, 246, 247; and joint management, 324; Noble brothers operations on, 230, 233–37; pollution in, 246, 287, 324; Prince's 1905 study of, 322–24; and regulation of fishing, 104, 107, 214, 215, 225, 226, 322–23; research about, 303–4; sea lampreys in, 330; and Squaw Island controversy, 268–69; and Tupper administration, 216, 217, 218, 223, 224, 225, 226; in wilderness era, 6. *See also* Georgian Bay Fisheries Commission; *specific species of fish*

Georgian Bay Biological Station, 304, 320, 322

Georgian Bay Fisheries Commission, 269, 304, 307–8, 322–24

Germans: as fishermen, 80, 81, 83, 84–85

gill nets: and Booth's expansion, 62, 64, 67–68, 70; and changing species in Great Lakes, 154, 161; and decline of mainstays in Lake Erie, 327; and destruction and waste of fish, 100, 101; and Dominion Fishery Commission report, 219, 220; and early state regulation, 181; and economy, 235; and ethnicity of fishermen, 84; and expansion of commercial fishing industry, 49–50, 51, 56, 58; and fishermen–dealer relationships, 67; in Georgian Bay, 322; and growth patterns of commercial fishing industry, 30, 38, 39–40, 41, 42; and harvesting technology, 38, 39–40, 41, 42, 49–50; and income of fishermen, 90; and Indians as fishermen, 77, 84; and industrial-urban development, 143, 144; and Joint Commission study, 245; in Lake Erie, 100, 189–92, 201, 245, 261; in Lake Ontario, 245; lifting of, 56–57, 97, 258, 260 (fig.); and Noble brothers operations, 234; and pound nets debate in Ohio, 189–92, 201; and Prince's 1905 study, 322; and regulation, 103–4, 107, 188–90, 201, 215, 225, 226; rise and decline of fishing with, 64; and roving fishing, 66–67; seizure of, 230, 309; and state fishery commissions–fishermen relationship, 188–92; and states–province cooperation, 327; and technology, 56–57, 258, 259; for trout, 68; and Tupper administration, 219, 225, 226; in wilderness era, 6, 7; and work of fishermen, 94, 97; and World War I, 276. *See also* nets

gill-net steamers: 41, 49–50, 254, 258, 260 (fig.), 276, 322, 325

Goderich, Ontario, 30–31, 81, 83, 134, 135

Gogebic-Penokee Range, 131, 132

gold mining, 134, 136, 283, 287

Gott, George, 144–45

Grace M (tug), 309–10

Grand River, 134, 165, 291, 292–93

Great Britain: and Bering Sea controversy, 228, 240, 241, 334; Booth's connections in, 61; and boundary between Canada and U.S., 9, 331; cultural attitudes about salmon in, 26; fishery policies of, 12, 14, 102, 178, 289–90, 305, 332; and growth patterns of commercial fishing industry, 34, 35; influence on Canadian policies of, 205; and Joint Commission study, 242, 247–48; and joint management/regulation, 239, 333; as market, 34, 35, 151; and opposition over negotiating treaties for Canada, 316; and Pelee Island incident, 231; and pollution, 287, 289–90; and survey of American fisheries, 199; and Treaty of 1908, 312–20, 324; U.S. negotiations with, 199. *See also* Joint Commission Relative to the Preservation of the Fisheries in Waters Contiguous to Canada and the United States

Great Depression, 253, 258, 272, 327, 330, 331

Great Lakes: changing species in, 149–71, 214, 257, 279, 330; division of, 9–12, 15; Euro–North American visions of, 15; evolution of new profile of fish in,

166–71; influx of fish not native to, 162–66; as means of transportation, 114; physical characteristics of, 113, 115 (fig.); reasons for decline of fishery resources in, 336–37; size of, 4. *See also specific lake or topic*
Great Lakes Fisheries Laboratory, 302
Great Lakes Fishery Commission, 333
Great Lakes Water Quality Agreements, 334
Green, Seth, 25, 147, 162, 163, 164–65, 239
Green Bay: and changing species in Great Lakes, 152, 155, 159–60, 168; and destruction and waste of fish, 100; fishermen on, 83, 263; and growth patterns of commercial fishing industry, 30, 41; harvesting in, 259; and harvesting technology, 41; ice fishing on, 86–87; and lumbering, 121, 122, 127, 152; night spearfishing on, 7 ; pollution in, 280, 296; trap nets in, 259; in wilderness era, 7, 8
groundwater, 281, 289
Gulf of Mexico, 114, 137, 285
Gulf of St. Lawrence, 210, 242, 303

Hamilton, Ontario: Canadian–U.S. game officials meet in, 142–43; and changing species in Great Lakes, 170; creditors of fishermen in, 236; enforcement around, 210; fishermen from, 87; and growth patterns of commercial fishing industry, 34; harbor of, 138; and industrial-urban development, 139, 141, 142, 146; international conference in, 193; pollution around, 279–80
Hancock, Michigan, 129–30
harbors. *See* docks/harbors
Harris, Edward, 219, 220
harvesting of fish: and American expansion into Canadian waters, 56; and anti-Americanism, 318; and cooperation in commercial fishing industry, 274; and dealers, 53; decline in, 57; and decline of mainstays of commercial fishing industry, 253, 324; and expansion of commercial fishing industry, 49–50, 51, 53, 56, 57, 255; experimentation with new ways of, 255; in Georgian Bay, 39, 49–50, 323, 324; in Green Bay, 259; and growth patterns of commercial fishing industry, 36, 37, 38–41, 42; and intergovernmental cooperation, 334; and International Fisheries Commission study, 318; in Lake Erie, 38, 39, 49, 50; in Lake Huron, 38, 40; in Lake Michigan, 39, 40, 41, 49; in Lake Ontario, 38, 40; in Lake Superior, 39, 40; and limnological survey of Lake Erie, 327; and markets and distribution strategies, 275; and Prince's 1905 study, 323; and production levels, 263; and regulation, 334; and research, 305; and structure and strategies of commercial fishing industry, 264; and technological development, 38–41, 42, 49–50, 57, 258–61; unevenness of, 93–94; U.S. Commission reports about, 49; and work of fishermen, 93–94; and World War I, 276, 278. *See also* production
hatcheries: and Booth's expansion, 72; and cooperation between Canada and U.S., 213; criticisms of, 214, 304–5; dealer-entrepreneur views about, 51; and expansion of commercial fishing industry, 51, 57; and federal–state cooperation, 182–85, 201; and federalism, 311; first federal, 199; increase in number of Canadian, 209–10, 237; and intergovernmental cooperation, 193; in Michigan, 183 (fig.), 200, 311; Nettle's work with, 208–9; in New York state, 201; Ontario as responsible for Canadian, 304, 307, 320; and policy balance sheet, 320; and pollution, 295; popularity of, 187; and public policy, 298; Put-in-Bay, Ohio, 300; and reasons for failure of nineteenth century conservation efforts, 186–87; and regulation, 107, 179, 214; and research, 298, 302, 304–5; for salmon, 208–10; and technology, 57; U.S. Commission's support for, 198–99, 201; violence against, 209, 211; for whitefish, 199, 210; Wilmot's work with, 198, 209–10
health issues: and Crisis of 1890s, 238; and enforcement through customs laws, 144–45; and industrial-urban development, 144–45, 146; and joint efforts, 334; and marketing and distribution strategies, 274–75; and pollution, 280, 284, 285, 288, 289, 290, 294, 296; as

health issues (*continued*)
trigger for regulation, 146; and World War I, 278
herring: and changing species in Great Lakes, 149, 154, 155–56, 162, 163, 167, 168, 169–70, 171, 279; and cooperation in commercial fishing industry, 273, 274; decline/devastation of, 27, 245, 251, 255, 286, 297, 302, 321, 324–26, 327, 330, 332; and decline of mainstays of commercial fishing industry, 256, 327; demise of era of commercial fishing of, 45; and destruction and waste of fish, 100; in Detroit River, 245; escalation in catch of, 254; and expansion of commercial fishing industry, 45, 56, 58; fishermen for, 76, 93; in Georgian Bay, 322; and growth patterns of commercial fishing industry, 30; ice fishing for, 86; and industrial-urban development, 144; and International Fisheries Commission study, 318; and Joint Commission study, 245; in Lake Erie, 27, 245, 251, 255, 261, 274, 275, 286, 302, 320, 321, 324, 325–26, 327; in Lake Huron, 294, 301–2; in Lake Ontario, 291; in Lake Superior, 76; as mainstay of commercial fishing industry, 27, 153, 154, 155–56, 327; marketed as salmon, 56; and markets and distribution strategies, 275; overfishing of, 58, 168, 332; and pollution, 279, 286, 291, 294, 302; predators of, 154, 155, 322; price of, 324; and Prince's 1905 study, 322; production of, 157, 169–70, 255, 256, 325; and regulation, 179, 188; research about, 299, 301–2; in Saginaw Bay, 294, 318; smoked, 155; and state fishery commissions–fishermen relationship, 188; and technological development, 56; in wilderness era, 5
hooks and lines, 5, 36, 67–68, 78, 84, 88, 176, 177, 231, 258
hoop nets, 6, 84, 225
Hubbard, Bela, 35, 150–51
Hudson River, 29, 162
Hudson's Bay Company, 31, 77
Humber River, 20, 22, 88, 141–42
Huron, Ohio, 37, 52, 53, 58, 106, 133
ice fishing, 36, 86–87, 88, 127
Icelanders: as fishermen, 83
illegal fishing: and American expansion into Canadian waters, 104, 208; and anti-Americanism, 308–11; and Booth company operations, 266; and changing species in Great Lakes, 152; and decline of mainstays of commercial fishing industry, 324; and discrimination in licensing, 223, 224; and Dominion Fishery Commission report, 220; and dominion survey of 1868–69, 210; fines and penalties for, 179; and fishermen–dealer relationship, 92; and Fishery Law of 1868, 206, 208, 210, 211; in Georgian Bay, 322–23, 324; and harvesting technology, 261; by Indians, 77–78; in Lake Ontario, 211; and Noble brothers operations, 233–37; and Pelee Island incident, 230–33; and Prince's 1905 study, 322–23, 324; and regulation, 104, 214, 225; and Tupper administration, 220, 223, 224, 225, 230–37. *See also* enforcement; overseers; patrol boats; poaching
Illinois, 11–12, 116, 117, 263. *See also* Chicago, Illinois
Illinois River, 139–40
immigrants, 34, 51, 80, 81, 83–85
Indians: and Booth company operations, 65, 266; and British–American relations, 10; Canadian laws as applicable to, 77–79; and commercial fishing industry, 19, 65, 266, 298; and discrimination in licensing, 223, 224; exploitation of, 78–79, 178, 214; as fishermen, 5–9, 76–81, 84; fishing methods of, 39, 76, 77, 78, 84; near Georgian Bay, 81; illegal fishing by, 77–78, 214; in Killarney, 233; near Lake Huron, 76, 79; near Lake Michigan, 76; near Lake Ontario, 19; near Lake Superior, 64, 76, 77, 81; lumbering's effects on, 77; population of, 76; and public policy, 77–79, 298; removal of, 331; salmon fishing by, 19, 21, 22–23, 24; near Sault Sainte Marie, 81; as source of knowledge, 84; spearfishing by, 7, 130; and sportfishing, 298; subsistence culture of, 7–9, 10, 15, 19, 23; torchlight fishing by, 7, 130; treaty rights of, 64, 79–80, 223, 298; and Tupper ad-

ministration, 223; and whitefish, 124, 150; in wilderness era, 5–9, 10, 20, 22, 23
industrial-urban development: and changing species in Great Lakes, 153, 167–68, 170, 337; and developing drainage basins, 136, 137–48; and Joint Commission study, 245, 246; near Lake Erie, 139, 143–44, 145, 146, 246, 325; near Lake Huron, 143–44, 146, 246; near Lake Michigan, 138, 139, 141; near Lake Ontario, 139, 141, 142, 143, 146; near Lake Superior, 139; legacy of, 325, 331, 337; and pollution, 279–86, 287, 289, 290, 292, 294, 295, 337. *See also* lumbering; mining
insecticides/pesticides, 117, 284
International Fisheries Commission, 312–20
International Joint Commission, 283–84, 285, 288, 289, 334
Irish: as fishermen, 81, 83
iron mining, 131–33, 134, 194, 283, 285, 287
isinglass, 56, 85, 159, 160
Isle Royale, 68–69, 72, 83, 84, 85, 98, 116, 130–31, 316

Joint Commission Relative to the Preservation of the Fisheries in Waters Contiguous to Canada and the United States: American reactions to report of, 247–48; and anti-Americanism, 248; appointments to, 242; and Booth company operations, 64–65, 66, 68, 69–70; and Canadian Department of Marine and Fisheries, 240, 248; Canadian reactions to report of, 248; and Canadian system of regulation, 244, 248; and changing species in Great Lakes, 150, 160, 161, 163, 164, 166; and commercial fishing industry, 333; creation of/charge to, 240–41, 243; and Crisis of 1890s, 238–40; criticisms of report by, 247–48; and destruction and waste of fish, 101; and developing drainage basins, 119, 125, 126–27, 128, 135, 143, 144; failure of, 333; findings and recommendations of, 241, 243–49, 274; as first attempt at joint management, 313, 333; and fishermen–dealer relationship, 92; gathering of information by, 242–43; and gill netters versus pound netters, 191; and pollution, 333; and regulation dilemma, 102–3, 105–8; and research, 299; and Tupper's administration, 221; and work of fishermen, 97
joint management/regulation: and Canadian Department of Marine and Fisheries, 203, 208, 240, 248; and commercial fishing industry, 332; and decline of mainstays of commercial fishing industry, 324, 327; differing American and Canadian views toward, 332–33; examples of European, 240–41; failure to achieve, 239–40, 248–49, 333–34; and federalism, 336; and Georgian Bay, 324; and health issues, 334; and international agreements, 312–20, 333; and International Fisheries Commission study, 289, 312–20; Joint Commission study about, 102–3, 105–8, 243–49, 312, 313; and Joint High Commission study, 312; lack of public support for, 332; and nationalism, 333; need for, 109, 292; and policy balance sheet, 320; and pollution, 292; and Prince's 1905 study, 324; problems/difficulties of, 332–33; and public policy, 312–20; and research, 332; and sea lamprey, 333; and state fishery commissions, 193; and states, 333; by states–province, 327; and Treaty of 1908, 251, 312–20; and treaty-making powers, 240; and Tupper administration, 218, 227–28, 237; and Waterways Commission, 312
Jones Island, 75, 83
Jordan, David Starr, 313, 314 (fig.), 315–16, 318, 319

Kate Wilson (tug), 267, 309
Kenosha, Wisconsin, 263, 280, 281
Kerr, John W., 180, 210
Keweenaw Peninsula (Michigan), 83, 129, 130, 131, 132, 200, 283
Killarney, Ontario, 52, 77–78, 214, 218, 223, 229, 233, 234, 235, 321, 323
Kincardine, Ontario, 83, 134–35
King, Larry, 86, 99
Kingston, Ontario, 4, 20, 280
Kittie Gaylord (steamer), 41

Kitty D (tug), 309
Koelz, Walter, 149, 254–55, 258, 262, 285, 295, 301–2, 324–26
Kolbe, W. F. *See* W. F. Kolbe and Company
Kumlien, Ludwig, 80–81, 83, 89–90, 94, 97, 198, 199

labor force, 47–48, 54, 55, 102–3, 261, 264
Lake Erie: and American expansion into Canadian waters, 55, 56, 219; and anti-Americanism, 227, 308–11; battle of, (1894), 232; and Booth company operations, 266, 267–68, 269, 271; and boundary issues, 9, 11–12; and changing species, 154, 155–56, 157–58, 159, 160, 161, 163, 165, 166, 167, 168, 171; characteristics of, 4; and cooperation between Canada and U.S., 212; and cooperation in commercial fishing industry, 273–74; decline of commercial fishing in, 321, 322, 324–27, 330; drainage basins around, 114, 116, 117, 118–19, 120, 129, 131, 133, 135, 139, 143–44, 145, 146, 246; early agricultural-commercial economy around, 10; enforcement on, 218, 230–33, 308–11; and expansion of commercial fishing industry, 49, 50, 51, 52–53, 55, 56, 253–54; and failure of reform, 192; and federalism, 311; fishermen of, 83, 86, 94, 154, 157–58; and growth patterns of commercial fishing industry, 28, 29, 30, 31, 34, 36, 38, 39; industrial-urban development near, 139, 143–44, 145, 146, 246, 325; and International Fisheries Commission study, 316; and Joint Commission study, 242, 244, 245–46, 247, 274; limnological survey of, 286, 295, 304, 326, 327; pollution in, 245–46, 280, 284, 285–86, 292, 295, 296, 324, 326, 327; production for, 202, 255, 256, 261, 325; public concern about, 326; rate of cleansing, 113; regulation of, 104, 105–7, 175, 180, 188–90, 192; research about, 299–300, 302; retention time for, 4; and state fishery commissions–fishermen relationship, 188–92; and technological development, 56; and Tupper administration, 218, 219, 226, 227, 228, 236; U.S. Commission reports about, 201, 202; in wilderness era, 4, 9, 11–12. *See also* Pelee Island incident; *specific topic*
Lake Huron: and American expansion into Canadian waters, 55, 56, 219; and Booth company operations, 68, 269; and Canada–U.S. boundary, 11; changing species in, 152, 154, 156, 163–64, 165, 167, 168, 171, 214; and cooperation between Canada and U.S., 212; and cooperation in commercial fishing industry, 274; decline of fishing on, 109; drainage basins around, 114, 116, 120, 121, 124, 125, 126, 127–28, 135, 143–44, 146; and expansion of commercial fishing industry, 51, 55, 56; fishermen of, 81, 86, 99, 128; and growth patterns of commercial fishing industry, 29, 30, 36, 38, 40; and industrial-urban development, 143–44, 146, 246; and International Fisheries Commission study, 318; and Joint Commission study, 244, 246, 247; lumbering around, 282; pollution in, 200, 246, 282, 287, 294, 295, 302; regulation of, 107, 214, 226; research about, 301–2; retention time for, 4; sea lampreys in, 330; and Tupper administration, 216, 217, 218, 219, 223, 226; U.S. Commission report about, 200; in wilderness era, 4–5, 6, 8, 11. *See also* North Channel; *specific topic*
Lake Michigan: and American expansion into Canadian waters, 56; beam-trawl trial on, 56, 61, 84; and Booth company operations, 269; and boundary decisions, 4, 12; changing species in, 149, 154, 155, 158, 160, 164, 165, 167, 168; drainage basins around, 114, 116, 117, 120, 121, 122, 125, 128, 129, 133, 138, 139, 141; exclusion from Joint Commission study of, 105, 242; and expansion of commercial fishing industry, 49, 51, 53, 56, 58; fishermen of, 77, 81, 83, 84, 85–86, 94, 141; and growth patterns of commercial fishing industry, 29, 30, 34, 36, 39, 40, 41; industrial-urban development around, 138, 139, 141; and International Fisheries Commission study, 318; labor force on, 47; Milner's study of, 39, 40, 41, 47; pollution in, 200, 280, 287; rate of cleansing, 113; reten-

tion time for, 4; and technological development, 56; U.S. Commission report about, 200; in wilderness era, 8, 12. *See also* A. Booth and Company; *specific topic*
Lake Nipigon, 158, 276, 286
Lake of the Woods, 57, 93, 99, 161, 229, 316
Lake Ontario: and American expansion into Canadian waters, 56; and Booth company operations, 269; and boundaries, 9, 11; changing species in, 149, 154, 162, 163, 164, 167, 168, 169, 170, 214; decline of commercial fishing on, 202, 332; and dominion survey of 1868–69, 210; drainage basins around, 114, 116, 117, 120, 127, 128, 134, 139, 141, 142, 143, 146; early settlements around, 10, 23–24; enforcement on, 210–11, 291–92; and expansion of commercial fishing industry, 56; and federal–state cooperation, 185; fishermen of, 84, 86, 143; and Fishery Law of 1868, 205, 208–11; and growth patterns of commercial fishing industry, 28, 29, 37, 38, 40; and industrial-urban development, 139, 141, 142, 143, 146; and International Fisheries Commission study, 316; and Joint Commission study, 242, 244, 245, 247; pollution in, 200, 245, 279–80, 282, 284, 285–86, 288, 291–92; production from, 200, 261; rate of cleansing, 113; regulation of, 19, 25–26, 27, 107, 175–78, 180, 208–11; retention time for, 4; sea lampreys in, 330; U.S. Commission reports about, 200, 201–2; in wilderness era, 4, 7, 9–11; Wilmot's programs for propagation and stocking of, 208, 209. *See also specific topic*
Lake St. Clair: and changing species in Great Lakes, 161, 165, 167, 168; and developing drainage basins, 136, 143–44; and growth patterns of commercial fishing industry, 30, 31; and industrial-urban development, 143–44; and Joint Commission study, 244, 247; pollution in, 286; and regulation as fair or foul, 226; research about, 299; sturgeon of, 78; and Tupper administration, 226, 227, 236
Lake Superior: and American expansion into Canadian waters, 56; and American versus Canadian policies, 229; and Booth company operations, 58, 62, 64–73, 265, 266, 269, 272; and Canada–U.S. boundary, 4, 11; changing species in, 149, 150, 152, 154–55, 158, 159, 160, 164, 169–70; characteristics of, 4; and cooperation in commercial fishing industry, 273, 274; drainage basins around, 114, 116, 120–21, 122, 125, 128–29, 130, 131, 132, 133, 134, 139; and expansion of commercial fishing industry, 51, 52, 56, 58; fishermen of, 76, 80, 81, 84, 85, 86, 94; and growth patterns of commercial fishing industry, 31, 36, 39, 40; and industrial-urban development, 139; and Joint Commission study, 244, 246, 247; pollution in, 155, 246, 280, 282; production from, 261; rate of cleansing, 113; and regulation, 107; research about, 299; retention time for, 4; and Tupper administration, 218, 229, 230; and U.S. Commission study, 200; in wilderness era, 4, 6, 8, 11. *See also specific topic*
Lamorandier, Pierre de, 234–35
Laurier, Sir Wilfrid, 236, 248, 291, 312, 322
lawyers. *See* bowfin
leasing of fishing grounds, 179, 190, 191, 199, 205, 207
lime, 117, 134, 179, 180, 181, 205, 290
limnological survey: of Lake Erie, 286, 295, 304, 326, 327
Lodge, Henry Cabot, 317
Long Point Company, 219, 222, 309
lumbering: and agriculture, 123; and changing species in Great Lakes, 152, 168, 169, 170; complaints about, 124–25; and Crisis of 1890s, 238; and dealers, 125; and destruction and waste of fish, 101; and developing drainage basins, 113–14, 116, 120–28, 130, 132–33, 136, 148; effects on Indians of, 77; and enforcement, 218; expansion of Canadian, 213; and fishermen, 81, 125; and Fishery Law of 1868, 211–12; near Georgian Bay, 104, 120, 121, 124, 125, 126, 128, 212, 213, 246; near Green Bay, 152; and growth patterns of commercial fishing industry, 35; impact on Great

lumbering (*continued*)
Lakes of, 125–26, 128; and Joint Commission study, 244, 245, 246; near Lake Erie, 120; near Lake Huron, 104, 120, 121, 124, 125, 126, 127–28, 212; near Lake Michigan, 120, 121, 122, 125; near Lake Ontario, 120, 127, 128; near Lake Superior, 120–21, 122, 125, 246; and mining, 130, 132–33, 134; mobile pattern characteristics of, 57; as more important than fishing, 211–12; and Ontario–dominion controversy, 306; and pollution, 124–25, 282, 286, 287, 289, 293, 295; production patterns in, 44; and regulation, 104, 213, 214; and salmon fishing, 26; and spawning, 152; and Tupper administration, 218; U.S. Commission reports about, 125; and whitefish decline, 200; in Wisconsin, 152

MacGregor, Alexander, 30–31, 32
Mackinac County, Michigan, 6, 77
Mackinac Island, 42, 150
Mackinaw boats, 40–41, 42, 74, 84, 90, 101, 141
Manitoba, 73, 161, 264, 266
Manitoulin Island, 52, 78, 81, 223, 224, 233, 235, 266, 268
Manitowoc, Wisconsin, 30, 128, 280
marine biological stations, 303–4
marine biologists, 320, 326–27
markets: American dominance in Canadian, 45; and American expansion into Canadian waters, 47, 54, 56; analysis of, 278; and anti-Americanism, 307, 308; and Booth company operations, 65, 267, 269; Canadian, 45, 307, 323; Canadian access to American, 272, 307; and changing species in Great Lakes, 155, 159; and dealer system, 52, 272; and decline of mainstays of commercial fishing industry, 332; and developing drainage basins, 137–38, 139; in early twentieth century, 255; and enforcement, 274; expansion of, 214, 253; and expansion of commercial fishing industry, 54, 56; glutting of, 215, 225, 267; and growth patterns of commercial fishing industry, 27–28, 33, 34, 36, 37, 42; and income of fishermen, 92; and industrial-urban development, 139; and marketing systems, 253; and policy balance sheet, 320; and Prince's 1905 study, 323; and production, 263; and regulation, 213, 214, 225; research about, 301, 305; and salmon in Lake Ontario, 27; and structure and strategies of commercial fishing industry, 264; and Tupper administration, 225; and World War I, 275–76. *See also* transportation
Marquette, Michigan, 132, 133, 258
Marquette Range, 131, 132
Marsh, George Perkins, 146–47, 197
Maumee River, 29, 119, 135, 295, 326
McKinley, William, 190, 191, 248
McKinley Tariff (1890), 55, 65
Menominee Range, 131, 132
Mesabi Range, 132
metal industries: as pollutants, 280–81, 282. *See also* mining; *specific type of industry*
métis, 81, 83, 233
Michigan: and agricultural development, 116–17, 118, 119, 120; and anti-Americanism, 310–11; antipollution provisions in laws of, 290; artificial propagation program in, 186, 311; boundaries of, 12; and changing species in Great Lakes, 150, 151, 160, 168; conservation in, 259; and decline of mainstays in Lake Erie, 327; and Detroit international conference, 185; and developing drainage basins, 116–17, 118, 119, 120, 121, 124, 128–29, 131, 132, 133, 134, 142; and federalism, 311; and growth patterns of commercial fishing industry, 29, 30; hatcheries in, 200, 311; Indians in, 8, 79; and industrial-urban development, 142; and intergovernmental cooperation, 184, 212, 327; and International Fisheries Commission study, 318; labor force in, 263; lumbering in, 121, 124, 132, 282; mining in, 128–29, 131, 132, 133, 134; and pollution, 281; regulation in, 12, 181–82, 188, 192, 263, 318; and research, 299; salt deposits in, 281; sportfishing in, 184; state educational institutions in, 186; and state fishery commissions–fishermen relationship, 188, 192; statehood for, 11–12; and U.S. Com-

mission survey, 199; whitefish decline in waters of, 200; in wilderness era, 12. *See also specific city/town*
Michigan Board of Fish Commissioners, 144, 168, 184, 185, 186, 188, 193, 199, 299, 312
Michilimackinac, 5, 8
Michipicoten Island, 66, 152
mills: and changing species in Great Lakes, 153; and developing drainage basins, 142, 143, 146, 147; and Dominion Fishery Commission report, 220; and Fishery Law of 1868, 205, 211–12; and Georgian Bay, 246; and industrial-urban development, 142, 143, 146, 147; and Joint Commission study, 246; and Lake Superior, 246; and patrol boats, 230; and pollution, 282, 283, 284, 287, 290, 291, 293, 294; and regulation, 176, 177, 181, 182, 214; and whitefish decline, 200. *See also* lumbering
Milner, James W.: artificial propagation and stocking programs of, 182, 196–97; on capital investment, 47; and changing species in Great Lakes, 150–51, 152, 153–54, 155, 157, 158, 159–60; on dealers, 51; and developing drainage basins, 141, 147; on harvesting technology, 38–41, 49; and industrial-urban development, 141, 147; on labor force, 47; and pollution, 198; and production figures, 46; and regulation, 182; report on commercial fishing industry of, 35–38; significance of 1872 report of, 41–43, 303; Smiley's review of reports of, 199; on spawning grounds, 93; and state fishery commissions, 182; and wasteful fishing practices, 198; and whitefish decline, 182, 198; and work of fishermen, 93
Milwaukee, Wisconsin: and Booth company operations, 62; and developing drainage basins, 127–28, 139, 141; fishermen from, 76, 84; and growth patterns of commercial fishing industry, 34; harbor growth of, 140 (fig.); ice fishing near, 86–87; international conference in, 193; pollution around, 280, 281
mining: and developing drainage basins, 113–14, 116, 128–36, 148; and fishermen as miners, 86; and growth patterns of commercial fishing industry, 35; near Lake Superior, 128–29, 130, 131, 132, 133, 134; and lumbering, 130, 132–33; in northern Great Lakes region, 282–83; open-pit, 132; and pollution, 282–84, 286, 287, 290; production patterns in, 44; and regulation, 194; shaft, 132
Minister of Marine and Fisheries: and cooperation with U.S., 212–13; and decline of mainstays of commercial fishing industry, 323, 324; and enforcement, 210–11; and Fishery Law of 1868, 205, 207; as head of Department of Marine and Fisheries, 206; and International Fisheries Commission study, 316; and marine biological stations, 303; and Prince's 1905 study, 323, 324; and research, 303–4; role of, 244. *See also* Canadian Department of Marine and Fisheries; *specific person*
Minneapolis, Minnesota, 62, 301
Minnesota: and cooperation in commercial fishing industry, 273; and Detroit international conference, 185; and developing drainage basins, 133; and early regulation for Great Lakes waters, 12; and federal–state cooperation, 184; and federalism, 311; fishermen of, 85; mining in, 131–32, 133; and U.S. Commission survey, 199; in wilderness era, 12. *See also specific city/town*
missionaries, 4–5, 7, 8, 15, 20, 22, 23, 114, 150, 154, 158
Mississippi River, 137, 150, 288
Mitchell, Peter, 210–11, 212
Montreal, Quebec: creditors of fishermen in, 236
Moore, H. F., 92, 135, 144, 161, 163
mullet, 168, 169, 322
muskellunge, 169

nationalism, 72, 227, 297, 333, 336
nationality: of fishermen, 81, 83–94
nets: and anti-Americanism, 309–10; Baird's views about, 197; and changing species in Great Lakes, 157; and decline of mainstays of commercial fishing industry, 322; and destruction and waste of fish, 99–100; and developing drainage

nets (*continued*)
basins, 126; and discrimination in licensing, 224; and Dominion Fishery Commission report, 220; and dominion survey of 1868–69, 210; drying, 97; and enforcement, 211, 214, 218, 230; and expansion of commercial fishing industry, 47, 49; and fishermen–dealer relationship, 67–68; and Fishery Law of 1868, 205; in Georgian Bay, 322; and growth patterns of commercial fishing industry, 30, 36, 37, 38, 39–40; and harvesting technology, 38, 39–40, 49, 259, 261; Indian use of, 39; and International Fisheries Commission study, 313; and Joint Commission study, 246–47; in Lake Michigan, 40; lending of confiscated, 224; lifting of, 49, 56–57, 97, 246, 258; linen, 30; and lumbering, 104, 126; mesh size of, 103, 104, 107, 108, 178, 181, 182, 190, 197, 199, 202, 205, 214, 219, 220, 225, 246, 318, 322; number of, 246; and pecking order among fishermen, 88; regulation of, 25, 64, 103–4, 105–6, 107, 108, 175, 178, 181, 182, 189–90, 197, 214, 225; research about, 304; for salmon fishing, 24, 25; seizure of, 230, 309–10; and state fishery commissions–fishermen relationship, 189–90; and technology, 258–59; treating of, 97; and Tupper administration, 218, 219, 224, 225, 230; U.S. Commission's reports about, 197, 199; in wilderness era, 5. *See also specific type of net*

Nettle, Richard, 25, 179, 208–9

New Brunswick, 26, 176, 209–10, 303, 317

Newcastle, Ontario, fish hatchery, 26, 208, 209, 302

New York City: and Booth company operations, 269; dealers in, 254; as distribution center, 37, 301; federal and state fishery commissions meeting in, 213; and growth patterns of commercial fishing industry, 29, 37; international conference in, 193; and markets and distribution strategies, 257, 272, 275

New York state: and agricultural development, 116; and anti-Americanism, 310–11; and changing species in Great Lakes, 164; conservation policies of, 14; and cooperation between Canada and U.S., 212; county enforcement in, 176; and decline of mainstays in Lake Erie, 327; and Detroit international conference, 185; and developing drainage basins, 116, 142–43; hatcheries in, 201; and industrial-urban development, 142–43; and intergovernmental cooperation, 327; regulation in, 12, 175–77, 178, 180–82, 192, 201; and salmon in Lake Ontario, 24, 25; in wilderness era, 12, 14. *See also specific city/town*

Niagara Falls, 127, 281, 285, 286

Niagara River: and changing species in Great Lakes, 170; fishermen of, 81; and industrial-urban development, 142, 143, 144; and International Fisheries Commission study, 316, 317; pollution in, 280, 285–86, 289, 291, 292; and regulation, 179, 180; and salmon in Lake Ontario, 20

nickel mining, 283, 284, 306

nightfishing, 7, 21, 22, 130, 178

Noble brothers, 77–78, 218, 223, 229, 230, 233–37, 321

North Channel (Lake Huron): and anti-Americanism, 307; and Booth company operations, 266; and changing species in Great Lakes, 160; and decline of mainstays of commercial fishing industry, 322, 324; developing drainage basin around, 114, 116; harvesting in, 324; and International Fisheries Commission study, 318; licensing for, 223, 224; pollution in, 283, 324; and Prince's 1905 study, 322; roving fishermen in, 99; and Tupper administration, 223, 224; in wilderness era, 6

Northville, Michigan, 185, 198–99, 200

Northwest Ordinance, 10, 11, 12

Norwegian boats, 41, 84

Oconto, Wisconsin, 122, 160

Ohio: and agricultural development, 116, 119, 120; and anti-Americanism, 310–11; antipollution provisions in laws of, 290; artificial propagation in, 189; boundaries for, 11–12; and cooperation in commercial fishing industry, 273; dealers in, 192; and decline of mainstays in

Lake Erie, 327; and Detroit international conference, 185; and developing drainage basins, 116, 119, 120, 135–36; gill-net versus pound-net debate in, 188–92, 201; hatcheries in, 185; Indians in, 10; and intergovernmental cooperation, 184, 185, 212, 327; and International Fisheries Commission study, 319; petroleum industry in, 135–36; regulation in, 12, 181, 182, 188–92, 201; and research, 299; and state fishery commissions–fishermen relationship, 188–92; and state universities' curricula, 186; statehood for, 11–12; and U.S. Commission survey, 199; in wilderness era, 12. *See also specific city/town*

Ohio Fish and Game Commission, 186, 188, 189, 190, 191, 201, 290, 299, 311

Oil Springs, Ontario, 135, 136

Ojibwe Indians, 6, 8, 9, 64, 76–77, 79, 82 (fig.), 130, 223, 235, 268

Ontario: and agricultural development, 116, 118; and American expansion into Canadian waters, 55; and anti-Americanism, 308, 312; and Booth company operations, 268, 269; boundaries of, 12, 306; and British colonial policies, 14; and changing species in Great Lakes, 161; conservation policies of, 14; and cooperation in commercial fishing industry, 274; and Crisis of 1890s, 239–40; criticisms of, 308; and decentralization of administration of policies, 237; and decline of mainstays in Lake Erie, 327; and Detroit international conference, 185; and developing drainage basins, 116, 118, 134, 135–36; Dominion of Canada's controversy with, 180, 269, 302, 304, 305–7, 312, 316, 319, 322, 323, 324, 336; enforcement by, 265, 308, 310, 320; and expansion of commercial fishing industry, 55, 254; and hatcheries, 304, 307, 320; and intergovernmental cooperation, 193, 327; and International Fisheries Commission study, 316, 317; and Joint Commission study, 242; and licensing, 261, 265, 308; management of fisheries by, 12, 304, 307, 320; markets and distribution strategies in, 276; mining in, 134; petroleum industry in, 135–36; pollution in, 281, 288; Precambrian shield in, 134; production in, 263; and public policy balance sheet, 320; and research, 302, 320; settlement of, 10, 134; stocking programs in, 320; studies of commercial fishing between 1896 and 1933 by, 261; trade associations in, 274; in wilderness era, 10, 12, 14; and World War I, 276. *See also* Dominion Fishery Commission for the Fisheries of the Province of Ontario; Upper Canada; *specific city/town*

Ontario Agricultural Commission, 119, 127, 134, 135, 146

Ontario Department of Game and Fisheries, 276, 291, 292, 293, 294, 306, 321, 326

Ontario Game and Fisheries Commission, 165, 166, 167, 193, 262–63, 268, 271, 304, 306, 308, 312

Oswego River, 20, 21–22, 143

Ottawa, Ontario: joint management/regulation conference in, 317; typhoid in, 288; in wilderness era, 12. *See also* Dominion of Canada

Ottawa Indians, 5, 8, 77

Ottawa River, 125, 212

overfishing: and anti-Americanism, 318; and Booth company operations, 66, 68, 72, 266; and changing species in Great Lakes, 162, 168, 171; and dealer system, 187; and decline of mainstays in commercial fishing industry, 324–25, 326, 337; and destruction and waste of fish, 101; and developing drainage basins, 142, 147; and divided jurisdictions, 332; and economic issues, 278; between 1896 and 1933, 251; and ethnicity of fishermen, 85; and expansion of commercial fishing industry, 58; fishermen's pressure to continue, 88, 199; in Georgian Bay, 91, 246, 322; and income of fishermen, 91, 92; and industrial-urban development, 142, 147; and International Fisheries Commission study, 318; and Joint Commission study, 244, 245, 246; in Lake Erie, 106, 201, 245, 324, 326; in Lake Superior, 246; official sanctioning of, 278; and politics, 334; and pollution, 286; and regulation dilemma, 106, 108; research about, 299; state fishery commissions' warnings about, 186, 192; U.S. Commission re-

overfishing (*continued*)
ports about, 200, 201, 202; of whitefish, 200, 299, 324; and World War I, 278
overseers: and anti-Americanism, 227; appointment of, 206, 207, 210; and Booth company operations, 265, 266; corruption of, 218; and discrimination in licensing, 223; and dominion survey of 1868–69, 210; enforcement by, 207–8, 217–18, 230; equipment and boats of, 208; and Fishery Law of 1868, 206, 207–8; functions of, 206; increase in number of, 210; and licensing, 206, 208; lighthouse keepers as, 218; and Noble brothers operations, 233, 234, 235; and pollution, 290–91, 292, 293, 294; and regulation, 213–14, 225, 226; and Tupper administration, 217–18, 222, 223, 225, 226, 227, 230. *See also* fish inspectors/wardens
oxygen, 117, 118, 169, 279, 295

Pacific Ocean, 198, 231, 242, 248, 272, 302, 316, 319, 334
packing industry, 274, 275–76, 336
Panic of 1893, 45, 58, 72, 102, 105, 221, 224, 247
part-time fishermen, 32–33, 67–69, 85–86, 88, 187, 263, 335
patrol boats: and anti-Americanism, 308–9, 312; armed, 230, 231, 309, 310; and Booth company operations, 265; as check on American poaching, 229, 242; and harvesting technology, 258; inauguration of, 217–18; on Lake Erie, 230; on Lake Superior, 230; and mainstays of commercial fishing industry, 152; and Noble brothers operations, 233, 234
PCBs, 283–84
Pelee Island incident, 230–33, 237
Pennsylvania, 12, 133, 310–11, 327. *See also specific city/town*
perch: blue, 171; and changing species in Great Lakes, 155, 156, 163, 167, 168, 169, 171, 279; ice fishing for, 86; in Lake Erie, 256, 324, 325; and pollution, 279; production of, 255; in St. Clair River, 83; stocking programs for, 198, 202–3; U.S. Commission reports about, 202; yellow, 86, 155, 156, 168, 169, 171, 257, 325
Peshtigo fire (Wisconsin), 122
Petrel (patrol vessel), 71, 144–45, 216, 218, 230, 232, 233, 267, 308–9, 310
petroleum industry: and developing drainage basins, 134, 135–36, 145; and Joint Commission study, 245, 246; and pollution, 280, 281, 282, 284–85, 286, 290, 291, 292, 294
Petrolia, Ontario, 135, 136, 281
pickerel: blue, 167, 171, 219, 325; and changing species in Great Lakes, 167, 168, 169, 171, 279; in Georgian Bay, 322; and herring, 322; increase in, 219; in Lake Erie, 325; market popularity of, 322; and Noble brothers operations, 233, 236; and pollution, 279; yellow, 171, 322, 325
pike: blue, 86, 101, 169, 171, 255, 257, 273, 324; and changing species in Great Lakes, 152, 155, 156, 167, 168, 169, 171, 279; and cooperation in commercial fishing industry, 273; and developing drainage basins, 119, 143; grass, 119, 169, 246; ice fishing for, 86, 87; increase in, 219; and industrial-urban development, 143; and Joint Commission study, 246; in Lake Erie, 246, 256, 324, 325; in Lake Huron, 5; and markets and distribution strategies, 275; northern, 152, 155, 168, 169; and pollution, 279; price of, 255; research about, 299; spearing of, 87; U.S. Commission reports about, 202; walleye, 5, 86, 155, 156, 168, 169, 257, 325; in wilderness era, 5
Pittsburgh, Pennsylvania, 61, 129–30, 301
poaching: and American expansion into Canadian waters, 33, 54, 229, 242, 336; and anti-Americanism, 307, 308–10, 312; and Booth company operations, 266, 267; and commercial fishing between 1896 and 1933, 266, 267; and enforcement, 153, 211, 213, 229, 242, 312; and Joint Commission study, 241–42, 243; on Lake Erie, 267, 308–10; and mainstays of commercial fishing industry, 152; and Pelee Island incident, 230; and policy balance sheet, 320; and pollution, 286. *See also* Pelee Island incident
Point Pelee, 31, 309
Poles: as fishermen, 81
politics: and anti-Americanism, 307; and

Booth company operations, 267; and conservation, 323; and decline of mainstays of commercial fishing industry, 323, 324; and discrimination in licensing, 224; and Dominion Fishery Commission report, 220; and failure of joint efforts, 248–49; and Joint Commission study, 247–48; and Noble brothers operations, 233–37; and pollution, 293; and Prince's 1905 study, 323, 324; and regulation, 214–15; and research, 305; and Tupper administration, 221–22, 224, 227–37

pollution: and agriculture, 118, 120, 284, 286, 287, 289, 295; air, 281–82, 289; and antipollution provisions in fishery laws, 289–90; and canals, 285; and changing species in Great Lakes, 153, 154, 155, 156, 162, 163, 170–71, 279; and conservation, 294, 311; and consumption, 279; cooperative efforts to control, 333–34; creators of growing, 279–86; and Crisis of 1890s, 238, 239; and decline of mainstays of commercial fishing industry, 139, 324, 326, 337; definition of, 244; and destruction and waste of fish, 101, 102, 290, 293, 295; and developing drainage basins, 113, 118, 120, 124–25, 126–27, 128, 131, 134, 139, 141, 142–43, 144–45, 146, 148; and Dominion Fishery Commission report, 219; and dredging, 281, 283, 291; and economic interests, 278, 287; between 1896 and 1933, 251, 279–96; and enforcement, 214, 218, 290–94; and federalism, 311; and fishermen, 291, 296; and Fishery Law of 1868, 205, 208, 211–12; growing importance of, 294–96; and hatcheries, 295; and health issues, 280, 284, 285, 288, 289, 290, 294, 296; impact on Great Lakes of, 296, 337; and industrial-urban development, 139, 141, 142, 144–45, 146, 148, 279–86, 287, 289, 290, 292, 294, 295; and International Fisheries Commission, 288, 289, 334; and Joint Commission study, 241, 244–46, 247, 333; from lumbering, 124–25, 126–27, 128, 211–12, 282, 286, 287, 289, 295; major factors causing, 239, 337; as menace to fish, 289; and mining, 131, 134, 282–84, 286, 287, 290; and overfishing, 286; and overseers/inspectors, 290–91, 292, 293, 294; and poaching, 286; and policy makers/politics, 288–90, 293; Prince's definition of problem of, 286–88; and production, 279; and progressives, 288–89; public indifference to, 296; and rate of cleansing, 113; and regulation, 105, 179, 181, 214, 215, 225, 294, 334, 336; research about, 287–88, 294, 301, 302; and southern Great Lakes, 279–80; and spawning, 286, 287, 289, 295, 296, 326; and sportfishing, 289; and state fishery commissions, 186, 290; and states–province cooperation, 327; and stocking programs, 292, 295; from tanneries, 128, 141; and Tupper administration, 218, 219, 225; and urbanization, 279–86, 292; and U.S. Bureau of Fisheries, 289, 294–95; U.S. Commission reports about, 196, 198, 199, 200, 202, 289; and wetlands, 284; and World War I, 280–81, 294. *See also specific lake/river/bay, species of fish, or type of pollution*

poor people, 88, 224, 228

Portage Lake and Lake Superior Ship Canal, 129

Portage River, 119, 129, 130, 135

Port Arthur, Ontario, 65, 67, 69–72, 104, 108, 265–66

Port Arthur Fish Company, 69–72, 265–66

Port Clinton, Ohio, 52, 53, 119, 135, 160

Port Colborne, Ontario, 231, 284

Port Dover, Ontario, 254, 274

Port Huron, Michigan, 121, 126, 127

Port Stanley, Ontario, 224, 254, 261

Pottawattomie (steamer), 41

pound nets: and American expansion into Canadian waters, 55; and Booth company operations, 62, 64–65, 66, 68, 69, 70, 71–72, 265; and capital investment, 94; and changing species in Great Lakes, 155, 161; and destruction and waste of fish, 100–101; and developing drainage basins, 124; and Dominion Fishery Commission report, 219, 220; and ethnicity of fishermen, 84; and expansion of commercial fishing industry, 50, 51, 52, 55; and fishermen–dealer relationships, 67, 68; in Georgian Bay, 322; and growth patterns of commercial fishing industry,

pound nets (*continued*)
38–39, 40, 42; and harvesting technology, 38–39, 40, 42, 49, 50; illegal use of, 71; and International Fisheries Commission study, 318; and Joint Commission study, 245, 246; in Lake Erie, 94, 95 (fig.), 189–92, 201; in Lake Michigan, 94; in Lake Superior, 66, 94; lifting of, 246; and lumbering, 124; and Noble brothers operations, 234; Ohio debate about gill nets and, 189–92, 201; performance record of, 68; and Prince's 1905 study, 322; regulation of, 71, 103, 105–6, 107, 181, 182, 188–92, 201, 214, 225, 226; rise and decline of fishing with, 64; and state fishery commissions–fishermen relationship, 188–92; and technology, 258; and Tupper administration, 218, 219, 220, 225, 226, 234; and work of fishermen, 94, 96

price: and American expansion into Canadian waters, 93; and anti-Americanism, 308; and Booth company operations, 69, 70, 265, 266, 267, 268, 269, 271; and changing species in Great Lakes, 161; and cooperation in commercial fishing industry, 273; and dealer system, 52, 272; and decline of mainstays of commercial fishing industry, 321–22, 324, 330; and dominion survey of 1868–69, 210; in early twentieth century, 253; and expansion of commercial fishing industry, 58; and fishermen–dealer relationships, 69, 70, 85, 93, 271; of herring, 324; and income of fishermen, 90–91, 92, 93; of pike, 255; and regulation, 214, 215; and tariffs, 70; of trout, 255; of whitefish, 151, 255; and World War I, 254, 255, 276

Prince, Edward E.: and American expansion into Canadian waters, 55; and anti-Americanism, 309; appointment of, 220–21, 303; and Booth company operations, 265–66; and changing species in Great Lakes, 161, 165–66, 171; criticisms of, 228–29; definition of problem by, 286–87; and developing drainage basins, 147; and expansion of commercial fishing industry, 55; Indian policies of, 79; and industrial-urban development, 147; and International Fisheries Commission study, 313, 315–16; loss of influence by, 324; 1905 study of Georgian Bay by, 322–24; research of, 303; and Treaty of 1908, 319; and Tupper administration, 222, 228

Privy Council: British, 261, 306, 309, 336; Canadian, 206, 231, 236, 267

processing, 36, 37, 254, 255, 275, 278

production: and American expansion into Canadian waters, 54, 55; in Canada, 46–47; of carp, 255, 256; changing profile of, 255–57; and changing species in Great Lakes, 169–70; and conservation, 278; and dominion survey of 1868–69, 210; in early twentieth century, 255–57, 261–63; and expansion of commercial fishing industry, 45–47, 49, 54, 55, 57; of herring, 157, 256, 325; and income of fishermen, 91; for Lake Erie, 202, 255, 256, 261, 325; for Lake Ontario, 200, 261; for Lake Superior, 261; of perch, 255; and pollution, 279; and regulation, 213; of rough fish, 256; of sturgeon, 160, 256; of trout, 155, 256; in U.S., 45–47; U.S. Commission reports about, 35, 46, 198, 200, 202; of whitefish, 151, 256; and World War I, 275–76; during World War I, 251, 253

progressives, 251, 288–89, 297, 306, 332

public: and commercial fishing during World War I, 276; concern about Lake Erie of, 326; and Crisis of 1890s, 239; and decline of mainstays of commercial fishing industry, 326; education of, 276; and fish as common property, 179, 332, 333; indifference to pollution issues of, 296; and joint regulation, 332; lack of support for regulation by, 193–94, 332

public policy: American compared with Canadian, 229; and American dominance, 307–11; and anti-Americanism, 307–11; balance sheet, 320; centralization of Canadian, 204–5; and conservation, 311–12; dealer-entrepreneurs' influence on, 57–58; and declining fish resource, 297–320; and developing drainage basins, 139; and expansion of commercial fishing industry, 57–58; and federalism, 305–7, 311–12; and Indians, 298; and industrial-urban development, 139; and joint regulation, 312–20; and Ontario–

Dominion of Canada controversy, 305–7; and research, 297, 298–305; and sportfishing, 297–98; and technological development, 56, 57–58; and Treaty of 1908, 312–20. *See also* regulation; *specific policy, policy makers, commission or agency*
Pulaski, New York, 21, 23, 177
Put-in-Bay, Ohio, 185, 299–300

Quebec, 10, 179, 208–9, 210, 316, 317

Racine, Wisconsin, 263, 280, 281
railroads: and Booth company operations, 62, 67, 269; and cooperation in commercial fishing industry, 273; and developing drainage basins, 121, 133, 138; and expansion of commercial fishing industry, 57; and growth patterns of commercial fishing industry, 34, 35, 36, 37, 38, 42; and hatchery programs, 184; and interconnecting waterway system, 138; and lumbering, 121; and marketing, 254; and markets and distribution strategies, 272, 275; and mining, 133; refrigeration cars for, 42
Rainy Lake, 57, 161
Raisin River, 295, 326
Rathbun, Richard, 64, 66–68, 127, 161, 170, 242–48, 299
refrigeration, 45, 57, 76, 256, 272. *See also* freezing techniques
regulation: and agricultural development, 193; and American expansion into Canadian waters, 54, 104–5, 214–15; and anti-Americanism, 307, 310–11; Baird's views about, 197; and Booth's expansion, 64–65, 72; in Canada, 44, 64, 65, 92, 177–78, 192–93, 203, 204–15, 237, 244, 248, 332; Canadian contempt for, 210–11; and capital investment, 105; commercial fishing industry's views about, 177, 181, 182, 187–94, 214, 247–48, 272, 278, 297, 320, 335; and competition, 108–9, 187, 189, 215; and dealers, 51, 108–9, 272; debate about state or federal, 107, 109; in decade of expansion (1879–88), 213–15; decentralization of Canadian, 237; and decline of mainstays in Lake Erie, 326–27; and developing drainage basins, 146, 147–48; Dominion Fisheries Commission study about, 102–5, 107, 109; and Dominion of Canada, 177, 179–80, 204–15, 336; and dominion survey of 1868–69, 210; early state, 180–82; and economy, 109; and expansion of commercial fishing industry, 44, 54, 57, 182; failure of, 173, 337; as fair or foul, 224–26; and federal–state cooperation, 182–85; and federalism, 311–12, 336; and first regulators, 175–94; and fish as common property, 179, 332, 333, 335; fishermen's attitudes about, 102–9, 227–37, 334, 335–36; gradual equalization of, 319; and growth patterns of commercial fishing industry, 29, 33, 36; and harvesting of fish, 334; and hatchery programs, 107; and income of fishermen, 92; Indians as means of circumventing, 178; and industrial-urban development, 146, 147; inequity in, 307; and International Fisheries Commission study, 318; lack of public support for, 193–94; laissez-faire, 44, 51, 181–82, 332–33; lawsuits about, 190; and mining, 194; need for American, 202; need for flexible, 244, 246–47; need for uniform, 243, 311–12, 316, 320; in 1940s, 320; and Ontario–dominion controversy, 306, 307, 336; and overfishing, 106, 108; and pollution, 105, 294, 334, 336; and Prince's 1905 study, 322–23; and research, 302, 327; and rivalry between Canadian and American fishermen, 104–5; of salmon in Lake Ontario, 19, 25–26, 27, 175–78; and state fishery commissions, 187–94; and states–Canadian relations, 192–93; and stocking programs, 104; and technological development, 57, 108; and Treaty of 1908, 312–20; during Tupper administration, 216–37; unfairness of, 247, 248, 335; U.S. Commission concern about, 197, 201–2, 203; and value of catch, 105; and World War I, 276. *See also* enforcement; illegal fishing; joint management/regulation; state fishery commissions; tariffs; *specific state, body of water, or type of regulation*
Reighard, Jacob, 299–300
Rochester, New York, 24, 25, 34, 139, 143, 147, 176, 193, 279–80, 281

Roosevelt, Theodore, 288, 312, 313
Root, Elihu, 312, 316
Roth, Filibert, 122–23
"rough, coarse fish," 166, 167, 169, 214, 219, 225, 255, 256, 263, 322, 324–25
roving commercial fishing, 66–67, 99
rowboats, 31, 38, 161, 208, 231, 258
Russians: as fishermen, 81

Saginaw, Michigan, 126, 127
Saginaw Bay, 38, 80, 134, 135, 156, 168, 294, 316, 318
Saginaw River, 126, 127, 134, 156, 168, 272, 295
sailboats: and Booth's expansion, 62, 69, 70; and dealer domination, 53; for enforcement, 208; and expansion of commercial fishing industry, 49, 50, 53; and growth patterns of commercial fishing industry, 30, 38; and harvesting technology, 38, 41, 49–50; on Lake Michigan, 97; and technology, 258; and work of fishermen, 97
salmon: artificial propagation of, 25, 208–10; Atlantic, 4, 5, 14, 19–27, 149, 201, 332; and Booth company operations, 60–61, 272; in California, 136; canned, 60–61, 275; and changing species in Great Lakes, 149, 151, 161, 169, 171, 279; commercial fishing for, 23–27; cultural attitudes about, 26; decline and destruction of, 25, 26–27, 134, 157, 201, 210, 321, 332; and developing drainage basins, 128, 134, 142, 143; and dominion survey of 1868–69, 210; and early agricultural-commercial economy, 14, 19–27; as easy to catch, 151; and ethnicity of fishermen, 84; in Europe, 241; and expansion of commercial fishing industry, 56; and Fishery Law of 1868, 205; and growth patterns of commercial fishing industry, 28; in Gulf of St. Lawrence, 210; hatcheries for, 179, 208–10; herring marketed as, 56; in Humber River, 142; illegal fishing for, 211; and industrial-urban development, 142, 143; and International Fisheries Commission study, 316; in Lake Ontario, 4, 14, 19–27, 28, 128, 134, 169, 175–78, 180, 205, 209, 210, 211, 332; and lumbering, 128; and markets and distribution strategies, 275; methods for catching, 20, 21, 22, 24, 25, 84; and mining, 134, 136; Nettle's work with, 208–9; in New Brunswick rivers, 26; in New England rivers, 26; off Pacific coast, 199, 248, 316, 319, 334; physical appearance of, 21–22; and pollution, 26, 279; population of, 20–21; regulation of, 19, 25–26, 27, 175–78, 179, 180; size and quality of, 21; sockeye, 334; spawning of, 19–27, 134, 176; stocking of, 26–27, 143, 208–10; and technological development, 56; threatened extermination of, 25–26; U.S. Commission reports about, 199, 201; in wilderness era, 4, 5, 19–20, 23; Wilmot's programs for propagation and stocking of, 208–10
Salmon River, 20, 21, 24, 25, 134, 177
salt, 117, 126, 127, 134–35, 281, 283
Sandusky, Ohio: and agricultural development, 117, 119; and American expansion into Canadian waters, 55–56; and anti-Americanism, 308; and changing species in Great Lakes, 155, 158, 159, 160, 161, 163; dealers in, 51–52, 53, 56, 57, 188–90; and debate about gill nets and pound nets, 192; and developing drainage basins, 117, 119; and expansion of commercial fishing industry, 49, 51–52, 53, 55–56; and exploitation of Indians, 78; fishermen from, 85, 106; and growth patterns of commercial fishing industry, 29, 34, 37; and harvesting technology, 49; hatchery at, 185, 186; and International Fisheries Commission study, 318; packing facilities in, 52 (fig.), 76; pound nets around, 106; regulations in, 29; and state fishery commissions–fishermen relationship, 188–90, 192; trap net fishermen in, 318
Sandusky Bay, 29, 51, 165
Sandusky Fish Company, 106, 191
Sandwich, Ontario, 210, 223
sardine, 163, 272
Sarnia, Ontario, 135, 226, 281
saugers, 169, 257, 324, 325
Sault Sainte Marie: and Booth company operations, 65–66, 71, 72, 266; canals at, 109, 124, 128–29; and decline of fishing, 109; and developing drainage basins, 124, 128–29, 130, 133; dynamiting

for canal at, 109; and expansion of commercial fishing industry, 52; fishermen near, 77, 80, 81; Indians near, 77, 81, 82 (fig.); leasing of land for hatchery near, 199; and lumbering, 124; and mining, 128–29, 130, 133; Noble brothers' tugs impounded at, 235; overseers at, 234; pollution around, 285, 288; whitefish at, 124; in wilderness era, 6, 8

sawdust: Baird's views about, 197; and changing species in Great Lakes, 153; and developing drainage basins, 125, 126, 147; and enforcement, 214; and Fishery Law of 1868, 205, 211; and Georgian Bay, 246; and Joint Commission study, 245, 246; and Lake Huron, 246; and Lake Superior, 246; Milner's views about, 182; and pollution, 287, 290, 291; and regulation, 214; and state–federal cooperation, 182; study about, 212; and Tupper administration, 217; and whitefish decline, 200

sawmills. *See* mills

Scandinavians: as fishermen, 80, 81, 83, 84, 85, 273

Schacht, Siemon, 84–85, 159

schooners, 30, 123

scientific research: academic, 297, 298–305; and artificial propagation, 304–5; on Atlantic coast, 197–98; and Canadian–U.S. relations, 305; and Crisis of 1890s, 239; and decline of mainstays in Lake Erie, 326–27; and federalism, 311; funding for, 297, 298, 299–300, 302, 303, 305, 327; and harvesting, 305; and hatcheries, 304–5; importance of, 336–37; increase in Canadian, 237; and intergovernmental cooperation, 193, 333; and joint regulation, 332; and laboratory to test fish products, 301; lack of, 239; at marine biological stations, 303; and marketing, 305; and Ontario–dominion controversy, 307; on Pacific coast, 198; and politics, 305; and pollution, 287–88, 294; and Prince's appointment, 220–21; and public policy, 297, 298–305, 320; and regulation, 302, 327; rise of, 298–305; and sea lamprey onslaught, 333; and Tupper administration, 218, 220–21, 229, 237; and U.S. Commission, 196, 197–98; and World War I, 301. *See also specific person, agency, or department*

scoop nets, 76, 109

Scots: as fishermen, 83

sea lampreys, 155, 163–64, 166, 170, 251, 286, 320, 328 (fig.), 329 (fig.), 330, 333

seals: in Bering Sea, 228, 240, 241, 334

seines: and Booth's expansion, 64, 66; and changing species in Great Lakes, 152, 161, 165; and destruction and waste of fish, 99–100; and discrimination in licensing, 224; and Dominion Fishery Commission report, 220; and growth patterns of commercial fishing industry, 30, 32, 38, 40, 42; and harvesting technology, 38, 40, 42; and Indians as fishermen, 84; and industrial-urban development, 142; and Joint Commission study, 245; regulation of, 25, 103, 175, 178, 225, 226; and salmon in Lake Ontario, 25; and Tupper administration, 220, 224, 225, 226; at Wellington, 32; and whitefish, 152

seizures: and anti-Americanism, 309–10; and Booth company operations, 267; of nets, 230, 309–10; and Noble brothers operations, 235, 236; and Pelee Island incident, 230–33; of tugs, 145, 309–10

set-line fishing, 56, 84, 161, 177, 230, 258

settlers, 30, 134, 175, 176, 177, 211

sewage: and changing species in Great Lakes, 156; and decline of mainstays in Lake Erie, 326; and developing drainage basins, 114, 126, 127, 130, 141, 142, 143, 144, 145; and industrial-urban development, 141, 142, 143, 144, 145; and Joint Commission study, 245; in Lake Erie, 326; and lumbering, 126, 127; and mining, 130; and pollution, 280, 285, 287, 288, 289, 290, 291, 292, 293, 295, 296; and salmon in Lake Ontario, 26

shad, 147, 162, 163, 199

sheepshead, 166, 169, 256, 257, 324, 325

Sheppard, O. B., 88, 141, 142

silt, 244, 284, 285, 289, 295

Smith, Hugh M., 124, 141, 161, 200, 201–2, 219, 225

smoked fish, 56, 85, 275. *See also specific species*

Snell, Merwin-Marie, 124, 141, 200

social class, 34–35, 72, 88
Southampton, Ontario, 109, 127, 128, 225
Spanish River, 126, 283–84
spawning: and agricultural development, 10, 118; Baird's views about, 197; and changing species in Great Lakes, 152, 153, 154, 156, 157, 158–59, 161, 166, 169; and decline of mainstays in Lake Erie, 326; and destruction and waste of fish, 100, 101; and developing drainage basins, 118, 124, 125, 126, 134, 145–46, 147; and Dominion Fishery Commission report, 219, 220; and dominion survey of 1868–69, 210; and Fishery Law of 1868, 205, 209, 210; in Georgian Bay, 323; and industrial-urban development, 145–46, 147; and Joint Commission study, 245, 246; in Lake Erie, 245, 246, 327; in Lake Huron, 246; in Lake Ontario, 245; and lumbering, 124, 125, 126, 152; and mining, 134; and Noble brothers operations, 233; and pollution, 286, 287, 289, 295, 296, 326; and Prince's 1905 study, 323; and regulation, 103, 104, 105, 107, 178, 179, 181, 189, 192, 226; research about, 302, 304; and state fishery commissions–fishermen relationship, 189, 190, 191, 192; and states–province cooperation, 327; and Tupper administration, 219, 220, 226, 233; and violence against Wilmot's work, 209; in wilderness era, 6; and work of fishermen, 93. *See also specific species*
spearfishing: and dominion survey of 1868–69, 210; and enforcement, 211; and Fishery Law of 1868, 205, 209; and growth patterns of commercial fishing industry, 36; and ice fishing, 87; and Indians as fishermen, 84, 130; and industrial-urban development, 142; in Lake Ontario, 7; and regulation, 177, 178, 225; for salmon, 20, 21, 22, 24, 25; in wilderness era, 5, 7; and Wilmot's work, 209
sportfishing: in Canada, 207; commercial fishing industry's views about, 297–98; and conservation, 335; and Crisis of 1890s, 238; and hatchery programs, 184, 187; and Indians, 298; influence of, 297–98; from Lake Erie, 230–33; and licensing, 207; and Long Point Company, 219; and Ontario–dominion controversy, 307; and Pelee Island incident, 230–33; and pollution, 289; and public policy, 297–98; and regulation, 176, 180, 181, 187, 225; and Tupper administration, 219, 225, 230–33; U.S. Commission reports, 202; and whitefish decline, 200
Squaw Island, 218, 268–69
Standard Chemical Iron and Lumber Company, 293, 294
state fishery commissions: activities and functions of, 184–86; commercial fishing industry's relations with, 187–94, 196; and competition, 190; conference of, 311; establishment of, 182, 184; and intergovernmental cooperation, 193, 212; and International Fisheries Commission study, 316; and pollution, 290; and pound nets, 190–91; and regulation, 187–94, 311; and research, 299; and state universities, 299; and stocking programs, 198; and U.S. Commission, 196, 197, 198, 201
states: antipollution provisions in laws of, 290; conservation policies of, 14; and Crisis of 1890s, 239; and decline of mainstays in Lake Erie, 327; and division of Great Lakes and rivers, 11–12; early regulation by, 180–82; and enforcement, 206, 319–20; and federalism, 311, 316, 336; Indian policies of, 79; and intergovernmental cooperation, 182–85, 186, 203, 212, 213, 239, 311, 333; and International Fisheries Commission study, 316; and Joint Commission study, 247; and licensing, 319–20; and regulation dilemma, 107, 109, 336; and state universities, 299. *See also specific state*
St. Clair Flats, 133, 144
St. Clair River: and changing species in Great Lakes, 161, 168; and developing drainage basins, 127, 135, 143–44; exploitation of Indians along, 78; fishermen of, 83; and growth patterns of commercial fishing industry, 30, 31; and industrial-urban development, 143–44; and Joint Commission study, 244, 247; and lumbering, 127; and mining, 135; perch in, 83; and regulation, 179; sea

lampreys in, 330; sunfish in, 83; and Tupper administration, 226, 227, 228
steam, 42, 45, 49, 50, 51, 65, 66–67, 258, 260 (fig.)
steamers: and American expansion into Canadian waters, 54, 55; and Booth's expansion, 62, 67, 69; and changing species in Great Lakes, 158; for enforcement, 208, 214; and ethnicity of fishermen, 84; and expansion of commercial fishing industry, 49, 50, 51, 54, 55, 56; fishermen's dependency on, 69; gill-net, 215, 258; and growth patterns of commercial fishing industry, 29, 36, 37, 41; and harvesting technology, 38, 39–40, 41, 42, 49, 50; on Lake Michigan, 41, 62; and mining, 130; as patrol boats, 217–18; pollution from, 295; seizure of, 230; and technological development, 56, 258; and Tupper administration, 217–18, 264; waste from, 154; and work of fishermen, 94, 97
St. Ignace Island, 69, 126
St. Joseph, Michigan, 84, 97, 98, 160
St. Lawrence River: and agricultural development, 116; and changing species in Great Lakes, 163, 170; and developing drainage basins, 116, 138; and enforcement, 211; and federal–state cooperation, 185; and interconnecting waterway system, 138; as means of access to Atlantic Ocean, 137; pollution in, 288; salmon in, 19, 20, 22, 25, 26
St. Louis, Missouri, 37, 61
St. Mary's River, 6, 76, 124, 129, 152, 285, 289
stocking programs: and anti-Americanism, 227; of Atlantic coastal rivers, 147; Baird's views about, 197; and Booth company operations, 64, 72, 264; and Canadian policies, 204, 237, 336; and conservation, 311; criticisms of, 229; dealer-entrepreneur views about, 51; and developing drainage basins, 143, 147; effectiveness of, 202–3; and expansion of commercial fishing industry, 51, 57; and federalism, 311; fishermen's views about, 334; and Fishery Law of 1868, 208–9; in Georgian Bay, 323; and intergovernmental cooperation, 182–83, 204; and Joint Commission study, 241, 247; need for, 203; in Ontario, 320; for perch, 198, 202–3; and pollution, 292, 295; and public policy, 298, 320; and regulation, 104; for salmon, 26–27, 143; for shad, 147; and state fishery commissions, 186–87, 198; and technological development, 57; and Treaty of 1908, 319; for trout, 202–3; and Tupper administration, 221, 227, 229, 237; U.S. Commission's support for, 182–83, 196–97, 198, 199, 200–201, 203; for whitefish, 198, 202–3; Wilmot's work with, 198, 208–9. *See also* artificial propagation
St. Paul, Minnesota, 61, 62, 301
Straits of Mackinac, 53, 62, 80, 126
sturgeon: and American expansion into Canadian waters, 93; and changing species in Great Lakes, 149, 157–61, 162, 168, 169–70, 279; characteristics and habitat of, 157–61; commercial worth of, 158; decline/demise of, 45, 161, 168, 169, 251, 255, 268, 297, 321, 322, 324, 330, 332; destruction/waste of, 27, 99, 157–58, 159–60, 161; as easy to catch, 159; and expansion of commercial fishing industry, 45, 49, 56, 57, 58; fishermen's attitudes about, 84–85, 99, 157–58; in Georgian Bay, 322; harvesting techniques for, 161; homing sense of, 159; ice fishing for, 86; and income of fishermen, 93; and Indian exploitation, 78; and industrial-urban development, 144; in Lake Erie, 324; in Lake Huron, 5; in Lake St. Clair, 78; as mainstay of commercial fishing industry, 27, 157–61; overfishing of, 58, 332; and pollution, 279; production of, 160, 169–70, 255; and regulation, 188; research about, 300; size of, 246; smoked, 85, 159, 160; spawning of, 78, 158–59, 161; and state fishery commissions–fishermen relationship, 188; and technological development, 56, 57; U.S. Commission reports about, 202; and whitefish, 159; in wilderness era, 4, 5
subsistence culture, 7–9, 10, 15, 19, 23, 28, 331
suckers, 166, 168, 169, 257, 279, 293, 322, 324, 325
Sudbury Basin (Ontario): ores from, 283–84, 306

sugar-beet factories, 287, 295
Superior, Wisconsin, 122, 129, 133, 139, 280
surveying and plating fishing grounds, 190, 191, 196, 199–200
swampland, 118–20, 123, 138, 246, 293. *See also* wetlands
Swiss: as fishermen, 81

Taft, William Howard, 319
tanneries, 126, 127–28, 141, 146, 287, 291
tariffs: and American expansion into Canadian waters, 55, 220; and anti-Americanism, 307; and Booth's expansion, 65, 70; and Canadian–U.S. relations, 220; and dealer–fishermen relationship, 70; and dealers, 51, 55, 272; and expansion of commercial fishing industry, 51, 55; and lumbering, 126; and markets and distribution strategies, 275; and price, 70; and regulation, 104; and Tupper administration, 220, 227
technology: as cause of degradation, 337; and changing species in Great Lakes, 171; and dealers, 51; and destruction and waste of fish, 101; and enforcement, 261; and expansion of commercial fishing industry, 45, 49–50, 56–58; and growth patterns of commercial fishing industry, 38–41, 42–43; and immigrants as fishermen, 85; and Joint Commission study, 244; and mining, 133; and production, 255; and public policy, 298; and regulation, 108, 215; and roving fishing, 66–67; and salmon in Lake Ontario, 27. *See also specific type of technology*
TFM (3-trifluoromethyl-4-nitrophenol), 155
Thessalon, Ontario, 86, 99, 104
Thunder Bay, 30, 85, 158
Toledo, Ohio: and changing species in Great Lakes, 160, 163; dealers in, 53, 160, 188–90; and developing drainage basins, 133, 135–36, 139; and expansion of commercial fishing industry, 53; fishermen from, 135–36; and growth patterns of commercial fishing industry, 28, 29–30, 31, 33, 34, 37; industrial-urban development in, 139, 281; and International Fisheries Commission study, 318; packing facilities in, 76; and petroleum industry, 135–36; and pollution, 280; and state fishery commissions–fishermen relationship, 188–90; trap net fishermen in, 318
Torch Lake, 129, 130, 283
Toronto, Ontario: and Booth company operations, 267; and changing species in Great Lakes, 170; creditors of fishermen in, 236; dealers in, 254; and developing drainage basins, 127, 138, 139, 141, 146; fishermen from, 88; fish markets, 33; and growth patterns of commercial fishing industry, 28, 33, 34, 37; harbor of, 138; and industrial-urban development, 139, 141, 146; National Expo in, 276; pollution around, 279–80, 288; regulation of fishing in, 33; and salmon in Lake Ontario, 23; and Tupper administration, 226; water supply for, 288; in wilderness era, 12. *See also* Ontario
Toronto Bay, 20, 226, 291–92
Toronto Islands, 29, 31, 226
transportation: and commercial fishing between 1896 and 1933, 258, 272–73, 275, 276; and dealer system, 272–73; and developing drainage basins, 114, 116, 120, 121, 123–24, 127, 128, 131, 133, 138, 139; and growth patterns of commercial fishing industry, 34, 37; and industrial-urban development, 139; innovation in, 57; and interconnecting waterway system, 138; and lumbering, 123, 127, 128; and markets and distribution strategies, 275; and mining, 131, 133; subsidies for, 276; of timber, 120, 121; and World War I, 276. *See also specific type of transportation*
trap nets, *frontispiece,* 25, 66, 181, 225–26, 230, 259, 261, 318, 319
trawls. *See* beam-trawl
Treaties: of 1908, 192–93, 249, 251, 289, 312–20, 324, 333; of 1946, 333; of 1954, 320; of Paris (1783), 10–11
Trent–Severn Waterway, 164
trout: and anti-Americanism, 308; artificial propagation of, 25; ban on exportation of, 308; and Booth's expansion, 68; brook, 25; and changing species in Great Lakes, 149, 152–56, 162, 164, 165, 168, 169–70, 171, 279; closed season

for, 324; clubbing of, 100; decline/demise of, 27, 45, 168, 202, 219, 245, 251, 297, 321, 322, 324–25, 329 (fig.), 330, 332; and destruction and waste of fish, 100; and developing drainage basins, 116, 142; and Dominion Fishery Commission report, 219; as easy to catch, 153; and ethnicity of fishermen, 85; and expansion of commercial fishing industry, 45, 58; and fishermen–dealer relationship, 68; fishermen's attitudes toward, 98; and Fishery Law of 1868, 205; as food fish, 165; in Georgian Bay, 322, 324; gill nets for, 68; and growth patterns of commercial fishing industry, 30, 37, 42; and herring, 154, 155, 322; hooks and lines for, 84; ice fishing for, 86, 87; and industrial-urban development, 142; near Isle Royale, 116; and Joint Commission study, 245; in Lake Erie, 324–25; in Lake Huron, 5, 330; in Lake Ontario, 202, 215, 245, 291; in Lake Superior, 4, 84, 100, 152–56; as mainstay of commercial fishing industry, 27; and markets and distribution strategies, 42, 275; Nettle's work with, 208–9; and Noble brothers operations, 233; in Ontario waters, 27; overfishing of, 58, 332; and pollution, 279, 291; as predators, 152–53, 154, 155; price of, 255; production of, 155, 169–70, 255; and regulation, 106, 179, 181, 215; and sea lampreys, 330; spawning of, 93, 154; speckled, 27, 181, 208–9; stocking programs of, 202–3; and technology, 258; and Tupper administration, 219, 233; U.S. Commission's reports about, 199; in wilderness era, 4, 5; and work of fishermen, 93

truck transportation, 272–73

True, Frederick W., 34–35, 53, 83, 97, 100, 198

tugboat captains, 88, 90, 145, 267–68, 309

tugs: and anti-Americanism, 308, 309; and Booth company operations, 62, 64, 65, 66, 69, 70, 71, 267–68, 269, 272; capital investment in, 254; and dealer domination, 53; and decline of fishing, 109; and destruction and waste of fish, 101; from Erie, Pennsylvania, 309; and expansion of commercial fishing industry, 49–50, 53, 56, 58; and garbage barges, 144–45; in Georgian Bay, 322; gill-net, 276, 322; and harvesting technology, 49–50; and income of fishermen, 90; and Indians as fishermen, 77, 78; and industrial-urban development, 144–45; and Joint Commission study, 245; on Lake Erie, 245; licensing for, 276; and Noble brothers operations, 235, 236; and patrol boats, 218; and regulation, 107; and roving fishing, 66–67; seizure of, 145, 230, 235, 236, 309–10; steel, 258; and technological development, 56, 258; and Tupper administration, 218, 230, 235, 236; and work of fishermen, 94, 97; and World War I, 276

Tupper, Charles Hibbert: and American expansion into Canadian waters, 222; and American versus Canadian system, 217; anti-Americanism of, 266; appointed Minister of Justice, 229; appointed Minister of Marine and Fisheries, 216; appoints Dominion Fishery Commission, 218, 219–20; and Bering Sea controversy, 240; and Booth company operations, 265, 266; and changing species in Great Lakes, 163; and commercial fishing industry's opposition to regulation, 193; criticisms of, 215, 221–24, 227–37; cruiser patrols inaugurated by, 217–18; early years of administration of, 216–21; and economic issues, 237; Indian policies of, 79; and joint Canadian–U.S. management, 218, 237; and Joint Commission, 240–41; and Noble brothers operations, 233–37; and Pelee Island incident, 230–33; and Prince's appointment, 220–21; style of, 220; and uniform policies for management of natural resources, 248–49

turtles, 119

Two Harbors, Minnesota, 131–32, 133

Two Rivers, Wisconsin, 74, 75–76, 83, 128

typhoid fever, 288

United Nations, 337

universities: of Michigan, 295, 299, 301–2; of Ohio, 299; of Toronto, 147, 303, 304; of Wisconsin, 186, 299

Upper Canada, 14, 24, 25, 175, 177–78, 179, 180, 207
urbanization, 34, 114, 136, 137–48, 167, 168, 170, 245, 279–81, 292. *See also* industrial-urban development
U.S. Bureau of Fisheries: artificial propagation program of, 256; conferences sponsored by, 305; and decline of mainstays in Lake Erie, 326, 327; ecology objective of, 301; and harvesting technology, 259; and hatcheries, 320; and International Fisheries Commission study, 319; and Lake Erie, 326; as part of Commerce Department, 255, 301; and policy balance sheet, 320; and pollution, 289, 294–95; and production, 257; and research, 301, 305, 320, 327; and stocking programs, 320; as successor to U.S. Commission of Fish and Fisheries, 254–55; and World War I, 276
U.S. Commission of Fish and Fisheries: and American expansion into Canadian waters, 54, 55; and Booth's expansion, 62; *Bulletin,* 196, 199; and changing species in Great Lakes, 151, 154, 161, 165, 168; and dealer system, 272; and Detroit international conference, 185; and developing drainage basins, 125, 141, 146; establishment/goal of, 195; and expansion of commercial fishing industry, 49, 54, 55; functions/activities of, 195–96; and income of fishermen, 90; and industrial-urban development, 146; and intergovernmental cooperation, 182–85, 212, 213; as part of the Department of Commerce and Labor, 300–301; and pollution, 289; reports/studies of, 184, 196–200, 201–3; research program of, 196, 197–98, 255, 299–301, 302; and state fishery commissions, 196, 197, 198, 201; survey of fishermen (1885) by, 81, 86; and surveying and plating fishing grounds, 190, 191, 196, 199–200, 201–2; U.S. Bureau of Fisheries as successor of, 254; views about Canadian policies of, 203; and work of fishermen, 97. *See also* Baird, Spencer F.; Milner, James W.; U.S. Bureau of Fisheries
U.S. Department of State, 145, 199, 212–13, 231, 232, 316, 317, 319
U.S. Food Administration, 276, 277
U.S. House of Representatives, 248, 300, 319
U.S. Steel, 138
U.S. Tariff Commission, 273–74, 275

Van Oosten, John, 294, 301–2
Vigilant (patrol cruiser), 258, 267–68, 309–10, 310 (fig.)

Wakeham, William, 161, 170, 242, 243, 244–47, 248
Washington, D.C.: Joint Commission meetings in, 241, 242; laboratory to test fish products in, 301; as market, 37
Washington Island, Wisconsin, 41, 69, 75, 83, 100, 263
waste: and changing species in Great Lakes, 170; and developing drainage basins, 116, 128, 139, 141, 146, 147; and early state regulation, 181; in Georgian Bay, 322; and industrial-urban development, 139, 146, 147; and pollution, 280, 281, 282, 287, 290, 292, 294; state fishery commissions' warnings about, 186; from tanneries, 128. *See also* dumping; *specific type of waste*
Waterloo, Ontario, 292, 293
Watertown, New York, 127, 143, 170
Waukegan, Illinois, 155, 263
weirs, 5, 25, 84, 175, 177, 178
Welland Canal, 29, 164, 285, 330
wetlands, 118–20, 132, 133, 165, 281, 284. *See also* swampland
W. F. Kolbe and Company, 254 (fig.), 274–75
Whitaker, Herschel, 144, 186, 299
whitefish: and American expansion into Canadian waters, 54, 93, 323; and anti-Americanism, 307, 308; ban on export of, 308, 323; and Booth company operations, 62, 64, 66–67, 69–70, 266; and changing species in Great Lakes, 149, 150–53, 155, 156, 157, 158, 159, 162, 163, 164, 165, 167, 168, 169–70, 171, 279; characteristics and habitat of, 150–53; closed season for, 324; decline/demise of, 45, 163, 167, 168, 169, 182, 198–99, 200, 202, 219, 239, 245, 251, 255, 268, 297, 299–300, 302, 307, 308,

321, 322, 323, 324, 330, 332; destruction and waste of, 27, 54, 64, 100, 101, 109, 124, 152, 153; in Detroit River, 245, 295; and developing drainage basins, 124, 126, 141, 142, 144; and Dominion Fishery Commission report, 219; as easy to catch, 151, 152; and expansion of commercial fishing industry, 45, 49, 54, 57, 58, 151; fishermen's attitudes toward, 98; and Fishery Law of 1868, 205; as food fish, 150–51, 154, 165; in Georgian Bay, 308, 322, 323, 324; and growth patterns of commercial fishing industry, 30, 34, 35, 36, 37, 42; harvesting of, 64, 259; hatcheries for, 199, 210; ice fishing for, 86–87; illegal fishing for, 230; and income of fishermen, 93; and Indians, 124; and industrial-urban development, 141, 142, 144; and intergovernmental cooperation, 182; and Joint Commission study, 245, 246; in Lake Erie, 200, 245, 324, 325; in Lake Huron, 5, 152, 200, 246, 259, 302, 330; in Lake Michigan, 30, 62, 141, 200; in Lake Ontario, 200, 202, 215, 245; in Lake St. Clair, 299; in Lake Superior, 4, 150, 200; and lumbering, 124, 126; as mainstay of commercial fishing industry, 27, 150–53; and markets and distribution strategies, 35, 42, 275; and Noble brothers operations, 233; overfishing of, 58, 168, 299, 324, 332; and pollution, 200, 279, 295, 302, 324; popularity of, 154; predators of, 152–53, 154, 155, 159; price of, 151, 255; and Prince's 1905 study, 323; production of, 151, 169–70, 255; and regulation, 106, 179, 181, 182, 188, 215, 302; research about, 299, 300, 301–2; at Sault Sainte Marie, 124; and sea lampreys, 330; and seines, 152; spawning of, 152, 246, 302; and state fishery commissions–fishermen relationship, 188; stocking of, 198, 202–3; and technological development, 57, 259; in Traverse Bay, 299; undersized, 64, 68; U.S. Commission reports about, 198–99, 200, 202; in wilderness era, 4, 5, 6, 150; and Wilmot's program, 208; and work of fishermen, 93

Whitefish Point, Michigan, 65, 66–67, 72

Wikwemikong (Manitoulin Island), 81, 223

Wilmot, Samuel: appointed Superintendent of Fish Culture, 209; and Canadian Department of Marine and Fisheries, 209–10; as chair of Dominion Fishery Commission, 219; and changing species in Great Lakes, 163–64, 166–67, 171; criticisms of, 229; and developing drainage basins, 125, 147; fish-breeding report of, 125; and fishermen–dealer relationship, 92; Indian policies of, 79; and industrial-urban development, 147; and lumbering, 125; personal and professional background of, 26; propagation and stocking program of, 208–9, 211; retirement of, 209; and salmon in Lake Ontario, 21, 22, 26–27; and Tupper administration, 219, 229; U.S. Commission's interest in work of, 198; violence against work of, 209, 211. *See also* Dominion Fishery Commission on the Fisheries of the Province of Ontario

Wilmot Creek, 21, 24, 25, 26

Wilson, Woodrow, 319

Windsor, Ontario, 223, 280

Wisconsin: agriculture in, 117, 284; antipollution provisions in laws of, 290; boundaries of, 12; canals in, 124; and changing species in Great Lakes, 152, 168; conservation in, 259; and developing drainage basins, 116, 117, 122–23, 124, 127, 131, 133; and federal-state cooperation, 184; and federalism, 311; Indian policies of, 79; lumbering in, 122–23, 124, 127, 152, 282; mining in, 131, 133; regulation in, 12, 181, 182, 188, 263; and research, 299; sportfishing in, 184; and state fishery commissions–fishermen relationship, 188, 192; statehood for, 11–12; stocking programs in, 184; and U.S. Commission survey, 199; in wilderness era, 11, 12. *See also* Green Bay; Lake Michigan; Lake Superior; *specific city/town*

Wisconsin Commission of Fisheries, 184, 186, 188, 192, 193, 299

women: as fishers, 226; and fishing industry, 75–76

Woods Hole, Massachusetts, 198, 302

World War I: and agriculture, 284; and Booth company operations, 264; commercial fishing during, 255; and cooperation in commercial fishing industry, 274; and dealer system, 272; and decline of mainstays of commercial fishing industry, 324; and Great Lakes fisheries, 275–78; and pollution, 280–81, 284, 294; and price, 255; production during, 251, 253, 275–76; and research, 301

Wright, Ramsey, 147, 303, 304